ALSO BY PHYLLIS LEE LEVIN

Abigail Adams
Great Historic Houses of America
The Wheels of Fashion

EDITH AND WOODROW

★ *The Wilson White House* ★

PHYLLIS LEE LEVIN

A LISA DREW BOOK

SCRIBNER

NEW YORK   LONDON   TORONTO   SYDNEY   SINGAPORE

♨

A LISA DREW BOOK/SCRIBNER
1230 Avenue of the Americas
New York, NY 10020

Designed by Colin Joh
Text set in Aldus

Manufactured in the United States of America

1   3   5   7   9   10   8   6   4   2

Library of Congress Cataloging-in-Publication Data

Levin, Phyllis Lee.
Edith and Woodrow: the Wilson White House/Phyllis Lee Levin.
p. cm.
"A Lisa Drew book."
Includes bibliographical references (p. 571) and index.
1. Wilson, Woodrow, 1856–1924. 2. Wilson, Edith Bolling Galt, 1872–1961.
3. Presidents—United States—Biography.
4. Presidents' spouses—United States—Biography.
5. Married People—United States—Biography.

E767.L57 2001
973.91'3'0922—dc21
[B]   2001041109

ISBN 0-7432-1158-8

For information regarding special discounts for bulk
purchases, please contact Simon & Schuster Special Sales
at 1-800-456-6798 or business@simonandschuster.com

As ever,
for Bill
for my children and theirs

Contents

I wish you could see my room as I write . . . there is a long couch on which I imagine you resting while I am at my big businesslike desk opposite, where I have orchids on either side of me to gladden my eyes when I have to turn away from you. . . . It pleases me to feel you are here and I find it hard to stay at my desk instead of coming over and kneeling beside you and whispering something you already know . . .

     —Edith Bolling Galt to Woodrow Wilson, May 24, 1915

And *then*, the loneliness! The loneliness of the responsibility because of the loneliness of the power, which no one *can* share. But in the midst of it I knew that there was one who *did* share—*everything*— a lovely lady who has given herself to me, who is my own, who is part of me, who makes anxieties light and responsibilities stimulating, not daunting, by her love and comprehension and exquisite sympathy . . . the whole divine partnership transforming everything, the Constitution of the United States itself included . . .

  —President Woodrow Wilson to Edith Bolling Galt, August 14, 1915

             Saturday, 8 P.M.

             The White House

Preface

The deathbed admonition of Woodrow Wilson's angelic, admiring first wife, Ellen, that her husband, a great man, should not become a *lonely* great man, paved the way to his remarriage. Enter Edith Bolling Galt— and the rest is "history," idealized, sanitized, and indeed, invented in her autobiography: a story played out in Washington and Paris and around the world, against the guns of World War I and the partisan cross fire over the eventual refusal of the United States to join the League of Nations. The story of Wilson's second marriage, and of the large events on which its shadow was cast, is darker and more devious, and more astonishing, than previously recorded.

From the morning of October 2, 1919, when Woodrow Wilson suffered coronary thrombosis, and a paralyzing stroke, Edith insisted that her husband, the twenty-eighth president of the United States, was yet a dynamic leader, an indispensable visionary, physically enfeebled only temporarily. Though she acknowledged that she studied every paper sent to her by various cabinet secretaries and senators and had tried to digest and present in tabloid form matters that in her view needed imperatively to go to the president, "I, myself," she protested, "never made a single decision regarding the disposition of public affairs. The only decision that was mine was what was important and what was not, and the very important decision of when to present matters to my husband." In fact, she could recall only one instance when she had acted as intermediary in an official matter, "except when so directed by a physician."[1]

As the White House became hushed and secretive, Edith Wilson assumed what she defined as her stewardship. When access became tantamount to power, however, the handful of statesmen, historians, and politicians who experienced her new authority tended to describe her in more formidable terms, as female regent, secretary of state, supersecretary, and ultimately, the first woman president of the United States. She had become keeper of the key to the now impregnable White House and to the president himself (Edith's turbulent handwriting conveys her invalid husband's mumbled and cryptic answers, such as they were, on all presidential correspondence of that period), while official Washington pleaded for her intervention on crucial domestic and international issues. Edith herself categorically repudiated the allegations concerning her exercise of power. It was always "others" who meddled with the truth, whereas she would set and keep the record straight. In writing her autobiography, *My Memoir*—a testament to the heroic presidency of her husband—she presumed to take an "oath to tell the truth, the whole truth, and nothing but the truth—so help me God."[2]

No one would prove more adept than she at publicizing this image of Woodrow Wilson and his Edith struggling valiantly and succeeding in the White House. In addition to writing her *Memoir*, which reflects her recasting of facts and prejudices, she subsidized the author whom she appointed to compile the eight-volume biography *Woodrow Wilson, Life and Letters*, and exercised her authority over every word uttered in the film *Wilson: The Rise and Fall of an American President*, produced in Hollywood in 1944. That film, a benevolent tour of the twenty-eighth president's life, depicts the melancholy scene, immediately following Wilson's severe stroke, in which his physician assures Edith there is no need for her husband to consider resignation in favor of the vice president. To the contrary, with certain precautions and support, administered by Edith, he is declared to be entirely capable of conducting the government of the United States. In conforming with this heartening prognosis, Wilson does, in the film, reappear on the White House veranda as an able, cheerful invalid. Though one might assume that the dialogue revolving around the momentous decision that Wilson remain in office should be attributed to the scriptwriter Lamar Trotti, its source is Edith Wilson's own *Memoir*. Her name fails to appear among the screen credits, but a deputy of Mrs. Wilson's was on the scene to affirm her story line. Ray Stannard Baker, her husband's anointed and openly partisan biographer, whose "absurd *scenario* picture" of the president "as a stainless Sir Galahad" was denounced by Winston Churchill, is listed as one of the two technical advisers.[3]

Baker did not disappoint Edith Wilson's confidence. The film was the fulfillment of her life's work to exalt her husband. Wilson without blemishes was to be compared to Washington and Lincoln, the rectitude of his position regarding the League unquestionable, his opponents in that pursuit indefensible, his physical disabilities negligible, and his intensely affectionate correspondence with a third woman, outside his two marriages, excluded.

Eluding the eyes of occasional skeptics of "the White House of Mysteries,"[4] Edith Wilson retained a host of acolytes, including several senior historians, who accepted her interpretation. Perhaps they knew her as a youthful widow and were of a generation too old (and too gentlemanly) to believe that the Southerner with the soft, musical voice might have deceived them, or that any such woman might arrogantly preempt power and deliberately distort her country's history. One of her prominent champions, for example, acknowledges that "Mrs. Wilson's memory is often faulty, colored by her preconceptions," while simultaneously insisting that her *Memoir* is an "essential document."[5] With such support, Edith Wilson has had her way with history—and might have continued to do so but for recently disclosed medical reports dating back to 1919, which refute the romantic story she assiduously devised. All turned to ashes on the Memorial Day weekend in Upperville, Virginia, in 1990, when the sons of Wilson's physician and confidant Cary Grayson— James Gordon Grayson and Cary T. Grayson Jr.—released the original diagnoses made by their father and his colleague Dr. Francis X. Dercum on the occasion of Wilson's stroke. These papers make it clear for the first time that on October 2, 1919, Wilson suffered a devastating trauma, so extensive that it precluded anything "more than a minimal state of recovery."[6] Given Wilson's beclouded presidency, the late Arthur S. Link, dedicated editor of sixty-nine volumes of *The Papers of Woodrow Wilson*, who regarded the task as a "divine call," and who had originally dismissed the idea that Edith Wilson ran the government after her husband's illness as "pure nonsense . . . more into the realm of legend than scholarship,"[7] would concede, on further thought and almost wistfully, that "Edith emerges as the master of the cover-up (such as it was), doesn't she?"[8]

Though Wilson, due no doubt to his frail health, never managed to write the history of his presidency, a multitude of surrogates—and one has the impression that everyone attending the Paris Peace Conference kept a diary—abundantly filled the void. Yet Wilson, who appeared to the world as a dogmatic idealist, more preacher than diplomat, did leave behind a confessional autobiography in his correspondence with three women. Those letters reveal throughout the seasons of his life the rise and fall of a narcissistic, ambitious, sensual, dependent, emotionally vulnerable, and physically impaired man, who led the United States during World War I. The intimate letters—to Wilson's treasured first wife, Ellen, and subsequently to his epistolary beloved, Mary Allen Hulbert Peck, with whom he maintained an extensive correspondence until his remarriage—help to prepare us for the whirlwind courtship and capitulation of the widower of eight months to the reverential Edith Bolling Galt. Flattering and possessive and physically attractive, she was soon his lover and trusted political adviser. Wilson met Edith Bolling Galt in March 1915; he proposed marriage in May. In June she acknowledged her joy in being taken into a "partnership as it were." By August, Wilson gave affirmation of their shared lives and work. By December, they were man and wife. There would be much to learn about his new partner, his "strange, lovely Sweetheart," and there is no doubt that Edith revealed her "secret depths" with style and imagination and, according to her whim, with more than a tinge of fantasy. By the time her formidable talent for fiction was disclosed, the damage was done. Her victims included her husband's closest and trusted adviser, Colonel Edward Mandell House, Senator Henry Cabot Lodge, Secretary of State Robert Lansing, and a renowned British ambassador; and of course, the president himself.

The revelation of the physical and mental condition of the invalid Woodrow Wilson alters history's pious perception of him as a star-crossed victim of other people's frailties, rather than as a deeply flawed man. Princeton's Arthur Link and his staff have accordingly cautioned biographers and historians who write of Wilson as, in those last years, a reasonably healthy and responsible person to reconsider his impulsive, irrational behavior "with some understanding of its causes."[9] The truth of his incapacity naturally poses grave questions of its consequences for world affairs. Link seems to imply that a healthier Wilson would have been a more conciliatory diplomat. Entry into the League of Nations could have transformed the record: "In a world with the United States playing a responsible, active role, the possibilities of preventing the rise of Hitler were limitless."[10]

We must therefore consider whether events leading to the Second World War might have been recast had Edith Wilson permitted the vice president, Thomas R. Marshall, to supplant her incapacitated husband in the White House in 1919. Given Marshall's reasonable temperament, is it not possible that he might have reached a compromise with Henry Cabot Lodge over the degree to which Americans ought to involve themselves in foreign wars, and have thus led the United States to membership in the League of Nations? Such great questions are central to my reconsideration, in the present book, of the role and influence of Wilson's wife during "one of the most extraordinary periods in the whole history of the Presidency."[11] Edith Wilson was by no means the benign figure of her pretensions; the president far less than the hero of his aspirations. On closer examination, their lives are a sinister embodiment of Mark Twain's tongue-in-cheek observation that he "never could tell a lie that anyone would doubt, nor a truth that anybody would believe."[12]

★ Part I ★

*A First Marriage, a Widower,
a Romance*

CHAPTER 1

"A great capacity for loving the gentle sex"

On Monday, August 3, 1914, as Woodrow Wilson's cherished wife of thirty years lay dying in the White House, Germany declared war on France. If not prepared, Wilson had been warned of a seemingly insoluble impasse. During the previous May, the president's personal overseas emissary, Colonel Edward Mandell House, had signaled Wilson from the American embassy in Berlin:

> Whenever England consents, France and Russia will close in on Germany and Austria. England does not want Germany wholly crushed, for she would then have to reckon alone with her ancient enemy Russia; but if Germany insists upon an ever-increasing navy, then England will have no choice.[1]

In such a climate of hatred and internecine jealousies, House concluded, "there is some day to be an awful cataclysm."[2]

On June 28, in the town of Sarajevo, in the Austrian province of Bosnia, the nationalistic terrorist Gavrilo Princip, craving Bosnia's freedom from Austria, had shot to death the heir apparent to the thrones of Austria and Hungary, Emperor Francis Joseph's great-nephew Archduke Francis Ferdinand, and his consort, the duchess of Hohenberg. In a matter of months, after four decades of mounting tension following the Franco-Prussian War of 1870, the entire continent was embattled. A "wave of madness"[3] had spread from Liège to Constantinople and to the peninsula of Gallipoli in the Dardanelles.

Last hopes for peace in Europe were extinguished by Germany's declaration of war on Russia on August 1. Ultimately, the so-called Great War, whether in the cause of patriotism, racism, power, freedom, or survival, leaving 10 million dead and 20 million wounded, would re-create and propagate the ancient, historic enmities it was intended to resolve.

Nor was it to be "the war to end war"[4] but a devastating prelude, with less than a quarter-century hiatus, to World War II.

On August 3, Great Britain's eminent foreign secretary, Sir Edward Grey, pleaded in the House of Commons for public and parliamentary support of France and Belgium. That evening, his sad, eagle eyes looking out on the summer greenery of St. James's Park, the veteran statesman took stock of the end of a nineteenth-century world of social order and imperial authority and sadly concluded, "The lamps are going out all over Europe; we shall not see them lit again in our lifetime."[5] Newly at war with Russia and France, Germany thundered into neutral Belgium on August 4, and in protest on legal and moral grounds, Great Britain declared war on the invader later the same day.

In Washington, as he sought to soothe the press regarding the effect of the news from abroad, Wilson maintained a calm exterior. "There is no cause for excitement," he cautioned, while acknowledging great inconvenience in the money market and in the exchanges, and temporarily, in the handling of crops, especially cotton. Provided "we all cooperate to see that nobody loses his head," Wilson was convinced that the nation could reap a "great permanent glory."[6] Sitting at his wife's bedside, however, bravado failed him. He could not conceal his private agony from his family. For the first and only time in her life, his daughter Eleanor saw her father weep. In future conversations Wilson referred feelingly more than once to Sir Edward Grey's loss of his own wife and spoke of himself as being "utterly alone."

Following Ellen's death on August 6, during his intense mourning, Wilson, having sent his daughters Margaret and Jessie to the family's rented summer home, Harklakenden, in Cornish, New Hampshire, found solace in remembering his life with Ellen. Tears came to his eyes as he talked to Ellen's brother Stockton Axson, and his cousin Helen Bones, of what this loss meant to him—he said he felt like a machine that had run down; there was nothing worthwhile left in him. The three sat in the rose-colored family room on the second floor of the White House. Axson, writing of those days, recalled the solitary figure of the president, his hair whitened, looking old and worn. Deeply dispirited, he occasionally read from Burton's enormous anthology of poetry.[7] However, the central theme was Ellen, and Wilson thought back to their first meeting in April 1883, when apple blossoms showered the rolling hills of northern Georgia like pink and white confetti, and he, at twenty-six, was a partner in the struggling law firm of Renick and Wilson in

Atlanta.⁸ Ellen, about to turn twenty-three, was five feet three inches, with a deep dimple, a bang of copper-colored ringlets to screen what she regarded as her too-high forehead, and pleading brown eyes. The pace of her Southern drawl was so slow that Wilson eventually came not only to mimic her, but also to tease that she "took longer than anyone else in the world to say things."⁹

Ellen Louise Axson was one of four children of Samuel Edward Axson, minister of the little First Presbyterian Church in Rome, Georgia. Her paternal grandfather was the president of the Greensboro Female College and the distinguished minister of the Independent Presbyterian Church in Savannah. She was born on May 15, 1860, her brother Stockton in 1867, followed by Edward in 1876. Their mother, Margaret Jane Hoyt Axson, died shortly after giving birth to her fourth child, nicknamed Madge, in 1881. Ellen was a graduate of the Female Seminary in Rome, Georgia, established by Elizabeth Caldwell, a protégée of the influential Emma Willard, who presided over the rigorous Troy Female Seminary. Ellen had studied algebra, philosophy, logic, natural history, and botany and was considered an outstanding student in French, English literature, and composition. She looked forward to a career as an artist and hoped to study painting in the North and, possibly, in Europe. Meanwhile, she earned a pleasant income drawing portraits in crayon.

Ellen's father suffered a nervous breakdown, and the Axson family moved from Rome to Savannah in the fall of 1883. The Reverend Mr. Axson, after episodes of physical violence, was confined to the Central State Mental Hospital at Milledgeville the following January and died there, very likely by suicide, on May 28, 1884.¹⁰ Money from her father's legacy sent Ellen north that year to Manhattan, where she lived at 120 West Eleventh Street, and then at 95 Seventh Avenue, while studying at the Art Students League. When she'd announced her engagement in September 1883 to "the greatest man in the world," Wilson confessed his "need of a sweetheart," saying that he had hardly dared to hope to win one on a four-month acquaintance, and that "even you, my darling, don't know yet how intensely I can love (though you shall know it some day)."¹¹ The two-year interval between the couple's engagement and marriage prompted a correspondence that gives enduring insights into their relations, and into the convolutions of Woodrow Wilson's personality. All of Wilson's letters during this period reflect his intricate and incessant self-analysis, his powerful ambition and preoccupation with work, and his awareness of his own excessive sensitivity. He constantly exhibits concern over his mental and physical health, fretting about his delicate eyes and ominous headaches, and guarding his lungs against consumption.

The ardent and angular groom-to-be was a shade less than five feet eleven inches tall. His searching eyes were sea-colored, and depending on his mood, their warm blue could turn cold, gray, and steely. His mouth was disarmingly generous, almost sensuous; a bold mustache accentuated the depth of a plunging jaw. Wilson was painfully aware that people often regarded him as "a rare bookworm" with no joy in his soul, "incapable of sentiment, smileless and given over to dead love." There seemed to be something about the cut of his jib, he said, that led people to take him for a minister or a missionary, "though I could myself never discover what it is."[12]

But he did not have to look further than his Scottish and Irish fore-bears to understand his heritage. He could reach back to the seventeenth-century Reverend Robert Wodrow (so spelled), author of *The Sufferings of the Church of Scotland*, to apprehend the strict claim the church laid upon his shoulders. Indeed, he needed to look no further than his father. At the time of Wilson's birth on December 28, 1856, Dr. Joseph Ruggles Wilson was pastor of the First Presbyterian Church of Staunton, Virginia. He moved with his wife, Janet, and their family, which included Woodrow's brother, Joseph Jr., and his sisters, Marion and Anne Josephine, to churches in Augusta, Georgia, in Columbia, South Carolina, and in Wilmington, North Carolina, and served for thirty-four years as permanent clerk of the General Assembly of the Presbyterian Church of the United States. He died on January 21, 1903.

Dr. Wilson, with his dark hair and trim beard, looked Lincolnesque in his middle years, though with softer features. Attesting to the affection-ate relations between father and son, Woodrow Wilson would explain that it was both for his own education and for the pleasure of being with his father that he helped prepare the Assembly's minutes. The father, in Stockton Axson's judgment, had a decided literary talent and was more like Samuel Johnson than any other man he had ever known in the flesh: "a man of books, but also of intimate contact with life" with "an extraor-dinary power for conversation and a robust personality." In Axson's opinion, the son was indebted to the father, both by inheritance and training, for "a very considerable portion of his great literary power."[13] But his idol, "shamefully neglected as a vital influence in stirring in Wil-son his 'Woodrow Conscience,'" was his uncle James Woodrow. Far ahead of his times in enlightening Presbyterians about Darwinism and a very able scholar, his devotion to "truth" as he saw it—at the expense of breaking up the Columbia Theological Seminary—nevertheless set a precedent "for his nephew's failure as president of Princeton, and of the United States in 1919." The men, it was said, were much alike in their "same unshaken determination of purpose once the mind was made up, the same instinctive aloofness."[14]

At his mother's death on April 15, 1888, Wilson told Ellen that he suffered unspeakable sadness and that memories of her "seem to hallow my whole life."[15]

Reared in a house of books and prayer, he was a "delicate, silent child, shy amid a group of noisy cousins who called him Tommie."[16] Wilson spoke frankly of his closeness to his mother, a reserved, proud, independent woman with firm ideas on the education of children—they were not to be shut up in a schoolroom until after they were ten. He had, admittedly, "clung to her," a derided "mamma's boy," until he was "a great big fellow" and wondered whether his love of the best of womanhood "came to me and entered my heart through those apron-strings." If he had not lived with such a mother, he questioned whether he would have deserved, in part through transmitted virtues, such a wife as Ellen—"the strength, the support, the human source of my life."[17]

In effect, at the time of his betrothal, in his demand for Ellen's total love and her unquestioning acceptance, he had revealed a craving for devotion and for woman's unreasoning tenderness that would persist throughout his life, never serving him well, and, in the end, taking its bitter toll.

But his mother, extremely anxious and worried about her son's health, ambitious for both him and for her husband, was often ill—probably, it has been speculated, on a psychosomatic basis—and, on "good evidence," suffered from chronic depression. In later years, her son attributed his tendency toward melancholy moods to his mother.[18]

Wilson was admitted to the Georgia bar on October 19, 1882, but his failure after less than a year to establish a successful law practice in Atlanta prompted his decision to attend Johns Hopkins University. Two days after his engagement to Ellen in September of 1883, Wilson arrived in Baltimore to pursue studies in history and political science. It was not the first detour in his educational odyssey. He had left Davidson College in North Carolina after his first year to go to Princeton and later was satisfied that quitting the University of Virginia Law School six months before his graduation had been the most prudent step he could have taken because—as he told a classmate—his digestive organs were seriously out of gear.[19]

Love was the key to Wilson's salvation—so he believed and asserted. Love was a cure that might soothe and ameliorate his strong passions and an intensity of mercurial feelings, which, he hoped, were not transparent and which he fervently tried to conceal. To Ellen, he confided that it was hard in his case to have to deal with his "unamiable feelings," his "crooked dispositions."[20] He prayed that none of his friends—or his enemies—would ever find out how much it cost him to renounce his own way. "I have the uncomfortable feeling," he admitted, "that I am carrying a volcano about with me."[21] There were also instances of near remorse when he thought that he had done Ellen, whom he called Eileen on occasion, a very questionable service in preparing her for life with a man not only sensitive but also restless, and of overwrought disposition; a man of "unappeasable ambition to produce something worthy of the world's reading," a man bent on compelling her "to hear and pass judgment upon what he does in the progress of the adventure."[22] Lightening his tone, Wilson asked Ellen, "How can a fellow in Baltimore write a lecture on Adam Smith when he's forever thinking of a girl in Georgia?"[23]

Wilson's early ambitions were thus directed not only at fame and position, but at achievements worthy of renown. His self-regard discovered faults of character that he was ready to acknowledge, at least to his indulgent young love. However, he would attempt, less and less, as years passed and power was attained, to discipline his egotism or to test, against principle and circumstance, an obdurate conviction of his own righteousness.

On the first of January 1884, Wilson described to Ellen his plan to write a book to be called *Congressional Government*. Reconstituting and expanding on papers he had published in college, he appeared to concentrate on a single topic with a spectrum of titles.

Six years earlier, in 1878, Wilson had written "Cabinet Government in the United States," which was, ironically, submitted to and accepted by a young Harvard-educated Bostonian and future antagonist, Henry Cabot Lodge, an editor of the *International Review*. In this article Wilson had proposed two of the most critical themes of his philosophy of government. One of these he would later ignore, and the other affirm, both with fatal consequences. Contradictory to his nonnegotiable stance on the League of Nations, in which he would prove intolerant of discussion and demeaning of his critics, Wilson, a senior at Princeton, had argued that frank and open debate is the essential function of a popular representative body. He also wrote—and subsequently underscored—that "American government is practically carried on by irresponsible committees"; there was "no more despotic authority under the forms of free government than our national Congress now exercises."[24]

In 1887, his essay "Of the Study of Politics"[25] would be followed by "The Study of Administration."[26] The rules, systems, and methods of governing, as he envisioned them, apparently did not have personal application. Wilson emphatically cautioned in the "Study of Politics" that "to know anything about government, you must see it alive—not merely as it appears in written constitutions and laws." Discounting his own advice, Wilson did not visit Washington before handing down definitive pronouncements. Only in 1897 would he actually attend House and Senate sessions.

Wilson's inspiration was the English critic and historian Walter Bagehot. Wilson thought Bagehot had, beyond anyone before him, made the British government much more intelligible to ordinary citizens. Similar treatment, if applied to the American Constitution, Wilson thought, would produce a measure of revelation for those who were still reading *The Federalist* as an authoritative constitutional manual. "The object that I have placed before myself," he wrote Ellen, "is so dear, so sacred in my eyes that anything that in the least obstructs or diminishes the chances of achieving it hurts me like a slap in the face."[27] The theme under discussion was the opportunity to contribute "something substantial to the political knowledge and the political science of the country, to the end that our forms of government and our means of administration may be perfected." Walter Bagehot was perhaps the principal literary figure who held Wilson in thrall and to whom he was indebted for the thrust of his own work. As a Princeton student, his idols included William Gladstone, Edmund Burke and his Whig opponent William Pitt, and John Bright, the English nineteenth-century orator, statesman, and champion of the middle class.

Wilson's father had hoped his son would follow in his footsteps in the Presbyterian ministry. As it turned out, the son, "born halfway between the Bible and the dictionary,"[28] had an undeniable desire to preach, but before a far less circumscribed congregation. A zealous student of the English orators, he had joined Princeton's debating club, the Whig Society, and cautioned against viewing oratory as an end rather than as a means. The object of oratory was, he said, "persuasion and conviction—the control of other minds by a strange personal influence and power."[29]

In an intimation of his future, he spoke of the careers open to orators, including the "bar, the pulpit, the stump, the Senate chamber, the lecturer's platform."[30] A card found in one of his books was signed, "Thomas Woodrow Wilson, Senator from Virginia."[31]

In perfecting his oratorical talents he became intolerant of those who did not meet his personal standards. In an outburst of scathing prejudice, he savaged a fellow student, "a greasy junk-shop Jew who had been partially washed and renovated and oiled that he might appear to less overwhelming disadvantage among decent people."[32]

To Ellen, Wilson was at last able to confide his deepest secret. His haunting sense of disappointment and loss came from an inability to fulfill, despite his gifts and inclinations, his heart's primary ambition: that of taking an active—if possible a leading—part in public life; to be, if not a guide to public policy, then a guide to public thought. Had he even modest independent means of support, he would enter politics and try to fight his way to predominant influence amid the hurly-burly of Congress. The sober methods of the scholar and the man of letters required constant and stringent schooling; he felt a much greater affinity for the busy rush and practical talk of the outside world than for subdued, monotonous, bookish society.

Wilson had never made such confessions before, but now it was as if he could not stop. He thought of himself, he told Ellen, as having a strong instinct for leadership, an unmistakably oratorical temperament, and the keenest possible delight in public affairs. He had no patience for the tedious toil of research but, instead, harbored a passion for interpreting great thoughts to the world. And even as he accepted Ellen's judgment that the writer's career is the highest, his prophetic dreams remained intact. He persisted in hoping that some combination of fortunate circumstances might open a public career to him and offer the chance to find out whether he really did possess the talents he sensed within.

Subject to doubt, illness, pessimism, depression, Wilson's hypersensitivity made him a vulnerable young man. Despite his emotional frailties, however, he enjoyed his work with the Hopkins literary society, a debating club. Endowing it with a new name, Hopkins House of Commons, together with a new constitution of his own composition, he wrote a set of bylaws and presided over the meeting at which his plans were accepted with unanimity. He confessed to a sense of power in dealing with men collectively that he did not always feel in dealing with them singly. Throughout the challenges and frustrations, and the achievements, of those two years at Johns Hopkins, Wilson constantly besought Ellen to "continue to love me as you do now."[33]

By the time of his marriage, he had completed, after months of deliberation, the two-year course at Johns Hopkins. Initially, he eschewed a degree, confiding to Ellen that both his mental and physical health would be jeopardized "by a forced march through fourteen thousand pages of dry reading," and that he would find books of his own choosing more profitable. Ever mindful of his physical frailties, he fretted about overtaxing his eyes and about dull headaches. He was not oblivious that he was sacrificing a great deal in giving up the degree, including the possibility that he would "fetch a bigger price with a Ph.D. label."[34] But he was sure, he explained, that in not pursuing a degree he would be guarding his lungs against consumption. However, one year later, he would present as his dissertation the heavily derivative, heartily praised *Congressional Government*, published by Houghton Mifflin in October 1885. Passing the departmental examination and receiving a Ph.D. from Johns Hopkins, he claimed that he had pursued the graduate degree for Ellen's sake; and she, in turn, was pleased that it would afford him more opportunity for advancement.

A scent of orange blossoms pervaded the manse of the Independent Presbyterian Church in Savannah, Georgia, where its pastor, the Reverend Isaac Stockton Keith Axson, grandfather of the bride, and the Reverend Joseph Ruggles Wilson, father of the groom, married Ellen Louise Axson and Woodrow Wilson at seven o'clock on the evening of June 24, 1885. There was no music, no bouquet for the bride, but Ellen did wear a white dress of her own making and her mother's lace veil for a wedding that was performed in a matter of seconds.[35] Three years younger than her twenty-eight-year-old husband, she looked vulnerable and pristine. She had suffered the death of both her parents and had accepted responsibility for rearing her orphaned siblings. Realistic about her family's medical history, she was burdened by her father's mental breakdown and her own possible fragility. Though she thought of herself as being strong as "India rubber," she spoke before marrying of having a thorough physical examination and of abandoning the thought of marriage in the event that she was not quite sound. Wilson responded by bringing up the matter of his own delicate health, asking her what right he had to beg her to marry him. At Ellen's suggestion, they then abandoned the discussion of medical problems.[36]

CHAPTER 2

"Among the foremost thinkers of his age"

An offer, in April 1885, to teach at the newly founded college of Bryn Mawr had made Wilson's marriage possible. Fortified with a salary of $1,500 annually for two years as an associate professor in history, and with permission to supplement his income by lecturing elsewhere, Wilson was able to tell Ellen that she would no longer need to turn her talents to moneymaking, and that her undivided attention was essential to his ambitions. Bryn Mawr College, with two or three buildings and forty-two students on an old farm ten miles northwest of Philadelphia, was intended to serve as the female counterpart to rigorous institutions of male education and was thought of as a kind of Miss "Jane" or "Johanna" Hopkins.[1] Yet teaching at Bryn Mawr seemed to leave Wilson immune to any visionary concept for women. In the not distant future, when the issue of women's suffrage loomed and he, as president, was first called upon to take a decisive stand, he was oddly without convictions.

Wilson was in agreement with Ellen's lack of sympathy for "that false talk about a woman's right to live her own life," if that meant the right of women to live apart from men.[2] The family was the foundation, the life and soul, of society; marriage ennobled women as nothing else could do, and if a woman could not preserve her individuality within the family, she simply had no individuality worth preserving. A creed that held otherwise—that claimed for women the independent rights enjoyed by men—would require the male to assume those duties abandoned by mother and housekeeper. "Oh, it is a shame so to pervert the truth!" Wilson said. Women did have a right to live their own lives, did have mental and moral gifts of a sort and of a perfection that men lacked, but with this fundamental distinction: "They have not the *same* gifts that men have. Their life must supplement man's life, and it cannot supplement man's life without being in closest wifely commune with it."[3]

To a remarkable degree, given her early aspirations, Ellen fulfilled his ideal. Married less than a year, she remained supremely content. Her husband could not possibly know, she told him, how he satisfied her pride and ambition, how she gloried in his "splendid gifts, his noble, beautiful character, that rare charm of manner and 'presence,'—indeed *every*thing" about him.[4] Instead of painting, she sewed, studied at Mrs. S. T. Rohrer's Cooking School in Philadelphia, bore three daughters— the first, Margaret Woodrow Wilson in 1886—within four years, and diligently read the books her husband brought to her, cheerfully noting that she would equal or exceed him in his contempt for French literature and particularly for Balzac. On the whole, Ellen seemed to think herself ennobled by marriage, as her husband assumed a woman might well be who recognized her duties. Ellen spoke of being privileged in her marriage to a man whom she alone, as yet, recognized as a genius. She felt honored to be chosen, as she repeatedly told him. She had one wish above all: "I want you to love *me*."[5] That he did so, we may judge from her response of August 27, 1902, to this ardent husband of seventeen years:

> How do you expect me to keep *my* head, you dear thing . . . when you lavish upon me such delicious praise? Surely there was never such a lover before, and even after all these years it seems almost too good to be true that you are my lover. All I can say in return is that I love you as you deserve to be loved—as much as you can possibly *want* to be loved.[6]

Woodrow Wilson's sentiments about the place of women in society, embraced by Ellen, were unmodified by his experience as a teacher. Never a warm admirer of higher education for women, Wilson made plain his convictions about his students' limitations. There was little question that young women did extremely well in their literary studies— Greek, Latin, and English. But he complained that, in his courses in economics and history, female students were too passive, too complacent ("they just sit and take it all").

Wilson was extremely restless at Bryn Mawr. Preoccupied with the demands of teaching and lecturing, he was all the while seized with ambition to write about the genesis and development of modern democratic institutions. By November of 1886, he was exploring ways to detach himself from the college and go abroad for one or two years. He asked a friend to estimate the cost of living in Berlin for a man, wife, and child who would not care "a peppercorn for style, but who would require for a while, perhaps, a nurse, and always comfort."[7] He wanted to learn the German language, essential to his research for *The State*, a college textbook on comparative government from antiquity through the nineteenth century, for which he had signed a contract the previous spring. He also required leisure to know, better than he could from any vantage point at Bryn Mawr, "the modern world."

To help her husband with his research, Ellen studied German so that she might translate and write digests of the *Handbuch des öffentlichen Rechts der Gegenwart,* edited by Heinrich Marquandsen, the essential source for Wilson's project.[8] However, the birth of their second daughter, Jessie Woodrow, in Gainesville on August 28, 1887, precluded the proposed venture abroad. A subsequent attempt to qualify for the post of assistant secretary of state in Washington came to nothing. Frustrated by his inability to find alternatives to his Bryn Mawr responsibilities, the thirty-one-year-old professor was despondent about his present situation and his future.

An offer to teach at Wesleyan University in the fall of 1888 promised a better salary and a chance that Wilson, who had "for a long time been hungry for a class of *men*," could at last fill that void in his life.[9] He broke his contract with Bryn Mawr on grounds that the college had not fulfilled a promise to provide him with an assistant. The family of four moved from the seclusion of the cottage in a deep ravine on Gulph Road, Bryn Mawr, Pennsylvania, into a colonial house at 106 High Street, facing directly the broad campus in Middletown, Connecticut. Wilson lectured juniors and seniors on political economy and on the Constitution of the United States, continually examining and analyzing his own philosophy of politics as he wrote "The Character of Democracy in the United States" for the *Atlantic Monthly* and lectured at Brown University on "state and social reform."

A popular professor now with a burgeoning reputation, his liveliness, enthusiasm, and earnestness were infectious. He founded at Wesleyan— as he had done elsewhere as an undergraduate and a graduate student— a kind of political laboratory, this time a British-influenced debating society known as the Wesleyan House of Commons. He continued his lectures at Johns Hopkins, begun in 1887, during his third year at Bryn Mawr—the same year Wake Forest College in North Carolina awarded him an honorary degree. He was elected president of the Johns Hopkins Alumni and was taken into Phi Beta Kappa. His message was spreading. He called, in messianic terms, for statesmen who would lead the forces of reconstruction and renewal, and he spoke and wrote of an America "obliged to pull herself together, adopt a new regimen of life, husband her resources, concentrate her strength, steady her methods, sober her views, restrict her vagaries, trust her best, not her average." He prophesied a time of great change.[10] He also played tennis and coached football. A third daughter, Eleanor Randolph, the "Yankee" daughter, was born in Middletown in 1889.

Wesleyan would prove to be only a way station on Wilson's road back to Princeton. He did not find its student body sufficiently stimulating—rather, the students seemed culturally deprived, owing to a parentage, for the most part, "of narrow circumstances and of correspondingly narrow thought." In 1890, Wilson achieved the post he had actively solicited, an appointment to the College of New Jersey (Princeton University after 1896) as professor of jurisprudence and political economy. Exhilarated by that recognition, he was proud to be selected by a college that he considered "a big institution of the first class, with superior facilities for work, with the best class of students, and affording a member of its faculty a certain academic standing."[11] If the Wilsons ever had tranquil years, they were the first five spent in Princeton—where he would serve on the faculty for twelve years, and as president for eight—with a constant flow of family visitors adding to the congenial atmosphere.[12] Wilson was never to seem so happy again, nor was he ever quite so well. Indeed, his chronically fragile health was evident even during the relatively untroubled Princeton years.

He lectured on American constitutional law, international law, English common law and administration, on public law and general jurisprudence, the philosophy of law and of personal rights. He was again hailed as a first-class lecturer, despite his somewhat distant personality, a certain dignity and distinction that held him aloof. He continued to lecture at Johns Hopkins and began to do so at the New York Law School. In 1892, at the age of thirty-six, he was offered the presidency of six universities. The seventh would be Princeton.

Wilson's soaring reputation could only reinforce Ellen's conviction of her husband's greatness. She marveled at "such strength and nobility of character combined with such ineffable tenderness, such unselfishness and thoughtfulness in things great and small, a nature so exquisitely gifted in power of sympathy, of understanding others." When she added to all this a "strength of purpose and of will and powers of application which result in achievements so great," she could only conclude that Woodrow, though still young, must be ranked "among the foremost thinkers of his age!"[13]

Effusive, tender, and protective, Ellen had allowed her critical abilities, once so helpful to Wilson, to lapse. In the seventh year of their marriage she had elevated him to the realm of an icon, to be worshiped as well as cherished. "To think of you, dear," she wrote in June 1892, "is a pleasure like that derived from a perfect picture or poem. It is as if a master artist had conceived a grand ideal, 'had seen it steadily and seen it whole,' and then with truly magic skill had been able to *realize* his vision."[14]

From his college days onward, Wilson had written constantly, ambitiously, authoritatively, and sometimes verbosely, not only to supplement his income but to enhance his reputation. He was at his most prolific during his Princeton years from 1893 through 1902, when he published nine volumes and thirty-five articles—including a variety of personal essays, two of which were entitled "The Author Himself" and "On an Author's Choice of Company." *Division and Reunion*, a political history of the United States between 1828 and 1893, from the age of Jackson through the Civil War and Reconstruction, was published in March 1893, followed by *An Old Master and Other Political Essays* and by *Mere Literature*. Wilson's treatment of *George Washington* in 1896 as "a great English statesman" was judged "far beyond *merely* clever brilliant work" by the reverential Ellen,[15] and as "the lowest point in his literary career" by a more recent critic, the historian Arthur S. Link.[16] *A History of the American People* was something of a best-seller when serialized by *Harper's Magazine* in 1901 and published in five volumes in 1902.

In his writings, Wilson is perhaps at his most revealing in his exclusion of Thomas Jefferson, Alexander Hamilton, and John Adams, among others, from "A Calendar of Great Americans," published in the *Forum* in February 1894. "I can find no man in history I should care to be like," he told Ellen. Possibly he thought of himself as the embodiment of his own definition of the true American spirit—as opposed to the "un-American" Jefferson.[17] Ingenuously casting himself as "optimistically progressive and hopeful and confident," he dismissed the third president of the United States as "unspeculative, unfastidious."

When discussion shifted from her husband's intellectual and professional accomplishments to the matter of his health, Ellen, aware since their courtship days of his physical frailty, was understandably protective and discreet. He had complained of a sharp attack of indigestion in the autumn of 1895, five years after his arrival at Princeton, and was diagnosed as having neuritis, which he called writer's cramp. When he lost the use of his right hand the following year, his father feared that Woodrow was going to die. He had probably suffered a stroke. It seemed that cerebral vascular disease would stealthily erode his health again in 1900, 1904, 1906, and 1907. In 1896, he compensated within days for the loss of the use of his right hand by forming perfect script with his left, a feat substantiating the diagnosis in his boyhood—supported by his being a poor mathematician—of "developmental dyslexia,"[18] a complex condition associated with a mixed cerebral dominance affecting language. A slow reader into adult life, he unknowingly described the symptoms of dyslexia (that is, of impaired reading ability) when he complained to Ellen that "steady reading always demands of me more expenditure of resolution and dogged energy than any other sort of work."[19] Dyslexia may have compounded the pressures that precipitated his departure from Davidson College after one year and from law school six months before graduation, as well as his procrastination over the completion of his doctoral thesis at Johns Hopkins.[20]

In that summer of 1896, Ellen, certain that Wilson needed a complete respite from his daily obligations—the "college thoughts and regrets" that crowded his mind hint at his habitually delicate and even tormented mental state—urged him to take a bicycle tour through Scotland and England. He sailed for Glasgow in June and returned in August. By July, the weakness and pain in his right arm had dulled to a slight numbness in the tips of his first and second fingers. The use of a pen with a large handle eased his remaining difficulties in writing. During his absence, Ellen acted as her husband's business agent in negotiations with Johns Hopkins about fees for a proposed three-year course of lectures. It went without saying, she told Hopkins's president, Daniel Coit Gilman, that her husband would not wish to embark on the first year without some definite understanding as to the rate of remuneration in successive years, and that he could simply not afford, having built a house, to lecture indefinitely at so low a rate. "I put it all very circumspectly and unobjectionably I think."[21]

Though he did not seem to complain of any specific ailment, Wilson was encouraged to go overseas again in 1899, and he sailed on June 17 aboard the *Furnessia* in the congenial company of his brother-in-law Stockton Axson. Wilson was frankly ashamed of letting himself be talked into this trip, for allowing Ellen to conspire in persuading him that he "*needed* this elaborate self-indulgence." For most of his early trips, there had been money for only one person's passage, and Ellen was convinced that sea voyages restored her husband. In 1903, Wilson took Ellen abroad ostensibly for a second honeymoon. The voyage, as with his other travels, was not only prompted but justified, it was said, by his need for rest and relief from daily challenges, namely overwork, disappointment, sorrow, and discouragement. In February of 1905, Wilson, joined by Ellen, spent five weeks in Florida recuperating from a hernia operation, following an attack of phlebitis in one leg. After another stroke, in 1906, the entire family accompanied Wilson abroad. Again needing respite from the tensions of Princeton, he traveled to Bermuda alone in 1907, 1908, and 1909. Ellen budgeted for his lone trips by skimping on her own needs. She seldom bought anything new. Her children teased her for years over the remark of an acquaintance: "Mrs. Wilson, every fall you look sweeter in that brown dress."[22]

Wilson frankly looked on his election as president of Princeton, on June 9, 1902, as helpful in settling his future. It also gave him "a sense of *position* and of definite, tangible tasks," he told Ellen, "which takes the flutter and restlessness from my spirits!"[23] Ellen's reaction to this advancement was ecstatic: "The letters and the newspapers are both wonderful; the Alumni seem mad with joy and outsiders almost as enthusiastic. As for the Professors, students and Princeton people generally,—well the scenes here were indescribable! It is enough," she wrote a friend, "to frighten a man to death to have people love and believe in him so and *expect* so much."[24]

She gloried in many aspects of the election: to be chosen unanimously by the twenty-six trustees on the first ballot was unique in the college's history. And wasn't it wonderful, she rejoiced, "especially when one thinks that Woodrow made no . . . effort to get it . . . !" In more sober moments, Ellen recognized the drawbacks of the appointment, the heavy sacrifices it imposed on people of their temperament. Her husband's literary work must suffer greatly—just how much remained to be seen. They must leave their dear home, and what she saw as a sweet, almost ideal life in which he was simply a man of letters, to live in that great, stately, troublesome "Prospect," the president's mansion, and be forever giving huge receptions and stately dinners. Both were rather brokenhearted about this move, she professed, although she tried not to let her mind dwell on that aspect of the change. It was up to her to fulfill these new duties and responsibilities to the best of her ability.

Wilson's appointment was unique in another respect. By tradition the university's president was an ordained Presbyterian minister. Instead, the Board of Trustees had now chosen a preacher by inheritance, instinct, and gift, a moralist and reformer who referred to his talks and speeches as his sermons. Six years earlier he had spoken on the topic "Princeton in the Nation's Service," declaring that Princeton must be a school of duty, that duty must rest on religion, and that "there is nothing that gives such pith to public service as religion."[25]

On the bright, clear day of Wilson's inauguration on October 25, 1902, with banners floating from turrets and towers above autumnal treetops, he stood slim, erect, keen-eyed, a secular preacher with a visionary message. "In planning for Princeton," Wilson said, "we are planning for the country. The service of institutions of learning is not private, but public. It is plain what the nation needs as its affairs grow more and more complex and its interests begin to touch the ends of the earth. It needs efficient and enlightened men. The universities of the country must take part in supplying them."[26]

There was not the least hint at this time that Princeton, in less than ten years, would be "supplying," first, the state of New Jersey and, subsequently, the entire country with the services of Princeton's president. Nor that in less than twenty years, pleading for support for the country's entrance into the League of Nations, he would echo the words he spoke now: "I ask that you will look upon me not as a man to do something apart, but as a man who asks the privilege of leading you and being believed in by you while he tried to do the things in which he knows you believe."[27]

On the morning of May 28, 1906, Woodrow Wilson awakened completely blind in his left eye. A blood vessel had burst and the patient was diagnosed as having arteriosclerosis, hardening of the arteries due to prolonged high pressure on the brain and nerves. Wilson's father had died of the same disease three years earlier. Ellen recalled her father-in-law's harrowing last months under their roof, crying and screaming "like a person under the influence of ether."[28] But she comforted herself that her husband's condition, "an awful thing—a dying by inches,—and incurable," had been discovered in an early stage and that it had already been arrested. The doctor, in his cautious diagnosis, told her that the patient should lead a quiet life, and that, while fifty-year-old arteries could not go back to an earlier condition, he expected Wilson to be as well as he needed to be for any work he could reasonably undertake the next fall. The doctor warned, however, that excess work was dangerous, and he supposed that Wilson had done too much in the last few years.

This first retinal hemorrhage in 1906 was a signal of the severity of Wilson's underlying condition—his youthful complaints of fatigue and indigestion imply even earlier symptoms—a warning that would inexorably lead, thirteen years later, to dire consequences. When Wilson was told to rest his eye for the entire summer, the family decided to rent Loughrigg Cottage at Rydal in the English Lake District, in the shadow of Loughrigg Mountain, a short walk from William Wordsworth's home. In fact, Wilson's vision in his left eye was impaired from that time for the rest of his life, and he would suffer temporary paralysis of his right hand in 1908, the combination "characteristic of occlusive disease of the internal carotid artery, the major supplier of blood to the brain."[29]

His family preferred to evaluate Wilson's physical state quite differently and with greater optimism. According to Eleanor, her father was in good health again by the time of his return to America. Vigorously attacking his work, he began his fight to rid Princeton of the evils of the club system he so despised because of its intrinsically elitist premise. He hoped that, under his new plan, the dining halls of the proposed residential quadrangles would not only draw students away from the socially divisive eating clubs, but would also save the university from the danger of developing "*socially* as Harvard did and as Yale is tending to do."[30]

Wilson's eyes turned steel gray, and his long, angular jaw tightened at the *Princetonian*'s annual dinner in 1906, when he deliberately called attention to his "lonely privilege, in gatherings of educated men, to be the only person who speaks of education." As president of Princeton, he envisioned concerns of the mind as rightly being the supreme consideration among the undergraduate body. His goal was threefold. In his reform of the curriculum he would adopt the Oxford tutorial system. In his effort to make Princeton an example of pure democracy, he dreamed of scholars and students mingling in the newly built quadrangles, of every student in this inspiring environment "bent upon the errands of the mind" with the ultimate goal of serving his nation.[31] As for the graduate school, he thought of it as the apex of what Princeton could offer: it ought to be at the heart of the campus; efforts to locate it on a pleasant old estate at Merwick one mile away had to be regarded as part of an intolerable separatist movement.

Wilson's uncompromising refusal of a bequest of $250,000 for the construction of a John R. Thompson Graduate College initiated a definitive struggle between him and Andrew F. West, professor of Latin and dean of the graduate school—a contest involving the faculty and the

Board of Trustees. While Wilson's primary interest lay with the under-
graduates, West was most urgently concerned with the graduate facility.
To Wilson's mind, the projects were interdependent, to be unified in
a location where the "windows of the graduate college must open
straight upon the walks and quadrangles and lecture halls of the *studium
general*."[32]

Wilson appeared the winner when a new offer of half a million dollars
by William Cooper Procter, class of 1883, toward building the graduate
school at a separate site was rejected. As of February 7, 1910, Wilson
could write, "At last we are free to govern the University as our judgments and consciences dictate!"[33] His great sense of relief ended three
months later. West, with the backing of former president Grover Cleveland before his death in Princeton, had gradually become convinced of
the impracticality of linking the two projects. Three years Wilson's
senior, a gifted scholar, a witty man with a robust physique and a sea captain's ruddy skin, hearty voice, and manner, West had turned down the
presidency of the Massachusetts Institute of Technology to remain at
Princeton. On May 18, 1910, he accepted an appointment as coexecutor
of a $2-million bequest from Isaac C. Wyman of Salem, Massachusetts,
class of 1848, for purposes of building the graduate school.

Wilson's response to West's action was sheer dismay. Thwarted in
the realization of his goals for Princeton, in which he had an immense
emotional as well as intellectual stake, unable to comprehend or even
allow for differing opinions regarding financial considerations, Wilson
declared "the game is up"; he was not interested in administering what
he referred to as a club, and he believed he could be elected governor of
New Jersey. His failure to win the battle at Princeton, as he saw it, fore-
shadowed facets of his personality in later years: his consuming belief in
his superior judgment, his intolerance of rejection, his utter inflexibility.

Wilson thwarted was a vindictive man. In a drastic move—another omen
of future behavior when denied goals he believed sacred—he sought,
unavailingly, Dean West's resignation. A critically wounding aspect of
this confrontation at Princeton was Wilson's sense that loved friends had
failed him in a crucial test of loyalty. He felt personally betrayed by
those who did not agree with his ideals—most profoundly by Professor
John Grier Hibben. Initially, the entire Wilson family considered Jack and
Jennie Hibben "good neighbors in the rare sense of the word, invariably
the first to appear when anyone was ill or help of any sort was needed."[34]
Hibben was the friend who had taught Wilson to play golf, the friend who

had accompanied him to Philadelphia in May 1906, to see an eminent ophthalmologist, Dr. George Edmund de Schweinitz, about Wilson's hemorrhaged eye. He was the friend whom Wilson had appointed acting president in 1906, when he himself was too ill to participate in Princeton's commencement. Seven years earlier, in September 1899, Wilson had told the Hibbens, "Our love for you both, has put you beyond the reach of competition."[35] Eventually, feelings about these two men became so polarized that Hibben's admirers would contrast the "conciliatory man" who came to manage the university with tact and wisdom with Woodrow Wilson, the "autocrat" and "unlimited monarch."[36]

Stunned and desolate, Wilson would claim that, as a result of his disappointment in Hibben, he had lost his faith in friendship and would always fear close relationships. When he spoke of the pleasure, among friends, of sharing thoughts on matters of lasting importance, Wilson did not touch on his own habitual intolerance of differing views, or on his need for absolute loyalty to his ideals and goals. His custom of holding his beliefs like a bulldog, as Stockton Axson said, was to have a tragically destructive effect not only on future friendships but on his service to the nation.

Perhaps it was a defensive posture in the face of his alienation, but two years before his official resignation on October 20, 1910, at one of the critical points of the controversy, Wilson professed to being bored with his presidency of Princeton. His confidante on this occasion was Mary Allen Hulbert Peck. Their close friendship would escalate to a rumored love affair during Wilson's presidential campaigns, and subsequently during his courtship of Edith Bolling Galt.

Significantly, it was in Bermuda—where Wilson felt that he found complete contentment—that he first met Mary Peck in 1907. The attraction between the two was the cause, Ellen Wilson was said to admit, of the only unhappiness in her entire marriage.[37] Perhaps he had turned to his vivid new friend, if not physically, at least in a notably affectionate correspondence, at a period when he could no longer depend on his wife to hear out every nuance of his innermost thoughts and longings. Ellen was heartbroken and withdrawn after the accidental drowning of her brother Edward and his family in 1906. For a time, she responded only in pathetic nods to attempts to involve her in conversation and looked so sad that her daughter Eleanor gave up trying to arouse her. Having weathered her daughters' serious illnesses and her husband's ill health and hernia operation, she was further distraught over her brother Stockton's chronic breakdowns, so reminiscent of their father's erratic mental condition. When Ellen retreated into a "marked depression lasting from 1906 to 1910," Wilson turned to Mary Peck as his confidante, to assuage his wants and wounds, explore his future, and plot the later years of his career and life. In Mary, he marveled, he had found just the friend he had wanted and needed, "a perfect chum, an ideal companion."[38]

Having, as he wrote to Mary Peck, nothing new or entertaining to say about his daily duties as college president, what interested him was an analysis of the nation's political parties. In a self-serving exegesis, Wilson tried to reconcile his asserted principles with his invincible ego and with his cause at Princeton, which was the source of painful concern to him. He spoke of his desire to turn to new ventures, dwelt on his prospective transformation from academic to politician, and recounted how a Washington newsman had referred to his unimpeachable character and high intelligence as having misled New Jersey's "highwaymen" politicians into thinking him an easy mark, and how he had the Wall Street crowd "scared stiff." The national political situation was, in his opinion, desperate; and he speculated on what sort of man would be willing to take on William Jennings Bryan, the perennial Democratic candidate, denied the presidency three times, in the elections of 1896, 1900, and 1908. Wilson protested that he himself was not the candidate, but he was prepared to help the right man and carefully described his method for fulfilling and financing this goal. He proposed an imaginary ultimatum: he would give the Princeton trustees just two years and no more to do what was their bounden duty regarding reform of the university. Otherwise, he counted on retiring on a grant of $4,000 from the Carnegie Foundation for the Advancement of Teaching together with $2,000 of his own money, at which time he would be glad "to lend my pen and voice and all my thought and energy to anyone who proposed a genuine rationalization and rehabilitation of the Democratic party on lines of principle and statesmanship."[39]

In this discussion, Wilson was transparently disingenuous. He had obviously given considerable thought to his own candidacy for elective office and had been sketching with precision a self-portrait, as the man who must devote himself to principles, to ideas, to definite programs, "a man with a cause, not a candidacy."[40] He would be willing to take the initiative, to venture into the field alone, but then yield it "with the best will in the world" to one of his rivals. The man who initiated such an adventure, he well knew, would be misunderstood and easily discredited by the forces of jealousy. He was even willing to offer himself, though "certainly," he insisted, "I do not want the presidency."[41] The more closely he studied the office, the more reason he saw not to covet it, as the sacrifice might be more than a man could physically withstand. Nevertheless, inclination was greater than reluctance. Confessedly born political, he chafed like a dog on a leash, he said, that he must sit in academic seclusion. And frail though he might feel physically, he admitted that he would enjoy the fray that would free him from the polite restraints of academic controversy and allow him to speak out.

In effect, Wilson had already begun his campaign for political office. Princeton, from the start, had afforded him a platform for impassioned pronouncements at lecterns from Orange, New Jersey, to Carnegie Hall; from Charleston, South Carolina, to the Waldorf-Astoria. In the winter of 1905–6 he had talked about the connection of the university to a world in progress, speculated on *what would Christ have done in our day, in our place with our opportunities,* pondered whether governments should supply an equilibrium rather than a disturbing force, and championed a "Newness of Spirit," defined as Americanism.

Some days before William Howard Taft took over the presidency on March 4, 1909, Wilson railed against a lack of leadership on burning national issues: the "tariff of abominations," the challenge to government authority by railroads and trusts, and life insurance company scandals. In Chicago on February 12, before an audience celebrating the hundredth anniversary of Abraham Lincoln's birth, Wilson virtually unfurled his open declaration for public office: "We have heat enough; what we want is light. Anybody can stir up emotions, but who is master of men enough to take the saddle and guide those awakened emotions? Anybody can cry a nation awake to the necessities of reform, but who shall frame the reform but a man who is cool?"[42]

By September 1909, Wilson was in invigorated spirits, immersed in an article to be published that October in the *North American Review* under the title "The Tariff of Make-Believe." Without inhibition, he relished sharing with Mary Peck every nuance of its creation. He was, he readily acknowledged, "trying to poison every arrow the article contains, subtly enough to conceal the poison but effectually enough to kill." Nor did he claim that he was writing in a judicial frame of mind: "I want to hit hard, and if I observe the rules of the game I hope I may be forgiven the zest and enjoyment with which I hit." Reluctant to return to Princeton and the constraints of academia, he yearned for the "rough and tumble of the political arena. My instinct all turns that way." [43]

Two months later, before the McCormick Theological Seminary of Chicago, on November 2, 1909, Wilson defined his position: he was determined to live up to what he considered to be the core of Christianity, to be an "indomitable individual." Every turning point in the history of mankind had devolved on the choice of an individual whose spirit stood stiff and who said, "I go this way. Let any man go another way who pleases."[44]

A few years earlier, on January 18, 1906, after his delivery of a bracing series of lectures, Wilson had been hailed by the editor of the *Charleston (S.C.) News & Courier*, Colonel J. C. Hemphill, as the most promising of Southern candidates for the presidency. Presently, on October 20, 1910, Wilson, backed by Colonel George Harvey, founder of the influential *Harper's Weekly*, took a decisive step toward that goal. The reasons given for his formal resignation from the university he had "so long loved and sought to serve" seemed reasonable and even gracious and screened his sense of struggle and discouragement. "In view of Princeton's immemorial observance of the obligation of public service," he claimed he could not have done otherwise than to accept his nomination for forty-third governor of New Jersey. He was elected on November 5, 1910, with 1,333,682 votes—almost double the number received by Vivian Murchison Lewis, his seasoned opponent. Wilson's inauguration took place on January 17, 1911.

The election was a triumph for the man who vowed he would be "an indomitable individual," for the "Presbyterian priest" who eluded the taint of boss dictation from New Jersey's high-powered Senator James Smith Jr. Thwarting party bosses who had elected him "for the job of window dressing," Wilson, without a qualm, "proceeded to clean up the shop."[45] Plunging into a plan for reform, which included new laws known as the Seven Sisters,[46] he proposed an innovative election law, a Corrupt Practices Act, laws regulating public utilities, and an Employers' Liability Act.

As though Wilson's election as governor of New Jersey were tantamount to his becoming president of the United States, Ellen—at the moment her husband left for the New Jersey Democratic convention— sensed imminent change: "I can see, that our beautiful private life is gone."[47]

CHAPTER 3

"Turn a corner and meet your fate"

Ellen was proud of this grand fulfillment of her husband's nearly for-saken ambition, but the possibility of Wilson's holding the highest office in the land stunned her. Having suffered keenly from the verbal assaults launched on him, she no doubt took pleasure in learning that his enemies at Princeton had unwittingly kicked him upstairs—even perhaps as far as the White House. Yet she dreaded the effect of politics on his delicate health. Responding to her fears, Wilson reasoned, "In politics you expect fights and enemies."

As Ellen deliberated her role exhaustively, her quiet demeanor belied her concern. Though gentle, she was at the same time exceedingly firm. An insatiable reader who had probed Kant and Hegel in a period of religious doubt, she betrayed a hint of skepticism in her search for truth. She was responsible in many ways, whether subtle or overt, for rounding the precise corners of her husband's intense convictions and stringent principles, for enhancing his life with her love of art and poetry. Wilson proudly hung her copy of Bouguereau's *Madonna* in Princeton, at the White House, and again in retirement at S Street. And he learned to share his wife's love of poetry—of William Wordsworth above all, and to a lesser degree, Robert Browning: poets whom they read aloud to each other and to their family. On one occasion, in Denver, on May 7, 1911, Wilson shrewdly expressed his debt to her before an audience packed with suffragists. His eloquent tribute to Ellen's influence was no less sincere for being pragmatic in his efforts to appease hecklers regarding his position on women's right to vote. "From Mrs. Wilson, not only have I learned much but have gained something of a literary reputation. Whenever I need a poetic quotation she supplies it, and in this way, I acquire the fame of possessing a complete anthology of poetry."[1]

If Ellen heightened Wilson's appreciation of literary and pictorial art, he reciprocated by educating her in history, economics, and political science. He introduced her, during their first acquaintance, to two of his favorite British authors, the social scientist Walter Bagehot and the essayist and critic Philip Gilbert Hamerton. Without being one of those horrid "advanced women," Ellen, as her brother Stockton Axson said, was astutely interested in politics and unquestionably her husband's firmest advocate. She read the significant newspapers of New Jersey and New York, clipping all references to Wilson and giving him those he ought to see—at the same time making suggestions that went into the little book he always carried in his vest pocket. That habit of scrutinizing newspapers would continue in the White House, encompassing greater breadth and involving helping hands. Large yellow sheets pasted with extracts from newspapers from all parts of the country were regularly submitted by Wilson's staff to Ellen and her family.

Ellen, reported to be in sturdy spirits once again, was engrossed by every question concerning her husband. Close observers, including Wilson's secretary—the blue-eyed, pink-cheeked former Democratic legislator and lawyer Joseph Patrick Tumulty, from Jersey City—would say that she was a better politician than the president, that her political judgment was shrewd and sound,[2] that she was the one who "furnished the faith and sticking quality." Tumulty claimed that it was Ellen Wilson who prevented her husband from withdrawing his name at the critical moment during the Baltimore presidential convention, in late June 1912. At one point it certainly seemed that her husband had lost the nomination for president to the Speaker of the House of Representatives, Champ Clark, from Missouri, whom Wilson called "a sort of elephantine 'smart Aleck.' "[3] While Wilson's political supporters were ready to throw in the sponge, Ellen insisted that the fight was not over.

Ellen smoothed her husband's route to the presidency at every turn in her genteel manner, acknowledging favors and paying homage where homage was owed. It was Ellen, unquestionably, who acknowledged her husband's debt to Colonel George Harvey, a powerful political journalist, editor of the conservative *Harper's Weekly*, and a future ambassador to Great Britain—the one whom she regarded as Wilson's ablest advocate. Revealing her political expertise, as well as her commercial aspirations in regard to her husband's literary output, she had thanked Harvey profusely in November of 1910 for all he had done for Wilson in his election as governor of New Jersey. She also confided her hope that the present limelight would help to sell Woodrow's writings, for it "is very inconvenient for a public man to be penniless."[4]

Two years later, with the presidency at stake, Ellen's grave concern about

Harvey's alienation was manifest. On January 12, 1912, she solicited her cousin, Judge Robert Ewing, to counteract rumors that Henry Watterson, editor of the *Louisville Courier-Journal,* had turned violently against Wilson because of the latter's alleged ill treatment of George Harvey. During a meeting with Harvey and Watterson, Wilson had requested that the Colonel remove the "For President: Woodrow Wilson" flyer on his conservative magazine's masthead as damaging to Wilson's more liberal reputation, and though acquiescent, Harvey was grievously and, as it turned out, irrevocably wounded.

Writing to her cousin in Louisville for help in regaining Harvey's support, Ellen gave the story of the meeting: Harvey had begged Woodrow to be candid in answer to the question of whether the *Weekly's* "constant booming of him seemed to him unwise or embarrassing (in view, of course, of *Harper's* alleged connection with Wall Street)"; Woodrow had responded "in his usual absolutely open, frank manner," and Colonel Harvey had appeared to take the presidential candidate's negative comments "in perfect good humor and said he would have to 'put on the soft pedal.'"[5] The men then parted in the most cordial manner, her husband never for a moment dreaming that Harvey and Watterson had misunderstood him, or that they had been hurt.

Ellen was at a loss how to reconstitute the relationship. Seeking some resolution of this politically hazardous situation, she told her cousin that her husband had, after all, been encouraged to speak up, but that she did allow for his possibly awkward presentation of his feelings. In this regard, she explained, Woodrow himself, trying to make amends, had written to Colonel Harvey and had received a friendly reply—yet the reply showed Harvey's wounds; and "I do not know when we have been more deeply distressed than at that discovery."[6]

In his brooding on the prospect of becoming president, Wilson seemed to have forgotten his early yearning for national power. "The thought of the Presidency annoys me in a way," he wrote to his friend Mary Peck.[7] He may have assumed this attitude because he considered the presidential boom to be premature, since he had hardly begun his term as state governor. However, he did insist, "I do not want to be President."[8] His motives were both reasonable and unreasonable. "There is too little play in it, too little time for one's friends, too much distasteful publicity and fuss and frills." Instead, he enjoyed going his own way. "I love the affairs of the world and want to handle them, but I do not want to wear their harness and trappings."[9]

Woodrow Wilson's greatest single challenge at the Democratic convention of 1912 in Baltimore was to win the support of William Jennings Bryan. Lawyer, orator, former editor, and representative from Nebraska, Bryan had led the now moribund free-silver movement: "You shall not press down upon the brow of labor this crown of thorns. You shall not crucify mankind upon a cross of gold," he had admonished a spellbound audience at the Democratic National Convention in Chicago in 1896. Despite Bryan's political prominence, Wilson had, in 1897, dismissed him as a hollow orator; ten years later, more skeptical than ever, he fervently wished "we could do something, at once dignified and effective, to knock Mr. Bryan once and for all into a cocked hat!" In the following year, 1908, Wilson conceded that Bryan was "the most charming and lovable of men personally but foolish and dangerous in his theoretical beliefs." Wilson also asked at that time to be excused from speaking from the same platform with Bryan at the Jefferson dinner. Wilson's victory as a Democrat who carried an Eastern Republican state in his election as governor in 1910 caught Bryan's attention. From that time, the two men were rivals for leadership of the Democratic Party, and it was thought that "a single mistake in that delicate relationship might have made all the difference in the world at Baltimore in June 1912."[10] Their first personal meeting had taken place the previous year, on March 12, 1911, Ellen being both instigator and participant.

When she learned that Bryan was to address the Theological Seminary at Princeton, she invited this most vital political rival to dinner. Then, with an eye to Wilson's interests, she telegraphed her husband, who was speaking before the Southern Commercial Congress in Atlanta, Georgia, to return home immediately to join them. As a result of a simple family dinner at the rambling Princeton Inn on Nassau Street, Wilson was unexpectedly struck with the visitor's extraordinarily forceful personality, and Bryan found himself altering preconceived notions. Instead of finding a solemn college professor, he was charmed by the "gaiety and nimble-mindedness" of Wilson and captivated by Mrs. Wilson.[11]

Exhilarated because the dinner had gone so pleasantly, Tumulty sensed that the two men, both idealists, both relentlessly sincere, had reached an understanding—"something deeper than a political entente." Turning to his hostess, Tumulty said, "You have nominated your husband, Mrs. Wilson." Ellen replied, smiling, "It was nothing at all." But Tumulty knew, as did Ellen's daughters, that this was one of many times when Ellen Wilson was of incalculable value to her husband. "She did things so quietly," Eleanor said, "that we seldom saw her hand until later."[12]

Wilson considered his nomination for the presidency at 3:30 P.M. on July 2, 1912, "a sort of political miracle." Due to Bryan's decisive support, Wilson was victorious on the forty-sixth ballot. The prospect aroused awe—and a sense of loneliness and melancholy. What he dreaded was not what would be really big and essential and worth while in the whole thing, but all that would go with it, especially the excessive personal burden of the campaign.[13]

He was pitted against the divided Republicans, the conservative President William Howard Taft, who had been renominated at the Republican National Convention, and the former president Theodore Roosevelt, candidate of the newly created Progressive, so-called Bull Moose, Party. Proclaiming overlapping philosophies of social and economic reform, Roosevelt touted the "New Nationalism" while Woodrow Wilson espoused the "New Freedom."

Near the end of August, Wilson mulled over his chances. He thought Theodore Roosevelt's strength incalculable and believed that Taft would run third. As for how Roosevelt and he differed: "Roosevelt appeals to [people's] imagination; I do not. He is a real, vivid person, whom they have seen and shouted themselves hoarse over and voted for, millions strong; I am a vague, conjectural personality, more made up of opinions and academic prepossessions than of human traits and red corpuscles." Wilson was also deeply troubled that the next president "would have a task so difficult as to be heart-breaking," and that, if elected, he would probably sacrifice his life to it. Still, all things considered, he concluded, "It would be a splendid adventure and it would make me solemnly glad to undertake it."

For Wilson, the issue of tariff revision was paramount. Another prime target was the "money-trust" managed by a random handful of financiers. (The money-trust would be under control within the first nine months of his administration—by December 23, 1913, the date of the passage of the Federal Reserve Act, which many considered the crowning achievement of Wilson's domestic legislation.) He demanded that the "old partnerships between money and power which now block us at every turn be forever broken up."[14]

At Wilson's presidential inauguration, on March 4, 1913, Henry Adams, the contentious and poetic historian, was relieved to be rid of the "blundering" Taft even as he claimed that the new president was "loathed in advance by everyone within my circuit, Democratic or Republican."[15] The issues confronting Wilson were daunting. Crippling strikes engulfed railroads, shoe factories, textile mills. United States marines occupied Nicaragua and Haiti. By autumn, Bulgaria, Serbia, Greece, and Montenegro would invade Turkey in the first Balkan war, only to have Bulgaria turn on her supposed allies, Serbia and Greece.

In late March 1913, just weeks after the inaugural luncheon at which Wilson first met Dr. Cary Travers Grayson—and was impressed by his treatment of Wilson's suddenly injured sister, Annie Wilson Howe—Wilson appointed the Virginian and Democrat as his personal physician. Grayson had served as assistant surgeon for two and a half years on a world tour aboard the USS *Maryland*, before reporting for a return assignment to the Bureau of Medicine and Surgery to serve during William H. Taft's administration (as he had during Theodore Roosevelt's) as aide to the president.[16] Well qualified—surprisingly so, perhaps, in view of his later evasive diagnoses during Wilson's grave illness—he was a Phi Beta Kappa graduate of the College of William & Mary in 1898, had studied at the Medical College of Virginia in Richmond for three years, and had earned an M.D. degree (and a Ph.G. in pharmacy from the University of the South in 1902).

Cary Grayson quickly won the absolute trust of Woodrow Wilson, whose family delighted in Grayson's company. Others were more critical of this expert horseman whose name had been romantically coupled with successive young inhabitants of the White House, including President Taft's daughter Helen. When Irwin Hoover, chief usher of the White House for more than four decades, from 1891 to 1933, referred to Grayson as a "certain little man" and "the attentive little Doctor," he seemed to imply a judgment beyond the physician's slight five-foot-seven-and-a-half-inch stature.

At the time of her father's election as governor of New Jersey, Eleanor Wilson had suffered from fearful apprehension that the office would kill him. Now, in Washington, observing her mother's outburst of tears in preparation for a preinaugural tea with the Tafts, she thought how white Ellen's face was, how helpless and tiny she looked. Eleanor felt that whatever lay ahead for her parents would be too much for them.

Shortly after one o'clock on March 4, rays of sun penetrated the gloomy, overcast inaugural day as Wilson confirmed his oath of office on

Ellen's Bible. Summoning "all honest men, all patriotic, all forward-looking men" to his side, "God helping me, I will not fail them," he vowed, "if they will counsel and sustain me."[17]

At her husband's inauguration, Ellen Wilson, age fifty-two, was a newcomer to Washington, having visited the city on only one previous occasion. At their most objective, strangers commented on her sweet, gentle manner and charming Southern accent. Partisan critics were more inclined to describe her as "short, round-faced, round-pompadoured, red-cheeked and not so becomingly dressed,"[18] as she presided over the prayer-meeting social atmosphere of the White House, where frugality had never been more scrupulously observed, nor entertainment more abominable. One cabinet member found her timid and shy, like a "good, gentle small cousin who might have been counted on to provide cookies in Rome, Georgia."[19]

Those who knew and worked with her were not misled, however, by the reticent ways of this small, plump woman with brown hair, sparkling brown eyes, and broad brow. They knew at first hand and attested to the vision and insight with which she guided her husband.[20] Ellen Wilson's reservations about moving into the large and rather garish White House seemed to evaporate. She appeared eager to fulfill the obligations of the president's wife. In her initial interview with the experienced social secretary Isabella Hagner, she had asked that Mrs. Hagner do for her what she had done for the Roosevelts. She was particularly anxious, Ellen said, that her daughters—small, intense Margaret, beautiful and deeply religious Jessie, and the fashionable Eleanor—should enjoy Washington while pursuing their individual interests.

Ellen proceeded to give the requisite teas, evening musicales, and dinners, and on one occasion when the president was confined to his room with a cold, she received the delegation of champion corn growers as well as the prizewinners in domestic science. She, far more than the president, keenly realized that the social side of the position was very much a part of the job, a strong asset when conducted with proper dignity and acumen. Observing the couple as she did, Belle Hagner sensed that the president never fully appreciated this aspect of his office, and that the time given to social affairs seemed, on the contrary, rather to irk him. Apparently it was difficult for him to feel that he could, with the same ease, entertain members of the Republican Party as freely as he did his Democratic brethren without being misunderstood by the public.

* * *

In early July 1913, a rest having been prescribed, Ellen went with her daughters to Harklakenden, in Cornish, New Hampshire, and Wilson invited Joe Tumulty and Dr. Grayson to live with him in a "dismantled, bescaffolded, and possessed" White House.[21] Virtually untouched since 1902, the White House was undergoing a drastic program of redecoration and reconstruction instigated by Ellen. Only the state rooms escaped. Ellen was resigned that little could be done about the Red Room, other than to fill it with fresh flowers. With magenta velour paneling, heavy velvet curtains, a hideous rug, and overstuffed furniture, it was voted by the family the ugliest of the salons. Improvement of the adjoining state dining room involved removal of the stuffed elk and deer heads favored by Theodore Roosevelt, mostly bought from a New York decorator.

Ellen had reserved radical changes for the family quarters. With an appropriation of $9,600, six rooms of the third floor were being increased to eleven, and three baths added to the original one on that floor. As she disliked dark colors, green burlap was peeled from the walls of the second-floor corridor, giving way to amber Japanese grass cloth. Turning her attention from the interior to the White House grounds, Ellen planned equally comprehensive changes.

The physical disruption at the White House during that summer of 1913 only intensified Wilson's inner conflict over his official responsibilities and his private life. He felt like a ghost in the naked White House, moving about the echoing rooms and corridors that were stripped of rugs, carpets, and hangings. He complained that the "persistently impersonal" aspect of his work was oppressive. It was not that Wilson was oblivious to the great office he was administering, but that he resented its inherent restrictions: "A President [has] to be careful, must indulge in nothing natural and inevitable, in nothing that is not official and dull and regular."[22] He seemed rather to envy his secretary, Joe Tumulty, who on Friday afternoons in the summer ran for the early train to take him to his family in Avon near Sea Girt, New Jersey—and even, on occasion, missed a train back on Sunday evening. Wilson wasn't sure of what his own impulse might have been, had Cornish been within a six-hour rather than an eighteen-to-twenty-hour ride.

August days of unbroken anxiety and constant responsibility left him feeling helpless and defenseless, and aware that he must not give in to despondency. Great and grim events were developing nationally and internationally. He must decide the nation's course regarding Mexico's murderous President Victoriano Huerta and consider the reform of the antiquated currency and banking laws, and a means of keeping peace between the nations of the world and the United States. Wilson felt that he could hardly dare divert his attention for even an hour. "It was a lonely business . . . lonely, very lonely . . ."[23]

By early autumn of 1913, Wilson had Grayson by his side continually. The little spell of indigestion he was suffering was due to the use of all the gray matter in his brain, he said. He admitted to terrible strain since Congress had convened in the past April. In his attempt to make all paths straight and carry every plan to its completion, he found himself depleted and "unable," he admitted to Mary Peck, "to run both my stomach and the government."[24] On October 12, he looked forward to his family's return within thirty-six hours. After months of self-imposed exile, with the exception of a mere handful of reunions, Ellen would once again be home to protect him. When he was tired, she would stand behind his chair and massage the back of his neck. A doctor had assured her there was no cause to worry about her husband.

The same was not true for Ellen. In the span between the wedding of the Wilsons' daughter Jessie to Francis Sayre on November 25, 1913, and that of Eleanor to the secretary of the treasury, William Gibbs McAdoo, less than six months later, on May 7, 1914, Stockton Axson was shocked to see how greatly his sister had changed, and how enfeebled she appeared. On the eve of Wilson's second year in office, on March 1, Ellen had slipped on the bedroom floor. At first, Wilson attributed her subsequent weakness to the shock and to the prolonged effect on her nerves of the exacting duties of an exhausting social season. By June, when Ellen could not retain food and was growing weaker, the doctors still assured him that nothing was the matter with his wife organically. However, Wilson seemed to arrive at his own diagnosis.

Unquestionably influenced by Ellen's family history of mental illness and especially by firsthand exposure to her brother Stockton's tragic depressions, the president spoke of how heavy his heart was—"a nervous breakdown is no light matter."[25] Dr. Grayson's report was grave but not without hope: "The chief cause of Mrs. Wilson's present critical condition is a chronic kidney trouble . . . developed as one of the results of a nervous breakdown." Overwork was the culprit, due, Dr. Grayson stated, to her fidelity to social obligations and to her philanthropic work regarding Washington's slums, and for education in the Southern mountain districts.[26]

Ellen herself, with her arm so disabled that she could no longer sign her name or make a mark of any sort on a typewritten note, assured her daughter Margaret that with the incentive of her love "how can I fail of coming back to life?"[27] Possibly, Dr. Grayson had grown so close to the family that he could not, through emotional involvement, face the truth of Ellen's fatal illness, that she was suffering from Bright's disease, incurable tuberculosis of the kidneys.[28] Perhaps a fear of endangering the president's spirits kept Grayson from acknowledging the blunt truth of Ellen's mortal disease. On August 2, four days before she died, Wilson still spoke of Ellen "struggling through the deep waters of utter nervous prostration."[29] It was not Grayson but their former family physician, Dr. Edward P. Davis, who revealed the truth to Wilson just hours from the end.

Before she became unconscious, Ellen knew that her concern for Washington's slum dwellers had not been in vain. Both Belle Hagner and Helen Bones had teased about her "slumming parties," her tours of blighted neighborhoods in places such as Goat Alley and Snow's Court, which helped to rouse Congress to action.[30] Ellen was told that the bill sponsored by Congressman Julius Kahn on May 26, 1913, had been adopted by the Senate. It was passed by the House on Friday, August 7, 1914, the day after her death. What had been kept from her, at Wilson's request, was any news of the war abroad, of Germany's declaration of war on France and on England in the past few days. William Howard Taft immediately sent his condolences to Wilson. With greater candor, Taft told a friend that "Mrs. Wilson was a very sweet woman and offered an antidote to his [Wilson's] somewhat angular disregard of other people's feelings. . . . The White House will seem very solitary to him without her for . . . there is a splendid isolation about it that makes sorrow keener."[31]

Wilson felt ill on his return to Washington on August 12, after his wife's burial service in Rome, Georgia, visibly suffering from the loss of Ellen. When Grayson had found him, one day, with tears streaming down his face, the doctor persuaded the president to remain in bed until noon. "It was a heart breaking scene, a sadder picture, no one could imagine," Grayson wrote a forty-one-year-old widow, Edith Bolling Galt. His ultimate diagnosis was that of a devoted friend rather than a physician: "A great man with his heart torn out."[32] The third-generation physician from Culpeper, Virginia, was not only a friend of Edith's but, at thirty-six, a serious suitor of her twenty-two-year-old companion, Alice Gertrude Gordon, called Altrude. Edith and Altrude, as residents of

Washington, had grown close, meeting each week for lunch, tea, or dinner. They sewed or shopped together and attended church or the theater or a baseball game or cruised the Potomac with friends. More than a year before, after a dinner party given by Edith Galt on December 19, 1912, Altrude continued on to a dance, later noting in her diary, "Wonderful time—met Dr. Grayson." By springtime they were often a trio, Grayson joining the two women at mealtimes, as well as for motoring. Edith had owned her own "electric" since 1904; the wealthy, spirited, and social Altrude had acquired hers in the past year. On May 5, 1914, Altrude lunched with Edith Galt, but the next day, she alone received a prized invitation to the circus with Dr. Grayson, Woodrow Wilson, his daughter Margaret, and his cousin Helen Bones, who lived at the White House.

Grayson was deeply affected by Ellen Wilson's death, and by the president's profound sadness. Before tragedy scuttled that summer's plans, the physician had anticipated, during his stay with Wilson, Ellen, and their three daughters at Harklakenden, catching a glimpse of Edith and Altrude on a camping trip across the border in Mt. Kineo, Maine. On August 5, Grayson was hardly exaggerating when he wrote Edith from Washington that the president was having a "very trying and hard time having to deal with so many complications both international and at home."[33] Only by mid-September could he reassure Edith that "things are going smoother and easier with me than they have for a long time."[34] Grayson thanked her for her support and loyal friendship during the bleak month of August and told her how much her care, kindness, and thoughtful friendship had sustained him during those trying days.

Cary Grayson was not the only one suffering in the gloom that shrouded the White House. The president's first cousin, the delicate, blue-eyed Helen Woodrow Bones, who had moved with the family from Princeton to act as a sort of confidante and personal-secretary-of-all-work to Mrs. Wilson—to pay her bills, to shop, to tend to her personal correspondence, and generally to take up where Belle Hagner's official social duties left off—was bedridden and in the care of two nurses. Despondent in her grief, she mourned not only for herself but for the president, "my dearly beloved brother since my babyhood."[35] In some respects, she may have been closer to Ellen Wilson during those waning months of Ellen's life than were the three Wilson daughters—Jessie and Eleanor having recently married, and Margaret now pursuing a singing career.

Helen Bones had been intimately involved in each day of the seventeen months that Ellen Wilson lived as the president's wife, and she could see Ellen's imprint everywhere, from the gardens to the upper reaches of the White House itself, the handsome legacy of this shy, quiet woman of deceptive strengths. One came to recognize, immediately or eventually, Ellen's central role in her husband's life, to admire her artistic sense and business astuteness; to realize how carefully she had managed the family finances, investing and watching over their slender savings of the Princeton days. Her judgment and vision called for respect, as did the quiet manner in which "she guided and shaped and moulded his career." Her death seemed to mark "the ending of Woodrow's best self." Helen Bones would come to believe that "he never seemed as great after she was taken away!"[36]

Losing Ellen plunged Wilson into a state of unreality. He felt, he said, as though he had lost his identity and was living in some new, unfamiliar world. The presidency had brought him no personal blessing—only irreparable loss and desperate suffering. He did not mean to complain. The loss had humbled him and he hoped it would make him more serviceable. In anguish he wrote, "There is nothing but the work for me now."[37] With his own country's skies overcast by the storm raging in Europe, he found himself mired in domestic problems—most immediately in the South, which stood on the verge of bankruptcy from drastic curtailment of the market for cotton, its single salable crop. Facing winter in a state of exhaustion, Wilson spoke of his barren days, of wanting to flee, to escape. He was reading detective stories to forget, "as a man would get drunk."[38]

Versions of how Edith Bolling Galt gained admittance in March 1915 to a White House in deep mourning for the first lady differ in details, but one thing is certain: the chief White House usher, the courteous Irwin Hood Hoover, loyally committed, with the rest of the household, to Ellen Axson Wilson's treasured memory, was instantly on guard. His droll account tells of the "impressive widow" entering under circumstances "most natural and yet no doubt with intentions that might lead to anywhere." The pining widower, facing the most critical challenge of his career, struggling to maintain his country's neutral position in the face of the war abroad, had apparently heard of Mrs. Galt: of her good looks and fashionable appearance.

Somewhat plump by modern American standards, Edith, with her opulent figure and commanding air, her musical voice and violet blue eyes, was, said Hoover, just the type of woman that the president would admire. Her wide, fleshy face was heart-shaped, her nose a trifle small in proportion and strictly linear—as though a countering note of discipline needed to be introduced. Her public smile was as lavish as her pastry-chef hats and feather boas, and the Paris wardrobe that encased her five feet nine inches in jet-embroidered, rose-festooned brocades and satins.[39] She craved bouquets of "beauty roses," crimson as blood; the prick of their thorns gave her exquisite pleasure; her ubiquitous corsages of orchids—"poems in The Culture of Flowers," she called them—nestled against her neck. Woodrow Wilson would tell her one day that she was the only woman who could wear an orchid, that on everybody else "the orchid wore the woman."[40] As for Wilson, more "Apothecary than Romeo," his granite jaw and prim eyeglasses masked a formidably ardent Don Juan, who had self-confessedly always had "a great capacity for loving the gentle sex."[41]

After their meeting, Hoover writes, "the ice was broken and from that time on it was a continuous automobile ride for this lady." Hoover's private journal notes one of the stories that would soon circulate about Mrs. Galt, "the interesting widow, living alone, with admirers too numerous for her comfort." Hoover writes that in response to suggestions that she should remarry, she was said to have remarked, "more in jest than otherwise, that none less than a president himself might look for favor at her hands."[42]

As Dr. Grayson recalled, Wilson had seen Mrs. Galt weeks before meeting her. During a drive together with the president on Connecticut Avenue near Dupont Circle, Grayson had waved to his widowed friend, and the president had asked, "Who is that beautiful woman?" But the matter ended there until a brilliant early spring afternoon in March 1915 after Edith and Helen Bones had finished a long walk on Rock Creek Park's muddy bridle paths. Months earlier, when Dr. Grayson had first suggested introducing the two women, Edith had protested that, as he knew, she was "not a society person . . . never had any contacts with official Washington, and don't desire any"; she was, therefore, the last person in the world to help the still ailing, inconsolable Helen Bones, "the poor little lady . . . starving for companionship" and in need of exercise. On further appeal from Grayson, however, Edith had relented, and the women had enjoyed walks together as often as three times a week. Edith had at first refused Helen's invitation to tea that March afternoon of their walk. "I couldn't do that," she demurred, "my shoes are a sight and I should be taken for a tramp."[43] Reassured that Cousin Woodrow was out playing golf and that he repeatedly asked why Helen never brought her friends back to the lonely old house, Edith relented. By coincidence, precisely as they returned to the White House, the president and Grayson came back from golfing, their boots as muddy as those of the women.

Meeting face-to-face, they laughed at their plight. Edith would have been less feminine, she insisted, if she were not secretly glad that she had worn a smart black tailored suit, made for her in Paris by Worth, and a tricot hat that completed the ensemble. She was sorry to find the men's golf suits were made by a cheap tailor and were not smart. Of the significance of this occasion she wrote: "This was the accidental meeting which carried out the old adage of 'turn a corner and meet your fate.'"[44]

CHAPTER 4

"Anyone can do anything they try to"

"What better time than spring," the White House usher, Ike Hoover, wrote, "for love to break forth from the shackles of gloom and lonesomeness that had reigned within the breast of the President in the previous nine or ten months."[1] What better time indeed. Intimate friends of Woodrow Wilson's, seeing him desolate, had often spoken of their wish that the president might remarry. Yet others, though recognizing his plight, felt that this was not the time for romance. As Wilson's lightning infatuation with Edith Bolling Galt intensified, there was anxiety that the recently widowed president, faced with a campaign for reelection, but more significantly with a grim decision on the degree of the country's involvement in a foreign war, should not continually be distracted by a love affair that threatened his concentration on the nation's affairs.

Following the "chance" tea party, Wilson suggested that Helen invite Mrs. Galt, not for lunch, which he always had to leave early, but for dinner, when the entire evening would be at his disposal. The night of March 23, the White House Pierce-Arrow called first for Mrs. Galt, then for Dr. Grayson. The principal guest did not disappoint. She was young and handsome and dressed "to fit the fashion of her form," as Ike Hoover records.[2] A single purple orchid was pinned on her left shoulder. After Dr. Grayson and Ellen's cousin Colonel Edward T. Brown had tactfully excused themselves, Wilson took coffee with Edith Galt and Helen Bones by the fireside in the Oval Room.

Edith found Wilson full of interesting stories and information, and unequaled in his reading of three English poems. Before she went to bed that night she wrote to her sister-in-law Anne Stuart Bolling, her brother Rolfe's wife, that the president was "perfectly charming and one of the easiest and most delightful hosts I have ever known." Then, without warning, the letter's girlish tone was subdued into that of the somber pragmatist. Much as she wished she could visit, business conditions were so uncertain "that I don't feel I should use a cent that I can do without."[3]

A little over a month after that first dinner at the White House and following several more encounters, Edith spoke of her relations with the president as a ripening companionship. On April 28 she received her first note from Wilson with a copy of a book by a favorite British author, Philip Gilbert Hamerton. The point of *Round My House: Notes of Rural Life in France in Peace and War* was to be one of the president's honored themes: that nations should come to understand each other. Hamerton was the author he had read in the year he graduated from Princeton, in 1879. He had given another Hamerton work, *The Graphic Arts*, to his wife, Ellen, at the time of their engagement.

Wilson, in the spring of 1915, presented the Hamerton volume to Edith on a note of urgency, as a suitor might lavish a precious jewel. The volume, after all, had not been easy to come by: he had emphasized to Hoover that it was to be obtained under any circumstances. "I want this book," he insisted. "Please buy it for me at Brentano's or anywhere else it can be had, and, if it cannot be had immediately, please get it for me from the Congressional Library until it can be ordered."[4] The note accompanying the Hamerton volume, from "your sincere and grateful friend," eloquently conveys his sentiments, making numerous references to Edith's sorrowful mood and the solace exchanged in their mutual state of bereavement. "It puts me in spirits again," he wrote, "and makes me feel as if my private life had been recreated. But, better than that, it makes me hope that I may be of some use to you, to lighten the days with whole-hearted sympathy and complete understanding. That will be happiness indeed."[5]

In Edith Galt, Woodrow Wilson had indeed found "a heaven—haven—sanctuary." He sensed that he could count on Edith, as he had on Ellen, for utter loyalty and worshipful adulation, for a passionate physical communion. In that spring of 1915, the fifty-eight-year-old widower pursued Edith with the ardor of a young man in love. He told Edith Galt, sixteen years his junior, that if he might have her by his side and pour out his thoughts to her, he could face the terrible days ahead. Crucial problems in Haiti and Mexico had to be resolved; the imperial government of Japan had to be reminded that the United States had large commercial and religious interests in China, which it would never abandon; America's precarious neutrality toward Europe had to be evaluated. "I need you," Wilson told Edith. "I need you as a boy needs his sweetheart and a strong man his helpmate and heart's comrade."[6] Wilson's dependence on love and sympathy almost overwhelmed his great responsibilities: his consuming desire was to take his love in his arms and smother her with kisses.[7] Central to this love story, which led to his swift remarriage following the death of his beloved Ellen, is Wilson's recognition of his innermost yearning for carnal love as much as for companionship, protection, and emotional support. "I suppose there never was a man more dependent than I am upon love and sympathy," he had early confessed to Ellen; or a man "more devoted to home and home life."[8]

Edith Galt's response to Wilson was as flattering as it was reassuring. She could think of nothing more restful than to have him read to her. Past unhappiness was dispelled by another "life giving" automobile ride. His taking time to send her a personal note was "only generous good measure with which you fill my goblet of happiness." His "pledge of friendship blots out the shadows that have chased me today, and makes April twenty-eighth a red letter day on my calendar." Mrs. Galt was henceforth a constant luncheon and dinner guest of the president and Miss Bones or Margaret Wilson and motoring companion to the two women. In that spring and summer the president's attention to her was publicly noted. Hoover, who had, with Helen Bones's assistance, become the discreet go-between in routing the lovers' letters, observed the soaring progress of the affair and would later boast that, from their first drive, he could tell which way the wind was blowing.[9]

The evening of Tuesday, May 4, 1915, turned warm. As dinner guests dispersed, Woodrow Wilson gently guided smiling Edith Bolling Galt onto the south portico of the White House. There, in moonlight, he proposed marriage—which gave her "almost a shock."[10] If it had to be yes or no at once, Edith said, it must be no. After midnight, the prospective fiancée sat by her own large, square window, staring into the night. Flattered, awed, thrilled, she was able at last, as she wrote to him, to pledge all that was best in her "to share these terrible days of responsibility . . . to help, to sustain, to comfort" him.[11] Five days later, still hesitating over a formal acceptance of his proposal, Edith told Wilson, whom she had known less than two months, that "if you, with your wonderful love, can quicken that which has lain dead so long within me, I promise not to shut it out of my heart but to bid it welcome—and come to you with the joy of it in my eyes."[12]

At midnight on May 11, Edith reported to Wilson on her noon interview with her friend and lawyer, Nathaniel Wilson (unrelated to the president), whose opinion she valued and who had long exhorted her to remarry. The lawyer had taken her hand in his, called her "Child," told her that without knowing why, he felt that she was destined to hold in her woman's hand a great power—"perhaps the weal or woe of a country." He had said she could be an inspiration and a force if only she did not willfully close her eyes to opportunity. "In order to fit yourself for this thing that I feel will come to you," he had advised, "you must work, read, study, think!"[13]

Edith Galt had already read, studied, and thought about the subject of Woodrow Wilson, far more than her lawyer knew or than she may have realized. She had read Wilson's volume of speeches, *The New Freedom*, pressed on her by her sister-in-law Anne Bolling, who had ardently campaigned for the former governor of New Jersey. She had not only caught a passing glimpse of him, in the company of Altrude Gordon, at the White House and at the theater, she had also gone to hear him address Congress. Most recently and by a curious coincidence, Nathaniel Wilson, a Republican, had developed a strong intellectual interest in the president. He read everything Wilson had written, forwarding the books to Edith not only so that she might be in touch with national affairs, but because of their literary merit.[14] At the same time, Edith could divine something of Wilson's emotional state through her friendship with Dr. Grayson and with her walking companion, Helen Bones.

It was not surprising that the couple formed an immediate bond. Both, as they discovered, had revered their fathers; both, as Southerners, Edith said, could speak about the poverty of their own people after the Civil War and of the fidelity of the old Negroes to their masters and mistresses. "He could rely on my prudence," she later testified, "and what he said went no further."[15] As president, in pursuit of a second wife, he was almost as anxious a lover as the impoverished, questing young lawyer who had courted Ellen Axson, the shy art student from Rome, Georgia. Burdened by affairs of state, he was nonetheless most intensely preoccupied with his new love. Her tantalizing ambivalence to his proposal of marriage was almost as provocative as the suffering personality she projected during this period of their courtship.

In her letters to the president, Edith repeatedly refers to the melancholy aspect of her life, to "dark shadows," and to her "valley of darkness." A widow in her early forties, she emphasizes her youth and inexperience, appears retiring, almost reclusive. Incongruously, given her considerable height and Junoesque figure, she refers to conversations in which both her lawyer and Wilson address her as "little girl." Choosing to emphasize her sorrowful past, she recounts, in a letter to Wilson of May 11, her lawyer's advice: "Don't shut yourself up in this house alone because you are afraid to go into the larger life."[16]

Her persistent depiction of this bleak self-portrait is at odds with her professions of a happy childhood, her dispassionate account of her first marriage, and her active widowhood with its references to her extensive travels and Parisian wardrobe, and even to the numerous telephone calls she received from admirers. Her ebullient mention of the president in letters to her family belies her moody responses to her suitor, suggesting that her sense of propriety or etiquette imposed equivocation rather than immediate acceptance of the president's marriage proposal. Too prompt acquiescence, she may have feared, would give an impression of unseemly eagerness. It is also possible that she suffered at times from depression, which may have combined with her policy of shy decorum. Her own account of her birth hints at a precedent for this strained behavior.

Edith was born at 9 A.M. on Tuesday, October 15, 1872, the seventh of the eleven children of Judge William Holcome Bolling. That autumn morning, the judge was late for work—but did not have far to go. He and his family lived on tree-lined, cobbled Main Street in Wytheville, Virginia, diagonally opposite the three-story brick courthouse. Their home was a maze of rooms above three street-level shops in the homely redbrick building next to the Farmer's Bank and across from the Wytheville Hotel. Edith recalled her revered father laughing as he related how her birth had delayed the opening of the court; and how he had concluded that she there and then began her career by "keeping gentlemen waiting."[17]

She repeated many other family stories with gusto—with much or little verisimilitude. A Southerner by birth, tradition, loyalty, and ancestry, she would remain supremely Virginian, perfectly willing, as President Woodrow Wilson's wife, to observe the Memorial Day tradition of laying wreaths on the graves of Union generals in the Civil War, as long as the Confederate generals Robert E. Lee and Thomas J. "Stonewall" Jackson were remembered as well.[18] Virginia had seceded from the nation in May 1861 and was readmitted in January 1870, less than three years before Edith's birth. Her family had nurtured her allegiance with tales of antebellum glory and of devastation during the Civil War.[19]

As for many Southerners, history, for Edith, seemed to stop in 1865, "then started again as memory."[20] Edith liked to speak of more spacious times before the family, "with everything swept away," had had to leave, and later sell, their plantation. The ancestral place that Edith does conjure up with nostalgia, and that had been her grandparents' home, was nine miles from Lynchburg, cradled in a gently sloping valley, and crowned at the far end with the ravishing horizon of the Blue Ridge Mountains. However, unlike the soaring, columned grandeur of the James River plantations, the Bollings' 250-acre property was furnished with a humble white wooden house, together with a smokehouse and several log cabins. Though his grandparents had been the recipients of a 20,000-acre land grant, Archibald Bolling, Edith's grandfather, had built his modest clapboard Rose Cottage on a tract of land presented to his wife, Ann, along with numerous slaves, at their marriage, on May 15, 1825, by her parents, Benjamin and Harriet Scott Wigginton, who were also owners of vast properties.[21]

One of the stories of the Civil War Edith remembered most keenly was her father's account of the family's loss of every valuable possession to the Northern troops except for the family silver, and of how, unable to afford the older Negroes who had stayed on after the emancipation, he had told them, "You are now free; you don't belong to us anymore, and you will have to work to provide for yourselves."[22] Particularly wrenching, Edith wrote, was the plight of old Henry, the guardian of the silver, whose plea to go along with the family to Wytheville had been difficult to refuse. Despite Henry's role in preserving the silver, it had apparently vanished, or its amount may have been exaggerated, since the only silver specified on the "Appraiser's List of the Personal Estate of Dr. A. Bolling" (Edith's grandfather) is a lone ladle and a watch, estimated at $21 and $40 apiece. The six thousand pounds of oats and one hundred bushels of corn amount to less than $900, not half the worth of a twenty-two-year-old man named Daniel. Appraised at $1,800, Daniel was one of nine on the "List of Negroes belonging to the estate of Dr. A. Bolling."[23] Seemingly oblivious to the causes or consequences of the Civil War, Edith's stories would revolve around an "old darky driver," or women smiling "as only darkies can smile, revealing the generous white teeth and something of the happy-go-lucky nature of the negro of the South."[24]

Edith's father, William Bolling, had settled in Wytheville in 1857, age twenty-one, to practice law. Two years later, he was able to advertise his partnership with William Terry in the *Wytheville Times*.[25] In February 1860, the year his father died, he and his mother, Ann, had bought at public auction the three-story building "with all the necessary out-houses"[26] that was to be Edith's birthplace. For this they paid $6,810 in expectation of an income of $1,100 to $1,200 yearly from the rent of three shops on the first floor and the prospect of a flourishing vegetable garden in the picket-fenced backyard. Acquisition of the family home in Wytheville had, in Edith's *Memoir* about her birthplace, a more genteel patina, conjuring up a charming dwelling and an easing of the financial burden. The "one light in the dark world"[27] of the Bolling family's impoverished post–Civil War existence was its assurance of a roof over its head in Wytheville due to the old house on Main Street, which Edith, in disregard or ignorance of the facts, stated that her grandfather had taken in payment for a debt.

Though Reconstruction took its toll, farming brought a degree of prosperity, and in Edith's youth, Wytheville, wreathed by the Allegheny Mountains, prided itself as a "healthy, intelligent and enterprising town"[28] embracing about two thousand people, four hotels, seven churches, and three weekly newspapers. In summer, passenger trains arrived daily with visitors headed for the town's native mineral waters. Even before it took its place on the railroad in 1856, a decent road from Pennsylvania to Kentucky had saved Wytheville from the isolation suffered by neighboring towns.[29]

Despite the inadequacies of the shabby Bolling household, Edith said that "understanding, sympathy and love made up for material deficiencies." Her world, bound by her own four walls and the picket fence that framed the back garden, provided space enough, she claimed, for what she regarded as her own "healthy development of body and mind."[30] The Bolling family expanded to include, at one period, both maternal and paternal grandmothers, two paternal aunts, a cousin, and seven more children: fifteen or twenty to feed at each meal.

Despite Edith's attempt to gloss over her family's impoverished state, a neighbor was left with the lasting impression of her "sad and poor early life,"[31] although another friend spoke of her happy, joyful home. There may have been truth in both those accounts. The Bollings resorted to boarders to supplement their slender means. Dr. Benjamin James Perry, who came from Montgomery County, Maryland, in 1870, to practice medicine in Wytheville, not only paid them a monthly rent of $20, but seems also to have served the family in his professional capacity on October 30, 1872, prescribing medicine for a baby who may well have been the two-week-old Edith.[32]

Edith speaks of her father as being older (he was born on May 20, 1837; her mother, January 5, 1843), as though to explain by a difference of six years, why her timorous mother should have deferred to her husband in everything. In portraits, William Bolling's dark, arched eyebrows, blunt mustache threaded with gray, and his dark beard heighten his stern demeanor. He would serve as a lawyer for the Norfolk & Western Railroad and was appointed to the prestigious Board of Visitors of the University of Virginia in 1888, although he had not graduated from the law school. His acceptance of this honor with its implicit financial obligations—it entailed donations to the university—puzzled those who wondered, seeing the Bollings' apparent impoverishment, whether Judge Bolling might have built a facade of prominence at great cost to his family.[33]

Edith would speak of her grandmother Bolling as an unusually capable and dominant person to whom an obstacle was merely something to be overcome; she scorned the word *can't* and held, instead, that "anyone can do anything they try to." Though Edith in her youth physically resembled her tall, gravely pretty mother, in all other aspects the influence of her grandmother, Ann Bolling, was greater. In portraying this tiny, stooped, lame woman enthroned on a rocking chair that was lined with dog skin, Edith worried that she may have given her "too much canvas." In repaying a loving debt of gratitude to this distinct personality, Edith inadvertently painted a double portrait: she and her grandmother shared a startling likeness of personality. She augments the comment of her grandfather—who, writing on December 7, 1841, feared that Ann was too industrious for her own good: he had often thought "it would improve us both if our habits could be by some means neutralized; giving me more energy, and crippling your over industry with a little of my super abundant Laziness."[34]

Edith Bolling, instinctively, from the most tender age, was evidently her grandmother's rapt convert. Ann Bolling also was "as strong in her likes and dislikes as she was in every relation to life. She simply did, or did not like you—and that was the end of it, and no compromise." Edith herself revealed an iron will in a bizarre anecdote about an occasion of her young Wytheville days when she and her sister were entertaining two brothers on the second-floor rear balcony of their house. These two "very boring young sons of the Episcopal minister," had overstayed their welcome, so Edith said to them:

"'I bet you can't jump off that balcony to the ground.'

"'Of course we can.'

" 'I dare you.'

" 'They went out on the balcony and getting over the rail they hung by their hands from the floor. At that point I trod on their fingers. They left!' "[35]

Ann Bolling would have nothing to do with Edith's older sister Bertha, but being the favorite was "not all a bed of roses." Edith was responsible for stoking the fire, around the clock, of her grandmother's large room—which was densely furnished with a couch, a lamp on the candlestand, some chairs, a huge four-poster bed, and a trundle bed in which slept a number of the children and several pet dogs. Edith's duties also included washing her grandmother's elaborate lace caps in a special tub and ironing them.

Fortunately, the girl found generous compensations in discharging her duties. Grandmother Bolling's pleasure—no inconsiderable asset when compared with her displeasure—provided the key to all advantages: physical, material, and spiritual. Edith gave Ann Bolling credit for teaching her nearly everything she knew. Her grandmother's steel knitting needles clicked relentlessly as Edith read long Bible passages, the catechism, *Children of the Abbey*, *Lorna Doone*, and *Tristram Shandy*, and attempted French. Edith also learned to sew, embroider, hemstitch, and crochet, and to cut and fit dresses (instruction that at least prepared her for assembling a wardrobe at the Paris salon of Frederick Worth, if not to cope with graver challenges).

Edith's father also contributed to her education. With Edith at his side, seated in Grandmother Bolling's room, reading by the lamplight of his student days, William Bolling unfolded Shakespeare's world, where Hamlet pondered existence, and Shylock demanded his pound of flesh. In general, Edith's concept of Jewish people apparently owed much to her early encounter with Shylock; yet she would always be effusive in her praise and trust of Wilson's friend, Bernard Baruch, the chairman of the War Shipping Board, seeking the financier's advice, enjoying his bouquets and hospitality, which included the gift of a voyage to Japan. However, writing home during a stay in France with her friend Altrude Gordon, Edith praised their French companion and guide for her thoughtfulness—and for being a "perfect Jew about getting everything as cheap as possible."[36] In latter years, in the company of Wilson cabinet members, including Josephus Daniels and Robert Lansing, the story was told of a woman who had two stars for her nephews killed in war. Edith responded with the tale of "a jew merchant who had 75 stars . . . not for his family

in war but [for] the 75 customers he had lost because of the war." [37]
Edith admired her mother's beautiful, round script, each character formed
"as though for an engraving," and regretted her own wayward handwriting, unruly and juvenile, an oddly untidy aspect of her otherwise fastidious person.[38] During Wilson's courtship, she was shamed by her
"drably written sheets where even his clear, legible writing bespeaks
perfection." His letters and hers, she concluded, were characteristic of
their personalities, and it was useless for her to attempt to impress him.
Resigned to her blots and faults, she concluded, "I am what I am," consoling herself that her strengths lay elsewhere.[39]

Though her three older sisters attended school in Wytheville, Edith preferred her grandmother's tutelage and was excused, on grounds of shy-
ness, from studying even with the itinerant governess she mentions as
having somehow met up with the Bolling household. Edith's decision to
forgo early formal instruction outside her home—and her family's
endorsement of her choice—doubtless contributed to the results of her
first exposure to systematic schooling. On her fifteenth birthday, she
was sent to study music at the Methodist-affiliated Martha Washington
College in Abingdon, Virginia. The four-year college and associated Con-
servatory of Music offered three years of preparatory studies; its curriculum was rigorous and extensive, its purpose and philosophy in regard
to women positively visionary. Four years of history were required;
stress was laid on the study of mathematics. Physics and chemistry,
Latin, French, and German were taught. The one-year commercial course
incorporated studies in civil government and political geography with
grammar, spelling, bookkeeping, and typewriting. Health, at Martha
Washington College, was the "essential condition of perfect mental and
physical development." During cold weather, Edith and her classmates
were expected to exercise indoors, to march and to run, work out with
dumbbells, clubs, and chest weights. In spring, opportunities included tennis and basketball, and walking the eight-acre campus of lawns and
groves.

Despite claims that the food was wholesome, the hall and buildings
heated by steam, the dormitories furnished with Brussels carpeting,
Edith complained of hunger and cold among other deprivations. Alien as
she was to the rigors of scheduled classes, mandatory dress, prescribed
social hours, and the obligations of community living, her unhappiness
was foreordained. She abandoned school after the first year. She spoke of
the cruelty of the school director, the epitome of everything narrow,

mean, and bigoted, "a man," she remembered, "whom Dickens could have chosen to head Dotheboy's Hall."[40]

Edith was not yet sixteen when, on the first June night of her return from Martha Washington College, she fell in love with a thirty-eight-year-old man who had come to call on one of her sisters. A wealthy New Yorker representing Northern capitalists, he kept fine horses and entertained in a more elaborate style than was customary for Wytheville's townspeople. He transferred his attention to Edith almost immediately, claiming to have fallen in love with her at first sight. Edith saw or heard from her suitor every day, initially assuming that his gifts of candy and flowers and his moonlight picnics on top of the mountain "represented merely acts of kindness of an older man to a child." Although in retrospect she referred to this as an imitation love affair, she must have been more than superficially involved. She declared herself entirely recovered from her "fascination"[41] during her second attempt at school during the following winter in Richmond, Virginia.

The Richmond Female Seminary, established by John Henry Powell and more widely known as Powell's School, at 3 East Grace Street, was an ample brick structure embellished with iron filigree porch pillars and balustrade. Instead of the black that had given Martha Washington College an air of perpetual mourning, Powell's students wore their prim versions of fashionable dress in a variety of colors. In their long, willowy-waisted, bustle-backed gowns, some with lacy jabots or ties at the neck, some covered with aprons, they looked far more domestic than blue-stocking.[42] Edith expressed great enjoyment of Powell's. When she left in May, however, at the end of her first year, her school days were over. By the following winter, her family, with her three brothers to educate, could not afford her continuance at the Richmond school.

Her fragmentary education was to be a regret in later years. When President Wilson was beset by crises in Europe, Haiti, Panama, Mexico, or in his own cabinet, she mourned her impoverishment. The weight of the president's burden saddened her. "Never before did I long for the wisdom of a well-informed mind half so much," she told Wilson, "for then I could be a staff for you to lean on."[43] Wilson, in reply, gallantly assured her that he loved her because she satisfied "everything that is in me," and that he "could not love or admire a blue-stocking or endure a woman politician."[44]

At seventeen, Edith accepted the invitation to visit her older sister Gertrude Bolling, who had married Alexander Hunter Galt of Washing-

CHAPTER 5

"A new world" for Edith Galt

In the years between her departure from Wytheville for Washington and until her introduction to Woodrow Wilson, Edith Bolling appeared to thrive. The implications of a heartbreaking earlier existence movingly conveyed to her sensitive suitor contrasted dramatically with her own reports of her life at home and abroad.

Edith's four-month stay with her sister and brother-in-law in Washington during the winter of 1890 was the first of several visits intended to clarify her nebulous prospects. A ripe Southern belle, a wholesome, if somber, brunette beauty now grown to her full height of five feet nine inches, Edith was ambitious, curious, flirtatious, and—if her dowry might be counted in ancestry rather than currency—eligible for marriage. Washington, as a kind of finishing school, was a place where she could browse at her own pace through the cultural worlds of opera and theater and observe the people and fashions of the day. The city offered the opportunity of extending her education, governed and limited as it had been by her mercurial temperament and by her parents' means. It also expanded the range of eligible partners.

While she stayed with Gertrude and Alexander Galt over prolonged periods, Edith's bustling social life in Washington was augmented by the company of friends from Wytheville. On their first meeting, Norman Galt made no particular impression: he was merely her brother-in-law's cousin. Yet she could not have failed to recognize, given her Galt connection, that Norman was an extremely eligible bachelor whose family, of English and Scottish descent, were prominent, affluent, discreet, and generous citizens of the capital city. Norman Galt was twenty-seven years old—tall, immaculately groomed, with dark hair, a small mustache, and keen gray-blue eyes. He had studied in Washington, first at the Misses Kerrs' school, then at the Emerson Institute on Fourteenth Street, and had subsequently graduated from Gettysburg College. The youngest of four children, he lived with his recently widowed father, ton, D.C. Galt was a member of a prosperous family-owned silver and jewelry business that took pride in having sold a silver tea service to President Thomas Jefferson in 1802. Edith left Wytheville in 1889, presumably to follow in her sister's footsteps: to find an eligible partner during the coming months when a new world was opened to her in Washington.[45] Differing a shade from Henry Adams's claim of having gravitated to the capital "by a primary law of nature," Edith's move, like that of small-town girls everywhere, was at this stage motivated merely by a primary law of opportunity.

Matthew, in a spacious brownstone house on fashionable H Street between Fourteenth and Fifteenth Streets and worked at Galt's. The significance of Norman's almost immediate attraction to her initially eluded Edith. She insisted at age eighteen, as she had at sixteen, on being "still very much of a child,"[1] interpreting his gifts and his visits to Wytheville over the next few months, as she had those of her earlier, older beau, as a usual attention paid to any Southern girl.

During this period when she was seeing several other men, Edith wrote notes to Norman that were polite, coquettish, and provocative. She was sorry not to thank him in person for the "Beauty," as she called the roses, and for the violets, which would certainly be "a living reminder of your sweet thought of me."[2] At the same time that she assured her suitor "the memory of last night still lingers with me most charmingly," she begged him "not to get cross like you did before but believe that my thoughts are yours." Four years later, Edith, saying she was overcome by his patience and persistence, consented to marry Norman Galt. She was twenty-two and he was nine years older at their wedding on the evening of April 30, 1895, at St. John's Church in Wytheville. Their monthlong wedding trip, "a lovely tour," took them to Washington, New York, and Canada.[3]

The Galts' son was born eight years after their marriage, on September 23, 1903, in Washington, D.C. It was a day of miracles as far as Edith's mother was concerned, and she wished she might express one-half the love and joy she felt. "Kiss each other for me," she asked Norman, requesting also that her son-in-law send daily word of her daughter.[4] The rest of the family were no less elated. Edith's brother Wilmer wished the baby "his father's fine figure and his mother's good looks."[5] And her sister Annie Lee said, "Of all the astonishing things that have happened," this birth of a dear nephew "knocks me more completely off my feet!"[6]

The correspondence at this period suggests that the baby was born prematurely, after a five-month pregnancy, which may account for its fleeting life. Congratulations for the new parents with "two such loveable dispositions" turned into condolences within three days, and by September 30, Edith wrote to reassure her saddened mother that she was "gaining."[7] Mrs. Bolling's special message for Norman affirms an affectionate relationship between mother-in-law and son-in-law: "Kiss him and tell him I understand his feelings and sympathize deeply and sincerely and prize his marginal note greatly."[8]

The loss of their infant (he seems never to be referred to by name[9]) appeared to bring the couple closer. Norman wrote daily during their separations, when the Galt business necessitated that he remain in Washington while Edith visited 1479 Fairfield Avenue, Bridgeport, Connecticut, where her mother and brothers Randolph, Wilmer, and Julian moved after the death of her father, in 1899. Norman was a sentimental man, deeply in love with his wife. He enjoyed reminiscing in his letters to her about their "dear talks" of bygone summers when they had sat on the porch under a beautiful moon. Fond of his sisters-in-law who lived in Washington, Norman affectionately reported on his visits with them, but the overriding message of his letters was always one of love—"with all my heart," and a "big kiss" to "My dearest Sweetheart."[10] Although Edith's part of the correspondence has not been found, Norman's ardent letters suggest that they were written to a responsive wife. On June 25, 1904, on a warm Washington night, reading one of Edith's letters, Norman rejoiced over "how happy it has made me feel to read all the sweet things you say about me and to know that you are safe and well."[11]

On July 27, 1907, Edith and Norman Galt, having visited Ireland two years before, embarked on their second and last trip abroad together. The journey had been postponed due to Edith's appendectomy the previous year, during which Norman was so solicitous of her that she praised him to her sister as "certainly a tender, sweet fellow."[12] Norman himself had not been well a few months before sailing, but appeared quite recovered.

The Galts toured Cologne, Heidelberg, Lucerne, and Paris—Norman alone made several side business trips. The opinionated Edith condemned most people in Heidelberg as "very stupid looking and exceedingly common looking." In truth, the only aspects of the trip that met her unqualified approval were the reverently observed mealtimes, the highlight of all being a special dinner Norman had chosen. Edith recalled all five courses in Proustian detail, from salad dressing to fruit sauce.

Edith's comments in her diary about having "a perfect trip and there must be no regrets," and her mention of taking a "last look at favorite places,"[13] are puzzling in view of her occasional petulance during the journey—and poignant in retrospect, given her husband's death the following year. After suffering a month with the grippe—or according to Edith, a liver infection—Norman Galt died at 12:30 A.M. on January 28, 1908, at their home at 1308 Twentieth Street in Washington. He was forty-five years old. An indication of gradually failing health might be an inquiry by Edith's mother less than two years earlier: "How is dear

Norman now?" One year later, Edith had written to say that "Norman is almost well again, I think . . ."[14]

On the whole, Edith chose to remember Norman Galt, after thirteen years of marriage, as one might recall a fond, fastidious uncle: he was "a lovely person," and a most immaculate person who changed his clothes daily, wore two clean shirts and took two baths. She acknowledged their close and delightful friendship before their marriage, allowed that he had a sense of humor and that they had many jokes together. She speaks also of her family's devotion to him, of his sound judgment, of his unfailing eagerness to help the younger boys in her family—in fact, of his readiness to do everything for anyone she loved.

Within the Bolling family, Norman would merit recognition not only as a devoted husband but as a magnanimous benefactor who thoughtfully employed three Bolling brothers at Galt's. However, any hint of physical affection or love was denied him in Edith's *Memoir*, as though she wished to preserve, at least mentally, her virginal state, or feared that such affirmation might invalidate the passion of her second marriage. At Norman Galt's death, the *Washington Star*, January 28, 1908, called him "one of the most prominent residents of the Capital city." In the family tradition, Norman Galt had served on the board of the Children's Hospital, of which his father was president for many years, on the Board of Trade, at the Chamber of Commerce, and as a director of the Arlington Fire Insurance Company and of the Commercial National Bank.[15]

As sole executrix of her husband's will, filed before the probate court in the Supreme Court of the District of Columbia, and as the sole legatee, Edith stated her desire to continue the business of jeweler and silversmith, known as Galt & Brs., carried on at 1107 Pennsylvania Avenue, Northwest.[16] She appointed Henry Christian Bergheimer to act on her behalf in recovering all payables due to Norman Galt or herself. This decision to maintain Galt's was arrived at after sleepless nights.[17] Though Norman Galt was its sole owner, he had not completed payment due his father's estate or his uncle when buying out the firm. Apart from wanting to continue to pay off the debt, another factor in keeping Galt's was Edith's consideration not only of venerable Galt employees of twenty and thirty years' service, but of more recent ones—her brothers Randolph, Wilmer, and Julian. In addition she thought of her mother and sister Bertha, who relied on the firm for their support.

Having decided to maintain Galt's, she arranged to award herself the minimum amount she felt she could live on in order to leave every cent possible in the business until it was paid for. Other plans included remaining at 1308 Twentieth Street, NW, the house rented from the estate of Norman's father. She pointedly mentions that, while her father-in-law had built houses for another son and for his daughter, he had not felt he could afford one for Norman at the time of their marriage. It was to her husband's credit—perhaps the most flattering reference she pays him—that he had worked for everything that was his, and that Galt's would not have continued but for him.

Edith claimed a very small role in the running of Galt's over the next ten years. The principal players were her manager, Henry Bergheimer, and her lawyer, Nathaniel Wilson. But she does talk of long and technical conferences, of keeping in touch with the conduct of the firm, of moneys made and owed. She was clearly involved in major decisions, and during one trip abroad she chose to lengthen her stay only after her manager cabled the news that a pending meeting had been postponed. Ten years after Norman's death, Henry Bergheimer paid $80,000 for Galt & Brs., Jewelers, Silversmiths and Stationers. The vendor, Edith Bolling Galt, also received the sum of $5,705.07 in cash, which represented the year's profits, minus $3,025.56 for payments and goods delivered to her during that period.

Edith was proud that she never lived beyond her means, never exceeded the amount of her self-imposed income. As the widow of Norman Galt, she understood that her position and expectations were vastly changed since her marriage. The impoverished girl from Wytheville was able to order her wardrobe in Paris, had driven her own car since 1904, employed a household staff of two, and stopped at luxury resorts on her holidays. Intensely pragmatic, Edith saw to it that her budget was sufficient to maintain the style of life to which she had adapted, including one Western trip and four abroad in the next five years, on two occasions accompanied by her sister Bertha, whose expenses she paid. Her accounts of her travels afford a kind of gossipy entertainment. More important, they reveal her tantalizing complexity, and the extremes of her character. Disarmingly adventurous and purposeful, she was at the same time frivolous and petty.

Edith and her sister Bertha sailed on the Red Star Line in the summer of 1910, disembarking at Antwerp en route to Munich and London. Edith thought the Hotel St. Antoine would afford her a retreat, after her sea trip. She loved the quiet dignity of the hotel, dining in the courtyard on excellent French cuisine, waking and dozing as the cathedral bells chimed across the way. But much as she appreciated luxury, she was willing to pay for it only up to a point. In her opinion, Munich's packed hotels charged an excessive rate to guests who hoped to attend the opera and the Passion play in nearby Oberammergau. Instead, Edith paid $4 to rent an immaculate apartment over the theater on Maximilian Strasse, two single rooms opposite a large bathroom, with three meals and the water tax on baths included. Edith enjoyed her economies. On a later stay at the resplendent Hôtel du Palais in Biarritz, the former summer palace built by Napoleon III for his empress Eugénie, she triumphantly bargained until the frock-coated clerk, reduced almost to tears, had had his price of $25 daily whittled down to hers of $10. Of the double room with balcony and bath she had fought for, she said she found it so pleasing that "it tempted one to sit and dream and live only for the beauty in the world."[18]

The following summer, Baedeker in hand, Edith traveled abroad with a new companion. Among the final requests of her close friend James Gordon, a wealthy mining engineer who had died just the month before, was that she look after his orphaned seventeen-year-old daughter, whose mother had died when she was only four years old. Accordingly, Edith boarded the SS *Laplander* on August 12, 1911, in the company of the comely Alice Gertrude Gordon, called Altrude. The two women, twenty years apart in age, bonded by their mutual plight of loneliness, were only slightly acquainted at the start. Five months later, they had forged a solicitous and influential friendship, sharing books by Robert Louis Stevenson and Washington Irving along with myriad adventures from Antwerp to Brussels, from Zermatt to Lugano, from Milan to Lake Como and then Paris at the last. Altrude's eventual romance with the White House physician Cary Travers Grayson—they married on May 24, 1916—would have crucial consequences for Edith's future.

Having traveled to Europe once more in 1912 with her sister Bertha, Edith was undoubtedly sincere in her frequent mention of improving herself. Being acquisitive rather than intellectual by nature, however, it was as though she expected to collect knowledge as she did her Worth dresses and her custom-designed feathered hats and corsets. In her transient quest, her textbooks were guidebooks such as the popular Baedeker; her lecturers were informal guides such as the casual passerby; her language tutor was meant to talk, not to drill. For example, Edith commended Madame Tussaud's gallery in London to her sister-in-law; though the "queerest place" she had ever seen, it was "a splendid place to brush up on English History, for all the Kings and Queens of England are there in wax—besides everyone else you ever heard of."[19]

In her accounts of travels or of her life in Washington prior to her marriage to Woodrow Wilson, the decorative and affluent widow seems to avoid almost all mention of the company of other men. She made one rare exception of an encounter in Toledo with a Russian and "the most *English* of Englishmen" who worked for the London *Times.* Otherwise, she only hints at the possibility of suitors when she speaks of her differences with her lawyer, Nathaniel Wilson, in regard to the telephone, the instrument that he called an abomination and she regarded as her watchdog and social secretary. She admitted to receiving numerous lectures from the lawyer on how unworthy of her dignity it was to allow young men to telephone her instead of writing a proper note.[20]

Men did pursue Edith Bolling Galt by writing not only proper notes but ardent ones. Several existing letters more than hint at Edith's intense romance with Warren Clark Van Slyke, a thirty-seven-year-old lawyer, a graduate of Rutgers College, and son of a retired minister of the Reformed Protestant Dutch Church in Kingston, New York. With Edith's sister Bertha and Van Slyke's friend Herbert A. Biggs, the foursome traveled together in Europe during the summer of 1910. The next year Van Slyke was ill and Biggs wrote to Bertha that it was "too bad the quartet would not be together that summer."[21]

The man Edith called Dr. Van was almost apologetic about his love for her. One July night in 1911, he wrote that he had to "ram on the brakes hard" to restrain himself from begging for her love. Looking into the star-studded sky by night and the far horizon by day, he wondered if she felt his arms closing right around her, and he confessed that he could not banish his longing for her, for her comradeship, for her sharing things with him, for their oneness in mutual interests. He wanted to draw her tired head down and hold her close until peace and rest came to her. Warren's moods of impatience gave way to resignation that "in the fullness of an appointed time," which he realized he could not hurry her, "you will tell me, My Lady," whether he could have her love or simply friendship.[22] The answer was apparently the latter, since Van Slyke married another widow, Ruth A. Hallowell, in 1913.

Though Edith ultimately rejected Warren Van Slyke and probably a number of other suitors, she seems to have taken the initiative as a young woman in regard to Dr. Sterling Ruffin, the trusted friend of the Bolling family and Edith's personal physician. Ruffin would be among the handful of distinguished doctors summoned to the White House at the time of Wilson's stroke. Her flirtatious series of limericks "To S.R. from E.B."[23] are undated and may never have been forwarded:

> A lady, in pity and love
> Thinks oft of these sad lines above,
> And at last doth decide
> (Even though he deride)
> It is her place *to fling down* the glove,
>
> Or *gloves*—for, indeed, it is *two*
> She commends to his masculine view,
> And begs that he take
> Them *both* up, and make
> To coldness a *formal* adieu.

In the autumn of 1913, Tangiers was the last stop before boarding the SS *Saxonia* in Gibraltar on October 22. Edith's regret about the past months abroad was concentrated on her millinery: having brought only a steamer trunk to Europe, she hadn't room to pack any new hats. In fact, that autumn of 1913, Edith had passed up her chance for a Paris hat not only for that season. "Though I could not have guessed it then," she recalled in later years, "that was my last glimpse of Europe for more than five years." She returned in December 1918, in the company of her husband, Woodrow Wilson, to attend the Peace Conference in Paris.[24]

CHAPTER 6

"There is such a thing as a man being too proud to fight"

In June 1915, when the Wilson-Galt romance was scarcely three months old, Edith's lawyer, Nathaniel Wilson, cautioned her that, though she might be in love with the president, she could not expect him, greatly burdened as he was, to have time or thought for such private matters. People closer to the man saw the thing far differently.

There were those who, while sympathetic to the solitary widower, still mourned Ellen Wilson and held her in vivid and affectionate memory. Those more intimate still, such as Cary Grayson and Helen Bones, could hardly believe what they had wrought and considered the situation beyond any control whatsoever. They were justifiably concerned that the public might not approve, but they were also helpless: the president's existence seemed centered on Edith Galt, and they found him incomprehensibly changed. He was like any other suitor among millions, and, Ike Hoover observed, "no mean man in love-making when once the germ has found its resting place."[1] No pressure from his hand on hers, no show of solicitude or of Wilson's need for her presence, apparently escaped those vigilant onlookers—the White House staff, the family, friends, and colleagues.

Yet the lovers would not be cheated of their privacy. It was understood that immediately after dinner the guests retired to the second floor, either to the west end of the hall or to the library, while Edith and Wilson secluded themselves in his study, which had become their "courting place." All that late May and June 1915, until Edith's departure for Cornish with Wilson's family on the twentieth, the couple corresponded on days when they were unable to see each other. When the household was asleep and the study door closed, and "the tasks of the day unable to exercise their tyranny" over him, Wilson was alone with his darling, free to talk and think only of her.[2]

In that quiet room, he could turn to her and "dream that her dear, beautiful form is close beside me and that I have only to stretch out my arms to have her come to them for comfort and happiness and peace . . ."[3] Edith had appeared in his life at a moment of supreme testing. He confessed that he loved her "with a sort of fierce devotion compounded of every masculine force in me," that he lay awake in his bed whispering endearments to her, that his arms were empty and his lips "can speak nothing worthwhile all day long for lack of your kisses."[4]

Together with his declarations of love, of "unutterable longings and delights," went Wilson's confessions of loneliness and overwork and of his sobering recognition of the alarms of state and world affairs. With his "Quixotic darling"[5] to whom he had introduced his spiritual and intellectual mentors, such as Philip Hamerton and George Washington, he shared innermost thoughts on a warring Germany and a disillusioned secretary of state. On June 18, his letter, hand-delivered as always, referred to other challenges, speaking of Mexico and its volatile people.[6] Politically, he faced the necessity to plan and raise money for the next presidential campaign and, more urgently, to replace the present chairman of the National Democratic Committee. Wilson's campaign manager in the 1912 election, William F. McCombs, had turned out to be "the most unconscionably jealous and faithless and generally impossible person,"[7] with whom no one was willing to work.

Edith responded to Wilson by offering support, affection, assistance, opinion, and advice. When he complained that he did not know what to say in a speech at the Treasury Department on Flag Day, she said that she wished she could help him write it but was confident that he would arrive at something "I shall glory in." Persistently curious about Wilson's presidential responsibilities, she initiated the collaborative effort that he ebulliently embraced in mid-August: "Much as I love your delicious love-letters, that would make any woman proud and happy, I believe I enjoy even more the ones in which you tell me (as you did this morning) of what you are working on—the things that fill your thoughts and demand your best effort, for then I feel I am sharing your work—and being taken in to partnership as it were . . ."

Edith knew, as she explained, there were many things Wilson did not care to put on paper, for fear they might fall into other hands. However, she felt particularly close when she knew what he was engaged in—and all this day she had been happy in having his confidence. "Please don't forget," she added, "to tell me about the Democratic Committee matter when we are together."[8] In pursuance of their proposed partnership, she had written two days earlier: "How I wish I could really help you—I mean in a practical way—but that is where I am so useless." Instead: "All I can do is to love you—and be a refuge when you are weary or disheartened." As his guardian angel, she wished to protect Wilson, she told him, to enfold him as in a "garment," to let her "take part of the weariness, part of the responsibility."[9]

Almost from their first meeting Edith had revealed her partisan positions. She wasted little emotion over the fate of the fallen, some of whom she had helped to alienate. Her reaction to the resignation of William Jennings Bryan, secretary of state since Wilson's election, foreshadows her ultimately fateful influence regarding Wilson's closest colleagues and friends, and most crucially, state affairs.

William Jennings Bryan, the most renowned orator of his generation,[10] was committed to America's remaining neutral and embracing neither the German nor the Franco-British side in the European conflict. At the outbreak of the war in Europe, the president himself, on August 19, 1914, had declared that "every man who really loves America will act and speak in the true spirit of neutrality, which is the spirit of impartiality and fairness and friendliness to all concerned."[11]

The inexorable tide of events had, however, widened the differences of these two men on foreign policy, until the gulf between them was insurmountable. America's case for impartiality and neutrality disintegrated in the face of the cataclysm. The British and Germans hardened their adversarial positions, the British in effect declaring a blockade of Germany or refusing to accept the Declaration of London, the international code for war at sea. Instead, contraband lists were extended, neutral vessels bound to or from neutral ports were interfered with, and the American flag was hoisted as protection against enemy submarines. The German Admiralty proclaimed on February 4, 1915, that the waters surrounding Great Britain and Ireland, including the whole of the English Channel, were to be considered within the zone of war. All enemy merchant vessels found in those waters after February 18 would be destroyed, and it might not always be possible to save crews and passengers. According to the German declaration, neutral vessels were endangered within this zone due to British misuse of neutral flags.

The vulnerability of seagoing Americans immediately undermined even the pretense of a neutral stance. On February 10, a note, drafted by Woodrow Wilson and Robert Lansing, then counselor of the State Department, and issued over the signature of the secretary of state,

William Jennings Bryan, wished to call attention to the serious consequences of the Germans' contemplated course of action: "In such a deplorable situation"—viewing with profound concern the threat to destroy any merchant ships in the waters around Great Britain and Ireland—"the Government of the United States would be constrained to hold the Imperial German Government to a strict accountability for such acts of their naval authorities" that threatened the lives and property of American citizens and "the full enjoyment of their acknowledged rights on the high seas."[12]

The first serious threat to Wilson and Bryan's unified stance on neutrality occurred when an American citizen, Leon C. Thrasher, drowned in the sinking of the British ship *Falaba* on March 28, 1915. Woodrow Wilson, only three days earlier, had spoken at the Southern Methodist Conference recommending that hotheads trying to rock the boat should bear in mind the wish of "the great steadfast body of self-possessed Americans not to be hurried into any unconsidered line of action, sure that when you are right you can be calm, sure that when the quarrel is none of yours you can be impartial."[13]

Now, with the loss of an American life, Wilson had to face a painful reexamination of his position in a war seemingly remote yet threateningly close at hand. He admitted to one audience on April 8 that "no man is wise enough to pronounce judgment [nor] has the key to this confusion."[14] On April 19 he said, "There are many tests by which a nation makes proof of its greatness, but it seems to me the supreme test is self-possession, and the power to resist excitement, to think calmly, to think in moments of difficulty as clearly as it would think in moments of ease."[15] The following day, declaring America "the mediating nation of the world," he claimed the basis of neutrality was not indifference, or self-interest, but sympathy for mankind, fairness, goodwill, "impartiality of spirit and of judgment." Furthermore, he was "interested in neutrality because there is something so much greater to do than fight; there is a distinction waiting for this nation that no nation has ever yet got. That is the distinction of absolute self-control and self-mastery."[16]

For two weeks, as he weighed the best response to Germany, Wilson complained to a friend that every hour of his time and every particle of his strength had been used and exhausted. Yet this sacrificial state made no inroads on his habitual lunches, dinners, drives, and a ball game in the company of Mrs. Galt during that same month of April.[17]

Bryan did not underestimate the gravity of the country's situation, nor the delicacy of the questions posed. In letters to Wilson, he constantly

raised questions involving convoluted British-American relationships—
about Americans traveling on British ships, and British ships sailing
under the American flag, and about British interference with American
shipping. On May 1, the German embassy posted a "NOTICE!" in the
New York *Sun* that "travelers intending to embark on the Atlantic voyage are reminded that a state of war exists between Germany and her
allies and Great Britain and her allies; that the zone of war includes the
waters adjacent to the British Isles; that in accordance with formal notice
given by the Imperial German Government, vessels flying the flag of
Great Britain or any of her allies, are liable to destruction in those waters
and that travelers sailing in the war zone on ships of Great Britain or her
allies do so at their own risk." That same day German submarines sank
the American tanker *Gulflight,* drowning several American citizens. And
on the next day, May 2, in spite of the Germans' warning, the *Lusitania,*
the 32,000-ton British Cunard liner that was the fastest and most luxu-
rious ship at sea, departed from New York for Liverpool with 291 women
and 94 infants and children among the 1,195 passengers, and a cargo
including 173 tons of rifle ammunition and shrapnel shells.

Bryan conferred with Wilson at the White House on May 3. Contest-
ing the right of Americans to risk travel on British ships, Bryan suggested
that the German warning was evidence of a desire to avoid trouble
between the two countries. Judging from a letter from Edith to Wilson
dated May 5–6, the president must have fully discussed with her his differences with his secretary of state, causing her to raise the seemingly
premature issue of Bryan's resignation. On the evening of his proposal to
Mrs. Galt, Wilson may have confided his doubts about maintaining a neutral position in the augmenting war between Britain and Germany. Interference with commerce was one matter, loss of life was another. With a
new and terrible phase of the war—the Germans' use of asphyxiating gas
in the battle at Ypres on April 22—Wilson sensed that his parting with
Bryan was inevitable. "If the British method was lawless," he concluded,
"the Germans seemed inhuman."[18]

Edith had immediately realized that the subject of "W.J.B." troubled
Wilson, and much as it engaged her, she had not pursued the discussion
at their latest meeting, but wrote instead. "It will be a blessing to get rid
of him," she advised—flippantly suggesting that she would like to be
appointed in his place. In that way, though she promised faithfully not to
interfere with Wilson's work, the two lovers would confer daily. While
aware of Wilson's loyalty "to this person," Edith could easily justify his
dismissal. "If he deserts you now he is entitled to small courtesy or con-

sideration and," she advised, "I would not hesitate to put myself on record if he does so scurvy a thing."[19]

On Friday, May 7, with a cabinet meeting concluded and a golf game scheduled, the president learned by cablegram of what Winston Churchill denounced as "the crowning outrage of the U-boat war": a German submarine had torpedoed the *Lusitania,* which had sunk in less than half an hour off the southwestern coast of Ireland. Among the 1,195 drowned were 128 Americans. That same day, America's ambassador to Great Britain, Walter Hines Page, wrote his son, "We live in hope that the United States will come in as the only chance to give us standing and influence when the reorganization of the world must begin."[20] The next day, the White House stated that "the President feels the gravity of the situation to the utmost, and is considering very earnestly, but very calmly, the right course of action to pursue."[21] On Sunday, May 9, as Wilson worked on a formal protest to Germany, he wrote Edith to tell her that she was not to thank him for speaking of the great problems he faced in "these terrible days (when I can think of nothing bright but you)"; and that, if he could but have her by his side to pour out his thoughts about them, he would thank God and take courage and bless her that she cared and comprehended and allowed him to make her his confidante.[22]

Wilson saw Edith briefly on May 10, prior to going to Philadelphia, where he told four thousand newly naturalized citizens, "The example of America must be the example not merely of peace because it will not fight, but of peace because peace is the elevating and healing influence in the world and strife is not." Then came those haunting words: "There is such a thing as a man being too proud to fight. There is such a thing as a nation being so right that it does not have to convince others by force that it is right."[23] Wilson was confused, he would tell Edith, as to whether he was in Philadelphia or New York because his heart was in such a whirl from seeing her. He did not know very clearly before he got up to speak what he was going to say, or remember what he had said when he sat down.[24] However, his political enemies at home and his critics abroad would taunt him at every opportunity for his suggestion, so perilously phrased, that Americans could be "too proud to fight."

Wilson wrote twice to Edith on May 11, at seven in the morning and at nine that night. On the second occasion, he reported on his note to Germany, "And, oh, I have needed you tonight, my sweet Edith! What a touch of your hand and a look into your eyes would have meant to me of strength and steadfastness as I made the final decision as to what I should say to Germany. You must have felt it. You must have heard the cry of my heart to you and known in every fibre of you that I needed you."[25]

With foreboding Secretary of State Bryan had signed Wilson's note in regard to the attacks on the *Cushing,* on April 30, and the *Gulflight,* on May 1, and on the loss of American lives in the sinking of the *Lusitania,* delivered to the Germans on May 13.[26] "This Government," Wilson had written, "has already taken occasion to inform the Imperial German Government that it cannot admit the adoption of such measures . . . to operate as in any degree an abbreviation of the rights of American shipmasters or of American citizens bound on lawful errands as passengers on merchant ships of belligerent nationality; and that it must hold the Imperial German Government to a strict accountability for any infringement of those rights, intentional or incidental."

It was Bryan's wish that Wilson, who had written in confident expectation that "the imperial German government will disavow the acts of which the government of the United States complains," would also send a counterbalancing protest to England against her continuing blockade. Clinging to the concept of neutrality, Bryan could not bring himself to the belief, he wrote, that "it is wise to relinquish the hope of playing the part of a friend to both sides in the role of peacemaker, and I fear this note will result in such a relinquishment."

The secretary of state maintained a position of absolute neutrality on grounds that "Germany was inhuman in her submarine attacks—inhuman to the last degree." Still, he asked, was England less culpable when she cut off food supplies from innocent women and children and made unauthorized use of the American flag? He feared that denunciation of one side and silence regarding the other would be construed by some as partiality.[27] On May 9, Bryan asked Wilson's consideration of a policy that ships bearing contraband be prohibited from carrying passengers. Again on May 12, Bryan, more apprehensive than ever that the concept of "strict accountability" might be misconstrued, suggested that owing to the long-standing friendship between the United States and Germany, it might be advisable to postpone until peace was restored any disputes that did not yield to diplomatic treatment.

In a dilemma concerning Bryan's fears, Wilson wrote the secretary two notes on May 13, one canceling the other. Initially, on thinking over Bryan's suggestion, Wilson proposed a "tip" to be leaked orally by the Executive Office and the note to Germany to be given out by the Department of State. The purpose was to encourage the belief that "there is a good deal of confidence in Administration circles that Germany will respond to this note in a spirit of accommodation . . . that it is expected that it will be met in good temper and with a desire to reach an agreement, despite the passions of the hour." But no sooner was the "leak" typed than Wilson asked that it be canceled. On the basis of what he had indirectly heard from the German embassy, he was convinced that all chances of bringing Germany to reason would be lost. Apologizing to Bryan for changing his mind, he had decided that if they were to say anything of the kind, it must be said later, after the official note had had its first effect, but it seems never to have been sent. [28]

On Friday, May 14, Wilson boarded the presidential yacht, the *Mayflower*, to travel to New York to review the Atlantic fleet. His party included Edith, Altrude Gordon, and Dr. Grayson. After spending Saturday with Edith, Wilson could not resist telling her "what a delight, what a solace, what a tonic to everything that is best and a source of happiness in me . . . to be near you all day!"[29] After dinner, on deck above the silvery Potomac, he did, however, confide to Edith that he was distressed that Bryan now felt it was his duty to resign as secretary of state essentially for reasons of his pacifism. At that time, Edith knew only that Bryan was called the Great Commoner and stood for extreme views on free silver, which had split the Democratic Party in 1896. She also knew that many people did not take him seriously, and she advised the president that Bryan's resignation, far from a calamity, struck her as a real benefit. When the president asked her what effect it would have, she said without hesitation, "Good"; she hoped Bryan could be replaced with someone able who would command respect for the office at home and abroad.[30]

Edith was exhilarated, proud, and awed by her outing on the presidential yacht. In a letter, she asked her sister-in-law Anne, her brother Rolfe's wife, how she would manage under similar circumstances to put pen to paper "if your 'adored Woodrow' was sitting just opposite writing a code message and every now and then paused to tell you something interesting or spoke in his perfectly delightful way?" Even for "unenthusiastic me," Edith admitted, this was pretty hard to do. Scheduled to dock the next day, in expectation of a grandstand view of festivities that would include the wonderful sight of the passing fleet as it gunned its salute, Edith confided in Anne, "I feel like I was living in a story—and fear to move, lest I wake up and find it a dream."[31]

Home again on May 24, she thanked Wilson, in a remarkably prescient letter, for exquisite orchids ("I have never had an entire box before") that made her feel "like a princess, so rich am I in prodigal loveliness." Naive in the revelation of her tastes and style, transparent in her ambitions, disturbing in her vision of Wilson in diminished health, she wished he could see her room as she wrote, the big square window with its broad window seat and many cushions, and the big chair where she curled up to think, with a table alongside bearing a light and some books. Beyond this, there was a long couch on which "I imagine you resting while I am at my big businesslike desk opposite, where I have orchids on either side of me to gladden my eyes when I have to turn away from you. Besides these things, the room is made livable by a wood fire and more books and a few household goods that I love. It pleases me to feel you are here and I find it hard to stay at my desk instead of coming over and kneeling beside you and whispering something you already know . . ."[32] Three days later, Edith admitted that she was worried about Wilson's reaction to the sinking of the U.S. steamer *The Nebraskan* off the coast of Ireland and by how weary and discouraged he sounded. She so wanted, she wrote, to put her arms about him and to whisper the tenderness and sympathy that was in her heart. She was pleased that Dr. Grayson thought she seemed to understand the president and to do him more good than anyone else, and that Grayson wished she would come whenever she was asked, "for he really needs all the diversion he can get."[33]

Germany's response of May 28 to the earlier protest note was considered a cool attempt to justify the sinking of the *Lusitania* on the ground that the vessel was in reality a British auxiliary cruiser, that she undoubtedly carried mounted guns, as well as Canadian troops and 5,400 cases of ammunition destined for the destruction of German soldiers. It also implied that the German policy of submarine blockade would continue. Germany contested America's assertion that the sinking was inexcusable.[34] Wilson worked late, haggard with worry for private as well as state reasons. Friday, May 28, had not only been a critical day in the presidency but one that found the suitor less secure about his marital prospects. Canceling his cabinet meeting and all his appointments, including one with Warren G. Harding, the newly elected Republican senator from Ohio, he took to his room.

The hopeful suitor who had proposed to Edith Bolling Galt on May 4 had still not received an answer at month's end. In the interim, betraying her mercurial moods, in one letter she professes to love him and long for him, and in another, she apologizes for the "shock and disappointment" she had given him. In response, in spite of his promise to be patient, to banish doubt and dismay, he finds himself sleepless with agonizing doubts. His position is intolerable: "For God's sake try to find out whether you really love me or not," he writes Edith on May 28, pleading that she remember that he needed strength and certainty for his daily tasks, and that he could not "walk on quicksand."[35]

Within twenty-four hours, the couple appeared to reach an understanding. Knowing that Wilson was in mental and physical pain, ashamed that she had added to his burden, Edith assured him of her love, "and found such happiness in the giving." As for Wilson, after "many hours of inexplicable illness, deep depression and exquisite suffering" that had brought on a sort of illness, "the light had dawned." A new certitude and confidence had come to him, he wrote Edith the next morning. At his desk by 7 A.M. (and again at 11:30 P.M.), he told Edith how he looked forward to these quiet morning hours alone with his darling, when he could sit and, without fear of interruption or thought of the outside world, envision holding her close in his arms, forgetting all but their love. There was no one else in the world for him now, and nothing worthwhile but love. He could tolerate the interim period, resigned that the day's solemn duties would probably invade this quiet place where he sat and interfere with his thoughts of her, consoled that at the end of the day they could tell each other of their love. He faced the fact that the German note had to be answered soon, but he knew, he said, "when I see your eyes alert tonight with the sweetest, holiest thing in all the world, and hold you close in my arms and kiss you, with pledges as deep as my soul, I shall be made fit for that and more."[36]

As it turned out, the German note and the fate of William Jennings Bryan were intertwined and resolved in operatic fashion. Wilson simultaneously played statesman and lover in response to Edith's inquisitive, proprietary, and sometimes moody interventions. When she heard that the German ambassador, Count Johann H. von Bernstorff, had made an appointment to see Wilson, she sent over a note that Wednesday morning, June 2, asking Wilson not to see him alone. "Please don't think me silly or afraid," she pleaded. "I admit I am a coward when I think any harm might come to you. I never realized so fully before how I love you. The world would be a blank without you." On the following morning, Wilson confided that he had smiled at her "little panic." How his heart "leaped at the revelation of that sweet little penciled postscript!" As for the unfortunate von Bernstorff, who had come to ask how he could assist in bringing his crass government to its senses, Wilson had liked him for the first time because he "dropped the Prussian and became the man."[37]

Wilson made mention again, on June 3, of trying to draft his second note to Germany. Now that his heart was at ease, he told Edith (he was certain of her love—"so much more than your words tell me"), he could do his work again and far better than before: it was "a different thing working here at this desk now that you preside over it."[38] While he was organizing his thoughts for the preparation of the crucial diplomatic message, he was conscious of the sweet lady, he said, who stood bending over him. "I feel her gentle caresses and the precious kisses she gives me, and everything is made easy—I am strong and happy because I am her own." Edith, in turn, was pleased to be invited to the president's office and asked to read his answer to Germany. She took the greatest delight in sitting in his chair, surrounded by all his workaday paraphernalia, to read "what is to be such pregnant history" and to be allowed to "share the vital things that are making you famous." Nevertheless, what she read did not satisfy her, and so she told him, in a brief note that evening—written so late, she said, that she could talk to him for only a minute, explaining that it was because of her love for him that she was hard to please.

Edith had prefaced this letter by saying that she had read George Washington's "Farewell Address" (perhaps at Wilson's suggestion) in conjunction with Wilson's note to Germany. In her opinion, Wilson's note suffered by comparison. As tactfully as possible, she explained her feeling that "there was nothing of you, yourself, in it and therefore it seemed flat and lacking color." However, she had just reread the first note to Germany and thought it so splendid "that it will go ringing down the ages." The new note "must be an echo, only in reiteration of principles and you must put some little of yourself in it." On Saturday, June 5, Wilson assured Edith, as a subordinate might reassure his chief, that he had worked for her all the previous evening revising his reply. He had simplified it and strengthened it in many ways and hoped that he had brought it nearer to the standard his precious sweetheart, out of her great love, would exact of him. The new note did please her; "I am quite content with the paper as it now stands," she told him. She was better able to follow matters that had seemed too involved before. She treasured his confidence, she said, and his "splendid acceptance of what was really ignorant criticism."[39]

Edith Galt, flirtatious, presumptive, and a reckless critic, and President

Wilson, a wary politician and besotted lover, exchanged seven letters between Monday, June 7, and Wednesday, June 9, the date of Bryan's resignation. On Monday at 3 A.M., Edith hoped that "W.J.B." would prove himself worthy of Wilson's trust and confidence, and that Wilson could get him "to do the wise thing." Little more than three hours later, Wilson told her that what had disturbed him even more than W.J.B.'s threatened resignation was her thought—to his relief, now relinquished—of letting Altrude Gordon live with her in the following winter, which would have monopolized her "to the inevitable exclusion of the man who loves you as, I believe, few women were ever loved before." He was the happiest man in the world to think that she loved "as prettily, as charmingly," as she did everything else, and "How I love to make love to you!" he told his "Sweetheart," his "delectable comrade," his "dear chum of my mind and my heart."

Wilson, for all his gallantries, also discussed with Edith his apprehensions about the serious effects of Bryan's resignation on the country and on his administration, and his conclusion that Bryan suffered from "a singular sort of moral blindness and is as passionate in error as in the right causes he has taken."[40] Stockton Axson would recall Wilson telling him, "I am more afraid of a sincere man who is mistaken than of a scoundrel who is trying to mislead us."[41]

The second *Lusitania* draft, issued on June 9 (the third on July 21), was said to be the joint work of the president and Lansing, although Secretary of Agriculture David F. Houston gave the impression that his own suggestions, offered in the cabinet meeting of June 1, were responsible for much of it. The note denied German charges that the *Lusitania* had been a British auxiliary cruiser and insisted that the United States was contending for "nothing less high and sacred than the rights of humanity." Among its many points, the note made clear the government's acceptance beyond question of the principle that the lives of noncombatants could not lawfully or rightfully be put in jeopardy by the capture or destruction of an unresisting merchantman.[42]

Germany's reply, handed to the U. S. ambassador in Berlin, James W. Gerard, only on July 8, again attempted to justify the sinking of the *Lusitania* and held no hint of apology or promise of reparation.[43] Germany's position was that England was responsible for violating principles, for declaring the North Sea a war area, for intercepting legitimate neutral trade with Germany, for aiming at the destruction of the armed forces and the life of the German nation, and by so doing, repudiating all the rules of international law and disregarding all rights of neutral citizens.

* * *

For both Edith and Wilson, the overriding issue of Bryan's resignation was more intensely a matter of loyalty than of disagreement about German submarine warfare. Alike in their desire to reach a peaceful solution to the problems arising out of the use of the submarines against merchantmen, "we find ourselves differing irreconcilably as to the methods which should be employed," Bryan wrote to Wilson on June 8. Unable to sign the note Wilson had prepared for transmission to the German government, Bryan gave in his resignation, which Wilson accepted "with much more than regret, but with a feeling of personal sorrow."[44] Edith thought this letter "much too nice" and could understand, she told Wilson, "why I was not allowed to see it before publication."[45] Wilson admitted that it was always painful to feel that any "thinking man of disinterested motive, who has been your comrade and confidant, has turned away from you and set his hand against you."[46] But he had decided to suspend judgment and to give precedence to immediate tasks. "I have been deserted before," he told Edith. "The wound does not heal, with me, but neither does it cripple." A few days later Wilson reluctantly admitted that Bryan's "defection" had touched him to the quick and that the past week had been "one of the hardest in these hard years."[47]

In contrast to the president's reflective mood, Edith's was triumphant. "Hurrah! Old Bryan is out! . . . I could shout and sing that at last the world will know just what he is . . ."[48] The *Washington Post* editorial did her heart good: "The people will support the President as against Mr. Bryan or any other man who proposes an ineffectual method of enforcing American rights. It is to the President's credit that he stood firm against what must have been insistent pressures from Mr. Bryan for the enfeebling of American policy." Nonetheless, and contrary to Edith's assurance that it would be the greatest possible relief to be rid of Bryan, the secretary of state's resignation provoked busy speculation.

While no mention was made of Edith Galt's influence on state affairs, she continued to offer her opinions and they continued to be most warmly welcomed, at least in one quarter. "I feel, and rejoice to feel," Wilson told her, that Bryan's desertion was an experience they had gone through together that had bound them "by a new and more intimate sympathy and sense of identification. How little the public knows of all it has meant to me, and of the sweet *solace* it has brought me, in my dear Love's sympathy and loyalty."[49]

Despite his admitted pain, Wilson made a somewhat oblique attempt—as though he wished that her reactions might not be as capricious or volatile—to explain to Edith that Bryan's motives were not sinister. Edith's response was graceful, but unyielding and unrepentant. While in this instance Wilson insisted on retaining some feeling for a man she so despised, she openly promised future battles that she would forcefully wage and win. "You are a very subtle, and a very adorable person," she told him. "You are a fencer so worthy of anyone's steel that fencing becomes a delight—and I just glow when you beat me at my own game. I don't know how many times I will try to parry your thrust before you get entirely under my guard—(and, I warn you that I am a good fighter, and stubborn beyond measure) but you have my heart on your side—which is a tremendous handicap to me—and I promise to be a good sport and acknowledge it if I am beaten."[50]

Weeks later, still preoccupied with the subject, Edith referred to Bryan as a traitor and said that her blood boiled when she thought of him. At the risk of being thought a "firebrand," she said she was afraid that if Bryan were left in her hands by inscrutable fate, she would put him where the world would never be troubled with him or his "'peace' sheep-clothing." Wilson, already bemused by "the lovely lady I know and love—and love partly for the enemies she makes for herself"—was clearly startled by the depth of Edith's prejudice: "My how I like you, Edith, my incomparable Darling. And how you can hate, too. Whew!" The stationery on which she wrote about Bryan he fancied hot under his hand, he wrote on August 13, 1915. "Isn't it rather risky to use mere paper," he added, "when you commit such heat to writing?" And yet Wilson had to confess, only to her and despite his teasing, that in his own secret heart Bryan was indeed a traitor.[51]

CHAPTER 7

The president's most trusted adviser, Colonel House

By the time William Jennings Bryan resigned as secretary of state on June 9, 1915, Wilson had already considered his replacement. He told Edith that he thought of appointing fifty-one-year-old Robert Lansing—to which she countered, "But he is only a clerk in the State Department isn't he?"[1] Wilson defended his choice of Lansing as an able counselor in the State Department who had been schooled under his father-in-law, old John W. Foster, who was "ripe in experience." The president believed that Foster would steer Lansing and that the combination would be of great help to him. He also told Edith there was a chance to do much constructive work within the State Department, a task for which Bryan had no aptitude. If only he were "free to *take* the best man for the place," Wilson added, he could openly pursue those objectives.[2]

Wilson did not speak of his underlying intention, which was to act as his own secretary of state. Initially, he had himself counted out Lansing, insisting that he "would not do, that he was not a big enough man, did not have enough imagination, and would not sufficiently vigorously combat or question his views," and that he was "lacking in initiative."[3] On further consideration, Wilson abruptly reversed his opinion and decided that Lansing was the best man at hand to cope with rapidly changing needs. Lansing could put diplomatic notes in proper form and advise on international law, while permitting the president to share in, if not assume, other responsibilities of the secretary of state. Few people considered Lansing an ideal candidate, and most were articulate in their reservations. The man had an air of being "meticulous, metallic and mousy," a "library lawyer" who kept people at a distance.[4] Quiet and undemonstrative, even phlegmatic, he seemed, though nominally a Democrat, to have no interest in politics. On the whole, people thought of him as a scholar rather than a man of action. Not a philosopher, but rather a well-bred, well-read, well-informed man of culture.[5] He was also an enthusiastic amateur artist who filled notebooks with witty sketches of his colleagues.

Objections were overcome, or muted, and Robert Lansing, who had read law in his father's office in Watertown, New York, was appointed secretary of state *ad interim* on the day of Bryan's resignation. He took office on June 23. Wilson had dispelled Lansing's own doubts about his lack of political prestige by assuring him that his experience and training equipped him to conduct the foreign affairs of the United States. Under present conditions, Wilson insisted, that factor was far more important than political influence. Those close to the White House at this time were under the impression that Lansing accepted his post with a distinct understanding that significant negotiations with foreign powers were to be carried out by the president. In certain circles, it was understood that Wilson was "one of those men made by nature to tread the winepress alone."[6] Wilson's own daughter Eleanor McAdoo spoke of her father always being his own secretary of state. Sir Edward Grey did observe that the affairs of the Department of State were "unofficially conducted over the head of the Secretary" and that the president, without consulting his secretary of state, dealt unofficially with foreign governments. Though Wilson would eventually complain bitterly of Lansing's limitations, and ultimately of how he had deceived him, he did not at the outset believe that he would have trouble with him. He had confided these thoughts to Colonel Edward Mandell House, who at this juncture in the president's career appeared to be not only his single most trusted adviser but a veritable cabinet in himself and an unofficial ambassador as well as closest friend.

The relationship of the two men in 1915 was almost brotherly, based on unlimited trust, complete respect, and acknowledged affection. White House usher Hoover believed that House "was simply the one, the exclusive one," on whom Wilson counted, the man whose judgment and advice he solicited, and with whom there was "nothing too big, too important, too secret or too sacred" to talk about. House was a constant visitor to the White House. His arrival gave satisfaction and his departure left regret.[7] When he was unable to travel to the White House, the president went to see him; wherever they met, they talked for hours. House's sphere of influence was universally recognized: changes in the cabinet or State Department, or even in the Supreme Court, could often be traced to those conferences. In the early years, Ellen Wilson herself and the Wilson daughters sought out Colonel House as a special ally and intermediary who might, on occasion, modify Wilson's fixed ideas. [8]

Historically, there was a tradition for such an association at the White House. Benjamin Harrison had had his Dudley of Indiana, McKinley his Mark Hanna, Theodore Roosevelt his Henry Cabot Lodge, Taft his brother Charles, and later Harding had his Harry Daugherty, Coolidge his Frank Stearns or Dwight Morrow.[9] But none, in Hoover's opinion, came close to Wilson's dependence on House. It was a unique friendship that embraced each other's family, and its eventual deterioration and estrangement was to arouse enduring speculation, the more intense for recognition of Edith Bolling Wilson's overt influence and covert responsibility in that decline. With time, innuendo and eager gossip straining the facts, the public image of House, the influential "noiseless millionaire" of "almost Chinese self-effacement," [10] would be radically debased.

To his admirers, House was "a man who has made history, and molded great affairs,"[11] an advocate of public diplomacy, a statesman, politician, a policy maker, free of "the cunning . . . treachery of Machiavelli, the masterful ambition of Warwick, or the sly insidiousness of Talleyrand."[12] Those who minimized his role of ambassador-at-large spoke of him as the president's "anointed adulator" and errand boy, demeaned him as a latter-day Sherlock Holmes snooping around Europe to find a clue to peace. Detractors called him "Mr. Smooth-It-Away" and "the sphinx in the slouch hat."[13] Rivals for Wilson's confidence belittled him as "the President's silent partner." He was pejoratively referred to as the "American Prime Minister."[14] Cary Grayson, Edith Wilson's unresisting supporter, would define the stylistic differences between House and Wilson as those between "a pacifier and a man with a single purpose—differences between a man with a receding chin and a man with a fixed and prominent jaw." "Thus," the historian Charles Seymour concluded, House both "disdained fame and achieved it."[15]

There was still another unofficial, and in this case self-appointed, role that House assumed. As dedicated diarist of the Woodrow Wilson era, he was one of its major if serendipitous and compulsive historians, "the faithfulness and frankness of his recordings" being considered invaluable to scholars before and in the fitful aftermath of World War I.[16] In September 1912, House became Wilson's Boswell—the chronicler who, from stamina, devotion, and privileged access, could provide a backstage view, illuminating the light and dark, the challenges and intrigues, and the intimate moments of the man and his administration. Dictated most evenings to the faithful

"Miss Fanny"—Frances Denton, who was House's secretary and confidante for fifty years—the diary roams from the upstairs study of the White House to the gilded salons of the Paris Peace Conference, telling of politicians and prime ministers with arresting immediacy. House believed that almost no conversation, opinion, or prejudice concerning the Wilson presidency, at home or abroad, was too confidential or sensitive to put on record. This indiscreet liberality encompassed hearsay and sheer gossip and excluded only "graveyard" subjects, such as compromise with Lodge.

House's sincerity is disarming. The waxen, enigmatic figure of his critics' invention (unfortunately countenanced by his photographs) emerges from the diary as a man of passionate commitment, frustration, and loyalty: patriotic, courageous, disciplined. As his role diminishes, as he feels his ground usurped without recourse, as he inexorably slips from the position of the president's alter ego to that of the first lady's nemesis, House will often sound self-important, self-righteous, arrogant, and even a meddler. With an immense stake in Woodrow Wilson's administration, he believed that his role was to stir the president's ambition "to become the great liberal leader of the world."[17] Even as his sense of insecurity deepens, he has his say. His diary, confounding the outcry of Wilson diehards who would canonize their president, conveys the image of Wilson as a flawed hero, at times a great and magnetic statesman, on other occasions petty, inaccessible, casual, uncommunicative, undiplomatic, rigid, and finally, woefully ill.

House, the youngest of seven children, was born on July 26, 1858, in Houston, Texas, and was schooled at Bath, in England; in Virginia; and after his mother died, at the Hopkins Grammar School in New Haven, Connecticut. Starting in 1877, he studied at Cornell University, but left in his junior year because of his father's death. Already an ardent Democrat at eighteen, he had memorized the names of nearly every U.S. senator and representative and the governors of all the influential states and had immersed himself in salient national issues. A college friendship with Oliver T. Morton, son of an Indiana senator, afforded him an invitation to the Ulysses S. Grant White House. A comment was made of House that "his rare capacity for picking the right kind of men to know was one of the secrets of his amazing success."[18]

On August 4, 1881, House married Loulie Hunter of Augusta, Georgia. They traveled for a year in Europe before moving from Houston to Austin and could count, when his father's estate was settled, on a yearly income of $20,000.[19] House's involvement in four triumphant gubernatorial campaigns and the opportunity to exercise electoral skill and political judgment in the ten years he served as unofficial adviser to a succession of Texas governors appeared to be sufficient reward in themselves. Maintaining a modest profile, he said that he had not sought, nor did he especially enjoy, the honorary title of colonel that was conferred on him by the grateful governor James Stephen Hogg. House's fragile constitution undoubtedly influenced his understanding that he would never attain high office himself. "My ambition has been so great that it has never seemed to me worth while to strive to satisfy it" was the explanation he gave for his willingness to occupy the influential, if not decisive, position where substance and shadow were to be forever confused.

In 1910, judging the Republican Party's philosophical base splintered between the Old Guard and the Progressive movement, and sensing that the Democratic Party's moment had come, House headed east from Texas and, "like Diogenes, sought a man."[20] The national candidate that House and other party members looked for must not be too Southern; if possible he should come from the East but be liberal enough to attract the West. House knew of Wilson's reform program in New Jersey and thought that his difficulties at Princeton had proved him an opponent of aristocratic privilege. David F. Houston, the former president of the University of Texas and chancellor of Washington University in St. Louis, Wilson's future secretary of agriculture, managed an introduction of House to Wilson through two intermediaries. One was Edward S. Martin, the editor of *Life*. The other was Walter Hines Page, whom Wilson had met when he himself was a struggling young lawyer in Atlanta. The editor of *The Forum* and *The Atlantic Monthly*, partner in the publishing house of Doubleday, Page and Company, Page was to be Wilson's future ambassador to England. On the advice of these two men, Wilson, then governor of New Jersey, called on House at the Gotham Hotel in New York City on the afternoon of November 24, 1911. House was fifty-three, Wilson almost fifty-five. The men were immediately drawn to each other in their hour's talk, the beginning of "the strangest and most fruitful personal alliance in human history."[21] In the briefest passage of time it was, Wilson said, as though "we have known each other always."[22]

House thought that their public policies and what he saw as their closely similar temperaments helped to cement the friendship. There were, also, their identical goals: "It was my desire to see him president. He very much wanted to be president."[23] In writing *Philip Dru: Administra-*

tor, a heartfelt political manifesto packaged as a clumsy amateur novel and published anonymously in 1912, House espoused reforms through his leading character—an expert tariff board, a graduated income tax, a banking law affording a flexible currency—that were a startling match for those conveyed the same year in Wilson's *The New Freedom: A Call for the Emancipation of the American People.* As president-elect, Wilson carried a copy of *Philip Dru* to his rented house, Glencove, in Bermuda, in November 1912. In the previous June of that year, Wilson, within months of becoming president-elect, had written to House: "I shall be careful not to act independently in any matter in which I am not perfectly confident"; in September: "Your advice is as necessary as it is acceptable"; and in November: "I have depended upon your friendship throughout."[24]

House ventured abroad in the summer of 1913 on a self-appointed mission. Given his belief that American isolation from Europe was an "outworn remnant of another age," he was determined to promote world peace through greater understanding among the European powers. As a kind of "kitchen" ambassador, prospering in intimate rather than formal settings and practicing personal diplomacy on a continental scale, he could not have been treated with greater respect by the British foreign office had he officially held the office of secretary of state.

House called his next, more officially unofficial mission abroad, on May 16, 1914, his "Great Adventure."[25] Traveling directly for Germany, he nurtured the illusion of helping "to make the ground fallow"—to bring about an understanding among the great powers that would prevent the war that already seemed inevitable. Though his great adventure was a failure, House believed as firmly as ever, as he later told President Wilson, that by powers meeting at regular intervals, and by concerted international action, wars would be made impossible.

On a subsequent visit to Washington, House would reaffirm an idea he had already suggested to Wilson, that foreign policy should be the focal point of his administration during the next two years: Wilson "might or might not have an opportunity to play a great and beneficent part in the European tragedy; but there was one thing he could do at once, and that was to inaugurate a policy that would weld the Western Hemisphere together."[26] Wilson reacted enthusiastically, and at this moment, the historian Charles Seymour suggests, was born the very wording of Article X of the League of Nations Covenant:[27] "Mutual guaranties of political independence under republican form of government" and "Mutual agreement that the Government of each of the contracting parties acquire complete control within its jurisdiction of the manufacture and sale of munitions of war."

During a twelve-minute conversation in Wilson's study the evening of January 12, 1915, it was decided that House should leave for Europe at the end of the month as the president's peace emissary. House had arrived in Washington that day ostensibly to confer on the Pan American Pact's "three-ring circus of negotiations." But he soon turned his attention to the situation in Europe. He worried that Washington, losing ground, was no longer in as close touch with the Allies as formerly and was possibly intensifying British and German distrust of each other and of the United States. These factors would preclude the peace negotiations fervently sought by the president. With Bryan's concept of neutrality a lost cause, the British were angered by America's protests against its interference with neutral trade—that is, seizure or detention of ships or cargoes destined to neutral ports—and the Germans were incensed over the export of American munitions to Allied nations. Furthermore, House thought possibilities of mediation among European ambassadors to Washington were exhausted, and that it was essential to take up these matters directly, in personal talks with London and then Berlin.

That same day, Wilson and House agreed on a code to be used in sending cable messages. House also suggested that Wilson write him a letter of instructions—to be shown only if necessary—and together they outlined its contents, which, in the interests of secrecy, the president proposed to type personally on his own machine. The letter was intended to emphasize that House was not attempting an official overture at mediation, but giving voice to the president's wish to serve as a channel for confidential communication through which belligerent nations might exchange views toward ending the present conflict and rendering future ones less likely. House's message would clarify the president's desired role as interested friend. There was no wish to indicate terms or adjudicate; there was only one objective: the peace of the world.

Wilson submitted to House a draft of his commission on January 17, 1915. In the note across the top he asked that House "please criticize it freely" and send it back to him to be put into final shape for their meeting the next week.[28] The letter embodies the apogee of Wilson's trust in House and their mutual idealistic vision of world peacemaking and peacekeeping. Wilson recognized that he was sending House abroad as his personal representative on a mission "fraught with so many great possibilities." The president hoped that House would provide a confidential channel for setting up preliminary talks toward determining the terms of peace. He thought that the European nations might be glad to avail themselves of such a service on the part of the United States, to provide a court of opinion in this great struggle. Wilson, embroiled in problems with the Senate, once again affirmed his closeness to House, confiding, "You are the only one in the world to whom I can open my mind freely, and it does me good to say even foolish things and get them out of my system."[29] Three and a half months later, however, with the destruction of the *Lusitania*, House had suspended his hopes for his country's role as peacemaker in favor of that of partisan. He sent a telegram, dated May 9, 1915, which Wilson read to his cabinet members and subsequently shared with Edith Galt: "America has come to the parting of the ways, when she must determine whether she stands for civilized or uncivilized warfare. We can no longer remain neutral spectators. Our action in this crisis will determine the part we will play when peace is made, and how far we may influence settlement for the lasting good of humanity."[30]

Eager to consult with the president, determined to persuade him to put all the strength of America into war so that Europe "might remember for a century what it meant to provoke a peaceful nation into war," House inquired about returning to the States and received a sincere and cordial response: "You have been so invaluable to me over there and can be of such great service to me here in these times of perplexity that I am at loss to advise but I am perfectly willing that you should act on your own judgment and it will be very delightful to see and extremely useful to counsel with you again."[31] House's letters, the president told him, "filled my thoughts with many suggestions that are of the highest value to me, and promptly become part of my thinking . . ."[32]

House returned home, after almost five months abroad, on June 13, and was immediately briefed on the prospect of Robert Lansing succeeding William Jennings Bryan as secretary of state, and also on rumors concerning the president's personal life by the attorney general, Thomas W. Gregory, and Cary Grayson, among others. In Grayson's opinion, the president's affections were "seriously involved,"[33] and sooner or later he would ask Mrs. Galt to marry him, unaware that he had already done so. The president himself raised the subject of his romance directly with House while on his way to Cornish, New Hampshire, to join Edith Galt and family members who had preceded him by a few days for a stay at Harklakenden. On June 24 in Roslyn, Long Island, House, as host with his son-in-law Gordon Auchincloss, greeted Wilson at the station on his arrival at 8:45 A.M., and the two talked for three hours on a range of subjects before reaching that of the president's future marriage. As House remembered their talk, he recalled Wilson's having asked his thoughts regarding marriage: Would such a step lessen the president's influence with the American people? And when would it be possible to take such a step? Wilson explained that, leading a lonely life, he felt the need for companionship, and he thought his dear dead wife would be the first to approve. He and Ellen had talked over that subject. He was sure, he said, he would be following her wishes.

House was moved by Wilson's confidence and did not betray that he already knew of Wilson's involvement with Edith Galt. In response to Wilson's question about when it would be advisable to marry Mrs. Galt, he suggested postponement of the ceremony, bearing in mind that a candidate recently widowed would be criticized for campaigning for reelection with a new wife by his side. In spite of political caution, however, House was immediately and—contrary to Edith's belief—entirely compassionate (he believed that Wilson's health "demands it").[34] Having realized that the president had already made his decision, House was genially conspiratorial regarding the couple's happiness. He did find it remarkable that the president left to him the decision regarding the timing of the announcement of the engagement.

In July, House grew restive. He felt oddly out of touch—possibly unaware of the extent to which Wilson had turned to Mrs. Galt for advice and counsel. House also fretted about reports from Washington telling of a curious inertia in government that was attributed to the president's being "so engrossed in his fiancée." House's loyalty to Wilson was unquestionable, but it was not blind. He hesitantly acknowledged that, despite his profound admiration for the president's ability and judgment, Wilson's self-characterization as "a man with a one track mind" was possibly all too true and that he did seem unable to "carry along more than one idea at a time."[35] He observed too that Wilson was a man of intense prejudice who liked few people and found difficulty in working with those he found incompatible. That Wilson "dodges trouble," that he did not face problems directly, House now speculated, was the probable explanation for some of his difficulties at Princeton.

Most disturbing of all, House found that unless he was with Wilson in person, he could not stir him into action. The United States was totally unprepared should the controversy over the sinkings by the submarines lead to war. Mexico also required more vigorous treatment. House was only one of many who yearned for greater action. On July 30, Cary Grayson telephoned House from Boston about seeing him concerning a "troublesome matter." When they met, Grayson spoke for several hours of the president's infatuation with Edith Galt. Wilson was so entirely absorbed in this love affair that he was neglecting almost everything else and was using House's approval as an excuse for forging ahead with a step—his remarriage—that Grayson feared "would be fatal." Concerned for the president's political future, Grayson mentioned that opinions differed as to the effect Wilson's romance would have on the country's voters. This much House was willing to record in his diary, but he noted cryptically that other things that Grayson had said were so disturbing that he could not bear to write them down. He did record his regret that the president had fallen in love at this time and predicted that he would be criticized for not waiting longer after Mrs. Wilson's death. Ultimately, House expressed his precise sentiments to the "Dear Governor" with "deep affection" from his "Devoted Friend": He did not believe anything was to be gained by delaying the announcement of the engagement. . . . It would be well to let it be known that Wilson and Mrs. Galt had met for the first time last spring. . . . House had a plan whereby the couple would be able to see each other as much as Wilson wished without public knowledge. "Please come to see me after the engagement is made public," House continued, "and let us all have a good time together." There were good plays that they could enjoy, and he was sure that both of them would have a happy time. If this plan met with Wilson's approval, House would go into details later.[36]

CHAPTER 8

"Fit for counsel as any man"

In the American summer of 1915, even as war with Germany loomed, Wilson spent nearly a month in Cornish, more time than in the previous two summers. His obsessive love for Edith had become embarrassing for those close to him.[1] He insisted that he was having a working vacation and issued a formal statement through the White House that he was "keeping constantly in touch with the Secretary of State and every source that could throw light on the situation."[2]

Wilson had interrupted his stay to return to Washington for a five-day interval from July 18 to July 23 to respond to the second *Lusitania* note, which was received from Germany on July 9. The many letters he wrote to Edith during this interval, and throughout their subsequent separation in August, reiterate his headlong capitulation. One must marvel at how swiftly she gained his trust, how freely she offered her opinions on issues and personalities, and how thoughtfully he pondered those views.

On July 20, Wilson worked on his critical third *Lusitania* note notifying Germany that further sinkings would be regarded as "deliberately unfriendly." The stakes were enormous. The torpedoing of the gigantic, 30,000-ton British ship vividly brought home the identity of the enemy and the proximity of the battle, three thousand miles away, that seemed to draw the United States ever closer to its vortex. On that same day, Wilson wrote twice to Edith as his confidante and his lover. He thought of her continually as he moved through the day, from 9:30 A.M. to 5 P.M. He revealed that Lansing and he had agreed upon the note to Germany substantially along the lines that he had talked over with her. How he wished that he could go over it now and discuss it with his sweet partner![3] He felt maimed and imperfect without her and pronounced her "the sweetest *lover* in the world, full of delicacy and charm and tenderness and all the wonders of self-revelation. You match and satisfy every part of me, grave or gay, of the mind or of the heart,—the man of letters, the man of affairs, the boy, the poet, the lover."[4]

At 6:50 P.M. the next evening, Wednesday, July 21 (he had already written her at seven-fifteen that morning), a weary Wilson was able to report to Edith that the note was complete and would probably go off that evening or early the next morning. He considered it "so direct and emphatic and uncompromising"[5] that he thought it signified a final parting of the ways—unless Germany yielded, which he feared unlikely. Wilson enclosed a copy of the note, the first of many official documents he would share with Edith during the next month's separation. The text would not be given out to the public until Saturday, but of course she privately might read it to family and friends at Harklakenden, "to the little circle of students of American history whose departure for bed used to be our introduction to paradise!"[6]

Though Edith had said that the days in Cornish banished any doubt of her love for Woodrow Wilson, she had not overcome her reluctance to marry him. And while she admitted that it was dreadful to leave without making a definite promise, on August 2 she decided to pursue earlier plans to visit her friends Mr. and Mrs. Hugh Lawson Rose in Geneva, New York. The party of three would motor on to Ocean City, New Jersey, on August 20 to meet Edith's mother and sister Bertha for a ten-day sojourn before returning to Washington. Wilson's letter to Edith on August 3 set the tone and texture for the rest of the month's correspondence, daily and sometimes twice-daily bulletins that mingled high romance with precipitous affairs of state. In this way, Wilson was sustaining the mood of their mornings together in Cornish when they had sat, either in his room or study or on the porch, working before lunch, and relaxing afterward, playing golf or a game of pool, taking long drives over the mountainous countryside. "I am always with you," Edith wrote from Geneva, "and love the way you put one dear hand on mine, while with the other you turn the pages of history."[7]

In truth, Edith had already begun to contribute to those pages of history. Accustomed to working with her the past month, Wilson sent official documents to her as readily as he would to members of his cabinet or to Colonel House. On the other hand, it was no simple matter to forward those frequently bulky papers, not only because of their size, but because of interested observers. "Those contemptible spies, the newspapermen,"[8] Wilson warned Edith, were curious about every special visit either he or Dr. Grayson or anyone in the family made to the post office. Though his big envelopes with messages of state would go out with other official mail carried down by Joseph Tumulty at 4 P.M., there might be a little irregularity about her receiving his personal letters because he preferred to avoid the messenger who carried out the routine house mail. In his anxiety to receive Edith's letters privately, Wilson repeatedly dispatched "the faithful Hoover whom [he would] always love and value as a personal friend" to the post office, having him report as late as ten o'clock at night as to whether the nine-thirty mail from New York brought him "what my heart waits for."[9] Among other endearments, he told her she was "as trustworthy and capable and fit for counsel as any man."[10]

Faithfully sending her the big envelopes as well as the letters, Wilson elaborated on important events. On August 3, in reference to the ongoing crisis in Mexico, "the most interesting and unexpected piece of news is that that unconscionable old scoundrel [Victoriano Huerta] . . . has appealed to the Imperial German government to protect him . . . from us!" Wilson added that he didn't doubt the German ambassador, Count Johann von Bernstorff, would have been delighted, "but didn't dare." The incendiary matter on Thursday morning, August 5, was Haiti, where the United States was holding Port-au-Prince until the situation was more fully known. He mentioned too a note from Germany regarding the January sinking of the *William F. Frye* in the South Atlantic, and Germany's refusal to consider it a violation of United States rights— "additional proof of how insincere and impossible they are." He was also forwarding on that date a letter received from Walter H. Page, the United States ambassador to London, which she might hold until she got back to Washington.

Edith thought it was "such fun keeping in touch with your work," and she was "so pleased that you trust me so utterly."[11] Or as she later wrote: "his letters kept me *en rapport* with the stirring things with which each day was crowded."[12] Confidante, consultant, and sounding board as well as lover, she sought details on issues and personalities and was an eager witness to Wilson's evolving opinion on America's role with the Allies abroad—as, indeed, he was to hers. Informed of Ambassador Page's advocacy of a U.S. entry on England's side, she was especially interested in House's recommendation that Page be brought home to become "American" again.

The attitudes in England and among the Allies were so negative, Wilson had responded, that it looked to him as though "Europe had finally determined to commit suicide."[13] Discounting Page's fear of Germany's expansionist ambitions, the only way America could help to save the Continent was by "changing the current" of Europe's thoughts. This was the only worthwhile reason, he told Edith, to write a note to Germany or to England, or to anybody else. Notes like these "alter no facts; they change no plans or purposes; they accomplish nothing immediate,"[14] but they might, if only unconsciously, affect opinion and set up a counter-current.

Some days later, after further thought, Wilson wasn't quite sure that he wanted Page to come home; but "House's judgment in the matter counts very heavily with me," and probably, after talking with Lansing, he would send for his ambassador. But Edith, irrespective of House's opinion, wrote back quickly to say that, "unless he is so steeped in the English point of view that he does not see straight," there seemed much more reason for Page to stay in England to keep the president informed. She also told Wilson that she had found a coded message from James W. Gerard, the U.S. ambassador to Germany, "good for thought, rather unlike other things he has sent." And again slighting House's opinion, she wrote sternly, "It seems to me if Colonel House had read the cipher message from our representative in Berlin he would advise a change of air for him as more necessary than to Mr. Page." She could get little out of House's message—it seemed to her, in fact, House was "not quite clear about it himself."[15]

Edith was also current with important matters before the secretary of state. At the end of the first week in August, Wilson wrote of Lansing's reply to Austria's protest over America's sale of arms and ammunition to the Allies. "But you know the points in that controversy,"[16] he reassured her, adding, "There's nothing vital or critical in it anyhow." In fact, the president thought a number of situations were critical. Haiti was one, and affairs in Mexico seemed increasingly dangerous. Neighboring Latin American countries, alarmed after four years of escalating internecine conflict among Mexican revolutionaries, began a series of meetings, with U.S. participation, in May 1915 to attempt to mediate the conflict. While the president confided to Edith that he ought to be down in Washington, Lansing preferred that he remain in Cornish, for fear that the newspapers might give the impression of a crisis in diplomatic efforts regarding Mexico. "Always the newspapers! They make the normal and thorough conduct of public business impossible,"[17] Wilson grumbled.

Though he authorized, on Lansing's judgment, sending the Atlantic fleet to Veracruz on August 10 and thought his secretary of state undoubtedly right in his recommendation, Wilson was uneasy with the decision and worried about the consequences. Three separate governments claimed Mexico City, bloodied by street fighting for the past twenty-four hours, as peace overtures of the United States and the countries of the Latin American Conference failed to bring order.

On August 12, the day of Wilson's return to Washington, headlines announced the dire message that the "carnival of massacre and loot in Mexico City is worse than the outer world feared" and that the "capital was ravaged by six successive bandits with the title of president leaving a trail of blood and famine with American lives in daily peril."[18]

Wilson claimed that he did not expect much from the conference on Latin America's critical state. Actually, he hoped for a great deal, principally that the United States play a part similar to that which he already aspired to in Europe—the role of altruistic, peace-loving mediator. All he hoped to exercise was "a certain valuable moral effect on Latin America as a whole, and, indirectly, on Mexico itself." All he hoped to transmit was "the *spirit* in which we are trying to act—not playing a role of selfish aggression, not even playing Big Brother to the hemisphere too arrogantly."[19]

Wilson had returned to Washington with a "heavy heart."[20] With Edith away, nothing but work awaited him "and the fussing and scheming and palavering of many minds—and that bare and empty house with its ghostly furniture . . ." He had little patience with the Southern congressmen fighting on behalf of their cotton-growing constituents who suffered under England's embargo against the shipment of their crop to Central Europe. Cotton, Mexico, Haiti, the Germans, and the Allies were only a handful of the current concerns of the administration. All was familiar ground to Edith Galt. Thanks to her "loved Lord's" determination that she keep step with him each day, the crowded envelopes bulging with official papers, treaties, dispatches, reports, and letters continued to arrive, incorporating Wilson's own comments or explanations on the papers themselves or on separate slips.

She supplemented Wilson's information with newspaper accounts. In her letter of August 13 from Geneva, New York, she inquired if it was true that he had asked the secretaries of war and navy to give him suggestions for preparedness for war—"and that you are planning how to finance the increase in war preparedness?"[21] Everyone in Geneva, she reported, said this was a splendid move on his part, and she wondered whether Wilson was really going ahead with the idea.

Perhaps in rereading her letter she worried that she had exceeded unspoken boundaries. "You know I do not mean this for inquisitiveness," she explained, "but just because I know you don't mind telling me, and I am so keen to know of everything you are doing." On Friday, August 13, just before midnight, she wrote:

> I felt so queer this afternoon reading all these reports from the different theaters of war, sitting here in my quiet room, away from everything, in a tiny little town beside a calm lake. I—an unknown person—one who had lived a sheltered, inconspicuous existence now having all the threads in the tangled fabric of the world's history laid in my hands—for a few minutes—while the stronger hand that guides the shuttle stops long enough in its work to press my fingers in token of the great love and trust with which you crown and bless my life.[22]

Wilson was generous, even gallant, in his assurance of esteem as well as love in response to Edith's occasional expressions of anxiety over her role or her perceived inadequacies. "Please, dear little girl," he begged, "don't speak of 'inquisitiveness'—or about anything else."[23] There could be no such thing on her part concerning his responsibilities: "Whatever is mine is yours, knowledge of affairs of state not excepted,—and that without reserve, except that, as you know, there may be a few things that it would not be wise or prudent to commit to writing . . ." Also, he assured her, she was talking nonsense when she spoke of wishing that she had "the wisdom of a well-informed mind." Along with her sweet love and the support of her fine character, he thought the capacity of her mind as great as that of any man he knew. "It's you who completes me with what she gives of tender love and instant comprehension and frank counsel and companionship that fills all the needs of my thoughts and my affections."[24]

He also begged her pardon, in his letter of August 15, for not having told her about the "preparedness business." He explained that it was understood by the cabinet for some time that he was to have a program for preparedness to propose to Congress in December, that the War Department's report had arrived the day before and was now on his table. He had not had time as yet to read it, much less to study and digest it and form his own judgment. Wilson also reported that, in Haiti, America was now "necessarily" in armed authority with the "present congress and president of the dusky little republic depending entirely on our mercies to keep peace and maintain them in control . . ." A treaty was being rushed down for ratification by the congress that would give America virtual control of the finances of the Haitian government. Then, as if critical of his own policy, Wilson told Edith that to ask for ratification now, when it could scarcely be refused, was nothing less than high-handed. Always anxious that his country be perceived as mediator rather than aggressor, he expanded, "The circumstances are unprecedented; the necessity for exercising control down there is immediate, urgent, imperative; it is earnestly and sincerely desired by the best and most responsible Haitians."

Colonel House's name surfaced a number of times in Wilson's correspondence with Edith. Presaging the Texan's waning influence, it was now apparent (though not yet to him) that House's rival as the president's adviser was none other than Edith Bolling Galt. Wilson made this perfectly clear to Dr. Grayson on their return from golfing one afternoon at the Chevy Chase Country Club. The president said that he could not help thinking aloud about his first sight of Edith. It had been on Connecticut Avenue just above Dupont Circle, and he remembered she was wearing a red rose and that he had asked Dr. Grayson who she was. And now, a mere five months later, when the doctor mentioned that probably no one ever had in a lifetime more than one such friend as Colonel House, "if he were fortunate to have one,"[25] Wilson could not resist naming Mrs. Galt as another.

On a Saturday night in mid-August, Wilson returned from a two-and-a-half-hour drive in time to stand at attention at his desk as he heard a band play "The Star-Spangled Banner." He stood alone, with tears in his eyes, "and had unutterable thoughts about my custody of the traditions and the greatest honor of that banner. And *then*, the loneliness! The loneliness of the responsibility because of the loneliness of the power, which no one *can* share."[26] In that moving moment he realized, he wrote Edith, that "there was one who *did* share—*everything*—a lovely lady" who was his own, who was part of him, "who makes anxieties light and responsibilities stimulating, not daunting, by her love and comprehension and exquisite sympathy . . . the whole divine partnership transforming everything, the Constitution of the United States itself included—and I thank God and took courage!"[27]

On August 19, he turned to Edith, his "sweet Counsellor" and "Noble

Darling," to discuss the shocking news and grim consequences of the sinking of the White Star liner *Arabic* off the Irish channel with two Americans among the forty-four drowned. And had she seen articles in the *New York World* about the dissemination of German propaganda in the United States? On August 24, Wilson warned Edith that the big envelope she would receive that day would contain an alarming dispatch from their consul, J. H. Snodgrass, in Moscow. It was "a bolt out of the blue"—so much so that Wilson believed him to be panicked by rumor—reporting that the Russian defense had gone to pieces and the Russian government itself was thinking of taking refuge in Siberia.[28]

Edith might have been analyzing her own Galt & Brs., Jewelers report as she commented on one document from the secretary of war. Before departing from Geneva, she told Wilson that she had read the document most carefully and "while it is interesting and practical as far as the necessity for greater increase [of the Army] goes, it offers no plan and gives no working basis for cost, etc." She agreed with Wilson that it seemed intended for publication and carefully avoided details of what was needed, which, of course, could not be given to the public. She concluded, "It is just about what I expected though, that you would have to do all the work . . ." It was perhaps inevitable that Edith's letters would assume a proprietary, authoritative tone.[29] What seemed "so marvelous a thing" as the president's acceptance of her counsel was increasingly taken by her as license to judge, with unreflecting candor, the members of his administration and his staff, and in particular his adviser, Edward Mandell House.

No special issue was at stake when she spoke of hoping to see Colonel House when he came to Washington—a visit implied in a letter of his to the president, and forwarded to her. Having been assured that she more than filled and even surpassed House's role, she reinforced her claim as Wilson's main confidante by suggesting House's frailties. She knew she was wrong, but she couldn't help feeling that House was not a *strong* character. She supposed her feelings were based on a comparison with Wilson, for really every other man seemed like a dwarf in that context (when she thought about them). She was aware what a comfort and staff Colonel House was to Wilson, "precious One," and knew that Wilson's judgment about him was correct. However, she wrote, "He does look like a weak vessel and I think he writes like one very often." She admitted that "it was perfectly unnecessary . . . to tell you this but it is such fun to shock you and you are so sweet in your judgments of people and I am so radical. Never mind," she concluded, with notable inaccuracy, "I always acknowledge my mistakes and take a secret joy in finding you right and stronger than I am in every way."[30]

With this approach, so flattering to the president, Edith initiated a discussion not only of House but also of the president's secretary, Joseph Tumulty, both of whom were accorded, by Wilson, an affectionate if patronizing defense. "You *are* a little hard on some of my friends, you Dear—House and Tumulty," Wilson wrote on August 28.[31] But he assured her that he understood and was able to see them, he thought, with her mind as well as his own. Besides, she did not know them and had not been faithfully served by them, and therefore her heart was not involved in the judgment as was his. Then, with genial patience and manifest arrogance, he submitted an appraisal of the character of Joseph Tumulty, who obviously fell short of Edith's standards: she felt the person who represented Wilson in his office transactions ought to be a gentleman with tastes and manners that would commend him to the finer sort of people who came to see Wilson.

Wilson's case for his secretary was conciliatory to the plaintiff rather than to the absent defendant, the Irish Catholic Tumulty from Jersey City, New Jersey. "To your fastidious taste and nice instinct for what is refined," he readily conceded, "he is common . . . he was not brought up as we were; you feel his lack of our breeding." All of this was true, Wilson admitted, and he shared her judgment up to a point, as if it were his own. He also attempted to appease her with the thought that the great majority of the people who came to his office were not of "our kind," and neither were the majority or even a considerable minority of the men at the Capitol, in either House, nor "I need hardly add, are a majority of the voters of the country," and that in all these instances "our sort of gentleman would not understand them or know how to handle them."[32]

Having explored the negative side of Tumulty, Wilson's brief took a more positive as well as pragmatic turn. "There are fine natural instincts in Tumulty and nice perceptions, which you have not yet had a chance to observe." The secretary was absolutely devoted and loyal to him and not only understood the majority of people but knew how to deal with them better than Wilson himself—though Tumulty hated what was crooked just as heartily as the president or Edith. Tumulty also told him "with almost unfailing accuracy what the man on the street—the men on all streets were thinking (for example, Theodore Roosevelt) and in this particular job of serving the country through political action, a great diversity of talents is indispensable as [is] the greatest possible variety of breeding." An administration manned exclusively by gentlemen could not last for a twelvemonth. The only uniform requirement for office, to be wisely insisted on, was morals—a sound character and enlightened principles, and Tumulty had these. "Moreover, he is only technically common, not essentially. Wait until you know him and like him," he urged Edith, "as you will."[33]

"And, then, dear House": Wilson granted that Edith was no doubt partly right in her criticism; she had "too keen an insight and too discerning a judgment to be wholly wrong, even in a snap judgement of a man you do not know." But he could not stem his true admiration and affection for House and, contrary to her estimation, insisted that the man had a strong character—"if to be disinterested and unafraid and incorruptible is to be strong." He had too "a noble and lovely character" capable of "utter self-forgetfulness and loyalty and devotion." And he was wise, could give prudent and farseeing counsel, discover what many men of diverse kinds were thinking about, and how they could be made to work together for a common purpose. He won the confidence of all sorts of men, and won it at once, by deserving it.[34]

Wilson nevertheless made concessions to Edith on her so-called "snap judgement." She was right in thinking that intellectually House was not a great man, that his mind was not of the first class. Rather, he was a counselor, not a statesman. And he had the faults of his qualities. His very devotion, his ardent desire that Wilson play a part in international politics, made him take the "short and personal view when he ought to be taking the big and impersonal view, thinking not of my reputation for the day, but of what is fundamentally and eternally right, no matter who is for the time being hurt by it." In his affection for House, Wilson argued, "We cannot require of every man that he should be everything." And he predicted to Edith, "You are going to love House some day,—if only because he loves me and would give, I believe, his life for me,—and because he loves the country and seeks its real benefit and glory." Wilson wasn't worried about the ultimate impression his friend would make on Edith, since he knew she had an instinctive love and admiration for whatever was true and genuine. Closing the discussion, he cautioned her that she "must remember, dear little critic, that Sweetness and *power* do not often happen together. You are apt to exact too much of what you are yourself and mistakenly suppose it easy and common to be."[35]

Edith responded in a somewhat subdued voice, but stubbornly clung to her point about House. She was "almost" sorry that she had written what she had about Colonel House, but, as she explained to Wilson, she could no more keep things from him than she could stop loving him, "and so," she said, "you must forgive me. I know he is fine and true, but I don't think him vigorous and strong. Am I wrong?" She probably was not aware of two significant letters written to House by Wilson within ten days of one another. Agonizing over "the calamity to the world" if the country was drawn into the European war, the president urgently sought his friend's advice, knowing that Lansing would also be as desirous of House's opinion on the consequences of the sinking of the *Arabic.* The letter of August 31 to House was entirely personal, an avid testimonial to a still cherished friendship, periodically in question by the press, who were in turn influenced by House's jealous detractors. Wilson's letter to him began "My dearest Friend" and was signed "Affectionately yours":

> Of course you have known how to interpret the silly, malicious lies papers have been recently publishing about a disagreement between you and me, but I cannot deny myself the pleasure of sending you just a line of deep affection to tell you how they have distressed me. I am trying to bring to book the men who originated them. The only things that distress me in the malicious work of the day against us are those things which touch, not me, but those who are dear to me.

On September 2, 1915, *Town Topics* speculated on a presidential romance, but the potential bride identified was not Mrs. Galt. During the president's recent auto trip to Philadelphia to consult his oculist, two hours were unaccounted for by Secretary Tumulty and, it was concluded, he had spent that time visiting a Mrs. Peck. "This is not the first time the lady has been mentioned as the next mistress of the White House and when gossips are so persistent there usually is an element of truth."

Another story followed, suggesting the possibility of a different bride. On November 9, Mrs. Norman Galt and her mother, Mrs. Bolling, were said to be back in Washington "and very much in the public eye because of the attention of President Wilson who is a constant caller and frequent host of parties at which Mrs. Galt is the honored guest." The president was chaperoned by his kinswoman, Helen Bones, a devoted friend of the "handsome and fascinating" Mrs. Galt, who came from the distinguished Bolling family of Virginia. Her marriage to Norman Galt of Washington, wrote the reporter, "was a distinct social step downward, for during her husband's lifetime she made no progress socially. Now a widow, she has a rosier outlook."

Wilson begged Edith not to attach too much importance to Washington gossip, which not only irritated her but worried those concerned for his political future. Regarding their love affair, Wilson, stammering away naively, was cautioning discretion on the one hand while pleading sexual freedom on the other. "If we keep within bounds, as we shall, and give them no proofs that they can make use of, we can and should ignore them." Also, he pointed out, their own happiness was not an ordinary matter of young lovers, but for him, "a matter of *efficiency* . . . I am absolutely dependent on intimate love for the right and free and most effective use of my powers and I know by experience—by the experience of the past four weeks [separation]—what it costs my *work* to do without . . ." He concluded, "And so, we are justified in taking risks."

On his return from New Hampshire, to judge from the whispered conferences and rumors of coded exchanges, Wilson's political associates and friends were found to be strongly averse to his apparent plans for remarriage—and quite helpless to reverse them. Not a soul could be found willing to "bell the cat."[36] When the Postmaster General A. S. Burleson nominated Secretary of the Navy Josephus Daniels to talk to Wilson about fears that the electorate would not tolerate his early remarriage, Daniels firmly rejected the role of intermediary, explaining that it was a mission "in which neither my heart or my head was enlisted and in the performance of which my official head might suffer decapitation."[37]

Joe Tumulty, the president's secretary, was still another who, undoubtedly out of lingering loyalty to Ellen Wilson, was extremely uncomfortable with the idea of Wilson's swift remarriage. The secretary's personal reservations coupled with his anxiety over its potentially damaging political repurcussions led him to bluntly urge postponement—predictably incurring Edith's hostility when Wilson recounted his suggestion. Irritated as she might be by other people's opinions, however, Edith was concerned about the gossip. She herself warned Wilson that, just when the country was under the impression that he was giving every thought to the "complications of Government, it might be particularly bad" to have his private life discussed.[38]

Action was taken, at last, by Secretary of the Treasury William Gibbs McAdoo—the tall, lanky "Royal Prince and Heir Apparent,"[39] husband of the youngest Wilson daughter, Eleanor. McAdoo believed that he had found the key to postponement in his father-in-law's alleged romance and correspondence with the elusive Mary Allen Hulbert Peck, who had been a figure of public innuendo since his first presidential campaign.

Most probably, McAdoo knew little of the truth of Wilson's relations with Mary Peck since their introduction in Bermuda in 1907. It is also unlikely that McAdoo would have been aware of Mrs. Peck's latest succession of letters to the president, in which on June 16 and September 3 and 7,[40] she had pleaded for help so that her dependent son, Allen, might embark on his most recent business venture in southern California. Inspired by information from Grayson about the $7,500 check the president had sent in response to the appeal, the energetic McAdoo invented a story that pierced the core of Wilson's confidence: the Treasury secretary claimed that he had received an anonymous letter from Los Angeles reporting that Mrs. Peck was showing the president's correspondence and doing him much harm. In this way, McAdoo precipitated a nearly cataclysmic incident that Edith Galt would refer to as "the awful Earthquake."[41]

CHAPTER 9

"The awful Earthquake"

The week of September 6, 1915, inaugurated new difficulties for the president. A German U-boat had torpedoed the British *Hesperian*, and though the lone American passenger escaped injury, American intervention was now the burning question. Twenty thousand peace telegrams choked the White House mailroom on a single day[1] as the navy announced a new shore station for submarines was to be built in New London, Connecticut, and Wall Street financiers publicized plans to lend $500 million to England and France. Overwhelmed with anxiety at having to make decisions that "may affect the history of the country more than any decisions a President and Secretary of State ever made before," Wilson suddenly felt ill. [2]

But through his love for Edith, he was still able "to face *any*thing with a steady heart."[3] Wilson was euphoric over his reunion with his "precious, incomparable Darling" in Washington on September 1. She was "the companion I want (nobody satisfies my mind or my fancy as you do), the counsellor I want (nobody steadies me as you do), the sweetheart I want (nobody delights me as you do), the wife I want (nobody can glorify or complete my life or give me happiness as you can)."[4]

If Edith was unable to return his rapturous sentiments, it was merely for lack of words, as she claimed, to express her pride, reverence, and deep adoration and the almost awesome wonder she felt whenever she realized that he had given her his splendid heart and self and, most extraordinarily, the right to help him. She seemed momentarily humbled by the awareness of her potential responsibilities and inadequate experience as she wondered if she could be "worthy of this position . . . in which I can be such a help—or such a hindrance." She urged him, "Help me Dearest to learn how to help you."[5]

Wilson continued to deliver the big envelopes for which Edith hungered. As confidante of the president of the United States, she found that no state document or opinion was too "Personal and Private" for him to share with her. Fuming over the news, on September 17, of Henry Ford's proposal to turn over $10 million to William Jennings Bryan for financing peacemaking in Europe, she told Wilson that the former secretary of state's "impertinence passes understanding, and, that should he embark on even an American vessel for Europe and get blown up," she would be the first one to beg the government not to insist upon indemnity from Germany, but to send, instead, "our highest commendation and decoration to the commander of the submarine. I suppose," she characteristically added, "it is wrong to wish for such a deliverance but it would greatly strengthen my belief in eternal justice."[6] As for news of Wilson's refusal of a request from von Bernstorff for an interview, she was "speechless at his manifold plots and underhand dealings and know your splendid patience is strained to the breaking point."

As in the early days of courtship, Edith acknowledged moments of doubt. Despite having made a pledge on June 29—"I promise with all my heart absolutely to trust and accept my loved Lord, and unite my life with his without doubts or misgivings"—she talked about "kinks" to be put straight, about wasting precious minutes chasing shadows, and about how sometimes she could run "faster than they can catch me."[7] At other times, unable to outdistance them, she yearned for Wilson's dear hand to steady and guide her. Then she would be safe and "nothing can really hurt."[8] Responsive to all shades of her moods, Wilson was ever reassuring, eager for Edith to know the real character of his love for her, eager to make her realize "its reality, its tenderness, its depths upon depths, its delight." Undaunted by her constant effort ("agonizing" might be the more accurate term, Wilson suggested) to prove to him that he was in love with another woman, he dismissed her confession, her "deep trouble and shame" as "merely the struggles of a noble heart with itself."

Whatever problems Edith posed, Wilson remained rapturous. "I love you more than ever," he told her, "with an unspeakable longing to give you love in such abundance and in such ideal, unselfish fashion that everything but joy and confidence will be driven out of your thoughts forever. For I love you," (the *you* twice underlined) he insisted, "not some ideal woman whom I have constructed out of my imagination or out of a silly, blind love—as an inexperienced boy might." He was a mature man, sensitive beyond measure to impressions of character and to her having revealed herself to him as she had to no one else and her having taken pains to put into words the innermost secrets of her nature. "And the result? Love, *love,* unbounded, joyous love! Explain it how you will, it is *you* I love, just as I have found you; and not only love but trust and admire and adore. I am so impatient to devote my life to you . . ."[9]

The rainbow took a darker hue on September 18. In reaction to McAdoo's bogus tale of Mary Peck's sale of his letters, Wilson wrote to Edith that Saturday afternoon "with a heart too full for words." He felt he must see her at once, and he was taking the extraordinary liberty of asking, instead of her coming to the White House for dinner, that he might go to her at eight that evening. He had something personal to tell her. She would understand when he had a chance to explain. He loved her with the full, pure passion of his whole heart, and because he loved her, he begged "this supreme favor."[10] Of course, he could come, but what was the matter, and would he bring Dr. Grayson with him? Edith answered. She knew the doctor would have intuition enough not to stay, and "it will look better if anyone should see you—and it is also a protection to you . . ."[11]

A sorrowful Wilson stood alone—Grayson played no part in that evening's drama—as he rationalized the situation in which he found himself, his feelings about himself, how he could not allow anyone to blackmail him, how any letter he had ever written might be published; while he might be humiliated in spirit, it would be preferable to having a sword continually hanging over him.[12] His meeting was inconclusive, and Wilson, the next morning at 7:20 A.M., apologized to Edith once again. When it was the deepest, most passionate desire of his heart to bring her happiness and sweep away every shadow from her path, he had brought her instead "mortification and thrown a new shadow about her." Surely no man was ever more deeply punished for a folly long ago loathed and repented of. . . . He had tried to expiate folly by disinterested service and honorable, self-forgetful, devoted love. He prayed that God might forgive him as freely as God had punished him. Bitter at having disappointed her, obviously fearful of the letters' publication, Wilson spoke of feeling defeated, "stained and unworthy."[13]

After Wilson's wrenching news, Edith sat the night through in her big chair by the window, where she had fought out so many problems. Dawn brought clearer perspective, and she could see "straight—straight into the heart of things," and was ready to follow the road "where love leads." She could pledge that she would stand by him "not for duty, not for pity, not for honor—but for love—trusting, protecting, comprehending love."[14] In their third communication within less than two hours that Sunday morning, a jubilant Wilson "could shout aloud for the joy and privilege of receiving such a pledge, conceived by such a heart," and that "a nobler, more wonderful, more altogether lovely, loyal, adorable [woman] there could never be."[15]

That Sunday night Wilson slept like a child. A new chapter had opened in their wonderful love story; "the meaning of the whole thing has deepened,"[16] he told Edith the next morning. They both could say "no matter whether the wine be bitter or sweet, we will share it together and find happiness in the comradeship," and if they could say that, they could say all.[17] That evening, Edith was anxious that they both try to sleep well and get back to a routine. She was determined that they think only that this earthquake had left their love untouched and that they must rebuild "their City of Dreams on such a firm foundation that no other can shake it—or cause the occupants to quake or tremble."[18]

On Monday, September 20, Wilson drafted in shorthand another apology of sorts that would long remain private. A summary of his feelings about Mary Peck, his wife, the obligations of a puritanical man in public life, it was found among his papers after his death.

Analysis of the Statement
Admission

Even while it lasted I knew and made explicit what it *did not* mean. It did not last, but friendship and genuine admiration ensued. . . .

These letters disclose a passage of folly and gross impertinence in my life. I am deeply ashamed and repentant. Neither in act nor even in thought was the purity or honor of the lady concerned touched or sullied, and my offense she has generously forgiven. Neither was my utter allegiance to my incomparable wife in any-way by the least jot abated. She, too, knew and understood and has forgiven, little as I deserved the generous indulgence. But none of this lessens the blame or the deep humiliating grief and shame I suffer, that I should have so erred and forgotten the standards of honorable behavior by which I should have been bound.

In his despair, while Wilson assumed that the infamous letters had been published, he gallantly defended Mary Peck's reputation in the process:

These letters are genuine, and I am now ashamed of them—not because the lady to whom they are addressed was not worthy of the most sincere admiration and affection, but because I did not have the moral right to offer her ardent affection which they express. I am happy to remember that the only thing that at all relieves the pain and shame with which this correspondence could ever in the least degree affect is the honor of the noble lady to whom I then had the distinction and happiness to be married.[19]

Though he wrote to Edith in a positive voice, Wilson was riddled with doubt and guilt over the dilemma raised by McAdoo. Wilson deliberated his next move, and a talk with Edith brought him, he said, to the "startling, humiliating discovery" that he had acted like a coward, permitting himself to be dominated by fear. He had dreaded the threatened revelation "because it might make the contemptible error and madness of a few months seem a stain upon a whole life."[20] Now he would no longer permit his fears to deprive him of happiness and peace of mind. The remedy surely lay in his own hands. There must be a right way and a wrong way, and he must find the way most just and honorable for all concerned. He thought now of turning to Colonel House, to consult with him candidly. Thereby Wilson fulfilled his promise to Edith to get another man's point of view.

On Monday night, Edith slept from 1 A.M. until five minutes after seven. "That tells the story Sweetheart," she wrote Wilson the next day, on September 21. But at midnight, before falling asleep, she suffered a severe reaction. In a letter penned at that hour she explained, "It *is* the awful Earthquake of Saturday night that has caused doubt of the *certainty* of anything."[21] Writing in an unusually ragged hand, even for her, her pen wavering in one direction and then another, she asked if he ever knew "a more inconsistent bundle of complexities than I."[22] Since returning home from her holidays, the doubts had vanished and she was relishing "the exquisite luxury of loving and being loved" when "a rocket from the unseen hand of an enemy" fell in the midst of this radiance.

But the shadow lifted once again and she was able to report: "Love was still on the throne, but pale and bleeding trying to smile through his tears—and say the blow did not really hurt." Still, she trusted that love would lead them and help her to a new and stronger knowledge of all the greatness and sweetness of his heart and make her discard the "Superman" her love had created for the "vital, tender, *normal* man in my precious Woodrow."[23]

*　*　*

One of the strangest aspects of this traumatic passage in their courtship is the fabricated version Edith chose to present in her *Memoir*. Contradictory to Grayson's and House's diary notes and her own letter of September 26 to Wilson, which undeniably places the president, not Grayson, in her presence, Edith switches identities and invents vivid dialogue, as though the actual episode lacked drama in its own right. According to her rendition, written twenty-three years after the fact, "suddenly something happened which changed the entire situation, and might have changed the current of our lives."

On the evening of September 18, 1915, she was alone in her house for dinner when Dr. Grayson, as her story goes, arrived alone, around eight o'clock, in evident distress. He told her that the president had sent him to tell her something that he could not bring himself to write. "It was this. Colonel House was at the White House, having just returned from a conference with Secretary McAdoo. Both had been told in confidence of our engagement and, the Colonel said, they had sounded out a few people, particularly newspaper men, who told them the gossip was that should rumors concerning our engagement be true, Mrs. Peck was going to come out against the President, saying she had letters from him which would be compromising; and that all the old whispered scandals of the 1912 campaign would be revived."

Edith went to see Wilson, and the doctor and she were strangely silent as they drove through the familiar streets; and when they left the elevator on the second floor of the White House, Grayson went quickly to a door, which he opened, and beckoned her to follow. The curtains were drawn and the room dark; on the pillow she saw "a white, drawn face with burning eyes dark with hidden pain. Brooks, the colored valet, was by the bed. No word was spoken, only an eager hand held out in welcome, which I took to find icy cold, and when I unclasped it we were alone. Strangely in these tense moments things are understood with no need of words. I never asked why he had not answered my letter, only had it reached him. He said, 'Yes.'"

Years afterward, when Edith claimed to have asked Colonel House to tell her where he had got such an unjust impression as he gave the president about Mrs. Peck, the colonel said he had never heard anything about it from anybody. He and Secretary McAdoo had planned it between them because they thought at the time that a second marriage of the president might prevent his reelection. Colonel House concluded his story: "In that I was mistaken, for I think you have been a great asset." When she asked Mr. McAdoo about it, he said that it was entirely the colonel's idea! "This shifting of responsibility between Colonel House and Mr. McAdoo was a matter I never mentioned to my husband because I knew it would make him see red."[24]

The kindest explanation for this gross distortion of the facts has been suggested by a neuropsychiatrist, Dr. Edwin A. Weinstein, in his book *Woodrow Wilson: A Medical and Psychological Biography*, published in 1981: "Edith's amnesia about Woodrow Wilson's visit to her home and her confabulation of a collapse brought on by love shielded her from the memory of the two most painful events of her life—Woodrow Wilson's confession of his sin and the incapacity which followed his massive stroke of 1919."[25] However, enough mention has been made of Edith's extraordinary memory to cloud Dr. Weinstein's benevolent theory. Helen Bones, for example, recalled that Edith "could give you details by the bushel—quote the exact words of anyone with whom she has ever conversed, and describe any scene she has ever witnessed."[26] Stockton Axson, Ellen Wilson's brother, spoke of how Edith Wilson had once told him of her early training, how her mother used to tell her that when she went out, she must observe everything and be able to tell it clearly when she returned to her invalid grandmother, and how "in this way, she had cultivated her unusually accurate memory."[27]

Given these attributes and the evidence on hand, there is reason to suspect her *Memoir* in many instances, particularly her claim to "revealing the truth concerning personal matters which has been often distorted by the misinformed." Her biographer Alden Hatch published her version of the confrontation over the Peck episode, as well as his thanks to Mrs. Wilson for checking the accuracy of his entire manuscript. [28]

Notwithstanding Edith's melodramatic account of the president's collapse and of her reaction to it, she appeared to be in brisk spirits on Wednesday, September 22, when she told Wilson of her wonderful morning of golf with Helen Bones, using his gift of clubs. She did not think she played well, but she considered the equipment an "untold joy" and meant to improve her game. She urged Wilson to go out that afternoon after he got through seeing "that Traitor," as she insisted on calling Bryan, for he would need "fresh, pure air" in his lungs after being with him.[29] Having learned from Helen Bones that Colonel House was arriving that evening, Edith also asked Wilson, "Please let him help you in every possible way—and remember we are both strong enough to do the *right* thing—no matter what it costs." She also promised that when she came to see him, he would find a "new spirit, more at ease and less 'imperious.'"[30]

* * *

Wilson's recovery from the threat of the exploitation of his letters to Mrs. Peck was arduous, and the intense September heat did not help. House came to dine with the president at 7:15 on the evening of September 22. They chatted until 10 P.M. with Helen Bones and Axson and touched on America's role in the war abroad, Wilson seeming to imply that the country ought not to take part. When the rest had retired, Wilson took House into his confidence with reluctance, "but with a determination to have it over."[31]

The story House was about to hear was not new to him, though he gave no indication that he had heard it in detail from McAdoo earlier in the day. Wilson repeated his version, having, of course, no clue as to its source or its bogus content. He understood that there was much talk about this friendship, and he wanted House to know the whole thing. How the family had met Mary Peck in Bermuda, how Wilson had gotten to know her quite well, and though, he admitted, he had been indiscreet in writing her letters "rather more warmly than was prudent," there had never been anything between them, other than platonic friendship.[32] While assuring House that he refused to respond to the present potential scandal or to any form of blackmail, he also defended Mary Peck in the belief that she must have fallen under some evil influence if she was disclosing his letters. In response, House told Wilson not to worry, that he did not believe, either, in the truth of Mrs. Peck's supposed blackmail. House must have felt more than a twinge of guilt, for he excused himself from telling Wilson the whole story in order to protect the president's son-in-law. When McAdoo had told him what he had done about the fictitious and anonymous letter, House had not realized "what a cruel thing it was to do."[33]

The prospective marriage was discussed that very evening. Responsibility for the time of the announcement, the character of the wedding, and many other details, House wrote, was "placed squarely" on him. His spirits lightened, Wilson was wholly enthusiastic and optimistic when he wrote to Edith, at 7 A.M. on September 23, of having had a *fine* talk with House the previous evening that "cleared things wonderfully." House, the president assured Edith, "is really a wonderful counselor. His mind is like an excellent clearing house through which to put one's ideas and get the right credits and balances."[34] Still disputing Edith's earlier doubts, Wilson also told her that he was sure that the first real conversation she would have with House would entirely dispel her impression that he lacked strength. Wilson described his friend as having "quiet, serene strength, but it is great and real . . . I wanted a perfectly cool-blooded judgment, and I'm sure I got it,"[35] he assured Edith.

House and Wilson agreed tentatively on an official announcement to be made in the middle of October, with the wedding to follow before the turn of the new year. House thought Wilson's remarriage an "extremely delicate subject." Though House was wary, he was, contrary to Edith's supposition, not unsympathetic. Loyal to Ellen Wilson's memory, he repeatedly consoled himself that prospects of a second marriage did not lessen Wilson's affection for his first wife and that he had "never seen a man more dependent upon a woman's companionship."[36] House concluded that, given the weight of Wilson's burdens, it seemed a small concession that public opinion might make on behalf of this man not to criticize him too much for doing "what one in a humbler station of life would be able to do without comment."[37]

Colonel House and Edith Galt met at the White House on September 23, 1915, and arranged to take tea together the following afternoon. Somewhat naively, in view of Edith's instinctive dislike of him, House claimed they became friends immediately, and they arranged to meet again the next afternoon at five. Of that meeting, he wrote: "She seems delightful and full of humor, and it makes me happy to think the President will have her to cheer him in his loneliness."[38] He was buoyed by their chat, and by Edith's assurance that the president spoke of him with affection and with admiration for his ability to place problems in perspective.[39]

During this meeting, House mentioned the delight it gave him to find that Wilson and he were of parallel minds on public issues. In his anxiety to please Edith, he assured her that if the president played the role of peacemaker in the European war—that war being "the greatest event in human history excepting the birth of Christ"—he would "easily outrank any other American that had yet lived." Then House and Mrs. Galt took a short drive together in her electric runabout, and he returned to talk to the president. House ended this otherwise confident paragraph in his diary on an unsettling note. After dinner he joined the presidential party, along with Helen Bones and Axson, to see May Irwin star in a play at the National Theatre. Before cabinet members, who largely filled the other boxes, Wilson insisted that House take a front seat "to emphasize, so he said, the fact that we were not at outs, as had been recently stated" in an article in the previous month's *New York Herald.*[40]

Edith could not have asked for a more enthusiastic report from House than that relayed to her by Wilson. House, Wilson added, was the true and loyal friend he loved more than ever because, from the moment of seeing and knowing her, House had become as much her friend and partisan as Wilson's own. Moreover, Wilson hoped Edith liked and admired and trusted House a tithe as much as he did her!

On that same day, Edith wrote to her family of her engagement to the president, which she knew "must come as the greatest possible surprise." They were thinking of making an official announcement in early October, but the precise date depended on political considerations. The next morning, his dream of their future nearly realized, Wilson was at his desk at 7:15 to tell her she had set him *free* and made his full happiness "not merely a confident hope, but a *plan*," promising him "unhampered, unembarrassed comradeship in the mean time."[41]

Before the week was over, however, Wilson grew wary. He was discouraged, felt himself on uncertain ground, and confessed to Edith that his pain was never so great as when he felt that something he had "blunderingly done" had thrown her for a little while "back into the toils of doubt and misgiving."[42] He feared his intuition, "generally infallible in understanding what is going on in your dear heart," had failed him.[43] He worried about the expression on her face, "half sad, half absent," that he had never seen before, that made her face "exquisitely beautiful and yet as though the beauty were not for me!"[44] Was he at fault, was his cousin Helen?

Edith explained her sudden silence of the previous evening. She had felt treated as a child when Wilson had agreed with Helen Bones that family friends, the sisters Lucy and Mary Smith, must be told before the engagement announcement appeared in the papers, and that the announcement must, therefore, await their arrival. For the melodramatic Edith, this was the final straw, the gauntlet flung to the ground in the ultimate challenge. Admittedly depressed and exhausted, she cried out in frustration, "Oh! I am so tired of having to ask people things—and now even to get the Smiths' permission to announce our engagement." She knew it was better to tell him plainly how she felt, though it would worry him, which she never wanted to do: ". . . while I know it must be different, when things are discussed and consulted over I get impatient and restless, and if I did not love you, would be off with the bit in my teeth and showing a clean pair of heels to anyone who dare try to catch me."

Even in her distressed state Edith was able to assure Wilson that she knew she loved him enough "to walk up to the harness and put it on."

But she warned him: "I may kick it all to pieces if you don't know the trick of handling the ribbons—so as to guide without my knowing it." Just to have told him this much made her feel better, and she promised at the last, "I won't sulk anymore."[45]

Though McAdoo's tasteless attempt to delay if not disrupt Wilson's marriage to Edith Galt was successfully aborted, the rumor of slander persisted. The riddle of Mrs. Peck's relationship would remain a source of permanent fascination to journalists and historians. Beginning with a tip on Thanksgiving eve, November 1915, Washington newsmen plumbed, though fruitlessly, the story that important court proceedings had been filed involving the president.[46] Attacks by newspaper and telephone continued and intensified, spreading rumors that Wilson's wife, Ellen, had really died of a broken heart because of her husband's affair with Mary Peck, whose breach-of-promise suit was settled by Louis Brandeis.[47] House too writes of the "scandal monger" talk about Wilson and the deliberate efforts to portray him as a "thoroughly immoral man."[48] Mary, conscious of having paid a peculiar penalty for her friendship with Wilson, felt herself to be the victim of "subterranean politics."[49]

The true story may never be known. While Mary's correspondence reflects unique insights into the personality, character, and concerns of the twenty-eighth president of the United States, its source has remained somewhat of an embarrassment, a captive of history's footnotes as well as the subject of abiding curiosity. Though only about fifty of her letters remain on record today, constituting most certainly less than one-quarter of her response to the correspondence initiated by Wilson, their humor, vitality, candor, and vulnerability are compelling. Mary was a problem to both of Wilson's wives. Even the thought of her letters was so hurtful that Edith Wilson in later years dismissed their importance on grounds "that there probably wasn't much of anything in them."[50]

CHAPTER 10

Mary Peck, the dear friend he found in Bermuda

It was in Bermuda that Wilson had first met Mary Allen Hulbert Peck and nurtured the lasting friendship that became a threat to both his wives and, eventually, to himself, and "the basis of salacious gossip for two political campaigns." Identifying the three women who had most influenced the president's life, the author and journalist William Allen White named Ellen as the first, Edith as second, and recognized the third as Mary Peck.[1] Mary, however, with her fondness for theatrical allusions, insisted that her role in Woodrow Wilson's life was small, "scarcely a speaking part," for there were many more letters from Wilson than meetings with him during their long friendship. They met on ninety occasions, including ten at the White House. But the number of letters was too abundant (about 227 on record), and the content too important, for such a dismissive assessment, for the letters intimately expose, from first to last, the heart and mind of Woodrow Wilson. The privileged content of those letters to Mary Peck was noted by Wilson's second daughter, Jessie, Mrs. Francis Sayre Jr.—one of many who disapproved of the woman. Jessie thought it was "hard that the only one of [her father's] fine women friends who was not quite worthy of his confidence should have received it most fully." She regretted that her father revealed so much of himself to Mrs. Peck, even as she conceded, "How else can one get the story in his own words?"[2]

This lonely man had told his story to the woman whose "great and noble friendship," at a time when the world appeared somber to him, had put him at ease, allowed him to be happily himself. "Released from bonds to enjoy the full freedom of [his] mind"[3]—thus, at the start of their correspondence, Wilson pays tribute to Mary's benevolent influence. To Mary—reverting to an enduring theme, a dominant power in his life, his almost visceral compulsion for consummate allegiance and unconditional affection—he could write as he "would not dare write . . . to any one who knew me less well." Allowing for the "selfish indulgences of friendship,"[4] nothing was too private to discuss with Mary during his eight-year progress from president of Princeton University to president of the United States. Depending on his moods, he talked openly of childhood longings, ambition, power, leadership, writing, the press, politics, political personalities, institutional and world challenges, and repeatedly, of the meaning of friendship. He also freely discussed his physical disabilities, his incidences of nervous indigestion, and touched on his dental afflictions ("systematically neglected for eight years").

Turning to Mary Peck during "strenuous and disheartening" times, he revealed his searing sense of rejection, of failure, of being "too angry . . . too disheartened, too disgusted, to think straight or with any sort of coolness about what I ought to do in the circumstances." His words differ in successive letters, but the tone grows increasingly plaintive and the message more emotional in the Princeton years. Though he fought stubbornly, the penalties exacted from a week with the trustees of the university, who wore out his spirits rather than his body, were severe for this Scots-Irishman.[5]

Wilson's letters to Mary Peck amount to a heartrending self-portrait of his entire physical and mental being. Without underestimating their romantic implications, the letters are of still greater significance for the insight they provide into a vulnerable, melancholy man who fought the "blue devils," while craving recognition, sympathy, and understanding: a man of rigid ideals, vaulting ambition, and marginal stamina, so weary at times that he stayed in bed on Sundays, "sleeping, sleeping, sleeping without stint or end."[6] He was, he feared, one who could exercise no sort of moderation, least of all in his emotions. Wilson acknowledged that, when he did have the blues, "I go in for having them with great thoroughness and fairly touching bottom."

Spirited Mary Peck and flowering Bermuda came to symbolize a refuge to which Wilson could escape, if not bodily, then in his imagination, assured of security from the realities of Princeton, of the governorship, of the presidency, of broken friendships, and of family illnesses. Bermuda and Mary undoubtedly afforded respite too from Ellen, his beloved but troubled spouse, whose "serious soul was racked by a thousand cares, a thousand dreads, a thousand duties—processioning through her life." Bermuda was also a welcome change from the dark, brooding manses of his demanding heritage. Wilson talked of the island's peace and gaiety, remembering "delicious hours" in which he lost "all of the abominable self-consciousness that has been my bane all my life."[7]

Wilson had sailed to Bermuda for a rest in mid-January 1907, arriving a few days later in mid-June weather. He had turned fifty the previous month and had been president of Princeton since June 1902. Prominent as an author, as well as a speaker and educator, he was already mentioned as a candidate for United States senator from New Jersey, and even for president of the United States.

That he was in Bermuda on his own spoke of the more troublesome facets of his seemingly enviable life. Given his years of poorly controlled high blood pressure, he would never wholly recover from his partial blindness in May 1906. The retinal hemorrhage in his left eye was most likely due to undiagnosed hypertension.[8] Complaining now of discomfort from what was referred to as a lingering case of neuritis, he was also emotionally depleted by recent and unexpected opposition to his ambitions for Princeton, which he envisioned as a more democratic, more intellectual, more unified college and graduate school. Though barely four months had elapsed since his return from an entire summer's vacation in England's lake country, he was badly in need of further rest. This time he sought, following his doctor's advice, the monthlong solace of Bermuda's warm, soft, and languid air.

He soon filled his days, riding his bicycle, outlining a series of lectures that would be published the following year as *Constitutional Government in the United States,* and delivering sermons on two separate Sundays. At solitary dinners, sitting in a quiet alcove of the dining room at the Hamilton Hotel, he amused himself by speculating about people at the nearby dinner parties, watching the crowd as one would watch a stage from a box in the theater. One woman in particular caught his attention. He called her "My Lady" and used to change his seat at his table so that he was better able to see her.

The first time Wilson saw her, arriving late to join a dinner party, she wore a gold lace dress, glittering among the military and naval trappings of the group, and he wondered what she said that so suddenly enlivened what had seemed to him a rather dull-spirited company. After their introduction—Wilson's mention of Mary Peck to Mrs. William T. James, wife of Hamilton's mayor, resulted in invitations to both to dine at the Jameses' home—Mary told Wilson with appealing humor that she loved his flattery but that her circle brightened at her arrival for an entirely mundane reason: "I was nearly always late—they were hungry—therefore grumpy; and I meant *Dinner!*"[9]

Prepared to find Wilson interesting, Mary was charmed by the fun of their lighthearted talk, about the marketing of the island's lilies and onions and potatoes, about its tennis club and yacht races, its ever-present, ever-changing British regiments. As Wilson's stay in Bermuda was soon to end, Mary Peck switched her invitation from tea to dinner on the very next evening, when the swiftly assembled guests included Chief Justice and Mrs. Gollan.

Mary, a native of Michigan with a husband in Pittsfield, Massachusetts, lived that winter with her mother and son at Inwood, a quaint old Bermuda house with an enclosed rose garden where the only sound to be heard was the rhythmic ebb and flow of the sea on the south shore. Wilson dropped by Inwood the day after the dinner to leave a note—he did not wish to go away without saying good-bye—and it was with honest disappointment that he had not found her at home. On February 20, back at Princeton, he wrote to tell her that he was indulging himself by sending her a copy of Walter Bagehot's essays and a volume of his own. Five weeks later, he wrote again to Mary to say that he had taken pleasure in her kind letter, and though he had not answered it promptly, he carried it in his mind. It had done a great deal "to keep me in heart amidst much unrewarded toil."

Wilson returned to Bermuda alone the next winter, despite his suggestion to Ellen on his previous visit that the "next time you shall come with me, and then it will be perfect." He returned to the island to recover peace and perspective from "somewhat too strenuous business and anxiety."[10] Though Mary had never answered his last note, he immediately set out to find her. He had already driven over to Inwood only to learn that she had moved to Shoreby, in Paget, a stout white house with columned porches presiding high over the turquoise waters, with a sweeping view from the edge of the bay to the shores of Hamilton beyond. He met up with her in the little township of Bermuda. Leaning on a cane, having sprained his knee on the rough sea voyage, he was immediately invited to visit Shoreby, to lie in the porch hammock, to take tea, to dine with her family whenever possible.

Wilson was at peace, writing to Ellen that February that Bermuda was certainly the best place in the world in which to forget Princeton as an organization and a problem, and that the island afforded him most soothing rest. He hoped to write two lectures and then work on arranging certain essays. He also reported to Ellen that he had seen Mrs. Peck twice, that she was "very fine. You must know her." (In fact, she insisted that they stay with her at her home in Pittsfield, Massachusetts, when they attended James Garfield's inauguration as president of Williams College, and he wished to do so as he thought Ellen would like her, "despite her free western manner").[11]

Wilson also noted with admiration that Mary "seems to know everybody that is worth knowing,"[12] and as she had so often wintered in Bermuda, it seemed that everybody turned up at her house, including Mark Twain. However, he was remembering, he assured Ellen, her injunction. This appears to have been a word of caution by Ellen in regard to Mary, but it seemed not to have dampened Wilson's spirits in any vital measure.

Wilson did not dance, did not smoke, did not play bridge or swim, but he was quite content to be one of the spectators on the wide porch of the Hamilton Hotel leading out from the ballroom, and to be anchored down with Mary's fan or scarf when she went in to dance. He had never known anyone like her, such an exuberant creature, such a "veritable child of nature," so open and direct that he linked her with wild things and yet said she was meant to be "taken into one's confidence and loved."[13] Later he would remember hours, obviously cherished, in a little house with bougainvillea on the road to the south shore, hours when, as he said, he "lost all of the abominable self-consciousness that has been my bane all my life and felt perfectly at ease, happily myself, released from bonds to enjoy the full freedom of my mind."[14]

Forty-four years old when she met the fifty-year-old Woodrow Wilson, Mary Peck appeared more intelligent than beautiful; her hair, combed neatly away from her face and knotted in back, emphasized the clarity of her features. Tall and ample, she dressed in the height of fashion, in Gibson-girl shirtwaist tops and flaring skirts, tucked and pleated cottons with fine lace. People, including Wilson himself, mentioned her brilliant vitality, though Wilson's cousin Helen Bones found her "seductive," adding that she used her beautiful purple voice "caressingly though lazily." Helen acknowledged Mary's charm but qualified her gift for making her companions feel brilliant—it depended on her "absorbing way of listening to the words of wisdom uttered by *a man*."[15]

Born Mary Allen in Grand Rapids, Michigan, on May 26, 1862, she was proud of her early New England ancestry. She seemed always to have lived on the fringes of wealth and privilege, the tides of family fortune shifting her back and forth between private homes and boardinghouses. She had studied music with a starry-eyed Englishwoman, French under a Swiss, and English literature with a former family governess. At age twenty-one, she married a mining engineer and explorer, Thomas Harbach Hulbert. In the winter, he worked in Canada, while she traveled abroad to Munich, Venice, Florence, and Rome to visit with his parents. She gave birth to their son, Allen Schoolcraft Hulbert, in 1888, was widowed one year later, and remarried the next, on December 29, 1890.

Mary's second husband, Thomas Douse Peck, five years her senior, was a widower with three children, a graduate of Williams College, class of 1880, who worked in his family's prosperous woolen mills in Pittsfield, Massachusetts. The second winter in Pittsfield, Mary suffered a depression that precipitated a journey to Bermuda, where she and her husband moved to Inwood in Paget. By 1907 she admitted that their marriage was a failure.[16] Dismissed as "extravagant, histrionic, flirtatious," as a "lovely butterfly playing in utter unconsciousness in a world that did not touch her," she was notorious in some circles for her "frank courting of susceptible males."[17] While Mary Peck's friendships with a variety of men incited sporadic gossip—supposedly, she had captivated such diverse experts on feminine charm as Admiral John Arbuthnot Fisher, Mark Twain, the oil magnate Henry Huttleston Rogers, the American vice-consul, W. H. Allen, and the widowed British governor of Bermuda, General Sir Walter Kitchener, brother of Lord Kitchener of Khartoum—the nature of her bond with Woodrow Wilson would ever remain a question. Concentrated between the last two months of 1909 and 1910, when Mary was living with her mother in Manhattan at 39 East Twenty-seventh Street, their relationship was in all likelihood innocent, but to the onlooker seemed compromising.

Mary disclaimed any notion of a love affair. Nothing, in fact, aroused her displeasure as much as the implications placed on her bond with Wilson. She said that Wilson was attracted to her by her zest for life. She also observed that he was unusually fond of an attentive audience, and that it was restful for him to talk to her about his tribulations at great length and intimately. At times she felt she was studying economics and even practical politics as surely as any student in his classes. Understanding of his moods, ideals, and inhibitions, and of what she referred to as his steely, if not great, mind groping for affection, she was sometimes sorry for him, thought him cheated of his boyhood and a victim of rigorous ancestors. She felt that the will for martyrdom was strong in him. Though Mary Peck and Woodrow Wilson addressed each other as "Dearest Friend" and signed their letters "Your devoted friend," their correspondence reflects none of the urgency of Wilson's overt physical yearning for the women he married, both Ellen and Edith. Mary sums up what was probably the true nature of the couple's relationship: "Tender, yes; but hardly erotic, nor by any means measures of passion."[18]

Before they parted in Bermuda in February 1908, Wilson and Mary Peck began to plan the meeting of their families in Pittsfield, arranged eventually for October 5 after what Mary refers to as "the first congenial exchange of letters" between Ellen Wilson and herself. That summer Wilson went abroad exceedingly restive about his future, brooding over the possibility of resigning from Princeton, and on the increasing pressure to enter active politics. Though he had traveled without Ellen on numerous occasions, the likelihood of a confrontation between the two on the subject of Mary Peck has been suggested as one of the reasons for this solitary voyage to revisit England's Lake District.[19] Mary's correspondence with Wilson himself seems to have halted for the seven months between his return from Bermuda and their family gathering in Pittsfield in October, though its loss or destruction is possible.

While Ellen's thirteen letters, and their daughters' fifteen to Wilson from Old Lyme in the summer of 1908 have not been found,[20] one of Wilson's to Ellen quite specifically conveys the anguished state of their marriage. Reference to "cutting and cruel judgment" may bear on a remark that Ellen had made about Wilson's feeling for Mary Peck. On July 20, 1908, he wrote Ellen that he had never longed for her more, that she was

> everything that sustains and enriches life. You have only to believe and trust me, darling, and *all* will come right,—what you do not understand included. I know my heart now if I ever did, *and it belongs to you.* God give you the gracious strength to be patient with . . . me! "Emotional love,"—ah, dearest, that was a cutting and cruel judgment and utterly false; . . . but I never blamed you for it or wondered at it. I only understood—only saw the thing as you see it and as it is *not*,—and suffered,—am suffering still, ah, how deeply!—but with excess of love. My darling! I have never been worthy of you,—but I love you with all my poor, mixed, inexplica-

ble nature,—with everything fine and tender in me. Suffering and thinking over here by myself, *I know* it! [21]

Regardless of these protestations, Wilson's need for Mary Peck's friendship seems to have intensified after their family gathering in Pittsfield. Almost as a formal recognition of what was to be their prolific correspondence, only occasional until now, Wilson wrote, on October 25, 1908, that he could not tell Mary what a privilege it was to hear from her and to know that she was generously willing that he should keep in touch with her. The "individual flavor and delightful force" that she put into her letters made him deeply her debtor. [22]

He commented repeatedly on Mary's electric personality, her spirit, her energy, probably because these were characteristics quite alien to him and to Ellen. Seeking an excuse to be in her company, he wrote in early November to ask her plans for sailing for Bermuda so that, if possible, he "may be at the wharf to say good-bye? It would be a melancholy pleasure." [23] As politics frequently required Wilson's presence in New York City, he and Ellen, who sometimes accompanied him, and also his daughters, would visit Mary Peck.

In the summer of 1909, when Ellen was in Old Lyme with her sister, Madge, and her daughter Margaret—Jessie and Eleanor were in Europe—a rapturous letter from Wilson, alone in Princeton, told Mary that he felt suddenly freed from the sense of the world pressing in on all sides. Instead, this was a time when "one's dreams are set free . . . when they run where they please," when he longed most for his friends. This was the time too, he told Mary, "that gives me a special heart-ache that I cannot see whom I will, cannot have my dearest friends at call, cannot fill the inviting leisure with the pleasures for which it was made." This was the time when his thoughts, consequently, "play constantly about the ones I most miss." [24] He spoke of admiration being "a very pure pleasure," and of how pleasant it would be if one could keep the selfish longing from following and displacing it. Apparently, he concluded, "both admiration and the longing are what friendship lives upon in absence."

Wilson's commitment to Mary Peck, bordering on dependency, would have surprised those numerous detractors who looked on "poor Woodrow" as a victim of Mary's connivance. Among them, no explanation of any sort could be mustered in favor of Wilson's attachment to her. His entire "Bermuda experience," as it was referred to, was deemed unfortunate because of his meeting with this adventuress. As for invitations Mary Peck received to the White House, about which it was said she lost no opportunity to imply deep intimacy—these were gained, according to Ellen Wilson's cousin Florence Hoyt, by giving presents to the Wilson family. Mary was also accused of overentertaining,[25] of more or less trapping Wilson into behaving like "a gallant fool" who did not understand her kind at all.[26]

The fiction of Mary Peck as a family friend was politely sustained a number of times in a number of places after the initial family encounter in Pittsfield. Mary's visits, to Princeton, Trenton, and Sea Girt, Wilson's gubernatorial summer seat, and to the White House two months after the presidential inaugural, were formally scheduled. Ellen and her youngest daughter, the twenty-one-year-old Nell, in New York City to see a matinee performance of *She Stoops to Conquer* at the Garden Theatre, decided on the spur of the moment to "run and 'say howdy'" to Mary Peck, who lived across the street. The unsuspecting hostess was not dressed and took all of fifteen minutes to do her hair. But just as her unexpected visitors had to fly back to the theater, she ran after them in the hall, in her wrapper, to ask them to return for tea after the play, resulting in almost an hour's "delightful little visit,"[27] as Ellen reported to Wilson.

Mary Peck was particularly fascinating to the Wilsons' daughter Nell. She described Mary as a "charming woman, with great intelligence and humor." Watching her daintily puffing at one cigarette after another, Nell concluded it was a mistake to think it wrong for women to smoke, "since it was so becoming."[28] On the whole, Nell insisted that the family had enjoyed Mary Peck immensely—though not without some reservation, as her constant suggestions about improving their appearance "got on our nerves at last." Nell also wrote most protectively of her father's several deep and lasting friendships with women, naming Mary Peck among the specific six, "all brilliant and charming women," he liked most. Though her father wrote long letters to them and spent hours in their company, he also, according to his daughter, shared these friendships with her mother, who never betrayed a trace of jealousy because she knew there was no cause for it. Her mother considered herself a grave and sober person and had said to her husband, "Since you have married someone who is not gay, I must provide for you friends who are."[29]

Outwardly, at least, Ellen was a cordial hostess, not to be underestimated as a practiced politician in dealing with Mary Peck. Ellen made a point of having her husband's friend visit the White House, but it wasn't by chance, Helen Bones reasoned, that Ellen was too busy to see much of her and left her secretary to entertain and chaperon Mary and Wilson on their afternoon drives. Nevertheless, Ellen Wilson was very sorry for "Woodrow's friend,"[30] said Helen, and did buy some of her expensive clothing to help her when she was in financial straits.

In the unlikely relationship Wilson forged for the two women, the tall, vibrant, aristocratic-looking Mary Peck, who could "never learn indifference or restraint,"[31] was always extremely generous in her reference to the tiny, plump, dutiful, and solemn Ellen Wilson. The latter made small secret of her opinion of her husband's Bermuda acquaintance: during her first summer in Cornish, she had told Woodrow, "Mary Hulbert notwithstanding," she had met piles of New England spinsters whom she liked. [32]

Mary Peck's marital status was publicly clarified when, on December 9, 1911, a brief article in the *New York Times* (its front-page prominence being undoubtedly due to rumors of her closeness to Wilson) reported that Mrs. Mary Allen Peck of New York had brought a suit for divorce against Thomas D. Peck of Warrenton, North Carolina. That summer, Wilson encouraged Mary—who would resume the name of Hulbert when her divorce was granted the following year—to confide in him. "At every crisis in life it is absolute salvation," he had assured her years earlier, "to have some sympathetic friend to whom you can think aloud without restraint or misgiving."[33]

Nine months later, as rumors regarding their relationship persisted, Wilson was the one who sought help over a scandal that was being "fabricated" about a judge in Pittsfield having been shown one of his letters, in connection with her divorce. Aware that the mere breath of such a thing would put an end to his candidacy, he despaired, "It is too deep an iniquity for words!" [34] But despite bitter rivalry between Wilson and Theodore Roosevelt, and Roosevelt's political manager's prompting during this, Wilson's first, presidential campaign, Roosevelt refused to stoop to slander, or to question his adversary's morals. "What's more it won't work," he squeaked in his treble-pitched voice. "You can't cast a man as Romeo who looks and acts so much like the apothecary's clerk."[35] In some quarters, however, Mary Peck was blamed for the notoriety of her friendship with Wilson, for sharing its details and possibly some items of their correspondence.

*   *   *

On February 19, 1913, two weeks before starting down to Washington and the White House, President-elect Wilson reassured Mary that Bermuda and their friendship could not be altered and would remain in the background of his thought "no matter what is in the foreground."[36] Their letters, particularly for the years 1913 and 1914, testify to Mary's truly supportive role as Wilson revealed his innermost concerns during the first term of his presidency. Under the critical challenges of the currency bill—his efforts to reform the national currency system—and of the Mexican crisis, he lay awake at night, suffered spells of indigestion, complained about being depended upon for leadership and expected to do everything. Repeatedly, an element of desperation had seeped into his letters as he earnestly pressed Mary to maintain their relationship. Their understanding was, in his view, so complete that words were superfluous: "But I need not tell you all this. The joy of a real friend is that one need not explain anything: it is known and comprehended already."[37]

Wilson spent eight days in July 1913 with his own "happy adorable family,"[38] who were summering in Cornish, New Hampshire. Once back in Washington, however, Wilson's satisfactory holiday in no way affected either the momentum or content of his correspondence with his friend. He spoke of loneliness as though he were bereft of any shred of family, more anxious than ever for news of Mary, whose silence nagged away as summer tapered into autumn. Near the end of September, having heard that she was hospitalized in Nantucket, his sense of uneasiness reached such a pitch that, not for the first time, he wrote asking if someone could drop him a note to tell him how she was so that "this anxiety may not gnaw at my thoughts while I strive to handle big things of state?"[39]

Apparently recovered, Mary shared with her son a small apartment at 49 Gloucester Street in Boston during the winter of 1913–14. Living in an old city with a dignity and character all its own and a long tradition, Mary seemed restored. By June 1914, Wilson confided in Mary his fear that Europe might indeed be plunged again into wars like those of the Napoleonic era. He told her of Ellen's continued illness and explained that he was unfit to write the cheerful letter that Mary needed and that he would love to write. On August 7, he sent news of Ellen's death: "Of course you know what has happened to me; but I wanted you to know direct from me." Mary's message of condolence was already en route. She always mentioned Ellen with great sympathy, understood the burden of her responsibilities in the White House, and also recognized her ability and her flair. With war looming, it was incredible to Mary "that this terrible thing has come to you now, when you need that sweet love to help you in this terrible time. I know I can say nothing that can really help any of you but just to take to yourself the comfort of remembering she had much—much that was beautiful in her life—much that makes life worthwhile."[40]

During this bleak period, Wilson felt inadequate to Mary's needs, drained as he was by personal troubles that left him "cold and heavy, and therefore with nothing to give."[41] Knowing the role he must play in Mary's life, he regretted that he was deficient in the energy, the rich store of things, intimate and strange, that would divert her mind: "The days sap me,—sap me easily and quickly."[42]

Though he claimed that he lacked Mary's "magic of sympathy,"[43] Wilson did set out with immense care to be of help to her in a decidedly positive manner. On December 12, 1914, he wrote to Nancy Saunders Toy, wife of a Harvard University professor, a rambling letter that ultimately eased into the subject of Mary Allen Hulbert. He wondered if Mrs. Toy was free to make new acquaintances or free to seek people out at all? He had a friend now living at 49 Gloucester Street in Boston whom he wished very much she might know, immediately proceeding to describe Mary A. Hulbert in terms remarkable for their understanding and candor:

> She has had a hard life, chiefly hard because it denied her access to the things she really loved and was meant to live by and compelled her to be (or to play at being) until she all but became a woman of the world, so that her surface hardened and became artificial while her nature was of the woods, of hearty unconventional friendships, and of everything that is sweet and beautiful: a born democrat . . ."[44]

Wilson's next letter to Nancy Toy, written little more than a week later, was more precise. He thanked her for having Mrs. Hulbert to tea and told her how sincerely Mrs. Hulbert had enjoyed the occasion. The present letter was prompted by the news she had just sent him that Allen Hulbert had dissipated his modest fortune to the point where they found themselves almost penniless. Did Mrs. Toy know anybody in Boston to guide Wilson in helping Mrs. Hulbert earn a living? He suggested the field of interior decoration, for which, he said, she had an extraordinary talent and for which he could give her unqualified endorsement.

A few days later, Wilson confessed to Mary the steps he had taken, knowing that she urgently wanted to get to work and earn money. He had written five friends of his wish to help, asking them for advice in return. "Do you approve," he asked, "or have I gone too far and too fast without your sanction or permission?"[45] He was so anxious to act and had thought of little else since receiving her note. To Mary's own effort to earn some money by collecting recipes and drafting an article, Wilson responded with guarded criticism.[46] He asked her to amplify the selections that she had sent him, offered to have them typed and to mail them to Edward William Bok, the editor of the *Ladies' Home Journal.* Wilson then wrote to Bok, asking also for his assistance in Mary's case, an approach that bore some fruit. By mid-February Mary's news was already in the mail. "A wonderful thing" had come out of the article—not, she feared, because of its real merit, but because of Wilson's kindness—a check from the magazine for $50 that looked very large to her and gave her "a sense of power out of all proportion" to her ability.[47] Though the *Journal* saw fit to print Mary's articles on the "Tea Table" and "How to Pack a Traveling Bag," her book of recipes and entertaining etiquette, *Treasures of a Hundred Cooks,* would wait until the war was over.

However, when one of Wilson's contacts, Arthur Tedcastle, did find a job for Mary at Jordan Marsh, the department store, at a "substantial salary," Mary refused it. Surprised and offended by her refusal, Tedcastle found that his negative opinion was confirmed by his wife's observations that Mary was "artificial," "superficial," "vain," and "melodramatic," though "she did not mean any harm." When the Tedcastles visited the White House in March, Wilson was said to have asked Mrs. Hulbert's reasons for not taking the position, as he thought she had wanted work. "Mr. Wilson, it wasn't work she wanted," Mrs. Tedcastle replied. Wilson looked at her sharply, according to her account, and remarked, "I think I understand."[48]

In February 1915, Allen Hulbert sailed to California, where he would take up a variety of far-fetched ventures. It was Mary's introduction to the "chapter of horrors"—the subsequent story of Wilson's damaging associations with the Hulbert mortgages and allegations and the attempt to buy her off "with huge sums of gold."[49] No matter what effort Mary made to send entertaining reports of her travels, after mid-March 1915 her correspondence with Wilson inexorably lost its equilibrium. Though Wilson encouraged her to keep writing "so that I can think about you and turn away from myself,"[50] by early April he would tell her with unusual formality, "It has been very good of you to write while I was unable to answer. For I really have been unable to answer."[51] Expansive and reserved all at once, he mused about "the tug of things that cannot wait" perpetually pulling at his mind, about being immersed in delicate situations known to the public or invented by the press.

On April 21, Wilson again protested that he had been trying for two weeks to get time and strength to write her a real letter but that every hour of his time, every bit of his strength, had been used, and more than exhausted, by their friends, the people of the United States. He assured her that he kept well, kept going with undiminished force, but "it is costing all the while, I imagine, just a little more than I have without drawing on reserves." Wilson would fail to mention, that spring, his engrossing love for a statuesque widow named Edith Bolling Galt, to whom he had been introduced in mid-March and proposed marriage on May 4.

Mary was expecting to end her visit with friends in Hot Springs, West Virginia, on May 24. An attack of "heart-nerves-circulation-something!" kept her back, but, she wrote to Wilson, she would give much to see him one more time before departing for California around July 1. On May 29, inexplicably, Mary received a telegram from the White House, signed Helen Bones: "Monday perfectly convenient. You must stop over. Will send car."[52] On her arrival, before Wilson went to Arlington Cemetery to make an address, she motored with him, Helen Bones, and Margaret Wilson to see the McAdoos' new baby. Earlier that day Wilson had written to Edith Galt to tell her that she had become indispensable to him and how happy he would be if he could somehow immortalize her.

Only weeks later, on June 16, in absolute desperation, Mary told Wilson, "There is no peace for my old bones this side the grave."[53] Allen needed $6,000 by June 25 or his business was lost. Her predicament was heightened by Allen's most recent request, this time for $7,500, once again having assured his mother of "large returns" [54] on what now amounted to their "all," as Mary put it. She now asked Wilson if he could see a friend of hers, apparently to represent her in possible negotiations, and added, "you must act—as you think best." Somewhat grimly she promised, "All will go well—It must."

In July, in Cornish, both a tense and idyllic time for Wilson—the second *Lusitania* note from Germany would arrive on July 9; Edith Galt had pledged to trust and accept him, her "loved Lord," ten days before— he wished Mary an "affectionate good-bye" on her departure for Los Angeles and said that he knew she was doing the right thing and the only thing consistent with her happiness. He left Cornish on July 18, and on the nineteenth he signed a document, in an effort to ease her financial plight, to purchase mortgages from Mary Hulbert in the amount of $7,500.[55]

During the first week in August, Mary, though weary after the journey west, remembered the anniversary of Ellen Wilson's death. She assured Wilson that her thoughts were with him during this sad time and wished she could do something to lighten the burden whose weight robbed him of the strength even for personal grief. On the other hand, though it was a difficult time for him, she assumed his and Ellen's "dear ones" were with him, "and that helps." Mary was probably oblivious to a passage in the August 5 edition of Washington's *Town Topics*:

A conspicuous figure in society of late is Mrs. Norman Galt of Washington. She is a cousin of the President, an intimate of his daughters, and staying at present with the Wilson family at Harklakenden House. It was for this guest's entertainment that Miss Wilson gave the notable tea which included all the lions, literary and artistic for miles around Cornish. Mrs. Galt's home is in a smart quarter of the city [Washington]. It has an attractive interior and she entertains in good style. A frequent guest at her board is the President, who wisely ignores the tradition that the chief Executive should not visit private houses and goes unannounced wherever and whenever he pleases to the confusion of his guards.

Wilson's purchase of the mortgages took two months to complete. Even in her desperate straits, Mary did not withhold from him that at least one real estate authority had reported that the properties in question were overvalued. On September 14, the negotiations officially concluded, Wilson wrote, "It gives me real pleasure to purchase the mortgages." He enclosed a draft for $7,500, declining Mary's request that he first deduct $600 of interest, explaining that he did not know how to and did not care to. Once again, he explained that his tardy response was owed to "imperative things" that demanded his attention, and of course he omitted any mention of his twice-daily communications with Edith Galt.

On September 26, 1915, Wilson wrote to a cousin of Ellen Axson Wilson's that "something very delightful has happened to me which I am not yet at liberty to tell others but which I want you to know among the first." This was the "great happiness and blessing" that had come to him in the midst of his loneliness, that Mrs. Norman Galt, "a lovely Washington woman," promised to marry him. A week later Wilson told Mary

of his plans.[56] Mary's bittersweet answer to her "Dearest Friend" is dated
October 11:

> I have kissed the cross. We are very very glad you have found hap-
> piness and that you had time to think of us in the midst of it. I need
> not tell you again that you have been the greatest, most ennobling
> influence in my life. You helped me to have my soul alive and I am
> grateful. I hope you will have all the happiness that I have missed.
> I can not wish you greater.[57]

As though momentarily distracted from news of the intended marriage, she reported that she and Allen were well, both working at the
business that the president's kind purchase of the mortgages had made
possible. Abruptly back on track in the very next sentence, undoubtedly
having seen Edith Galt's photograph in a newspaper, Mary conceded,
"She is very beautiful and sometime perhaps I may meet her." Implicit
in the letter was her profound sense of abandonment.

A curious letter follows that attests to Wilson's commitment to Mary
Hulbert, even in the dwindling days of their long and close attachment.
Perhaps it was loyalty, perhaps guilt together with genuine affection,
that spurred him to write "a hasty line," awkward in its graceless flattery. He pointedly omitted any reference to his son-in-law William
McAdoo's story of alleged rumors that their correspondence was being
shown in public. He also assured her that his thoughts followed her constantly and explained that he wrote about his engagement "as early as I
did announce it to anybody." Just below the White House engraving on
Wilson's letter, to the side, as though silently crying out for an answer to
the unfathomable, Mary wrote, "Why?" adding her initials, M.A.H., in a
more subdued hand.[58]

News of Wilson's engagement to Edith Galt was a severe blow to
Mary, protest as she might. She and Wilson, she would write, had discussed the subject of marriage just once, at which time she teased the
president about his preference for a "doormat wife." Mary insisted that
"by no power of reasoning" could Wilson and she have been mated; Wilson's sense of correctness in the most minute things—one's grammar,
one's clothes, the lie of a rug—"was warranted to drive certain temperaments to the verge of consideration of brutal murder."[59] Besides, even if
he had thought about marriage to her, politics, she recognized, would
have automatically ruled out any consideration of a divorced first lady.
Despite misgivings, she did congratulate the bride-to-be, who responded

with thanks for the "very charming note, good wishes and expressions of friendship."[60] Mr. Wilson had told Edith of his long friendship with Mary, and Edith looked forward to knowing her in the near future. There was no hint at this moment of the turmoil that would precede their meeting briefly at luncheon in Los Angeles four years later.

CHAPTER 11

A wedding on December 18, 1915

The atmosphere at the White House on October 6, 1915, was solemn, the president subdued and uncommunicative. Secreted in his study most of the morning, he emerged only to take a brief lunch, and to wander about the second floor. He was standing in his study when Irwin Hoover answered his bell. Wilson wanted the chief usher to be among the first to know that he was going to marry Mrs. Galt. In response, Hoover was "both glad and sorry,"[1] words Wilson fully understood to imply concern for himself and affectionate memory for the first Mrs. Wilson. Hoover was silent for some moments before he said that he believed that Mrs. Wilson, if she could know, would approve.

News of the impending marriage now flared through the White House, bringing with it apprehension of change and disruption in the orderly way of life re-created in the aftermath of Ellen's death. There was quiet rejoicing and some anxiety: goodwill toward the bride-to-be alternated with sympathy for the family that, as Hoover bluntly put it, "would have to take a back seat."[2] Wilson spent the rest of the day in seclusion, awaiting the public response to the announcement, composed with two fingers on the Hammond typewriter in his study and made official at eight o'clock that evening:[3]

Mrs. Norman Galt is the widow of a well known business man of Washington who died some eight years ago. She has lived in Washington since her marriage in 1896. She was Miss Edith Bolling and was born in Wytheville, Virginia, where her girlhood was spent and where her father, the Honorable William H. Bolling, a man of remarkable character and charm, won distinction as one of the ablest, most interesting and most individual lawyers of a State famous for its lawyers. In the circle of cultivated and interesting people who have had the privilege of knowing her Mrs. Galt has enjoyed an enviable distinction, not only because of her unusual

beauty and natural charm, but also because of her very unusual
character and gifts. She has always been sought out as a delightful
friend, and her thoughtfulness and quick capacity for anything she
chose to undertake have made her friendship invaluable.

It was Miss Margaret Wilson and her cousin Miss Bones who
drew Mrs. Galt into the White House circle. They met her first in
the early part of the present year, and were so much attracted by
her that they sought her out more and more frequently and the
friendship among them quickly ripened into an affectionate intimacy. It was through this association with his daughter and cousin
that the President had the opportunity to meet Mrs. Galt, who
spent a month at Cornish this summer as Wilson's guest.

Wilson added and then crossed out

It is, indeed, the most interesting circumstance connected with the
engagement just announced that the President's daughters should
have picked Mrs. Galt out for their special admiration and friendship before their father did.[4]

Another "interesting circumstance" of that day's events did not go
unnoticed: Wilson's coupling the announcement of his wedding plans
with his intention to vote for women's suffrage in New Jersey. It was
thought odd in some circles. Indeed, it was considered an "antidote statement,"[5] among those aware that a few years earlier, in 1911, he had made
no secret of his bitter opposition: women of what he regarded as extreme
independence were contrary to Southern tradition. "How he did detest
newspaper women and women in business generally," the journalist
Frank Parker Stockbridge observed,[6] and his years with Martha Carey
Thomas, Bryn Mawr's formidable dean, had only reinforced his aversion. To his eyes, she was "the apotheosis of the 'advanced' woman," and
though he conceded her intellectual brilliance, he "cordially detested her
and all she stood for," despised her point of view and deplored her mas-
culinity. Uncomfortable with bluestockings and independent women, he
bowed at last to the issue of female suffrage when its political value
could no longer be ignored.

Headlines proclaimed Wilson's intentions to marry Edith Galt. Only
two other presidents had married while in office, John Tyler to Julia Gardiner in 1844, and Grover Cleveland to Frances Folsom in 1886. The

Washington Post claimed knowledge of the romance for the past three months; telegrams, letters, and telephone calls saturated the White House. Some, like Senator Henry Cabot Lodge, looked askance at the prospect of Wilson's "vulgar marriage."[7] Others, such as Edith's own family, were nearly ecstatic.

The official family engagement party took place that evening, October 6, at the White House. Guests included Edith Galt; her mother, Sallie Bolling; her sister Bertha; her brother John Randolph; Helen Bones; Wilson's son-in-law and daughter, Secretary of the Treasury and Mrs. McAdoo; the Misses Lucy and Mary Smith; Ellen Axson's first cousin Colonel Edmund T. Brown; and Dr. Grayson. Wilson had already met Edith's mother and sister Bertha, at tea one month earlier. The White House usher was riveted by the proceedings. The president was a courtly suitor and, in his courtesy to Edith's mother and sister, left "not a stone unturned to make them at home and comfortable under circumstances that are trying for the hardiest."

In the eyes of the Bolling family, Wilson was indeed "no more the President but a prospective son-in-law and brother-in-law." The family that entered hesitantly "left confident and understanding and full of approval," their departure comparable to the "conquest of a powerful army who had just been thru battle and come out victorious." All in all, the Bollings "had seen the light of future possibilities and became engulfed in the prospects."[8] Wilson was impressed by the approval he received from them. According to the chief usher, the words and looks of these relatives "swayed this great man just as it would have done to the plainest of everyday individuals."[9]

One week after the president's announcement, *Town Topics*, on October 14, presented its biting version of his engagement:

So much has been published about the President and Mrs. Galt since the prediction of the engagement, that little remains to be said. From an obscure position in Washington society—obscure because her husband was in trade—Mrs. Galt becomes Mistress of the White House. It is only a short time back that matrons of the exclusive Cave-dweller variety were wont to raise their lorgnettes whenever Mrs. Galt's name was mentioned and icily ask: "Who is this lady? She does not mingle in our set." Affiliation with trade was too severe a jar for the delicate susceptibilities of the dames of that rarified atmosphere. The Misses Bollings of Wytheville, Virginia—

three of the four daughters—had chosen their husbands from Washington merchants—a leather man, a flour man, a purveyor of jewels—and although they came from good Virginia stock, such alliances proved insurmountable obstacles. Now all is changed. The tradesman's widow is exalted to the first position in the land. She bears the transition with a dignity and poise that indicate a fine and stable character and experience in life. To her credit—she won the affection and respect of the President's daughter . . .

For a couple of generations the Galts have been the Tiffanys of Washington. Upon death, Norman Galt left the business to his wife, and she has managed to run it successfully, with her brother as active manager. Whether or no she will sell her interest, now that she is to become first lady of the land, is a matter that interests everyone.

The issue of Edith Galt's inferior standing—because of her association with the retail trade, "which alone here is a social bar sinister"—remained a source of "keenest interest and not a little trepidation," the *Washington Post* reported on October 23, 1915. How Edith might pay off old snubs when she became chatelaine of the White House was the question. It was thought that the whole social structure of Washington might have to be rebuilt:

> Persons in trade who never before have been able to reach even the outer fringe of society may find themselves leading the procession to the White House dinners, teas and musicales. . . . If they are recognized by the first lady of the land they will have to be accepted by society and put on charity boards, dance committees and patron lists.

Every aspect of Edith Galt was of public interest, and the president's conduct was no less so. The couple chatted on the private telephone newly installed the second week in October between the White House and Edith's home. They saw each other at lunch and dinner, met at the theater and on the golf course, took drives together; and their correspondence continued to flourish. "Eyes rolled" over the president's newly faultless tailoring and over his late hours. Noted too was how little time he had for family and affairs of state, how he spent hours in his second-floor study writing to Edith in the morning, and at noon (before revising the secretary of war's statement on national defense), and after a cabinet meeting. How, after returning to the White House past midnight, he shut himself up in his study to write what the chief usher surmised to be "fiery words of love and admiration"[10] to be delivered early the next morning.

Security was now a particular challenge as Secret Service men, who privately referred to Edith by the code name Grandma, attempted to adapt to the president's new routine. Each innovation was a matter of concern, including the first of the many times Wilson joined Edith for dinner with her mother and sister, who lived at the Cordova Apartments. The inability of the bulky White House Pierce-Arrow to negotiate the narrow driveway required Wilson to get out of the car on the outside curb and walk up to the entrance, to the anxiety of his security guards.

Now that the president himself fetched his fiancée and escorted her home, his schedule posed special challenges. Earlier in the courtship, when the agent Edmund Starling was assigned to follow the couple as they strolled through Rock Creek Park, he had felt like an intruder and had had to resist the temptation to look away. Now, he often escorted the president home at midnight and even at later hours, Wilson often choosing to walk, especially during those clear and crisp October and November moonlit nights. Though often weary and self-conscious, the Secret Service men were on the whole a romantic lot, "glad," as Starling put it, that "the boss had made good." Starling welcomed their walks, especially after a four-or-five-hour wait outside Edith Galt's house; but he relished the president's mood, grinned at his antics, his laughing, his "acting like a boy in his first love experience."[11] Once, waiting on the sidewalk as an occasional milk truck passed by, Wilson seemed to dance a jig.

Everyone in his immediate presence clearly knew that Wilson was "simply obsessed."[12] Even the most sympathetic observers were disturbed that affairs of state had become secondary, that he seemed to shrug off most of his duties, or just dealt "with the most important of doings and then only partially." Requests for appointments were postponed with the suggestion that Wilson was preoccupied with important business, with of course no hint that the business was Edith Galt. Cabinet officers, senators, officials in general, were all treated in the same way. In the past, it had been hard to obtain appointments with this president, but now matters of state were held in abeyance while he wrote "letters of love and admiration for the lady of his choice."[13] The president seemed to be staking everything on this romantic attachment while the war raging in Europe created ominous possibilities for the United States, and a campaign for reelection loomed for the following year.

The ability to reach Wilson was and always would be an issue of his presidency and of his personality. There were critics of his isolation, and then there were defenders, who insisted that the record showed days of crowded appointments and concentrated labor, of meeting an unending train of visitors and delegations. The *New York Times*, on December 2, 1915, perhaps provoked by Wilson's critics, elaborated on the president's availability. On Mondays, Wednesdays, and Thursdays Wilson was scheduled to receive those who "merely want to pay their respects, then senators and congressmen who have no engagements"; he also allowed thirty minutes for signing public documents and an hour and a half for special engagements. On Tuesdays and Fridays, after an hour devoted to appointments, he planned to spend from eleven to one o'clock with his cabinet.

On this schedule, Wilson complained, "Congressmen are rushing upon me from every quarter,"[14] and it was hard to say when, if at all, he could have a moment of his own. Yet he did take extended time for his daily automobile rides and golf games, these outings being scrupulously justified. "His extraordinary intensity as a worker," Ray Stannard Baker would write, "made necessary a stern adherence to a daily programme of rest and exercise, lest his burdens break his health." Along with this grim apology, it was admitted that Wilson's days "were not, however, without relaxation and delightful interludes; intimate friends or relatives were often at luncheon and dinner, and in these months the President was spending many of his evenings with Mrs. Galt."[15]

Interest in the presidential wedding plans for Saturday, December 18, was naturally unbounded. Hoover anticipated with apprehension the culmination of "this most extraordinary and embarrassing ordeal." He admitted frankly that "the sooner it was over, the sooner would all be relieved from the strain under which they were laboring."[16] Rumors churned about the date and place of the wedding, and Edith's trousseau, which consumed much of her time, was soon to become a controversial issue, reflecting the current divisive sentiments at home and abroad about the war.

Edith Galt stayed with Altrude Gordon at 12 West Tenth Street in New York City while she shopped for her bridal wardrobe. Always keen about fashion, she appeased her lavish purchase at the stylish furrier A. Jaeckel, a charcoal caracal coat bordered in white fox, by explaining to Wilson, the donor of this elaborate gift, that though the regular price of the coat was

$1,000, the store offered to make it for her for a bargain price of $475. "Don't faint or think I have gone crazy," she entreated him, "but it was so pretty I couldn't help it!" Despite her imposing frame, she metamorphosed into the "little girl" he referred to so frequently and lovingly as she proclaimed her desire to come and sit in his lap "and have you tell me you love me even if I am extravagant."[17] He was, he assured her, "*so happy*, Sweetheart, about the fur coat," adding, "You are *not* extravagant—you are only doing what I begged you to do!"[18]

No president, however, could protect her from a severe if ephemeral backlash against orders placed with Julius Kurzmann on West Fifty-seventh Street for a wardrobe largely to be sewn abroad in Paris. Initially, the French refused to work for the German proprietor of the exclusive Manhattan dress shop; in a more conciliatory mood, the Syndicate of Paris dressmakers, in recognition of Mrs. Galt's international prestige, offered to make a complete trousseau without cost to her, an offer that was not accepted.[19]

As Edith was an Episcopalian and Wilson was an elder of the Presbyterian Church, she would ask Dr. Herbert Scott Smith of St. Margaret's Episcopal Church and Dr. James H. Taylor of the Central Presbyterian Church to officiate at the wedding. But they were second choices. Her first, for sentimental reasons, had been the Virginia-born Right Reverend Dr. Lucien Lee Kinsolving, missionary bishop of the Protestant Episcopal diocese of southern Brazil, who happened to be touring the United States. However, the bishop, the son of the late Reverend Ovid A. Kinsolving, who had married her parents, fell victim to Edith's refusal to have her authority questioned or tempered, not even by the bishop himself.

In asking him to officiate, Edith had imposed her terms. Because she had asked no one outside the immediate families, she had not invited the bishop's wife and as the latter did not live in Washington, it did not seem to Edith a discourtesy to omit her. The morning of December 16, however, Edith received a letter from Bishop Kinsolving stating that he and his wife had arrived at the Shoreham, that they were sailing in a few days for England, where it would cause his wife "much chagrin to acknowledge to her titled friends that she had not been asked to the marriage of the President where her husband had officiated,"[20] and that, therefore, she had decided to come with him and would, he felt sure, be welcome at the ceremony.

On receiving the bishop's letter, Edith could hardly believe she had read it correctly. She at once wrote her answer. She thanked the bishop for letting her know of his wife's embarrassing situation regarding the wedding, but reminded him that several weeks before she had explained why she could not include her among the guests. As it was impossible to add to the list, her only other course of action was to excuse him from his promise to perform the ceremony, which she was doing at once. Edith then called on her private wire to the White House, where she found the president alone in his study. She read both letters to him and admitted that Wilson was "far more tolerant than I."

"Why not wait and think it over a little," he had suggested. But Edith, "hurt to the quick that a head of our church should have so affronted the President of the United States," was incapable of making any concession. "No, this letter goes to him right now. I will postpone our wedding rather than be bludgeoned into a thing of this kind." "Yes," came the voice over the telephone. "I was afraid of that. But, after all, the poor fellow has enough to stand with a wife like that."[21]

Adhering rigidly to the restrictive guest list, Edith Galt had not invited Colonel and Mrs. House to the wedding, for which she was apologetic. After dinner in Washington on Wednesday, December 15, she told House that it did not seem right, but House reassured her that it was impossible to make an exception without hurting others' feelings. That same evening the president discussed with House the details regarding the latter's prospective trip abroad. This fourth journey overseas was a matter of urgent consideration since an Austrian submarine had torpedoed the Italian ocean liner *Ancona* during the past month, with twenty Americans lost at sea. Since early autumn, House had sensed that the time was near when the United States must intervene; on November 10, resolute for the cause of the Allies, he suggested the concept of an embryonic League of Nations to his "Dear Governor." It seemed to House

that we must throw the influence of this nation in behalf of a plan by which international obligations must be kept, and in behalf of some plan by which the peace of the world may be maintained. We should do this not only for the sake of civilization, but for our own welfare—for who may say when we may be involved in such a holocaust as is now devastating Europe?

Must we not be a party to the making of new and more humane rules of warfare, and must we not lend our influence towards the freedom of both the land and sea? This is the part I think you are destined to play in this world tragedy, and it is the noblest part that has ever come to a son of man. This country will follow you along such a path, no matter what the cost may be.

That December evening, House reviewed plans for his trip abroad, including his proposed conference with British diplomat Sir Edward Grey, who already referred to the general idea of a League of Nations as the "pearl of great price."[22] The president, aware of some opposition to House's acting on behalf of the government without due legal authority, promised to write the colonel a letter of his appointment as special agent to be put to use simply for protection in the event of trouble with the Senate. Wilson's confidence in House was all-encompassing. "You need no instructions," he wrote on December 17. "You know what is in my mind and how to interpret it, and will, I am sure, be able to make it plain to those with whom you may have the privilege of conferring." By sending a letter special delivery, written on December 24, which was valued by House "in some ways as important a letter as he has ever written to me,"[23] Wilson reinforced his faith in his emissary:

> Your own letters . . . exactly echo my own views and purposes. I agree with you that we have nothing to do with local settlements,—territorial questions, indemnities, and the like—but are concerned only in the future peace of the world and the guarantees to be given for that. The only possible guarantees, that is, the only guarantees that any rational man could accept, are (a) military and naval disarmament and (b) a league of nations to secure each nation against aggression and maintain the absolute freedom of the seas. If either party to the present war will let us say to the other that they are willing to discuss peace on such terms, it will clearly be our duty to use our utmost moral force to oblige the other to parley, and I do not see how they could stand in the opinion of the world if they refused."[24]

Questions about Wilson's position would, in hindsight, only multiply. Was it ever possible to secure the "future peace of the world" and "have nothing to do with local settlements," and couldn't such a position lead to serious trouble at a peace conference? And hadn't Wilson's letter omitted any hint of agreement to the implication, perhaps unintentional, of House's earlier talks with Grey to intervene with armed force against Germany if she refused the proposals put to her? Assuredly, Wilson meant mediation; the United States was to use only "our utmost moral force" and appeal to the "opinion of the world." There was, in December 1915, no intention to take up arms on behalf of the Allies.[25]

On Thursday, December 16, two days before the wedding, Irwin Hoover rode the streetcar from the White House to the Supreme Court (soon to become the Superior Court) of the District of Columbia, where he was issued marriage license No. 72225, cost $1, in the name of Woodrow Wilson, fifty-eight, of 1600 Pennsylvania Avenue, and Edith Bolling Galt, forty-three, of 1308 Twentieth Street.[26] Hoover had given much thought during past months as to where the ceremony would be held. He knew that the president was compliant on matters of a personal nature, and Hoover was more resigned than pleased at the final decision that the marriage take place at Mrs. Galt's modest, six-room house. His sense of the dignity of the presidential office was offended: ample facilities at the White House, he thought, made it easier and "so much more appropriate to one in high exalted position." Charged with planning the wedding, he would try to comply with the president's desire for simplicity even as he knew it to be an impossible request. Mrs. Galt's cramped quarters inevitably created problems for Secret Service men, policemen, aides, secretaries, ushers, butlers, maids, and valets—not to speak of the guests.

Hoover's responsibilities entailed the choice of flowers and caterer, and the disposition of the wedding presents and of Mrs. Galt's personal furnishings. According to the list typed by the president, Mrs. Galt would be moving into the White House with her dressing table, two chests of drawers, a pier glass, a brass clothes tree, a piano and bench, a large rolltop desk and desk chair, a wicker rocking chair, an Indian seat with cushions, a couch with pillows, a big club chair, some photographs, bookends, and a sewing machine. As Hoover commented, "Sentiment must have played considerably, for surely the White House contained a most complete assortment of articles of this kind."

Hoover oversaw the transformation of Edith's snug brownstone into an elaborate garden, a tempest of ferns, trailing vines, Scotch heather, and pyramids of American Beauty and pink Lady Stanley roses. At minimum five species of orchids shading from purple to pink banked the hall mirror, the mantels, the white satin prie-dieu, while the customary purple would appear as usual on the bride's shoulder. The ceiling-high fern wedding bower with its rose-strewn, shell-shaped canopy was lined in white blossoming heather and centered with an orchid-edged mirror that reflected the wedding party. The Marine Band played on the upper bedroom floor as guests below walked, after an 8:30 P.M. ceremony, from parlor to dining room for supper provided by a leading Washington caterer.

At least ten cars of newspaper reporters were soon lost in their attempt to follow the president and his new wife that evening. Escorted by the Secret Service, the limousine, with drawn shades and covered presidential door crests, sped over the bridge into Alexandria, lights flickering from shore to shore, as the occupants boarded their private parlor car on the train bound for Hot Springs, Virginia. Once arrived at The Homestead, they were ensconced in a suite that included a living room filled with carnations and crimson roses, a dining room, two bedrooms, two baths, and two porches. Edith's only complaint referred to the "overpowering" dining room staff. Otherwise, she assured her family, "The weather is cold but radiant and so are we," and "Woodrow sends his love with mine and says we are as happy as children off on a holiday."[27] The couple started each morning after their baths, in wrappers and slippers, tending to their correspondence. Deluged by mail forwarded from the White House, they opened letters and innumerable telegrams and Christmas cards, as well as packages that included a Christmas tree with electric lights. They then dressed, golfed, lunched, rode in their car, and returned to write and work for an additional hour or more. They dined at 8 P.M., after which Wilson read aloud to Edith until, she admitted to Bertha, "I sometimes revert to my old habits and go to sleep—but otherwise I behave."[28]

Often, as Wilson worked at his typewriter or dictated to his secretary, Charles Swem, Edith wrote her notes, inquired of her mother as to whether she had received two baskets of flowers and cake, presumably mementos of the wedding, and sent Hoover a check in "loyal appreciation"[29] of his interest and assistance. Diligent as she was about her mail, she was nevertheless available to the president at any moment, explaining to Bertha and other relatives, "Now, I must stop—for the most wonderful person in the world has a free minute."[30]

Edith received a letter from Helen Bones that was especially generous and memorable, since Helen had so loved Wilson's first wife. Miss Bones wrote "To Beautiful Bride" to tell her the chief reason everyone at home had enjoyed such a "perfectly delightful Christmas is because we have had the consciousness all day of how happy our dear blessed Man is—down there with you!" If any man ever deserved happiness, certainly it was Wilson, and it was "a very great thing to know he has it now." By her own admission something of a pessimist, Miss Bones now told Edith that she felt "so far that you are going to make his life a truly joyful one from now on," that "I can't see a cloud in his sky."[31] Even the relationship between Wilson and House seemed serene that December as the president and his bride, "two grateful friends," joined in sending the colonel and his wife "their most affectionate Christmas greetings."

★ Part II ★

President and Mrs. Edith Bolling Wilson, Wartime

CHAPTER 12

"The world is on fire"

The perfect honeymoon ended two days earlier than planned. Wilson treasured his hours with Edith at Hot Springs, so secluded that it seemed "as if we had nothing to do with the great world,"[1] until a telegram from Joseph P. Tumulty plummeted him back into the reality of war-struck Europe. Wilson received his secretary's warning on January 2, 1916:

> In view of critical situation here arising out of *Persia* case think it would be unwise for you to prolong your vacation. Hope you will pardon this suggestion.[2]

By return wire Wilson told Tumulty that he was consulting the secretary of state, Robert Lansing, about the December 30 sinking, off the coast of Crete, of the British liner in which two Americans had died. In response, with two more ships foundered without warning, Lansing judged that it would be well if the president could return to Washington at once as Lansing personally was "very much alarmed over the seriousness of the situation."[3]

The Wilsons left Hot Springs on the night of January 3, arriving in Washington early the next morning. By eleven o'clock, the president was in his office to confer with Missouri's Senator William J. Stone and Virginia's Representative Henry D. Flood about a Congress in turmoil. Its members were still disturbed over the eight-month-old case of the *Lusitania,* over the destruction of the *Arabic,* the *Hesperian,* the *Ancona,* and now the *Persia,* and by repeated American casualties and endangered commerce, particularly in regard to cotton and wheat. Two days later, Senator Thomas P. Gore of Oklahoma, in echo of William Jennings Bryan, proposed two bills to curb the loss of Americans: one, he would prohibit U.S. citizens from traveling on vessels of a belligerent country, and two, forbid American vessels to carry U.S. citizens and contraband of war at the same time. Wilson's policy toward the festering Mexican situation was also in question. Some weeks earlier, on December 21, Venustiano Carranza's soldiers had raided American villages and Pancho Villa's men had shot at American soldiers. Now, on January 6, Senator Albert B. Fall of New Mexico hotly called for investigation of Wilson's theoretical nonintervention stance on Mexico and of his quest for "cooperative understanding" among all nations of the Western Hemisphere. The president's proposal of a pan-American peace pact that same day, declaring that the friendship of American nations must be "founded on a rock,"[4] would receive a profound setback when Villa's men crossed the border into Columbus, New Mexico, and held up a passenger train on January 10 and murdered one of the seventeen American passengers. As a result, legislators condemned Wilson's policy of watchful waiting for its "uncertainty, vacillation, and uncontrollable desire to intermeddle."[5]

Mexico, however, would have to defer to the most critical challenge of the day—the conundrum of "preparedness," which was the provocative act of arming for war in the name of peace. Tumulty, among others, warned Wilson of the urgency of this volatile issue. "I cannot impress upon you too forcibly," he wrote the president on January 17, "the importance of an appeal to the country at this time on the question of preparedness."[6] Tumulty sensed, and heard, the indifference and skepticism, the lack of enthusiasm in the Congress on that subject and understood its origin in the country's inability to grasp its urgency. Resistance, he thought, came, on the one hand, from the preachings of the pacifists, particularly William Jennings Bryan, and on the other, from the fomenting militarism of Theodore Roosevelt.

To reinforce his position, Tumulty quoted from the January 16 edition of the *New York Times:* "Unless the large personal popularity of the Chief Executive is exerted and his eloquence and logic are employed to induce the people to overcome the apathetic indifference or unreasonable hostility to preparedness exhibited in Congress, we cannot hope that the matter will be settled before adjournment."

Heeding Tumulty and others, Wilson inaugurated a six-day presidential tour on behalf of national preparedness in Pittsburgh, at Memorial Hall, on Saturday night, January 29, 1916. As president, amazed to hear men speak as if America stood alone in the world and could follow her own life as she pleased, he had come to warn of a world "on fire, and there is tinder everywhere ... the sparks ... liable to drop anywhere." Amid the fanfare of flags, of trumpets and applause, he announced his theme, in essence that "new circumstances have arisen which make it absolutely necessary that this country should prepare herself, not for war, not for anything that smacks in the least of aggression, but for adequate national defense ... an army necessary for the uses of peace." Acknowledging that Republicans were just as deeply and just as intelligently interested as he was in this question, he asked that he be backed up by the whole force of the nation, not as a partisan, but as the representative of the national honor.[7]

Crusading for preparedness, traveling hundreds of miles west and back, to Pittsburgh, Cleveland, Chicago, Des Moines, Kansas City, and St. Louis, the president returned to Washington on February 4. It was difficult, he said, to keep the United States out of the war, and he felt, triumphantly, that he had proved he was a man of peace "when possible."[8] By coincidence, Wilson's archrival delivered an almost identical message. In Brooklyn, on Sunday, January 30, Theodore Roosevelt told a gathering of the Brooklyn Institute of Arts and Sciences that he stood for "ample preparedness in order to avert war and in order to avert disgrace and disaster if war should come."[9]

"The Star-Spangled Banner" hailed the president, and his wife, Edith, followed her husband into the great halls along the tour route to the tune of "Here Comes the Bride." Newspaper headlines to the contrary, "the cynosure of every eye was not the president, but Mrs. Wilson." [10] She was "stately as a duchess,"[11] her beauty, her graciousness, her charm, fascinating reporters, who declared the first lady's dominant characteristic to be "love."

Missing the mark, the reporters doubted that Mrs. Wilson discussed weighty affairs of state and vast international problems or indulged in intricate metaphysical speculations. Instead, the guess was that a president did not want exhausting arguments from his wife, but sympathy, sensibility, admiration, appreciation, and emotional responsiveness. Given Mrs. Wilson's priceless heritage of humor, it was certain that "she laughs at his jokes and will keep on laughing to the end of time, no matter how many times she has heard them. How few wives," a columnist lamented, "possess this rare gift."[12] Another spoke of naturalness being Edith's chief charm and of how "she did not make any effort to be brilliant," but was simply "a modest, gracious woman with plenty of small talk, like anyone else."[13]

It was not only Edith Wilson's amiable personality and her striking brunette beauty that awed interviewers. They enthused over her complexion, her eyes, her "overflowing femininity," and were barely less enthralled by how she saw that the president had his rest, and how she judiciously bowed from the platform of the traveling White House train and returned inside to her sewing and to one of Owen Wister's books. No measure of reporting on Edith was complete without a detailed account of her wardrobe.

Some months later she was appraised more objectively, as a "good business woman," who sold her own car during her first year in the White House, who knew "how to look after her own affairs."[14] That she was preoccupied daily with the business of government might have been guessed earlier. At this juncture, her possible impact on the careers of her husband's colleagues was even more faintly perceived. No longer dependent on Wilson's courtship letters that had primed her on state events, Edith now actually worked at the president's side in his White House study, fulfilling roles from confidante to secretary to encoder and decipherer of secret messages.

A new routine prevailed. The president was called at 6 A.M. and ate from a small plate of sandwiches and a thermos of coffee waiting on a small table outside his door. Afterward, according to the season, joined by a Secret Service agent or an aide, the couple golfed for an hour—when they played eighteen holes, Wilson scored around 115, Edith approximately 200[15]—before returning for an eight-o'clock breakfast together. Edith accompanied him to his study, where they checked what she referred to as the Drawer to see if anything had "blown up" overnight. If there was time, she placed routine papers before the president for signature, blotting and removing them as fast as possible.

At the arrival of the obliging and expert stenographer Charles Swem, at 9 A.M., Edith lingered when possible to listen to Wilson's dictation. "It was a delight and an education," she said, "to hear the lucid answers that came with apparently no effort from a mind so well-stored."[16] Secret messages, however, were attended to in private sessions. It was a three-stage effort, for example, that succeeded in dispatching Wilson's coded telegram, dated January 11, 1916, informing Colonel House in London that "it now looked as if our several difficulties with Germany would be presently adjusted." First, the president wrote his message by hand; next Edith converted the letters by hand into clusters of code numbers, which Wilson, last of all, typed out on his White House stationery.

* * *

Colonel House had arrived in London on January 5, fortified with Wilson's unofficial instructions to convey the interest of the United States in the future peace of the world and in its guarantees. The latter included military and naval disarmament and a league of nations to secure each nation against aggression and to maintain absolute freedom of the seas. There was also, and not incidentally, a political edge to House's lofty mission, inspired by the Senate's pressure on Wilson to compel England and her allies to remove their restrictions on neutral trade.

Aware of British skepticism toward America's foreign policy, House turned to the White House for reassurance. Wilson obliged him with a cable that "may well be regarded as historic,"[17] marking as it did the president's first official commitment to a league of nations, his declaration that he was "willing and glad, when the opportunity came, to cooperate in a policy seeking to bring about and maintain permanent peace among civilized nations."

That January 1916, Colonel House saw as many people as could be crowded into the waking hours. These included soldiers, sailors, politicians, and members of the press. At the pinnacle of diplomatic circles, he met with Britain's prime minister and foreign secretary and spent an hour with King George V. In Germany, he again saw top-level government officials, contenting himself with mineral water as Germany's Chancellor Theodore von Bethmann-Hollweg downed copious amounts of beer during one of their talks.[18] From Paris, after conferring with the French prime minister and the American ambassador, among others, he predicted that "hell will break loose in Europe this spring and summer as never before"[19] and reported that he sought to impress upon both England and France the precarious gamble involved in a continuance of the war. As for the president's efforts to arouse people to the necessity for defense, he could not "put it too strongly, for the dangers are greater than even you can realize."[20]

The colonel stopped off to see the king of the Belgians before returning to London, where he had left Britain's Edward Grey with the impression, recorded in a memorandum dated February 22, 1916, that President Wilson

> was ready, on hearing from France and England that the moment was opportune, to propose that a conference should be summoned to put an end to the war . . . and, if it failed to secure peace, the United

States would leave the Conference as a belligerent on the side of the Allies, if Germany was unreasonable . . . Should the Allies accept this proposal, and should Germany refuse it, the United States would probably enter the war against Germany."[21]

Colonel House returned to Washington on March 6 and elaborated on his most recent mission in a two-hour automobile ride with the president and Mrs. Wilson. The men conferred again before dinner, studying Grey's memorandum of his conference with House, the president inserting the word *probably* in the ninth line, which read "the United States would [probably] leave the Conference as a belligerent on the side of the Allies, if Germany was unreasonable." The president then congratulated House, telling him, as the latter recalled, "It would be impossible to imagine a more difficult task than the one placed in your hands, but you have accomplished it in a way beyond my expectations."

Altogether, this and repeated visits to Washington seemed to reinforce House's belief in his unique position with both the Wilsons. Uneasy over the favorable publicity he had received on his recent trip abroad, he worried about Wilson's reaction. London's *Nation* pronounced the colonel's visit a "landmark in the war"; it was well for the world to have "at least one carrier of ideas and intelligence." *Collier's* contended that there were "a good many thoughtful folk who think that the best thing about President Wilson is Colonel House" and "quite a few of the discriminating who think the team would work with equal success if the positions were transposed."

House both relished and suffered this praise. At the close of his visit, in the second week in April 1916, House told Cary Grayson that he was disturbed by complimentary articles appearing about him in the press, feeling that they might give annoyance at the White House. Grayson had reassured him that he did not believe anything could shake the president's affection for and confidence in him. Grayson also relayed to him that Mrs. Wilson had told Miss Bones that Grayson and House were "the only two friends the President had who were serving him without a selfish motive."[22]

House's standing with the president's wife, however, was a different matter, given Edith's mercurial attitude toward her husband's close consultant. Although she had insidiously demeaned House before their introduction, she had, in a fleeting moment of cordiality, told House's wife, Loulie, in March 1916 that she wished the couple would come to live in Washington and regretted that the colonel did not spend more time with the president. That reversal did not long endure. Edith would soon be urging House to serve overseas—though not before enlisting his assistance, fruitlessly, in deposing both the secretary of the navy, Josephus Daniels, and Joseph Tumulty, as a way of being helpful to the president.

Edith's principal interest in the White House drama, far more than in its themes and issues, was in its casting. Her supreme preoccupation as protector of her husband's leading role was the evaluation of his supporting players. From the first days of their courtship, Edith had aired her thoughts to Wilson on them. Pronounced in girlish outrage or insinuated with coy humor, her declarations had both shocked and charmed the president into venting his own vitriolic antipathies.

Robert Lansing was a special case, more or less doomed from the start, and eventually despised by both husband and wife. Perpetually struggling for status, Lansing recognized that matters that were entirely within his province were not only attended to by the president but also by House. Lansing could hardly have been aware, however, of Edith's role—for instance, in regard to the note he wrote on March 25, 1916, concerning the sinking of the *Sussex*. All three had had their say: Wilson, having discarded Lansing's effort as too combative, wrote his own response in a more conciliatory mood; House objected to the last page as being inconclusive; Edith Wilson declared the end "weak and unsatisfactory."[23] But the president feared stronger words would signify a declaration of war, and he could not declare war, he said, without the consent of Congress. Though he disagreed with his wife and House, he readily discussed and defended his position with them.

House added the word *immediately* to the opening clause and suggested that the last sentence be dropped as it might open up the entire question for further argument. The note was further amended by Lansing and concluded:

> Unless the Imperial Government immediately declares that it abandons its present method of submarine warfare against passenger and freight-carrying vessels, the Government of the United States can have no choice but to sever diplomatic relations with the German Empire[24] . . . This action the Government of the United States contemplates with the greatest reluctance but feels constrained to take in behalf of humanity and the rights of neutral nations.[25]

* * *

Though Lansing considered this final draft somewhat of a compromise, lacking the force of his original note, he judged it to be "in the nature of an ultimatum for which I had so earnestly pressed."[26] Edith's reaction was less than conciliatory; the negotiations had only further weakened her opinion of Lansing. To House she confided her lack of confidence in Lansing's judgment, that he had gotten the president "into two or three bad situations."[27] William McAdoo was also Edith's target. She told House that she had always disliked the president's son-in-law; she considered him thoroughly selfish to the point of allowing "nothing to stand in the way of his ambition."[28] When she asked House his opinion of McAdoo's chances for the next presidential election, she was told "better than they had been, but it was too far off to speculate." Still later, Edith told House of the president's growing irritation with McAdoo and his insistence on offering unsolicited advice.[29]

Despite her early complaints about House to Wilson—he was "inept," looked and wrote like a "weak vessel"—Edith appeared to trust him, or at least had need enough of his conspiratorial help. Given his grand design for the president and consequently for himself—"Our places depend entirely upon how large a part he plays in history"[30]—it was logical that House should try to cultivate a close friendship with the president's wife and court the approval of this woman who shared his lofty goals for her husband. After their private talk on April 6, during Wilson's absence at a banquet, House wrote in his diary, "She undertakes to eliminate Tumulty if I can manage the Daniels change. I do not know which is the more difficult feat, but I shall approach it with some enthusiasm and see what can be done."[31]

Colonel House, it would seem, made his injudicious pact with Edith not only as a way of ingratiating himself with the president's wife but because, so he said, of a conviction that Josephus Daniels was the "weak seat in the Cabinet" and that the president ought to get rid of him. The secretary of the navy, a Southern newspaper proprietor, politician, and pacifist, was thought to be less interested in the fighting qualities of the navy than in its morals and way of life. Even during the initial rounds of discussion of cabinet appointments, according to House, Daniels had been found wanting. He not only fell short of being cabinet timber, but he was denounced as "hardly a splinter."[32]

It was Daniels's involvement with the painfully prolonged effort to promote Cary Grayson that drove Edith to seek his removal from office.

Both the press and the Senate took exception to the president's proposal, officially initiated in a letter on July 2, 1915, in which he asked if the secretary of the navy would be

> kind enough to tell me whether there is anything I can properly and legitimately do to set forward Cary T. Grayson's chances of promotion? I mean any such thing as, for example, ordering him to an examination or facilitating the process by which he may qualify.
>
> I need not say that he has not spoken to me about this and that the question has arisen in my own mind merely out of the desire to reward an uncommonly faithful and serviceable man. It would embarrass him if I were to do anything irregular and I myself would not desire to do anything of that kind, but I thought that it was possible that I might legitimately increase his opportunities in some way that would be above criticism.[33]

Intensely protective of Wilson, and weary, by January 1917, of the political ramifications of this issue—her husband was held guilty of inexcusable favoritism for attempting to promote his medical attendant and golf partner over the heads of 114 senior officers—Edith pounced on Daniels for handling the Grayson promotion with such ineptitude that the resulting controversy disturbed her husband's sleep. In this, even Grayson did not escape her wrath. Her husband's insistence to the contrary, she maintained that Grayson had been pushing for the passage of the navy personnel bill of 1915 that gave, for the first time, the rank of rear admiral to officers in the Medical Corps and that he had solicited her help with his promotion before she had ever met the president.[34] Years after Grayson's confirmation, a genial Josephus Daniels refuted any suggestion that the doctor owed his promotion to his close friendship with the second Mrs. Wilson. "There was no foundation for the flippant statement," Daniels stated, that "most men got their four stars from participation in war, but Grayson's came from the boudoir."[35]

The plot to get rid of Daniels was a failure. In hindsight, it was claimed that the displacement of Daniels would have caused political damage during Wilson's campaign for reelection. Later, Mrs. Wilson would vigorously deny her participation, insisting that House's story of her involvement was "absolutely false."[36] In the case of Tumulty, she made no secret of her distaste for the Catholic secretary—who, however, would refuse, politely but adamantly, to be removed from the office he cherished until the end of Wilson's presidency. The offer of supposedly more prestigious appointments was never a temptation for Tumulty, a staunchly sentimental man who chose and held fast to his place, and who had his defenders.

When the campaign for reelection began in earnest—Wilson's Republican opponent was the associate justice of the Supreme Court Charles Evans Hughes—there remained nevertheless the regular work of the White House. The study at the columned Shadow Lawn,[37] the forty-four-acre summer White House, a colonial-style Parthenon in Sea Girt, New Jersey, was stacked with army commissions to be signed. Wilson and she were a comfortable partnership in this autumn of 1916, Edith noted. They had to dispatch at least one hundred of these documents a day, and in her attempt to place and blot them as fast as Wilson could sign them, they "made a sort of game of it, seeing how many we could do in stated moments."[38]

Wilson, who at times was openly derisive of the press, shrewdly courted its members when it suited him. Barely less than one month before Election Day, on October 10, Wilson invited Adolph S. Ochs, publisher of the *New York Times,* to lunch with him on Tuesday, the seventeenth, and to bring along the newspaper's editor in chief, Charles R. Miller. Wilson said that he would greatly enjoy seeing them both and getting any advice they might have to give him about the many difficult and interesting things the White House was handling daily. Having accepted the president's invitation, the two journalists took a public surrey from the railroad station for the mile-and-a-quarter ride to Shadow Lawn, where they were ushered into a spacious reception room and waited ten minutes until the president arrived. Soon joined by Edith Wilson, her mother, her sister Bertha, and Helen Bones, they lunched in the breakfast room around a marble-top table.

Somewhat confused by the composition of the party—no doubt because he believed the nature of the occasion called for greater privacy and formality—Adolph Ochs seemed puzzled by Wilson's female entourage. Ochs thought Edith Wilson was a handsome woman with a perfect nose, and teeth good and large ("but turned in"). Though gracious, she did not strike him as having a brilliant mind. Wilson mentioned his disappointment that his rival, Hughes, in the presidential campaign, had failed to raise questions that would have given Wilson some intellectual exercise; but mostly the conversation was light and frivolous and consisted largely of anecdotes about golf. Edith had contributed one about asking her caddy if she, when about thirty yards from the hole, could make it with a midiron and being told, "Yes, if you hit it often enough." Ochs thought Mrs. Wilson had not fully realized the humor of this story, although it provoked much laughter.

After lunch the women departed and the three men moved to the corner of another large room where Wilson touched on many issues, both international and domestic, spoke about Great Britain, his great admiration for the French, his refusal to consider an early armistice if there was any suspicion that the time of truce might be used to formulate new plans for continuing the war, and of his feelings that he was considered as unfriendly to big business. The president described the former secretary of state and senator from New York Elihu Root as "intellectually dishonest"; Brandeis as "a tower of strength as an adviser and counselor, and not at all radical"; and Mexico's President Carranza as "a little, cheap country lawyer." Beguiled into believing that Wilson wished to talk very openly, Ochs said (after "apologizing and hoping he would pardon me for a very frank expression at which he interrupted to say " 'Certainly' ") he had not liked the president's speech of the day before. Instantly, Ochs realized he had been too blunt. Wilson's expression changed, his jaw set, and his face showed a little color as if he was about to make a tart reply. Ochs allowed that this might have been imaginary, since his colleague, the editor, Charles Miller, said he did not notice the change.

The talks ended, the newspapermen left at 4 P.M. Ochs, in summing up his impression of the meeting, was equivocal. In regard to his respect for Wilson's abilities and his patriotism and his desire to do the best for the country, the president had gained nothing and lost nothing in Ochs's esteem because, the publisher concluded, Wilson was at a disadvantage in the presence of Charles Miller. Wilson did not express himself as well, as intelligently, or as impressively on any subject as expected—he used many commonplace expressions—and Ochs concluded that Miller was the preeminently superior intellect and "Wilson was not as profound."[39]

That the *Times* was supportive of Wilson during both elections was enthusiastically acknowledged by Wilson. "My dear Mr. Ochs," he would write on November 20, 1916. "May I not tell you what I hope you know already but what it gives me pleasure to put into words, how deeply I have appreciated the support of the editorial page of the *Times*?" Five years later, ill and embittered, Wilson would refuse to contribute to the commemorative volume honoring Ochs's twenty-fifth anniversary as publisher on grounds that Wilson knew so little of the publisher's conduct of the newspaper that anything he would write would be vague and insignificant.[40]

Adolph Ochs's thought that Wilson had some misgivings about the possibility of his reelection was confirmed two days before actual votes were cast. On November 5, Wilson wrote to Robert Lansing in deep secrecy about a matter that he said he had thought about throughout the campaign, the question of what his duty would be if Hughes was elected and, given the war abroad, how to assure that some official would have moral standing to decide the direction of the nation's foreign policy in the four-month interval before the new president would take office in March. To solve this problem, Wilson told Lansing, he had devised a plan that was dependent, admittedly, on the consent and cooperation of the vice president. If he gained Marshall's consent, he proposed to ask Lansing's permission to invite Mr. Hughes to become secretary of state, while he would join Vice President Thomas R. Marshall in resigning, thus opening to Mr. Hughes the immediate succession to the presidency. That Colonel House had originated this astonishing plan in a letter to Wilson on October 20 was not mentioned to Lansing.[41]

Fifteen years later, when Wilson's proposed resignation surfaced in the second volume of the *Intimate Papers of Colonel House*, the *Times*, on June 6, 1931, was incredulous and dismissed the idea as a "Political Romance" that ought to take high rank "as a piece of political imagination."[42] However, on receipt of a copy of Wilson's actual letter, Ochs's successor at the *Times*, his son-in-law Arthur Hays Sulzberger, pronounced the revelation "a great story, almost unbelievable," and sought permission for its publication. After two months of negotiations, the *Times* request was refused, undoubtedly after consultation with Edith Wilson, on grounds that "this whole episode is of so much importance and the circumstances surrounding it were so unusual, that a premature publication would seem to arouse rather than to allay misunderstanding."[43]

On the stormy Sunday night two days before the actual election, Edith too was having second thoughts about her husband's success. She was dubious that "we" could win a majority of the electoral votes for, though the masses seemed to be for him, the Republicans had the money. In addition, she worried that the Mexican policy was still being attacked and that the European war was breeding new and greater problems every hour. Critics were calling his concept of "watchful waiting" a "vacillating un-American, unpatriotic foreign policy." As to the lack of statesmen in his cabinet to whom he might turn for counsel, it was suggested that Wilson, prompted by vanity and a belief in his own transcendental wisdom, considered he would need no counsel. Edith makes no mention of another obstacle threatening the reelection, the intrusion of devastating gossip about Wilson's relationship with his Bermuda friend, Mary Peck. With justification, Edith began to speculate on what they might do should they have to leave the White House in four more months.

On Election Day Edith drove with Wilson to Princeton. Waiting for Wilson outside the old engine house was the closest Edith ever came to voting for a presidential candidate. As a woman, she did not have the right to vote in 1916. After women's suffrage became law in 1920, she did not choose to vote that year and forfeited her right as a resident of the District of Columbia. Only when the butler, Brooks, delivered a wireless at 7:30 A.M., Thursday morning, November 9—Wilson had won by 277 to Hughes's 254 electoral votes—was she certain that the past tormenting days had ended in her husband's reelection.

The campaign, and the imminent first anniversary of her marriage, had apparently spurred fresh interest in an appraisal of the president's wife. Daisy Fitzhugh Ayres wrote in the *Louisville Courier-Journal*, "She is first in war, first in peace, first in the hearts of her countrymen. We endorse her thoroughly."[44] Edith Wilson, according to the *Washington Post*,[45] was first in another area, the first wife of a president to sit beside the chief justice when her husband delivered his inaugural address, and the first to stand beside him when he took the oath of office. She was the second wife of a president, after Mrs. William Howard Taft, to ride beside her husband to the Capitol and back again at the head of an inaugural parade.

In nearly a year as mistress of the White House, Edith had already made a distinctive place for herself. "Curious at first, this nation-wide scrutiny has become one of admiration, as Mrs. Wilson has accompanied the President everywhere on his campaign trips," wrote the *Star* of Washington.[46] Another attribute was now beginning to be noted: Edith's involvement with her husband's national and international concerns and her apparent conjugal influence. "Omnipotence," it was suggested, might be her middle name.[47]

CHAPTER 13

"A peace without victory"

Edith Wilson was now monitoring the nation's events in person. She was accustomed to sitting in on the president's conferences. James W. Gerard, America's ambassador to Germany, noted that during his five hours with the president at the White House, she was not only present but "at times asked pertinent questions showing her deep knowledge of foreign affairs."[1] Less ceremonious was her "attendance" at Wilson's conference with Poland's president, the great pianist Jan Paderewski. Excluded, she resorted to kneeling in the hall above and gazing down on Paderewski's face, "so fine, so tragic, so earnest," his hair "like a nimbus around his head." As he pleaded the cause of his nation, she felt she was witnessing through his eyes all the suffering and degradation of his countrymen.[2] Less fortunate another time, on an August evening in Magnolia, Massachusetts, when the president wished to meet privately with Colonel House and Sir William Wiseman, chief of the British Secret Service in America, she resented being asked to go off with Mrs. House, a reaction that did not go unremarked.[3]

Exclusion grew increasingly rare as Edith, with privileged access to government documents, began to work steadily by her husband's side. December 12, 1916, was the night of the first formal entertainment of the winter season, a dinner for the cabinet, but the president was preoccupied by the Germans, who, heartened by recent victories ("in the conviction that we are the absolute conquerors," as the kaiser told his troops), announced their readiness to talk about peace.[4] At first Wilson regarded the German note as "a very welcome surprise because it seems to . . . promise at least a beginning of interchanges of view."[5] On second thought, he was wary. He feared that the offer served to emphasize the uncompromising position of the beleaguered Allies—the battles of Somme, Verdun, and the Marne were yet to be won—and he was concerned that what might superficially seem favorable to a discussion of peace might actually breed a grim determination to prolong the war. Ignoring a White House full of guests, Edith chose to sit in his study while Wilson reworked his note to the Central Powers, the coalition of Germany, Austria-Hungary, Bulgaria, and Turkey.

Dated December 18, 1916, the day of their first wedding anniversary, the much-edited note informed the Germans that Wilson was proposing neither mediation nor peace but an exchange of views and, ultimately, a conference. He also assumed that the goal on both sides was virtually the same: "to make the rights and privileges of weak peoples and small states as secure against aggression or denial in the future as the rights and privileges of the great and powerful states now at war."[6] On December 21, to appease the Allies in their scornful objections to this message and their doubts about America's allegiances and intentions, Robert Lansing stepped clumsily into the breach. "The sending of this note," he grimly told the press, "will indicate the possibility of our being forced into war. That possibility ought to serve as a restraining and sobering force safe-guarding American rights. It may also serve to force an earlier conclu-sion of the war."[7]

Lansing's statement was interpreted as a signal that the United States was abandoning its neutral position and about to enter the war, and Edith noted in her diary, "Woodrow dreadfully worried."[8] Wilson wrote immediately to Lansing, asking if it would not be possible for him to issue another statement, saying that he found himself radically misin-terpreted; his intention was merely to suggest the neutral nations' direct interest in the question of possible terms of peace.

Lansing, in his frustration, wondered whether Wilson grasped the full significance of the great war or of the principles at stake. Perhaps the president had not sufficiently realized that "German imperialistic ambi-tions threatened free institutions everywhere."[9] Though he did make the second statement requested by Wilson,[10] the damage was done.

With this turn of events, Lansing's status (in jeopardy from the out-set) plummeted further. Observers of both men believed that the most amazing feature of their relationship was that it had lasted so long, Lansing being far more pragmatic and far less sentimental or moralistic than the president. In the next year the president repeatedly considered replacing his secretary of state, hoping that he would resign rather than wait to be dismissed.[11] House claimed to have talked Wilson out of ask-ing for Lansing's resignation on grounds that House doubted Wilson would do better with anyone else.

*   *   *

Germany's response on December 27, 1916, to the president's note of December 18 was so infuriatingly vague that Britain's Prime Minister David Lloyd George thought that to enter a conference on Germany's terms without any knowledge of that nation's proposals would be suicidal.[12] Yet, on the slender basis that the Central Powers were willing to meet merely to discuss peace terms while the Entente—France, England, and Russia—to the contrary insisted on discussion of specific issues such as guarantees and acts of reparation, Wilson was encouraged: "We are that much nearer a definite discussion of the peace which shall end the present war." He discussed with both his wife and Colonel House—who, at the president's invitation, arrived in Washington on January 11, 1917—the contents of the speech that he would deliver on the afternoon of January 22, defining before the Senate the "essential terms of peace in Europe." The speech, which Edith had carefully read aloud so that Wilson might record it on his typewriter, was hailed by the *New York American* as an "epoch in history."[13]

Addressing the American role in the peace effort, Wilson argued that it was inconceivable "that the people of the United States should play no part in that great enterprise." No covenant of peace that did not include the peoples of the New World could keep the future safe against war. As for the terms of peace, they implied, first of all, that it must be a "peace without victory." Victory would mean peace forced upon the loser, accepted in humiliation and under duress, at an intolerable sacrifice, "and would leave a sting, a resentment, a bitter memory upon which terms of peace would rest, not permanently, but only as upon quicksand. Only a peace between equals can last."

Peace, if it was to be lasting, must be founded on equality of rights, Wilson continued. Applying the Monroe Doctrine (the interpretation of which was to be at the heart of his ultimately crucial differences with Senator Henry Cabot Lodge), "no nation," he said, "should seek to extend its policy over any other nation or people, but that every people should be left free to determine its own policy, its own way of development, unhindered, unthreatened, unafraid, the little along with the great and powerful."[14] Notwithstanding the care Wilson had taken to analyze what he had feared might be controversial, the concept of peace without victory was the subject of both tumultuous praise and overwhelming scorn. Some dissenters wondered whether there had ever been a diplomatic policy that called for so many explanatory communications as that of the administration of President Wilson.

* * *

Relations between the United States and Germany were so uncertain that, in January 1917, an incident involving Joseph Tumulty once again emphasized the challenge of serving in a position of influence in the White House—particularly in the eyes of many Protestants, who not only believed Tumulty to be an agent of the Catholic Church but suspected that he had driven away a large Protestant vote.[15] Tumulty was the original of the contemporary White House press secretary, and under his aegis Wilson became the first president to hold regular, formal press conferences open to all accredited correspondents. (These were suspended during the war.) Although Tumulty would come to Wilson's rescue when the president was at his most vulnerable, protectively and effectively as his ghost speechwriter and letter writer and editor, Tumulty's hold on his job was always extremely tenuous.

Attorney General Thomas W. Gregory reported that Tumulty had indiscreetly told half a dozen friends that the United States had tapped the wires of the Germans both at their consulate in New York and at their embassy in Washington. Tumulty was also suspected of trying to exert pressure on the Department of Justice to drop its investigation of a friend, one of the members of the excise court of the District of Columbia, an Irishman who had been appointed on Tumulty's recommendation.[16] This would not be the first time that Wilson had heard strong charges against the Roman Catholic Tumulty—he himself had been canvassing his colleagues for many months to find a tactful way to rid himself of a secretary whom he, among others—most certainly including Edith—now regarded, largely because of his religion, as a political burden.

Years earlier, following his election as governor of New Jersey in 1910, Wilson had vowed that he was going "to ram" Tumulty's appointment down the throats of people who objected to him on religious grounds.[17] By 1916, however, and throughout his campaign for reelection, Wilson worried about how to dispose of him. During a discussion with House of possible cabinet changes, Edith had asked, "What about Tumulty?"

Wilson had first met Joseph Tumulty during his campaign for governor of New Jersey in 1910. Tumulty was then thirty-one years old, one of eleven children, the grandson of an emigrant from County Cavan, Ireland, born to and reared in the labyrinthine quirks of Jersey City's machine politics. No matter how far back his memory went, growing up above his father's grocery store on 260 Wayne Street, Joe Tumulty could not recall when he had not heard politics discussed. His father, Philip Tumulty, was the leader of an independent caucus of Irish Democrats and an elected member of the State Assembly; the son was admitted to the bar in 1902 after clerking at the Jersey City law firm of Bedle, McGee, and Bedle. As a police court lawyer, he climbed the steep and precarious ladder of the Fifth Ward Democratic Club to become its financial secretary before following in parental footsteps as assemblyman. After serving four terms, Joe Tumulty felt he had outgrown the office and chose not to run again and, in fact, thought of retiring from politics, at least temporarily. Shortly after witnessing Wilson's formal acceptance of the nomination for governor of New Jersey, he nevertheless volunteered to assist the candidate.

The editor of the Trenton *Evening Times,* James Kerney, was the first to suggest that Tumulty might help Wilson through the maze of New Jersey politics. Once exposed to the breadth of Tumulty's political talents and personal charm, the candidate knew he had found the close adviser, with intimate knowledge of the grinding complexities of the Democratic Party and of the state, so essential to the successful conduct of his affairs. Though Tumulty's politics were never dainty, they were considered essential and successful, the "indispensable weapons of a political realist" without whom Wilson's reforms in New Jersey would have been unattainable.

One thing was certain about his job with the governor—he knew his duties would be more political than clerical. The newspapermen who covered Wilson's headquarters in New Jersey liked Tumulty and thought he balanced Wilson's frigid antipathy to reporters. His appointment by President-elect Wilson as secretary was encouraged by William Gibbs McAdoo and Colonel House, both of whom felt that Tumulty's political instincts would be an essential asset. His detractors, who accused him of favoring fellow Catholics with an excessive amount of patronage, predicted the "recrudescence of that religious fanaticism which blazed out a generation ago"[18] and feared that he would reveal vital state secrets to the Vatican. The voices of McAdoo and House prevailed, however, among others who regarded Tumulty as Wilson's natural political complement. The issue of Catholicism was, though it remained combustible, temporarily filed away.

On March 5, 1913, Tumulty was named personal assistant to the president of the United States, to advise on patronage, politics, and public policy, with direct responsibility for supervising the executive office and for establishing contacts with Congress and the public, including the press. He thus served as a kind of press officer and chief of staff, assisted by, among others, a head correspondence clerk, a head letter clerk, a chief of the telegraph and telephone system, and a corps of stenographers and filing clerks. Attempting to define Tumulty's role in the Wilson White House drama, one journalist pictured him as both the stage manager and stagehand, as director and set designer, "raising the curtain and pulling the strings."[19] Others described his work as acting as the president's interpreter of public opinion, as his guide to mass psychology. "I try [a speech] on Tumulty, who has a very extraordinary appreciation of how a thing will 'get over the footlights.' He is the most valuable audience I have," Wilson told the journalist Ida Tarbell.[20]

Much would be made of the differences between Wilson and his secretary, who was portrayed as a genial, lighthearted Irish Catholic, gregarious, volatile, compassionate, and admired for his charm, tact, and good humor.[21] In contrast, Wilson was a shrewd but idealistic Scotch Calvinist, a man of flinty temperament, intolerant, impatient, willful, strangely aloof. He was seen at heart as a solitary man, his own favorite confidant. The distances between the men narrow surprisingly when it comes to discussing their heritage, ambitions, and education, and even their demeanor and dress. Like Wilson, Tumulty was inculcated with a stern moral code, but of Jesuit rather than Presbyterian persuasion. As a student of St. Bride's Academy, St. Bridget's School, and St. Peter's College, he had studied English literature, Latin, and rhetoric and had read Cicero and Demosthenes, Plato and Thucydides. He also read and spoke Italian. The winner of a gold medal for elocution, he would become known for spirited oratory.[22] Late in the presidency, it would be suggested that Tumulty was the one who grew in stature. With his energy, willingness, intelligence, and sometimes wisdom, strong moral conscience, and sharp sense of injustice, he read widely in American history and listened; Wilson, after 1912, read little and listened impatiently.

Two weeks after the reelection of 1916, the president told his secretary that he wanted him to run for the Senate from New Jersey. Tumulty took Wilson's suggestion to be an alarming signal of his wish for a new secretary and repeated this news to several members of the press, including David Lawrence, who had been an undergraduate at the time when Wilson was president of Princeton. A respected journalist, Lawrence went to the White House on Sunday afternoon, November 19, and sent in word that he urgently wished to see the president. During their meeting, Wilson suggested that it might be better to have a non-Catholic secretary; but Lawrence countered that Wilson's letting Tumulty go would

represent an appalling case of ingratitude. The press would not counte-
nance further estrangement from former political allies (Watterson and
Harvey to name two) who had cleared Wilson's path to the presidency.
Privately, Lawrence was of the opinion that Edith Wilson had poisoned
the president against his secretary and wished for him to be replaced by
House's colleague, Democratic Party activist Robert Woolley.[23]

Destined to remain the most enduring figure of Wilson's political
life—there were to be in all "ten years, two months, four days of . . . intimate, official, personal association"[24]—Tumulty would keep his job not
only because the president feared a backlash of unfavorable publicity,
but because, as he tried to explain to Edith, even as he acknowledged her
initial complaints about his secretary's lack of breeding, "your heart is
not involved in the judgment as mine is."[25] Wilson's ultimate humanity,
frequently swayed by Edith's demands, in this instance did not fail him.

Despite his popularity with the press and with Wilson's own family,
Tumulty was always vulnerable on religious grounds, demeaned as
"awfully Irish," as that "little Irish Catholic," accused of being a papal
spy. He was also unpopular with extremists in his church as well.
Maintaining—as he tried to do on all national issues—a secular position
regarding a turbulent Mexico, he defended the president's backing of the
regime of the aspiring reformer Venustiano Carranza in opposition to
that of the reactionary Victoriano Huerta, champion of propertied interests and of the Catholic Church, and to the menacing chieftan Pancho
Villa. Tumulty had shocked the church, he was told in February of 1916,
by ignoring—in order to please his Protestant president—the violence
done to members of his faith. He was said to have profoundly outraged
16 million Catholics in the United States.[26] Weeks later, however,
incensed by Pancho Villa's cruelty, his pillaging and burning of Columbus, New Mexico, and his murder of eight American soldiers and nine
townspeople, Tumulty could no longer maintain a position of neutrality.
With Carranza powerless to stop such raids and opposed to American
soldiers crossing the border in retaliation, Tumulty warned Wilson, as
others did, that it would be humiliating to the country if he did not send
in troops after Villa.[27]

Brigadier General John J. Pershing led those troops across the border
on their futile mission on March 15; twenty-three American soldiers
were taken prisoner by Carranza on June 21. Three days later, Tumulty
pleaded in letters to both Wilson and Lansing, and in three separate telephone calls to Lansing, that an ultimatum be given Carranza for the sol-

diers' release, which ultimatum was issued and honored. Nevertheless, in the autumn of 1916, members of the church, unaware of his intervention, portrayed Tumulty as a Catholic in public life who had betrayed Catholicism, as "one who seems to think that they are baptized politicians, not Christians."[28] On the one hand he could not please those Irish Catholics who despised his principles that separated country and party from religion. On the other, *Protestant* magazine claimed that Tumulty prevented any of its communications regarding the Catholic Church from reaching the president. His Catholicism was indeed a political football.[29]

Prejudice against the Roman Catholic Irish reached its zenith in the fall and winter of 1916–17. Tumulty was now definitely considered a political liability. In virtually demanding that Wilson remove him from his office, Edith had deep grudges to settle. Gossip about the secretary's indiscreet behavior, about his acting "perfectly crazy" and talking constantly against the president's remarriage on the grounds that it would ruin him politically, was thought to have reached both Wilson and Edith, and to have hurt Tumulty greatly.[30] His stature was further diminished on grounds of temperament, character, and judgment by Grayson, House, and McAdoo in what was judged to be a "political cabal."[31]

On November 14, 1916, the *New York Times* reported that Tumulty was to be appointed to the Board of General Appraisers, a financially beneficial but routine political position that would permanently remove him not merely from the White House and Wilson's side, but also from Washington itself. Tumulty responded to Wilson's offer two days later. He had thought it over most carefully, realized the kindness of the president's motives, but after deep reflection could not accept the appointment. Poignant in both his honesty and humility, he dreaded that his departure would be misconstrued as a reflection on his loyalty, which had been unquestioned. He knew, as Wilson did not, that rumors had been flying thick and fast in the past months as to the imminence of his removal and even the identity of his successor. Resigned to leaving if Wilson wished him to do so, Tumulty wrote that the president "could not know what this means to me and to mine. I am grateful for having been associated so closely with so great a man. I am heart-sick that the end should be like this."[32]

In the end Wilson capitulated to his teary-eyed suppliant, and as a result, Edith and the colonel failed, as they had with Josephus Daniels, to remove Tumulty, though his position was weakened. While she did not act alone, Edith's role in this episode possibly contributed most to the impression among the president's colleagues that she "exercised a powerful influence over the president with often unpleasant conclusions."[33]

A prime target now for relentless criticism from all sides, partisan, nonpartisan, Catholic, Protestant, Irish, and German, as well as from members of the president's immediate circle, Tumulty saw his name catapulted into headlines. In the company of Bernard Baruch, William McAdoo, Robert Lansing, and Edith Wilson's brother Rolfe E. Bolling, he stood accused of exploiting what would be identified decades later as "insider information." What came to be known as the "leak" investigation was spearheaded by zealous Republicans including Congressman William R. Wood from Indiana and Thomas W. Lawson, a New England muckraker who had eager support from Theodore Roosevelt.[34] The case against the five alleged that they had manipulated their stock holdings for financial benefit based on private knowledge of the content of notes exchanged between Wilson and the German chancellor. It had been, in fact, the latter's questionable peace overture during the second week in December 1916 that was the catalyst. Shrewd speculators, noting rumored negotiations in daily newspaper stories, and fearing that the war's termination would send Wall Street crashing, especially in steel commodities, began to sell short, continuing to do so until Wilson's note was released to the press on December 20, when prices soared again. After testimony before the Rules Committee of the House of Representatives and a maze of investigations, all of the accused were found innocent. Bernard Baruch, the financier, candidly admitted that based on his own assessment of the political situation he had sold short and profited substantially. With wry humor Tumulty was able to write a friend that even though Andrew Carnegie, John D. Rockefeller, and J. Pierpont Morgan should vouch for him, he had never been able to deal in stocks of any kind for the simple reason that "I haven't any money."[35]

The issue of Catholicism would never be resolved in Tumulty's lifetime. "Rome in the Government," the editorial in the *National Catholic Register*, reprinted in Louisville, Kentucky's *Baptist Western Recorder* on January 9, 1919, did not escape Edith Wilson's watchful eyes. President Wilson's friendship for the Catholic Church was the essence of the message; his unique relationship with Joe Tumulty was stressed in the first of five paragraphs:

God has doubly blessed the Catholic Church of America by placing one of its most faithful sons at the right hand of President Wilson. Next to the President, Hon. Joseph Tumulty, Knights of Columbus fourth degree, wields the greatest political power of any man in America, and as a true Catholic he is exercising the great trust which God has given unto his hands for the glory of the holy church. Through his tact and holy zeal he has created a warm friendship between the Catholic Church and President Wilson, together with the Democratic party . . .

Edith forwarded the editorial to Tumulty, assuring him that she knew it to be absolutely false. "Perhaps," she suggested, "you know of some way your priest or personal friend in your church could stop it." [36]

By January of 1917, Colonel House, influenced by Edith's momentary disloyalty to Grayson over the physician's struggle for promotion, wrote in his diary: "The little circle close to the president seems to have dwindled down to the two of us, Mrs. Wilson and myself."[37] Complacently, the colonel does not appear to question her enthusiastic recommendation that he succeed Walter Page as ambassador to the Court of St. James. It had not taken him three minutes, he said, to persuade Wilson that the post would be too confining, would limit his activities to Great Britain and prevent him from going to either France or Germany.[38] Undeterred, Edith Wilson raised the subject two months later, again soliciting House for the job.[39] Apparently oblivious of his own problematic status with the president's wife, House does not appear to wonder whether the offer of the diplomatic post might be her attempt to collapse the circle entirely.

CHAPTER 14

"Nothing less than war"

In the "second winter of her queenship," the Louisville, Kentucky, newspaper the *Courier-Journal* cheerfully concluded that Edith Bolling Wilson's "magnetism and personal appearance have won universal recognition." Her fashionable tastes enhanced her reputation. However, the press's general perception of the president's wife as frivolous—"like a glorified, big pansy . . . a flower picture, all aglow, in rich pansy purple"[1]— would change with the onset of war.

On March 8, 1917, Edith sent a message via Irwin Hoover to Secretary of the Navy Daniels. She told him that the president was suffering from a cold and declined to speak with or see anybody. When she and Daniels met, she would explain that she had been delegated to discuss the matter of arming ships, the regulations involved, and the decision to keep this matter secret.[2] As to the resolution of conflicting systems of promotion between the regular navy and the reserve, it was her hope, she said, that the U.S. Naval Academy might graduate its men in less than three years, or that they might be made junior lieutenants so as not to be outranked by members of the reserve. She also told Daniels an anecdote that once again emphasized the mercenary aspect she attributed to the Jewish people: The father of a Jewish boy in training at Fort Myer who would soon be an officer was asked, "Will he get a commission?" "No," the father replied, "he will get the full price."[3]

Monitoring domestic and foreign events, including critical news about Russia and Germany, Edith noted in her diary:

March 13, 1917:
There is a streetcar strike in the City [Washington] and a [national] railroad strike threatened to begin on Saturday. W. saw several people and telephoned others to see if it could be averted.

March 15:

Thrilling news from Russia ... Overthrow of the Government and taking control by the people.

In Edith's opinion, the cable from David R. Francis, the U.S. ambassador in Moscow, reinforced hope for a democratic Russia. News about the Germans, on the other hand, was horrendous. The president's "valley of decision, the most critical, the most heart-breaking of the entire period of his leadership," dated from the sinking of the American ship *Algonquin* on March 12, when he ordered the arming of ships to meet attacks by German submarines (three more ships went down on the eighteenth: the *City of Memphis,* the *Illinois,* and the *Vigilancia,* on which fifteen lives were lost), to April 2, when Wilson asked Congress to meet over "grave questions of national policy which should be taken immediately under consideration." "The war," Edith sighed, "is stretching its dark length over our own dear country."[4]

Colonel House caught a morning train to Washington on March 27. He found the president waiting for him and for his advice as to whether he should ask Congress to declare war, or whether he should say that a state of war existed and ask for the necessary means to carry it forward. House advised the latter, fearing acrimonious debate in Congress over a declaration of war. Wilson struggled with the message he was to convey on April 2—the most important he had yet delivered, in the colonel's opinion—whose contents Wilson refused to discuss with his perturbed secretary of state or any members of his cabinet. The subject of such great anxiety, Wilson had already—probably a week earlier—sought the opinion of Frank I. Cobb, editor of the New York newspaper the *World.* Arriving at the White House, the newsman found a tormented president waiting in his study. Wilson entreated, "If there is any alternative, for God's sake, let's take it."[5]

On the spring night of March 31, the president sat by himself on the south portico of the White House to type his speech by the light of an electric lantern that hung between tall, fluted columns. Edith remained alone upstairs. When she thought her husband was striking the keys slowly, as though weary, she went down to the kitchen to find milk and crackers and delivered these on a silver platter, to the little table by his side.

Wilson played golf with Edith on the morning of April 2. That after-

noon he read his speech in private to House and was encouraged to eliminate "until the German people have a government we can trust," a
phrase Wilson already had some doubts about. Edith wrote of April 2:
"Momentous day. Congress convened at 12 noon; called in special session to declare war." When the Wilsons reached the Capitol, the crowd
outside was almost as dense as on Inauguration Day, but perfectly
orderly. Troops were standing on guard round the entire building, which
stood out white and majestic in the indirect lighting used for the first
time on that eventful night. When she reached the gallery, after leaving
her husband in the room reserved for him, Edith found every seat taken
and people standing in every available place both on the floor and in the
galleries. She sat with her mother and her stepdaughter Margaret in the
first row, and she could hear the audience breathing, so still was this
great throng. When the president came in and everyone rose to their
feet, her heart seemed to stop.[6]

Wilson's voice was firm: "There is one choice we cannot make, we are
incapable of making: we will not choose the path of submission and suffer the most sacred rights of our nation and our people to be ignored or
violated." It was, therefore, with "unhesitating obedience" to what he
deemed his constitutional duty, but "with a profound sense of the solemn
and even tragical character of the step," that he advised "that the Congress declare the recent course of the Imperial German Government to be
in fact nothing less than war against the government and people of the
United States; that it formally accept the status of belligerent" and "exert
all its power and employ all its resources to bring the Government of the
German Empire to terms and end the war."

To counteract Germany's subversive activities in the United States, its
intrigues and its plots, as evidenced in a conspiring note to Mexico from
Arthur Zimmermann, the German secretary of foreign affairs,[7] the whole
force of the nation must be spent "to check and nullify its pretensions and
its power." In regard to the recent events in Russia, would not all Americans feel their hopes reassured by their most recent allies, that addition
of the "great, generous Russian people . . . in all their naive majesty and
might" to the forces that were fighting for freedom in the world, for justice, and for peace? "Here," Wilson said, "is a fit partner for a League of
Honor."

The president warned his audience of the need to fully equip the navy,
to raise an army of a half million men, and of the many months of fiery
trial and sacrifice ahead. "But the right is more precious than peace, and
we shall fight," he promised, "for the things which we have always car-

ried nearest our hearts, for democracy, for the right of those who submit to authority to have a voice in their own governments, for the rights and liberties of small nations, for a universal dominion of right by such a concert of free peoples as shall bring peace and safety to all nations and make the world itself at last free." The day had come, the president concluded, "when America is privileged to spend her blood and her might for the principles that gave her birth and happiness and the peace which she has treasured. God helping her, she can do no other."[8]

Shortly after 3 A.M. on Friday, April 6, Congress passed the war resolution, voting 373 to 50 that "the state of war between the United States and the Imperial German Government which has been thrust upon the United States be hereby formally declared." With the resolution already signed by Vice President Thomas R. Marshall and the Speaker of the House, Wilson added his signature at 1:18 P.M., using, at his wife's request, the gold pen he had given her as a gift. Wilson left the White House at two o'clock for meetings, returned, and spent the evening alone with Edith. The step having been taken, Edith wrote, "We were both overwhelmed."[9]

The country had officially been at war for only eight days when Edith took to her bed. The emotional drain combined with a working day that began at 5 A.M. and ended at midnight had, she conceded, been too much for her. She also worried that it was almost too much for her husband. Wilson had forgotten the railroads in his appeal for the cooperation of American industry, and when reminded of his omission, he had apologized that his brain was "just too tired to act."[10] She knew at once what was to be her most significant war work: she must safeguard her husband's health. When Dr. Grayson suggested horseback riding as a supplement or alternative to golf, she found herself in borrowed habit at 5 P.M. on the afternoon of his proposal. While her early-morning canters alongside her husband through suburban bridle paths became almost a daily occurrence, she was less successful as a novice cyclist.

Because, even now, Wilson talked of a future that might encompass a bicycle tour of Europe, Edith practiced indoors, hidden from passersby, with the help of two Secret Service men and her husband. Though she fell off her bicycle several times, nicked the enamel, and never learned to ride, the humor of the cycling interval did not escape her.

On June 30, Edith Wilson was hailed as the first woman of the land to sign one of the women's registration cards and send it to the office of the United States Food Administration, organized by a future president,

Herbert Hoover. As a member she pledged "to carry out the directions and advice of the Food Administrator in the conduct of my household insofar as my circumstances permit." By July, she and Helen Bones were able to turn over the products of one month's sewing, including four dozen pairs of pajamas and an equal number of sheets and pillowcases, for distribution among Red Cross societies of England, France, Italy, and Canada. Mrs. Wilson, the *Washington Post* reported on July 6, 1917, had taken the lead among women in official and diplomatic circles who used their own hands to supply the Red Cross, and her example had inspired cabinet and Senate wives to sew as well.

Edith was also recognized, somewhat ludicrously, as a shepherdess, at least in a supervisory capacity, for another successful war effort introduced months earlier on April 30, 1917.[11] Borrowing a flock of Shropshire black-faced sheep from the Bel Air Farm in Maryland, she turned them out to pasture on the White House lawn, having a shelter built for them in the rear of the White House. At shearing time, Will Reeves, a White House caretaker, was able to cut ninety-eight pounds of wool and send two pounds to each state, eventually auctioned for a total of $53,828 to benefit the Red Cross. When Edith invited Colonel House to come to Washington, she spoke of giving him "a pastoral sight of 14 sheep and 4 lambs—to graze on the lawn—and they really are awfully pretty."[12] The sheep remained on the grounds until the Wilsons moved out of the White House on the day of Warren Harding's inauguration.

The Wilsons' return from attending a July 14 wedding coincided with a demonstration planned by members of the Woman's Party to commemorate the fall of the Bastille. Three groups of women hoisted banners bearing the French national motto: "Liberty, Equality, Fraternity." The first group crossed Lafayette Square and took its station at the upper gate of the White House; the second group positioned itself at the lower gate; the third followed behind. All three groups were immediately arrested. At the police station the sixteen women were booked for unlawful assembly. Three days later, additionally charged with obstructing traffic, the women chose sixty days in the Occoquan Workhouse to alternative penalties of $25 fines each. Edith thought the suffragettes' banner outrageous. Though Edith and Joe Tumulty had both opposed leniency, Wilson, after a round of golf with Dr. Grayson, signed for the women's dismissal from jail.

Edith Wilson was challenged by the seemingly constant presence of the "detestable suffragettes," those "disgusting creatures" at the White

House gates.[13] Her references to the suffragettes' eighteen-month siege, begun on January 10, 1917, vary from tight-lipped objectivity to outspoken fury. To believers, their rainbow splash of yellow and white banners and their Woman's Party tricolors of purple, white, and gold were trumpet calls for recognition. To Edith and her fellow opponents of the issue, they might as well have been flags of red. In quest of the right to vote that had eluded them for seventy-nine years—since the 1838 Women's Rights Convention at Seneca Falls, New York—more than two and a half million women, influenced by the British militant suffrage movement, mounted an all-out campaign to pressure the president and Congress to pass a constitutional amendment. It was right and fair, they contended, that those who must obey the laws should have a voice in making them; those who must pay taxes should have a vote. More pointedly, it was argued that suffrage was not only a measure of justice and democracy, but also an urgent war measure.

Unless the government took at least this first step, suffrage champions asked, how could it ask millions of American women to accept conscription, giving up their men and domestic happiness to a war for democracy in Europe, while they were denied the right to vote on the government policies that imposed such sacrifice? Thus far, women had the right to vote in twelve Western states, but elsewhere in the country they were barred from the ballot box. Edith remained implacable. The only speech of her "Precious One that I ever failed to enjoy" was the address he gave at a suffrage meeting. (As she explained in her diary, "I hated the subject so it was acute agony."[14]) Nothing in the course of those tragic years of war, as battles raged and men and ships were lost, as the country struggled with mobilization and the vicissitudes of the League of Nations, seemed personally to repel Edith or Wilson so much as the women activists who picketed for suffrage. The activists sensed the couple's opposition and taunted the president in return.[15]

Before taking action at the White House gates, the suffragettes had painstakingly reviewed Wilson's seesaw record, in all its ambivalence. As a Princeton student, he declared in 1876, "Universal suffrage is at the foundation of every evil in this country." As a professor ten years later, he was "opposed to woman suffrage." As governor of New Jersey in 1911, his personal judgment was "strongly against" equal suffrage.[16] In 1913— though it was difficult by then to ignore the influence on congressional elections of enfranchised women in nine Western states—he at one time said that suffrage was a question to which he had given no thought and on which he had no opinion; at another time, he said the congressional agenda was too crowded. By the end of that year, he could take no action on the suffrage amendment until commanded by his party. In 1914, he could not act because of party commitments. Later, he excused himself on grounds of states' rights. In 1915, he voted for suffrage in New Jersey but refused to support it in Congress. In 1916, in June, in the most acrimonious debate of the Democratic convention, he was responsible for recognition of the principle of suffrage in the party platform—"We recommend the extension of the franchise to the women of the country by the States upon the same terms as to men"—but neither he nor the party endorsed an amendment to the Constitution.[17]

Throughout his campaign for reelection in 1916, he differed from Charles Evans Hughes, the Republican candidate, who favored a constitutional amendment granting the franchise to women on the same basis as men. The president, it was said, adhered "with good-humoured inflexibility" to the position he had always held on suffrage, "that the thing can best and most solidly be done by the action of the individual states, and that the time it will take to get it that way will not be longer than the time it would take to get it the other way."

In January 1917 the picket line circling the entrance to the White House was established after the Woman's Party concluded that the president was beginning to realize that the suffrage amendment must ultimately pass, but because he was safely in office for four more years, he felt no pressure to take immediate action. Once they started, the suffragettes picketed the White House in rain, sleet, hail, and snow, and Edith Wilson bemoaned their presence at either side of the gates parading great banners urging "Votes for women." Patronizing in his tentative approach to members of Congress about the appointment of a committee on women's suffrage in the House of Representatives, Wilson nevertheless appreciated its inherent political advantage. On May 14, 1917, Wilson advised Congressman E. W. Pou of North Carolina, "On the chance that I may be of some slight service in this matter, which seems to me of very considerable consequence, I am writing this line to say that I would heartily approve. I think it would be a very wise act of public policy, and also an act of fairness to the best women who are engaged in the cause of woman suffrage."[18] Finally, on June 13, obviously feeling some pressure, he suggested to Congressman J. Thomas Heflin of Alabama that "it would be a very wise thing, both politically and from other points of view," if the congressman and others of his opinion would consent to the formation of the proposed special committee of the House on women's suffrage.

When emissaries of the new Russian republic, which had just enfranchised its women, drove to the White House on June 20 to keep a 12:30 P.M. appointment with the president and with representatives from England, Belgium, France, and Italy, the suffragettes' message was printed on a giant yellow and white banner, to be known as the Russian banner:

> We women of America tell you that America is not a democracy. Twenty million women are denied the right to vote. President Wilson is the chief opponent of their national enfranchisement.
>
> Help us make this nation really free. Tell our government that it must liberate its people before it can claim free Russia as an ally.[19]

Learning of the pickets for suffrage and their message, Edith Wilson was indignant—but no less so, she said, than the crowd of onlookers who tore down the offending banner.[20] On June 26, owing to "suffragette disturbances," police patrol was increased at the White House.

Regardless of insistent and visible pressures, Wilson discounted the efforts of the women at his White House gates. He was angered by the suffragists who had picketed, and he did not doubt that their punishment matched their tactics and that they merited their jail sentences and ensuing deprivation. But on October 13, he assured Carrie Chapman Catt of his deep interest in the campaign for women's suffrage in New York. He added, however, that he hoped no voter would be influenced by anything the "so-called pickets" might have done in Washington. They represented, he was sure, such a small fraction of the women of the country that it would be most unfair to allow their actions to prejudice the cause.[21]

On January 3, 1918, Theodore Roosevelt would write to the chairman of the Republican National Committee to urge that everything possible be done to get Republican congressmen to vote for the suffrage amendment and to advocate adding a woman from every suffrage state to the National Committee.[22] Six days later, on Wednesday afternoon, January 9, Wilson, seemingly a convert to a constitutional amendment for woman's suffrage, if only for political expediency, spent an hour talking about the subject with a number of Democratic members of the House.

The day after that meeting, the House voted in favor of the suffrage amendment 274–136. In a pleasant but slightly oblique exchange on the subject, when Mrs. George Bass noted that Theodore Roosevelt's suggestion that a woman be added to the Republican National Committee was "turned to good account by the Democratic National Committee," Wilson wrote back, "I am particularly interested in the way you have dished Colonel Roosevelt."[23]

With the adoption of the suffrage amendment by the House, a congressman's wife, Ellen Maury Slayden, observed, "Political sensations even outdo the weather." In her perceptive story of the events on January 23, 1918, she noted that the president's "flying leap—or was it a double back handspring?—by federal amendment has brought laughter or tears according to your enthusiasm for 'the Cause' or your respect for the Constitution." She said it was fun to see Wilson's thick-and-thin followers who had opposed the suffrage, even by permission of the states, just a few weeks before trying now to adjust their positions. She loved stirring them up by casually remarking, "Evidently the pickets knew what they were about; they brought the President to terms." According to Mrs. Slayden's poignant account:

> For months past women have stood like wooden Indians, one on either side of the two White House gates. . . . The public never complained, but somehow they got on the President's nerves, and he ordered their arrest for obstructing traffic and [they] were hustled off to the workhouse at Occoquan. They were denied the simplest toilet articles of their own, dressed in filthy prison clothes, given beds that were unspeakable, and seated at the table with the lowest drunkards and prostitutes, black and white, arrested on the streets of Washington. The conditions at the place are so outrageous that that publicity this affair gave it may save many a poor wretch in future. . . . I was at headquarters when our culprits came in and could hardly believe my eyes. They looked ten years older, unkempt, dirty and ill for want of the commonest conveniences and decencies of life.

Given this background on the suffragists, Mrs. Slayden considered the "President's flop more absurd." Pro-administration papers and friends had been calling the pickets "traitors" and "pro-Germans" among other names. Only a week before Wilson's change of heart, Mrs. Slayden had heard the secretary of commerce, W. C. Redfield, attacking the women, his whiskers fairly shivering and shaking as he protested that he "would not believe one of them on oath," that they had "entered into a conspiracy to injure the honorable *gentleman* who kept the workhouse."[24]

On Edith's birthday, October 15, 1917, Wilson gave her a ring of black opal, her birthstone. Two days later, John Singer Sargent arrived from London to paint Wilson's portrait. Its disappointing execution was attributed, by the most circuitous reasoning, to Senator Henry Cabot Lodge. Sargent had offered to paint a portrait for the benefit of the American Red Cross in London. The sponsor, Sir Hugh Lane, subsequently died in the sinking of the *Lusitania*, and to settle on the subject of Sargent's portrait, the estate executors took a popular vote in the British Isles, resulting in the choice of Woodrow Wilson. The portrait, begun on October 17, was completed after about ten sittings, on November 3. It was exhibited, for one month each, at the Corcoran Gallery, the Metropolitan Museum in New York, and the Pennsylvania Academy of Fine Arts in Philadelphia. Wilson's old friend Bobby Bridges viewed the Sargent portrait three times and liked it "hugely." He felt that he could see the president getting ready to tell a story, with the quirk to the right side of his mouth. Wilson responded that he did not know how to judge it for himself, "but the family like it and that is a pretty good test."[25]

Possibly Wilson did not know at the time that the portrait had failed in one crucial instance: it fell critically short of his wife's standards. Perhaps Edith's reaction was negative only in hindsight, an example of her inclination to recall in an unflattering light incidents involving people who to her mind wronged her sacrosanct husband, either by daring to differ with him or by appearing to compete with him. Her account of Sargent's rendering of the portrait, and of a nervous and dull artist whom she found extremely courteous and well-bred though uninteresting, serves merely to introduce the duplicitous villain of her *Memoir*, Henry Cabot Lodge, her husband's most powerful political enemy.

Edith would not have minded the trouble she had taken to arrange things if a fine portrait had been the result. The four-poster bed was draped with dark curtains brought from the attic; a platform was erected so that Wilson would be level with the artist's eye; a chair that would "paint well" was brought down from a corner of the upstairs hall. But Edith was uneasy from the start. Sargent told her at the outset that he had never been so nervous over a portrait in his life. "That is surprising from the great Sargent," she said. "Well," he responded, "I only hope I can do it." All of this, she would recall, had struck her as peculiar, for surely painting a portrait was nothing for Sargent to be nervous about.

Wilson said that he had never worked harder than he did to entertain the painter while posing for him. For all this effort, Edith found the finished work a disappointment. She thought it lacked virility and made her husband look older than he was at the time.

Soon after the portrait was painted, Edith discovered, she claimed, a clue to the artist's initial nervousness. Thanks to Henry White, a rather unctuous flatterer, occasional confidant, and apparently, intimate of Sargent's as well as of Lodge's, she learned that the artist had dined with Senator Lodge the night before going to the White House and was told by his host that the artist's commission afforded him a great opportunity to serve the Republican Party. As everyone knew Sargent's ability to find the counterpart of animals in humans and thus reveal some hidden beastly trait, so Lodge looked to the painter to reveal to the world the sinister element he knew to be hidden in Wilson. But contrary to Lodge's expectations, having "therefore studied the man and tried to probe his very soul," White told Edith, the painter "could find nothing hidden or unworthy." Completing her story of intrigue, Edith Wilson assured readers that she had told the story "exactly as Mr. Henry White told it to me. Unfortunately all three men—White, Sargent and Lodge— are dead, but perhaps there are others still alive who know of it."[26]

CHAPTER 15

Fourteen Points

Wilson was perceptibly weary in the summer and fall of 1917. The war abroad, and what he considered the madness in Washington, took their toll. General John J. Pershing, commander in chief of the American Expeditionary Force, had reached Paris on June 13 to plan the buildup of port facilities, supply lines, and store depots, and ultimately to train more than 1 million soldiers for battle.

Suffering from fatigue, and from heat that was exceptional even for Washington, Wilson liked to cruise with Edith for a day or two at a time on the *Mayflower*. In this way—although he brought along his papers as well as his stenographer, Charles Swem—he could at least escape, he said, from "the *people* and their intolerable excitements and demands."[1] Edith was delighted when her husband appeared at noon on September 7 to say that he could get away for a few days' rest in a cooler climate. Taking the midnight train, they reached New York by morning and immediately boarded the *Mayflower* at Twenty-third Street. Rain gave way to sunshine, and on a clear, crisp September 9, the Wilsons paid a surprise visit to Colonel House and his wife, Loulie, at their home at Coolidge's Point in Magnolia, Massachusetts.

The couples met at the president's yacht in Gloucester Harbor and motored along the rocky coast for more than two hours before dining aboard the yacht. On the second day, the Wilsons attended a luncheon given in their honor by the Houses at the Essex Country Club. Wilson agreed to have his picture taken with Colonel House, but declined to do so in the act of shaking his host's hand. Mention in the newspapers of this was followed by an inept "explanation": "Those who have heard the recent weird rumor that the President and his confidential adviser have had a 'break' need not take this as an indication that the rumor was true." Wilson had declined to pose because, as he explained to the photographer, he never let anyone photograph him in that way: "It looks too foolish."[2]

The incident only intensified chronic rumors of discord between him and House that had probably been revived by the three-month separation caused by House's habitual summer retreat from the heat of the city. In fact, the colonel was entirely cordial in reference to the Wilsons, and at the colonel's departure for Magnolia, the president had written to him on June 1 to say he was "both glad and sorry that you have got off to the Massachusetts shore; glad for your sake, sorry for ours, who would wish to be much nearer to you."[3]

Probably no president had sought or depended on advice from a more singular source over a period of seven years. "Nothing in history is comparable to the peculiar part which I played in the Wilson Administration," House himself acknowledged in later years.[4] Wilson, a formidable loner, trusted House's ability to think as his alter ego and to act as his spokesman and emissary during their earnest seven-year quest to lead the United States and to establish peace among nations. To cite the florid praise of an eminent colleague, House's mind was "like a sleeve valve: no friction! His thoughts come clearly to one, through simple words directly spoken. This is not craft but art and genius. Yet W. too had an altogether extraordinary character: he was a genius, a very great man."[5] House also thought Wilson a genius, but in hindsight felt that Wilson's supreme contempt, the contempt of genius for routine, "bore within it the seed of much trouble."[6]

Physical separation of Wilson and House by no means precluded their intense exchanges on state matters. Far from estrangement, the tone of the succession of letters and telegrams is one of intimacy, in continuance of innumerable discussions in which the president requested and valued House's opinions. Wilson probably wrote at least a dozen times between June and October 1917; House, as observer, adviser, and intermediary, wrote far more frequently. House also conferred in person with the president a second time on board the *Mayflower* on September 16.[7] Even before they met in Magnolia, House had reminded Wilson of the call from pacifists in America, England, and Russia for a statement of Allied terms on indemnities and territorial encroachments. These people were being told and believed that Germany wished for peace on any terms, when actually the German military hierarchy envisioned a settlement solely on the basis of conquest. It seemed essential to House that people in Germany and elsewhere know the truth of the issues involved; and House hoped Wilson would think it advisable to make some early intervention to that end. The next day, the president told House, "Your letter chimes exactly with my own thoughts," and asked that House follow it up with advice on specific points. And when should he make such an address?—on Flag Day possibly?[8] Flag Day, which fell on June 14, would do, House replied, if the president arranged for wide publicity. "I would get the world on tiptoe beforehand, and then arrange to have what you say cabled in ungarbled form to the ends of the earth. You have come to be the spokesman for Democracy, as indeed the Kaiser is the spokesman for Autocracy."

Wilson delivered his speech on the grounds of the Washington Monument to a patient audience standing in soaking rain under umbrellas. At one with House, the president declared that "we are not the enemies of the German people and they are not our enemies. . . . They are themselves in the grip of the same sinister power that has now at last stretched its ugly talons out and drawn blood from us." With the military presently controlling Germany and southeastern Europe—in combination with Germany's immensely expanded commercial and industrial power—the establishment of a stable peace was out of the question. Peace from such a source could not be taken seriously. America would be menaced, and therefore, "we and all the rest of the world must remain armed, as they will remain, and must make ready for the next step in their aggression." But if they retracted their aggression, he concluded, "the world may unite for peace and Germany may be of the union."[9]

The appeal of the pope, Benedict XV, for peace, in the second week of August 1917 provided both House and Wilson with an immediate challenge. The chief British intelligence agent in the United States, Sir William Wiseman, advised Colonel House of the pope's initiative. While cautioning House about many difficulties, Wiseman told him that Arthur James Balfour, the British foreign secretary, would like the president to give him his thoughts on the subject in private.[10] On the thirteenth, House forwarded Wiseman's cable to Wilson, followed by House's letter of August 15, asking how the president thought it best to respond to the pope. In a situation "full of danger as well as hope," it was more important, House presciently stated, to help Russia weld herself into a virile republic than to beat Germany to her knees: a disordered Russia could lead to German domination. House also discussed prospects of aiding Austria and sustaining Turkey as an independent nation, and he warned that the problem of dividing Asia Minor among England, Russia, France, and Italy was "pregnant with future trouble."

All of this led House to hope that Wilson would answer the pope's appeal in such a way as to leave the door open for negotiations, and to throw the onus on Germany. This, House advised, could be done if Wilson would state that America's peace terms were well known, but that it was useless to discuss peace until the Prussian militarists showed themselves accessible. Further, it was hardly fair to ask the populations of the Allied countries (the Entente included England, France, Italy, and Russia) to discuss terms with a military autocracy. If the peoples of the Central Powers (the coalition in World War I of Germany, Austria-Hungary, Bulgaria, and Turkey) had a voice in the settlement, an overwhelming majority would probably be found willing to make a peace acceptable to the other nations of the world—a peace founded upon international amity and justice. On the whole, House thought that the occasion presented the president with an opportunity "to make a notable utterance and one which might conceivably lead to great results."[11]

Wilson responded immediately. On August 16, he told his adviser that he had not yet decided whether he would reply at all to the pope, but that he would be glad to let Mr. Balfour know what his attitude would be were he eventually to answer. On reflection, Wilson felt that appreciation should be expressed for the pope's humane purpose; but among Wilson's grave reservations it had to be noted that the present German imperial government was morally bankrupt; that no one would accept or credit its pledges; and that the world would be living on quicksand until it could be confident of dealing with a responsible government.[12]

On Thursday, August 23, 1917, Wilson sent House a first draft of his response to the pope, with the comment that he was sure his message should be as brief as possible and that he had therefore centered it on one point: "We cannot take the word of the present rulers of Germany for anything." Wilson asked that House tell him exactly what he thought of it; he would await House's views "with the deepest interest, because the many useful suggestions you have made were in my mind all the while as I wrote it." The president thought of House "every day with the greatest affection."[13] By return mail, House congratulated the president on writing "a declaration of human liberty" by insisting that "America will not and ought not to fight for the maintenance of the old, narrow, and selfish order of things. You are blazing a new path, and the world must follow, or be lost again in the meshes of un-righteous intrigue."[14]

That same Friday, House telegraphed Balfour (Wilson having already written House of his hope that the associated governments will "say ditto to us"[15]) to suggest that the Allies accept the president's reply to the pope as their own. By Monday, House had telephoned the coded

response from London to his son-in-law Gordon Auchincloss, assistant
to the counselor of the State Department. Auchincloss sent the sheet of
numbers to the White House, where Edith Wilson was not only privy to
this secret message of extraordinary importance but was also charged
with deciphering it. Her penciled transcription reads:

> Following from Lord Robert Cecil who is acting for Balfour:
>   My view is that it would be very desirable for British and other
> Allied Governments to accept. Is however one of such importance
> that I shall have to consult the cabinet and also our allies. I assume
> the President's reply follows the lines already sketched out. But I
> should be very grateful if it were possible to send me a summary of
> it if the President sees no objection. In order to get cordial coopera-
> tion it would seem advisable to give your reply to the governments
> in advance. It would be particularly desirable in case of Russia.[16]

It was said that, in drafting this reply to the pope, Wilson came to believe
that the time was ripe for him to define clearly America's peace program.[17] He was beginning to think now that work ought to be done as
systematically, and as fully and precisely as possible, to learn what final
peace arrangements might be acceptable abroad in order to formulate
the U. S. position at home—"to prepare our case with a full knowledge of
the position of all the litigants." "What would you think of quietly gathering about you a group of men to assist you to do this?" he asked House
on September 2, 1917, precisely five months after the country had gone
to war. House not only accepted the request immediately but had to
some extent already rehearsed it to serve an earlier need. To fortify
William Phillips, first assistant secretary of state, who had complained
the past May of being inadequately prepared for a peace conference on
the Balkan and Near Eastern situation, House had, during the summer,
initiated a special study in the U.S. embassy in London.[18]
  Within weeks of its conception, the discreetly named Inquiry emerged
publicly on the front page of the *New York Times*. A precursor of Franklin
Delano Roosevelt's celebrated brain trust, the Inquiry, meant to gather,
evaluate, and digest facts for prompt and handy use, was a university in
miniature with a staff of fourteen academics culled from Harvard, Yale,
Cornell, Columbia, Haverford, and the University of Wisconsin: authorities on geographic, economic, and legal questions, who would research,
write, and advise on the basic tenets of an equitable peace settlement. In
its earliest stages, the Inquiry was set up in Manhattan, where the Amer-

ican Geographical Society offered its offices, library, and mapmaking facilities. Dr. Simon E. Mezes, president of the College of the City of New York, and son-in-law of Colonel House, was appointed director; the lawyer David Hunter Miller (a law partner of Gordon Auchincloss's) became treasurer; and the journalist Walter Lippmann of the *New Republic* was secretary (to be replaced, on his departure for France to work in army intelligence, by the Society's Dr. Isaiah Bowman, chief territorial specialist).

The Inquiry's eight regional specialists, who divided the globe into areas of concentration, included Yale University's Dr. Charles Seymour, charged with Austria-Hungary, and Harvard University's Dr. Charles H. Haskins, dealing with western Europe; Columbia University's Dr. James T. Shotwell was listed under the less specific title of librarian and specialist in history. The collective studies of the group evolved into the Inquiry's report, completed early in January 1918, which helped Wilson to crystallize his so-called Fourteen Points. Reestablished in Europe, where it was known as the territorial and economic section of the American Commission to Negotiate Peace, and then the Territorial Section of the Peace Conference, the group contributed a definitive study of boundaries before its demise in February 1919. In characterizing the work of the Inquiry, Sir William Wiseman valued the earnest scholars as a group of men who gave "deep and impartial study to the tremendous and complicated problems arising from a war which shattered the remnants of the Holy Roman Empire, dissipated the dreams of Bismarck, and left the great Russian Empire chaotic and impotent."[19]

On September 29, when the front page of the *New York Times* enlightened its readers about the Inquiry—"America to Speak in Her Own Voice at Peace Table"—Wilson was angered by the publicity. He was personally annoyed also that the press had criticized him for giving to a single man—the name of Colonel House was implied rather than spelled out—the responsibility for gathering data for the peace program, rather than consulting prominent men of all political parties and various views to achieve a true consensus. The president bluntly reprimanded the reporter David Lawrence: "I think you newspaper men can have no conception of what fire you are playing with when you discuss peace now at all, in any phase or connection."[20] At this stage, Wilson was convinced that the Germans, if they could instigate a discussion of peace at this time, would insist on terms entirely favorable to themselves. He thought it "very indiscreet . . . and altogether against the national interest to discuss peace from any point of view."

Wilson's acute sensitivity to the difficulties of coping publicly with Germany's peace overtures was understandable considering the array of communications he received within three days in early October. On October 5, House forwarded a peace offering, which would come to be one of many initiated by the Germans, Austrians, and Bulgarians during the autumn-winter of 1917–18. House also passed on word from a Spanish diplomatic representative who had "officially reported German Government would be glad to make a communication to us relative to peace." Three days later, on October 8, the American ambassador Walter Page cabled a three-and-a-half-page evaluation from his London vantage point: the German peace inquiry was regarded as "the beginning of the end but the end is hardly expected soon."[21]

On Saturday, September 22, 1917, having gone to Keith's Theatre the previous evening, Edith fell seriously ill with a severe grippe. On the following Monday, Wilson apologized to House for postponing their planned meeting. He was spending every minute he could spare from his work with Edith, hoping each day that her headaches would subside, that she would feel better so that he might have a free mind for the many things "we must talk over, you and I."[22] Edith, treated by her friend Dr. Sterling Ruffin and confined to her room for two weeks, took comfort, she said, from the lights she saw from her dressing room windows gleaming from the State, War and Navy Building (the present Executive Office Building). The lights always cheered her, she said, and after watching them she would go to bed feeling more hopeful.[23]

On October 8, Wilson wrote House that Mrs. Wilson could now manage well enough, and his mind was therefore free to take up important matters of state. House records attending, on October 13, an executive session with the president until ten, "Mrs. Wilson making it a threesome." One immediate issue on their agenda was the question of House going abroad to represent the United States at an Allied War Council. In early September, Britain's Prime Minister David Lloyd George told House that he thought it essential to the cause of the Allies that an official representative of the first rank from the United States should come promptly to take part in the deliberations of the Allies over their future plans: "Needless to say it would be a source of the utmost satisfaction to us if you were to come yourself."

On October 14, the British foreign secretary, Arthur Balfour, cabled that he was authorized by the French and British cabinets to extend to House a most cordial invitation to take part in conversations and conferences on all questions of war and peace, and that it was with the greatest gratification that they had learned of the probability that this invitation might prove acceptable. Balfour could not speak officially for the Italians and Russians, but House might safely assume that those countries shared the same interests. [24]

Though House had told Wilson that he was willing to represent him abroad, House reminded the president of the pressing importance, also, of his work at home with the Inquiry. House even suggested that the president send two cabinet members, William McAdoo, secretary of the treasury, and Newton Baker, secretary of war, in his place, enabling these men to gather much information that would be useful in their two departments.[25] Wilson, however, unyielding in his choice, spent Wednesday morning, October 24, secluded in his study, immersed in the technical problems of defining House's credentials for recognition in formal diplomatic circles abroad.

Wilson's choice of House, who still lacked any official title, once again illuminated, according to his critics, the president's aversion to traditional diplomacy. "Nothing was further from Wilson's habit and cast of mind," the latter-day ambassador George Kennan would write, "than to take the regular envoys into his confidence, to seek their opinions, or to use their facilities for private communications with foreign governments . . ." In the rare instance when it did occur to Wilson to pursue his objectives by the traditional diplomatic methods—that is, attempting to influence the attitudes of foreign governments through private persuasion or bargaining—Wilson, as Kennan remarked, chose his "irregular agent" instead of a permanent envoy.[26]

The president outlined a letter for House's presentation in Great Britain, France, and Italy. After consultation with Lansing, Wilson then asked his secretary of state to write a letter informing the French ambassador, who had initiated the invitation to participate in the War Council, of his acceptance and of his commission to House to represent him. On further consideration of House's credentials, and in view of the regard for formality among European governments, Lansing suggested that it would simplify matters if Wilson would give his delegate a formal designation. Thus House would be referred to as "Head of the American War Mission and Special Representative of President Wilson in Europe."

Before leaving, House wrote to tell Wilson that he would think of him and "dear Mrs. Wilson constantly" while he was away and would "put forth the best" there was in him to fulfill Wilson's trust. He was sure the president knew how happy he had made him by giving him this great opportunity to serve. He also reminded Wilson that one of the highest duties imposed on the president was to care for himself, and that House did not put it too strongly when he said, "You are the one hope left to this torn and distracted world. Without your leadership God alone knows how long we will wander in the wilderness."[27]

The American War Mission with Colonel House at its head secretly left for Halifax on October 28. Wilson sent House a personal message on the day of his departure: "I hate to say good-bye. It is an immense comfort to me to have you at hand here for counsel and for friendship. But it is right that you should go. God bless and keep you both! My thoughts will follow you all the weeks through,—and I hope that it will be only weeks that will separate us. Mrs. Wilson joins in all affectionate messages."[28]

Ordinarily the president's foreign communications were handled by the State Department's code room; but for matters of greatest secrecy, Wilson and House would keep in touch privately. House was to code his outgoing messages and decode incoming messages, and Edith was entrusted to perform similar duties for her husband. This meant that from November 7, when the members of the American Mission arrived in London at the stroke of midnight, to their "mole-like" evening departure from Paris on December 6, Edith was witness to and partner in a private intelligence service run by two men dedicated to the supposition that they had been given the opportunity to serve mankind by settling the entire world in permanent peace. In his address to the American Federation of Labor on November 12, 1917, Wilson would define his position in the war:

> What I am opposed to is not the feeling of the pacifists, but their stupidity. My heart is with them, but my mind has a contempt for them. I want peace, but I know how to get it and they do not.
>
> You will notice that I sent a friend of mine, Colonel House, to Europe, who is as great a lover of peace as any man in the world, but I didn't send him on a peace mission yet. I sent him to take part in a conference as to how the war was to be won, and he knows, as I know, that that is the way to get peace if you want it for more than a few minutes.[29]

In this "black winter of the war" House and his party could not have arrived in London at a more catastrophic moment. On that same November 7, the Russian revolutionist who was sympathetic to the Allies, Alexander Kerensky, escaped from Petrograd. By ten o'clock that evening, Lenin proclaimed the overthrow of the provisional government. Within three weeks, with the Bolshevik government firmly in power, the Allies faced Russia's imminent withdrawal from the war. The Italians, devastated by the German and Austrian onslaught at Caporetto in the previous week, had abandoned their entire line along the Tagliamento River; their morale depleted, their cabinet collapsed. The day after his arrival, House lunched with Arthur Balfour and was pleased to be told that his coming at this time meant much, not alone to Great Britain on account of the debacle in both Russia and Italy.

Colonel House and his distinguished colleagues on the American Mission, as the London *Spectator* noted on November 17, "have arrived at the critical moment. . . . Their influence will be invaluable in the somewhat perturbed councils of the Allies." The following day the *New York Times* hailed House as the bearer of encouragement and reassurance to all civilized Europe: "Never in history has any foreigner come to Europe and found greater acceptance or wielded more power. Behind this super-Ambassador, whose authority and activities are unique, stands the President . . . and behind the President stands the country whose measureless resources and unshakable will are counted a sure shield against the successful sweep of Prussianism."[30]

In almost daily cables House reported on his meetings, scheduled at a breathtaking pace during a two-week period, from November 7 to November 22. He dined with the British prime minister, Lloyd George, and lunched with Balfour, the foreign secretary, and with Bonar Law, chancellor of the exchequer; he met with Sir George McDonough, director of military intelligence, and other British officials. He discussed the war's possible termination, and its aftermath, at Downing Street with Lord Robert Cecil, the acting foreign secretary. He spent an hour with the king at Buckingham Palace; on another day in a purely social visit, he and his wife, Loulie, lunched with the king and queen. Sir Edward Grey, the former foreign secretary, Balfour's distinguished predecessor, came from Northumberland to talk with him; and House found General Jan Christiaan Smuts from South Africa one of the few men he had met in the government who did not seem tired. The Houses entertained Balfour and Lady Essex at dinner. House met with Lord Northcliffe, editor of *The Times* of London; and the lord chief justice of England, Lord Reading; and with the first lord of the admiralty, Sir Eric Geddes.

On November 13, House cabled the president that French and British troops were being rushed to the front and should be ready for action by November 20. It was not probable that another offensive would be made on the French front until the spring—that is, before the Americans were strong enough to give material assistance, or the Russians recovered sufficiently to resume combat in the East. All in all, "It looks like a waiting game."[31]

That same day in Washington, the president played golf in the morning with Dr. Grayson, met with his cabinet, and joined Edith Wilson and a party at the National Theater to hear the Philadelphia Symphony Orchestra.[32] Also on that Tuesday, more than three years after the death of Ellen Axson, a simple ceremony at the Myrtle Hill Cemetery in Rome, Georgia, commemorated the placement of a sculptured gravestone at the burial plot of the president's first wife, beside her mother and father.[33]

On November 22, at Wilson's bidding, House's Mission crossed the Channel, headed for Paris. On the following day, he warned the president, "I foresee trouble in the workings of the Supreme War Council." House had just met alone with the French premier, Georges Clemenceau, who was earnestly in favor of unity of plan and action, but of the opinion that Lloyd George had nothing in mind. The premier wished, he told House, that America would take the initiative. He promised that he could be counted on to "back to a finish any reasonable suggestion."[34]

In Paris, House conferred with the prime ministers and foreign secretaries of England, France, and Italy and continued his thoughtful, informed, candid, and fretful letters and cables to Wilson. He reported daily and sometimes twice daily, advising and asking for advice. In regard to the continuing acrimony over the organization of the Supreme War Council, he told the French prime minister that it was hard enough to fight the Germans without fighting among themselves. Ever mindful of Wilson's ideology and of his own sense of his mission, House refused to be drawn into the Allies' controversies, particularly those concerning war aims of a territorial nature, and insisted, he told Wilson, that "we must hold to the broad principle you have laid down and not get mixed in the small and selfish ones."

Asked to advise on the Russian situation, House cabled that it was, as of November 23, "hopeless at the moment," that no responsible government was in sight; and he advised making no more advances or permitting any further contracts for purchases. On reading statements made by American papers to the effect that Russia should be treated as an enemy, House wired home on November 28 that it was "exceedingly important that such criticism be suppressed. It will throw Russia into the lap of Germany," he warned, "if the Allies and Americans express such views at this time."

On December 2, House cabled Wilson that there had been long and frequent discussions about Russia, but the result had not been satisfactory to him. In substance, the Allies were willing to reconsider their war aims in conjunction with Russia as soon as she had a stable government with whom they could act. At the same time, House told the president that the Russian ambassador at Paris believed it of great importance that the United States send a message to Russia affirming the disinterested motives of the United States and its desire "to bring a disorderly world into a fraternity of nations for the good of all and for the aggrandizement of none."[35]

In his hope of persuading the Allies to issue a joint statement of war aims, House cabled Wilson for approval of the resolution he intended to offer at the inter-Allied conference:

> The Allies and the United States declare that they are not waging war for the purpose of aggression or indemnity. The sacrifices they are making are in order that militarism shall not continue to cast its shadow over the world, and that nations shall have the right to lead their lives in the way that seems to them best for the development of their general welfare.[36]

He ended the cable by asking that Wilson answer immediately, should he have any objection to raise. It was of vast importance that this be done. The British had agreed to vote for it. The president's endorsement went out by cable the next day:

> The resolution you suggest is entirely in line with my thought and has my approval. You will realize how unfortunate it would be for the conference to discuss peace terms in a spirit antagonistic to my January address to the Senate. Our people and Congress will not fight for any selfish aim on the part of any belligerent, with the possible exception of Alsace Lorraine, least of all for divisions of territory such as have been contemplated in Asia Minor. I think it will be obvious to all that it would be a fatal mistake to cool the ardour of America.[37]

House was deeply discouraged when he found it impossible to persuade the conference to agree to such a mild resolution. When, in fact, he saw it tossed into the "scrap-heap,"[38] he cabled Wilson that he would arrive in Washington on December 17 and said that he hoped "you will not think it necessary to make any statement concerning foreign affairs until I can see you. This seems to me very important." The reasons for this message are noted in his own handwriting: "I sent this cable to the President because I had in mind his making a statement giving our war aims. I tried to get this done at Paris, but failed. The next best thing was for the President to do it."[39] On December 3, House received Wilson's cable telling him, "Sorry impossible to omit foreign affairs from address to Congress. Reticence on my part at this juncture would be misunderstood and resented and do much harm."[40]

Working far into the nights, Wilson had been preparing since late November for his annual message, to be delivered on December 4 before the second session of the 65th Congress. Edith sat with him, often decoding House's cables or coding her husband's answers as he wrote at his desk. The morning of December 4, she insisted that he play nine holes of golf, the first exercise he had allowed himself in days. They left the White House promptly at 8:30 A.M., rode twenty minutes, played roughly twelve holes, and were back in their car less than two hours later. Wilson continued to play the rest of the week with Ellen's cousin Colonel Edward T. Brown.

The couple left the White House for the Capitol at 12:15 P.M. The entire ceremony, Edith acknowledged, gave her a thrill. She was fascinated by its power and protocol, and she paid homage, as her eyes swept the audience, to its many-tiered powers: to the vice president and members of the cabinet; to the black-robed justices of the Supreme Court in front seats; to the Senate and House members circled behind them at their desks; to the Secret Service men at each door and surrounding the rostrum; to reporters lining the press gallery.

Introduced to the hushed throng, Wilson noted that eight months, crowded with events of immense and grave significance, had elapsed since his last address. He did not choose to debate the intolerable wrongs done and planned against America by the sinister masters of Germany, but he did think it important to ask, and answer, the question: When shall we consider the war won? He found the nation united in spirit and intention and paid little heed to those who told him otherwise. He admitted to hearing voices of dissent and criticism and the clamor of the noisily thoughtless and troublesome. He also saw men (perhaps those who had voted for him in the belief that he would keep the country out of war) here and there fling themselves in impotent disloyalty against the calm, indomitable power of the nation. He had also heard men debate peace who understood neither its nature nor the way in which they might attain it with uplifted eyes and unbroken spirits. He knew that none of these spoke for the nation, and he dismissed them: "They do not touch the heart of anything. They may safely be left to strut their uneasy hour and be forgotten."

On the other hand, he did think it necessary to say plainly what those here at the seat of action considered the war to be for and what part the country was meant to play in the settlement of its issues. The peace America would make must deliver the once fair lands and happy peoples of Belgium and northern France from the Prussian conquest and the Prussian menace. It must also deliver the peoples of Austria-Hungary, the peoples of the Balkans, and the peoples of Turkey, alike in Europe and in Asia, from the impudent and alien dominion of the Prussian military and the German commercial autocracy. There was, he pointed out, one embarrassing obstacle to peace as conceived by him: the United States was at war with Germany but not with Germany's allies. Having raised that dilemma, he now offered its solution. He would, therefore, earnestly recommend that the Congress immediately declare the United States to be at war with Austria-Hungary, which was simply the vassal of the German government.

At the end, Wilson, preacher, professor, and president, reassured his congregation and classroom, the citizenry of the United States, "Our present and immediate task is to win the war, and nothing shall turn us aside from it until it is accomplished. Every power and resource we possess, whether of men, of money or of materials is being devoted and will continue to be devoted to that purpose until it is achieved." And in the end, America would be free to base peace "on generosity and justice, to the exclusion of all selfish claims to advantage even on the part of the victors."

With his recommendation of a declaration of war on Austria, cheers swelled to a roar. Despite the many times Edith had gone over the words of this speech with her husband—she could repeat them almost line by line—the sentences came out, that noon on December 4, "in new colours." With Russia out of the war, with Romania crushed and Italy virtually beaten, all in the space of two months, Edith was cheered by "an unshakable faith," she said, "in America's ability to win."[41]

The way the American Mission had slipped out of Paris on the evening of December 6 was the culmination, the *New York Times* reported, of all the molelike activities of Colonel House. Only two persons knew the mission's departure hour or destination. The reporter Charles Grasty had wondered whether the colonel had made a quiet bet with himself on his ability to take a party of fifteen or twenty people out of the most conspicuous setting in Paris without anybody being the wiser.[42] Embarked the next day for home on the USS *Mount Vernon*, the group talked, as the shores of France faded into the mist, about personal adjustments to be made after keeping such heady company abroad.

On December 15, still aboard the USS *Mount Vernon*, House forwarded a summary for Wilson's information and one for the State Department, with the help of his son-in-law Gordon Auchincloss. He also gave notice of his planned arrival at 4:40 that same afternoon, to which the president responded by telling him of his delight at his safe return; Wilson was looking forward "with the utmost pleasure" to seeing House, and was hoping that he would stay at the White House. Two days later, House arrived at five o'clock and found Wilson waiting for him in his study, where they talked for two hours, in Edith's presence, about the workings of the Supreme War Council, its inefficiency, and House's recommendation to send over General Tasker H. Bliss as soon as possible to act as military adviser. Wilson also discussed the feasibility of sending an American political representative to sit in the Council with the prime ministers, a proposal finally accomplished in the fall of 1918. His choice was the colonel, he explained, because he trusted him to make essential quick decisions without needing advice at every stage of the negotiations.

On their second anniversary, December 18, Edith chose to celebrate that "happy, busy day" by sitting in the study with the president, Colonel House, Secretary of War Baker, and General Bliss. At that morning meeting, House described his unsuccessful effort abroad to persuade the Allies to make a unified declaration of their war aims in a way that would unite the world against Germany, help solve the Russian problem, and "knit together the best and most unselfish opinions of the world." At all cost, he said, it was imperative that Germany not be allowed to pose as the victim of Allied imperialist aspirations. At this moment, Wilson stepped in, deciding that, in lieu of an inter-Allied manifesto, he would formulate a declaration on American soil that might prove to be the moral turning point of the war. At this stage, the determination of the Fourteen Points regarding the aims of the war was discussed for no more than ten or fifteen minutes. House returned briefly to Manhattan, but was back in Washington on Sunday, December 23, arriving at the White House around six-thirty. He brought with him material researched by members of the Inquiry, bearing on the Fourteen Points that Wilson would announce to Congress and the world just two weeks later, on January 8.[43]

On December 26, the president issued a proclamation assuming control of the transportation systems of the country. Under the threat of strikes and walkouts, he publicly appealed to railroad executives and the brotherhoods alike to settle their differences "in this time of national peril."[44] The situation had become so acute that Wilson appointed William Gibbs McAdoo as director general of the railroads under a single authority on condition that he resign as secretary of the treasury. As Edith Wilson analyzed the problem, the railroads had "fallen down . . . neither materials nor troops were moving as they should."

On January 4, 1918, subsequent to issuing the takeover proclamation, Wilson addressed Congress on the subject of the railroads and recommended legislation.[45] That evening at nine, House arrived at the White House, ate lightly of the dinner saved for him, and reviewed with Wilson for more than two hours reports and maps, largely the work of the Inquiry, pertaining to the imminent Fourteen Points address. On January 5, a "remarkable day," the president was waiting for him at quarter past ten. Fifteen minutes later the two were at work—and finished, "as we would have it, at half-past twelve o'clock," remaking the map of the world.[46]

Though indebted to the Inquiry for much of its spadework, the concept and philosophy of a League of Nations, far from originating with Wilson, was credited to many sources, including an international women's congress that had met at The Hague under the presidency of the social worker Jane Addams in 1917. Even as Wilson and House worked, David Lloyd George assured a delegation of trade unionists gathered in London that "the settlement of the new Europe must be based on such grounds of reason and justice as will give some promise of stability . . . that government with the consent of the governed must be the basis of any territorial settlement in this war."[47] Suggesting that Wilson was indebted to Lloyd George, George Harvey published "The Genesis of the Fourteen Commandments" in the *North American Review* in February 1919. Whatever the diverse foundations of the Fourteen Points, however, Wilson was given credit for having evaluated and codified existing opinions and facts in the light of what he believed to be "practical idealism and clothed them in convincing phrase."[48] The president checked his speech with Secretary of State Lansing before delivering it at noon, in Congress, on Tuesday, January 8.

Speaking of America's aims in the war: "It is that the world be made fit and safe to live in; and particularly that it be made safe for every peace-loving nation which, like our own, wishes to live its own life, determine its own institutions, be assured of justice and fair dealing by the other peoples of the world as against force and selfish aggression." Succinctly conveyed, the fourteen paragraphs embraced open covenants of peace, openly arrived at, absolute freedom of navigation, removal of all economic barriers, guarantees of reduction of national armaments, impartial adjustment of all colonial claims, the evacuation and restoration of Belgium, the freeing of all French territory, readjustment of the frontiers of Italy, and autonomous development of Austria-Hungary. The relations of the several Balkan states were to be determined by friendly counsel along historically established lines of allegiance and nationality. Turkish portions of the existing Ottoman Empire were to enjoy a secure sovereignty, and other nationalities now under Turkish rule were to exercise autonomous development. Poland was to be independent. Point XIV stated that a general association of nations must be formed under specific covenants for the purpose of affording mutual guarantees of political independence and territorial integrity to great and small states alike. Having spoken, Wilson said, "in terms too concrete to admit of any further doubt or question," he noted the principle that ran through the whole program: "the principle of justice to all peoples and nationalities, and their right to live on equal terms of liberty and safety with one another, whether they be strong or weak."[49]

In Edith's opinion, "no public utterance Mr. Wilson had ever made was received with such general acclaim."[50] His words, the *New York Tribune* announced, offered a second Emancipation Proclamation; as Lincoln had freed the slaves of the South half a century before, Wilson now pledged his country to fight for the liberation of the Belgian and the Pole, the Serb and the Romanian, for the long-suffering populations of Alsace-Lorraine and the Italian Irredenta. Without a selfish ambition, without hope or covert thought of selfish advantage, the United States had entered a world war to restore justice, honor, and liberty to a world assailed by German barbarism and German ambition. "The President's words are the words of a hundred million," the *Tribune* asserted. "Today, as never before, the whole nation marches with the President, certain alike of the leader and the cause."[51]

Years later, though Edith identified House as having been her husband's only confidant for the four days before his delivery of his Fourteen Points address,[52] she steadily perpetuated the image of House as an indecisive, unproductive, fawning, and intellectually dishonest amateur. In this, she appeared oblivious to having raised profound questions about her husband's judgment—if, indeed, his most trusted counselor, emissary, and sounding board at this period of his presidency was to any degree as spineless, inadequate, and superficial as he appears in her persistently derogatory sketches.

CHAPTER 16

"She knows what her husband knows"

"*The nation is at war and all the forces of the nation, martial and material, are being mobilized for war. . . . Within eight months, peaceful and industrial America has turned into a military camp, by what is probably the most complete material and psychological transformation of a nation in the history of the world, for no other mighty state was ever so founded in antagonism to militarism and so deliberately dedicated to the pursuits of peace. . . .*

"*At the centre of all this agitation is the President on whose word the nation waited to begin its preparations, at whose word the nation began—when he said that the hour had struck. . . . Yet, in outward aspect, there is no quieter home in the land than his home, the White House. . . .*

"*The household life within is very domestic. . . . Whether [the President] is reading or conversing, the women of the family are busy with their incessant knitting. Other women less informed than Mrs. Wilson may have been temporarily misled by false rumors about the unimportance of knitting. Mrs. Wilson knows too much not to know how greatly needed knitting is. . . . She knows what her husband knows, what Secretary Baker and Secretary Daniels know, that for every reason this work must go on.*" "An Evening with the President: The White House as a Home," by Stockton Axson, *New York Herald*, January 27, 1918.

"She knows what her husband knows" is the phrase that echoes in memory after Stockton Axson's homage to the wartime White House is put aside. If Colonel House was considered an "irregular" diplomat, how might one define the role of the president's wife as other than an "irregular" confidential assistant and intelligence operative? A presence at the most confidential and rigorous discussions, every evening she accompanied the president to his study to check the Drawer, whose contents Wilson immediately reviewed. In his manifold role as confidant, adviser, and courier, the third member of that unorthodox diplomatic triumvirate was assuredly Colonel House.

It was Edith who telephoned House to invite him to dinner at the White House on Sunday, January 27, 1918. Wilson was suffering from a severe cold, and the three sat by the fireside in his study to discuss the size and composition of the commission to attend the peace conference envisioned to take place in Paris at the end of the war. Wilson, anxious about the issue, was eager for House's advice on candidates. The president told House that he was "so nearly official" and so closely wrapped up with the administration that his appointment would be expected and would serve as an excuse for excluding William Jennings Bryan, who thought himself in the running. As to numbers, Wilson believed that a five-member commission would be sufficient, though House preferred seven, allowing for four Democrats and three Republicans. House's prior experience in Paris had taught him the necessity of having sufficient members to serve on different committees to discuss items and to formulate policies. Wilson, however, made it clear that he would appoint no more than two Republicans, and Edith Wilson announced that she was disappointed to learn that there would be anyone going other than the president and the colonel.

To House's surprise, Wilson said that he thought Secretary of State Robert Lansing would have to go. To represent the War Department Wilson settled on General Tasker H. Bliss, reputed to be calm, trustworthy, broad-gauged, farsighted, and astute, and especially admired by the president for his "robust good sense."[1] Edith Wilson wondered about Elihu Root and ex-president William H. Taft; House said that he preferred the latter for reasons of geography and personality. As Lansing and Root were from New York, House did not advise sending both men, and he thought Taft, from Ohio, was more flexible and tractable, being good-natured and easily led.[2] House would question Wilson's final choices.

On January 31, 1918, Colonel House warned the president that "the situation is so delicate and so critical . . . it would be a tragedy to make a false step . . ."[3] Every embattled nation was torn between the passion to continue the war and the hope of ending it. Only now, forty-two and a half months after the first hostilities, newly recruited American soldiers would be landing weekly in France—six hundred fifty thousand in all by the coming April. Victory in late May of a brigade of four thousand Americans at the village of Cantigny on the Somme would evoke "the first cold foreboding" among the Germans that this was not, as they had hoped, "a rabble of amateurs."[4] Even as the Supreme War Council met at Versailles on June 2, General Pershing would be negotiating the arrival of over three hundred thousand American soldiers.

Much was known and far more was unpredictable. The intricate and cumbersome matters at stake were subject to the impact of personalities, and to ancient loyalties and enmities—the balance of the whole made vulnerable by secret treaties as well as open if fluid allegiances among the nations of the Entente and those of the Central Powers. Grave consideration had to be given to a rising socialist party in Germany, and to its million strikers, who had stalked out of their factories on January 28, as well as to its pacifist factions.

Bolshevik domination in Russia, Russia's traumatic withdrawal from the Entente, and the fallen nation's signing of the peace of Brest Litovsk on March 3 not only fired Germany's territorial aspirations but raised the question of Japanese intervention in Siberia. Months after the *New York Times* had predicted Russia would take the place of the Balkan states "as a chessboard of international chicanery,"[5] Wilson confided to House that he was "sweating blood over . . . what is right and feasible (possible) to do in Russia. It goes to pieces like quicksilver under my touch . . ."[6]

The question of the moment was how far the United States might encourage the peace movement and reform forces in Central Europe without weakening the Allies' will to fight to the end for a just peace.[7] House dined again with the Wilsons on Monday, January 28, and also conferred with the president the next day. In the brief interim, House forwarded telegrams from the American ambassadors in Italy and France reporting Europe's fear that America was becoming too potent and unsympathetic to European interests and of growing resentment of the president's firm and "directive" position. The telegrams, the letters, and House's own diary refute Edith's depiction of House as a "jelly fish" and reveal, instead, a man of strong, candid opinions, loyally, sincerely, and conscientiously fulfilling Wilson's mandate to act as his deputy at large, with the multifaceted duties of witness, steward, broker, and intelligence agent.

Having in effect created a brand-new post in the diplomatic realm, a secretary of the world, Wilson asked his appointee, Colonel House, to follow events in enemy territory as recorded in the socialist press and in speeches, as well as in reports from Berne, Copenhagen, Paris, and London, in order to fortify the president's arguments against German imperialists.[8] Presumably to circumvent the State Department, House was also to funnel secret messages to and from Wilson to the former first lord of the British admiralty and the present foreign secretary, Arthur James Balfour; to relay opinions from the new British ambassador, Rufus Daniel Isaacs, Lord Reading; and to consult with Sir William Wiseman, the chief British intelligence agent in the United States, as well as with Thomas G. Masaryk, president of the Czecho-Slovak Committee and future first president of the Czecho-Slovak Republic, among other prominent officials.

As yet another illustration of how diversely House served the president, Wilson asked him to convey a message to his publisher, Harper & Brothers, in response to their question regarding his plans for literary works at his term's expiration. He wanted them to know that he wished to be absolutely free of any commitment at this time, though he was none the less appreciative of their generous suggestions.[9]

Dissatisfied with German and Austrian responses, which questioned a number of his Fourteen Points, Wilson chose to clarify his terms publicly, before Congress. House, at Wilson's invitation, arrived on February 8 to work on a speech in which Wilson dismissed the terms of the newly appointed chancellor, Count Georg F. von Herling—the German maintained that certain points should be settled by his country's allies, or later, by negotiation—as being as archaic as those of the Congress of Vienna. "We cannot and will not return to that," Wilson assured his audience on February 11. "What is at stake now is the peace of the world. What we are striving for is a new international order based upon broad and universal principles of right and justice—no mere peace of shreds and patches." Furthermore, peoples and provinces were not to be bartered about from sovereignty to sovereignty "as if they were mere chattels and pawns in a game, even the great game, now forever discredited, of the balance of power."[10]

Again at Wilson's request, House returned to Washington on February 23 to discuss the less than secret peace offer of Emperor Karl of Austria routed through the king of Spain. The message to the president had been intercepted by British intelligence, and Wilson asked that House contact Balfour for comments and suggestions as well as for his opinion as to the necessity of informing other members of the Entente of its existence. Suspicious of the sincerity and motivation behind the peace offer, the president asked House to tell Balfour that he would not close the door to further discussion, but would rather "develop and probe what the Emperor of Austria had in mind."[11]

With Europe seemingly on the fringes of peace, Lord Robert Cecil, Britain's minister of blockade, had begun to think beyond the concept to the actual structure of a league of nations. In this vein Cecil chose to write to House, who, he knew, had been "specially charged by the President with the superintendence of all questions which need preparation in connection with the Peace Conference." The league was bound to be among those questions, Cecil told House. The British had appointed a committee to inquire, particularly from a juridical and historical standpoint, into the various schemes for establishing, by means of a league of nations or other device, some alternative to war as a means of settling international disputes. The British did not at present intend to publish the fact of the formation of this committee, but Cecil hoped that House would accept a copy of *Three Centuries of Treaties*, whose author was the committee chairman, Sir Walter Phillimore, formerly lord justice of appeal and a well-known authority on international law. Should House's staff be engaged in a similar task, Cecil believed it would be of mutual benefit to share their ideas.[12]

It was too soon, and the American studies too new, House responded to Cecil, to warrant such a mutual exchange. House's subsequent suggestion that a committee might be formed to work out ideas for the peace conference was initially rejected by Wilson, who feared that the moment questions of organization arose, "all sorts of jealousies come to the front which ought not now to be added to other matters of delicacy." Wilson was disdainful of irritating peace "butters-in" and "woolgatherers," such as members of the League to Enforce Peace, the Carnegie peace group, and the World Court; but he did grudgingly acquiesce in the colonel's proposal to invite certain peace advocates—William Taft, Elihu Root, and Harvard University's President A. Lawrence Lowell— to join him at luncheon with the British archbishop of York on April 11. As to how the League should evolve, Wilson touched on what was to become the sticking point of the troubling document:

My own conviction, as you know, is that the administrative *constitution* of the League must *grow* and not be made; that we must *begin* with solemn covenants, covering mutual guarantees of political independence and territorial integrity (if the final territorial agreements of the peace conference are fair and satisfactory and *ought* to be perpetuated), but that the method of carrying those mutual pledges out should be left to develop of itself, case by case. Any attempt to begin by putting executive authority in the hands of any particular group of powers would be to sow a harvest of jealousy and distrust which would spring up at once and choke the whole thing. To take one thing, and only one but quite sufficient in itself: The United States Senate would never ratify any treaty which put the force of the United States at the disposal of any such group or body. Why begin at the impossible end when there is a possible end and it is feasible to plant a system which will slowly but surely ripen into fruition?[13]

Almost a month having passed since they had seen each other, Wilson was now eager to meet with House, who had been ill. The last paragraph of his letter extended a cordial invitation on March 22: "When you feel wholly fit, come down (we shall not need more than an hour's notice) and we will have one of our clearing talks, which I stand in much need of. We are happy that you are getting well, and all join in affectionate messages."[14]

Contrary to Dr. Axson's well-meaning account, Edith Wilson did put aside her knitting to join the Red Cross and wore a blue and white uniform to work on the afternoon shift at the canteen near the old Baltimore & Ohio freight depot. She also joined forces with Dr. Anna Howard Shaw in an open letter to the women of the Allied countries, urging united effort toward protecting the morals of the soldiers and war workers. Furthermore, she took on the task of naming one thousand or more ships.

The White House observed not only wheatless and meatless days, but gasless Sundays. Following the fuel administrator's request to conserve gasoline, the Wilsons abandoned their official limousine to set out for church in an ancient victoria found in the White House stables and hastily polished. Secret Service men followed in an old-time surrey with fringe around the top, escorted by police, who, in the name of patriotism, abandoned motorcycles for bicycles. Though official entertainment dwindled to a minimum, the Wilsons received visits from such motion picture stars as Mary Pickford, Marie Dressler, Charlie Chaplin, and Douglas Fairbanks. On Saturday, April 20, Wilson saw Edith off for Philadelphia to spur on the Liberty Loan bond campaign. This occasion of her review of twenty-five women led by a group on horseback marked her first attendance at a public function independent of the president. On May 15, Edith drove to Potomac Park for the inauguration of the first airmail route between Washington and New York.

Another event remote from her war efforts was to absorb her attention during the spring of 1918. This was the serial publication in *The Saturday Evening Post* of an impassioned defense of "The real Colonel House"[15] against the purported "tommy-rot . . . tootings" of slanderous journalists who misinterpreted and reviled his manner, his character, his finances, his role, and his missions. The author, Arthur D. Howden Smith, asserted that people who knew the real Colonel House considered him "an astute politician, yes, the cleverest politician the country ever saw. But they do not stop with that. They believe that his greatest attribute is his statesmanship, his diplomacy in handling men and pushing measures." Rounding out his portrait of House as a man who had made history and molded great affairs, Smith concluded, "He is the President's principal counselor, probably the only man upon whose advice Woodrow Wilson leans with implicit trust, and anyone who is acquainted with the upstanding character of Mr. Wilson, his stern self-confidence, will appreciate what this means."[16]

One object of the articles on House was to resolve "the vexed question" of the so-called secret sources of the colonel's millions. House's yearly income of $20,000 stemmed from his inheritance at his father's death, and from his investments. As for those skeptics and cynics who questioned what satisfaction House received from his work, who talked of his connection with Wall Street and the big banking houses, who seemed to think he must receive some shady rake-off for his services, all were dismissed by his biographer. "How foolish they are!" he concluded. House had never craved wealth "as it is understood in the East." It was apparently to a breadth of interests, to his vast acquaintance—far wider, actually, than the president's, since it reached through all strata of society and included hundreds of men and women outside official circles—that House owed his phenomenal grasp of public sentiment.

However honorable in intention, the articles emerged as a court biography that embarrassed its subject and offended members of the press. *The Real Colonel House* was weighted by excessive praise of its hero as the instigator of every successful move made by Woodrow Wilson. Critics sought to account for the publication of the articles, and in particular for the self-effacement of the president, "who has not hitherto been regarded as handicapped by excessive modesty, or as disposed to concede to others the credit justly his." Wilson, keenly sensitive as he was, would be more than human if he were not to resent an effort to convey to the public that he owed everything to the Texas colonel, in reality the "power behind the Throne and confidential advisor of the one of all our long line of Presidents who is least amenable to the advice of others, no matter how well equipped for the task."[17] These critics suggested, almost as an afterthought, that the articles were meant to prove to his detractors how well fitted House was for the mission of principal representative of the United States abroad.[18]

Wilson was apologetic about his tardy reply to House's letter regarding the biography. The president hoped that House understood why he did not hear from Wilson more frequently; entering an English tank on exhibit he had burned the inside of his right hand on grasping a nearly red-hot pipe.

The letter was also reassuring. Wilson now told House that he regretted the annoyance caused to the colonel by the biographical articles. While he had realized that House would squirm at certain passages, he concluded that on the whole the writer "has tried to treat you fairly and he certainly has treated you in the most friendly spirit. We just have to grin and bear it," he advised, "when these things happen."[19] That same day Edith wrote, "We have just read your letter and had to laugh over your agony of being in print—although we realize along with your fun over it—there is real annoyance." She had been cutting out the articles as they appeared, intending to wait to read them all together, but in the end read them individually, finding them all interesting and finding no serious objections. "Your letter to the *Evening Post* I am going to keep if you don't mind—for it is so characteristic in its fury and fairness—Love to you both from us. E.B.W."[20] Though both letters from the Wilsons appear sincerely affectionate, House remained sensitive about the publication of his biography. During dinner with the Wilsons in the following September, when Edith's sister Bertha told House how people were saying he was a "maker of men," the president smiled dryly and remarked, "He ought to change his pattern." House noted in his diary: "He said this with himself in view in order to be facetious."[21] Still later, when George H. Doran, the publisher, sought the president's approval before promoting the hardcover version of the articles, also published in 1918, Wilson told Tumulty that he did not think this was the time to publicize the colonel and felt sure that the colonel would concur "in advising that the book be let rest for the present."

While both Colonel House and Ray Stannard Baker omitted reference to its publication, Howden Smith's volume was eventually the subject of intense speculation, not on literary grounds but about its effect on the friendship of the two men. It was, according to its author, "the original cause of the rift that ended in a rupture."[22] Considering the critical mission Wilson entrusted to House in the months ahead, the immediate impact of *The Real Colonel House* was apparently negligible. In the summer of 1918, Wilson told House, "I hail your letters with deep satisfaction and unspoken thanks go out to you for each one of them, whether I write or not, and the most affectionate appreciation of all that you do for me."[23]

Most significantly, the president forwarded to House the British preliminary draft, grounded on the Phillimore committee report, of the proposed League of Nations "constitution" (Wilson initiated the term *covenant* on July 16). Would House rewrite it as he thought it ought to be rewritten, along the lines of his recent response to Lord Robert Cecil's inquiries? "This will be the best means," Wilson explained, "of expressing a definite judgment and furnish me the full basis for the comment and opinion . . . which the British Government is asking."[24]

On a day's notice, House was able to arrange for the Wilsons, who were arriving at the Magnolia station on the morning of August 15, 1918, by special train, to occupy the home of Mrs. T. Jefferson Coolidge, a fine colonial house that stood on a point between the Manchester and Magnolia beaches, a few hundred yards from the colonel's own dwelling. The purpose of the president's visit was to discuss the proposed League of Nations. Seated in the pleasing loggia overlooking the sea, Wilson explained to House how he had revised his draft of the League's Covenant, and how he thought a league of nations might be incorporated in the peace treaty. All three of Wilson's drafts—the second on January 10, 1919; the third, ten days later—affirmed the president's two great central convictions: a league was necessary, and its need immediate. Evaluating Wilson's role, his official biographer, Ray Stannard Baker, has written that Wilson would be credited not with originating a single idea but rather as having served as "editor or compiler" of the final Covenant of the League, "selecting or rejecting, recasting or combing the projects that came to him from other sources."[25]

Wilson and House continued their talks while a company of marines kept the public at a respectful distance. The men visited back and forth, discussing not only the framework of the League of Nations but also the Allies' economic policy, the president's Mexican policy, England's politics, and the meaning of Germany's peace efforts. House differed with Wilson on the issue of smaller nations joining the league on equal terms with the larger ones. Of the fifty-odd possible members, not more than twelve at most would fight seriously in the event of a great war, or be of service in financing it; and yet, as the plan stood, forty could overrule decisions made by the twelve. The difficulties were so apparent to House that he worried that the concept of a league would become nothing more than an idealistic dream.

House was also concerned about the president's health. Prompted, perhaps, by Wilson's ready admission of fatigue ("I am very tired, for there never were so many problems per diem"[26]), House made some discreet inquiries and observations that only deepened his unease. When he asked whether the president could stand another term, Dr. Grayson said, "He might go for another ten years if nothing untoward happened."[27] When House recalled the president's reference to his "leaky" mind, and his failure to remember the conclusion of one conference, Edith was dismissive. In response to his criticism of the president's method of conducting his work—he paid too much attention to detail and did not sufficiently delegate to others—Edith said bluntly, "When he delegated it to others he found it was not well done." House believed—and it is not clear whether he explained himself further to Mrs. Wilson or reserved his remarks for his diary—that the president "should give himself ample leisure to think clearly upon the big problems that confront him and not have his mind wearied with detail someone else could do."[28]

During that long weekend in Magnolia, the entire party, including House's son-in-law Gordon Auchincloss, and their British visitor, Sir William Wiseman, enjoyed the clear, crisp weather, the automobile rides, and golf, taking lunch at the Houses' home, while dinner was served at the Wilsons'. The president spoke openly on a number of subjects. Wiseman came away with the impression that Wilson was "a pretty extreme radical with that curious uninformed prejudice against the so-called governing class in England." Nor did he appear to harbor much sympathy for Italy but thought she entered the war as a cold-blooded business transaction and showed a similar indifference toward Bulgaria and Turkey.

Wilson did, however, speak with conviction of genuine liberal elements in Austria and even in Germany who sincerely wished to follow democratic ideals, though admittedly they were too small a minority to influence their people as a whole. Wilson's personal hatred of the kaiser, whom he had never seen, struck Wiseman as almost amusing, causing him to comment, "The elected autocrat can see no good in the hereditary tyrant."[29] The president appeared to have little detailed knowledge of continental politics, relying in those matters on House's advice.

In the weeks following that intense intimacy of the five-day discussions in Magnolia, House felt curiously neglected. He maintained a one-way correspondence with Wilson, forwarding pertinent mail regarding the resolution of the war, and on September 3, in a notably thoughtful and prophetic letter, asked if Wilson did not think the time had come to commit the Allies to as much of his program as possible. As the Allies succeed, he warned, "your influence will diminish. This is inevitable. By the time of the Peace Conference you will be nearing the end of your second term and this, too, will be something of a challenge to those, both at home and abroad, who have the will to oppose you." Regarding the most immediate threat of the Republicans to Wilson's plans, House predicted that if their party came to the Congress flushed with victory at the polls in the midterm elections two months away, no appeal the president could make would be successful. He also cautioned Wilson that while there would be men of vision and loftiness of purpose who would rally to his support, they would be in the minority.

With no response from the president after a five-day interval, House, despite his accustomed equanimity, felt himself nearly abandoned. It was difficult, he complained to McAdoo, to advise Wilson, who not only expected House to keep abreast of both domestic and foreign situations but also to read the president's mind and divine its conclusions. Though House was sure that his influence with the President was as strong as ever—or so he was encouraged to think by friends in whom Wilson had confided—the situation was "hardly fair to me, and less fair to him." If his advice was as necessary as Wilson seemed to think, "it would be more valuable if he informed me oftener as to his reactions upon what I advise."[30]

A call from the White House and a conference with the president after breakfast at the White House on Sunday, September 22, seemed wholly to restore the colonel's confidence. With the Allies, reinforced by American troops, stemming the Germans in France and Belgium, the Turkish army shattered, the Bulgarians disarmed, and the prospects for peace increasing, Wilson had been thinking about House's letter. He was impressed by House's argument that the time had come to pledge the Allies to his principles and to that end had written a speech, which he now asked that the colonel review.

Five days later, the Houses accompanied the Wilsons to the Metropolitan Opera House in New York for the opening of the fourth Liberty Loan bond drive, an occasion for the presidential address. It was Wilson's intent to convey as never before a vivid sense of the great issues involved, in order that the audience might appreciate and accept with enthusiasm the duty of supporting the government. To achieve a secure and lasting peace, Wilson told his audience, "it will be necessary that all who sit down at the peace table shall come ready and willing . . . to create in some virile fashion the only instrumentality by which it can be made certain that the agreements of the peace will be honored and fulfilled. . . . That indispensable instrumentality is a League of Nations formed under covenants that will be efficacious." He proposed a general alliance, as differentiated from special and limited alliances, to avoid entanglements and clear the air of the world for common understandings and the maintenance of common rights. As for Germany, there would be no terms, no bargains, and no compromise. The world does not want terms, he concluded. "It wishes the final triumph of justice and fair dealing."[31]

House was unsure about the reaction to the speech, thinking it was perhaps over the heads of the audience. But Wilson had accomplished his goal, at least as it was recognized by the London *Daily News* on October 8, 1918:

> We can no longer dwell in the atmosphere of vague phrases. We must say whether President Wilson speaks for us or for himself alone. . . . There is no policy before the world except that of the President, and there is no other policy that would be tolerated by the democracy of any allied country. Its immediate endorsement is vital.[32]

Edith would remember the next four weeks of negotiations as the most hectic of the entire war. As she saw the situation, the Germans were suspected of proposing an armistice in order to re-form their armies and fight to better advantage, and the Allies' task, while avoiding this pitfall, was to put an end to the fighting permanently and at the earliest hour.[33] On Sunday, October 6, promptly after receiving the German government's informal request to the United States to "bring about the immediate conclusion of a general armistice on land, on water, and in the air," Wilson telephoned House for advice on how to word his guarded response to this suspect peace overture. On Monday morning, the Swiss minister delivered the German government's formal request for an immediate armistice; Germany accepted the President's terms on the thirteenth. The next day, Wilson wrote a letter of credentials for House, which was followed, on October 16, by a second document of still more exalted terms:

> Know Ye, That reposing special trust and confidence in the Integrity and Ability of Edward M. House, of Texas, I do appoint him a special representative of the Government of the United States of America in Europe in matters relating to the war, and do authorize and empower him to execute and fulfill the duties of this commission with all the powers and privileges thereunto of right pertaining during the pleasure of the president of the United States . . .[34]

In preparation for House's departure for Europe, Wilson again devised a secret code between them. House was struck by the fact that the president deliberately avoided giving him any instructions, saying, "I feel you will know what to do." Pondering this, House wondered at the strangeness of their relationship. He was undertaking a mission of crucial importance without having received a word of presidential direction, advice, or discussion. He consoled himself that Wilson knew where their minds ran parallel, and also where they diverged. "I will follow his bent rather than my own," he vowed.[35] He never ceased to find those circumstances remarkable, the more so as Wilson's whole reputation was at stake at the time.[36]

On Thursday evening, October 24, Edith entered her husband's study just as he was getting up from his typewriter. He had in his hand an appeal for the choice of a Democratic Congress in the coming election and read it aloud to her. "I would not send it out," she advised. "It is not a dignified thing to do." Wilson's response was tinged with fatalism: "That is what I thought at first . . . but it is too late now. I told them I would do it." He rang the bell and gave the message to Hoover for delivery.[37] The president's appeal was issued the following day.

> I have no thought of suggesting that any political party is paramount in matters of patriotism. I feel too deeply the sacrifices which have been made in this war by all our citizens, irrespective of party affiliations, to harbor such an idea. I mean only that the difficulties and delicacies of our present task are of a sort that makes it

imperatively necessary that the Nation should give its undivided
support to the Government under a unified leadership, and that a
Republican Congress would divide the leadership.

The leaders of the minority in the present Congress have
unquestionably been pro-war, but they have been anti-administra-
tion . . .

I need not tell you, my fellow countrymen, that I am asking
your support not for my own sake or for the sake of a political
party, but for the sake of the Nation itself, in order that its inward
unity of purpose may be evident to all the world. In ordinary times
I would not feel at liberty to make such an appeal to you. In ordinary times divided counsels can be endured without permanent
hurt to the country. But these are not ordinary times . . ."[38]

The drive for a Democratic Congress was not news to Edith. It had
been under discussion with Tumulty early in September and as recently
as a week before the president's appeal, when Wilson had been peti-
tioned by an "avalanche" of both House and Senate Democrats to support their campaigns. Wilson's advisers in this instance, Vance C.
McCormick, head of the War Trade Board, and Homer S. Cummings, the
Democrats' campaign manager, thought his initial draft too strong, too
bitter, reinforcing Edith's fear that it betrayed her husband's irritation
with partisan attacks.[39] In the editing, despite deletions of specific names
of offending Republicans such as Henry Cabot Lodge, the intent of the
message remained intact and the reaction to it was even angrier than
anticipated. "This is not the President's personal war," the Republicans
protested, and Theodore Roosevelt wrote Lodge, "I am glad Wilson has
come out in the open; I fear Judas most when he can cloak his activities
behind a treacherous make-believe of nonpartisanship . . ."[40]

Dismay was not merely a partisan reaction. Even the most influential
and highly placed Democrats recognized the president's appeal as his
first fatal blunder, perhaps his "greatest mistake."[41] Reviving every partisan animosity, his appeal was also criticized, though he explicitly said
this was not the case, for its implication that the Democrats enjoyed a
monopoly of patriotism from which Republicans were excluded. It was
predicted that his manifesto would drive those Republicans who had
criticized Theodore Roosevelt for his attacks on Wilson into siding with
the former president. Worse, a possible defeat of Wilson's divisive quest
would weaken his image abroad—for which, critics said, the "president

will have no one to thank but himself and his indiscreet and wholly unnecessary appeal against the Republicans."[42]

In some circles there was speculation that this disastrous turn of events might have been avoided if House had not gone abroad. Those who had come to regard him as Wilson's greatest confidant and "sagacious, useful and very necessary counsellor" regretted his absence from Washington.[43] House himself affirmed this concept, maintaining that he was greatly disturbed by the president's appeal for a Democratic Congress and that, had he been at home, he would have counseled against this "needless venture."

The facts, however, speak of his missed opportunity to advise the president during an earlier discussion at the White House. He was so absorbed with the German notes at the meeting on Sunday, September 22, that he brushed the question aside, perhaps because he failed to recognize its volatility. When the president told him of his earnest desire that a Democratic Congress be elected and of his intentions of making a speech or writing a letter to that effect about two weeks before the elections, House "did not express any opinion as to the wisdom of this."[44]

A Republican majority was elected to Congress on Tuesday, November 5. Across the ocean, French and British evaluation of the election found it quite remarkable that the president, knowing the American Constitution required ratification of all treaties by the Senate, had not seized the opportunity to become a national rather than a party leader. Years later, scornful of Wilson's judgment, Winston Churchill denounced the American president for his strong party feeling and for the sense of personal superiority that led him to reject working with both parties. "Peace and goodwill among all nations abroad, but no truck with the Republican Party at home. That was his ticket," Churchill said, "and that was his ruin, and the ruin of much else as well." Calling him the very name Wilson would have most rejected, Churchill stated that the American president was "in every main decision a party politician, calculating and brazen." He elaborated:

A tithe of the fine principles and generous sentiments he lavished upon Europe, applied during 1918 to his Republican opponents in the United States, would have made him in truth the leader of a nation. His sense of proportion operated in separate water-tight compartments. The differences in Europe between France and Germany seemed trivial, petty, easy to be adjusted by a little good sense and charity. But the differences between Democrat and Republican in the United States! Here were really grave quarrels. [45]

Wilson's failure to recognize the importance of cultivating Republican support and the significance of the party's sweep of Congress had been baffling. If the Republican Party had no voice in the matter, how could the Senate majority be expected to validate any agreements to which the president and his plenipotentiaries might see fit to commit the United States at the council table of the powers of the Entente?[46] Compulsively, Wilson seemed to ignore suggestions from Attorney General Thomas Gregory and Colonel House that he choose two qualified Republicans and one independent, thereby ensuring Senate approval of whatever treaty he received, as well as preventing organized opposition. Henry Cabot Lodge, chairman of the Foreign Relations Committee of the Senate and Wilson's nemesis, was one Republican overlooked for membership on the commission. At Wilson's announcement of his final choices, which included Bliss, House, Lansing, and the single, somewhat token Republican, Henry White, Senator Lodge commented, "The President has appointed himself four times and Henry White."[47]

Wilson's choice of Henry White, over at least a dozen more qualified candidates, as the sole and not quite "full-blooded" Republican, was bitterly denounced.[48] The president, it was concluded, was going abroad not as the spokesman of the American people, nor of a majority of those people, nor even of an overwhelming proportion of his own minority party, but of himself alone. Henry White was a mystery choice; by all accounts, he gave no evidence that he had ever voted a Republican ticket, and his complaisance toward the present administration, which retained his son in the diplomatic service, was notorious. Formerly American ambassador to Rome and to Paris and engaged in diplomatic life since he was seventeen, White gave the impression of being more Gallic than American.

With the president under fire, Colonel House's unofficial position once more became an issue. There was, it was true, no one who so completely enjoyed the confidence of Woodrow Wilson or was so thoroughly acquainted with his views or better qualified to win over the president to the Allies' decisions. Equally, since House had witnessed the indescribable horrors of German devastation in France and Belgium, there was no reason to take exception to his presence. However, political adversaries continued to criticize Wilson for being represented by a "mere private citizen," bereft of Senate approval and of the sanction required by law for all who serve and represent the United States abroad.

From October 26, when House went to live at the handsome residence at 78 rue de l'Université in Paris, to represent the president, cables clicked back and forth between the two, and Edith worked early and late coding and decoding them. The tension was not lessened by the knowledge that the end of the war was near—and that its conclusion signaled the start of perilous negotiations. Subject to doubt and suspicion, the European statesmen, it was said, all believed that Wilson's program was a wild dream, quite outside the realm of practical politics. They gave it lip service but were privately irritated by the American president's diplomatic dominance, and by the manner in which he took responsibility "upon himself of a kind of arbiter of the world's destiny."[49]

For House, Paris, at least superficially, appeared to be the same old gay, heedless city, crowded, busy, with stores ablaze and cabs swarming the streets—although one could hardly ignore the exhibition in the Place de la Concorde, extending well up the Champs-Élysées, of captured German artillery, flying machines, tanks, hundreds of guns of all sizes. For House himself, dispatches to the president in Washington demanded an exacting routine: written at evening, then tediously coded, they were picked up between 3 and 4 A.M. by embassy messengers on motorcycles.

The daily and twice-daily exchanges, from October 27 through December 9, when Wilson was in midocean bound for France, reveal how intimately these two worked together and how exhaustively they discussed the terms of the armistice, the conditions of peace, the interpretation of the Fourteen Points, the location of the Peace Conference, and the character, temperament, and mood of its participants. Responding to House's constant inquiries, Wilson informed him of his preference for some neutral meeting place, such as Lausanne. Wilson also thought that they should throw their whole weight behind as moderate and reasonable an armistice as possible, to prevent a renewal of hostilities by Germany. Otherwise, it would make a genuine peace settlement exceedingly difficult, or even preclude it.

House assured Wilson that he was prepared to take bold measures, almost to the brink of unveiled threat, should the peace terms of the foreign leaders with whom he met at the Quai d'Orsay differ essentially from those of the president. House stood ready to remind the Europeans of the possible penalties for differences that would give rise, in Congress, to the question as to whether the United States should continue to champion the aims of Great Britain, France, and Italy. Affable and complimentary, Wilson told the colonel he depended on his "discretion to insist at the right time and in the right way," and also that he was "proud of the way" House was handling things.[50]

Just after midnight on November 7, the German government had notified Marshal Foch by radiogram that representatives to receive terms had been chosen and were ready to depart. Twelve hours later, at 7 A.M., the train carrying the German delegates pulled up near the station of Rethondes in the Compiègne Forest. Thus, with negotiations for the armistice under way, House encouraged Wilson to read the terms to Congress and use the occasion to give out another message to the world:

> You have a right to assume that the two great features of the Armistice are the defeat of German military imperialism and the acceptance by the Allied Powers of the kind of peace the world has longed for. A steadying note seems to me necessary at this time. A word of warning and a word of hope should be said. The world is in a ferment and Civilization itself is wavering in the balance.[51]

On November 11, Wilson sent government employees on holiday and announced to the people of the United States:

> The armistice was signed this morning. Everything for which America fought has been accomplished. It will now be our fortunate duty to assist by example, by sober, friendly counsel and by material aid in the establishment of just democracy throughout the world.[52]

With news of a genuine armistice, Edith could not bear to be excluded from the celebrations. In the company of her mother and her sister Bertha, she rode down Pennsylvania Avenue in an open car. Though immediately recognized and overwhelmed by throngs of people, she was still glad that she had gone out, regretting only that her husband was not at her side. That same night, Wilson, in white tie and tails, and Edith—dressed "in one of the costumes which matched her mounting sense of majesty"[53]—appeared without notice at the Italian embassy. Ambassador and Countess di Celere were giving a ball to celebrate the birthday of the king of Italy, and though it was not the custom to invite the president to foreign embassies, Wilson, in the exhilaration of the moment, had suggested that he and Edith should go. The ball was in full sway when the couple arrived unannounced at the embassy on Sixteenth Street. They stayed for an hour, during which the president toasted the health of the king. On their return to the White House on that momentous day, they were much too excited to sleep. Instead, they kindled a fire in Edith's room, sat on the sofa, and talked into the early hours of the morning. Wilson then read a chapter of the Bible and went to bed.

Edith Wilson, age 13.
(Library of Congress)

Edith Wilson was first married to
Norman Galt in 1895. *(Woodrow Wil-
son House, a National Trust Historic
Site, Washington, D.C.)*

Edith Bolling Galt Wilson's mother,
Mrs. William Holcome Bolling.
(Courtesy of W. R. Chitwood, M.D.)

Edith Wilson's father,
Judge William Holcome Bolling.
(Courtesy of W. R. Chitwood, M.D.)

Edith Wilson's birthplace, Wytheville, Virginia. She lived with her family,
the Bollings, on the two upper floors of the three-story brick building
(right) adjacent to the mansion with the columned porch, then occupied by
Governor E. Lee Trinkle. *(Woodrow Wilson House, a National Trust
Historic Site, Washington, D.C.)*

Edith Wilson's first husband, Norman Galt. *(Woodrow Wilson House, a National Trust Historic Site, Washington, D.C.)*

Edith Wilson as the wife of Norman Galt. *(Woodrow Wilson House, a National Trust Historic Site, Washington, D.C.)*

Edith Wilson, as Norman Galt's wife, purchased a Columbia Electric Victoria Phaeton in 1904. *(Woodrow Wilson House, a National Trust Historic Site, Washington, D.C.)*

Edith Wilson *(upper left)* with her mother, father, and two sisters. *(Woodrow Wilson House, a National Trust Historic Site, Washington, D.C.)*

Ellen Axson Wilson
(Library of Congress)

Woodrow Wilson in
Bermuda, Mary Peck is
to the left of Wilson,
Mark Twain is in the
center, circa 1908. *(The
Mark Twain House,
Hartford,
Connecticut)*

Ellen and Woodrow Wilson, circa 1910. *(Library of Congress)*

Ellen and Woodrow Wilson with their daughters, Jessie, Eleanor, and Margaret, circa 1913. *(Library of Congress)*

Woodrow and Edith Wilson, newly married. *(Library of Congress)*

Woodrow and Edith Wilson leaving a Daughters of the American
Revolution meeting, Washington, D.C., April 17, 1916.
(Library of Congress)

Woodrow and Edith Wilson with
Rear Admiral Cary T. Grayson, M.D.
(Woodrow Wilson House, a
National Trust Historic Site,
Washington, D. C.)

Woodrow Wilson and Joseph P.
Tumulty. *(Woodrow Wilson*
House, a National Trust Historic
Site, Washington, D.C.)

Joseph P. Tumulty at his White
House desk. *(Library of Congress)*

Suffragettes at the White House gate. *(Library of Congress)*

Alice Roosevelt Longworth
buying Library Bonds, July 12,
1918. *(Harris and Ewing
Library of Congress)*

Sir Edward Grey (Viscount Grey of
Fallodon). *(George Gratham Bain
Collection, Library of Congress)*

Major Charles Kennedy Craufurd-Stuart (in uniform) with
Archbishop Cosmo Lang, circa 1918. *(Harris and Ewing,
Library of Congress)*

President and Mrs. Wilson with Colonel Edward Mandell House, October 1918.
(Edward M. House Papers, Manuscripts and Archives, Yale University Library)

Rear Admiral Cary T. Grayson, M.D., and President Wilson on the bridge of the U.S.S. *Washington* en route to the Paris Peace Conference, December 10, 1915. *(Courtesy of Cary T. Grayson)*

Irwin Hood Hoover, White House chief of staff, en route to the Peace Conference. *(Woodrow Wilson House, a National Trust Historic Site, Washington, D.C.)*

Greeting President Wilson on the rue Madeleine in Paris, December 14, 1919.
(Woodrow Wilson House, a National Trust Historic Site, Washington, D.C.)

The Wilsons with the British royal family in the garden of Buckingham Palace,
December 28, 1919. *(Library of Congress)*

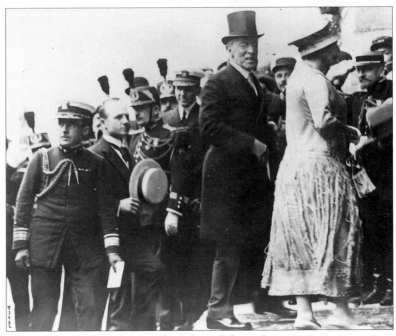

Rear Admiral Grayson *(far left)* and the Wilsons in Paris, 1919.
(Library of Congress)

Mrs. Robert Lansing, Edith Benham Helm, Robert Lansing,
(Woodrow Wilson House, a National Trust Historic Site, Washington, D.C.)

Colonel Edward Mandell House and his wife, Loulie, leaving Versailles. *(Edward M. House Papers, Manuscript and Archives, Yale University Library)*

Senators William Borah, Henry Cabot Lodge, and Reed Smoot outside the White House, May 7, 1924. *(The National Photo Company Collection, Library of Congress)*

Sir William Wiseman on shipboard with Douglas Fairbanks and Mary Pickford. *(Edward M. House Papers, Manuscript and Archives, Yale University Library)*

President and Mrs. Wilson out for a drive in the White House Rolls Royce.
(Library of Congress)

Woodrow Wilson at the door of 2340 S Street NW, November 12, 1923.
(Woodrow Wilson House, a National Trust Historic Site, Washington, D.C.)

Bernard M. Baruch at Hobcaw Plantation, South Carolina, circa 1930s. *(Princeton University Archives)*

Bernard M. Baruch. Background portrait of Woodrow Wilson painted by Sir William Orpen in 1919. *(Princeton University Archives)*

★ Part III ★

*Paris and Round-Trips on
the SS Washington*

"Such a Cinderella role"

"We were the 'troops' who were going to the front—to the Peace Conference in Paris," Edith Wilson exulted, ignoring the controversy surrounding that fact. Even as she and her husband boarded the midnight train out of Washington on December 3, 1918, the hazards of Wilson's attendance at the Peace Conference were being examined and exploited to a disturbing degree. Edith's conviction that it was the president's duty to be in Paris had prevailed, her advice having much to do with her husband's taking this controversial step.[1] Edith herself had not escaped criticism. The European venture, enabling her to play "First Lady of the world," incensed the president's critics. They protested that he ought to do his "junketing" after he was out of office, that "messiahs should travel alone," and that the decision to travel to the solemn Peace Conference accompanied by a loved one was certain to add an aura of frivolity, and to be misunderstood as "more provincial than kingly."

The author H. G. Wells took exception not only to Wilson's failure to draw on the moral and intellectual resources of the members of the Republican Party, and to his inclination to surround himself with "personal adherents," but to Edith Wilson herself, who would add, he said, "a social quality, nay, almost a tourist quality" to the peace settlement.[2] Worse, the editor George Harvey, Wilson's once ardent supporter and now his fierce foe, suggested that the president was going abroad largely because of his profound conviction that Europe could not get along without him, and because his wife, having been long confined to attending official functions, had earned a bit of recreation.[3] Harvey also suggested that Wilson was going abroad not as president of the United States but as a candidate for "President of the League of Nations, or President of Humanity, or President of the World."[4]

The many adversaries of Wilson's travel plans argued that the American president would lose all the power that emanated from distance and detachment, the very mystery and uncertainty that were held to be among his strongest weapons. He would become merely one among many, with only one vote, his protests dismissed as those of a thwarted and disappointed negotiator, with the significance of his powerfully worded messages lost in translation. Europe's leaders, already jealous of Wilson's influence and recognition abroad, might play him off, one against the other, in a game of diplomacy in which they had been schooled since the days of Metternich and Talleyrand, a game that Wilson, the novice, could not afford to play. To escape lurking dangers, the president was advised to remain safe and effective in Washington, where he had the ear of all the world, with Congress affording him the great public stage from which he could bypass the Peace Conference with his own appeal for world peace.

Wilson had revealed the magnitude of the role he expected to play: the governments of Europe "very reasonably desire my personal counsel" and it was "highly desirable" that he give it, he informed Congress on December 2. He also assumed that he would be the one to preside over the conference. House tried at first to discourage him, rephrasing as tactfully as he could the fears already expressed by Americans abroad that Wilson's attendance would involve a loss of dignity and a diminution of his commanding position. House explained to Wilson that precedent and courtesy would prevent him from being chosen as president of the conference, that Clemenceau would preside if it was held in France. House also had to tell him of Clemenceau's hopes that the American president would not sit at the conference because he would be the lone head of state among the French, English, and Italian prime ministers. He tried to palliate the unwelcome advice by intimating that the main issues could be settled in preliminary, informal conferences at which the peace terms would be worked out, as they had been with the armistice.

Though House labored to choose his words cautiously, Wilson was annoyed, hurt, and suspicious that jealousy was the root cause of attempts to relegate him to what he saw as a lesser role. "Your [message] upsets every plan we have made," he complained, "we" undoubtedly referring to his wife. It was clear to Wilson that the French and English leaders wished to exclude him for fear that he might lead the weaker nations against them. As for attending only the preliminary conferences, that was simply a way of "pocketing" him. He did not understand the distinction being made between premiers and foreign secretaries on the one hand and monarchs or presidents. He saw himself as a peer of prime ministers, who were "directing heads" of their governments. "I play the same part in our government," Wilson insisted, "that the prime ministers play in theirs. The fact that I am head of the state is of no practical consequence. No point of dignity must prevent our obtaining the results we have set our hearts upon and must have." Furthermore, he held, it was "universally expected and generally desired" in Washington that he attend the conference, and he did not believe that anyone would wish him to sit by and try to steer from outside.[5]

On the brink of his departure for the Peace Conference, Wilson was tragically unaware that though he was the choice of his party, he was no longer the choice of the nation. He appeared not to recognize the diminution of his power imposed by the recent election of a Republican Congress. He also chose to ignore that his journey to Paris was neither universally expected or desired. He was, in effect, a year too late. Twelve months earlier, on November 15, 1917, the reporter Marguerite Cunliffe-Owen feared that without Wilson the conference "might come to grief and even result in another war." He was "the one great master statesman produced by the present war," the one, irrespective of political parties, to enjoy extraordinarily extensive powers, greater than those of any constitutional monarch or even autocrat in the Old World, almost without dissent.[6] Now, however, in December 1918, the public had grown restive, wanting fewer abstractions and more facts, questioning the platitudes and "sob stuff" of the last eighteen months, wanting to know precisely how ardent was the Allied countries' desire for Wilson's presence and, more precisely, "the form of their importunities."[7]

A tentative role was found for the vice president in Wilson's absence and defined while the president was at sea. By radio to the ship's newspaper, *The Hatchet*, it was announced that Thomas Riley Marshall had presided at a cabinet meeting in obedience to the president's request, but that he had assumed no official duty. An appealingly open and frank man, Marshall took pains to clarify his delicate standing. "In order that my action shall not be misunderstood or misinterpreted," he explained with humility, "I am acting in obedience to the request preferred by the President upon the eve of his departure. I am here informally and personally. I am not undertaking to exercise any official duty or function. I shall simply preside in an informal way over your meetings out of deference to your desires and those of the President."[8]

Still another protest had been lodged against the choice to transport the Wilsons on the *George Washington*, formerly the third-largest vessel of Germany's merchant fleet and now lavishly remodeled. Staffed with a maitre d'hôtel, two chefs, and a full complement of waiters from the Biltmore Hotel, the ship, it was noted, contrasted with the Jeffersonian simplicity with which the Democratic administration had started out in 1912. The Wilsons were protected from the vulgar herd by having a separate dining room and promenade deck; Secretary of State and Mrs. Robert Lansing and a select few others had still another dining room; the "masses"—the college professors, and every variety of professional expert the occasion was thought to require—were herded apart from "the classes" into a common ship's dining saloon.[9]

Inspecting her quarters, Edith delighted in finding that the presidential suite, warm and comfortable with English chintzes and cretonnes, included, together with the private dining room, a sitting room with closets, an ivory-colored bedroom and large bath, a workroom, and a study across the way—every room being filled with her favorite crimson roses. The servants, Brooks and Susie, were waiting to stow all belongings. Before noon, Edith stood beside her husband on the ship's bridge, having taken time to tuck a message under the wing of a carrier pigeon to thank Rear Admiral Albert Gleaves for the thoughtful dockside arrangements he had made on their behalf.[10]

Observation of the president as he occasionally waved his hand, and thoughts of his "tremendous grip on the hopes and affections, not only of America but of the world," brought tears to the eyes of his former student and fellow passenger, Raymond Blaine Fosdick, liaison in matters of morale between the War Department and General Pershing. In that moment, all criticism seemed momentarily suspended as good wishes prevailed. The president was pardonably delighted to read the *New York Times* editorial, reprinted in the ship's newspaper on Saturday at sea, to learn that "he was saluted by more varied tumultuous expressions of good wishes than ever fell upon the ears of a departing traveler—universal, genuine, hearty, unmistakable."[11]

The pleasure of this tribute was clouded by *The Hatchet*'s front-page story from London noting that Prime Minister Lloyd George, in a political address in London on December 7, "continues significantly quiet regarding the proposed League of Nations with its accompanying general disarmament."[12] Specific on other issues, Lloyd George had said, in sum, that the kaiser must be subjected to the doctrine of personal punishment for personal guilt, that all responsible for the murders at sea and maltreatment of prisoners of war must answer for their crimes, and that the Central Empires must pay the cost of the war. The prime minister's glaring failure to clarify Great Britain's position on the League of Nations angered the London press. The endorsement of the League was, according to the owner of the London *Times*, Lord Northcliffe, the most important matter to be decided to ensure justice, repress wrongdoing, and guarantee the sense of international security that would obviate the need of competing armaments.

Edith was quite visible during the voyage and admired, at age forty-six, for her excellent figure and blooming looks. Pretty, trim, and rather girlishly dressed, she walked by herself on the deck that first day when her weary husband, suffering from a cold and a hoarse voice, chose to remain in his stateroom. (Luckily, neither she nor the president attended the ship's movie that evening. When its title, *His Second Wife*, was first announced on the screen, it elicited a half-suppressed gasp from an embarrassed audience.) When Wilson did emerge from his stateroom, he walked briskly, arm in arm with Edith, followed by four Secret Service men and a marine officer, appearing to listen with interest to his wife's conversation, often calling her "sweetheart."

Although Wilson dined alone with his wife and most often worked in his stateroom, he did see various members of his entourage, including the group of professorial advisers known as the Inquiry, as well as the press and the French ambassador, Jean Jules Jusserand. Wilson's shipboard conversation with Robert Lansing defined their starkly incompatible personalities: the contrast between the president, drawn "as if by keenest scent to the solution of political rather than legal problems,"[13] and the secretary of state, who was the consummate legal professional. Lansing, with twenty-two years of practice as an international lawyer and nearly three years as counselor and secretary of state, was quiet and unassuming, meticulous and methodical. He was also, according to some colleagues, plodding and dull. Yet his eloquent defender, the diplomat and historian George Kennan, has challenged these critics: Lansing's "stuffy correctness and legal precision" tended, according to Kennan, to camouflage his powers of insight, exceptional understanding of the diplomatic process, and qualities of thoroughness "that lie at the heart of the diplomatic profession"—his "light somewhat obscured by the contrast between his quiet, unassuming nature and the President's overriding personality."[14]

In their single conference aboard ship, on December 8, Wilson's general explanation of the League of Nations was found wanting by Lansing, much too diffuse for the secretary of state's tidy, lawyerly mind. Lansing considered Wilson's plan impractical, and his idea of a mutual guarantee of independence, and of territory backed by united force or economic pressure, a dangerous proposition. If the plan was to be based on unanimity, Lansing feared that it would amount to nothing.

Wilson brushed Lansing's objections aside, and the secretary of state felt that he could not insist at that time. He suspected House was at the bottom of the scheme, having "a great imagination and the mind of an inventor." Convinced that on this occasion House had "flown his kite too high," Lansing vowed, once he reached Paris, to check or at least to modify the folly, which was certain, in his opinion, to cause endless trouble. He determined that when he next saw the president, he would not only point out the weakness of his plan, but be prepared to offer a practical substitute. At the end of their hour's conference, Lansing left feeling "rather depressed," predicting that "there are rocks and breakers ahead I fear."[15]

The last night aboard ship, following a movie starring Geraldine Farrar and just before the lights went up, a group of fifty bluejackets, gathered unseen in a corner of the dining room, sang softly to the standing audience, "God be with you till we meet again." The president bowed his head and there were tears on his cheeks, and at the end everyone joined in "Auld Lang Syne."[16] Edith, who had continued to read the official papers that came her husband's way on shipboard, had loved the voyage.[17] Life was serene on the calm sea; the ship was steady and she felt better with every new day. She spoke of the ten days aboard the *George Washington* as a real holiday, and though Wilson worked every day (as she herself had, in a sense), it was "life-giving to my husband."[18]

At noon on Friday, December 13, the mists that had shrouded Brest's harbor had evaporated, unveiling the president's ship, the *George Washington*, at the head of a long double column of American warships, French cruisers, and a flotilla of destroyers, steaming through the narrow strait under a canopy of hydroplanes and a dirigible. Greeted by thundering salvos of artillery ashore and afloat, and by a delegation of American admirals, French officialdom, and Wilson's daughter Margaret, the presidential party went ashore by tender at three that afternoon. The band played "The Star-Spangled Banner" and the crowds cheered as Edith, carrying a vast bouquet and an American flag, walked down the gangplank on the arm of General Pershing, followed by the beaming and bowing president, silk hat in hand "amid a perfect whirlwind of cheers."[19]

As the quays, hills, and terraces of the old Breton city rang with cheers for the first American president to make personal contact with Europe and its affairs, Edith heard the mayor of Brest, flanked by generals and admirals, diplomats and ministers of state, compare her husband's present mission with that of the first president of the United States. Not only was Wilson *"le grand successeur de Washington,"* but *"l'apôtre du Droit."* Newspaper headlines at home cheered Wilson's momentous journey with equal enthusiasm and pride: "Wilson Steps on Foreign Soil Amid Thunders of Guns and Cheers."[20]

Arriving at the train station, the Wilsons stepped from the crimson carpet that ran the entire length of the platform into their flower-festooned compartment and settled back in rose-brocaded furnishings to view the countryside from a broad window. The train moved slowly out of Brest at 4 P.M. and stopped at seven, to allow three hours for a formal dinner for eighteen to be served in the dining car, as well as a walk on the platform, before the couple retired to an ample suite.

In Paris the next morning, the Wilsons were greeted by the president of the French Republic, Raymond Poincaré, and by members of the French cabinet and representatives from the American embassy. After still another formal welcome and response, Wilson with Poincaré entered an open victoria drawn by well-groomed horses. Edith followed in a double carriage, accompanied by Madame Poincaré, who presented her with orchids. Madame Jusserand, wife of the French ambassador to the United States, and Margaret Wilson made up the party. Exultant over the reception accorded them along their triumphal way down the Champs-Élysées to the Place de la Concorde, Edith was astonished by the sheer volume of people who not only lined the streets and leaned from the windows, but perched like sparrows at the very top of the horse chestnut trees. Nearly buried under flowers that rained on their carriage, Edith grew giddy trying to respond to the bursts of welcome that "came like the surging of untamed waters."[21] It was touching and bewildering, she acknowledged, "the many ways in which [the French] tried to express their feeling."[22] After they turned into the Place de la Concorde, they rode past the Madeleine and halted, at last, at the palace of Prince Joachim Napoleon Murat at 28 rue Monceau, which had been lent to the Wilsons for their coming two months in Paris.[23]

Prince Murat, a descendant of Napoleon's sister, Caroline Bonaparte, was at hand to greet them and their party, and to show them through his splendid mansion poised in the center of an entire block in the heart of Paris. Secluded by a ten-foot wall topped by an ivy-covered iron trellis of more than two feet, the property included several other houses, an enormous stable, and a garage filled with twelve large limousines. Touring the beautiful drawing rooms on the first floor, and a dining room about equal in size to that of the White House, Edith admired the tapestries and walls, which were either wood-paneled or hung with old brocades or green silk embroidered with Napoleonic wreaths of gold. The marble staircase led to second-floor suites, with a drawing room, two bedrooms and bath, a study for Wilson, and a boudoir for his wife where satin-lined closets, armoires, and cabinets could easily encompass "everything you ever owned." The floor above was reserved for the domestics, Susie and Brooks, while the basement accommodated seventeen servants. If Edith, who had toured palaces but never resided in one, attempted some reserve in her admiration for Prince Murat's magnificent establishment ("a real Napoleonic house," in which the emperor was represented everywhere), members of the White House staff were less inhibited.

Hoover had unqualified praise for the meals, and he marveled too at the linens, china, and crystal. He was fascinated by the printed menu at each plate as well as by the footmen dressed in full livery who tended each diner. He conceded that altogether everything was done to make one comfortable, including food and wine in your room every night, slippers and robes at the side of your bed, shoes shined every night, disposal of your clothes and hats, but he begrudged that tips were expected in return for these courtesies. Charles Swem, Wilson's stenographer, wrote home to tell his wife, Daisy, that he was "living like a bloomin' King."[24]

Amid all this glory, the person who had been most involved in masterminding their first hours and days in France was not at the president's side. In mid-December, Colonel House came down with a severe case of influenza that would be followed by a critical case of gallstones, igniting rumors of his death, affording him "the interesting experience of reading his own obituary notices and eulogies."[25]

Sporadically seeming to recover, House was again severely stricken on January 9 and incapacitated for ten days. His presidential assignment to work with the British on behalf of the League of Nations was, at his suggestion, turned over to his legal adviser, David Hunter Miller. His illness during this crucial formative period in the Peace Conference, and the loss of his guiding influence, was regarded by Wickham Steed, the British editor, as a "serious misfortune—which proved to be a disaster." Even *Town Topics* rallied readers' attention to Colonel House's illness:

... it has been observed that every error in judgment made by the President on the eve of the last election, has occurred when the sane advice of the Colonel from Texas was unavailable, either through illness or absence. That Woodrow Wilson should be deprived of his services at this particular juncture in Paris is most unfortunate and adds to the misgivings which already prevail as to the part which is to be played at the Congress of Versailles by the President in our name.[26]

"Paris Meets the President and Takes Him to Her Heart," the *New York Herald* proclaimed on December 15. Edith's coronation followed two days later: "In Purple Velvet Gown, Mrs. Wilson Captures Crowd."[27] She was dressed in violet velvet with a matching violet hat for the reception at the Hôtel de Ville at which Wilson was welcomed as a citizen of Paris, and when she threw violets from the balcony, "the people below went wild with cheers."[28]

Certainly there was never any question on Edith's part as to her role. Embarked officially on the grandest of grand tours, she regretted there was no time to keep her Line-a-Day notebook but decided that newspaper clippings, "the published record," would be a substitute diary. Breathlessly happy, she rode from ceremony to ceremony in flower-filled open carriages, in furs and feathers, proud witness to the resounding applause that paid tribute to her husband wherever he went—at the American embassy, at the French Academy, at the Franco-American Club, at the British embassy, and at the Sorbonne, where he received an honorary degree.

As a change of pace, Sunday was given over to the American Hospital in Neuilly and the French Hospital in Paris. Finding it a severe trial to see the badly wounded, Edith was buoyed by the same splendid spirit, she wrote her family, "that makes all those boys the admiration of the world." Another afternoon, with Dr. Grayson and her secretary, Edith Benham, she visited the Lighthouse for the Blind, a place that left her speechless with pity, but thankful that those with the ability to discern light could be taught a trade and given new inspiration.

Less than a week before Christmas, Wilson asked House to arrange a meeting with Clemenceau, which took place on the morning of December 19. Wilson did most of the talking at this session, while Clemenceau "in a mild way" agreed that a League of Nations should be attempted, although he acknowledged that he was not confident of success either in being able to form it, or of its being workable once formed. Two days later, Wilson and House held a meeting with the heads of the Italian government, Premier Vittorio Emanuele Orlando and Foreign Secretary Baron Sidney Sonnino, which proved equally inconclusive. Sonnino reaffirmed his country's confidence in the Treaty of London, meant to shore up Italy's vulnerable frontiers, which had been established on April 26, 1915, in partnership with Great Britain, France, and Russia.

The Wilsons spent Christmas Day with General John J. Pershing, commander of the American Expeditionary Forces,[29] reviewing troops stationed at headquarters in Chaumont, surrounded by fields of snow, in the mountains of the Vosges, and in the Argonne Forest. Wilson was frustrated that the Peace Conference, intended to start on December 17, was now scheduled instead for January 18. Due to British elections, David Lloyd George was preoccupied in London and was awaiting the election results before naming a delegation to the Peace Conference. Clemenceau had yet to clarify his position before the Chamber of Deputies, which he would do on December 29. Resigned to the postponement, Wilson decided to complete his ceremonial visits to both Great Britain and Italy in the interim.

Four French cruisers accompanied the president's ship out of Calais and were relieved halfway across the straits of Dover by six magnificently beflagged British warships, who led the rest of the way to the British shore. Arriving at the Charing Cross Station, the Wilsons were greeted by the king and queen of England and by David Lloyd George. The prime minister was not alone in his curiosity about the American president. All of Europe's designated peacemakers were inquisitive about Wilson, concerned to know what he was like personally as well as to probe his goals and terms. Among themselves, the Europeans were well acquainted, having met during the trials of the war. Intrinsically practical men, they did not always agree, but their disagreements were national rather than personal. They could only act, Lloyd George reasoned, within the limits permitted by the opinions of the people they respectively represented, whose exigencies, difficulties, aims, traditions, and prejudices would have to be taken into account.[30]

Wilson was quite different, Lloyd George thought: the product of another hemisphere, another world. While the British and their allies had dealt daily with tragic realities, visible and audible on land and sea, Wilson, it seemed to him, had soared in clouds of serene rhetoric. When Allied troops were dying by tens of thousands, it had been difficult to reach Wilson, to bring him to earth, to convince him that cumulative and prolonged slaughter might bury their cause in irreparable disaster.

Lloyd George's concerns about Woodrow Wilson would be augmented by the British minister of munitions, Winston Churchill, then forty-five years old. Living simply and frugally in the bosom of his domestic circle, inaccessible except to friends and servitors, and very sparingly to them, towering above Congress, the cabinet his mere implement, Wilson seemed "untempered and undinted in the smithy of public life." As a result, in all of his strength and in all his weakness, in his nobility and in his foibles, in spite of his long academic record and great authority, Wilson was "an unmeasured quantity to the mighty people who made him their ruler in 1912. Still more was he a mystery to the world at large."[31] The British were not alone in questioning the visitor from America.

In France, Clemenceau had already commented on Wilson's idealism and his Fourteen Points with the wry observation that "even the *Bon Dieu* got along with Ten Commandments."[32] And at home, according to George Harvey's *War Weekly*, the unqualified spontaneity of Wilson's reception abroad did not dispel America's doubts about the president's judgment in his choice of a "commission of manikins" and in his display of the rankest partisanship in his futile demand for the defeat of Republican candidates for Congress on grounds that they were pro-war and antiadministration.[33]

"Two Million Londoners Give Wilson Reception of His Life," the *London Daily Mail* reported of one of the greatest crowds ever seen, on December 27, 1918. The president's visit was hailed as a happy omen for a fuller understanding between the two great English-speaking nations. Wilson rode in the first carriage with King George; Edith with Queen Mary and her daughter, Princess Mary. Passing through Pall Mall, the Dowager Queen Alexandra, widow of the late King Edward, and her sister, Queen Maude of Norway, came down to the footpath to greet Wilson, who rose and waved his hat in response. Wilson then joined King George and Queen Mary on the balcony of Buckingham Palace overlooking a crowd of thirty thousand people, including soldiers and sailors, the orphaned and the wounded, who cheered until Wilson was forced to speak out to "honor you men who have been wounded in this fight for freedom," and to warmly thank them for their friendly welcome. Edith Wilson, dressed in a black suit with sealskin collar, stepped forward. She waved a small American flag at first and then a small Union Jack plucked from the corner of the balcony, a gesture that aroused sustained cheers until she and her husband withdrew inside the palace.

Edith reveled in the grandeur of her next three days in England. While the British insisted on referring to Edith's secretary, Edith Benham, as her lady-in-waiting, it was Edith's maid, Susie Booth, who was said to be the most popular person in Buckingham Palace—so much so that the Queen had sent for her.

Wilson and King George were reported to have talked pleasantly at the evening's informal dinner. On the following day, the president conferred with David Lloyd George and Arthur Balfour, touching on the Peace Conference, the question of freedom of the seas as it was affected by a League of Nations, the urgency for an international labor policy, the necessity of curbing Italy's extravagant territorial ambitions, and the "grave menace of the Irish problem." Satisfied with the proceedings, the president found both men agreeable and apparently willing to aid him in setting a program for the Peace Conference that would make for a minimum of friction.[34] That same day, at a luncheon given by Lloyd George, Wilson was introduced to England's significant political and labor leaders and was able to discuss briefly with the latter a proposed international labor agreement. Edith, meanwhile, lunched with Lady Reading, the wife of the ambassador to the United States, took tea with Mrs. Lloyd George, and paid scrupulous attention to royalty's dress code—to glove lengths and tiaras—as she prepared for the state dinner honoring her husband.

At this first elaborate dinner given since the outbreak of war, the guest list of 125 embraced eminent figures of every facet of British life—of finance, politics, diplomacy, and literature—and included the commander in chief of the British army, the British Grand Fleet, and the authors Rudyard Kipling and Arthur Conan Doyle. Irrespective of the queen's brilliant jewels and the male chests resplendent with orders and medals, the supreme attraction of the evening for Edith Wilson, Hoover, and Grayson was the $15 million display of solid gold in the form of hundreds of plaques, shields, and plates, some as large as tea trays, glowing from the walls of the great court dining room. The yeomen of the guard, standing like statues at the rim of the room, reminded Edith of the men seen at the Tower of London, who wore medieval hats and pointed beards and were armed with halberds. Hoover summed up the evening at the palace most succinctly: "Honestly it was so gorgeous it was vulgar."[35]

* * *

Wilson spoke at Buckingham Palace on the night of his arrival in London on December 27, and twice the next day, at London's Guildhall and Mansion House. After a midnight departure on the king's private train bound for the Scottish border—and for a sentimental journey to his mother's birthplace in Carlisle and to his grandfather's church and home—he stopped in Manchester to speak twice the afternoon of December 30. A single thread laced together five messages: his assumption that in the aftermath of war there could be unity of ideal and purpose in the peace settlement yet to be made. "There is," he assured his audience at Buckingham Palace, "a great tide running in the hearts of men. The hearts of men have never beaten so singularly in unison before. Men have never been so conscious of their brotherhood." Referring implicitly to America's Monroe Doctrine, Wilson admitted that the United States had always felt, from the beginning of her history, that she must keep herself separate from European politics. And frankly, even now, on this December afternoon, she was interested not in European politics, but in the partnership of "right" between America and Europe, interested not merely in the peace of Europe, but in the peace of the world. He recognized that the settlement just ahead was something more delicate and difficult than ever before attempted, necessitating a "genuine concert of mind and of people." In conclusion, he told his audience, he wished to emulate his stern ancestors, those very determined Covenanters. He wished, not only for Great Britain and the United States, but for France and Italy and the world to enter into a great league and covenant, "declaring ourselves first of all friends of mankind . . . uniting ourselves together for the maintenance and the triumph of right."

His championship of a new order of world government aimed at the demise of the old, "that unstable thing called 'balance of power'"—the thing in which the balance was determined by the sword, by jealous watchfulness and antagonism of interests; the men who fought this war were men from free nations who were determined that "that sort of thing should end now and forever."[36] Days later, as though these words had personally been directed across the straits of Dover to Paris, France's Premier Georges Clemenceau on December 29 before the Chamber of Deputies put Wilson on notice: "I pin my faith to the principle of the balance of power, and it will be my guiding principle throughout the Peace Conference." In speaking of the *"noble candeur"* of Wilson's ideas, Clemenceau intended to emphasize how simplistic they were, and therefore impracticable.[37]

Immediate reaction to the visit to Britain was, however, quite pleasant. On Saturday, December 28, which was Wilson's sixty-second birthday, King George, accompanied by the duke of Connaught, arrived at the president's apartments to congratulate him and to present him with a set of books on the history and description of Windsor Castle. Later, at the American embassy, the president was visited by the archbishop of Canterbury and by Sir Edward Grey, the distinguished former minister of state for foreign affairs. Still later, the Wilsons' carriage was led by a troop of the king's household cavalry on the way to the Guildhall while the great chimes of Westminster Cathedral caroled the American and British national anthems on what Wilson called "the greatest day of my life."[38]

Though it was rainy and gloomy as they left London, bidding goodbye to the king and queen, David Lloyd George, and the duke of Connaught at the flag-draped Victoria Station, Edith and Woodrow were satisfied and happy. However, there is some evidence that the Wilsons' sentiments were not entirely reciprocated by the king. Having planned his first holiday at Sandringham Castle in four years, he was annoyed when Lloyd George insisted he remain in London over Christmas to welcome the president of the United States. He was bothered further by Wilson's failure at the state banquet to refer to the part played or the sacrifices endured by the British Empire in the recent struggle. "I could not bear him. An entirely cold academical professor—an odious man," King George was said to have told his private secretary.[39]

On the way to Italy, Edith noted with enormous pride that the day she left England was the occasion on which she rode on the trains of three heads of state—of the king of England from London to Dover, of the president of France from Calais to Paris, of King Victor Emmanuel from Paris to Rome. Now, on January 3, in radiant sunshine, under a sapphire sky, it was King Victor Emmanuel and Queen Helena who greeted the Wilsons at the station in Rome, along with the mayor, municipal counselors, and crowds from end to end of Via Nazionale, vigorously waving American and Italian flags and shouting, "Viva Wilson." Once again enthralled by palace treasures, brocades and tapestries, bejeweled and decorated royalty and aristocracy, Edith marveled at fate's having chosen her "for such a Cinderella role."[40]

On his visit to Italy, Wilson made ten official speeches. As he had in England, he spoke in Rome, Genoa, and Milan of the lofty unity of ideal and purpose and moral obligations, with significant embellishments.

Without deviating from his principal theme, he inserted critical references to Germany, to the Balkans, and again to the need for a moral substitute for the balance of power. In Rome, accepting honorary citizenship, he said that he would not have been at liberty to leave America if he had not felt that the time had arrived when, forgetting local interests and purposes, men should unite in this great enterprise "which will ever tie free men together as a body of brethren and a body of free spirits." He spoke in Turin of the recent struggle as not merely a European struggle, but a struggle for the freedom of the world and the liberation of humanity.[41]

While there was great applause for these speeches, there were also questions concerning his reference to the country's "most tender topic—Jugo Slavia"—which, he had been forewarned, posed a dire threat to Italy's supremacy in the Adriatic.[42] Nevertheless, Wilson forged ahead. The great difficulty among such states as those of the Balkans was their accessibility to secret influence and intrigue. Now that this intrigue was checked, they must learn to be independent. "Our task at Paris," he continued, "is to organize the binding force and the friendship of the world—to see to it that all the moral forces that make for right and justice and liberty are united . . ."

In his appraisal of the visit to Italy, Ike Hoover noted what was remarkable was Italy's partiality to Wilson, how "wild" the people were about the president. They seemed to consider him another Savior come to earth. Frankly amazed, Hoover believed that Wilson could at this moment have been elected to anything—could be king if he so chose. The French were also wild about Wilson, Hoover said, but not to the same degree as the Italians.[43]

CHAPTER 18

"Is it a League of Nations or a League of notions?"

In Paris, Edith herself was frustrated by the delay in initiating the Peace Conference, which was, as she said, the real business of their trip. She consoled herself that her husband, though weary from his recent tour, was doing quiet, effective work that "will count tremendously in the ultimate result."[1] Meanwhile, the household at 28 rue Monceau had settled in comfortably, with Edith Wilson's secretary, Edith Benham, and Cary Grayson as part of the inner circle. Though they were showered with ceremonial invitations, certain evenings at Prince Murat's palace were remarkably similar to those at the White House. After dinners that included Edith's brother Wilmer, and Helen Bones's sister, the president read aloud from the work of the British essayist A. G. Gardiner—on one occasion, Gardiner's sketch of Theodore Roosevelt; on another, the sketch of Wilson himself, an immensely flattering portrait said to be based on information provided by Colonel House. On yet another evening, Wilson read several chapters from this favorite author's *Pebbles on the Shore.*

One evening, when the conversation drifted to the Peace Conference, Wilson spoke with feeling about the French effort to oblige him to visit the devastated regions of France—convinced, as they were, that an immediate tour of their shattered land would influence Wilson's attitude on the bill of indemnity owed to France by Germany. When, on January 26, Wilson did journey to Château-Thierry and the Belleau Wood and saw the shell-torn ruins of the great cathedral, the Gothic masterpiece of Rheims—a city of 250,000 shriveled to 3,000, who survived in cellars amid horrible debris—his concession was too late for critics, who held that he was prejudiced in favor of Germany and cowardly about facing the realities of ravaged France. However, he was not to be moved by this argument. The whole question of peace, he maintained, had to be

approached with detachment. Hatred could not be the basis for a just settlement: such a peace would lead to another war and a still more terrible
reckoning. Asked if he did not believe in punishment, he replied that the
German people had incurred their own penalties and would be shunned
for generations to come.[2]

As a member of the presidential household, Grayson found his intimacy
with the Wilsons deepened to the point where he was entrusted with
responsibilities quite apart from his medical duties to the president: he
had now become both special emissary and press official. At dinner one
evening, Wilson asked him to deliver to the prime minister of South
Africa, Jan Smuts, the most recent draft of the League of Nations constitution, which contained Wilson's additions, with House's emendations,
to what was, in origin and essence, Great Britain's Phillimore Report.
Noting Grayson's debut as Wilson's liaison with French newsmen, the
American press commented that "the most discreet and assiduous of
physicians . . . led by the atmosphere and new environment of the French
capital, had blossomed forth in the Light of Boswell . . ."[3]

In a rhapsodic account of his eminent patient, Grayson informed
Parisians of Wilson's pretty tenor voice, and of the president's love for
the theater and for sports, literature, and music. Grayson also assured
the French press that the president was in reality sentimental, notably
loyal to his friends, and enjoyed getting together with his former com-
rades of college days. Owing to his timidity, Wilson refrained from
speaking the French language, though he understood it well and read the
French classics in their original text. In all this, however, Grayson had, as
Wilson's critics said, left out one important detail: "the requisite Rembrandt shading was missing."[4]

The president held his first formal meeting with the premiers, Lloyd
George, Clemenceau, and Orlando—together they would be known as
the Council of Four—on January 12, 1919. That evening, Wilson and
Edith entertained at dinner two members of the American Commission,
Robert Lansing and General Bliss and their wives, as well as the advisers
of the American Economic Commission, Bernard Baruch and Herbert
Hoover. Colonel House, who had dined with Wilson on January 8, the
day before he fell critically ill, was absent from the party; he did not
recover for ten days. Meanwhile, with her husband in conference and his
days increasingly arduous, Edith shaped her own accordingly.

As she was now disengaged for most of the day, she relied for company on her secretary, Edith Benham. Settling into a routine of sorts,

Mrs. Wilson began each day by accompanying her husband to his 10:30 A.M. meeting, usually by car. Sometimes, the secretary joined the couple on this morning route, but more often met the president's wife afterward, for a shopping excursion. Having by now spent about five weeks with the Wilsons, Edith Benham thought them most unusual: always the most devoted lovers, with never a cross word between them. Mrs. Wilson was unusually self-contained, though always wonderfully gracious, her smile and charm proverbial. "Very quiet about her dislikes, but a very loyal friend" was an opinion the secretary would come to revise later in her life. [5]

Mrs. Wilson, cheered by receiving "the dear home news" of her family's Christmas, recounted in turn her own routine. Inveterate shopper that she was, she came away "sadder and wiser" as she found that hardly anything was available for less than 1,500 francs, equal to about $300. A simple meal in a hotel restaurant came, she was told, to $10 a person, and an elaborate one could run as high as $20 or $30. [6]

Ike Hoover was one of President Wilson's "immediate party of nine," which included clerical and domestic help whose arrival in Paris had been compared to the "landing of the pilgrims." [7] Culture shock, owing to differences of custom, comprehension, and interpretation, afflicted the entire group with varied and even humorous results—symptomatic, perhaps, of a fundamental disparity between people, nations, and continents.

Among European customs alien to his sensibilities, it was probably the pace, or lack of it, that bothered Wilson most of all. Committed to punctuality, as was Edith, he preferred everyone to be ready at the appointed hour. Certainly, as far as his early meetings in Paris were concerned, he found the rhythm distorted. He was in the habit of arriving promptly; others straggled in. When the Peace Conference eventually got under way in serious discussion only to be interrupted by afternoon tea, that time-honored European custom was begrudgingly dismissed by Wilson as being "just like an old ladies' party." [8]

At three o'clock on the afternoon of January 18, the Peace Conference was officially launched in the gilded Salle de la Paix of the French Foreign Office. That gathering of the Old and New Worlds in the name of peace and reconstruction included two presidents, nine premiers, innumerable foreign ministers, emirs of Arabia, maharajas of India, and representatives of China, Japan, Siam, South Africa, Australia, Poland (freshly reinstated on the political map after centuries of oblivion), the

newly conceived Czechoslovakia, and the new Balkan confederation
of Yugo-Slavia. Stepping to the podium, French president Poincaré
reminded the assembled throng of an infamous period in his country's
history. Precisely on this day, forty-eight years past, on January 18,
1871, the German army had marched victoriously through the streets of
Paris, France had ceded Alsace and most of Lorraine to the invader—who
demanded an indemnity of 5 million francs—and William I was proclaimed emperor of Germany at Versailles. Born in injustice, the German empire had ended in ignominy: "You have assembled," Poincaré
cautioned the audience, "to enact measures which shall forever prevent
such brutal wrongs."

At the start of this comprehensive gathering, Wilson proposed that
Clemenceau be appointed permanent chairman. He made the proposal,
Wilson said, as a matter of custom and as a tribute to the French Republic, but he wished to do so for another reason: as a tribute to a man held
in genuine affection and to honor France in the person of its distinguished servant. From their frequent consultations in recent days, Wilson knew how warmly Clemenceau focused on the goal to which all
faces were turned. Wilson could, therefore, attest to the Frenchman's
"brotherhood of heart." Outlining the program to be discussed, Wilson
named, first, responsibility for the war; second, war crimes; third, international labor legislation; and fourth, the formation of a League of
Nations, an item that should lead the agenda of the next session of
the conference. Expressing fervent confidence in Clemenceau, Wilson
assured his audience, "He feels as we feel, as I have no doubt everybody
in this room feels, that we are trusted to do a great thing ... in order that
the hearts of men may have fear lifted from them and that they may
return to those pursuits of life which will bring them happiness and contentment and prosperity."[9] Wilson spoke on, of kindred spirits, bound by
a kindred goal, of a general treaty of peace incorporating the healing
concept of a League of Nations, of ensuring the future and permanent
peace of the world.

As he spoke, Wilson was both hero and suspect. He was a puzzle to the
audience, who wondered whether the representative from America, full
of strange ideas and new principles, could sit in with the family of
Europe. As an honored guest, politely accepting Europe's ancient customs and its tradition of rivalries and alliances, could he, they asked,
comprehend European deprivations and anxieties and, in France's case,
the perpetual trauma of invasion? Was the American to be regarded "as

a rich and powerful pioneer son, returned from far lands, who had just saved the old home from foreclosure and now proposed to banish antique furniture and change the plumbing?"[10]

With the conference under way, Edith was concerned about her husband's hours and troubled because he worked until near midnight and was not free even on Sundays. She so hoped, as she wrote to her family, "that he can put through all the splendid things he is striving to do for the world."[11] At the start he seemed to be standing the strain wonderfully well. As he wearied, however, of the protracted negotiations for incorporating the Covenant of the League of Nations in the composition of the Peace Treaty, she resented those who would appear to him to deny him his dream. She began to see her husband as the lone visionary amid a set of gravely flawed colleagues. Clemenceau, she would later recall, was "an avowed cynic, distrustful of humanity's ability to rise to unselfish heights." David Lloyd George was "a political weather-vane shifting with every wind that blew across the Channel lest it affect his personal fortunes." Signore Orlando kept his ear to the ground "for fear Italy should not get all she hungered for."[12]

February 17 was the date originally set for the Wilsons' return to Washington for the closing session of the 65th Congress. "In order not to have to come back [to Paris]," Edith wrote her family, "every minute must count."[13] Wilson's eventual change of heart, his plan to return to Europe for a second time, provoked concern among many of his sympathizers, who feared such a move would prove anticlimactic. Wilson, in response, claimed that he understood the risk involved in his return to Europe but dismissed it as the view of the press—which he personally did not consider representative of America, controlled as it was by large moneyed interests and out of touch with the views of the populace. When asked how he assessed national opinions if not from the newspapers, he said that he got them from different sources and pieced them together as one would a mosaic. Also, it had to be kept in mind that he had been a student of American political history for years and "had saturated himself in it."[14]

The president conferred with Colonel House and Premier Orlando at the Hôtel Murat on the evening of January 30, to compare the American version of the Covenant for the League of Nations with that of the Italian. Wilson emerged from that meeting in high good humor, saying that Orlando was a "fine fellow and most reasonable"—which meant, according to a staff member, that "he agreed with the President," but that, in reality, all was "not so rosy as is pictured," and there were "stormy times ahead."[15] Wilson was beginning to show fatigue. He complained that the French had instructed Leon Bourgeois, their representative on the League of Nations Commission, to delay and obstruct proceedings as much as possible. Wilson was annoyed for another reason. He declared the French "unsportsmanlike" in their wish to impose new and harder conditions on Germany each time the armistice was reviewed.[16] France seemed to him almost compulsive in its terror of Germany, and in its fear that Germany was rearming. Wilson believed that the German people were exhausted by war, and that the Allies controlled three-fourths of German raw materials, preventing Germany from manufacturing arms. He saw no need for the French to set up a buffer state, the proposed Rhenish republic. He spoke of the selfishness of the French, who, forgetting Belgium, Serbia, and Poland, seemed to feel that they were the only nation that had suffered in the war.

At the second plenary session of the Peace Conference, the afternoon of Saturday, January 25, Wilson "executed a Napoleonic stroke" when he put through a resolution binding together, hard and fast and forever, the Peace Treaty and the League of Nations Covenant.[17] Within a fortnight, there were ominous rumors of "dark clouds gathering" and of a "general atmosphere of distrust and bitterness." The fate of the League Covenant was still very much in doubt. The resolution that incorporated the League of Nations as an integral part of the general treaty of peace was openly resented. Clemenceau warned that France was being sacrificed in the attainment of high but vaguely general ideals. Convinced that Wilson's persistent focus on the League was obscuring the far more significant issue of a renascent German military, the editor of *Le Figaro* sounded an open alarm on Monday, February 10: "President Wilson has lightly assumed a responsibility such as few men have ever borne. Success in his idealistic efforts will surely place him among the greatest personages of history. But failure will plunge the world into chaos, and will make the . . . author of this chaos one of the most pitiful figures ever presented by history.[18]

Wilson's reaction to the criticism, implicit and overt, of his policies was acute. While insisting on his most cordial feelings toward the French, he abruptly instructed Dr. Grayson to announce the possibility of moving the Peace Conference out of Paris, away from partisan intrigues and gossip, to more neutral territory such as Geneva, Switzerland. Though the warning was dismissed as a trial balloon, Clemenceau was disturbed and hurried to American headquarters to see Colonel House, who was apparently charged with calming the storm.

On Tuesday, February 11, for the first time, the possibility emerged that Wilson might fail to carry home an approved draft of the League of Nations. Congress alone had the power to direct American military and naval forces into warfare; yet the French were insisting on the creation of an international army, with an international general staff, as an adjunct to the League of Nations, to guard their country from the menace of another German invasion. With the conference virtually deadlocked over this issue, Wilson, dejected, left at 7 P.M. Since the next meeting was set for two days later, and only four days remained before his own sailing—now scheduled for February 15—affairs seemed to an American journalist "ominous of disaster for the President."[19] At the morning session on February 13, the situation still appeared hopeless. After two hours, during which time only six articles out of the total of twenty-seven of the Covenant had been adopted, Wilson, tired and despondent, announced that he would not return to the meeting. He would leave the proceedings to Lord Robert Cecil.

As the meeting continued without Wilson, Cecil proved an adroit tactician. By "a sudden *coup de théâtre* " two major obstacles dissolved: the French issue of an international army was abandoned, and the Japanese provision for racial equality was temporarily withdrawn. Thus out of a clear sky, and at the moment when defeat stared him in the face, Wilson learned of his apparent success. After ten contentious meetings, the Covenant of the League of Nations had gained the unanimous vote of fourteen nations. As chairman of the committee to prepare a Covenant for the League of Nations, an "astounded and delighted" president was then invited to make a report, to read the Covenant, and to give a speech at the plenary session of the Peace Conference at the Quai d'Orsay at 3:30 P.M. the next day—that is, immediately before his departure for Brest to sail home on the SS *George Washington*. The meeting would provide him with the opportunity to make his final bow before leaving. That accomplished, it was predicted, "he will depart in triumph with his Covenant in his pocket."[20]

Edith, who naturally longed to hear her husband speak at this momentous meeting, was aware that only members of the conference were invited to attend. She sensed that his speech would be not only the culmination of all his work in Paris in past months, but also the climax of their visit. Intimately informed on the issues, she always tried to be at home when Ray Stannard Baker, as head of the press bureau of the American Commission, made his daily visit to the Hôtel Murat to brief the president, to report on the news at the end of the day, as well as to decide on material to be furnished to the press.[21]

With Wilson's tacit approval, she approached Grayson about asking Clemenceau for permission to attend the meeting and learned that the doctor was keen to go himself. Pledged to discretion, the two found themselves at the far end of the grand Salon d'Horloge, sitting together in a tiny alcove muffled with red brocade curtains. When her husband rose to speak, Edith forgot any discomfort. She could see that he was making a deep impression on the audience as he dwelt on one of the most satisfactory advances of the Covenant: "We are done with annexations of helpless people. . . . We recognize in the most solemn manner that the helpless and undeveloped people of the world . . . put an obligation upon us to look after their interests primarily before we use them for our interest . . ." While Wilson admitted that many terrible things had come out of the war, so had some very beautiful things: "Wrong has been defeated, but the rest of the world has been more conscious than it ever was before of the majesty of right. . . . The miasma of distrust, of intrigue, is cleared away. Men are looking eye to eye and saying, 'We are brothers and have a common purpose. We did not realize it before, but now we do realize it, and this is our covenant of fraternity and of friendship.' "[22]

The response of Henry Wickham Steed, editor of *The Times* of London, exalted Wilson's most fervent aspirations. "The old dimensions of national individualism, secrecies of policies, competitive armaments, forcible annexations for selfish purposes and unqualified State Sovereignty, were raised, if only for an instant, to a higher plane on which the organized moral consciousness of peoples, the publicity of international engagements and of government by the consent of and for the good of the governed, became prospective realities." Then, his hope tinged with doubt, Steed asked, "How long will the instant last?"[23]

The French journalist writing for *L'Illustration* was plainly skeptical: "In the emptiness and silence of this room called 'of the clock,' so ostentatious with its great drapes of red damask and brilliant gilding, three strokes resounded from the henceforth historic dial. And the delegates began to file ceremoniously through the heavy fog which the high windows opening on the Quai d'Orsay permitted to penetrate the room.

Mon Dieu, how opaque it was, that fog which surrounded the birth of the League of Nations."[24] Across the ocean, Americans were asking, "Is it a League of Nations or a League of notions?"[25]

Wilson's choice of Colonel House over Robert Lansing to "stoke the fires" while he was gone until mid-March was painfully embarrassing to the secretary of state. Lansing did in candor differ with Wilson. He believed that the president's obsession with the League of Nations blinded him to everything else, that an immediate peace mattered little to him compared with the adoption of the Covenant. "The whole world wants peace. The President wants his League. I think that the world will have to wait" was Lansing's bitter conclusion.[26] Convinced that Lansing was unsympathetic to the League, Edith interpreted the secretary of state's plausible difference of opinion as a deliberate act of disloyalty to her husband.

Disapproval of Lansing did not, however, signify wholehearted approval of Colonel House. Professing to like the colonel, she consistently managed to temper her flattery with complaints about his being colorless or overready to agree with the president. She clearly took no pleasure in his selection to represent her husband in his absence, but she was resigned that "in public life, however, one often is obliged to use the instrument readiest to hand."[27] Another detractor of House's was Ray Stannard Baker, who, by selective reporting and through his claim that the colonel was not in touch with the "inner strategy," would manage to warp the breadth of Wilson's leave-taking message and instructions and, thereby, to distort House's responsibilities.

On February 12, two days before Wilson left Paris for Washington, he met with his four fellow peace commissioners in Monsieur Pichon's room at the Quai d'Orsay and informed them that he thought it possible to frame the conditions of Germany's disarmament before settling the terms of peace. He was encouraged in this belief by the assurance that the military advisers could produce such a plan in forty-eight hours. When Clemenceau demurred at some length at the idea of discussing a matter of such importance during Wilson's absence, the president was modest in his response: the French premier had paid him "an undeserved compliment." He assured Clemenceau that in technical matters most of the brains he used "were borrowed: the possessors of these brains were in Paris." He would, therefore, go away with an easy mind if he thought that his plan had been adopted in principle . . . and leave it to his colleagues to decide whether the program drafted by the technical advisers was the right one. He did not wish his absence "to impede so essential a task as the preparations of a preliminary peace." He hoped to return by the thirteenth or fifteenth of March, allowing himself only a week in America. However, Wilson assured Clemenceau that he did not wish during his unavoidable absence that "such questions as the territorial question and questions of compensation should be held up."[28] It was also at this meeting that Wilson announced that he had asked Colonel House to take his place during his absence.

Wilson was glad to be going home, even for a few days. With the Covenant in hand, he felt that he had kept faith with the people. On the morning of his departure from Paris, Wilson called on Colonel House in his private study at the Crillon Hôtel for a twenty-minute tête-à-tête in which they agreed to communicate in a private code.[29] When House told him, "We could button up everything during the next four weeks," Wilson appeared "startled and even alarmed at this statement." House explained that the plan was not actually to bring these matters to a final conclusion but to have them ready for such a conclusion on Wilson's return. An essential item on the agenda was the arrangement of a preliminary peace with Germany to settle key issues: the reduction of the German army and navy to peacetime strength; the delineation of the boundaries of Germany including the cession of Germany's colonies; the amount of time required for payment of reparations; the economic treatment of Germany. House also asked Wilson to bear in mind, while he was in Washington, that it was sometimes necessary to compromise to get things through; not a compromise of principle, but a compromise of detail. House had made many such concessions while he had been in Paris. He was ready, as he put it, "to yield the things of today in order to obtain the things of tomorrow." He did not wish the president, as House wrote in his diary, "to leave expecting the impossible in all things."[30]

House, in his oblique way, was acknowledging that Wilson's cherished League was far from secure. Though the French appeared to accept the draft proposals for the League of Nations, they did so without any confidence. They would distinctly have preferred an undertaking of more substance for their future defense than the experimental Covenant: for example, a direct commitment of American arms and power. On the night that Wilson left for America, Lansing, anguished over the tedious, time-consuming negotiations, predicted that while the president had launched his Covenant without much difficulty, "he will find it harder to steer it into port."[31]

House accompanied the Wilsons from the Hôtel Murat to the station, where they walked on a carpeted path bordered with palms and ever-greens all the way from the curb to the train. The surprising turnout of seemingly all of official France included President and Madame Poincaré and Clemenceau and his entire cabinet. The British ambassador was also present. The president bade House a fervent good-bye, shook his hand, and put his arm around him. House, though guarded about the treaty's future negotiations, was protective of Wilson. Given their burdensome work—"almost killing since it continues day and night"—he hoped that the president, as House wrote to Edward S. Martin, the editor of *Life,* would be able to rest on his way home before he had to take up his duties there.[32] As for Edith, she cheerfully noted that, after much kissing of her hand, clicking of heels, and speeches, they were on their way home.

CHAPTER 19

Paris to Washington, and back...

Bound for home aboard the SS *George Washington*, Edith Wilson took pleasure in the presence of Eleanor and Franklin Roosevelt. She found the youthful couple—Eleanor was thirty-five; Franklin, assistant secretary of the navy, was thirty-seven—"very delightful companions."[1] The women, Eleanor a gaunt Gibson girl, Edith a cluttered Renoir, had previously served at the same Red Cross canteen at the Washington railroad station that daily provided as many as ten troop trains of soldiers with soup, coffee, and sandwiches. Initially, Eleanor seemed pleased that Wilson's daughter Margaret worked on her shift, that Edith showed up, in uniform, with fair regularity, and that the president came in person to express his interest in their efforts. However, Eleanor soon grew impatient. Mrs. Wilson's appearance, together with the wives of a prominent ambassador and a cabinet member who had come to look rather than to serve, "rather tries my soul but it is good for my bump of deference."[2]

In Paris in January 1919, Eleanor Roosevelt had helped to allay complaints over the Wilsons' failure to tour France's devastated battlefields by sweeping Edith into her own project of visiting the war wounded in the hospitals.[3] Eleanor was most complimentary about the president's wife: "Mrs. Wilson left a few flowers at each boy's bed," she wrote, and "I was lost in admiration because she found something to say to each one. I stood tongue-tied and thankful that all that could possibly be expected of me was a smile."[4] Eleanor was a discerning observer of the president, judging that in the ordinary things of life he made continual blunders, was a poor judge of men and affairs, self-conscious, shy, and uncertain. She was nevertheless moved by his ardent insistence that the United States must join the League. Otherwise, "it will break the heart of the world," Wilson explained, "for she is the only nation that all feel is disinterested and all trust."[5]

*   *   *

After stormy hours at sea, with the ship off course by seventeen miles and horns incessantly lamenting the fog, the SS *George Washington* escaped a hazardous sandbar to dock safely in Boston on the morning of February 24, 1919. On this "marvelous day" Edith would remember thinking their reception almost equal to and as warm, if not as picturesque, as those abroad. Escorted by the Republican governor of Massachusetts, Calvin Coolidge, the presidential party wove its way to Mechanics Hall, which was packed to suffocation, with hundreds more wanting admission. "If Boston were a representative nation," Edith said, "the pulse of the Nation beat steady and true for what the President was working to attain."[6]

Though Boston seemed a surprising detour on the Paris–Washington axis, its mayor, Andrew Peters, had solicited Wilson's visit for over a year. The plan had crystalized when Joseph Tumulty, early in January, had urged the president on his return to consider a stopover in Boston, instead of New York, to strike in favor of the League of Nations, a move that "would make ovation inevitable throughout New England and would centre attack on [Henry Cabot] Lodge,"[7] the president's despised political adversary. The consequences of Wilson starting a backfire on the senator's own premises, should Lodge decide to "turn on the hose," were the subject of immediate speculation.[8]

In strained circumstances, Governor Coolidge proved a conscientious but awkward diplomat. As Republican to Republican, as governor to senator, Coolidge judged that he and Lodge were in substantial accord. In order, however, that Lodge's action should be "timely and effective"—in other words, not an embarrassment— Coolidge would have him recognize that the Massachusetts public was in favor of some kind of a league, though probably not in favor of its proposed form. "Our party is not an opposition party but a constructive party," he reminded Lodge, advising that "a negative never satisfies." Concerned that, despite its careful phrasing, his message might be overemphatic, Coolidge concluded in his letter to the senator: "Do not pay too much attention to my suggestions. We are all very proud of you here and confident of the soundness of your views."[9]

Wilson's coming to Boston was complicated by another maneuver: an invitation he had issued to members of the Senate Foreign Relations Committee to join him for dinner on his arrival in Washington. Originally, he had intended merely to address Congress formally on the results of the Peace Conference, but Colonel House had vetoed the plan as wholly inadequate, one that would only reinforce a prevalent and not very flattering image of him as schoolmaster-lecturer and preclude discussion, consultation, or explanation. Immediately before leaving Paris, Wilson had rejected House's suggestion. On reconsideration, however, he cabled Tumulty on February 14 to send out invitations with the request that he be permitted to review with his guests, article by article, the League's Covenant before it was subject to congressional debate. He added one caveat: that members refrain from comment in Congress on the proposed League of Nations until he had a chance to discuss it with them.[10] Surprised by the news that the president now intended, in spite of their prior conversation, to make an important speech on landing in Boston, House telegraphed Wilson in midocean on February 18 urging him to take a conciliatory approach. In view of the dinner the president would be giving to the Foreign Relations Committee members, "I hope," House advised, "you will compliment them by making your first explanation of affairs over here to them and confine your Boston remarks to generalities."[11]

On the morning of February 24, eight thousand people crowded into Boston's Mechanics Hall to hear Governor Coolidge, effusive host rather than proverbial "Silent Cal," welcome Wilson with a reception, as Coolidge said, "more marked even than that which was accorded to General George Washington; more united than could have been given at any time during his life to President Abraham Lincoln." In response, in challenge to the unnamed senator from Massachusetts, Wilson told his cheering audience, "We set this nation up to make men free and we did not confine our conception and purpose to America, and now we will make men free. If we do not do that, all the fame of America would be gone and all her power would be dissipated. She would then have to keep her power for those narrow, selfish, provincial purposes which seem so dear to some minds which have no sweep beyond the nearest horizon." Then, as if he were personally lecturing Lodge, Wilson said, "Any man who thinks that America will take part in giving the world any such rebuff and disappointment . . . does not know America. I invite him to test the sentiments of the nation."[12]

The next day the Associated Press reported that Wilson had been on American soil not more than three hours before "he threw down the gauntlet to those who distrust the proposed concert of governments based on the American ideals which had won the war for justice and humanity."[13] Ignoring the tension provoked by what she called "his clear, charming address," and concentrating instead on the ovation given her husband, Edith would recall that day in Boston as one of sunshine and great happiness, when "every wind for ratification of the Treaty when it was submitted to the Congress blew from favorable quarters."[14] Bound for Washington, Edith looked forward to the busy week ahead.

In Washington, on the evening of February 26, the White House glowed with hospitality, illuminated inside and out for the first time in two years. Edith Wilson was the lone woman to join her husband and thirty-four members of the U.S. Senate (the supposedly irreconcilable Republicans, William E. Borah and Albert B. Fall, having sent their refusals). After dinner, Henry Cabot Lodge escorted her from the table into the East Room, where she remained only long enough to exchange pleasantries. The guests then seated themselves in a semicircle, like a school class, with the president, in front, answering questions in an exchange that appeared to Dr. Grayson as "more or less of a free and easy character."[15] Yes, the nation would relinquish some of its sovereignty, but every other nation in the League would make a similar surrender and sacrifice for the good of the world. And no, the Monroe Doctrine was not forgotten. Where once the Monroe Doctrine announced to the world that America would not permit foreign aggression in the Western Hemisphere, now those preparing to set up the League of Nations were recommending that the Monroe Doctrine be extended to cover the world, making all nations a party, proposing thereby to broaden its scope and strengthen its application.

Wilson also touched on issues of disarmament, peace-threatening disputes, American representation on the executive council, and German representation in the League. Before the conference ended, near midnight, the president voiced his fervent hope that the present draft of the League Covenant would become effective without radical changes, emphasizing the difficulty of making amendments to the draft already accepted by fourteen nations in its present form.

The next day the *New York Times* complimented the president on his appealing impression, his being "remarkably frank,"[16] and concluded that, altogether, the dinner had been everything that could have been expected. Neither party sought to embarrass or heckle the president but showed in their attitude their realization of the momentous character of the occasion and approached the issues and problems involved as serious men seeking enlightenment. The article, most flattering to Wilson, not only described the breadth and complexity of the discussion but also cast the president as a judicious, practical, optimistic executive.

By contrast, the New York *Sun*, an entrenched Republican paper, reported a statement of the Republican from Connecticut, Senator Frank B. Brandegee, which signaled the problems ahead. Brandegee took deadly aim at his host (and possibly his host's wife): "I feel as if I had been wandering with Alice in Wonderland and had tea with the Mad Hatter."[17] Lethal and prophetic, Brandegee claimed that with the "wide-open eyes of an ingenue, the President met every legal, constitutional, or commonsense question with glittering generalities. Even more interesting were totally unexpected admissions the President was induced to make. It is the opinion of a number of Senators that unwittingly, perhaps, he has slain the infant of his dreams by these confessions."

Fortunately, the Wilsons were spared the senator's scathing private opinion, confided to Chandler Anderson, that the dinner at the White House was a miserable affair, just about the most uncomfortable and uncongenial dinner he had ever attended. There had been nothing to drink except iced water and a half glass of the sparkling water Apollinaire; and the one small cigar given afterward was of mediocre quality. Brandegee also passed on a detail regarding Edith Wilson's person: Senator Lodge had told him he was amazed to find that when the president's wife had laid her hand on the table "her finger nails were black with dirt."[18]

Others, recalling that dinner, described Edith as "beautiful and gay," handsome but not as tactful as she might have been, talking to Lodge enthusiastically and innocently (so her husband later claimed) about their magnificent reception in the senator's native city.[19] The Virginian had mistaken the Bostonian's cordiality for approval or, at least, acquiescence.

At a distance of twenty years, when Edith looked back on that week in Washington, she still found the sniping at the League incomprehensible. Promise and betrayal by Henry Cabot Lodge appear to be the theme of her reconstruction of the after-dinner conversation between her husband and the senator on the subject of the League and the Covenant. As nearly as she could remember, the president had said to Lodge :

"Of course you understand, Senator, I will have to go back to Paris and resubmit [the League and Covenant papers] to the Conference, for while it is not essentially changed, it is not what they accepted the day I left; and I have some pretty stubborn men to deal with.

However, I am going to do my best, and if this draft as it stands is accepted, do you think it will go through the Senate?"

Mr. Lodge replied: "If the Foreign Relations Committee approves it I feel there is no doubt of ratification."

"Very well then," my husband answered, "I consider that, armed with your approval, I can go back and work feeling you and your associates are behind me."

Lodge bowed his head in assent.

Edith acknowledged that, only with hindsight, reflecting on that reference to Foreign Relations Committee approval, did she sense its threat and power and detect "a very subtle difference from its apparent meaning."[20]

Lodge's account of the evening, dated October 26, 1919, hardly allows for a substantive conversation with the president and once again suggests the inventive turn of Edith's mind. Lodge tells of a large and pleasant dinner, and of a president who was civil and showed no temper, but did not seem to know very thoroughly the draft of the Covenant of the League of Nations. Lodge adds "as a matter of very vivid recollection" that, while he asked Wilson one or two questions, the principal interrogation was conducted by Senator Knox and, more particularly, by Senator Brandegee. In Lodge's judgment, the president's performance under Brandegee's keen and able cross-examination was anything but good.[21]

Edith eventually conceded that the facts validated the impression that Lodge, in the light of his speech before the Senate two days later, had already intended to block ratification in the committee and on the Senate floor. To justify her initial optimism regarding the League, Lodge's opposition did not, at this time, appear to represent the sentiment of the country. Edith cited William Taft's speaking tour on behalf of the League, and a favorable press, as evidence of Wilson's expected triumph. The essential fact remained, however, that the Republican Party prevailed in the Senate.

What Henry Cabot Lodge considered the inequitable premises of the invitation to dinner at the White House, added to the president's tactless presence in Boston, only steeled his resentment of Wilson. He denounced the entire performance of the president—landing in the senator's own city and addressing a mass meeting, while Lodge and his colleagues were reduced to silence on the terms of the League Covenant until after their dinner in Washington—as "a piece of small cunning in which [Wilson] is fond of indulging."[22] Angered though he was, Lodge accepted Wilson's invitation and would not have done otherwise because he wished to observe, he wrote Henry White, "what I think is required of an honorable man."[23]

While promising silence and compliance with the president's request, he also warned Governor Coolidge on the day of Wilson's arrival in Boston that he would speak on the following Friday "if I live until that day." He left no doubt about his position on the League. He recognized that many excellent people favored a league of nations to bring peace to the world, but he did not believe these same people had examined the propositions or considered the difficulties. All he desired, he insisted, was that the American people study the provisions of this agreement before they bound themselves to it. It certainly deserved consideration; but it would not be settled by hurrahs or by emotion or passion. It must be settled by calm and most thorough examination. "I shall be very careful in what I say," Lodge promised Coolidge, "but I cannot for a moment give my support to things which I believe will not make for the peace of the world."[24]

The morning of the publication of the *Sun's* offensive article on the White House dinner, Lodge made good his threat to Coolidge that he would have his say that Friday, February 28. Before the Senate he spoke at length, thoughtfully, exhaustively, passionately. He examined the articles of the League with a watchmaker's eye for detail, pronounced its design flawed, its parts imprecise, and concluded, "Uncertainties [which] . . . cloud this instrument from beginning to end . . . give a rich promise of being fertile in producing controversies and misunderstandings." Lodge's fastidious mind, drilled in taut logic and legal language, resented what he judged to be airy provisions for the League's mandated territories (he was wary of the suggested jurisdiction of the United States over Constantinople, for example) and was dubious of the treaty itself. He pleaded for "consideration, time and thought" and insisted on "facts, details and sharp, clear-cut definitions" as he demanded that the Covenant of the proposed League of Nations contain a definite statement as to whether it would have a military force of its own or the power to summon the forces of its members.

Meanwhile, Lodge vowed to keep on suggesting that before the United States bind itself in any way, the extent of such commitment should be made clear—for "what we are bound to in honor we are bound to do." Until some better constitution for a league could be drawn, it seemed to him that the world's peace would be much sounder, much more surely promoted, by allowing the United States to go on under the

Monroe Doctrine, responsible for the peace of this hemisphere, without any danger of collision with Europe. If, he continued, a league was desired, it might be made up by the European nations whose interests were chiefly concerned, and with which the United States could cooperate fully and at any time when cooperation was needed. He supposed he would make himself the subject of derision for quoting from George Washington's "Farewell Address," but it stated so momentous a truth that he could not refrain from citing it:

> Europe has a set of primary interests which to us have none or a very remote relation. Hence she must be engaged in frequent controversies the causes of which are essentially foreign to our concerns. Hence, therefore, it must be unwise in us to implicate ourselves by artificial ties in the ordinary vicissitudes of her politics or the ordinary combinations and collisions of her friendships or enmities.

Lodge wished to emphasize another point: if the United States entered any league of nations, it did so for the benefit of the world at large, and not for its own benefit, having no boundaries to rectify, no schemes, and no desires for the acquisition or conquest of territory. There was, therefore, no gain for peace in the Americas to be found by annexing them to the European system. Whatever we did there, we would do from almost purely altruistic motives, and therefore, we were entitled to consider every proposition with the utmost care, to make sure that it did not do us injustice or render future conditions worse instead of better than they were at present.

The whole subject was admittedly "one of enormous difficulties." Striving to make real advances toward the preservation of the world's peace would take time, Lodge predicted, and care, and long consideration. A world constitution could not be hastily constructed in a few weeks in Paris, when it had taken fifty of the ablest men in the United States, if not the world, three months to achieve a Constitution of the United States, which, despite its clarity, precision, and excellence, left volumes of questions to be answered by the Supreme Court. Besides, "passion and emotion are not going to perish or die out of men because we sign an agreement for a league of nations."

There was only one solution for this moment in history, Lodge said, and this was to make peace with Germany on terms that would prevent her from "breaking out again upon the world." Peace with Germany could not come soon enough for the senator. Much time had been wasted and the delays bred restlessness and confusion everywhere. Germany, he argued, was "lifting her head again, the whining after defeat changing to threats." Her fields, after all, had not been desolated, nor her factories destroyed. Menacing once again—wanting to annex 9 million Germans in German Austria, reaching out in Russia and reviving her finances and commerce everywhere—Germany, he predicted, "in the future as in the past" was the only source of a great war.

A segment of his speech that embodied the senator's most personal message was unquestionably designed for Wilson's ears: that men differed as to the best method of securing the world's peace in the future did not signify that anyone was against permanent peace. "No question," Lodge concluded, "has ever confronted the United States Senate which equals in importance that which is involved in the league of nations intended to secure the future of the world."

On that same eventful February 28, Wilson spoke at the White House to members of the Democratic National Committee; his denunciation of the Republican senators, undoubtedly exacerbated by the *Sun's* insulting indictment and hearsay regarding Lodge's speech, was injudicious and self-demeaning. He played into the hands of his worst adversaries. Initially, and inimitably, he talked in lofty terms about America's position as the only nation in the world that could accept the mandate of Constantinople as "a work of disinterested philanthropy" and stated that it would be a most serious matter for the confidence of the world in this treaty if the United States did not accept its mandate.

His concentration seemingly lapsing, he veered to the personal, inadvertently revealing his tortured state of mind, his lack of emotional control, and his inability to fortify himself against his presumed enemies. Speaking extemporaneously—and, as he believed, confidentially, though his words were being recorded and transcribed by a government stenographer—Wilson exploded into a petulant diatribe against his adversaries, all those blind, provincial people down to "the littlest and most contemptible." It was not so much their character for which he had contempt, though that contempt was thoroughgoing, but for their minds. They had not got even good working imitations of minds. They reminded him of "a man with a head that is not a head but is just a knot providentially put there to keep him from raveling out." These men were of no use; and Wilson, in his fury, declared that, if he could really say what he thought about them, "it would be picturesque."

These men (he did not name them) had horizons that did not go beyond their parish, not even to the edges of the parish. The gibbets on which they were to be erected by future historians would be so high they would scrape the heavens, and he did not know any fate more terrible than to be exhibited in that future catalog of men who are utterly condemned by the whole spirit of humanity: "If I did not despise them, I would be sorry for them." One thought sometimes cheered him, he continued. On the fifth of March 1921, he would begin to be a historian instead of an active public man and would have the privilege of writing about these gentlemen without any restraints of propriety and repay them for the abuse suffered, to which he could not respond, without shocking the sense of propriety of the entire country. Which made it very fortunate, Wilson thought, that the term of the president is limited (i.e., not legally but physically), believing as he did that no leader could stand such pressure; he was liable some day, if his own experience was standard, to burst by merely containing restrained gases.[25]

Wilson was to endure further setbacks and frustrations in the week before his return to Paris. Near midnight on March 3, Lodge again rose before the Senate to read what would be called the round-robin petition, initiated by Brandegee. The document bore thirty-nine signatures of members who would have the Senate resolve that it was the sense of that body that, while it was their sincere desire that the nations of the world should unite to promote peace and general disarmament, the constitution of the League of Nations, in the form now proposed to the Peace Conference, should not be accepted by the United States. The petition would also declare the sense of the Senate that the negotiations on the part of the United States should immediately be directed to the urgent business of negotiating peace terms with Germany. The proposal for a League of Nations would then be taken up for careful consideration. The vote on March 4 was significant because it put Europe on notice that more than one-third of the Senate would not accept the Covenant of the League of Nations as it appeared in the first draft. Lodge took satisfaction in that it would teach Europeans who had ignored the startling result of the recent American election that their vision of Wilson as all-powerful "was as indefensible as it was stupid."[26] According to former president Theodore Roosevelt, Mr. Wilson's leadership had emphatically been "repudiated" by the American people.

Still another trial awaited Wilson. A Republican filibuster on March 4 prevented the passage of pending bills, postponing their review until the instillation of the new, victorious Republican Congress. As a result, the president abandoned one planned statement for another. The conciliatory first, unpublished, acknowledged, "The 65th Congress, now adjourning, deserves the gratitude and appreciation of a people whose will and purpose I believe it has faithfully expressed."

His splenetic second statement, published in the New York *World* on March 5, was aimed at a "group of men in the Senate [who] have deliberately chosen to embarrass the administration of the Government, to imperil the financial interests of the railway system of the country and to make arbitrary use of powers intended to be employed in the interest of the people." He took for granted, he continued, that the men who had prevented the passage of necessary legislation had considered all the consequences and were willing to assume responsibility for the impaired efficiency of the government and the embarrassed finances of the country during the time of the president's enforced absence.[27]

Even the loyal and admiring Secret Service man Edmund Starling, weighing Wilson's bitter reaction, would conclude that the president had no one to blame but himself for his predicament. His initial failure to appoint men like former president Taft or Elihu Root to the Peace Commission was one blunder. His electioneering call for a Democratic Congress that had "stirred up a hornet's nest" was even more serious. "That mistake—for it was a mistake—was the handwriting on the wall for Wilson, but none of us recognized it as such at the time."[28]

Colonel House was in contact with Wilson during the president's stay in Washington and on his return journey to Paris. To keep him abreast of League negotiations, in accordance with their agreement, House had cabled to Wilson aboard the SS *George Washington* and repeatedly to the White House. To more than a dozen cables from House, Wilson responded on three occasions.[29] The number and urgency of House's messages definitely negate subsequent charges that he acted on his own and failed to alert the president to the decidedly ephemeral nature of the agreement that Wilson had signed on February 14, a day before his departure from France. During Wilson's transatlantic journey, House cabled him that the shooting and wounding in the shoulder of French premier Georges Clemenceau was symptomatic of France's general unrest and discontent, that the country had changed her position and was now anxious to sign the peace treaty, possibly due to the realization that her own army was becoming demoralized.

On February 23, House reported his meeting with Clemenceau and relayed the French premier's insistence on the creation of a Rhenish republic on the west bank of the Rhine. This was in response to Wilson's earlier cable, cautioning that the determination of the geographic boundaries of Germany involved the fortunes and interests of other peoples and should not be arrived at purely from the official French viewpoint. He knew he could trust House and their mutual colleagues "to withstand such a programme immovably," and Wilson was willing to have the strictly military and naval terms decided immediately and presented to the Germans, but could agree at present to nothing beyond those terms. The president concluded with "warm thanks for full information you are sending."[30]

When Wilson landed in Boston on February 24, he had received word from House elaborating on the text—which he assumed the president had secured from government sources—of separate resolutions regarding the preparation of preliminary peace terms with Germany, Austria-Hungary, Bulgaria, and Turkey. House also reported his discussion on the critical subject of the Rhenish republic in which France's high commissioner and military adviser André Tardieu said that his country would be willing to have the republic set up for only a limited period of years, at the end of which the population would be permitted to decide their future for themselves. In this way, the breathing space would afford France protection until she recovered from the present war and, Tardieu concluded, the principle of self-determination would be safeguarded.

House had also informed the president of the plan to give priority to the work of committees involving a peace treaty with Germany: reports should be available by March 8, in time for the president's consideration on his arrival in Paris. After Wilson had approved them, they would be submitted to a plenary session of the conference for agreement. If this procedure was followed, it ought to be possible to summon the Peace Conference to reconvene at a date not later than the first week in April 1919.

On February 25, House's message suggested that the president ask Taft to see him at the White House, as he "is the leader of those in the United States who are trying to sustain you in your fight for a League of Nations."[31] On the twenty-sixth House told Wilson that Tardieu had submitted a memorandum on the French position respecting the left bank of the Rhine and that House would cable Wilson fully when he had had the opportunity to study it.[32] On February 27 House informed Wilson of Arthur Balfour's and Lord Robert Cecil's approval of House's own recommendation that they make an effort to start the League of Nations functioning at once, with the original committee members acting as a provisional executive council.

Meanwhile, the proposal was made to call in the neutrals and explain the Covenant to them and say that an invitation was soon to be extended to them to become members. However, House promised Wilson that there would be no meeting unless the French, Japanese, and others agreed not to offer any amendments to the Covenant until the president's return.[33] On March 1, House informed the president of his telephone conversation with David Lloyd George in which the two had drafted a timetable for action. Based on the president's arrival in Paris by March 13 or 14, it might be possible to settle the preliminary peace terms with Germany by March 23 and to name a day on which the Central Powers were to participate.[34]

Wilson's objections, cabled before leaving Washington on March 4, reflect the dissonant thoughts of a president whose goals for his Covenant had been spurned in Washington. Though upset by House's proposal, he managed to temper his disapproval.[35] "Your plan about starting the League of Nations to function at once," he wrote, "disturbs me a little." On the contrary, if the strategy Wilson had in mind could be followed, with the explicit and public understanding that this machinery was being used provisionally and merely for the purpose of facilitating the processes of the Peace Conference, perhaps, Wilson speculated, this danger would disappear. The people of the United States were undoubtedly in favor of the League of Nations by an overwhelming majority, but many forces, particularly those prejudiced against Great Britain, were exercising a considerable influence against it, and "you ought," he cautioned House, "to have that constantly in mind in everything you do."[36]

House's wire, both reassuring and problematic, crossed that of the troubled president. "We have not yet found a satisfactory way to make the League of Nations function as I suggested and nothing will be done until after your arrival. In the meantime we will try to shepherd the neutrals into the fold." House also advised Wilson that the situation in Germany, particularly in Bavaria, was extremely precarious, and that he had tried to impress both the British and French with the necessity of getting food into those areas immediately. Clemenceau and Balfour had agreed to bring up the question of supplies, and Clemenceau asked that, meanwhile, he be given time to bring the French public to a realization of the importance of sending food into Germany. "Everything has been speeded up," wired House, and he felt confident that by the time of Wilson's arrival "all questions will be ready for your approval."[37]

Given the detail and depth of these cables, and the urgency and frequency with which they crossed the Atlantic Ocean, their evaluation by Ray Stannard Baker, the president's press officer and future authorized biographer, was irresponsible and misleading. At one time he would claim that, during Wilson's absence from Paris, House kept up only "fragmentary communication with the absent President." At another juncture, Baker wrote, in 1922, that House had sent the president long cablegrams on developments in Paris, the ultimate effect of which was to "confuse everything, serve exactly the contrary purpose from the one the President had in view."[38] Baker's malignant pronouncements on this so-called interim period were to be harshly augmented by Edith, who viewed House's handling of the peace treaty negotiations as nothing less than catastrophic on personal terms and to the cause of world peace. In her *Memoir*, published seventeen years after Baker's volume, she bitterly condemns the colonel for having "given away,"[39] during her husband's absence, the terms of the peace treaty as perfected by him, which, she erroneously implies, were immutable, rather than subject to the temperament of the participating leaders and to such contemporary vicissitudes as France's critical financial state and England's labor difficulties.

The Wilsons' train, bound for New York City, pulled out of Washington's Union Station on March 4 at 1:56 P.M. En route the president reviewed with Edith, Tumulty, and Grayson details of recent events in Congress. He then wrote his speech to be given that evening at the Metropolitan Opera House. In its delivery he more than fulfilled Senator Frank Brandegee's judgment that concession was not Woodrow Wilson's line: his vanity having suffered a traumatic jolt, "he will go to any length for revenge upon those who have humiliated him before the world."[40]

Encouraged by former president William H. Taft's enthusiastic introduction, Wilson ignored his dubious reception in Washington as he promised his Manhattan audience that the first thing he was going to tell people abroad was that the overwhelming majority of the American people were in favor of the League; he knew this to be true because of unmistakable intimations from all parts of the country, "and the voice rings true in every case."

With Congress his obvious target, he spoke of being amazed, not alarmed but amazed, at the comprehensive ignorance in some quarters as to the state of the world. He did not know where these men had been closeted, or how they had been blinded, but he did know they were out of touch. Shaming these nameless Americans "who set up a doctrine of careful selfishness thought out to the last detail," he threatened that the next time "there would be so many threads of the treaty tied to the covenant that you can not dissect the covenant from the treaty without destroying the whole vital structure."[41] He suggested that an individual might often be found selfish and confined to his special interests, but Americans in mass were willing to die for an idea. "The sweet revenge therefore is this, that we believed in righteousness and now we are ready to make the supreme sacrifice for it, the supreme sacrifice of throwing in our fortunes with the fortunes of men everywhere."[42] Edith was especially effusive about his reception at the Metropolitan Opera House. "My husband never failed to get his audience and on this night they seemed really to go wild," she said. "I have never seen a more representative crowd and they stood and cheered and would not leave."[43]

Like her husband, who said he was puzzled "by the fact of criticism,"[44] Edith not only castigated but dangerously underestimated the opposition. The mirror the couple now held up to themselves obscured all blemishes. They saw themselves as emissaries on a mission—Wilson hoping to lead the world out of chaos, and to be hailed as the Messiah.[45] They were unable to conceive of their reverse image as a "pretentiously imperial pair making what they obviously felt was an almost apocalyptic pilgrimage."[46]

Edith dismissed the possibility that Lodge's differences with her husband might have some logical foundation. The passing years would intensify her resentment to the point where, losing control of her emotions, she made a public declaration in her *Memoir* of her hatred of the Bostonian. The eventual defeat of the treaty, in the Senate, was attributed by Edith to that squall that came out of the blue, instigated by the jealousy of one man, by Henry Cabot Lodge "and his sinister hate." When Edith thought of Lodge, she was reminded of Robert Ingersoll's lines at Napoleon's tomb: "I would rather have been a peasant and wear wooden shoes than this imperial monarch who covers Europe with blood."[47] Though she did not mistake Lodge—"by the mercy of God"— for an imperial monarch, she pronounced him "a venomous serpent crawling through dirty paths—leaving poison as he followed his slimy underwater awful course."[48]

CHAPTER 20

The preacher and the Brahmin

Edith Wilson underestimated the gravity of Lodge's differences with her husband, misread Lodge's character, and knew little of his Brahmin history or the tenets of his education. Like his professor, mentor, and friend, the legendary Henry Adams, twelve years his elder, Henry Cabot Lodge "stood up" for his eighteenth-century heritage, his Plymouth Pilgrim forebears, his Constitution of 1789, his Harvard College, and his Boston.[1] Nearly six feet tall, slender, and pink-cheeked (thus "Pinky" to family and close friends), with the piercing eyes of an amiable raccoon[2] and a fashionable Edwardian mustache and goatee, Lodge was a patrician figure. Called the Duke of Nahant, after his summer place on the Massachusetts coast, he wore high-button jackets, bow ties, straw boaters, plush felt bowlers, and spats. Of Norman and English lineage, he was a descendant of the first minister of the Massachusetts Bay Colony, Francis Higginson. His grandfather George Cabot, a charter member of Boston's "Salt Fish Aristocracy,"[3] who had sailed to wealth in transatlantic trade, had served as Massachusetts's first full-term senator. The grandson, born on May 15, 1850, in his grandfather's granite mansion on Winthrop Place off Sumner Street in Boston, had graduated from Harvard College in 1871, and from Harvard Law School in 1875.

As an undergraduate, Lodge joined the Porcellian and Hasty Pudding Clubs and studied medieval history with Henry Adams in his senior year. As one of Adams's first three doctoral candidates, Lodge produced a dissertation, "Anglo-Saxon Courts of Law," for which he received the degree of doctor of philosophy in 1876. He taught American history at Harvard for the next three years. His professor's advice and guidance were to be a seminal influence on the evolution of his own austere standards. "The first step," Adams counseled Lodge, "seems to be to familiarize one's mind with thoroughly good work; to master the scientific method, and to adopt the rigid principle of subordinating everything to perfect thoroughness of study."[4]

With Lodge's election to the Massachusetts legislature in 1880, Adams—as the descendant of two presidents, John Adams and John Quincy Adams—would impart wisdom burnished by ancestral exposure. "If you can make friends with the most influential members, including the Speaker, if you can occasionally bring one home to a family dinner, or to a talk in your library; if you can, in short, make yourself important or agreeable to the leaders, you will next be in a position to claim a good committee and be a leader yourself."[5] At the end of Lodge's sophomore year at college, Adams had cautioned, "There's only one way to look at life, and that is the practical way. Keep clear of mere sentiment whenever you have to decide a practical question. Sentiment is very attractive and I like it as well as most people, but nothing in the way of action is worth much which is not practically sound."[6]

Much as he valued Lodge, Adams took greatest pleasure in the company of his protégé's wife, Anna Cabot Mills Davis. The clever, queenly, violet-eyed, and hospitable Nannie, an admiral's daughter, tossed off classical quotes, Adams said, with as much aplomb as a university man. She softened her husband's intimidating Brahmin image, his case of "Bostonitis," accentuated by an impenetrable crustiness and by his chill, cultured, rasping voice and "la-di-dah accent."[7]

Adams had known Lodge intimately as a scholar, teacher, assistant editor of the *North American Review,* and political reformer from 1873 to 1878. Later he spoke wryly of Lodge's having suffered from the misfortune of becoming not only a senator but a senator from Massachusetts, a singular circumstance fatal to friends and, apparently, friendships. Happily, Adams knew another side of the man—had regarded himself as his elder brother or uncle since Lodge's marriage in 1871.[8] The men long remained close, and years later, during August 1895, when they were together in Normandy, at Caen, Coutances, and Mont-Saint-Michel, Adams allowed that "in the thirteenth century, by an unusual chance, even a Senator became natural, simple, interested, cultivated, artistic, liberal—genial."[9]

Lodge would prove far less engaging on the subject of Woodrow Wilson, a theme on which he could become offensive even to Adams. As early as February 1915, Henry Adams, exposed to Lodge's seething comments about Wilson, found the senator "off his balance, and his hatred of the president . . . demented."[10] At a heated dinner-table discussion just after the president's declaration of war against Germany on April 2,

1917, Adams, the host, pounded the table to silence as he cautioned "Cabot" that he had "never allowed treasonable conversation at this table and I don't propose to allow it now."[11]

With the death of Nannie Lodge on September 28, 1915, "the love and light" of Henry Cabot Lodge's life "went out in an instant." His namesake, his engaging, cherished son, nicknamed Bay, a poet and one of three children, had died suddenly five years earlier. Melancholic over the deliberations of America's entrance into the war, finding "the times . . . very evil" in the early spring of 1917,[12] Lodge was still less sanguine two years later. Given the critical issues at stake in the peace settlement, he loathed the president for his "spirit of petty tyranny and his determination to have his own way."[13] Never having expected to hate a political adversary with the hatred he felt toward Wilson,[14] he regarded him, in agreement with Theodore Roosevelt, as "the most dangerous man that ever sat in the White House"—with the sole exception of James Buchanan, who had been dangerous because he was weak, unlike Wilson, who was dangerous because he was determined "to have his own way, no matter what it costs the country."[15]

By February 1919, mourning the death of Henry Adams, Theodore Roosevelt, and the British ambassador Cecil Spring-Rice, Lodge spoke of himself as "chilly and grown old."[16] He was sixty-seven. Conceding that he was lonely and confused, he grew increasingly intolerant of the "general and sloppy demand" to stand by the president. He could not bear talk of Wilson's "noble idealism,"[17] and as for Wilson's declaration immediately prior to U.S. entry into the war, favoring "peace without a victory," Lodge did not see "how there can be any peace worth having in Europe unless the Allies win a decisive victory."[18] He pointed out, in his own defense, that he had stood by the president when he was right and had backed him on the Nicaragua treaty, the Haitian treaty, and the Danish island purchase—all Republican policies and all sound. Lodge admitted that he had stood against him just as steadily when he thought Wilson was doing harm, and "my standing by him," Lodge had told Roosevelt, "consists in trying to force his hand and push him forward along the path he does not want to follow."[19]

Lodge was appalled to think that Wilson would be exalted to posterity as the upholder of democratic ideals. The barrier between the men soared higher and firmer with each passing month and year as the senator became increasingly suspicious of the president's motives and intolerant of his contradictions, of what he perceived as Wilson's lack of generous emotion, his entire subjection to his personal animosities.

Lodge took some comfort in the hope that a future historian would compare the president's war message, which was excellent, with all his preceding and contradictory messages and criticize his inconsistencies.

When Lodge had first called on Wilson a few days after his inauguration in 1913, Lodge reminded him of their initial encounter, which he thought the president might have forgotten. With a pleasant smile, Wilson acknowledged their introduction at a Harvard commencement and assured Lodge that a man never forgets the first editor who accepts one of his articles. Wilson would not have mentioned, though undoubtedly must have known, that Lodge, editor of The International Review, had marked Wilson's second article "R.R.R.," received, read, rejected.[20] Their relationship had deteriorated sharply by 1917, when the senator learned that because he was to speak at the celebration of the hundredth anniversary of the Church of St. John in Washington on January 12, the president had refused to attend. Lodge, whose offer to withdraw was turned down by the rector, claimed to be amused by the incident, which he believed to be retribution for his disapproval of the president's attitude ("too proud to fight" being an unacceptable concept) toward the sinking of the Lusitania. He found Wilson pompous in perceiving his great mission to humanity was that of pacifier of the warring nations.

By 1919, the harsh differences between the men—Lodge the Pilgrim and Wilson the preacher—were entrenched: their distrust, disdain, and dislike of each other was consummately mutual.[21] The president accused both Lodge and Elihu Root of wanting to bring back days of private influence and selfish advantage and was determined to hit these men "straight in the face, and not mind if the blood comes."[22] As for Lodge, he had long supposed that Wilson was "either alarmingly ignorant of conditions abroad or temporarily unbalanced by the flush of political success."[23]

The senator's disagreement with Wilson's action in Mexico had provoked the first notable rift in their relations. Wilson's use of force, on April 21, 1914, in the bombardment of Vera Cruz, resulted in the deaths of 19 Americans and 126 Mexicans and brought Mexico and the United States close to war. A far more critical issue was the Ship Purchase Bill, which Wilson championed and Lodge feared would force America into war: the senator regarded the purchase of German ships interned in American harbors as an unneutral act, almost an act of hostility to the Allies, that vitally affected the honor and welfare of the country and far transcended any question of ordinary party politics.[24] Lodge suspected the bill owed its inspiration to Secretary of the Treasury McAdoo's business connections with the banking house of Kuhn Loeb, which was allied with leading German steamship lines.

The thought that the American government did not comprehend the repercussions from such an act, did not anticipate the immediate threat—that England, France, and Russia might refuse to recognize the transfer flag and capture the former German ships—compounded by Wilson's refusal to promise that they would be kept out of the North Atlantic trade, prompted Lodge for the first time to attack the president personally before Congress. Weeks later, taunting Wilson further, Lodge said that the first thing Wilson did with a new subject was to make up his mind, any subsequent information being regarded as a mere impertinence. He compared him to the Oxford don who claimed, "My name is Benjamin Jowett / I'm the master of Balliol College / Whatever is known, I know it / And what I don't know isn't knowledge."[25]

Lodge was disdainful of Wilson as commander in chief, considering him all words and otherwise empty. He knew for a fact that Wilson—except to see General Pershing for a few minutes before his going overseas—had not spoken with any officers of the army or navy. "Think of a commander-in-chief who never talks with those in charge of his soldiers," Lodge exclaimed to Theodore Roosevelt.[26] Lodge believed that Wilson avoided such meetings from fear of outspoken opinions from officers. "He does not want the truth told to him. It wearies him and makes him nervous to see people." As a whole, Wilson scarcely saw anybody, not even members of his own cabinet. Lodge had it from their own lips that they communicated with him in writing.

The senator also took exception, with House in mind, to "this business of using personal agents"—whereas representatives charged with negotiating treaties were normally confirmed by the Senate.[27] Graver still than his estimate of Wilson's executive ability—the president surrounding himself with "wooden-headed bureau chiefs"[28]—was his charge that Wilson was determined to make America's intervention a party war, shutting out prominent Republicans. "He is a mean soul," Lodge concluded.[29] This meanness about political parties he laid directly at Wilson's door. During the war, House and Senate Republicans and Democrats were working together on committees and on the floor as one party; but the president, his "pettiness beyond belief," was intolerant of political ecumenism. How different, the senator lamented, was the Republican president William McKinley's conduct during the Spanish War, and his appointment of Democrats such as Burton K. Wheeler and FitzHugh Lee to positions of importance.

There was still another division between Lodge and Wilson. This concerned the latter's journey abroad, which Lodge had been convinced, prior to Wilson's departure in December 1918, would do him no good, whatever the warmth of his reception. Little more than a year later, the senator pronounced Wilson "on the down-grade."[30] He allowed that it was perhaps too much to hope that he himself might live to see the president found out; but he thought the truth was gradually rising to the surface.[31] A historian might see all Wilson's blemishes, had only to read his papers and messages to seize the truth. Unfortunately for Lodge, this conviction was not justified. His own reputation as hangman to Wilson's white knight was to be perpetuated by Edith Bolling Wilson and countless others who portrayed the senator as the spoiler and villain who deliberately, unreasonably, and cruelly victimized the blameless Wilson by thwarting his visionary designs for a League of Nations and world peace. Cruelty there was; but penetration also.

Possibly no imaginable circumstances could have fostered a respectful relationship between the second-generation Southerner, child of preachers and frugal parsonages, and the Northerner, steeped in decades of affluent New England ancestry. Even aside from their opposed personalities and heritage, their differences of philosophy were profound. Given the polarized theories of government that the two had codified as young men, their enmity seemed foreordained. Wilson signaled, as early as his Princeton senior-year essay, a warning of his disdain for Congress and for its power and constituents:

> There is no one in Congress to speak for the nation. Congress is a conglomeration of inharmonious elements; a collection of men representing each his neighborhood, each his local interest; an alarmingly large proportion of its legislation is 'special'; all of it is at best only a limping compromise between the conflicting interests of the innumerable localities represented.

Five years later, as a lecturer at Johns Hopkins, Wilson had belittled congressional power and had left no doubt, in his essay "Constitutional Government," of his admiration for a uniquely empowered president who need disclose no step of negotiation until completed, at which time the government "is virtually committed. Whatever its disinclination, the Senate may feel itself committed also."

Contrary to Wilson, Lodge believed that the ambitions or fate of presidents or presidential candidates were "infinitely small" compared to the power of Congress in treaty-making matters. He looked strictly to the patriots and founding fathers for a pattern of government. Lodge's principles were profound, considered, and distinguished. His confirmed belief was that the system of treaty-making established by the Constitution made it clear, by practice and precedent, that "it would be neither possible nor safe to level the vast powers of treaty-making exclusively to one person."[32]

Beyond the explosive issue of treaties, Lodge's distrust of Wilson was compounded by what he considered the president's inconsistencies—which included his failed promise to keep the country out of war, his misinterpretation of the Monroe Doctrine, his insistence on combining the peace treaty and the League Covenant, and his going to Europe and "meddling abroad." More intimately, and unfairly, there was the matter of Wilson's early remarriage, a haste that Lodge pronounced "vulgar."[33]

Before Wilson set sail for Europe on March 5, friends and critics quite other than Lodge also questioned the wisdom of his going abroad again. Given his first emotional reception and the extravagant expectations that were impossible for any man to live up to, his return was bound to result in anticlimax. Skeptics saw little hope that by going to Paris he would succeed in imposing his impracticable and idealistic League on other nations. Mention was made of his impatience with any contradiction, his belief in his own infallibility. And all the while, there were many matters of surpassing importance and urgency at home.

None of these comments by friends or foes surprised Lodge. Prolific communications from abroad convinced him that the Peace Conference was losing its hold on the public overseas, and time was now working for Germany.[34] The novelist Edith Wharton, writing to Lodge from Hyères, reiterated the theme of French disenchantment, specifically on the vulnerable topic of Wilson's visits to the battlefield—or lack of them. Someone who had not been in France throughout the war and heard the tone in which the French pronounced certain names—Verdun, Lille, Sens—could not imagine, Wharton said, the affront caused to all that was deepest and finest in French national sentiment by Wilson's evident indifference to the nation's suffering and sorrow. That Wilson had never, as far as she knew, uttered a word in public in praise for the French or British armies was not calculated to endear him either. "With a people like the French nothing offends more than tactlessness, and his has been on a rather monumental scale."[35]

Word from across the Channel was no less negative. The English editor L. J. Maxse of the *National Review* pronounced himself bewildered by events in Paris, and by the behavior of certain leaders who seemed to have completely lost their grip on the problems confronting them, and to be "wandering in the clouds."[36] In Maxse's opinion, the English were in difficulty because of their desire to do honor to the president of the United States, partly on account of his position, partly because he was a guest; but, he wrote Lodge, "we really cannot afford to compromise our whole position in order to support his attractive but unworkable theories."

Rudyard Kipling, whose only son, Second Lieutenant John Kipling, had died in battle in 1915, was skeptical of Wilson on several counts. "It strikes people," he wrote to Lodge in mid-March 1919, "that if the world had settled first with the Hun and had considered the League of Nations later, it might have been a happier world than it is. The chief thing that is worrying the powers of Europe now is whether Mr. Wilson has authority from the U.S.A. (who one gathers from the Constitution, though not from his language, employs him) to deliver any goods in her name."[37] Still another friend wrote the senator from England that sensible people were inclined to think that Wilson was "cold-blooded and an egoist but with some large and sincere visions and extreme cleverness of a rather dangerous kind."[38]

Transcending personal bitterness, Lodge's candid and feeling response to his European correspondents reflects a principled man whose world was in crisis, whose sense of logic rejected Woodrow Wilson's interpretation of and power over the clamorous issues at stake. In his intense frustration, the senator did not mince words on what he considered the inflated, inaccurate, and dissembling accounts of Wilson's accomplishments abroad, or his standing with Congress at home. In regard to Wilson's enlistment on his side of a Democratic Congress, "It was refused, emphatically refused," Lodge assured Kipling. As for the delayed peace with Germany, it had produced a situation that, at the present moment, "seems to me alarming."[39]

Pursuing a single theme throughout his correspondence, Lodge repeated his commitment to the idea that without Wilson's resistance, the treaty with Germany could have been disposed of by Christmas, 1918, and could have been made so strong that she would forever be fettered against another outbreak upon the world. Had that been achieved, the Allies might have gone on to discuss a League of Nations; but months would not have been wasted on endless questions that detracted from what Lodge regarded as the essential task of making peace with Germany.

One of the most critical items of Lodge's voluminous correspondence is his declaration to Edith Wharton: "I am in favor of a League of Nations if so constituted that it will promote and secure the peace of the world so far as possible and not endanger or imperil the United States." What troubled Lodge was not the principle of the League, but the draft of its Covenant that Wilson had produced and submitted to the world. In Lodge's opinion, that draft fulfilled neither of his stipulated conditions, was loosely and obscurely drawn, was full of doubtful points over which nations could easily quarrel, and impaired certain policies of the United States that were regarded as essential. Constantly examining and justifying his thoughts about the League, Lodge assured Mrs. Wharton, "I am as anxious for the establishment of world peace as any man can possibly be and will do anything to promote it, but if you would examine that [draft] thoroughly or could go over it with me I think I could show you how extremely dangerous it is."[40]

It was of enormous consequence, in taking the most momentous step ever made by this country, that no mistake be made. All Lodge asked, he insisted, was that the American people should consider carefully this draft before they decided to commit to it. Lodge chose, as an example, Article 10, which destined the country to guarantee the territorial integrity and political independence of every member of the League. This would mean, of course, every nation on the face of the earth. It seemed to him this was grave enough not to be lightly dismissed; before the senators agreed to anything of such importance they ought to be very sure that the instrument would produce the general peace of the world and not lead to dissension and the breeding of controversy and, possibly, of war.[41]

Lodge summed up the situation for his nephew Moreton Frewen: most of the Senate strongly favored a League of Nations that did not interfere unduly with the settled policies and rights of the United States.[42] In March, with Harvard University's President A. Lawrence Lowell at Symphony Hall, Boston, in a "Joint Debate on the Covenant of Paris," the senator argued that he was not against any league of nations, but was for one put in proper shape, one that did not disregard George Washington's advice to avoid permanent alliances, one that did not contradict the Monroe Doctrine, or was not basically unconstitutional—since only Congress had power to regulate armament and commerce, and to declare war. His fear was that in trying to do too much, "we might lose all."[43]

The Wilsons again boarded the SS *George Washington* in Hoboken on March 4, 1919, to sail the next day. In the opinion of the chief usher, Ike Hoover, things not only seemed but were different this time, and he wrote of having "queer feelings." Despite the salutes, the convoys, the cruisers, the destroyers, and the squadron of airships hovering above, people were not so demonstrative as the first time, nor were the crowds as large nor the noise as boisterous. To be honest with himself, it was a feeble send-off compared with that of December 4, 1918. Hoover sensed that even the president standing on the bridge appeared to feel the lack of enthusiasm as the ship pulled out of the dock at eight-fifteen the morning of March 5.

During the voyage over a rough, rolling sea, Wilson was visible for the first time only on the third day. He was having trouble with his teeth, looked worn and gray, and ran a temperature. On the sixth day out, he was able to play a little shuffleboard with Edith, and their favorite card game of Canfield. Wilson's spirits improved, and he told Grayson that he usually had respect for the doctor's diagnosis, but had this time decided he was wrong. True, Wilson had a headache, neuralgia, a sore throat, a toothache, fever, and a chill, and his equatorial zone had been on strike, but he had worked out his trouble himself. According to his own diagnosis, he was suffering "from a retention of gases generated by the Republican Senators—and that's enough to poison any man."[44] Hoover regarded Wilson's luncheon invitation to the newspapermen aboard as a sign of his recovery.

Even on shipboard, Wilson could not escape challenges to his League. Just before sailing, he had weathered an ugly exchange with a delegation of Irish-Americans who questioned the League's lack of provision for Ireland's independence from England. Now, he read in the ship's paper, *The Hatchet*, that Sinn Fein threatened to influence Irish-American voters to kill the League unless their claims for the establishment of an Irish republic were agreed to by the Peace Conference. Angry and belligerent, Wilson told Grayson he would "go to the mat with them—show them where they got off in America."

The president was still on the high seas on March 7 when he learned of a conference among Colonel House, Lloyd George, and Clemenceau in which they discussed, among many problems, the distribution of Germany's payment to the Entente, the question of feeding Germany, the dismemberment of the Turkish Empire, and acceptance by the United States of mandates for Armenia and Constantinople and, again, the critical question of land along the left bank of the Rhine.[45] In a stern response of March 10, four days before docking at Brest, Wilson hoped, as he cautioned House, that "you will not even provisionally consent to the separation of the Rhenish Provinces from Germany under any arrangement, but will reserve the whole matter until my arrival."[46]

House's reports from Paris to Wilson did hint at his own profound disappointment over the negotiations in which he was so responsibly involved. It was now obvious to him that the peace would not be along the lines he had hoped for. He was disturbed over conditions in Germany and Austria, and especially in Germany. He saw a definite risk of having those countries turn Bolshevik if they were not sent food. Yet the Entente governments ignored his repeated warnings, sat by complacently, and blocked every move the Americans tried to make to remedy this dangerous condition. House had concluded that scarcely a man in Paris in authority, other than the president of France, had a full and detached understanding of the situation, or the capacity to settle the infinite number of challenges. Then again, House also admitted to reservations about the French president—that, in some measure, he lacked executive ability for coping with "this supreme task." The others would fail as well, he predicted, owing to their own prejudices and selfishness, too engrossed by their own affairs to see beyond their own nation's boundaries.

Noting the number, variety, and complexity of the difficulties, House wrote: "It is Archangel and Murmansk at one moment, the left bank of the Rhine the next, Asia Minor, the African colonies, the Chinese-Japanese differences, the economic situation as to raw materials, the food situation as it affects the various countries of Europe, enemy and neutral, and the financial situation as it relates to the United States, and the Allies." Basically, House concluded, he disliked "to sit and have forced upon us such a peace as we are facing."[47]

Despite her husband's problems, political and physical, Edith chose to commemorate this episode most fondly. Brimming with optimism, ignoring the frigid reception in Washington and House's worrisome cables, which her husband undoubtedly shared with her, she insisted there was every reason to believe that, in spite of conflicting national ambitions, the League of Nations as part of the peace treaty would provide the peaceful means of readjusting any mistake. In an odd contradiction, Edith allowed, in virtually the same breath, a more pessimistic glimpse of Wilson, less secure and even faintly resigned to compromise. As though he had come to terms with his critics, or at least recognized the existence, if not the validity, of their arguments, Edith wrote that one day, as they walked the deck together, he said, "The best we can hope for is not to satisfy any one entirely—strange as that may seem; for only so, with give and take, can we come to an agreement."[48] Possibly Wilson was speaking not of his own need to compromise, but of his expectations that the others involved would agree to do so.

In truth, Wilson's prospects were a puzzle. Eleanor Roosevelt, among others, fretted about his and the country's future. The tension between the president and Congress during this period was very great, she would write, and thoughtful people both in the United States and abroad were pondering a situation in which the executive, charged with the duty of dealing with foreign nations, might come to an agreement that would be turned down by the Senate, as had been done before.[49]

CHAPTER 21

A different president . . . a different Paris

It was an altered President Wilson who headed east over the Atlantic on the SS *George Washington* for the second time. After his month's absence, the American president also faced a different Paris and the "gaunt realities," envisioned by Winston Churchill, "which prowled outside."[1] Behind him lay the sullen veto of the Senate; before him, the entanglements of the Europeans. His White House dinner for the Senate Foreign Relations Committee had revealed to him implacable party rancor, the spirit of Lodge pitted against the League of Nations. On his previous voyage, all his moral indignation had been concentrated upon the Old World. On the second journey, he was largely preoccupied by the New. His original purpose had been to convert Europe to his views; now, the Senate of the United States stood in need of discipline. Branded as a partisan rather than a national leader, he found himself having to reassure French and English skeptics of his authority, "while producing world salvation in a form acceptable to political enemies whom he had deeply and newly offended."[2] Still smarting from the repercussions of his flawed mission at home, he would blame Colonel House almost immediately on meeting him at Brest: "Your dinner was a failure as far as getting together was concerned."[3]

Wilson's criticism of House was muted compared to Edith's. Her aggrieved account in her *Memoir* of the disastrous shipboard reunion of the two men on the moonlit Thursday night of March 13 would put into permanent question the contribution, character, and loyalty of her husband's closest colleague and trusted adviser, if not "his most intimate friend,"[4] denying him a respected resting place in history. Transforming frustration into condemnation in the intervening years, she explicitly damned House with responsibility for Wilson's shattered health and foreshortened span of life, and for nothing less than the denial of her husband's vision and hope for the world.

That she herself might bear some responsibility for the damage for which she blamed House—"the wreckage of [Wilson's] plans" and "tragic years that have demoralized the world"—would not have occurred to her. Yet it was she who shielded the president of the United States from a timely perspective that might have moderated his ultimately fatal position regarding the League. She could not understand or appreciate House's matchless role in Wilson's life for the past seven years, his ability to enlighten her husband as to the realities of politics both at home and abroad, and to penetrate somewhat the president's strangely private domain.

Belittling House as "small and unimpressive," Edith Wilson ignored the fact that others valued him as an artful negotiator who, if allowed to continue in his role, might have helped her husband to achieve, at last, the peace terms of his vision. But for her "prejudiced influence," which prevented House from exercising his skill in compromise, the historian Arthur Walworth concludes, the League of Nations might have had greater acceptance in the American Senate.[5] In 1924, when Sir Edward Grey spoke of the serious consequences of the break between Wilson and House, he was sure, he told House, that if the two had remained together, the history of the previous four years would have been a different story.[6]

After an interval of twenty years, Edith, in her *Memoir*, recalled arriving in Brest, being met by a large group of French officials and many Americans coming aboard from a tender, and the surprise of seeing Colonel House. The welcoming officials having departed, the passengers gone to bed, Wilson and House talked on while Edith remained in her adjoining stateroom. She would not join the men because she knew that they were engrossed in serious talk. She waited. It was after midnight, and very still, when she heard her husband's door open and the colonel take his leave. She opened the door of their connecting rooms to find her husband standing, looking almost ill. He seemed to have aged ten years, and his jaw was set in that way it did when he was making superhuman effort to control himself. Silently he held out his hand, which she grasped, crying, "What is the matter? What has happened?" Wilson smiled bitterly. "House has given away everything I had won before we left Paris. He has compromised on every side, and so I have to start all over again and this time it will be harder, as he has given the impression that my delegates are not in sympathy with me." By way of explaining his compromises, Edith wrote, House had told Wilson that as the hostile press in the United States was opposed to the League of Nations as a part of the peace treaty, he had thought it best to yield on other points lest the conference withdraw its approval of the League altogether. So he had yielded, and her husband, "aghast when he learned what House had done," told Edith, "there was nothing left."

Edith Wilson's drama of the midnight meeting was not only confirmed but embellished by the Secret Service man Edmund Starling. According to Starling, House boarded the ship accompanied by his son-in-law Gordon Auchincloss. When the president saw House, he asked him to his suite. Starling followed the two men and took up his watch outside the door. There he encountered John Edward Nevin, a reporter with the International News Service, who gave him news of the conference, including the rumor that Colonel House "was letting the water out of the dam which the president had erected." The reporter left; House emerged looking disturbed and walked rapidly away. As Starling stepped into the cabin to close the door, he saw the president standing, his eyes fixed on Starling but showing no recognition, his arms hanging loosely at his sides. Something in his appearance made Starling pause. Wilson's face was pale, drawn, and tired. His whole figure expressed dejection. Starling closed the door, "mentally cursing Colonel House."[7]

These alarming accounts by Wilson's intimates would be affecting were it not for the fact that Colonel House never did board the SS *Washington*. Nor was his presence at Brest a surprise. The president's earlier cable informing House of his late arrival, probably reaching Brest at 8:30 P.M. and dining before going ashore, shows that he expected to meet with House that evening and regretted the inconvenient hour.[8] On that night of March 13, the Wilsons disembarked after dinner as planned and boarded a special train that left Brest at 10:30 P.M., arriving in Paris at noon the next day.

House, who had gone up to Brest on the president's train, found it a hard trip in foul weather. He had inspected some camps en route—the Red Cross, the YMCA, and other American organizations connected with the army. Eager to have the president to himself that evening on the train to bring him up-to-date on developments in Paris during his absence, House was exasperated to find the French ambassador to the United States, Jean Jules Jusserand, intruding on those valuable hours.

Cary Grayson would claim that Wilson confided to him the content of his conversations with both House and Jusserand before retiring aboard the train that Thursday at midnight. According to the physician, House warned the president of the apparent desire of the French authorities to sidetrack the Covenant and have a preliminary peace treaty signed that would include the complete disarmament of Germany and the creation of a Rhenish republic and, in effect, "do what the president had declared on a number of occasions he would not countenance, absolutely denude Germany of everything she had and allow Bolshevism to spread throughout that country." In the president's conversation with Jusserand—if accurately recounted by Grayson—Wilson abruptly cut short the Frenchman's assertion that everyone was in favor of the League of Nations, "but, of course, there were a number of changes that would have to be made." "Hold on, Mr. Ambassador," Wilson had insisted. He too had relinquished a great many conditions he had desired: the resulting agreement was the best to be achieved under the circumstances. Though it did not go as far as he would like—much had been eliminated from the Covenant he had drafted—"if we had not accepted what we have here we would not have a League of Nations."

After breakfast the next morning in his railroad car, Wilson resumed his conference with Colonel House, who showed the president various reports that had been prepared to inform him of matters to be faced immediately on his arrival in Paris.[9] The president also took time to discuss his bitter experience in Washington. He complained of the insulting manner in which he was treated by certain senators on their visit to the White House, describing how Philander Knox and Henry Cabot Lodge had remained perfectly silent, refusing to ask questions or to act in the spirit in which the dinner was given. Attempting consolation, House said that he considered the dinner a success because it had dispelled criticism of the president's supposed dictatorship and refusal to consult the Senate about foreign affairs. Conscious of Wilson's darkened mood, however, House noted that "The President comes back very militant and determined to put the League of Nations into the Peace Treaty."[10]

Since numerous historians of the period concede that Edith's reminiscences are not always reliable, some skepticism should be expected in regard to her account of the House/Wilson meeting upon the president's return to France. Instead, House's own account is dismissed as inconsequential.[11] The possibility is scarcely entertained by historians of the period—with Arthur Walworth among the rare exceptions—that Edith Wilson's version might be a partial if not gross invention. She could not acknowledge the realities or legitimacy of other people's views or accept less than reverence for her husband and his purposes. Edith, psycho-neurologist Dr. Edwin A. Weinstein has written, was given to invention and untruth when she was under stress.[12]

Undoubtedly her refusal to recognize Wilson's faltering powers warped her memory of an increasingly unsympathetic French and British press and a rebellious U.S. Senate and provoked her lament that there was "all to do over again." Possibly, as Arthur Walworth suggests, the failure of the League to attract the political support essential on both sides of the Atlantic stimulated Mrs. Wilson's inclination to make a scapegoat of House.[13] The American president who now traveled up to Paris was merely the equal of three other prime ministers, who expressed growing impatience with his little "sermonettes" on issues that they had fought for on the battlefield during the years Wilson proclaimed himself too proud to fight.[14]

Rather than hold Wilson in any way responsible for his beleaguered position, Edith charged his deputy Colonel House with having surrendered her husband's gains during Wilson's four-week absence. She ignored that Wilson's position had been critically modified by intervening circumstances. The changed attitude of the conference had been fully reported to Wilson not only in House's cables but, also, by accounts he had received of the meetings at the Quai d'Orsay from members of the Commission to Negotiate Peace. It does not appear that House was culpable of fatal and binding decisions regarding the League. On the contrary, he was properly deferential, as reflected in his cable of March 4, which assured the president, "By the time of your arrival all questions will be ready for your approval."[15]

An insight into House's true role during the interim period that loomed so darkly in Edith Wilson's *Memoir* was provided by David Lloyd George. The British prime minister wrote that he could give no better idea of the variety and scope of the conversations that took place outside the council chamber than by publishing "Notes of an interview between M. Clemenceau, Colonel House and himself held at the Ministry of War, rue Dominicq, at 10:30 A.M., 7th March, 1919." Discussion was far-ranging, including the subject of peace with Germany, its navy, and the question of indemnity. When House was asked whether America would contribute to a permanent army of occupation, "he expressed great doubts but said he would put it to the President." When pressed for America's view about taking a mandate for Armenia and Constantinople, House replied "that America was not in the least anxious to take these mandates, but that she felt she could not shirk her share of the burden."

Despite their significant content, Lloyd George wrote, "talks of this kind did not represent final agreements between the principal delegates of France, the U.S.A. and Great Britain, or even definite conclusions at which any one of them had individually arrived." Another defender of House was General Tasker H. Bliss, the military representative of the United States on the Supreme War Council, who dismissed rumors that House had neglected to protect the League while the president was at home as being "without grounds of support."[16]

Far from being isolated in her opinion, however, Edith had numerous supporters among Wilson's uncritical followers who helped propagate her hostile judgment of House. "They've double-crossed the Chief, " Frank I. Cobb of the New York *World* would tell his wife.[17] For decades historians have echoed Edith's account of House's betrayal of Wilson, his habit of compromise, and his vanity. More obliquely, they undermine him with faint praise. Grayson spoke of House as a quiet, modest, unassuming, clearheaded man whose face was "unmarked and unseamed by heavy lines of thought."[18] Ray Baker, Wilson's press officer in Paris and subsequent biographer, allowed that House was as truly liberal as the president and a loyal supporter of the League of Nations, but that "there was nothing hard, clear, sure, definite, in his intellectual processes." The colonel, Baker concluded, "would make peace quickly by giving the greedy ones all they want."[19]

Baker wrote emphatically of the coldness that grew between the president and House from the time of their meeting at Brest.[20] The coldness, he said, was not due to trivial personal differences or small jealousies, as popularly reported; although it did have personal and trivial aspects, it was based on far deeper failures. Baker, in truth, loathed House. Privately, the journalist dismissed him as superficial and unimportant, a bright, lively little man, optimistic in the presence of tragic events—in contrast to Wilson, the serious man of the conference, gray, grim, and lonely, fighting a losing battle against heavy odds.[21] Dismayed by Baker's generally flawed and prejudiced history of the era, which was eventually disseminated in multiple volumes, Winston Churchill would find it disquieting "to think how many conscientious citizens of the United States must have drunk from his infected fountain."[22]

Contrary to Baker's account, the jealousies were not irrelevant but insidious, and immensely influential. The president's shrunken inner circle would seal him off from the very problems of the Peace Conference that House had tried tactfully to convey. David Lloyd George was keenly aware that House had his rivals and enemies in the American camp who resented the position accorded to him.[23] House, in Lloyd George's opinion, was like an accomplished family lawyer, thoroughly loyal to his client, about the only man really trusted by Wilson himself, who was chronically beset by misgivings about his fellow beings. "The voice of House was the voice of Wilson" until repeated insinuations of the colonel's disloyal and willful decisions gradually but relentlessly crippled the relationship between the two men. As Lloyd George saw it, "The president was intensely jealous of his personal authority. He had at least one divine attribute: he was a jealous god."[24]

The canny and observant White House usher, Ike Hoover, in speaking of the "cabal," specifically mentions envy and jealousy motivating those who conspired against House. Hoover was surprised at how well the conspirators worked in consensus. He implicates a third party and "sad to relate" one who had unlimited access to the president's mind and understanding. Though he does not name him, he can be referring to none other than Dr. Cary Grayson. The physician is repeatedly cited as the source of some of the most potent arguments against Colonel House and his "efforts to separate the covenant from the treaty."[25]

In early June, when Grayson would complain to Lansing that "things were certainly muddled," he said that House was to blame: he had always advised giving up for the sake of harmony whenever hard-pressed. "He is certainly a great little agreer all right," Grayson told Lansing.[26] Grayson's remarks fell on the receptive ears of the secretary of state, sensitive to his exclusion from the Wilson inner circle. Embittered and frustrated, Lansing incorrectly assumed that House had proposed Wilson's coming to Europe and privately accused the colonel, along with the president, of pride of authorship of the League of Nations when, in fact, both General Jan Smuts and Lord Robert Cecil had initiated the concept.

There is no evidence whatever of Grayson's presence at the meetings on which he vividly reports. Grayson's source was likely Mrs. Wilson, if not the journalist Herbert Bayard Swope of the New York *World*, or the physician's close friend Bernard M. Baruch. None of these was known to be friendly to House.[27]

*   *   *

Compared to the bleak December journey from Brest to Paris, the countryside in mid-March appeared to Edith "a vast paradise." The grass was green, the cherry trees and flowers were in bloom, and her first feeling on arrival at their new residence in Paris was that people had been happy in that house. This she took as a good omen. She admitted that her spirits needed lifting in the spring of 1919.[28]

The house, which she described as more homey than the palace of Prince Murat, was 11 place des États-Unis. The vast, splendid, mid-nineteenth-century mansion had been built by a Second Empire tycoon, the banker and patron of the arts Ferdinand Raphael Bischoffsheim.[29] L'Hôtel Bischoffsheim, lent by family descendants to the Wilsons, included a ballroom imported from a palace in Naples, painted ceilings and paneling, mirrored walls, period furniture, marble statuary, Renaissance bronzes, works by Rembrandt and Rubens, Frans Hals and Géricault, among other artists, and a spiraling white marble main staircase carpeted in red.[30] The second-story ballroom was soon transformed into an office.

As House candidly acknowledged, he had arranged for Wilson to meet with David Lloyd George and Clemenceau in his own rooms at the Crillon on the afternoon of the president's arrival because he wanted to keep his hand on the situation. From three to five o'clock, the discussion centered on the crucial French–German boundary question and the amount of reparations Germany should be forced to pay. An impatient witness, House wrote that the prime ministers skirted around the different questions long enough for him to vow to settle them, troublesome as they were, "that same week, if possible."[31]

Grayson's version of the meeting, from which he was absent, was exceedingly unflattering to House and has been widely quoted by partisan scholars. According to the physician's diary, Wilson, on the afternoon of March 14 at the Crillon, was told by Lloyd George and Clemenceau that they and their colleagues in the inner council, in which House sat by Wilson's direction, had mapped out a program calling for "the sidetracking of the constitution of the League," and that "Colonel House had practically agreed to the proposition."[32] Wilson, already alerted by House's telegrams and letters to high feelings over the peace treaty, which were now confirmed in these disillusioning talks with Clemenceau and Lloyd George, decided that he must again clarify the American goals. His concern was certainly heightened by one of Joseph Tumulty's numerous cables during this period, advising Wilson "your most critical time in setting forward America's position at the conference has come. Opposition to League growing more intense from day to day. Its bitterness and pettiness producing reaction."[33]

The purpose of Wilson's statement to the press, dictated to Ray Baker on the morning following the Crillon meeting, was to rescue without delay the League of Nations "so compromised by Colonel House during his absence," as Edith stated in her *Memoir*. Wilson authorized the statement that there had been no change in the original plan for linking together the League of Nations and the peace treaty in accordance with the decision made by the Peace Conference at its plenary session of January 25, 1919, "and there is no basis whatever for the reports that a change in this decision was contemplated."[34] Wilson's statement was posted at American headquarters and then circulated to all other delegations. Edith relates with satisfaction that "the statement caused a sensation."[35]

The president also sent a cablegram to Tumulty in Washington announcing that "the Plenary Council has positively decided that the League of Nations is to be part of the Peace Treaty; there is absolutely no truth in any reports to the contrary."[36] On March 16, in response, France's foreign minister, Stephen Jean Marie Pichon, called in representatives of the foreign press and declared that the Covenant could not under any circumstances be made a part of the peace treaty. Possibly, he said, the principle of the League might be stated in some general way in the peace treaty, but certainly not the League as a whole. Chaos ensued. Under pressure, Pichon declared himself misunderstood; Clemenceau sent a soothing message; and Tardieu, the military adviser, after talking with House, made the rounds of the press and prevented Pichon's statement from being printed. The situation was now reversed: the Covenant was once more to be included in the treaty, but with some redrafting and with consideration given to amendments proposed by American senators.[37]

Wilson's study became the daily meeting place of the so-called Big Four (named the Olympians by the *Daily Mail*), comprising Clemenceau, Lloyd George, Orlando, and Wilson. The room, hung with huge maps on which new boundaries were to be traced, bustled with experts passing in and out of the study and up and down the stairs. Pressure was on the president to satisfy domestic demands in the United States without impairing the League's structure; another task was to meet foreign opposition. Increasingly disheartened by French intransigency, Wilson told Edith that the French were behaving so badly that he really thought they wanted to begin the war again: that they wanted to do in reverse what Germany had done in 1870—that is, to annex some of that country.[38]

Sessions lasted far into the night. Nothing ever stayed settled; new issues arose at every moment, with "every problem supposedly decided requiring reconsideration."[39] Edith saw her husband, with rare exceptions, only at meals, or when she sat in his office while he was writing letters home. He seemed to grow thinner and grayer as he remained determined to hold the delegates to their pledge to incorporate the League Covenant into the peace treaty and to achieve a formula for acceptable amendments. What Edith refers to as "the dread disease" therefore struck with some warning.

CHAPTER 22

Wilson suffers a "flareback"

Wilson was being treated for a cold. He had already suffered much pain in his left eye and his nose, and Grayson had diagnosed an abscess developing in his nostril. During the four or five days prior to his physical collapse on April 3, the president's actions appeared erratic at times as he reversed his positions on salient issues. On March 27, he surprised House by deciding to accept Clemenceau's demand for a separate security treaty between France and the United States. A few days later, Wilson proved equally unpredictable to his fellow commissioners when he agreed to the Anglo-French scheme for reparations. Also, he unexpectedly declared that he did not feel bound by considerations of logic or compelled to settle matters in accord with strict legal principles. On March 28, by virtually all accounts, the president, visibly worn and extremely impatient, could not resist the opportunity to tell the French ambassador to the United States just what he thought of him. This was the day of a notorious row between Clemenceau and Wilson over France's claim to the left bank of the Rhine.

On the following day, March 29, Wilson officially agreed to France's annexation, pending a plebiscite to be held in fifteen years, of the valuable Saar coal mines, in recompense for Germany's destruction of France's northern coal mines during the war. A day later, Wilson was "vituperative and rigid" in his reaction to the British journalist Henry Wickham Steed's suggestions for compromise on that issue. A stormy conference on the morning of April 2, concerning the Polish army transport problem and French restrictions on German couriers, so completely disturbed the president that Edith Benham said she had never seen him "so irritated, so thoroughly in a rage." House, who conferred frequently with him by private telephone, commented that Wilson, never a good negotiator, was becoming stubborn, angry, and unreasonable, and that nothing was being run coherently. A commission to Syria, though appointed, was still awaiting instructions, as were innumerable other matters. "It could be done so easily that it is maddening," House wrote on April 1, "to see the days go by and nothing decided."

Secretary of State Robert Lansing, depressed himself, told friends that the high hopes for the Covenant were vanishing and that "black pessimism broods over Paris." Unless the Germans were summoned to the council table, there would be no German government with which to make peace. Meanwhile, Bolshevism was becoming the refuge of despair, and moderate elements of society were growing radical while radicals were becoming bitterly hostile to governments that did not give them peace. Noting the mounting military strength of Great Britain, the United States, Serbia, and Russia, Lansing wrote to John Davis, American ambassador to the Court of St. James, "the effectiveness of the League of Nations, as a preserver of peace may at least be viewed with skepticism."[1] Lansing feared that "so much time has been given to get the bandage ready that the patient might bleed to death" before it was applied.[2]

On Thursday, April 3, Wilson spoke by telephone with House about his conversation with André Tardieu regarding the Saar Valley. At 2 P.M. Wilson conferred with King Albert of Belgium and then resumed an earlier meeting with the English and French premiers. Toward evening Wilson could continue no longer. He fell violently ill at six and coughed so intensely that he could barely catch his breath. Running a fever of 103 and plagued with diarrhea, Wilson spent one of his worst nights in Grayson's memory. When word spread that the president had been ordered to bed, supposedly with a cold and sore throat, cynics suggested that he might be suffering instead from a diplomatic illness as an antidote to fruitless discussion; or that the presidential collapse might be interpreted as a warning to his colleagues.

The next morning, aware of the gravity of the president's condition, Grayson faced the question of what should be said to the public. Wilson, it turned out, had no objection to Grayson's announcing that he was sick in bed. In fact, he advised that this be done, since he did not want to be thought of as quitting when only the fact that he could not sit up prevented him from continuing the work of the Peace Conference. By April 5, his temperature had dropped to 101, and he showed signs of improvement, though his bronchial tubes were filled with mucus and he wheezed as he breathed. Grayson, who had first thought the president was ill from food poisoning, told the press that Wilson had come very near to having a serious attack of the prevalent and dangerous influenza, but, by going to bed, had apparently escaped it.

Too ill to continue at this critical juncture of the talks, Wilson appointed House—again to Secretary of State Robert Lansing's intense humiliation—to sit in for him as the Council of Four resumed their meetings. This was done at the suggestion of David Lloyd George, who reasoned that if Lansing was present, the foreign ministers of all the other countries would deem it their duty to attend. There was of course the possibility that Lloyd George preferred House not only because he had already worked with him and respected him, but also because he dismissed Lansing as "a mere cypher." The most significant aspect of Wilson's appointment of House touches on the question of the feelings between the two men. That the president was willing to entrust House with his chair at the negotiations strongly indicates that their relations were far from the shambles described by Edith Wilson following their encounter at Brest.

On April 7, ill in bed, Wilson precipitated an acute diplomatic crisis by insisting that orders be cabled to the Navy Department at Washington to return the SS *George Washington* to Brest at once. The president was said to call for his ship from frustration that his Fourteen Points were steadily being eroded by the French and British. He was weary of what he considered the needless discussion of petty details and the constant shifting of positions, so that the gains of one day were lost the next. When the news spread, skeptics said he was "going home to mother," and that his departure would provoke "a great sigh of relief."

Wilson rescinded his order almost immediately. He changed his plans, Edith said, because statesmen large and small entreated him to remain, and small nations looked to him as their one hope. Once more it was apparent that, without the president and the fight he was making for a just peace, the treaty would be less acceptable. If there was still a chance for terms he could sanction, Wilson did not intend to leave Paris.[3] According to Grayson, the SS *George Washington* incident had a "castor oil effect" and more progress was made within two days following Wilson's order than in the previous two weeks. Although Wilson's call for his ship had been made on petulant impulse, the gesture was generally thought to have been effective.[4] Lansing believed that the president's order for departure had sent cold shivers down the spines of illustrious statesmen. "A withdrawal at this time," Tumulty cabled Grayson, "would be a desertion."[5]

Though Wilson was well enough to hold a meeting at his house on the place des États-Unis on April 8, Edith maintained her vigil. Her concern over his depleted health—she had seen him utterly spent by his burning fever—was further agitated by an increasingly hostile press. American newspapers, reflecting the recent Republican senatorial debacle, attacked the amendments to the League Covenant. One afternoon when President Wilson had gone to Lloyd George's apartment, Edith opened a newly arrived batch of newspapers from home to read the Philadelphia *Public Ledger*'s reprint of Henry Wickham Steed's editorial in the April 7, 1919, London *Times*.

"In so far as there is a real improvement in the prospects of the Conference," Steed believed it to be "attributable chiefly to the practical statesmanship of Colonel House, who, in view of President Wilson's indisposition, has once again placed his *savoir faire* and conciliatory temperament at the disposal of the chief peace makers." Furthermore, during the absence of Mr. Lloyd George and President Wilson, House, "who has never found difficulty in working with his colleagues, because he is a selfless man with no personal axe to grind, brought matters rapidly forward. The delay that has occurred since the return of President Wilson and Mr. Lloyd George has been due chiefly to the upsetting of the good work done during their absence." In conclusion, "if there is now a chance that the Conference may be hauled back from the brink of failure on to relatively safe ground," Steed maintained, "it is mainly due to the efforts of Colonel House and to the salutary effect of the feeling that the Allied peoples are becoming seriously alarmed at the secret manipulations of their chief representatives."[6]

As Edith interpreted Steed's article, the sole constructive work of the American delegation had been done in her husband's absence while Colonel House, she writes in her *Memoir*, was in charge as "the only brains of the Commission." Just then a tap at her door interrupted her thought, and Colonel House appeared. He was there to see the governor, as he always called the president, and finding he was out, House thought they might talk until Wilson returned. Feeling he would be as distressed as she was over the article she had just finished reading, Edith picked it up and asked, "Colonel, have you been reading these awful attacks on Woodrow, or have you been too busy?" She read several paragraphs aloud. The colonel's face turned crimson and he asked, "Has the Governor seen that article?" "No, it has just come," she replied, "but did you ever know of anything so outrageous?" The colonel sprang up, took his coat in one hand, held out the other, and said, "Please let me have that to read—after all I will not wait for the Governor." "Why," Edith recalled saying, "I thought you said you wanted to see him!" By this time House had reached the door, through which, she wrote, he fled as though pursued.[7]

Shortly afterward, Dr. Grayson arrived and she told him of the funny way in which the colonel had acted. Grayson said, "everyone is talking about these articles and the gossip is that House's [son-in-law] Gordon Auchincloss is inspiring them on the Colonel's behalf. Several of our friends among the newspaper people have told me that the man who writes these articles is always in the Colonel's room and gets all his tips from him."

When Edith told Wilson about the paper, his answer was "Oh! I am sorry you hurt House—for I would as soon think of doubting your loyalty as his." Recalling this incident, Edith insisted, as she had in regard to other crucial passages in her life, "I have told this exactly as it happened for it is stamped indelibly on my memory . . ." She said her husband believed that House had shown the gravest error in judgment during the time of their return to America, and that Wilson saw his deputy's "capitulation" during those weeks as evidence of weakness and lack of backbone to stand up against men with whom he preferred to be on intimate terms. That conduct, Wilson held, according to Edith, never involved personal vanity or disloyalty to Wilson himself, or to the cause he had at heart. In response to Edith's pronouncement that House was "a perfect Jelly fish" for not standing firm, Wilson replied, "God made Jelly fish . . . don't be so hard on House. It takes a pretty stiff spinal column to stand against all the elements centered here."

Some weeks later, when Edith was herself ill with a badly infected foot, the colonel sent her a cluster of her favorite orchids, for which she thanked him by telephone.[8] "Strange as it may seem," she said, that afternoon when the colonel fled from her sitting room was the last time they spoke, "and absolutely the last time he ever came to our house except for formal meetings where many others were present and I never saw him."

Dr. Grayson was concerned that Wilson's illness could be treacherous, especially in the Parisian climate. His fear of the president's suffering a "flareback" was soon realized. Though the medical records have been destroyed, evidence suggests that, less than three weeks after his earlier bout of illness, "something very serious did happen to Wilson . . . so serious that, at times, it rendered him incompetent."[9] Based on documents of the original diagnoses, doctors have concluded that he suffered some kind of vascular accident,[10] probably a small stroke, on or about April 28. That was precisely the period of stormy negotiations over Italy's campaign for Fiume, the Adriatic seaport of northwest Yugoslavia, a campaign that Wilson emphatically vetoed; and of Japan's demand to retain the already captured former German province of Shantung in China, to which Wilson painfully acquiesced.

According to Grayson—his only reference to this illness surfaces in connection with a medical report written on October 15, 1919, but revealed only in 1991—Wilson was "subjected to a terrific strain in Paris." As a result of lack of exercise, work in ill-ventilated rooms, and unfavorable weather conditions, "general physical impairment" developed, which, Grayson concluded, "prevented him from obtaining his usual sleep."[11] Even fifteen years after the fact, Grayson was unable to admit to Wilson's illness. Asked at lunch by David Lloyd George if it was true that Wilson had suffered a stroke while in Paris, the doctor said, "Definitely not." The president had only a touch of influenza, which he had caught from Clemenceau; and the slight twitching of his face, Grayson insisted, was the remains of a nervous condition from which Wilson had suffered years before, and which eventually showed under great strain.[12]

Dr. George De Schweinitz, Wilson's ophthalmologist from Philadelphia, was "commissioned," together with Dr. John Chalmers Da Costa, to examine the president in April in Paris with reference to a neurologic episode. Dr. Da Costa, professor of surgery at the Jefferson Medical College in Philadelphia, and a lieutenant commander in the Naval Medical Corps, initially denied that he was rushed to Paris to examine Wilson. Instead, he said, he went to see the president on April 24 to pay his respects. However, the New York Times, as well as the papers in Da Costa's personal files, attests that the surgeon had made the trip to Paris specifically to treat the president.[13] Dr. Malford Wilcox Thewlis, a neuropsychiatrist who saw Wilson at that period, probably on April 29, visited the president "on the sad day he wakened with a little stroke so destructive that it had made of him a changeling with a very different personality and a markedly lessened ability." Wilson had told Dr. Thewlis that morning that his hands were so shaky he was unable to shave himself. Later, Grayson admitted to the author Gene Smith that Wilson had several minor strokes before he left Paris.[14]

Wilson was afflicted with hypertension (high blood pressure) at a relatively early age—causing small strokes in 1896 and 1906, and until the middle of his presidency—which can account, Dr. Bert E. Park has written, "not only for virtually all aspects of his poor health, but also for more of his later behavioral and cognitive changes." The disease not only affected his conduct but predisposed him to what is now conclusively diagnosed as a cerebrovascular accident in late April 1919, and his devastating large-vessel atherosclerotic strokes in September and October of the same year.[15]

Historians have generally supposed that Wilson's health had little impact on his thinking during his few days in bed. After his quick recovery, he was said to work with his normal drive and acuity, with the possibility of one mistake during this period of his illness. This "might have been to appoint Colonel House to represent him on the Council of Four," when he fell ill during the first week in April—a judgment that the Princeton University editors of Wilson's papers now acknowledge as "a subjective editorial comment."[16] His chronic elevations of blood pressure might conceivably account in part for his becoming more and more secretive, suspicious, and defensive, for his impaired memory and judgment, for his being unreasonable and fussy; and for much of his intransigence and personality transformation from 1918 onward. In the opinion of Supreme Court justice Louis D. Brandeis, Wilson began to break in the summer of that year.[17]

The use of official automobiles by the staff unexpectedly infuriated Wilson; he blamed House for the French servants who, he claimed, were spying on him; and he buried in a strongbox some of the papers he normally kept in his desk. After lunch one day, he complained that the red and green furniture was all mixed up and asked Grayson for his assistance in rearranging the reds in the American corner, the greens for the Britishers, and the odds and ends in the center for the French, together with a high-backed, purple-covered chair that looked to him "like a Purple cow strayed off to itself." Dr. Grayson noted how pleased and relaxed Wilson became after they repositioned the furniture.[18] By June 1919, even House, usually somewhat reverential in his comments on Wilson, spoke of the president as "one of the most difficult and complex characters I have ever known. He is so contradictory that it is hard to pass judgement upon him."[19]

Wilson's illness might also explain certain of his political and diplomatic blunders—his earlier deliberate choice of a nearly one-party commission to the Peace Conference, his relative disdain for detail, his lack of sensitivity and consideration for others, including Lansing, during the entire conference, and toward House during its latter half.[20] His stark black-and-white perception of the Peace Conference as a crucial debate between moral America and the wicked, self-interested English, French, and Italians (he could not recognize that Clemenceau in particular was terrified of another war) had threatened his success from the start.[21] The most astonishing change in his behavior following his acute illness, in the opinion of neurologist and historian Dr. Edwin Weinstein, was the reversal of his attitude toward the Germans. [22] The day before he was stricken, on April 2, Wilson objected to the introduction by Lloyd George and Clemenceau of a resolution to bring the former German emperor to trial because, he reasoned, a dangerous precedent would be established if the victors in a war were also the judges. The day after he returned to the meetings, he opened with a resolution to bring the ex-kaiser to judgment for "a supreme offense against international morality and the sanctity of treaties."

That Woodrow Wilson fell ill in April did not surprise his European colleagues. Given his personality and the strained circumstances, they believed his physical collapse in the middle of the conference was almost inevitable. The reversals he had endured since his initial reception were radical and defeating. The intoxicating grandeur of his original welcome (streets named after him, applause from the crowds, in the press, in the Chamber of Deputies) had all but evaporated in a blizzard of criticism that must have withered his self-confidence. Despite Wilson's apparent calm and impassive countenance, Lloyd George judged him to be an extremely sensitive man and felt that there was no knowing what pain he suffered from the rancorous disparagement of his opponents in America or from spiteful caricatures in the Parisian press.[23]

Like all the European delegates, Lloyd George had frankly eyed the American president with "a measure of suspicion not unmixed with apprehension." The British prime minister believed Wilson to be inexperienced, untrained, and untutored in the vagaries of foreign political life, unable to allow for differences of tradition, language, antecedents, temperament, and environment. Ultimately, Wilson had to learn that the chronic troubles of Europe could not be settled by hanging round its neck the phylacteries of abstract justice. Abstract principles did not settle frontiers that were so intricately involved, historically and traditionally.

When Wilson appeared at Europe's councils, he was there on equal terms, Lloyd George said, and his training had never qualified him for that position. Unlike Europeans, who had dealt every day during the war with ghastly realities on land and sea, Wilson appeared to be "soaring in clouds of serene rhetoric," to shun "the sight or study of unpleasant truths that diverted him from his foregone conclusions."[24]

Clemenceau, at seventy-eight, wrinkled, a fringe of white hair escaping his black skullcap, his hands gloved in gray suede, was amused by Wilson the idealist, so long as he did not insist on incorporating his dreams in a treaty that Clemenceau had to sign. If the president carried a dispute beyond what the French premier judged relevant, Clemenceau would open his great eyes in twinkling wonder and turn to Lloyd George as much as to say: "Here he is, off again."[25]

Unaccustomed to conferring with equals, Wilson found it exceedingly difficult to adapt—so the Europeans thought. Everywhere, he found that decisions based on his conception of right and wrong carried him away from a real settlement, and that practical expediency demanded compromise on every side and on every question. Compromise, which was the watchword of the entirety of the League's negotiations but anathema to Wilson, wrung an impassioned defense from Lloyd George. From his desk at the White House it all looked so easy. But the Old World was a different world. He could not measure accurately with his rigid yardstick—timber gnarled and twisted by the storms of centuries. Those who would say that President Wilson's exalted principles were somehow beyond their vision misunderstood the situation, Lloyd George answered indignantly. "We were just as truly there to frame a treaty that would not dishonor [the slain soldiers'] memory as was the President of the United States."[26]

Wilson's proprietary concept of the peace treaty and the Covenant was striking—and irritating. Queen Marie of Romania found Wilson "very convinced of always being right" and slightly patronizing, "certain that he will always have the last word, always intrenched in his superior, detached attitude."[27] Ambassador Jusserand described Wilson, in June 1919, as a man who, had he lived a couple of centuries earlier, would have been the greatest tyrant in the world "because he does not seem to have the slightest conception that he can ever be wrong."[28] John Maynard Keynes, who attended the Peace Conference as the representative of the British Treasury—resigning when it became clear to him that reasonable modifications would not be made to the peace treaty—provides, in *The Economic Consequences of the Peace,* published in 1919, an illuminating exegesis of Wilson's conduct, personality, and human limitations:

> There can seldom have been a statesman of the first rank more incompetent than the President in the agilities of the council chamber. A moment often arrives when substantial victory is yours if by

some slight appearance of a concession you can save the face of the opposition or conciliate them by a restatement of your proposal helpful to them and not injurious to anything essential to yourself. The President was not equipped with this simple and usual artfulness. His mind was too slow and unresourceful to be ready with *any* alternatives.[29]

Wilson's face, halfway through the conference, revealed to Lloyd George the wear and tear that ultimately ravaged and undermined his health and wrecked his cherished schemes and ambitions. "A disillusioned prophet is an abject spectacle," the British statesman concluded, as Wilson emerged out of the ordeal a shaken man.[30]

Cary Grayson began to follow and fill House's footsteps and, in meaningful ways, to replace the colonel, short of taking his place during the actual negotiations. Even though Wilson, during his illness in the first week of April, had officially appointed House as his substitute, Grayson made it a point, as he later revealed, to see Lloyd George after a meeting of the Big Four to ask him if he had any information to convey to the president. Grayson also boasted of his successful collaboration with Tumulty, against House's recommendation, to fill the opening left by the retiring attorney general, Thomas Watt Gregory.

The physician not only echoed Mrs. Wilson's discontent with House but reinforced it with his own adverse opinions of the colonel's words, motives, and actions. Grayson's diary, by means of snide observations and near accusations, portrays House as weak, sly, and even dishonest. House was the "Great American Acquiescor"; House was "naturally putty in the hands of the newspapermen when they get him to talk"; he was "not pulling squarely"; House's "YES, YES and NO, NO to Lloyd George and Clemenceau and Orlando had had a very serious effect in handicapping the President in dealing with these gentlemen." Colonel House's greatest success, Grayson concluded, "was when he was known as the sphinx. In the early days when the President utilized him for special investigations and other matters he was able to absorb the situation, return with it and explain it to the President and decline to talk for publication at all. The result was that his reputation for wisdom grew, as it always does when a man is known to be silent."[31]

On evenings when Edith Wilson worked on a crochet pattern and the president played Canfield and talked of "the decisions which may make or unmake the world," it was Grayson's role to read aloud published comments concerning the League.[32] As the president's confidant, he was dispatched on special missions, such as calling on Bernard Baruch at the Hôtel Ritz. When the president was too fatigued to brief his press officer, Ray Baker, and did not feel that he could recall the events of that day, he asked his physician to substitute for him: "You know briefly about what occurred. Won't you go out and explain the situation."[33]

The president's physician, as Wilson's trusted spokesman, was flattered that Charles H. Grasty of the *New York Times* asked him for editorial comment to cable back to the newspaper. Though he had been caustically critical of House's closeness to Steed and to other newsmen, Grayson himself now openly courted the press. He was in constant touch with the INS reporter John Edward Nevin and conferred with Grasty daily. He wrote Joseph Tumulty that he was spending all the time he could in guiding correspondents and showing them every attention.[34]

Grayson seems particularly to have appreciated Edith Wilson's tale of her encounter with House concerning the Steed editorial. Grayson returned to it in 1926 in an article called "The Colonel's Folly and the President's Distress," published posthumously—he died in 1938—in *American Heritage*, in October 1964.[35] Echoing Baker (or perhaps it was the reverse?), he noted that, while House's methods were adroit, diplomatic, and never corrupt, the colonel viewed himself as a sort of kingmaker who wished to exert power without incurring responsibility, who regarded politics as a game and delighted in moving the pieces on the board. Grayson claimed that too many trips to Europe, too much association with the great folk of the world, too much delegated responsibility, and too many adulators had spoiled the Colonel House of the early years of the Wilson administration.

Grayson had only highest praise for Edith Wilson: "She was a perfect angel."[36] Her detractors described her quite differently. Weary of her persistent talk about her Indian ancestry "proclaimed by the cockatoo feathers invariably waving from her hats and the clashing colors of the startling gowns she wears," one critic called her "Mrs. Sitting Bull."[37] But whether one admired or ridiculed her, that no one was more protective or solicitous of Wilson was indisputable. Her devotion to the president during his April illness enabled her to nurse him in a way that made professional help unnecessary. Her only thought was for his comfort; her days were shaped by Wilson's. If possible, she walked with him to his meetings, lunched and dined with him, and would not leave the house if there was a chance of inducing him to go for a stroll or a drive. The occasional respites included attendance at the horse races and a twenty-minute motor ride out of Paris to lunch with Bernard Baruch.

In her spare time, Edith kept up a chatty and concerned correspondence with her family. She also confided to her mother that May 7, 1919—a glorious spring day with fruit trees and purple and white lilacs in bloom—was somewhat of a disappointment. This was the day the peace treaty was presented to the Germans, and Edith had hoped to go to Versailles with the president to witness the presentation. However, space was available only for the delegates and five representatives of the press of each of the large countries and two of the small ones, and Wilson felt that it would be more tactful for her to forgo attending.

The Germans, given fifteen days to reply to the 214-page peace treaty, protested that the German government and people were unwilling to sign a treaty that they would not be able to fulfill.[38] They were not the only ones to quarrel that its terms were harsh and impractical. On May 22, the prime minister of South Africa, General Jan C. Smuts, warned England's Lloyd George that he would decline to sign such an unjust treaty, which the French, he said, had larded with needless humiliations and irritations. Eight days later, Smuts presciently informed Wilson that the treaty was "against the letter and spirit of your points," and that "this Peace may well become an even greater disaster to the world than the war was."[39]

Some days earlier, four members of the recently formed American Commission to Negotiate Peace—a kind of extension or subsidiary of the original peace delegation, which included the future historian Samuel Eliot Morison and future U.S. ambassador William C. Bullitt—resigned on principle from foreboding that the treaty was so punitive that it would make Germany eager for revenge. Another member, Lieutenant George B. Noble, wrote to Joseph C. Grew, secretary-general of the commission, on May 15, that he felt that the peace, as proposed, "will be an exceedingly dangerous settlement,—if it could be called a 'settlement,'—of world affairs . . . provocative of future wars, rather than a guarantee of world peace."[40] Bullitt sent Grew a copy of his note to the president saying that instead of arriving at a permanent peace based on unselfish and unbiased justice, the government, in his opinion, "had consented now to deliver the suffering peoples of the world to new oppressions, subjections, and dismemberments [leading to] a new century of war."[41]

Edith Wilson herself comments that on the matter of reparations, her husband believed France and England had gone too far. They had imposed indemnities beyond Germany's capacity to pay, especially in view of industrial restrictions that would hamper the defeated nation's economic recovery. Implying that this question had been discussed, she indicates that Wilson had assured her that all these matters would properly come before the League of Nations for adjustments "after the passions engendered by the War had cooled somewhat."[42]

The deadline for replying was extended as a new delegation of Germans continued, in Edith's word, to "haggle" over the terms, and to offer counterproposals to the disputed document. "Observations on the Conditions of Peace" were handed in by the German delegation on May 29, and the "Reply of the Allied and Associated Powers" was delivered on June 16. With no date set for signing the peace treaty, the Wilsons decided to accept the invitation of the king and queen of the Belgians for a visit on June 18 and 19. Traveling with a party of seven or more, which included Wilson's daughter Margaret and Herbert Hoover, Edith commented on the evidence of destruction in war-worn Belgium, noting the shattered library of Louvain and that Ostend was quite unlike the gay resort of her prewar visit.

After a German cabinet crisis, and a sharp ultimatum from the Allies, the signing of the treaty was set for Saturday, June 28—the fifth anniversary of the assassination of Archduke Ferdinand of Austria, and the date of the Wilsons' departure. Following intricate negotiations and insistent refusals, the president capitulated to the French president's invitation honoring him at the Élysée Palace two days earlier. Diplomatic interests having muted private grudges, the Wilsons rose to the elaborate occasion, their arrival in the palace courtyard heralded by rolling drums. Edith, aware of her husband's resentment of Poincaré's differences of opinion, gave scant attention to the dinner, attended by ambassadors and ministers of all the Allied countries, and the most illustrious members of French official circles. She did, however, leave a clear description of her dress from the designer Worth. With the sequin-embroidered heavy silk gown, shading from sparkling white to grays to black, ending in a fishtail train, she wore a tiara of sequins and rhinestones and a pin of diamond doves of peace given to her by the City of Paris.

Two days later, the Wilsons, with Dr. Grayson, left their temporary White House at two o'clock to stop at the Élysée Palace for a farewell visit to President and Madame Poincaré before traveling on to the Palace at Versailles for the signing of the peace treaty. The sun broke through clouds as they mounted the steps to the Hall of Mirrors, where the signing would take place. Wilson was followed by stalwarts of the original Peace Commission: Colonel House, General Tasker Bliss, in uniform, Robert Lansing, and Henry White. Clemenceau sat at the center, Wilson on his right, Lloyd George on his left. The delegates and press crowded the rest of the room, whose right extreme was reserved for distinguished guests. There, Edith Wilson shared the front seat, a tapestry-covered bench, with Mrs. Lansing and Mrs. House, while Edith Benham and Margaret Wilson sat farther back.

The silence was broken by the entrance of the Germans, who, in Edith's opinion, looked uniformly stolid and uninteresting. When the Americans were called upon to sign, Loulie House pleaded to stand long enough "to see my lamb sign." The president whispered afterward to Lansing, "I did not know I was excited until I found my hand trembling when I wrote my name." Walking back to their seats, Wilson smiled at his wife, and Henry White stopped, bowed to Edith, and passed on. By three-fifty that afternoon the last of the Allied and associated delegates had finished. The cannons roared. The war was over.

Despite his insistence that there was ground here "for deep satisfaction, universal reassurance, and confident hope," Wilson immediately touched on the problems of the peace treaty as well as the critical question of its acceptance by the U.S. Senate. In the statement addressed to "My Fellow Countrymen," cabled to Tumulty, the president said, "The treaty of peace has been signed. If it is ratified and acted upon in full and sincere execution of its terms it will furnish the charter for a new order of affairs in the world. It is a severe treaty in the duties and penalties it imposes upon Germany, but it is severe only because great wrongs done by Germany are to be righted and repaired; it imposes nothing that Germany can not do."[43]

House too was anxious about the peace treaty. It was "not the best in the world, but good enough for the purpose and probably as good as could have been done under the circumstances." He still thought that Root and perhaps Taft should have been among the commission members, not because they would have done better, but because their influence would have ensured good treatment in the Senate and inspired confidence in a larger number of people. "We are too close to the Treaty to judge it fairly. It is like looking at a painting with your face against it. Only time can demonstrate its virtues or defects," House wrote to Ralph Martin, the editor of *Life* magazine. [44]

*   *   *

That night all Paris was delirious.[45] People sang, danced, dragged cap-tured German guns through the streets, and reaped a rich harvest of sol-diers' caps as souvenirs. Lansing left the Hôtel Ritz at 9:15 P.M., after dining with the Paderewskis, to go to the Gare des Invalides to join French president Poincaré, Premier Clemenceau, General Pershing, Arthur Balfour, and the cheering crowd that waved the president and his party away on their journey. Half an hour later, the train steamed slowly out of Paris, to arrive in Brest near noon, Sunday, June 29. "The work of seven months finally accomplished," Grayson sighed.

A small tender carried the Wilsons to the SS *George Washington*, which was anchored outside the breakwater. Both were understandably weary. Wilson, pale and haggard, stumbled aboard. It seemed to his loyal Secret Service man Starling that the president lacked the coordination of mind and body that had always been his outstanding characteristic.[46] House concurred with Starling as he elaborated on his own painful situ-ation. Years later, moved by both loyalty and pride, House would tell a reporter that the president was not perfectly well in Paris or else the mischief makers could not have made trouble between them. When it was suggested that the three reasons for the estrangement in Paris were Mrs. Wilson, Cary Grayson, and Bernard Baruch, House cautioned against attributing to any one of these an ignoble motive. With the equanimity that so irritated the critics who disparaged him for being pli-ant and conciliatory, House reasoned that Mrs. Wilson, "like every wife, desired to shield her husband. She undoubtedly resented stories deliber-ately printed in order to cause dissension between her husband and myself."[47] House would speak of the "bedside cabinet" and its members, Grayson, Baruch, and Edith Wilson, who had desired to elbow him out because he was "too potent a factor."[48] He also said that he understood Edith's wish to be her husband's sole adviser. "There was in this the jeal-ousy which so frequently exists between a wife and her husband's best friend. She believed I was getting credit that belonged to her husband. I do not blame her."[49]

CHAPTER 23

A Congress "frothing at the mouth"

On an unusually cool, windy, exhilarating July 8, 1919, at the end of an unprecedented presidential absence, a procession of battleships, airplanes, and dirigibles hailed the return of President Woodrow Wilson and his wife, Edith, to American shores. If not precisely a conquering hero—since the reaction of Congress to the Versailles Treaty he had in hand was the urgent question—Wilson was welcomed as one. As tugboats nudged the SS *George Washington* into shallow waters at the Hoboken Army Dock, New York's governor and mayor, Alfred E. Smith and John Hylan, waited to accompany the couple through flag-festooned streets and cheering mobs to their first stop at Carnegie Hall. There, the president would assure his eager audience that it was "a wonderful thing for this nation, hitherto isolated from the large affairs of the world, to win not only the universal confidence of the people of the world, but their universal affection."

The Wilsons then boarded a train at Pennsylvania Station, arriving at midnight in Washington's floodlit Union Station. Standing on the sidelines, Alice Roosevelt—daughter of Theodore Roosevelt, the president's old political rival—took satisfaction in reporting to friends that the crowd that greeted Wilson was somewhat sparse: the sort of crowd that any president commands, but nothing special. She also rejoiced that there was little cheering. She and a friend hurried past the Capitol and up Pennsylvania Avenue, where Alice parked her car, stood on the curbstone, and noted that no more than three hundred people had followed the "sanctimonious" Wilson and his wife to the White House. Staring into the car as it passed through the gates, she crossed her fingers, conjuring a favorite imprecation of her childhood repertoire of black magic in prayer that Wilson might forever be plagued by evil tidings. Alice was heard to mutter aloud, "A murrain on him, a murrain on him, a murrain on him."[1] Even she might have felt a twinge, had she known that her darkest wishes would be fulfilled within three months.

"Princess Alice," the beautiful, poison-tongued daughter of Theodore Roosevelt, was even more disdainful than her father of Wilson's concept of "watchful waiting," and his laggardly entry into the recent war. Alice's dislike for the president's second wife was almost as vehement. She thought of Edith as a formidable-looking woman and spoke sarcastically of her huge, carnivorous-like orchid corsages, suggesting that she must eat them before going to bed.[2]

The rest and diversion on the boat had apparently done Wilson good. The president was quite himself again, in the view of Ike Hoover. Wilson seemed to feel that he had left many of his troubles behind, was looking to the future with confidence, and talked of returning to Geneva as the head of the League of Nations. His emphatic orientation to international problems was nevertheless an anxiety to those aware of dangerous domestic problems to be faced on this homecoming—a pending railroad strike, race riots and lynchings, and the consequences of prohibition. Despite the resolution against mob action adopted by the thirty-ninth convention of the American Federation of Labor, twenty-six blacks had been lynched in the United States between March and June 1919. Riots between whites and blacks had erupted in Georgia and South Carolina, and worse was soon to come in the heart of Washington.[3]

Viewed from Robert Lansing's perspective, Wilson's prospects seemed no easier. Lansing felt that Wilson was insufficiently prepared to face a Congress "frothing at the mouth in real or assumed rage," whose members were "licking their chops in anticipation of the full meal which they intend to make off the administration."[4] On the other hand, he allowed that, with the president seemingly never more pugnacious or bellicose than now, the meal might prove "rather indigestible when . . . served up."[5]

Edith Wilson, married nearly four years and now accustomed to European grandeur, was surprised by her pleasure in coming home. It was good to reach Washington, and to see the White House limousine, with Robinson at the wheel. It was reassuring to be surrounded once more "by the simple dignity of the White House, spick and span with cool linen on the chairs and flowers everywhere."[6] During the two years of U.S. participation in the war, the White House had been open to the public just ten times. Throughout the months of the Wilsons' absence, not a single member of the presidential family had been in town, not even "the wandering minstrel," the musical Margaret Wilson, nor "the pretty Wilson," Jessie Sayre.[7]

The Wilsons settled into a familiar schedule. They golfed at 8:30 A.M., lunched with members of the Bolling family, Professor Axson, or cousin Colonel Edward Thomas Brown and his wife, and the omnipresent Dr. Grayson. They took their daily automobile ride in late afternoon, rested, dined with family, and on occasion, went off to the latest musical at Keith's. For the first two weeks, it was like living in an inferno—the weather did not break until early August—and Edith spoke of most of *smart* Washington being out of town in the tremendous heat—"only the slaves of the people remaining to work,"[8] presumably herself and the president included.

On the morning of July 10—a torrentially rainy day less than forty-eight hours after his arrival in Washington—Woodrow Wilson met with approximately one hundred members of the press at a conference in the East Room of the White House before proceeding to the Capitol. He readily answered reporters' questions about trade relations with Germany, about Russia, about demobilization, about the Fiume and Shantung settlements, and about his plans for a trip west. He stopped short when asked if he would be willing to discuss criticism of Article X of the League Covenant, which committed the United States to "respect and preserve" the territorial integrity and political independence of all members of the League and to fulfill its obligation according to the decision of the Executive Council. "No," he responded, "only to say that if you leave that out, it is only a debating society, and I would not be interested in a debating society. I have belonged to them and have found them far from vital."

Standing before the Senate at noon, his tone seemed more conciliatory as he acknowledged possible skepticism among some of his audience, though only as a tentative aberration on the path to complete conversion. He was taking the earliest opportunity, he said, to lay the treaty before Senate members for ratification, a treaty that "constitutes nothing less than a world settlement." He mentioned the difficulties of grafting the new order of ideals on the old, but added that even the most practical and most skeptical had turned to the League as an "all but universal adjustment of the world's affairs." Statesmen, he continued, now found the newly planned League "as the main object of the peace, as the only thing that could complete it or make it worth while. They saw it as the hope of the world, and that hope they did not dare to disappoint. Shall we or any other free people hesitate to accept this great duty? Dare we reject it and break the heart of the world?" In conclusion he declared, "The stage is set, the destiny disclosed. . . . We cannot turn back. We can only go forward."[9]

On the following morning, the _New York Times_ reported, "Ovation to the President but Most Republican Senators Fail to Join in Applause." The disappointed audience of opponents and supporters had expected a masterpiece; instead of the raw meat they craved, a critic observed, Wilson had "fed them cold turkey." On finishing his speech, he had laid the bulky Versailles Treaty on Vice President Marshall's rostrum and left the Senate chamber "oblivious to the failure of his address."[10] He had failed to give arguments in support of the League or to explain obscure portions of the Covenant. He had failed to answer vital questions: Why was the Shantung Peninsula awarded to Japan when it is the Chinese Holy Land? What about the meaning of Article X? Why does Ireland's seven-hundred-year struggle for independence go unrecognized while Poland and Czechoslovakia are set up as independent states? How can the United States withdraw from the League? What mandates does the country assume?[11] The stage, as arranged by Wilson, was, obviously, far from set. Antagonized by the president's address, Senator Lodge would spend the next two weeks reading aloud in the meeting room of the Senate Foreign Relations Committee, before a negligible audience (eventually dwindled to a lone clerk), the entire text of the 268-page treaty—an effort that could be explained "on no other rational basis than a desire to play for time."[12]

Edith Wilson dismissed the querulous and even insulting reception on grounds that partisans were already at work, bent on the president's destruction by defeating the treaty at any cost. It was inconceivable to her that some people in Washington cared little "for the heart of the world or for Wilson either"; or that some people were so cruel as to scoff at him as the "haggard smiling object which crept into Washington," who seriously thought he could put the League of Nations through the Senate while ignoring that even its loyal supporters William Howard Taft and Charles Evans Hughes favored reservations.[13]

That Wilson began on Monday, July 14, to hold quarter-hour discussions with individual congressmen prompted speculation that he intended to be a little more liberal than in the past in granting appointments to members of the legislative branch. If so, the new policy was expected to win him considerable popularity at the Capitol, especially, it was said, among members of his own party, who often found themselves embarrassed because they were not able to go freely to the White House to talk the issues over.[14] That Monday night, the Wilsons paid a call at the French embassy, their only social venture since their return—a visit that, Edith thought, despite bitter differences in Paris, appeared to please Ambassador Jusserand, and which she herself seems genuinely to have enjoyed.

Wilson's plan to hold daily conferences with members of Congress had been in operation for only a few days when, on the weekend of July 18, he again fell ill. On that Friday, he was unwell when he went to the Capitol to confer with Senator Gilbert Monell Hitchcock, the ranking Democratic member of the Foreign Relations Committee and acting minority leader of the upper house. On Saturday night, when Wilson boarded the *Mayflower*, he was supposedly suffering from indigestion. Ill throughout the damp and stormy trip on the Chesapeake Bay and Potomac River, he also contracted a cold. He was ordered to bed on his return to the White House on Monday morning, his ailment now being described by Grayson and reported in both the *Washington Post* and the *New York Times* as acute dysentery rather than indigestion.[15]

Not for the first time, Dr. Grayson was protective of his patient and guarded, if not dissembling, about his physical state. Evaluation at a later date by Dr. Bert E. Park, a neurosurgeon and author of "Wilson's Neurologic Illness during the Summer of 1919," concludes—contrary to Grayson, and despite the lack, then, of accurate medical records—that it was "reasonably certain" that the president had again suffered a small stroke. Park also strongly suggests that Grayson, desperate to keep Wilson's condition secret, had hustled his patient aboard the *Mayflower* in spite of warnings of an impending storm. "Certainly being placed aboard ship in rough waters would not have been beneficial for a patient suffering from an upset stomach and diarrhea."[16]

Edith, like Grayson, tried to make light of her husband's illness. In answer to solicitous inquiries from Henry White, she assured the American commissioner in Paris that the illness was not serious, and that she thought it was the result of the long strain he had been under rather than the effects of the chilling weekend cruise. She stressed that he was in bed only one day, but even then he had had to work as things were even more hectic in Washington than in Paris, and twenty-four-hour days seemed too short for the disposal of the demands made upon him. Despite her reasonable explanation, she betrayed some pessimism about the situation. "Of course I believe it will all come right in the end, but the partisan spirit seems armed to the teeth—and it may take a long time to conquer."[17]

This exchange between Henry White and Edith Wilson was significant not only for its reference to the president's illness in July 1919, but also as evidence of Edith's increasing authority. White, in cultivating Edith's friendship—"august lady," he flattered her—was quite aware of its benefits in access to the president. In the previous May, White had written in confidence to Assistant Secretary of State William Phillips of his "very friendly relations" with Mrs. Wilson, whom he found "a very valuable channel of communication with the President." White also reported that he was on good terms with her secretary, Miss Benham. He had been surprised, he added, to find in Mrs. Wilson a much keener perception than anticipated "in respect to questions more or less complicated."[18]

In July, effusively apologetic for talking shop, but deliberately circumventing Dr. Grayson's order that Wilson be kept quiet, White told Edith that he hoped he did not cause interference by sending directly to her a long cablegram, "one alas of several recently," in urgent need of an answer. He ought to know immediately the position that Wilson wanted taken in the Council of Five relative to the claims of Bulgaria upon Western Thrace. Unclear in his own mind as to the wisest course, he awaited presidential enlightenment.[19]

In a sign of his debilitating health, Wilson had great difficulty with his address to a joint session of Congress on August 8. "One of the poorest on record," that lengthy and diffuse message on the cost of living was alternately cautionary and evangelical and vaulted unpredictably from food prices to international obligations. Perhaps the most striking and outwardly visible sign of the president's eroding faculties was his loss of memory, painfully apparent in a frustrating exchange of letters that prefaced his interview with members of the Foreign Relations Committee on August 19.[20] As chairman of the committee, Henry Cabot Lodge tried on July 15 and again on July 22, in an effort to clarify some points of the treaty, to pry relevant papers from Wilson.[21] On July 22 he specifically asked Wilson to send along the agreement with Germany, referred to in Article 237 of the treaty, regarding the distribution of German reparation payments, in the event that such agreement had been decided by the allied and associated governments. In a vague response—either having forgot or ignoring his own signing of such an accord on the past May 1, and a letter he had written to Lodge on the subject—Wilson said that an attempt was being made to reach such an agreement, but he had not yet learned of one "having been arrived at."[22] Increasingly forgetful, unable to recognize the necessity of accommodating the Senate's growing reservations, and obsessed with the need for the Senate's acceptance of the treaty "as is," Wilson was, by mid-August, "so set in his beliefs and his ways," according to the neurosurgeon Dr. Park, that "he had become a veritable caricature of his former self."[23]

Technical evaluation of Wilson's illness and its consequences both personally and for the nation—the "be-all and the end-all"[24] question of whether the president's impaired health had affected his judgment and, even more to the point, whether his underlying condition had led to overt disability as the nation's chief executive—would come later. Based on the ravages of Wilson's illness, his forgetfulness, his difficulty composing his speeches, his failure to acknowledge the reality of the opposition, Dr. Park would decide affirmatively on both counts. "That Wilson would lose his ability to shift reflectively with changing circumstances," Dr. Park concluded, "was an event of considerable significance for the United States and the world."[25]

Robert Lansing's testimony before the Senate Foreign Relations Committee on August 6 only bolstered Lodge's opinion that Wilson was "one of the most sinister figures that ever crossed the history of a great country."[26] Lansing had returned to his Washington office toward the end of July torn between "Duty Versus Inclination," as he entitled his lawyerly, pedantic, and confused analysis of his humiliating experience abroad. Among his memorandums of that period, one of August 2, 1919, was headed, "The Danger If the President Insists on Ratification Without Changes or Reservations." On August 11, he wrote, "No Compromise, No Ratification." Lansing could only hope that the president would realize that he could not by sheer dominating force compel the Senate, which was hostile to him personally, to accept this document. "Now is the time to catch flies with honey and to throw away the vinegar. Unfortunately," Lansing concluded, "the President seems to have no taste for honey."[27]

Lansing was questioned by the Senate Foreign Relations Committee for four hours on August 6 and for two and a half hours on August 11. Perceiving Lansing's lack of actual knowledge of the negotiation of the Covenant, the senators had reveled in his ignorance and blamed the president by innuendo for not consulting his secretary of state. "'I do not know' was his most frequent answer," the New York *Sun* reported. "We trust," the *Detroit News* said, "Mr. Lansing enjoyed the scenery around Versailles . . . while waiting the arrival of the American newspapers to read what the peace conference was doing."[28] British observers regarded his performance as a helpless confession of ignorance on important questions, "on second thought pitiable." It was hardly necessary to point out that these proceedings were really an attack on Wilson, their object to discredit him by showing that, for his principal minister, "he had chosen a man who in matters of the most supreme importance could be compelled virtually to admit ignorance and incompetence."[29]

Henry Cabot Lodge was in a testy mood. The president had not sent the documents he had repeatedly requested. Lansing appeared to know nothing about the treaty generally and was unable to add anything to what the Senate already knew. "The Shantung business," as Lodge referred to it, was even more troublesome. Lodge, who justly considered it morally indefensible, thought the ceding of Shantung to Japan dangerous in the last degree. Aggravating the situation was a secret agreement that France, Great Britain, and Italy had negotiated with Japan in which Japan had agreed to enter the late war and clear the Pacific of German fleets. Her reward was to be the German rights in Shantung, which meant giving her practical control of the railroad system of north and south China. Still worse, Lodge thought, was the letter from the British ambassador in Tokyo, agreeing to Japan's demands on the understanding that Britain acquire all the islands in the Pacific.[30]

It seemed to the senator that all the Allied nations had sought advantages in coming into the war. By contrast, Americans had wanted nothing except the defeat of Germany. With the five great powers in control, he concluded that the League was to be a "mere ornament," delaying and endangering the treaty. Unfortunately, the two were indissolubly linked. The United States was itself beset by labor problems, high prices, and the challenges of the newly enacted prohibition laws, and Lodge was wary of this invitation, in the form of the League, to plunge America into the troubles of Europe, including many questions that were, he felt, of minimal concern to Americans. Given the country's grave anxieties, he thought the treaty could not possibly be agreed to by the United States without strong reservations in regard to the League.

Frustrated, impatient, angered, Lodge was openly critical of the president in his letters to friends and colleagues. He wanted facts and information, rather than Wilson's opinions. Members of his committee were wearied by the president's chatter about "voices in the air" and "visions" and "lights on the path" and "the dawn of a new day." Lodge did not even believe Wilson capable of explaining his own treaty—not that any-one could, but least of all the president, of whom he said, "He has no mind for details. His mind is too large to think of them."[31] Meanwhile, Lodge had crystallized his own goal. "I am seeking to make the League safe for the United States and release us from obligation which might not be kept and preserve rights which ought not to be infringed," he wrote on August 18, the day before meeting with Wilson. The senator was inclined to think that when the League went into operation, if it ever did, it would be a helpless failure, except in paying large salaries to a large number of persons. He saw in it the threat of great dangers, and those "I wish our country to avoid."[32]

On August 14 members of the Senate Foreign Relations Committee voted to see Wilson at his convenience to discuss the treaty. Five days later, on August 19, the scene was extraordinary. "Nothing like it had ever happened before," wrote the newsman David Lawrence. The giant iron gates of the White House, locked during the greater part of the war, were thrown open to admit sixteen of the seventeen committee members.[33] The senators came in groups or individually, some in their motors and limousines, some on foot.

"Perhaps the most remarkable debate in Washington in many generations" began at 10 A.M. and lasted for three hours and twenty-five minutes. The committee members and six stenographers, five of the Senate's and the president's own Charles L. Swem, gathered in the East Room while nearly one hundred news correspondents were stationed in the room below.[34] The *New York Times* called it "epoch-making."[35] And no single event was as yet so revealing of the vulnerable president's diminishing faculties. He was found to have made "at least sixteen overt errors, misrepresentations, and self-contradictions" involving dates or documents he did or did not possess and concerning the secret agreement with Japan and her claim to Shantung, the fulfillment of international obligations under Article X, and questions on reparations. His mistakes did not pass unnoticed by Lodge.[36] Nor did his provocative message. The president did not object to interpretive reservations, but he was unalterably opposed to any substantive reservations or amendments—Wilson possibly exaggerating here the dire consequences of additional clauses that would require recommitting the treaty to the signatory powers.

Hoping that the present conference would expedite the senators' consideration of the peace treaty, Wilson gradually but inexorably found his way to the capital challenge of the meeting—the quicksilver issue of Article X, which, he stated, was "in no respect of doubtful meaning, when read in the light of the covenant as a whole." The United States would indeed undertake under Article X to "respect and preserve as against external aggression the territorial integrity and existing political independence of all members of the league." He reminded his audience, "That engagement constitutes a very grave and solemn moral obligation. But it is a moral, not a legal, obligation, and leaves our Congress absolutely free to put its own interpretation upon it in all cases that call for action. It is binding in conscience only, not in law. Article X," he added firmly, "seems to me to constitute the very backbone of the whole covenant. Without it, the league would be hardly more than an influential debating society."

The conference, said the *New York Times,* was characterized by an entire lack of antagonism on the part of the senators, and the president, throughout, and was the picture of amiability. Only when pressed on the issue of moral as opposed to legal obligations imposed upon the United States "did the Chief Executive appear to lose patience." "Not less binding; but operative in a different way because of the element of judgment" was his curt reply to Senator Warren Harding.[37] But civility did not signify agreement or capitulation. The president remained adamant. His intransigence was in fact a classic symptom of brain damage, leading to Dr. Park's fateful conclusion that "Wilson was impaired in the strictest medical sense of the word during the summer of 1919."[38]

Wilson was not unaware that he faced a dilemma, although he failed to envision or accommodate a practical solution. When Wilson had asked whether there was any change in the sentiment of the Senate toward the ratification of the treaty, Democratic senator Key Pittman had reported that the contrary was true—that the desire on the part of a number of Democratic senators to pass the treaty with reservations was steadily, if not rapidly, growing. Furthermore, if Wilson made any statement that revealed his own determination to have the treaty ratified without any reservations, Pittman predicted an immediate and definite alignment in the Senate and that "a number of Democratic Senators will come out openly for reservations."[39]

On the day after his conference with the senators, Wilson spoke with considerable heat to Lansing of his inclination to refuse to permit the United States to become a member of the League of Nations and "to throw up the whole business and get out,"[40] since the negotiating process depended on such intriguers and robbers. Again, the disturbing evidence of his petulance and eroding memory, his adamant refusal to make the one move that might break the impasse, and the reversal of his own recent stand on interpretive resolutions confirmed that Wilson's "biological clock was clearly winding down." He had indeed become "a veritable caricature of his former self."[41]

Diminished by illness, Wilson had long forgotten the wisdom of his youth. Otherwise, he might have been guided by his address of 1890, "Leaders of Men," where he had written that compromise was "the true gospel of politics" and had asked, "Do we not in all dealings adjust views, compound differences, placate antagonisms?" "Uncompromising thought," he had said, "is the luxury of the closeted recluse."[42] In 1908, eleven years before his struggle with the Senate, his comprehension of the coming rivalry was prescient:

> When, as sometimes happens, the Senate is of one political party and the President of the other, [the President] may himself be less stiff and offish, may himself act in the true spirit of the Constitution and establish intimate relations of confidence with the Senate on his own initiative, not carrying his plans to completion and then laying them in final form before the Senate to be accepted or rejected, but keeping himself in confidential communication with the leaders of the Senate while his plans are in course, when their advice will be of service to him and his information of the greatest service to them, in order that there may be veritable counsel and a real accommodation of views instead of a final challenge and contest.[43]

On August 28, Joseph Tumulty announced to reporters that the president would set out, on September 3, on a twenty-five-day trip to the West. Tumulty was not in favor of this trip. He saw, in the place of the vigorous, agile, slender, active, and alert man of earlier years, an old warrior who had not only grown grayer and grayer but grimmer and grimmer in his determination to fight to the end. It did not take a trained eye to see that the president was on the verge of a breakdown. Lansing too was distressed by Wilson's plans. For reasons of policy rather than presidential health, Lansing had one month earlier advised the president strongly against this speech-making trip, fearing that the senators would resent the seeming attempt to go over their heads to the people. However, permitting himself a glimmer of optimism, Lansing added that, if Wilson took the right tone in his speeches, "it may be all right, but if he does as he planned originally, that is go for Senators in opposition hammer and tongs, he will not help the cause."[44]

At this juncture, two people were more intimately aware of Wilson's vulnerable state. Neither his wife nor his physician wished him to go west. Exhausted by the protracted daily and weekly conferences, oppressed by Washington's deadening heat, Wilson was obviously a sick man. His face was drawn and pallid and he frequently twitched in a pitiful reaction to shattered nerves. Grayson did not think Wilson was strong enough to make it "without disastrous consequences" and in numerous talks pointed out the discomfort of a month of train travel, the perpetual strain of speaking and handshaking, and the endless luncheons, dinners, parades, and receptions. In response, the president said that it was his duty to go to the country and explain to the people what failure to ratify would mean; and to express his hope that an aroused public would force the Senate to yield.[45]

On August 29, Edward House read of Wilson's plans in a London newspaper. That House should learn indirectly about the president's planned trip said something about the declining relations between the two men. House wrote at once a courteous, thoughtful letter to wish the president well. From his perspective it seemed that hostility to the League in America was almost wholly based on Article X and its requirement that the United States defend the political independence of all members of the League at the decision of the Council. Wilson would best know after his tour, House continued, whether the American people responded to the argument that we were, for the first time, making order out of anarchy in international relations and laying down the principle that territory was no longer to be acquired by force of arms.

At the president's request, House had left for London to work with the commission appointed by the Peace Conference to draft definite conditions for the operation of mandates. Though long an advocate of the development of a system of international supervision of colonial areas, House, by July 15, had found the work "mere child's play" compared to what he had been through and was eager to go home. His letter of August 26 told Wilson of his plans to sail on the *Lapland* on September 16.

House also mentioned, in a postscript to his letter to Wilson, that "our annual falling out seemed to have occurred." This news, gleaned from colleagues and friends, did not surprise him, but its glaring amplification in newspapers posed a challenge that he meant to meet graciously. He was referring to the New York *Sun's* August 27 story, reported from Paris, proclaiming "Wilson-House Break Is Near." There was no open break, the story acknowledged, but for the first time the two men were no longer *en rapport* and the colonel had ceased to function as the president's unofficial diplomatic agent. Reasons given for his sudden effacement stemmed from the president's learning of the conditional agreement that the colonel had made in Wilson's absence with Premier Clemenceau and Prime Minister Lloyd George to postpone the League of Nations until peace had been made with Germany. Other purported offenses included House's poor advice on the Shantung decision and on negotiations with Italy.[46]

Wilson responded by cable on August 29 that he was deeply distressed over the malicious story about the break between them and advised, "The best way to treat it is with silent contempt."[47] Wilson's telegram of the previous day had brought disappointing instructions to House, asking him to remain abroad and proceed to Paris on grounds that it would be a mistake to return to America before the Senate ratified the treaty, since it might be construed as a breaking up of the American Mission. The colonel immediately cabled news of his changed plans to his son-in-law Gordon Auchincloss, as "an urgent request from earth" (presumably Wilson's code name) asked that House remain in Europe at least until after October. "He evidently does not relish the idea of my leaving with everything in such an uncertain condition," and of course House would do as the president wished.[48]

Auchincloss, independent, irreverent, and often indiscreet—he privately called Wilson the "White Father"—was loyally solicitous of House and suspected motives other than those described by his father-in-law. Anticipating Wilson's orders after speaking to Grayson and Tumulty, Auchincloss had already cabled House advising him against changing his plans, and expressing his belief that the president wished to delay House's return to prevent his being called to testify before the Senate. Auchincloss assumed, he assured House, that he would have no difficulty with the Senate, and that his testimony would have "a distinctly good effect."[49] Lansing was of similar opinion, that the president did not wish to have the colonel in Washington while the treaty was being considered by the Senate, and that his being summoned before the committee might prove embarrassing. However, Wilson was so insistent that House return to Paris until affairs there had crystallized that the colonel had to yield. He crossed the Channel on September 3, the date on which the president left Washington to tour the West.

Three months later, House was to be under siege again. In response to the sensation caused by a blistering attack from the partisan New York *World*, the London *Times* noted on December 12 that "both the State Department and the immediate entourage of the president are known to resent the friendship and confidence which Colonel House so long enjoyed in the highest quarter."[50] The *Times*, refuting the *World*'s "obvious misstatements and perversions," was eloquent in praise of House. In Britain, the *Evening Standard* assumed "it is quite natural that, when the President found that he was being severely criticized for the text of the Treaty, his displeasure should vent itself on the people who persuaded him to do the things for which he has been himself attacked."[51]

Wilson worked all day in preparation for his 7 P.M. departure on September 3. Before starting out, he conferred with Nebraska's Senator Hitchcock regarding the status of the treaty in the Senate, once more expressing his fervent hope that it would be ratified without any change requiring reconsideration by the Peace Conference. He also told Hitchcock of his emphatic intention to point out in all his forthcoming speeches that, if amendments or drastic reservations were made, they would lead to interminable delays and to eventual rejection of the treaty by the Allied powers. Should the United States be excluded from participation in the treaty, this country would be forced, Wilson feared, to make an individual peace with Germany.

Departing from Union Station, Wilson wore a white straw boater, a blue jacket, white trousers, and white shoes; Mrs. Wilson, dressed in navy, with a matching hat, smiled broadly. They were traveling on the private presidential railroad car, *Mayflower*, with Dr. Grayson; Wilson's secretary, Joseph P. Tumulty; Wilson's stenographer, Secret Service men, twenty-one newsmen, and five photographers. The possibility that this journey might have met the president's goal of bolstering the faltering peace treaty and the incipient League of Nations will always be in question.

Given the national atmosphere, and his own health, Wilson's decision to go to the American public over the heads of the Senate in September 1919 was irrational and "bound to be futile."[52] "It was Wilson's prideful belief," Samuel Eliot Morison has written, "that God and the people were with him—the hubris which in Greek tragedies always destroyed the proud—that led him to make a direct appeal to the electorate."[53] Weighing her husband's determination against her concern for his health, Edith admitted, "Neither Dr. Grayson nor I could find an answer."[54]

CHAPTER 24

Wilson's greatest publicity campaign

With each revolution of the wheels of the presidential train, Edith's anxiety intensified. As the *Mayflower* steamed onward—through the Middle West, across the northern plains and beyond the Rocky Mountains, over the Pacific Northwest, and down the Pacific slope, turning eastward at last—her husband seemed to grow thinner before her eyes, his headaches becoming more frequent and severe until, in one instance, he was almost blinded and saw double when he rose to speak in an increasingly husky voice. Edith hoped against hope that his distress would prove temporary, but he continued to lose his appetite. Because he was under such great nervous pressure, he could not even digest the little that he did eat, and Dr. Grayson fed him liquids and soft foods as Edith stood anxiously by. Soon he could not sleep, and in Montana, as a result of hot, dry weather and dust, developed a throat infection and an asthmatic condition, which the doctor sought to alleviate by spraying his nose and throat, often in the middle of the night.[1]

Edith's pride prevailed. In contrast to her fearful assessment of her husband's physical state, recorded in her *Memoir*, her report of his political prowess was overwhelmingly positive. She would hear only hyperbolic praise for his speeches and their reception, insisting, "It is no imagining on my part when I say that the crowds grew larger and more enthusiastic." Indifferent to discrepancies that might in any way impair Wilson's heroic image, she claimed that his first meeting in Columbus, Ohio, on September 4 "met with a tremendous response"—an assertion contradicted by Dr. Grayson, himself no mean apologist for the president. The doctor reported that a small attendance made the meeting "very unsatisfactory." He attributed the poor turnout to the Thursday-morning scheduling, a railway strike, and the fact that the president had spoken in the city before.[2]

Embarked on the greatest publicity campaign of his career, Wilson exhaustively defended the peace terms with Germany, the Shantung amendment, the searingly controversial Articles X and XI, and his interpretation of the Monroe Doctrine. Repeatedly he disputed Italy's claims in the Adriatic. From the outset, verdicts on his message were polarized. On September 3, the *Los Angeles Examiner* declared people weary of his "sentimental theorizing and glittering generalities"; tired of Europe and its affairs, they wanted food, money, and men at home. "The people wish that the Senate would take the Versailles treaty out on the floor, knock it in the head, join with the House in a declaration that the war is over, tell England, France, Italy and all the rest of the world to paddle their own canoes and so make an end of the whole tiresome business."[3] Wilson's supporters, on the other hand, were "elated beyond expression." They were astounded by the way the president could change his style to appeal to his audience and were convinced that his punches were "bound to tell."[4]

Wilson's range was undeniably remarkable. Professor, prophet, and impassioned circuit rider, he castigated the unruly, unobliging, and illiterate, conjured agnostics to see the light of the League, and complimented the devout. He even invited his audience to forget parties. In his present office he saw himself as much the servant of his Republican fellow citizens as he was the servant of Democrats. He was trying to be, he said, "what some gentlemen don't know how to be—just a simple, plain-thinking, plain-speaking, out-and-out American." Though he claimed to set aside party politics, the "pygmy minds" and "contemptible quitters" whom he denounced were undoubtedly affiliates of the Republicans.

His voice thick, suffering from a severe headache at the opening of the tour, Wilson assured audiences that he had long chafed at the confinement of Washington, long wished to fulfill his full-hearted purpose—to go out and report to his fellow countrymen about a document "unique in the history of the world." He professed himself astonished by certain statements about the treaty: the truth was these were made by persons who had not read it or had not comprehended its meaning and argued against it out of radical misunderstanding.

Wilson's unnamed target was ex-president Taft's secretary of state, Pennsylvania's Republican senator Philander Chase Knox, who had in recent days urged Congress to reject the Versailles Treaty because its terms with Germany were so harsh that they would only lead to even bloodier conflicts in the future.[5] In the president's defense of the treaty (severe but not unjust, as he saw it), its purpose was to punish "one of the greatest wrongs ever done in history . . . and there ought to be no weak purpose with regard to the application of the punishment."[6] As for those who feared unwanted obligations inherent in membership in the League of Nations, "if the treaty were wrong, that might be so, but if the treaty is right, we will wish to preserve right." He had not the slightest fear, given the purpose, that arms would be necessary.

On the evening of September 4, the *Mayflower* pulled into Indianapolis but waited outside its berth for half an hour until Wilson finished his dinner. At the Fairgrounds, the president implored an audience of more than sixteen thousand to comprehend Article X of the Covenant of the League of Nations: "Article X speaks the conscience of the world. Article X is the article which goes to the heart of this whole bad business. . . . You have heard it said, my fellow citizens, that we are robbed of some degree of our sovereign independence of choice by articles of that sort. Every man who makes a choice to respect the rights of his neighbors deprives himself of absolute sovereignty, but he does it by promising never to do wrong, and I cannot, for one, see anything that robs me of any inherent right that I ought to retain when I promise that I will do right."

Article XI was Wilson's favorite. "It says that every matter which is likely to affect the peace of the world is everybody's business, and that it shall be the friendly right of any nation to call attention in the League to anything that is likely to affect the peace of the world or the good understanding between nations . . ." In contrast to the present situation in which "we have to mind our own business," the situation would change dramatically. "Under the Covenant of the League of Nations, we can mind other peoples' business and anything that affects the peace of the world, whether we are parties to it or not, can be brought by our delegates to the attention of mankind."[7]

On Friday, at their third stop, Grayson hailed the president's lunchtime address before the St. Louis Chamber of Commerce as "exceptionally brilliant." Wilson, the fervent evangelist, assured his audience that he had heard gentlemen draw a distinction between nationalism and internationalism, and he did not follow the distinction. For him, the greatest nationalist is the man who wants his nation to be the greatest nation, and the greatest nation is the nation that penetrates to the heart of its duty and mission among the nations of the world. The nation that has that vision is elevated to a place of influence and power that it cannot get by arms, that it cannot get by commercial rivalry, but which it can get by that spiritual leadership that comes from a profound understanding of the problems of humanity.

In such a light he conceived it a privilege to discuss the great questions of the world. One was pan-Germanism and what lay between Bremen and Baghdad. After you got past the German territory, there was Poland; Bohemia transformed into Czechoslovakia; Hungary, now divided from Austria but not sharing Austria's strength. There was Romania, Yugoslavia, vanquished Turkey, then Persia and Baghdad. "The route is wide open, and we have undertaken to say, 'This route is closed!'"

After lunch, Wilson, plagued by now relentless headaches, in need of exercise, and reassembling his energies for that evening's talk, slipped away from the hotel with Edith and Grayson to drive to a park where he would take a brisk walk. He had clearly not recuperated from his stroke in July. Fatigue as well as sheer pain contributed to the increasing burden of speeches whose inaccuracies, untruths, generalizations, and "ragged array of learned locutions" were duly noted.[8] Wilson's claim in Columbus that he was privileged to "have been bred, and am proud to have been bred, in the old Revolutionary stock which set this government up" was definitively challenged by the *New York Herald*. His mother had been born in Carlisle, England, and emigrated via Canada in 1833, and every one of Wilson's four grandparents was born and reared in the United Kingdom long after the Revolutionary War. "Just what led President Wilson to claim Pilgrim forebears," the article concluded, "is not clear."[9]

Not only Wilson's would-be ancestry but his geography and his dates were called in question. He had placed Baghdad in Persia, instead of Iraq. He was mistaken when he referred to the Austrian crown prince's assassination in Serbia rather than in Sarajevo, Bosnia. When he confused the dates of the secret treaties—those between Japan and Great Britain in 1914 and those between Japan and the Allies in 1917—Senator George William Norris complained that "the President has not got his history straight."[10] Though Wilson thanked Norris for correcting him, he would repeat this "unintentional inaccuracy," along with others.[11] Less than two weeks after boasting of his Revolutionary ties, he abandoned them. By the time he ventured into Portland, Oregon, on September 15, he proudly claimed a different set of forebears: "I come of a race that, being bred on barren hills and unfertile plains in Scotland, being obliged to work where work was hard, somehow has the best zest in what it does when the job is hard."[12]

* * *

Only rest, complete rest and escape from the crowds, Edith realized, would restore her husband, and she was as protective of him as the rigorous circumstances permitted. Assisted by Grayson, she was no doubt responsible for the telegram Tumulty sent in the president's name only four days out: a naive request, considering the critical domestic and international issues of the moment and the intensely controversial nature of the peace treaty, that both the White House and the State Department limit their contact with him, that the White House forward only "absolutely essential" mail, and that the State Department, in place of dispatches, simply present him with questions that needed his decision.[13]

Edith was nearly frantic with fear for her husband's health and prospects. The depth of her concern was probably known only to Grayson at the outset of the journey. To the public she was a decorative woman with a baroque wardrobe—beaded, befurred, feathered, and silver-buckled—and a tantalizing way of seeming at once forthcoming and withdrawn, accessible and guarded. As Maud Murray reported in the *Columbus, Ohio, Dispatch,* "When she looked one straight in the eye and says 'I am happy to meet you,' you have a feeling that she means it. But she certainly does keep herself close to impersonal things, such as flowers and the sunshine, or rain."[14] In confirmation of earlier impressions, the *Kansas City Post* observed on the fourth day of the tour that "Mrs. Wilson talks little and smiles much." It was concluded that there was little more to remember of Mrs. Wilson "than a warm handclasp and a gracious smile."

Of course, there was more. The way she listened to her husband's speeches left a strong impression of her admiring devotion. In Kansas City, Edith, shielded by a drooping black velvet hat, was described as sitting in her usual attitude, her head uplifted and slightly to one side, listening attentively, smiling now and then at one of the president's sallies or turning to her companions with a quick glance of appreciation. "If Mrs. Wilson had heard the president make that speech before she gave no evidence of it. She looked as interested and as concerned as if he were a country preacher delivering his first sermon. One almost felt she was prepared to get up and prompt him if he had hesitated at a line."[15]

By September 9, in an attempt to conserve Wilson's strength, Grayson advised against rear platform speeches. With Nebraska, Minnesota, North Dakota, Montana, Idaho, and sixteen addresses behind him—there would be nearly forty in all—the wished-for respite was not to be found in Seattle. The crowd that packed the streets on September 13 included five thousand members of the Industrial Workers of the World protesting the imprisonment of Eugene V. Debs, Tom Mooney, and others under the Federal Espionage Act. Though the demonstration was silent, there was no question about the message conveyed on each man's hatband, "Release Political Prisoners," or the intermittent impression of "a sinister note."[16] At the sight of five blocks of men standing silent on both sides of the street in the Woodley district and staring past him, Wilson looked physically stricken.[17]

The president's spirit would carry him through that evening's talk, but the terrific strain that he had been under for more than a year was telling.[18] Grayson hoped that the president would reboard his train after the Saturday-night speech and proceed to Mt. Rainier for rest through Monday. However, after church on Sunday, Wilson met with a delegation of the labor leaders who had confronted him the day before. He intended to work at full capacity.

On the edge of his inevitable breakdown,[19] several events conspired to exacerbate Wilson's vulnerable state. He had to contend with three Republicans who, like a "wrecking crew," haunted his footsteps and negated his messages before large and susceptible crowds. The president had received ample warning of these "irreconcilables." Referred to, also, as the "bitter-enders" and the "battalion of death," they had made known their plans immediately following the announcement of his intention of touring their home states of Washington, Idaho, and California. James A. Reed of Missouri joined William E. Borah and Hiram W. Johnson in opposition to the president's "covenanting crusade," this "hippodroming excursion," this "cavorting and gallivanting" at the taxpayers' expense.[20]

Trying as it was for Wilson to endure enemies from the opposite camp, he was more "incensed and distressed beyond measure" by a conviction that he harbored a nonbeliever on his own turf. His long-smoldering suspicions of his own secretary of state's disloyalty became, in his view, confirmed. During his journey from Seattle to Portland, he learned of Robert Lansing's negative feelings about the treaty from a former employee of the American Peace Commission, William C. Bullitt, whose testimony before the Senate, according to the *New York Times*, "supplied fresh capital for the political enemies of the Treaty and of the President."[21] "Here he was in the heart of the West," Tumulty would write of Wilson, "advancing the cause so dear to his heart, steadily making gains against what appeared to be insurmountable odds, and now his intimate associate, Mr. Lansing, was engaged in sniping and attacking him from behind."[22]

In testimony before the Senate Foreign Relations Committee about his own activities during the war and at the peace conference, Bullitt stated, on September 12, that it was no secret that Mr. Lansing objected vigorously to numerous provisions of the treaty. Bullitt quoted Lansing as saying, "I consider that the League of Nations at present is entirely useless. The great powers have simply gone ahead and arranged the world to suit themselves. England and France in particular have gotten out of the treaty everything that they wanted; and the League of Nations can do nothing to alter any of the unjust clauses of the treaty except by unanimous consent of the members of the league, and the great powers will never give their consent to changes in the interests of weaker peoples." The worst was yet to come. Lansing, according to Bullitt, in discussing the possibility of ratification by the Senate, had also said that he believed "that if the Senate could only understand what this treaty means, and if the American people could really understand, it would unquestionably be defeated, but I wonder if they will ever understand what it lets them in for."[23]

The immediate response of his critics was to demean Bullitt, to call him a fool, liar, impertinent. It was hard to imagine the Senate or the public "taking seriously statements which, even if true, were obviously the grossest possible breach of confidence," Henry White wrote from Paris to Henry Cabot Lodge. Bullitt, White advised, was suffering from wounded vanity, was retaliating because his urgent advice that the American delegation should enter, and immediately persuade other great powers to enter, into diplomatic relations with the Bolshevik government of Russia had been rejected. Not among the regular experts of the delegation, Bullitt was merely an attractive and rather striking personality who had temporarily been taken on by the State Department.

White assured Lodge that he liked Bullitt personally and appreciated his keenness and zeal, but regretted that a man of such brilliant possibilities should show himself to be so entirely unworthy of confidence. White could not have been consoled by Lodge's reply. "You had better read a copy of Bullitt's testimony before you say that it counts for nothing," the skeptical Bostonian advised. Though Lodge did not defend Bullitt's breach of confidence, he insisted the latter's statements were fortified with papers at every stage and were true: whatever White thought of Bullitt's lack of discretion, this did not affect the strength of his testimony.[24]

On the night of September 13, Lansing was at his family cottage in Henderson Harbor on Lake Ontario when he received a telegram from Acting Secretary of State William Phillips, suggesting that he might consider giving out a statement roughly on the following lines: "The course of William C. Bullitt, a former employee of the American Peace Commission, in violating confidential relations . . . is too contemptible to warrant dignifying with a statement in reply." Beyond that many of the assertions were false, Phillips continued, everyone to whom he had spoken, including most representatives of the press, felt that Bullitt's act was wholly contemptible. However, no one could come out and brand his conduct as it should be branded except "you who were his chief. It is hard for me to know what to suggest. I feel that something is called for which will in the mind of the public denounce such conduct."

Two days later, after a talk with Democratic senator Hitchcock, Phillips telephoned Lansing to suggest another approach. The senator was inclined to believe that, unless Lansing categorically denied Bullitt's statement, "your course of silence is the best." Hitchcock, however, thought it would be advantageous if Lansing would give him some statement expressing himself on the desirability of ratification of the treaty that Hitchcock could use during the Senate debates in case the opposition attempted to use Bullitt's remarks.[25] Lansing obliged Hitchcock. He wired Phillips to tell Hitchcock that he declined to make any comment on Bullitt's statement but that he believed the important question at issue was the ratification or nonratification of the treaty and that he was "strongly in favor of immediate ratification of the treaty without modifications as the whole world demands the restoration of peace."[26]

Privately, Lansing realized there was just enough truth to Bullitt's violation of confidence to make things difficult. The secretary admitted he had discussed the treaty with some frankness, and when Bullitt had come to say good-bye, Lansing had told him some provisions in it were bad but, in view of the conflicting claims, it was difficult to make them all good. "You see how a slight variation made my remarks antagonistic to ratification and Bullitt unhesitatingly made the variation." When Bullitt said that Lansing was not enthusiastic over the League of Nations, "well, there he came pretty near the truth as you know," Lansing wrote to his friend John W. Davis, the U.S. ambassador in London.[27]

* * *

Though he preferred not to make an official statement, Lansing did attempt to reach the president on his tour. Eleanor Lansing Dulles remembers her uncle calling on the wall telephone just inside the porch of a neighboring farmhouse near Lake Ontario, only to be rebuffed by Mrs. Wilson and Tumulty.[28] The secretary offered another explanation on September 17, in a coded telegram sent to the State Department to be forwarded to the president in San Francisco. Lansing's message told Wilson that he was greatly distressed by Bullitt's public disclosure of a most confidential interview: Bullitt's conduct was "most despicable and outrageous." Lansing methodically traced the circumstances of Bullitt's resignation, the reasons, and Lansing's own advice. In view of Bullitt's statements, did Wilson think it wise for Lansing to respond to the printed report on the Bullitt hearing? Lansing assured Wilson that he desired to do everything he could to help in the ratification of the treaty and deeply regretted his conversation with the disloyal young man who was "seeking notoriety at the expense of the respect of all honorable men."[29]

Wilson was heading toward Los Angeles on Saturday morning, September 20, when he read Lansing's telegram. Grayson was so alarmed by the president's reaction—saliva formed at the corners of Wilson's mouth, his lips trembled, and his pallor increased—that the doctor began contemplating a means of canceling the balance of the trip.[30] Wilson did not acknowledge the telegram nor did Lansing make a public statement. After sharing the telegram with Tumulty, the president told his secretary that Lansing's disloyalty must not go unchallenged, and that, were he in Washington, he would at once demand the secretary's resignation. That action, Tumulty was convinced, was forestalled only by the president's illness a few days later.[31]

Lansing, having been temporarily spared, seems not to have understood his own perfidy. He thought "the Government and its officers ought not to be at the mercy of unscrupulous and irresponsible young rascals whose sense of duty disappears when an opportunity for notoriety arrives!" he told John Davis. [32] It did not occur to him to think of himself as a fifty-five-year-old rascal who had repeatedly undermined the president's policies in conversation and in correspondence. Emotionally and perhaps intellectually dishonest, Lansing's impregnably starched public facade hid the incorrigible caricaturist and plaintive diarist, who was also an unhappy public servant. In Paris he had suffered so severely from Wilson's studied neglect that his beloved wife, weeping, had wanted him to resign.[33] What he could not ignore he chose to rationalize, while clinging to his endangered and inauspicious, though prestigious, career as secretary of state.

Lansing sought solace by pleading his case against Wilson and the treaty in letters to friends and officials, and in random encounters. He found excuses for continuing to work for a president from whom he felt personally estranged, and with whom he critically differed on the most profound issues of the day. "Descended in an unbroken line of Democratic ancestors since the foundation of the Republic," he had "inherited a devotion to the Democracy, which I put before all personal interests."[34] Nevertheless, with his raw Parisian wounds, he continued to contemplate resignation until he was abruptly relieved of the decision and the position.[35]

The *New York Times* followed not only Lansing's involvement with Bullitt, but also pondered Colonel House's connection with that quasi–State Department employee. The paper chose not to censure Bullitt for making use of opportunities that were put in his way. Rather, it questioned Lansing's judgment and the extraordinary freedom and frankness with which he had discussed the work of the Peace Conference in private conversation. The *Times* also wondered that Bullitt had been "strangely enough a trusted employee, certified by Colonel House." The New York *Sun* reported that it was difficult to shed the impression that much of Bullitt's version was true, "particularly that which concerned the domination of the work of the American delegation by Colonel House, with whom, as every one at the Hôtel Crillon knew, Bullitt enjoyed unusually close relations."[36]

House's son-in-law Gordon Auchincloss called Bullitt a "jackass" and pronounced his testimony "a nasty piece of business." Though he believed House was in the clear, but for his questionable judgment in having trusted Bullitt at all, Auchincloss urged his father-in-law to counteract the young diplomat's "misstatement" with a short statement of his own. House, however, did not wish to enter the controversy: Bullitt was "practically right," he allowed, though he had not given the whole story. House sounded at once philosophical and wistful in his response to Auchincloss: "So as always are we sacrificed in the house of our friends. . . . I have always told you that it was not our enemies that needed watching but our friends."[37]

After Los Angeles, the presidential party would head home—in Edith's opinion, not a moment too soon. She had hoped that her husband might count that Sunday, September 21, as a day of rest. Instead, there were to be innumerable visitors, including Mary Allen Hulbert Peck, whom Wilson had invited to lunch at one o'clock. He had spoken briefly with her son, Allen Schoolcraft Hulbert, in Washington recently and now looked forward to seeing her. She had declined, saying the time was impossible; but when Wilson called to ask if one-thirty was better, she accepted. Recalling the attempts, by scandalmongers, to make an intrigue of Wilson and Peck's friendship, Edith declared that she was glad to receive Mary Peck and to show her disdain for slander.

Wilson's vein of elusive but persistent humanity appears here. That this ailing, exhausted man, a foremost figure of the world, should have given thought and time to the now obscure connection with Mary Peck—arranging for her to be received by his wife, and offering her their assistance—defies cynical interpretation. Wilson found it easier to extend kindness where he could also condescend and was least at ease with equals and independent minds. Consideration for others, however, never completely deserted him.

On that Sunday, Mary, in the four-year-old dress she had worn on her last visit to the White House, rode a streetcar to the Alexandria Hotel, where she was greeted by Grayson in uniform. She found Edith Wilson the *maîtresse femme*, a woman of strong character. In Mary's opinion, Edith played well "that most difficult role" of third party to the reunion of two old friends endeavoring to explore the incidents of years in a single afternoon. Edith would describe Mary as "a faded, sweet-looking woman who was absorbed in an only son."

At Wilson's urging, Mary told of her life since their last meeting in Washington on Memorial Day, 1915, when he was still a widower. The president was very quiet; Edith said nothing. Mary told him how she had been approached by that alleged "representative of the Republican party" who had said that a member of the Wilson cabinet and his wife were ready to testify against the president if there were impeachment proceedings; and Mary mentioned other incidents of harassment. Wilson expressed his deep regret that she had suffered from the gossip of his political enemies. They also talked about the League of Nations, and apparently still smarting from the challenges posed by Lloyd George, Clemenceau, and Orlando, Wilson complained that they had all failed him, "all of them, all of them!"

Had she not coveted every free moment for her weary husband, Edith said, she would have enjoyed Mary Peck. When Wilson left the room to meet with a committee of the League to Enforce Peace, Mary said she would wait until he returned. She stayed too long, until dark: "Poor woman, weighed down with her own problems," Edith said, "of course she did not understand." Later, when Edith Wilson disappeared to tell the valet to fetch Mary Peck's wrap, Wilson asked, "Is there nothing we can do?" "Not for me," Mary said. "But you can help Allen." Edith then escorted Mary to the elevator, bade her a kindly farewell, and as Mary told it, "the elevator quickly dropped me out of the life of my friend Woodrow Wilson—forever."[38] Edmund Starling, a declared admirer of Edith Wilson, wrote later that he thought Mary Peck "a drab, faded woman of middle age and how anyone could have cast her in a romantic role" was more than he could imagine.[39]

Wilson's two days in San Francisco and Oakland, the *New York Times* reported, were good evidence that the country would turn in resentment on any group of men who balked at the treaty or "render impossible America's effective participation in a League of Nations."[40] California's response to the president proved that the people were behind the treaty. But Wilson's triumph was tempered. In modest space, the *Times* noted that "although the President's health is said to be excellent, sixteen days of travel and speechmaking have been very fatiguing and Dr. Grayson insists on more opportunity for rest whenever possible." There was the suggestion of a slight cold. On September 22, the paper expressed universal admiration for the president's qualities as a stayer who did not spare himself in his mission to arouse people to the significance of the treaty. A two-day splitting headache was mentioned. Thousands cheered him in Salt Lake City as he acknowledged them partisans of the treaty. Again, on Thursday, September 25, he was given a generous reception in Cheyenne, but looked drawn and nervously clutched and unclutched his hands as he spoke, as though the effort to concentrate on his subject was an additional strain.

Breathing with difficulty for the past two weeks and lapsing into frightening fits of choking, the president now slept, or tried to sleep, propped up with pillows in a chair. He delivered a faltering but stirring speech in Pueblo, Colorado, the last of almost forty on this tour. Grayson, however, greatly concerned, proposed, a few miles out, that they stop the train, get some fresh air, and walk. By now, Starling, who had stayed close to Wilson in the past weeks for fear that he might collapse at any moment, pronounced the president "on his last legs. Nothing but courage kept him going." Starling found Wilson's speeches repetitious and believed that Wilson sometimes lost the thread of his thought. His voice was weak, and every phrase was an effort for his whole body. Once he wept. [41]

Late in the evening of September 25, Edith's maid, Siegrid, came to brush her hair and to give her a massage. Thinking Wilson asleep in the neighboring compartment, the women were quiet, and were surprised when he knocked at their door and said he was very sick. At 2 A.M. Grayson found that his patient could hardly breathe, that the muscles of his face were twitching and he was extremely nauseated. The next morning, one mile out of Wichita, a haggard Tumulty announced "the tour's off" due to a "severe nervous attack" that had kept Dr. Grayson and Mrs. Wilson up with the president until 4 A.M. Eliminating stops in Oklahoma City, Little Rock, Memphis and Louisville, orders flashed to clear the tracks, to rearrange the seventeen-hundred-mile run to speed the *Mayflower* back home. [42]

Fearing that he would be called a quitter, Wilson wanted to finish the work he had started. Told, however, that he must stop before his condition deteriorated further, he relented. "If you feel that way about it, I will surrender," he told Grayson. To Tumulty he said, "I don't seem to realize it, but I seem to have gone to pieces." With this admission, as he turned to look out the train window, large tears fell from his eyes. [43]

The train heading for Washington was expected to arrive on Sunday at 1 P.M. Wilson remained secluded in his stateroom with Edith and Grayson in constant attendance. He telegraphed his daughters Jessie Sayre and Margaret Wilson that he was "returning to Washington. Nothing to be alarmed about." A day later John Edwin Nevin reported in *The Denver Post* that Admiral Grayson, who normally rode in one of the other cars of the train, spent Friday night in the president's car, so that he would be close to his patient. To offset wild rumors, Grayson insisted that the president's condition was not alarming, but that he had suffered a complete nervous breakdown, a condition the physician seemed to believe less onerous than the truth of his ailment. Nevin added that the doctor, who knew the president's physical condition better than any other living person, did give warning that only complete rest for some time would restore his distinguished patient sufficiently for him to resume charge of the nation's affairs.

Nevin also informed readers that plans for the president to confer with the senators leading the fight for the confirmation of the Treaty of

Versailles had been canceled as were all his engagements and official functions for the coming two or three weeks. Admiral Grayson intended to keep his patient in the White House, where everything that might be needed for his care would be available at instant notice. "Mrs. Wilson remained in complete charge of the nursing of the president, however."[44]

As people gathered at every station to see the train, it seemed to Edith like a funeral cortege. She tried to do some knitting and to divert her husband with small talk. The hours dragged on: "the air was so heavy with unspoken agony that all seemed a travesty."[45]

The *New York Times'* headline on Saturday, September 27, announced, "The President Suffers Nervous Breakdown." The condition was not life-threatening. It was said to date back to an attack of influenza in Paris the preceding April and was caused by overwork. The special message to the disappointed people of Wichita, who had shut down their businesses for the day, explained that some of the president's distress was due to his exposure to high altitudes and to a loud San Francisco orchestra playing ragtime that affected his nerves. Also, the *Times* pointed out, the president's lack of exercise on the tour had caused blood to go to his head at the expense of his stomach and other organs.[46]

There had been an undercurrent of apprehension about the president's health ever since the trip started. Correspondents on the train suspected for several days that something was wrong. David Lawrence observed that Mrs. Wilson, usually all smiles, had looked anxious in the last few days. The reporter noted that in Pueblo, as Wilson had talked eloquently but in a weak voice of his visit to the Suresnes cemetery in France where American soldiers were buried, the audience had wept. So had Edith Wilson, hearing her husband say that he wished "some of the men who are now opposing the settlement for which those men died could visit such a spot [so that] they could feel the moral obligation . . . not to go back on those boys, but to see this thing through to the end and make good their redemption of the world." Edith's tears gave the impression, as she watched the president, "that she feared he might break down during his speech."[47]

Bulletins proliferated as the train lumbered toward Washington. The *Mayflower* pulled into Union Station on Sunday morning, September 28. The president emerged three hours later as his daughter Margaret ran to meet him. Because of a chill in the air, Edith Wilson insisted that Wilson wear a warm overcoat. Edith, up most of the night, looked tired that morning, but she smiled as she left the train. Wilson's visibly "extreme nervous condition" was noted, and he looked worn and shaken as he said good-bye to the engineer and the conductor and waved his hand to the newspapermen. He managed to walk through the station without support and raised his hat several times to the crowd of more than one thousand anxious onlookers. When wounded soldiers on a bench in the Red Cross canteen applauded him, he smiled and nodded.[48]

Word circulated that no one should attempt an engagement with the president or bring to his attention the contest over the peace treaty or any other issue. It had been assumed, until this breakdown, that the president, on completion of his Western tour, would take personal charge of the pro-treaty forces and that he would campaign extensively to win over the Covenant's critics to unconditional acceptance. Now his close advisers would insist that he accept their decision that the treaty situation could be handled during the next two weeks by Senator Hitchcock and other leaders in the Senate.

The *Times* eulogized the president: "The figure that will stand out in the memory of the Western people is that of a man burning with a restrained passion for a great purpose, for the accomplishment of which he would gladly lay down his life."[49] He had not had a vacation since the fleeting two weeks he took in 1915. Given the nation's current problems—the demands of labor, the high cost of living, the war, ratification of the peace treaty and acceptance of the League of Nations—he could be considered "as truly wounded as a soldier on the Battlefield."[50]

Once back in the White House, where it was possible to protect the patient, Grayson took steps to effect the rest cure, which was, in his view, the only means of restoring Wilson to health.[51] Grayson also took the precaution of asking two specialists to see the president. Dr. George De Schweinitz, the ophthalmologist, was expected Friday, October 3; Francis Xavier Dercum, the neurologist, the following day.[52]

Edith Wilson was lauded as an indefatigable nurse. Members of the presidential party paid her high tribute for watching her husband night and day, and being "ready to answer any call."[53] Following Grayson's instructions, Edith spoke of how she had twice turned away Sir William Wiseman, the chief British intelligence agent. When he said that he had important information for the president and would like to see him privately, she told him that her husband was ill but promised, if Wiseman returned that afternoon at two, she would have the president's answer. As Edith had never liked "this plausible little man," she was glad that her husband had then decided his information was not important enough for Wilson to receive him. "This was the one instance," she claimed in her *Memoir,* "that I recall having acted as an intermediary between my husband and another on an official matter, except when so directed by a physician."[54] The disclosure of seventy-year-old papers would reverse this interpretation of her role as go-between. They would prove that, far from heeding the advice, quoted at length, of the various physicians called in to aid her critically ill husband, Edith Wilson was quoting herself. In fact, it would be discovered, the president's wife had invented their supposed instructions.

⋆ Part IV ⋆

Illness

CHAPTER 25

"The beginning of the deception of the American people"

The full story of October 2, 1919, of the morning that turned the president of the United States "from giant to pygmy," could be truthfully told by only one person: Edith Wilson. Ike Hoover, the chief usher, troubled by so much guessing over the event—and by the fact that, though some guessers hit close to the mark, they could not offer a correct historical record—was prompted to write "The Facts about President Wilson's Illness."[1]

Hoover emphasized repeatedly that he regarded Mrs. Wilson as the "fountain source from which all information of necessity had its beginning." As it seemed to him, however, that her lips were sealed, he recorded what he knew in the light of his opportunities to hear and to see, at the time and on the premises. Lauded for his efforts as "an intelligent and sturdily honest witness," Hoover presented an account, historians say, that has the ring of truth.[2]

At ten minutes to nine that morning, Edith Wilson had rushed along the upper hall of the White House to phone down to the usher's room. To avoid switchboard gossip, she remembered, even in emergency, to use the private line and requested Hoover to "please get Dr. Grayson, the President is very sick." After alerting Grayson and ordering a car for him, Hoover raced up the stairs to see if he might do anything for the stricken president and his wife, only to find the bedroom door tightly closed. He waited helplessly for Grayson's arrival a few minutes after nine. The doctor knocked gently on the locked door, was admitted, and emerged ten minutes later to pronounce, with an anguished cry, "My God, the President is paralyzed." This was the only time that the word *paralyzed* was mentioned, to Hoover's knowledge, in regard to the president. By afternoon, doctors seemed to be everywhere and a consultation was under way. That day an "air of secrecy" enveloped the White House, and those outside the sickroom could learn nothing. This was "the beginning of the deception of the American people," and never, in Hoover's opinion, was a conspiracy "so pointedly and so artistically formed."[3]

Eventually, Hoover was called into the president's room to assist Grayson and two nurses to rearrange some of the furnishings.[4] The president lay stretched out on the vast Lincoln bed. He looked dead. There was not a sign of life. His face bore a long cut about the temple, still bloody these many hours later; a wound on his nose, unbandaged, was red and raw. Looking at him, Hoover thought Wilson "was just gone as far as one could judge from appearances." Hoover accurately surmised that Wilson, when stricken, had fallen from the bathroom stool, hit his head on the sharp bathtub plumbing, and collapsed on the floor. Mrs. Wilson, hearing her husband's groans, had raced to the bathroom, where she found him unconscious, and dragged him, with amazing strength, to his bed.

Irwin Hoover's story, published posthumously in 1934 in his book *Forty-two Years in the White House*,[5] was extremely displeasing to Edith. She strenuously disagreed with the White House chief usher's "rather remarkable account." Preceding her *Memoir* by four years, it beclouded her own version of her husband's shattering illness and raised epic questions about his ability to govern as an invalid. She had no recollection that the president had suffered a single cut or even a bruise, nor, she said, did Grayson. She also said that Cary Grayson had helped her to lift the president onto his bed. Though she admitted in her *Memoir* that her husband had suffered a stroke that paralyzed the left side of his body, leaving an arm and one leg useless, "thank God," she said, "the brain was clear and untouched."[6]

After a consultation among Francis Dercum, the respected Philadelphia neurologist who reached Wilson's bedside at four-thirty that afternoon, Dr. Sterling Ruffin, professor of medicine at George Washington University; Rear Admiral Edward Rhodes Stitt, head of the Naval Medical School; and Dr. John Benjamin Dennis, director of the Naval Dispensary, a consensus was reached, unsurprisingly, that absolute rest was essential for some time. Edith also noted that Dr. Dercum and Dr. Grayson "were not quite satisfied" with Wilson's condition—a breathtaking understatement; or, perhaps, a shocking lie, since the president was "seriously disabled, both in a medical and constitutional sense," and that, due to previous physiologic insults to his brain, "neither Wilson's thought processes nor his conduct in office would ever be the same again."[7]

In the late evening of October 2, in contrast to the wary bulletins of previous days, Grayson conceded that "the President is a very sick man." His condition was less favorable and he had remained in bed throughout the day."[8] The gravity of the sickroom was captured in terse daily notations in the White House appointments diary in which the names of visiting physicians were the only variants on those of Wilson's daughters: "A.M. Mrs. McAdoo left; P.M. Mrs. Sayre left." Beginning with October 10, Hoover typed "All just the same" day after day, the high point of the week being Edith's two automobile rides. After Monday, October 20, 1919, he gave up entirely on the diary for the next two months. There were to be "no further entries in 1919 . . . from Monday, October 20th, 1919, to Wednesday, December 31, 1919."[9]

"The news of the serious illness of the President fell like a pall on all hearts," and Joe Tumulty was in tears. "We must all pray," he said.[10] The worst was feared, and all the world—including foreign as well as American diplomats, cabinet officials, and the vice president himself—clamored for information about Wilson's health. Robert Lansing, immediately on his return from New York City, where he had welcomed the king and queen of the Belgians, telephoned Admiral Grayson for details. Asking the nature of Wilson's trouble, Lansing was told only that the president's condition was "bad" and that he could see no one. The next morning, scanning Friday's alarming headlines, Lansing left for the Executive Office of the White House to talk to Joseph Tumulty, who appeared nervously excited and very much depressed. Informed by Tumulty that Wilson had taken a turn for the worse, Lansing asked, "In what way?" Tumulty did not answer in words, but put his right hand to his left shoulder and drew it down along his left side. Lansing concluded that Wilson's left side was paralyzed.[11]

During this talk with Lansing, Tumulty telephoned Grayson to come to the Executive Office. On Grayson's arrival, the three went to the Cabinet Room, where they discussed for nearly an hour what course should be taken if the president's disability continued. Grayson was extremely reticent, specifying only that the president's malady was a nervous breakdown. In view of what Tumulty had implied, Lansing did not press the matter. The discussion, apparently led by Lansing, turned to the possibility of calling in the vice president, Thomas Riley Marshall, to act in Wilson's stead as soon as possible. Lansing also talked about the absence of precedents as to what constituted disability, produced a copy of Thomas Jefferson's "Manual," and offended Tumulty deeply by reading the specific clause in the U.S. Constitution on presidential succession: "In case of the removal of the President from office, or of his death, resignation, or inability to discharge the powers and duties of the said office, the same shall devolve on the Vice President."[12]

After a brief pause, an outraged Tumulty, in a cold and deliberate voice, informed the secretary of state that "the Constitution is not a dead letter with the White House." He too had read the Constitution and made it clear that he did not find himself in need of any tutoring. Tumulty, according to his account, then asked Lansing whom he had in mind to certify the president's disability. When Lansing suggested that neither he himself nor Grayson would be the ones to do the job, Tumulty lost patience completely. He would not serve a day under Marshall. "You may rest assured," he told the secretary of state, "while Woodrow Wilson is lying in the White House on the broad of his back I will not be a party to ousting him. He has been too kind, too loyal, and too wonderful to me to receive such treatment at my hands." If anybody outside of the White House circle attempted to certify the president's disability, he and Grayson, Tumulty added, would stand together and repudiate that person. Furthermore, Tumulty continued, if the president were in a condition to know of this episode, he would, in Tumulty's opinion, take decisive measures. "That ended the interview," Tumulty wrote. "It is unnecessary to say that no further attempt was made by Mr. Lansing to institute ouster proceedings against his chief."[13] Lansing vehemently condemned Tumulty's account as "entirely untrue": he had not sought Marshall to serve as president, although, in retrospect, he thought he should have done so.[14]

Meanwhile, the sixty-five-year-old vice president was himself bewildered and close to tears. The former governor of Indiana, whom Wilson had grudgingly accepted as his second-choice but politically prudent running mate during his first presidential campaign, was the survivor of the "Dump Marshall" movement during Wilson's second. When the vice president came immediately to the White House to inquire about the president's health, he was turned away, unenlightened. In fact, Marshall felt keenly that he ought to have officially been informed about Wilson's health, and that the tragedy of assuming the duties of president would be especially trying if he had to do so without warning. Instead, he depended on the newspapers, and the journalist J. Fred Essary, Washington correspondent of the *Baltimore Sun,* was delegated to tell him that Wilson had suffered a stroke on Thursday, October 2.[15]

Marshall, a slight man with a limp, would habitually be described as genial and portrayed, accompanied by his wife, as a prized Washington dinner-party guest. His sole bulwark against oblivion was his remark, taken out of context, that "what this country needs is a good five-cent cigar."[16] Critics were persuaded that he was somewhat inept, too timid, too indifferent, incapable, and ill-equipped to aspire to the presidency. In more objective quarters, Marshall was highly regarded. A kindly man of wisdom and humor, and an experienced and skillful, if not dynamic, politician, he was appraised by Josephus Daniels as "a real statesman of patriotism, ability, originality and devotion to the public weal," who added distinction to a great office often underrated.[17]

Marshall was a lawyer whose earlier experience, at the time of Wilson's departure for the Paris Peace Conference, had alerted him to the stark fact that the framers of the Constitution had left a void in the ground rules for defining presidential "inability." In response to those who urged him to undertake the duties of the absent president, Marshall made his terms perfectly known: if either Congress or the court directed him to assume the office, he would obey.

As the president lay prostrate, Marshall was humiliated by aspects of his ambiguous position. With the country leaderless and convulsed with rumors, he spoke with some bitterness of the standing joke regarding his duties, that "the only business of the vice-president is to ring the White House bell every morning and ask what is the state of health of the president."[18] Feeling ignored and ill-treated, the so-called "small calibre man" revealed the sensibilities of a first-class temperament when he wrote of his dilemma to Robert Lansing. What became of him as vice president was quite unimportant, but, when he traveled in the name of the president, he expected to be treated accordingly. In view of his experiences going to New York City to represent the president in welcoming King Albert of Belgium, he desired to notify the State Department that, if called upon again, "a complete schedule of the way in which I am to be treated as his representative must be furnished to me."[19]

To those who urged him toward the White House during Wilson's illness, Marshall would say that he never wished to be accused of being a usurper. There was, in fact, little chance that the vice president might be so stigmatized, given the character of the self-elected "bedside government" that had instantly fallen into place, and which remained mysterious and impenetrable. Theoretically a triumvirate, it was rather the case of two deputies, Tumulty and Grayson, whose first loyalty was to the third and presiding member, the president's wife, rather than to the government they were sworn to serve. Edith Wilson would dismiss Marshall's name as abruptly as she broached it in a purported conversation with Dr. Dercum when her husband fell drastically ill. Marshall appeared to understand the situation. He was determined not to get entangled with Edith Wilson, he told Arthur Krock of the *New York Times*: "No politician ever exposes himself to the hatred of a woman, particularly if she's the wife of the President of the United States."[20]

In the three or four days following Wilson's stroke, the White House metamorphosed into a hospital, as doctors, nurses, and equipment poured in. There were still no details, and no explanations beyond Grayson's misleading bulletins. The lack of specific information was extraordinary, as Hoover considered that the president lay on his bed, a wreck of a man who could not speak above a whisper and swallowed with difficulty, his mind enfeebled. From beginning to end, Grayson's reports on the president's health, substantiated publicly by Dr. Dercum, avoided mention of a stroke in any of its permutations. His medical bulletins never ventured beyond a description of Wilson's collapse as "nervous exhaustion," a condition he later promoted to a functional, not organic, "fatigue neurosis." On October 3, the *Washington Post* informed readers that "the President's illness is diagnosed as 'nervous exhaustion,' but the danger is that the present attack of neurasthenia may develop into nervous prostration, in which case it would be many months before the President would be able to resume his duties." Dr. Dercum, on his return to his home at 1719 Walnut Street in Philadelphia, "merely confirmed Dr. Grayson's diagnosis made previously, and found the President very much in need of rest. He is very cheerful and takes an interest in what is going on. This is an encouraging indication."

Thereafter, White House bulletins on Wilson's health were couched in classic physician's language, deliberately opaque, obtuse, simultaneously suggesting danger and hope. There was no immediate fear, but there was always the possibility of fear; fluctuations in his condition should not necessarily be regarded as alarming and yet they could be alarming; there was a good chance that he would fully recover from his nervous breakdown in a reasonable time, and then again, it might take months of enforced rest. That Wilson was able to eat and sleep with more regularity was considered a particularly promising sign, since his chronically sensitive digestive organs and his respiratory system, weakened by the last spring's attack of influenza, had initially interfered with his ability to sleep soundly during his present illness. Whatever his physical impairments, he was a man whose mind "was alert and clear," who chatted and joked with members of his family about his illness and was eager to get back to his desk. Furthermore, Dr. Grayson claimed that he had managed to frustrate Wilson's call for a stenographer on October 5 by reminding the president that it was Sunday and that he was a good Presbyterian.[21]

Once Edith determined her husband to be out of immediate danger, she faced the crucial question of how he might best serve the country, preserve his life, and if possible, recover. Her compelling account of how she wisely sought and received the compassionate and constructive advice that shaped the course of history was universally echoed by scholars and biographers for decades. Invalidated by recent disclosures, her story of the decision that her ill husband should remain in office, and of the evolution of her own stewardship, reveals a boundless, and unconscionable, imagination.

She had asked the doctors to be frank with her, she recounted, because she must know the probable outcome so as to be honest with the people. Recovery depended, they said, on the president's release from every disturbing problem during these days of recuperation. Yet how could that be accomplished in a form compatible with the duties of the chief executive? How could she protect her husband from national problems when the country looks to the president as its leader? In her account, the sixty-three-year-old specialist who was most familiar with her husband's case stepped forward with the answer. This was Francis Dercum, listed in *Who's Who* as professor of nervous and mental diseases at Jefferson Medical College, on the staff of the Philadelphia Hospital, consulting physician to the Asylum for the Chronic Insane, Wernersville, Pennsylvania, and editor of a textbook on nervous diseases.

For Mrs. Wilson, Dr. Dercum was not only consoling but optimistic. He recounted the history of Louis Pasteur, who, having been stricken in a similar manner, not only recovered but later accomplished his most brilliant discoveries. In the case of her husband, to afford him the protection essential to his recovery, Dr. Dercum proposed a solution to Edith: "Have everything come to you; weigh the importance of each matter, and see if it is possible by consultations with the respective heads of the departments to solve them without the guidance of your husband. In this way you can save him a great deal. But always keep in mind that every time you take him a new anxiety or problem to excite him, you are turning a knife in an open wound. His nerves are crying out for rest, and any excitement is torture to him.'"

"Then," Mrs. Wilson describes herself as asking, "had he better not resign, let Mr. Marshall succeed to the Presidency and he himself get that complete rest that is so vital to his life?"

"No," Dercum said, by Edith's account, "not if you feel equal to what I suggested. For Mr. Wilson to resign would have a bad effect on the country, and a serious effect on our patient. He has staked his life and made his promise to the world to do all in his power to get the Treaty ratified and make the League of Nations complete. If he resigns, the greatest incentive to recovery is gone; and as his mind is clear as crystal he can still do more with even a maimed body than anyone else. He has the utmost confidence in you. Dr. Grayson tells me he has always discussed public affairs with you; so you will not come to them uninformed."

"So began my stewardship," Mrs. Wilson explains. "I studied every paper, sent from the different Secretaries or Senators, and tried to digest and present in tabloid form the things that, despite my vigilance, had to go to the President. I, myself, never made a single decision regarding the disposition of public affairs. The only decision that was mine was what was important and what was not, and the *very* important decision of when to present matters to my husband."[22] According to Edith Wilson, her husband asked her thousands of questions, insisted on knowing everything, particularly about the treaty, dictated notes, and told her which senators to write to or send for. At the physician's direction, she was the one to convey messages to cabinet members and others so that the president might be relieved of the nervous drain of seeing them in person.

Edith Wilson's epic rendering of her conversation with Dr. Dercum would, despite some skepticism, still prevail were it not for the startling revelation, in June 1991, of the existence of Dr. Dercum's actual and wholly contradictory clinical papers, more than seventy years old, dated October 20, 1919, as well as those of Grayson, undated. These lengthy and detailed reports "make it clear for the first time that Wilson, on October 2, 1919, suffered a devastating trauma, one so extensive," the editors of *The Papers of Woodrow Wilson* have concluded, "that it would be impossible for him ever to achieve more than a minimal state of recovery."[23] It has been suggested that Grayson prepared his medical reports in anticipation of a congressional inquiry into the president's health, and the same reason presumably accounts for the existence of Dercum's. No such inquiry took place. And these reports, never submitted to the public, were exiled to Grayson's private files.[24]

It is obvious, however, that Grayson, like Edith Wilson, could neither face nor acknowledge the harsh realities of the president's sickness. He would insist, in a letter of October 9, 1919, to the reporter Louis Seibold, that the president was not affected mentally. He could sincerely say that Wilson's mind was "as good as it ever was," that it was his hope that in the not far distant future it would be considered safe to permit the president to resume his work. In fact, Grayson wished that he himself might be "similarly afflicted if I could be as mentally alert as the President."[25] On the same day, he called the Washington urologist Dr. Harry Atwood Fowler concerning the president's alarming new medical problem, a swollen prostate gland, which barely escaped surgery and required additional treatment from Dr. Hugh Hampton Young, clinical professor of urology at the Johns Hopkins Medical School.

Two of Grayson's unpublished and newly retrieved statements pertinent to Wilson's health again evade any mention of a stroke. Instead, on October 15, 1919, Grayson once more insisted that intensely hard, incessant work had depleted Wilson's physical and nervous energy, caused his lack of muscular development, his obstinate neuritis, and the relaxed condition of the mucous membranes of the nose and throat. After a thorough physical and neurological examination of the president, Grayson would not admit to any evidence of a large or serious lesion of any important organ, announcing only that Wilson was steadily and slowly gaining. At present, Grayson wrote, Wilson's mind, clear, keen, logical, incisive as ever, and at times showing evidence of accustomed humor, was in a condition "where any question of international or national importance could be submitted to him for his counsel, advice and decision."[26]

As late as October 29, 1919, Grayson was writing still another fictitious diagnosis, probably an aborted public statement, that tells something about the conspiratorial atmosphere of the White House. He asserts that there was no foundation whatever for fears that the president's exhaustion might have impaired his mind, that his blood pressure and heart action were normal, that his eyesight showed no deterioration in comparison with a year ago, "and the degree of physical exhaustion which was the natural reflex action from the drain on his nervous energies has happily almost entirely passed away."[27] By contrast, after studying Wilson's medical history, the neurosurgeon Dr. Bert E. Park notes that already in the summer of 1919, Wilson's memory loss, difficulty in composing a speech, and above all, his untreated hypertension and cerebrovascular disease took "their toll on the president's intellect and behavior."[28]

Grayson's continually misleading references to the president's ailments as influenza and nervous breakdown might appear to be the obtuse findings of an ill-trained physician. On the contrary, Dr. Grayson was sharply aware of Wilson's waning health and, from the start, prescribed a sensible diet and constant exercise. When essential, he had conferred with the most renowned specialists of the day.

Grayson's third diagnostic paper recovered from his sons—the undated memorandum he is thought to have written in case Congress chose to investigate the extent of Wilson's disability—reviewed the president's ailing health from the time of his Western tour. Continuing to dissemble about the complexity of Wilson's condition on Thursday morning, October 2, the doctor stated only that the president's complaint "of some numbness and weakness" on his left side led to the summons of various consultants, who confirmed over ten days that Wilson was suffering "from a thrombosis involving the internal capsule of the right cerebral hemisphere."[29]

In consultation with Grayson, Dercum forwarded to the physician his "final and complete" medical statement on October 20.[30] His report begins with his first examination of Wilson on the afternoon of October 2, when he found the president's left leg and left arm in complete paralysis and the lower half of the left side of his face drooping. Conscious throughout, though somewhat somnolent during the examination, Wilson answered questions a trifle slowly, but was articulate. The left side of his face, head, neck, and trunk, and his left arm and leg were numb; his vision, already faulty in one eye, was noticeably impaired in both. Three more examinations, on October 4 (participated in by Dr. De Schweinitz), 11, and 18, confirmed the initial diagnosis, that of a severe organic hemiplegia, or in layman's terms, paralysis of one side of the body, probably due to a thrombosis of the middle cerebral artery of the right hemisphere. Dercum specifically states that at the time of the first consultation the full diagnosis of the president's illness was communicated to Mrs. Wilson and Margaret Wilson. The subsequent course of the case revealed the hemiplegia to be persistent, but, Dercum cautiously states, "because of the improvement noted at various times, Dr. Grayson thought it wise to issue general statements only."[31]

Grayson too is specific on this point. He says that the diagnosis "was at once communicated to Mrs. Wilson and Miss Margaret Wilson and without any reservations."[32] In relaying Edith Wilson's response, Grayson quite plainly says that it was not merely lingering optimism for the president's health that suggested the wisdom of general rather than specific statements. "Further," Grayson acknowledges, "Mrs. Wilson, the President's wife was absolutely opposed to any other course."[33] The consultants, faced with the reality that Wilson was beyond improvement, were prepared to make a truthful statement of his condition to the public, but, Grayson writes, "in view of the wishes of——this was deferred."[34] The identity of "——" is hardly a mystery. The doctor's acknowledgment was undoubtedly prompted by the necessity of protecting himself against accusations of disseminating false information, in the event of an official investigation. In his discreet omission of Edith Wilson's name, he was, as always, attempting to treat the president's wife as tactfully as possible, having already conspired with her to suppress the truth of her husband's feeble health in Paris and again in Washington, and virtually concealing him aboard the *Mayflower* in the previous July, to be free from prying eyes.

Perhaps, given his furtive negotiations with Edith Wilson, Grayson might have hazarded some thought that the president's first wife would have coped differently. As Wilson's future bride, Ellen had openly discussed her family's medical history, including her father's breakdown. As Wilson's wife, she had nurtured him through mental as well as physical trials of his own. Wisely encouraging him to travel far from the sources of his grievances, in both academic and public life, it might have occurred to Grayson that Ellen, contrary to Edith, would willingly have sought refuge for the stricken president far from the confines of the White House.

Edith Wilson's stirring account of her bedside exchange with Dr. Dercum illustrates once again her lack of compunction in adapting history to her own obsessive purpose. Her ingenuous declaration that Woodrow Wilson was, above all else, the beloved husband whose life she was trying to save—fighting, as it were, with her back to the wall—and after that, the president of the United States,[35] was apparently intended to justify the position she assumed and to defuse possible accusations of her own ambitions to act as president. Since Dercum immediately recognized the gravity of the president's health, however, it is hardly likely that he would have advised Edith that her husband could do more for the country with a maimed body than any other man in full health. It is also "extremely unlikely," as the neurologist and historian Dr. Edwin Weinstein points out, that Dr. Dercum would have used language so similar to Mrs. Wilson's own. By the time her book was published, Dr. Dercum was dead.[36] Grayson was not unaware of the hoax that he had helped to perpetrate. Initially, when Josephus Daniels suggested that he tell the truth, Grayson had agreed that a great wave of sympathy would have poured into the White House. He wished that he could have done so, he told Daniels, but he was forbidden to speak. The president and Mrs. Wilson, he said, had made him promise to that effect.[37] On another occasion, after lunch at the White House, Grayson discussed with Ray Stannard Baker his "secret report," a document apparently so private and of such significance that Baker did not dare refer to its content in his own diary. He did, however, record that Grayson was obviously troubled and sought his judgment as to what he had done. Baker, in response, assured the president's physician that he was absolutely right, that it was a stupendous responsibility he had had to assume. In Baker's view, the doctor had both wisdom and courage and was "a fine, brave, simple man if ever there was one."[38]

Wilson's entire cabinet attended a special meeting on the morning of Monday, October 6, Secretary of State Lansing presiding. The next day, headlining Tumulty's denial of the rumor that Marshall might be asked to act as president, the *New York Times* printed Admiral Grayson's report to the cabinet to the effect that the president's condition was "encouraging, but suggested that only urgent matters be brought to his attention, in order that his rest be made as complete as possible. The state of business in the departments is such," he had added, "that there is little requiring the president's immediate attention." The meeting, intended to soothe and reassure the public, raised instead the question of whether the vice president should be called upon to act as president during the president's disability or whether members of the cabinet could assume the powers and undertake the duties of the presidency until his recovery.[39]

In his private notes of the meeting Grayson wrote that Lansing appeared "somewhat astounded" when, in response to the secretary's direct questions, Grayson declared the president's mind was not only clear but very active and that he was very much annoyed when he had found out that the cabinet had been called and had wanted to know by whose authority and for what purpose. The war secretary, Newton D. Baker, seems to have intervened at this awkward moment. He thought it would meet with the approval of the cabinet to say that they had only gathered as a mark of affection, that there was nothing for the president to be concerned over at present, and that they were all looking out for his interests as best they could. "Please convey our sympathy to the President," he added, "and give him our assurance that everything is going along all right."[40] Considering the cabinet's inaccurate and falsely optimistic picture of Wilson's condition, as well as Tumulty's commitment to Wilson and Cary Grayson's total capitulation to Edith Wilson, it seemed to be implicitly understood that no one would be permitted to take Wilson's place in office. Members of the president's bedside government bitterly resented Lansing for having proposed a meeting of the cabinet, let alone for raising the question of succession. Under these curious circumstances, there was an element of realism to the thought that, to assume the presidency, Vice President Marshall "would have had to lay siege to the White House."[41]

CHAPTER 26

"The President says"

In the days following her husband's stroke on October 2, Edith Wilson was vastly offended by gossip directed at her conjectured ambition to act as president and her rumored refusal of all advice on matters of state. Determined to defend herself, Edith vowed that she would do so as if she had taken the oath "to tell the truth, the whole truth, and nothing but the truth—so help me God."[1]

She asked the public to imagine the circumstances in which her husband had been stricken: with his tour a success, with public sentiment once again in favor of the treaty, and with pro-treaty senators eager to push that advantage, the president had suddenly been laid low, ruled out of the fight that he would have continued though he knew it might cost him his life. Because he had immediately regained consciousness and was able to speak clearly at all times, she herself could work with him in greatest harmony. He would ask thousands of questions, insist on being fully informed, dictate his responses, and tell her which senators she should send for and what suggestions he had to make to them. She, carefully taking notes, would read them back to him, to avoid any mistake in transmitting his views.

Edith's evaluation of the president's capabilities at that time differs radically from other accounts. Ike Hoover wrote that, for the first chaotic month, at least, the president was completely incapacitated mentally and physically—indicating that no official could see him. Wilson resumed dictating three or four letters daily to his stenographer, Charles Swem, only four months later, on February 2. Pathetically impaired, he would start a letter, but shortly his voice would grow indistinct, and at last he would lose the thread of what he was saying and stare into space as though in a trance. Reminded, he would start again. Eventually, when urgent matters required his signature, the relevant documents were read to him; and with a pencil, his hand steadied and pointed, he would sign where his hand had been placed—signatures that were mere scribbles compared to his normal endorsement.[2] He was pronounced well enough to ride out in public on a balmy day in March. To say that, as time passed, Woodrow Wilson's condition improved was not, in Ike Hoover's opinion, to say much.

It would be about six weeks before the president could be lifted from his bed, placed in a chair by the bedside, and moved to another part of the room. The first rolling chair proved a failure as Wilson could not sit upright. Perceiving that more rigid braces were required for the president's "poor old deformed body," Hoover suggested trying out a chair on wheels, similar to those used on the boardwalk at Atlantic City. First rented for a weekly fee of $5, then acquired, this soon proved essential to the president's daily routine. Its footrest raised to extend directly from the seat to avoid the strain of bending the knees, it would be used every time he got out of bed during his remaining time in the White House.

Hoover was to push the chair day after day, roll it into the elevator on Wilson's few excursions out of the White House as spring approached, and practically carry him the rest of the way to the waiting automobile. Hoover pointed out that Wilson never rode now in the rear seat of the car where he would have slid down or toppled over, as the car rolled along, but was always placed in the front with the driver, where the seat was braced. He wore his cape coat, as he could not get his limp arm into the sleeve of an overcoat. On eventual trips to the theater, initiated after sixteen months of illness on February 1, 1921, shortly before the end of his second term, the president would be driven to the rear entrance of the playhouse and, with much assistance, helped to his seat.

In these tragic circumstances, the chief usher privately concluded, there was no real head of the government. Commenting on the optimistic reports on Wilson's health that appeared in the papers day after day, Hoover said flatly that there "never was deception so universally practiced in the White House as it was in those statements being given out from time to time." As no photographers were permitted in the White House, there would be no physical evidence to give the lie to the imposture.

Out of the bedlam of the earliest days, a routine did evolve. Wilson would be taken from his bed about ten o'clock, placed in his chair, and rolled to another room, or to the White House porch or south grounds for an hour or so, weather permitting. Of the papers and letters forwarded by the trusted Grayson, mostly from Tumulty, only those of Edith's choice were read to him, with decisions, such as they were (his ability to speak remains in question), conveyed back through the same channels. In the last year of Wilson's residency, until he went out of office in March 1921, he regularly saw a movie in the East Room at noon—and so that he might have a different one each day, Hoover "scoured the universe."

Though it was said that Grayson had limited influence on Mrs. Wilson, it was Tumulty whose position was the most exposed. By her own admission, Edith had never liked Tumulty. For one thing, he could copy her husband's signature so perfectly that no one could detect the difference. This made her nervous, in spite of Wilson's assurance that Tumulty would never commit any impropriety. Possibly because she sought to protect Wilson from the stress of public affairs, or more probably because she did not trust Tumulty, Edith permitted him to see the president only three weeks or so after his stroke.

Tumulty was willing to undertake any task he thought to be in the president's best interests, such as writing or arranging to have written letters sent out over Wilson's signature, as well as state messages such as those delivered on Armistice Day, on Thanksgiving, and to Congress. Tumulty went to work on a note of welcome to the Industrial Conference, which Wilson had earlier initiated in the hope of bringing capital and labor into closer cooperation. Sent in the president's name to a meeting held on the afternoon of October 6 in Washington, the greeting, written in Tumulty's practiced Wilsonian manner, conveyed the president's deep regret over his absence and encouraged "a searching investigation for a policy which will carry us forward upon lines of fair dealing."[3]

With Edith Wilson dominating the uneasy triumvirate of herself, Grayson, and Tumulty, it was not simply a matter, as one historian wrote, of her building a "Chinese wall" around the president: she was, in fact, the wall. When asked how she decided problems were sufficiently important to require the president's attention, she said, "I just decided." She added, "I talked with him so much that I knew pretty well what he thought of things."[4]

Mrs. Wilson's assumption of the responsibilities of the incapacitated president would not have come as a surprise to those who had observed her authoritarian manner and her determination. The press, having been closely exposed to Edith during the recent Western tour, had noted that, when she saw the president tiring, she would put her foot down on interviews. Admiral Grayson would speak of Edith as an "executive genius," as one of the most practical women who took on the responsibilities and burdens of many.[5] Despite Grayson's mollifying references to an unencumbered president, for example, at the October 6 cabinet meeting, Edith Wilson and Joseph Tumulty knew differently. There was much that needed urgent attention; and these two, in their uneasy collaboration, were not found wanting in energy, confidence, or audacity.

On October 6, as her husband lay helpless, Edith coped with an official request from the Senate for facts concerning the newspaper report of a landing by American sailors or marines on the Dalmatian coast that had occurred without the knowledge of the president, the secretary of the U.S. navy, or any other competent American authority.[6] Her handwritten memorandum, with its agitated penmanship and ragged spelling, is a seismograph of her emotional state. Contrary to her claim of acting in one sole instance as intermediary between her husband and another on an official matter except when directed by a physician,[7] the tone and content of Edith's memorandum display a daring assumption of presidential responsibilities. The document, undated, addressed to the secretary of the navy, Josephus Daniels, on White House stationery, is purportedly from the president—whom others have described as being, at this time, "in grave danger,"[8] and "hardly able to do much besides sleep."[9] The note contains explicit instructions as to how Daniels must respond:

> If the Congress should ask questions concerning the employment of our nava [*l* omitted] forces in the Adriatic and Meditarea [*sic*] please refer the questions to me at once informing the Congress you have done so by my direction and that the replys [for replies] will be forthcoming in due course unless indeed the Executive should find that it was not compatible with the public interest to convey to the [*Public* crossed out] Congress at this time the particular information desired [period omitted][10]

Next, Edith telephoned Daniels to say that she was sending over, by the hand of the White House stenographer Charles C. Wagner, the memorandum dictated by the president, but that it was unsigned because Dr. Grayson did not wish any business brought before her husband. Daniels, in turn, reassured the president's wife that he had already taken care of the matter, and that he was enclosing a copy of his letter to the presiding officer of the Senate stating that a senior American naval officer had found it necessary to land a small guard from the USS *Olympia* to protect Italian soldiers on Serbian territory at Trau from counterattack. On that same day Edith wrote—or more accurately, scribbled—another note to Daniels: since his letter had already been sent to the Senate before he received her communication, that is "the Memorandum dictated by the President and taken to you in person," she considered the matter "finished business" as far as his files were concerned. She would not at present submit his response to the president "as the Drs insist all business shall be kept from him."[11]

Given this circuitous, almost farcical way of conducting government business, it wasn't surprising that the British journalist Arthur Willert, looking back to the fall of 1919, judged the next six months as "surely the most bizarre that Washington has ever experienced."[12]

By October 12, the thirtieth misleading bulletin released by the White House to the press announced that the president still suffered from "nervous exhaustion." Rather than soothing the public's doubts, these bland reports aroused deepening anxiety about the condition of the man in the White House. Demoralized by the mystery and misrepresentation attending Wilson's collapse, the secretary of war, Newton D. Baker, said that he felt he had aged a year in just a few weeks.[13] When a letter from Senator George H. Moses, published in the *New York Times* on October 12, declared the president a very sick man who had suffered some kind of a cerebral lesion, who "will not be any material force or factor in anything," Dr. Grayson commented to the press on the following day that "Senator Moses must have information that I do not possess."[14]

With Grayson's official denial, rumor and gossip flared through Washington and across the country. The *San Francisco Bulletin* expressed dissatisfaction with repetitive official announcements of "no noticeable change in the President's condition. . . . The secrecy and even the deception practiced by court physicians in the case of a monarch similarly afflicted have no place in the procedure of an orderly republic. We are a grown-up people and if told everything will be better prepared to face the worst if there is really no hope for an improvement."[15]

A few weeks later, suspecting the truth, *Harvey's Weekly* declared Dr. Grayson's conduct "flagrantly stupid from the beginning." To conceal the president's actual condition "was an impropriety and an injustice so gross and at the same time so stupid as to defy temperate description." Such things might not be regulated, but some unwritten law of courtesy, of propriety, of decency, should make it impossible for functionaries ever again to treat the president of the United States as though he were emperor beyond the law itself.[16]

* * *

With the president enfeebled, official Washington now sought access to him through Joseph Tumulty. The secretary of the interior, Franklin Knight Lane, convinced that he needed a letter from the president to resolve the problems of the current Industrial Conference, wrote directly to Tumulty, not only enclosing a letter to the president, but a proposal for his response. In his cover letter, he told the president that he was "sorry to annoy you, but I must." On the strength of Lane's draft, read to the participants of the Industrial Conference over Wilson's signature on October 22, 1919, the *New York Times* announced that the president was again in touch with the affairs of that conference, that he had sent a message in writing to Secretary Lane through Tumulty, and that subsequently "the President's physicians insisted that he do no more work during the day, and the President spent the afternoon resting."[17]

Abroad, the Bolsheviks' capture of Petrograd raised the urgent question of feeding the populace of Russia and precipitated Robert Lansing's "Memorandum to Be Read to the President" regarding the Russian embassy's request to buy twenty-nine thousand tons of wheat flour at an estimated cost of $3.7 million from the United States Grain Corporation. The draft letter that was enclosed, dated October 22, prepared by the State Department, authorizing Julien Howland Barnes, wheat director, to effect the transaction was retyped in the White House and bore the president's signature.[18] When Barnes then made a similar request on behalf of the Polish government, Edith Wilson invented what she considered a more official presentation of the combined efforts of herself and her husband. While Wilson lay nearly comatose—according to the testimony of Hoover and a series of physicians—Edith prefaced messages with "The President says" firmly inked below the engraved letterhead of the White House stationery. She used this phrase repeatedly throughout Wilson's official correspondence during this period. With this heading and in response to Barnes's request regarding Poland, she directed Tumulty to "tell Mr. Barnes to draw up the proper form of authorization and send it for the President's signature." The message was initialed EBW.[19]

Either Tumulty or Newton Baker wrote the Armistice Day statement issued by Wilson "To my Fellow-countrymen." The Thanksgiving proclamation, drafted by Robert Lansing on Wilson's behalf on November 3, was returned to the secretary of state two days later stamped with the U.S. seal and without a single change, a fact that distressed its author. Lansing was concerned that Wilson had either not been permitted to read the document or was not in a mental state to do so critically. The secretary could not conceive how the president, if he were able to review the statement at all, had permitted it to be issued without some addition of his own phrases. He also thought Wilson's signature, so severely distorted and almost illegible, a shocking manifestation of the president's physical state.

The pending delivery of Wilson's State of the Union address to Congress in December was a triumph of teamwork between Joseph Tumulty and Edith Wilson. Given his consuming urge to maintain the facade of the Wilson presidency, Tumulty was apprehensive that Congress was to convene in a new session on the first day of December, and that the president would be required to forward his message on the following day. "Will you please remind him of this?" Tumulty asked Edith Wilson on November 10.[20] Two weeks later, with the help of Charles Swem, Tumulty sent her a twenty-five-page draft of a proposed message to Congress by the president. "You will notice," he told her, "that I followed the spirit at least of the president's Western speeches in many of the things I say. There are some repetitions in it that we can, of course, take care of."[21]

Presented to Congress on December 2, 1919, in a heavily edited version (Edith's handwriting runs throughout the original), its authorship seemed suspect to many. The style was Wilsonian, and Lansing recognized sentences and phrases of previous addresses—though, detecting another hand at work, he said "the loose stones are there but not the cement usually used by the President." The reporter David Lawrence, however, did not doubt that the long and intricate message was written by Wilson "as it is in very much his language which nobody can imitate." And Tumulty proudly forwarded to Edith the editorial of the *Washington Star* commenting on how, in view of the president's illness, from which he "is now happily recovering," his message "commands attention by its felicity and strength of phraseology, so familiar to those who have studied the Presidential state papers."[22]

Undoubtedly due to yet one more of Dr. Grayson's delusory bulletins, the *New York Times* on December 3 reported that "according to those close to President Wilson, the condition of his health is improving steadily," commenting that Wilson had worked on his annual message and had written and dictated letters; that his shorthand notes for this message and other writings were said to be extremely clear and unwavering, which, with other evidence, showed that his nerves were well under control. Also, in spite of all reports to the contrary, "those in a position to know the President's condition of health insist that he is getting along excellently . . . that the serious aspect of his illness has disappeared and that his gradual complete recovery is assured."

On some occasions, Edith Wilson was remarkably responsive to the president's obligations and, in clear-cut cases, had no choice but to allow speeches and letters to be ghosted in her husband's name, reserving the right to edit them as she saw fit. Bills coming before Congress presented a greater difficulty, which she could influence only negligibly during Wilson's enfeeblement. During the special session of the 66th Congress, between September 30 and November 18, 1919, twenty-eight acts would become law by default because of the president's failure to respond within the requisite ten days.[23] These included acts pertaining to the Cincinnati, New Orleans and Texas Pacific Railway Company, to the authority of the secretary of war, to the Idaho National Forest, to national security and defense, to Treasury appropriations, and to the granting of citizenship to certain American Indians.

Though Wilson was credited with a decision on the Volstead Act, his veto of that bill prohibiting the sale of intoxicating beverages (overturned in both the House of Representatives and the Senate on October 27 and 28, 1919) was in reality written by Tumulty with the obvious approval of Edith Wilson, and with a distinct possibility that the president knew nothing about the message sent in his name.[24]

Edith's intrinsic hostility toward Robert Lansing might account to some degree for her negative response to his numerous and urgent attempts to reach her husband. Fundamental to this tortuous relationship was her contempt for the secretary of state, no doubt intensified by William Bullitt's alarming testimony concerning Lansing's views on the treaty and the League. That testimony had also recharged rumors of Lansing's resignation and of the likelihood that, but for the president's grave illness, the secretary of state would have been jettisoned long ago. Robert Lansing, however, was tenacious. In answer to pressing inquiries from overseas, Lansing had warned the undersecretary of state, Frank Polk, who was winding down the work of the American Mission abroad, that the president was seriously ill and unable to attend to any business: "You should not therefore for the present forward to him personal communications," Lansing cautioned on October 3, 1919, "since they cannot be answered."[25] Nearly two weeks later, obviously still unclear about the facts of the case, he informed Polk that he was seeking the president's advice "about nothing because his health is the first consideration."

Again on November 14, Lansing reported to Polk that the president remained seriously ill and that "Grayson does not desire him to have questions submitted which require constructive thought."[26] Still later the secretary was in a quandary as to how the government was to continue to function. He felt like a man trying to swim with his feet tied: "Of course we will manage some way but it presents many embarrassments," he wrote to the American ambassador to Great Britain, John W. Davis.

Though decisive on many aspects of government, Lansing recognized the limitations of his authority. He was not too proud to humble himself before Edith Wilson, pleading and cajoling to attract her husband's attention. He turned to the White House on November 4 for advice on the recognition of the provisional government of Costa Rica—a move that he recommended. In view of the president's desire to assist struggling constitutional governments, Lansing felt that his chief would personally prefer to pass upon this proposed action. Tumulty forwarded the note to Edith Wilson with a painstaking one of his own:

"When you think an opportune time has arrived, will you not be good enough to present the attached letter to the President from Secretary Lansing?"[27]

Relaying the president's disappointing answer, Edith was oblivious to the civilities usually accorded to correspondents—let alone to the secretary of state. Rather than responding to Tumulty or Lansing or others personally, she continued to prefix directives in her husband's name, emblazoning "The President says" across the pages, as though these words of authority emanated from a White House throne instead of Wilson's pitiful bedstead—if, indeed, their authenticity was not open to question in the first place. In answer to Lansing's request regarding Costa Rica, Edith Wilson wrote:

The President says it is impossible for him to take up such matters until he is stronger and can study them.

So if an answer must be made—the Sec. of State can say he (the Sec.) cannot act without the President's consent and that the P. directs the matter be held in abeyance until he can act[28]

Lansing wrote to Wilson again on November 5, convinced he had a duty to call the president's attention to the friction between the United States and Great Britain precipitated by the retention of the *Imperator* group of ships by the U.S. Shipping Board in retaliation for alleged arbitrary

THE WHITE HOUSE,
WASHINGTON.

The President says it is impossible for him to take up such matters until he is stronger & can study them —

So if an answer must be made — the Sec. of State can say he (the Sec.) cannot act without the Presidents' consent to action by Great Britain concerning German tankers. While it was unanimously agreed that holding the *Imperator* ships was indefensible—and tended to discredit the honor of the United States and the pledged word of its president—Lansing advised, in a cabinet meeting, that no action could be taken on account of the Shipping Board's position that it was responsible for its actions to the president alone. Considering the matter of urgent importance in the conduct of international relations, he asked that the president empower the cabinet or himself to require the Shipping Board to transfer the *Imperator* and other ships of the group to Great Britain or to the lawful owner.

Lansing enclosed a three-page memorandum on the U.S. Shipping Board controversy, including a comprehensive history of its background and the names of seven of the boats in question. Tumulty appears to have forwarded this communication with a memo dated November 11, saying that he had been advised by Ambassador Davis that the United States ought to consent to the immediate return of only the *Imperator* and to hold the others for what Davis called "trading purposes on the other side." By way of answer, Edith, on the bottom half of this memo, continuing onto the lined page of a pad, issued another message, theoretically a direct pronouncement from Wilson:

> The President says he does not know enough about this matter to act upon it and [crossed out] that no action be taken until he is well enough to act upon it.[29]

Unable or unwilling to accept repeated rejection, Lansing sent a letter of two paragraphs to the president on November 12. "I venture to lay before you," he wrote Wilson, in sending a summary as well as copies of telegrams the State Department had received from Paris and London regarding the political and military situation of Syria, the general question of the Turkish Empire, and of the matter of mandates. "I venture to suggest," Lansing continued, "should it meet with your approval," instructing the ambassadors to England and France to inform the Peace Conference and the British government that since the United States Mission was not prepared to take part, Washington would have no objection to other powers proceeding with those negotiations. He "should be very grateful," he concluded, "for an expression of your views." After a week's silence Lansing once again sought Tumulty's intervention. And once again Tumulty wrote to Edith Wilson asking that she speak to the president about the enclosed memorandum from his secretary of state.

Lansing's next "Memorandum: For Mr. Tumulty" pleaded for positive answers to previous communications on November 4, 5, and 12. Matters urgently requiring immediate decision, he pointed out, included participation of the United States in negotiations for a treaty with Turkey; the status of the *Imperator*; recognition of the Costa Rican government. On a sheet that was undated and marked for reference and "Not for signature," Mrs. Wilson held her ground and sent this roughly inked message:

> The President says please inform the State Dept. he will not act on these until he is stronger.[30]

Lansing had better luck, or at least received a more positive reaction, with another letter to the president, first sent in an unsealed envelope for Tumulty's approval, with the request that, if he had no comment to make, he should seal and deliver it. Before complying, Tumulty wrote cautiously, "Dear Mrs. Wilson: I leave it to your judgment as to what to do with this letter." This time Lansing offered elaborate apologies to the president for disturbing him with a lengthy letter—but, he explained, he felt he should know the president's views in order to carry out his policies. Lansing also assured the president that he would endeavor, so far as he was able, to avoid annoying him with the vexatious questions that seemed to multiply rather than decrease due to the inexcusable delay in the ratification of the peace treaty and, even more, because of the disturbing political and economic state in many countries. In her response, initialed EBW, Edith told Lansing:

> The President says he agrees with the Secretary as regards to withdrawing our representatives in Paris and of retaining our member of the "Supreme Council."
>
> About the signing of the Treaty with Bulgaria he thinks if the American Representatives are sett [*sic*] in Paris they could sign— but does not advise their remaining for that purpose.[31]

Within the secrecy in which the White House now operated, or failed to operate, only Edith Wilson and Cary Grayson knew the truth of the president's pronouncements, comments, or decisions. In the early weeks of his illness, Edith's memos would have represented, at most, rough interpretations of Wilson's spasmodic episodes of clarity. However, to maintain the fiction of his capabilities after his stroke, she immediately banished Gilbert Close, his confidential secretary since Princeton days, and one of his two chief stenographers (Charles Swem was the other). Close, in fact, never saw the president during all those months, until one or two days before his own resignation on January 30. "I just had nothing to do, and I got awfully tired of doing nothing," he would explain; and it seemed to him that "Mrs. Wilson apparently ran the whole show during that period."[32]

Close was mistakenly under the impression that Wilson sometimes dictated to his wife and to her secretary, Edith Benham—whose typist, he believed, took care of all the president's personal dictation and typing. Had he been able to look at the most significant bulk of the White House correspondence, he would have understood how expendable his services had become and how economically Edith worked in his stead. From the time of Wilson's stroke until months afterward, she simply scrawled succinct directives in his name under "The President says" at the bottom or top or side of the incoming official memorandums and of those select letters she chose to open, leaving Tumulty to respond in some more official form. She sometimes used a lined piece of paper and, occasionally, the official stationery.

Edith seldom left her husband's side, if she could help it. She exercised by walking on the south side of the White House where she could be reached at a moment's notice and occasionally went for a short drive in Rock Creek Park. Accommodating the needs of the nation to the needs of the president, she ensured that he have absolute quiet and saw to it that the White House and its grounds were all but sealed. Her attitude toward the president's condition was disturbing to many. Even the most sympathetic, who recognized that his life was endangered by a breakdown resulting from overwork and from cruel disappointment over his cherished aspirations, questioned the nature and duration of his dissembled illness. Comparisons were made with the country's plight during the two-month lapse between the fatal shooting of President Garfield and his death, when Garfield's secretaries had carried out his duties or, having no power to sign or act in his name, had gone through the motions. In that tragic interim, however, it was pointed out, the problems of domestic and foreign policy had not been so "multifarious and exacting" as they now were in the aftermath of the Great War.[33]

A sense of momentary optimism flared when Wilson was quoted in the *New York Times* on October 26 as characterizing a proposed general strike of all U.S. bituminous-coal miners and mine workers as "one of the gravest steps ever proposed in this country affecting the economic welfare and the domestic comfort and health of the people." *Harvey's Weekly*, like others, took Wilson's "admirable intervention" in the coal strike as a sign that he was again an active force in government, "to the pleasure and the profit of the nation."[34]

Wilson's published statement regarding the coal strike was, however, in no way indicative of his health. Fortunately, Tumulty had the ability to anticipate and fulfill certain of the president's obligations during the agonizing complexities of a nation in transition from war to peace—in regard to its fundamental industries, where railroads and steel and coal industries were in turmoil, and its discharged veterans angered by rampaging inflation and lack of employment. In the absence of any government blueprint for a postarmistice, boom-to-bust nation, and in the wake of a precipitous drop in farming and land values, and in the abrupt decline of the metal, textile, and chemical industries, the February 1919 estimate of 3 million unemployed would swell to 4.754 million for the year 1920–21. Negotiations between coal operators and representatives of the miners, begun on March 31, 1919, were halted in a deadlock on April 27. In the same month, wildcat strikes of railway workers erupted throughout the country. And in the coming October, in Alabama alone, eleven thousand coal miners would go out on strike.[35]

Tumulty himself drafted the statement about the strike, which was attentively edited by the director general of railroads, Walker Downer Hines, and the Secretary of the Interior Franklin Lane, among other members of the cabinet. Wilson undoubtedly never saw the statement on the coal situation with which he was so enthusiastically credited.[36] Tumulty met with less success in regard to the peacetime adaptation of the country's railroads and their transition from government to private hands. He forwarded the message prepared by Walker Hines to Edith Wilson on November 11 with the assurance that he himself had reviewed it carefully. As all advisers considered it urgent that it go to Congress that day, Tumulty asked that Wilson sign the two copies enclosed so that Tumulty could deliver it promptly. Obviously, Wilson was not well enough to address this potential crisis and Edith wrote Tumulty:

> The President says he cannot do anything with the R.R. situation until he can write something himself to send or deliver to Congress.[37]

THE WHITE HOUSE,
WASHINGTON.

The President Says
he cannot do any
thing with the R.R.
Situation until he can
Write something liter
ally to Send or
deliver to Congress.

111969

Praise for Wilson was ephemeral. Questions about his health burgeoned. Edith was perhaps too successful in achieving her purposes, for it was said that the degree of mystery shrouding her husband's illness "promotes exaggeration." *Harvey's* flatly stated, quoting the Constitution, that in an emergency in which the president could not discharge the powers and duties of his office, whether brief or protracted, "the Vice-President is to act." If Edith read that statement, its cautionary message regarding presidential succession fell on deaf ears. Public business, as she acknowledged, was not her primary concern. Instead, speaking as though the White House were her private domain, she felt that "a house of sickness could not be judged by normal standards." Perhaps at this juncture her perspective on the office of the president of the United States could not be judged by normal standards either. Otherwise, she might be deemed ruthless, presumptuous, and shallow in her regard for the highest office in the land. Her horizons did not extend beyond her husband's sickbed; and she frankly asserted that "to have good nurses was almost as important as to have good Cabinet officers."[38]

CHAPTER 27

Lodge's olive branch

The real effect of the peace treaty, and above all of the Covenant, would depend on the spirit in which it was executed, and on public opinion. It would be the quality of statesmanship and public insistence brought to bear on preventing war that would either make the League of Nations a vital force for peace, and mark the beginning of a new era, or abandon the world's peoples once again to the cycle of conflict. The breadth of commitment on the part of the United States—and thus of the New World—was central to any positive outcome. In November 1919, fulfillment of this grand ideal was impeded by the gargantuan struggle over the Covenant's Article X and the bitter disagreement fomented by the varying interpretations—by Wilson, Lodge, and Gilbert Monell Hitchcock—of the Monroe Doctrine and domestic autonomy.

President Wilson's Article X: *The Members of the League undertake to respect and preserve as against external aggression the territorial integrity and existing political independence of all Members of the League. In case of any such aggression or in case of any threat or danger of such aggression the Council shall advise upon the means by which this obligation shall be fulfilled.*[1]

Republican senator Lodge's proposed reservation on Article X: *The United States assumes no obligations to preserve the territorial integrity or political independence of any other country or to interfere in controversies between nations—whether members of the league or not—under the provisions of article 10, or to employ the military or naval forces of the United States under any article of the treaty for any purpose, unless in any particular case the Congress, which, under the Constitution, has the sole power to declare war or authorize the employment of the military or naval forces of the United States, shall by act or joint resolution so provide.*[2]

Democratic senator Hitchcock's proposed reservation on Article X:

That the advice mentioned in article 10 of the covenant of the league which the council may give to the member nations as to the employment of their naval and military forces is merely advice which each member nation is free to accept or reject according to the conscience and judgment of its then existing Government, and in the United States this advice can only be accepted by action of the Congress at the time in being, Congress alone under the Constitution of the United States having the power to declare war.[3]

For weeks, the city of Washington bristled with speculation about the president's collapse and his "exceedingly personal Government." House was out of the saddle, Lansing was in, and then again, the White House was dominated by Tumulty. Edith Wilson's name was conspicuous by its absence. For practical purposes, the work in Paris was lost, and America was seen creeping into its old shell of provincial isolation. The policy and power of the Senate Republicans were acknowledged, as was the president's mismanagement of the Senate. The London *Times* correspondent Arthur Willert commented that "he will be cramped in every direction. Fancy talking about the possibility of the U.S. not ratifying the alleged crystallization of the Presidential 14 points! What a mess that man in his megalomania has made of things."[4]

As for the American Raymond Fosdick, the devout Wilson loyalist who had been charged with surveying morale in American army camps in France, he was shocked to learn the extent of the president's unpopularity. It was alarming to discover that vitriolic feeling at home, where Republican dislike of the president had changed to open hatred; to realize that, in spite of Wilson's desperate illness, there was no sympathy for him. Comments at the Capitol or in the hotel lobbies were hair-raising: "To hear people talk, one would think Wilson was the chief enemy of his country." An impression of impending disaster could not be dispelled.

The situation in Washington seemed daily more chaotic and unpredictable. The Republicans were determined, for their part, to drive their objections through unmodified. On the Democratic side, a moribund president, dissension within his party, and a lack of positive leadership left little to hope for. The country had wearied of the squabble and was more urgently seized with the looming industrial discord. The drama being played out with regard to the peace treaty and the League appeared to Fosdick as part tragedy and part farce: tragedy because the Senate had no comprehension of the colossal stakes involved in its attempt to humiliate the president; farce, because it was "as flagrant an exhibition of small politics as we have ever had in the Capitol."[5] As for the Covenant, Wilson's concept of the League's fourteen-point charter, it was "misunderstood and misinterpreted everywhere and altogether things look rather gloomy."[6]

Her first battle, Edith believed, was to save her husband's health. As to that other battle—the passage of the peace treaty on her husband's absolute terms—she was bitterly offended by "that stinking Lodge," that "snake in the grass," and by the amendments by which the despised senator planned to cripple her husband's historic document.[7] To her mind, the struggle had narrowed down to a personal vendetta against her husband by the Machiavellian senator and his supporters, and she blindly repudiated any concession to their opposing view. Realists were, however, aware that choices had to be made and compromises achieved.

Friends and colleagues, convinced of the inevitability of compromise, flooded the White House with recommendations. The Chicago newsman H. H. Kohlsaat, a strong believer in the League of Nations who had previously enjoyed unusual access to the president, was alarmed at the change. He pleaded with Wilson, to whom he wrote on October 20, to accept the Lodge reservations rather than have the treaty rejected entirely. He enclosed his letter in an envelope addressed to Mrs. Wilson. On October 23, Edith, not disposed to ignore the more congenial members of the press, politely explained to Kohlsaat that she was returning his note addressed to the president because the doctors "insist nothing be brought to him which is not absolutely essential and not knowing the purpose of your message I think you will appreciate the wisdom of their precaution."[8]

Given the national and global complexities of the moment, and the urgent challenges to government, Edith's judgment of what was worthy of her husband's time appears grotesquely subjective. On October 30, Attorney General A. Mitchell Palmer was one of the first members of the cabinet permitted to see the president. On that same Thursday afternoon, Edith confidently permitted Wilson a second interview: "Our patient improved so that on October 30th we could receive informally the King and Queen of the Belgians," she explained.[9] As Ike Hoover observed, "Every effort was made to save the President from coming in contact with people or considering anything except what appealed to Mrs. Wilson as being important persons."[10]

The visit to the United States of King Albert and Queen Elizabeth of Belgium and their son, Prince Leopold, had been scheduled since the pre-

and that of the pr
or to the presiden
White House had
lerks had been added to t
rrespondence on social topics.[11]
tions concerned with the Belgian visit
discussion of Lansing's participation—a
at Edith Wilson's insistence. When, on the appoi
turned up unexpectedly with the king and queen of Be
left him standing in the hall as she moved with the royal co
into the Green Room. Embarrassed by this outright snub to the secre
tary of state, Edith Benham urged an aide to have him join the others.
Afterward, sealing Lansing's doom, Edith told her secretary that had she
known Lansing was coming, she would have refused to see him.[12]

The Belgians behaved like all considerate friends who find themselves
inadvertently in a house of sickness. King Albert spent ten minutes with
Wilson, the queen five. The president, sitting up in bed, suddenly realized that he was wearing an old gray sweater rather than his dressing
gown. However, Edith was relieved to find the queen so understanding
that one could not feel embarrassed in her presence. As for King Albert,
she thought him gentle as a woman in his sincere sympathy and solicitude for the president. He was also reassuring, telling Wilson of his hope
"that your ideas and ideals will be carried out. My feeling is that they
will be."

Not surprisingly, Edith Wilson designated another royal personage as an
essential visitor. On November 13, with two of the president's daughters, Margaret Wilson and Jessie Sayre, Edith stood at attention as the
boyish, blue-eyed, golden-haired, twenty-five-year-old Edward Windsor, prince of Wales, entered the White House. The prince's visit had
alternately been canceled, postponed, reconsidered, and reinstituted ever
since the Americans' confidential wire of October 7 informed the Foreign Office that "there is a disturbing complication."[13] On October 24,
the State Department, weighing those complications, announced its final
decision that His Royal Highness should proceed, but that in consequence of the president's illness, his visit should be curtailed so as not to
exceed the duration of that of the king of the Belgians.

After tea, Prince Edward took the elevator to the second floor and proceeded to the sickroom, where he found the president propped up in the
Lincoln mahogany bed. Awkward at first at the sight of the ailing presi-

prince comple*tely* won over Edith, s
nner in whi*ch he* deferred to her husba
his later ye*ars* as the duke of Windsor, this
nce of Wale*s was* hailed as a personal success,
service, and *an* unqualified triumph. That heartenin
e young prin*ce cheered* not only the British but also the
mbassador to *Great* Britain, John Davis, who would intro-
a factor in the *crucial* question as to whether the U.S. govern-
would join the *League*.

The royal visi*ts were* essential, if not to the president, certainly as a boost to his wi*fe's* morale. Momentarily diverted from the wreckage of life at the *White* House, eluding those whom she neither liked nor trusted, *as* well as problems that defied solution, Edith Wilson, in a forlorn re*collection*, noted that "all this made the time slip away."[14]

Edith was now obliged to confront the fight for reservations to the Covenant, the body of rules by which the League was to be regulated, being pressed in the Senate. Contemptuous of Henry Cabot Lodge, she refused to admit the possibility that his arguments could be rooted in valid philosophical as well as political differences. Though the senator's private correspondence and public statements during that period would have displeased her, they reveal Lodge as a man of conscience with rational doubts about the effectiveness of the Covenant that held hostage the signing of the peace treaty. His letters articulate his anguished resentment of the president's position and, above all, his doubt that the League was likely to be either enduring or successful.

Contrary to Edith's caricature, he was informed and patriotic—zealous, certainly, but sincere. "We are not so ignorant as you may think," he sternly advised Henry White, the sole Republican on the U.S. delegation to the Peace Conference, on October 2, 1919. That Lodge and his colleagues had given months of study to this matter, White, his friend since youth, certainly knew for a fact. White had written the senator almost weekly of his hopes and fears regarding the maneuvering in Paris. Lodge stressed brusquely that the Republicans had other sources as well, from which they had obtained information refused to them by the president. Lodge was angered by the repeated delays. Peace with Germany would have been achieved during the past April but for the president's insistence that it be tied to the League and its Covenant: "The result was a misfortune to the world. It is not our fault," Lodge told White.[15]

Given his terminal distrust of the Covenant's Article X, Lodge was vious summer. Their visit and that of the prince of Wales were—according to Washington gossip prior to the president's stroke—to be the most stately functions the Wilson White House had ever attempted. It was rumored that three new clerks had been added to the State Department to deal with related correspondence on social topics.[11]

In early deliberations concerned with the Belgian visit on October 30, there had been discussion of Lansing's participation—a suggestion abandoned at Edith Wilson's insistence. When, on the appointed day, Lansing turned up unexpectedly with the king and queen of Belgium, Edith left him standing in the hall as she moved with the royal couple into the Green Room. Embarrassed by this outright snub to the secretary of state, Edith Benham urged an aide to have him join the others. Afterward, sealing Lansing's doom, Edith told her secretary that had she known Lansing was coming, she would have refused to see him.[12]

The Belgians behaved like all considerate friends who find themselves inadvertently in a house of sickness. King Albert spent ten minutes with Wilson, the queen five. The president, sitting up in bed, suddenly realized that he was wearing an old gray sweater rather than his dressing gown. However, Edith was relieved to find the queen so understanding that one could not feel embarrassed in her presence. As for King Albert, she thought him gentle as a woman in his sincere sympathy and solicitude for the president. He was also reassuring, telling Wilson of his hope "that your ideas and ideals will be carried out. My feeling is that they will be."

Not surprisingly, Edith Wilson designated another royal personage as an essential visitor. On November 13, with two of the president's daughters, Margaret Wilson and Jessie Sayre, Edith stood at attention as the boyish, blue-eyed, golden-haired, twenty-five-year-old Edward Windsor, prince of Wales, entered the White House. The prince's visit had alternately been canceled, postponed, reconsidered, and reinstituted ever since the Americans' confidential wire of October 7 informed the Foreign Office that "there is a disturbing complication."[13] On October 24, the State Department, weighing those complications, announced its final decision that His Royal Highness should proceed, but that in consequence of the president's illness, his visit should be curtailed so as not to exceed the duration of that of the king of the Belgians.

After tea, Prince Edward took the elevator to the second floor and proceeded to the sickroom, where he found the president propped up in the Lincoln mahogany bed. Awkward at first at the sight of the ailing president, but later relaxed, the prince completely won over Edith, she said, with the courtly, easy manner in which he deferred to her husband. In contrast to the tenor in his later years as the duke of Windsor, this visit of the youthful Prince of Wales was hailed as a personal success, an important public service, and an unqualified triumph. That heartening response to the young prince cheered not only the British but also the American ambassador to Great Britain, John Davis, who would introduce it as a factor in the crucial question as to whether the U.S. government would join the League.

The royal visits were essential, if not to the president, certainly as a boost to his wife's morale. Momentarily diverted from the wreckage of life at the White House, eluding those whom she neither liked nor trusted, as well as problems that defied solution, Edith Wilson, in a forlorn recollection, noted that "all this made the time slip away."[14]

Edith was now obliged to confront the fight for reservations to the Covenant, the body of rules by which the League was to be regulated, being pressed in the Senate. Contemptuous of Henry Cabot Lodge, she refused to admit the possibility that his arguments could be rooted in valid philosophical as well as political differences. Though the senator's private correspondence and public statements during that period would have displeased her, they reveal Lodge as a man of conscience with rational doubts about the effectiveness of the Covenant that held hostage the signing of the peace treaty. His letters articulate his anguished resentment of the president's position and, above all, his doubt that the League was likely to be either enduring or successful.

Contrary to Edith's caricature, he was informed and patriotic—zealous, certainly, but sincere. "We are not so ignorant as you may think," he sternly advised Henry White, the sole Republican on the U.S. delegation to the Peace Conference, on October 2, 1919. That Lodge and his colleagues had given months of study to this matter, White, his friend since youth, certainly knew for a fact. White had written the senator almost weekly of his hopes and fears regarding the maneuvering in Paris. Lodge stressed brusquely that the Republicans had other sources as well, from which they had obtained information refused to them by the president. Lodge was angered by the repeated delays. Peace with Germany would have been achieved during the past April but for the president's insistence that it be tied to the League and its Covenant: "The result was a misfortune to the world. It is not our fault," Lodge told White.[15]

Given his terminal distrust of the Covenant's Article X, Lodge was emphatic in stressing, as he did to the Right Honorable Viscount Bryce on October 8, 1919, that Congress, and not the League Council, would make decisions for the United States regarding war and peace, that it was "not only our right but our duty to decide what burdens we should take."[16] Lodge and a majority of the Senate stated and restated that they thought the League to be a political alliance that gave no assurance of promoting world peace and menaced the safety and sovereignty of America. The requirement of a unanimous vote from the nine members of the Council, and the agreement of a majority in the Assembly, seemed to make the amending provision unworkable. Altogether, his analysis was carefully deliberated, and quite inconsonant with Edith Wilson's accusations of wanton antipathy.

Early in that troubled October, Lodge grew confident that the treaty could not pass the Senate unless reservations were made to relieve the United States from certain obligations and to leave the Monroe Doctrine and the settlement of domestic questions wholly within the exclusive jurisdiction of the United States. This would not defeat the League and would allow other member states to accept its present terms, if they chose.[17] At the same time, he added his own supporting opinion to speculation abroad that a League of Nations without U.S. participation would be ineffectual. "Of course the League cannot get along without us. I have never had the slightest doubt that they will very gladly accept the reservations," he wrote to Henry White on November 3.[18]

Consistent in private and in public, he once again enlisted the inspirational figure of George Washington to fortify his cause. On October 9, he reminded his audience that America's first president had "warned against foreign alliances," not because he held to selfish isolation but because he was convinced that anyone who votes to make this government a part of an international government or a constituent member of a supergovernment not devoted to the identical purposes and clearly expressed aims of our Constitution "has cast a vote to destroy this country."[19]

Lodge's reputation remains that of the ruthless, calculating spoiler, whose central goal was to embarrass Wilson. Nevertheless, in one expert's opinion, what were known as the "Lodge Reservations" were of a wholly minor character that left the League's structure intact and "would have interfered with its workings not at all."[20] It seems that the senator did explore some vein of compromise that might have made a crucial difference, had Wilson been permitted to consider it. The historian Thomas A. Bailey has written, "Wilson's vice-regents shouldered a grave responsibility in keeping it from him—granted that they did. If such a decision was made on the ground of the president's ill health, this was further proof that he should have resigned. If the decision was made on the ground that Mrs. Wilson disliked Colonel House and distrusted his advice, as we know she did, then she should have resigned along with her husband."[21]

Lieutenant Colonel Stephen Bonsal, interpreter abroad for both Wilson and Colonel House and recently home from Europe, called on Senator Lodge in Washington on October 28 at the request of the ailing Colonel House. Bonsal, a schoolmate of the senator's late son-in-law, Augustus Peabody Gardner, admired Lodge, whom, politics apart, he affectionately considered "the most interesting man in the Senate." During their talk Lodge frankly and repeatedly stated his anxiety about Article X, which President Wilson consistently referred to as the heart of the Covenant. Bonsal thought he detected that Lodge was not as confident as he was rumored to be, but seemed, rather, in a mood to compromise.

Reviewing the Covenant article by article, Lodge penciled in on an official copy of the treaty a number of what Bonsal thought unimportant verbal changes that ran to about fifty words. It seemed to Bonsal that these changes, largely concerned with verbiage, were milder and differed sharply from the reservations Lodge had introduced in the Senate, and which now blocked the path to ratification. Lodge thought that his penciled changes, if accepted, would smooth the way to ratification, and Bonsal telephoned Colonel House after his second talk with the senator on November 2. That news came, House would remember, "like a rainbow in a lowering sky. The situation is brighter, much brighter." Within the hour, Bonsal forwarded the copy of the Covenant with what he called Lodge's "olive branch," his "slightly diluted" notations, which the elated colonel sent on to the White House.[22]

Two weeks later, on November 16, in an entirely despondent mood, Bonsal made a sad entry in his diary: "Not a word has come to House from the White House, not even an acknowledgment that the important communication has been received." Lodge's olive branch having been rejected, all hints of the senator's willingness to mediate vanished. Evaluating the aftermath, Bonsal supposed that Lodge, a man of enormous vanity, might well have thought that Wilson, with his "accustomed arrogance," had snubbed him. Bonsal also blamed the "blackout in Washington." There was a strong possibility, he guessed, that the olive branch may never have reached Wilson—"altogether an unfortunate mess." Years later, at a loss to explain what had happened to Lodge's paper, Bonsal speculated that probably, with the exception of Mrs. Wilson and Admiral Grayson, "no one knows, and as they never showed the slightest appreciation of its importance, whatever they may have known, they have probably forgotten."[23]

House remained suspicious of the odd circumstances of Lodge's supposed concessions and questioned the senator's good faith and the motivation that induced him to take this apparently conciliatory step. The colonel was wary of doing Lodge an injustice, but even more cautious of wronging the stricken president by holding him responsible for ignoring an opportunity that had, perhaps, never been presented to him. Given the sincerity of his quest and its faint but inestimable possibilities, House was understandably hurt, as he said later, when Edith Wilson wrote that "by conferring with Lodge, his arch-enemy," House "broke the president's heart." "How unfair this is," House told Stephen Bonsal.[24]

The aborted delivery of Lodge's notes on the Covenant was neither the first nor the last instance of Colonel House's frustrated attempts to reach Wilson. It was a striking example of how remote he appeared in Edith Wilson's estimate of essentials. Virtually marooned in Paris, fighting abandonment as tactfully as possible while the president was barnstorming the West on behalf of the League, House had sent cables and letters to Wilson. On September 20, he noted that the British had withdrawn their plenipotentiaries, with one man only remaining in Paris, and House therefore advised that the presence of four American commissioners not only seemed unnecessary, but might lead to criticism in the United States. On September 29, he telegraphed from Paris to Wilson, who had been rushed back to Washington just the previous day: "We are greatly distressed to hear of your illness. Our love and good wishes are always with you." The next day he forwarded a letter on the fraught question of Fiume, but urged the closing of the Hôtel Crillon offices and the reduction of representation to a minimum to avoid criticism that was already rife. He was counting on sailing in the first week in October, unless he was wanted sooner.

House sailed on October 6 on the *Northern Pacific*, arriving at Hoboken on October 12, so severely ill with a recurrence of kidney stones that he was carried down the gangplank on a stretcher, his general condition so poor that the doctors would refuse to operate at this time. On October 22, House wrote to Edith Wilson. He was responding to the first word he had received from the White House in two months, however indirectly—a letter Edith had written to thank his wife, Loulie, for her sympathy and concern for the president. When her husband was better, Edith promised to tell Wilson of Loulie's letter and the colonel's message, and also about the latter's illness. At the moment, however, "as we keep every thing from him (which it is not important to have his advise about, & which would annoy or distress him, I have not yet told him of the Colonel's illness or that he has left Paris—for I knew how anxious he was that he remain there for the time."[25]

House was troubled by this message. That Edith had not told the president of House's return indicated to him that Wilson was either much sicker than he had thought, or that more importance was laid on House's remaining abroad than had seemed possible. Having no correct idea of the extent of Wilson's incapacity, he wrote to Edith, "I take it that for some reason he has not read these letters or cables." Reiterating for her benefit the gist of his communications over the past month, he said that his work was entirely finished, his continued presence had begun to raise unpleasant comment, and all the commissioners had agreed that it was best for him to return home. What he had not mentioned previously was that he was so unhappy and uneasy about the president's condition before he'd left Paris that "I should have come in any event even if there had been no understanding." House also wrote that his own doctors had advised him to keep quiet for some time, but if Edith felt he could be of any service whatever, he would be glad to come to Washington whenever she indicated. He was sure that she knew how deeply distressed he was "and how willingly I would do anything in my power to serve either the President or you."[26]

Edith Wilson responded one day later, her studied vagueness disheartening if not insulting. She was sorry that her letter to Mrs. House had caused him unhappiness. She really did not know whether the letters and cables he spoke of had ever reached the president for the party was moving so fast—she was obviously referring to their Western tour—the president had had almost no time except that which he devoted to preparation of his two and three speeches a day. When they did reach home, Dr. Grayson had forbidden his looking at the vast accumulation of mail. Also, the president's progress necessarily had to be slow, and his ignorance of House's return could therefore do her husband no harm. Furthermore, implying that House was guilty of disobedience, she said that if Wilson did think the colonel should remain in Paris ("that I knew he did . . . some time ago"), it might have caused him to worry to learn of his return.

A cable from abroad from Sir William Wiseman provided Colonel

House with another excuse to reach out to the president. In a note to Mrs. Wilson, House enclosed Wiseman's message that the U.S. Senate's delay in ratification of the peace treaty, and general use of the vital international situation for party purposes, "has aroused strong feeling of irritation among general public here as well as political circles." House, in his second enclosure, a brief personal one to Wilson, wrote that he was glad that the president was getting on well, that it was good to have his steady hand at the helm once more, and that House hoped "no further mishaps may come to you." He added in the next paragraph that after many weeks of painful illness, "I find myself practically well and of course you know I am always at your service."[27]

Edith responded to House immediately, telling him that she had read the president his letter and Wiseman's cable and "oh! poor fellow I am so sorry," her husband had said, when he learned of House's illness. Her note was not quite as ingenuous as that report might suggest. She alerted House that he was not to be allowed into the White House sanctuary. The president "did not ask me where you wrote from, so I fancy he still thinks you are in Paris." She also mentioned owing Mrs. House a note but excused herself. "My hands now are so full that I neglect many things. But I feel equal to anything that comes now that I see steady progress going on, although it is very, very slow."[28]

Edith Wilson did not overstate her responsibilities. She was in fact the self-appointed censor as well as the sole liaison between the bedridden president of the United States and the Congress during those weeks when the country's membership in the League of Nations trembled in the balance. The stakes were historic; yet she showed no hesitation in assuming such a role. In her autocratic way, she elected Senator Gilbert Monell Hitchcock, Democrat from Nebraska, former publisher and present minority leader, to the minuscule category of persons permitted, along with royalty, to see her husband.

During their interview on November 7—with his predictable sentinels Edith Wilson and Grayson standing by[29]—Wilson brightened when Hitchcock reported that the Democrats were defeating the dangerous amendments one by one and would soon have them all out of the way. The president grew anxious again when told of the significance of the reservations. He then asked how many votes could be gotten for ratification without reservations. When Hitchcock said "not over forty-five out of ninety-six," Wilson groaned, "'Is it possible, is it possible.'"

As a result of this interview and at Edith Wilson's suggestion, Hitchcock sent the president's wife a typewritten letter on November 13 bringing her up-to-date on Senate negotiations. The Republicans, Edith learned, were solidly supporting the "Lodge Reservations," while the Democrats were offering substitutes that they, with three or four exceptions, were supporting. Already the Senate had adopted the first and second reservations, not as unacceptable as previously drafted, to win the support of four or five "mild reservation" senators. "Still it is bad," Hitchcock warned as he outlined the party's plan.

At the appropriate time, the Democrats would offer a resolution of unqualified ratification of the peace treaty as a substitute for Lodge's resolution of ratification with reservations. Republicans outnumbered Democrats and could carry motions that required only a majority vote. But ratification of the treaty—whether on Lodge's terms or on Wilson's— required a two-thirds vote in favor. Neither side, on its own, had the numbers to assure that. With every expectation of being beaten on the motion for unqualified ratification, the Democrats would next offer what Hitchcock called interpretive reservations to take the place of the supposedly drastic reservations proposed by Senator Lodge. Again expecting "of course, to be beaten also on this vote," the Democrats would find solace in having made the Democratic record clear. Next, it was expected that Lodge would present for final vote a resolution of ratification that included his reservations, which the Democrats would oppose to prevent the mandatory two-thirds vote for ratification.

Having outlined their strategy, Hitchcock allowed that the plan was subject to modification, in case the president advised them to vote for the Lodge Reservations to salvage what would be left of the treaty. As some Democrats felt they would like to have the president's guidance, the senator proposed to submit the matter to him, perhaps in a week's time. Their choice posed a dilemma—whether it would be worse to reject Wilson's sacrosanct treaty altogether rather than to accept the Lodge restrictions on use of U.S. forces, or to accept the Lodge Reservations in order to preserve the rest of Wilson's plan. At the heart of the Democrats' problem was the urgent concern that a negative vote on ratification of the treaty with the Lodge Reservations might wrongly suggest to the public a Democratic disavowal of all Wilson's work in Paris.[30]

At this time Hitchcock also enclosed the two pages he had written of "Proposed Substitute Reservations" to the treaty to take the place of those proposed by Senator Lodge, an altogether reasonable document doomed by Hitchcock's subservience to a defiantly implacable president. Hitchcock told Edith that the first four were "in substance" in accord with Wilson's memorandum of September 3, written prior to his Western tour, and the last one, "I think, in accordance with [Wilson's] own views on the true meaning of the League's Covenant."[31]

Two days later, on November 15, Hitchcock informed Edith by letter that the vice president had announced that he, as presiding officer of the Senate, would rule that if the Lodge resolution failed to receive a two-thirds vote, other resolutions of ratification might be offered. The hour was close at hand when Hitchcock must learn from the president definitely whether the friends of the treaty should vote against the resolution of ratification containing these Lodge Reservations, thus defeating it. Recognizing the bleak prospects of the proceedings, Edith scrawled a message lengthwise on the back of an envelope, presumably for Hitchcock: "program you outline has his approval—He could not accept ratification with Lodge Reservations in any case."[32]

Hitchcock was invited to call at the White House on the morning of November 17. Wilson, with Edith and Dr. Grayson standing guard, lay on his back, appearing very weak as he confided to Hitchcock that it tired him to read or discuss important matters. He was also aware that he was in the dark to some extent, except for what Mrs. Wilson and Dr. Grayson chose to tell him, and that "they have purposely kept a good deal from me." Hungry for news, he wanted Hitchcock to tell him all that had taken place since he fell ill. Later that day, Hitchcock forwarded to Mrs. Wilson a four-paragraph, typewritten draft of a letter, embodying the content of the morning's discussion. Modestly titled "A Suggestion"— presumably a response to inquiries about how Democratic senators ought to position themselves on the upcoming vote on the treaty—the document left no doubt about Wilson's stance: he hoped that all true friends of the treaty would refuse to support the Lodge resolution; he warned that "the resolution in that form does not provide for ratification, but rather for defeat of the treaty."[33] In consultation with her husband, Edith Wilson crossed out "A Suggestion" and wrote "To Senator Hitchcock" at the top, and "My dear Senator" at the start of the body of the letter, and replaced Hitchcock's original word "defeat" with "the nullification." Four out of six lines were slashed away in the third paragraph. The thought that "the door will probably then be open for a possible compromise" was altered to allow only for the probability that the door would be open "for a genuine resolution of ratification."[34] With this editing, Hitchcock's surrogate letter was to be read in the president's name before the Senate on the day of the crucial vote.

To. Senator Hitchcock   463A

My dear Senator

You were good enough to bring me word that the democratic
senators supporting the treaty expected to hold a conference
before the final vote on the Lodge resolution of ratification
and that they would be glad to receive a word of counsel from
me.

I should hesitate to offer it in any detail but I assume
that the senators desire my judgment upon the all-important
question of the final vote on the resolution containing the many
reservations by Senator Lodge. On that I can not hesitate, for
in my opinion the resolution in that form does not provide for
ratification, but rather for defeat of the treaty. I sincerely
hope that the friends and supporters of the treaty will vote
against the Lodge resolution of ratification.

I understand that the door will probably then be open for a
possible compromise agreement on a resolution that will make
ratification possible. At least the democratic senators will
have made a record in support of the treaty by bringing forward a real resolution of ratification while those who
oppose it will be compelled to bear the responsibility.

I hope therefore that all true friends of the treaty will
refuse to support the Lodge resolution.

* * *

Edith's version of the genesis of that critical letter reveals that, however much she may have guarded her husband against all forms of pressure, she herself was not immune to overtures on the subject of the League. She could not be unsympathetic to friends—especially to such a valued and persuasive one as the financier Bernard Baruch, who entreated that Wilson compromise, and who insisted that "half a loaf is better than no bread." The bitter negotiations had taken their toll: she admitted that the long, drawn-out fight was "eating into my very soul." In her anxiety and her love for Wilson, she now felt that nothing mattered but to get the treaty ratified. As a result, after Hitchcock came to tell her that the struggle had narrowed down to a personal fight against the president by Lodge and his supporters, and that, unless the administration accepted the Republicans' reservations, the treaty would be beaten, she went in desperation to her husband. For her sake, would he "accept these reservations," she pleaded, "and get this awful thing settled?" She recounted that, turning his head on the pillow and stretching out his hand to take hers, he had answered in a voice she would never forget:

> Little girl, don't you desert me; that I cannot stand. Can't you see that I have no moral right to accept any change in a paper I have signed without giving to every other signatory, even the Germans, the right to do the same thing? It is not I that will not accept; it is the Nation's honour that is at stake.

It was "better a thousand times to go down fighting than to dip your colours to dishonourable compromise," he told Edith, and she agreed. In fact, she said, she felt like one of her husband's betrayers to have ever doubted his position. For the first time, she felt that she saw things clearly, and she vowed that she would never ask him again to do what would be manifestly dishonorable.[35]

On the same day that Wilson sent Hitchcock his emphatic opposition to Lodge's position, the senator again wrote Edith Wilson to tell her of his developing negotiations with Lodge. After it was intimated to Hitchcock that Lodge was willing to confer about a possible compromise on the League, the two men had met and Hitchcock had made a proposal. Following the expected defeat of the Lodge resolution, Lodge would support a motion for reconsideration, to be followed by Hitchcock's proposal for a resolution of ratification with interpretive reservations.

Then the Senate would recess for a day to allow for conference on whether compromise was possible.

Lodge listened, consulted with his associates, then advised that he could not accept the proposition unless Hitchcock could state in advance what compromise could be offered. Hitchcock was at a loss here. He explained that he could not answer at once because he had to consult not only the president but the Democratic members.

On that same November 18, the day before the final vote on the treaty, a statement by the Washington bureau of the Committee of the League to Enforce Peace, which included Harvard president A. Lawrence Lowell among its members, was read in Congress: "The treaty, even with the reservations . . . can accomplish this purpose and should be ratified. . . . The world waits. Delay is perilous."[36] Tumulty sent Mrs. Wilson a newspaper clipping from the New York *World* of a message from South Africa carried by the Associated Press in which the prime minister of South Africa Jan Christiaan Smuts appealed to the United States to adopt the League Covenant and "not to blast the hopes of the world."[37] In a three-page telegram, Herbert Hoover, then chairman of the American Red Cross, assured Wilson that he was "impressed with the desperate necessity of early ratification," even with the opposition's reservations. Its operation could repair mistakes in its building.[38]

Lodge, as though he found it necessary to reaffirm, clarify, or defend his point of view, prepared a form letter and a statement, either for his constituents or for himself. Though it is possible that neither was ever dispatched, both the documents clearly codify his position. In essence, the form letter cautioned that "no step be taken without the most thorough consideration of the agreements." His formal statement insisted that the Senate has equal power and responsibility with the president in the making of treaties and "would not obey the orders of the President who undertakes to command the Senate to ratify the treaty without reservations adopted by a large majority of the Senate . . ."[39]

On November 19, Senator Henry Ashurst of Arizona breakfasted early and went directly to the Capitol to attend the caucus called by the Democratic leader Hitchcock on the Lodge resolution of ratification. "The breeze from my motor-car stirred the dead leaves strewn about, and I knew that President Wilson's Treaty would soon be as dead as those leaves," he wrote in his diary. As far as he could judge, the pro-Leaguers had "sinned away their day of grace."[40]

Hitchcock's caucus was attended by every Democratic senator who favored the treaty with the exception of Senator Culberson of Texas, who was ill. Senator Oscar Underwood of Alabama moved that the Democratic senators negate the Lodge resolution of ratification. Then Hitchcock read and passed around Wilson's letter that counseled friends and supporters of the treaty to vote against the resolution that, as he saw it, did not provide for its ratification, but rather for its nullification. Examining the letter, Ashurst noted that it was not signed by the president but that a facsimile of his signature had been stamped on the letter in purple ink.

At noon, the Senate convened, Vice President Marshall presiding. The chaplain prayed for the spirit of wisdom and counsel "that we may do our duty." Of the ninety-six senators, ninety-four answered the roll call (Culberson was absent; there was a vacancy in Virginia). Within ten minutes, Lodge announced that the press had sent him a copy of Wilson's letter to Hitchcock. As the senator from Nebraska had not offered it, Lodge said, he thought it should be read at this time and he proceeded to do so. This done, Lodge told the president of the Senate, "I think comment is superfluous, and I shall make none."

The Democratic senators were astounded that the letter had been sent to the press, and the mild reservationists were enraged by its content. After five and one-half hours of debate, at five-thirty in the afternoon, the roll call on the Lodge resolution with its strictures on the use of U.S. forces followed: thirty-nine ayes and fifty-five nays. Republicans and four Democrats who preferred ratification with reservations to total rejection voted in favor. The rest of the Democrats, following Wilson's directive against a modified treaty, combined with the thirteen irreconcilables in opposition to the League in any form, accounted for the paradoxical outcome. After furious parliamentary maneuvering, two more votes were taken (with a few voters lost in the process) on reconsideration of the treaty with Hitchcock's reservations and with Lodge's: the first was defeated forty-one to fifty, the second forty-one to fifty-one. Senator Underwood then appealed for unanimous consent to vote on the treaty without reservations, with the result that the Versailles Treaty, which had been ratified by all Allies abroad, was voted down in the Senate, thirty-eight to fifty-three.[41] Had the Democrats ignored Wilson and voted along with the Lodge reservationists, the treaty would have been ratified. The coalition of Wilson's partisans and the absolute opposition, the anti-League irreconcilables, the so-called bitter-enders, spelled its demise. The treaty having failed to command a simple majority, much less the necessary two-thirds vote, the Senate adjourned until the new session scheduled to begin on the first Tuesday in December.

On November 19, the day of the Senate vote, "A Draft of a State-ment" was prepared in Edith's handwriting. It was apparently a falter-ing, incoherent attempt by the president to organize and analyze his thoughts on the significance of the treaty:

> This Treaty not a particular compact between us & the other Signa-tory Powers but a general (chiefly European) settlement with the Central Powers, which the associated governments by high valor & the unutterable sacrifices of their people won the right to exact but whose terms they determined in constant conference with us, with unfailing deference to our views & with an honest effort to make them square with the principles we had laid down as the guiding principles of the conflict.
>   Reservations in effect redefinitions of responsibilities & duties undertaken by us under the Treaty.
>   This is the field & function of negotiation not of ratification.[42]

Parallel, yet in sharp contrast to Wilson's feeble attempt to order his thoughts on the treaty, is the form letter that Lodge drafted shortly after its rejection—again, perhaps, for his own record. The taut paragraph lends credence to the belief that Lodge was not altogether opposed to the treaty—his resolution for ratification with reservations was itself proof of this point—but he was determined to protect his turf and fiercely. "Reser-vations were placed upon the treaty that a decisive majority of the Sen-ate felt were necessary for the protection of the independence, the sovereignty, and the peace of the United States. The President's followers in the Senate, under his direction, refused to ratify the treaty with those reservations. The treaty can be ratified with those reservations, but not without them; and it is for the President to determine whether he is will-ing to accept them in order that the treaty may be ratified."[43]

At this point, Lodge had lost all patience with Wilson and what he viewed as "the loose and general way" in which the president had talked about idealism and liberalism and vision. The senator said and wrote this bluntly, both in private and publicly. Such men as Wilson forgot that others had ideals but also knew the importance of wisdom and tolerance in converting ideals into realities. In Lodge's opinion, if Wilson were a true idealist, he would have saved his Covenant and secured its adoption in the Senate of the United States by accepting some modification of its terms, on grounds that the principle was more important than its details and qualifications. Then, as a true idealist, Wilson would have succeeded in large measure, as had Lincoln when he put aside for a time the emancipation of the slaves, on which his heart was set, in order to preserve the Union, which to him was the highest ideal and, at that moment, the dominant purpose.[44]

Edith Wilson said that she could scarcely bring herself to tell her husband that the treaty had been defeated in the Senate both with and without Lodge's reservations. As she sat by his bedside to give him the news, she worried that the shock might have serious consequences. According to her account, the president was silent for a few moments, then said, "All the more reason I must get well and try again to bring this country to a sense of its great opportunity and greater responsibility."[45]

CHAPTER 28

The "Smelling Committee" pays a visit

Reactions to the failure to pass the peace treaty were vindictive, sarcastic, and disbelieving. "There never was another great international transaction so perniciously befogged with misrepresentation," *Harvey's Weekly* raged on November 22. "And Damned Be He" Wilson was cursed the very next week.[1]

There was no question in the mind of the editorial writer, undoubtedly Colonel George Harvey himself, that the president was responsible for the defeat of his own treaty and Covenant. This Harvey considered the more remarkable as the president had devoted a year to the negotiations process and, at the end, through his own crass ineptitude and arrogance, had brought the whole thing to ruin. Up to the very last moment it was almost impossible to believe reports that the president would dispatch "the beloved offspring of his acute mentality through the traditional slaughter house to an open grave. But he did." A check of the sequence of events made the outcome even more implausible.

The *Weekly* noted that the Senate had rejected the treaty, for approval without reservations, by a vote of fifty-three to thirty-eight. It reviewed the subsequent votes, noted the Democratic defectors, and concluded that the forty-two remaining loyalist Democrats voted against ratification "by explicit request of the President." If, on the other hand, "the President had expressed a desire for ratification or if he had remained silent, the entire forty-two would have voted aye and the treaty would have been ratified by a vote of eighty-one to thirteen. "The President," an incredulous Colonel Harvey concluded, "prevented ratification. Those are the facts. There is no getting away from them."

And still the *Weekly* was not done with the president but concluded "Mr. Wilson Should Resign." To strengthen the case against him, and to highlight his contradictory nature, the ever-resourceful *Weekly* reminded readers of how differently the youthful Wilson, a student at Johns Hopkins back in 1885, assessed matters, when he wrote: "The President really has no voice at all in the conclusions of the Senate with reference to his diplomatic transactions, or with reference to any of the matters upon which he consults it. . . . He is made to approach that body as a servant conferring with his master, and of course deferring to that master . . ."[2]

Observing the ruins of the treaty, Henry Cabot Lodge was more dismayed and bewildered than vengeful. Mulling over the results, he complained openly that the president had delayed the treaty with Germany by yoking it to the League, that he had ignored both the powers of the Senate and that the overwhelming majority of the populace insisted on reservations protecting the United States. Lodge explained and defended his own position—sufficiently insecure to make him ardently appreciative of Elihu Root's praise of his leadership. Lodge was especially heartened that it was the wish of this distinguished former senator and Nobel Peace Prize laureate that all the friends of the treaty could understand that Lodge had given the treaty its only chance for ratification, "a chance which the President in his willful self-sufficient pride has rejected."[3]

Lodge's response shed some light on his earlier efforts to reach a compromise on the League. On December 3 he wrote:

In the closing days of the past session of Congress we gave Hitchcock [the Democratic leader of the Senate] opportunity to make any proposals for modifications which he desired. He declined to make any at that moment, saying the time was not sufficient. We then went to the vote, with the results you know. After his refusal to make any proposals there was no opportunity for further change. I could not then break my line. It would have thrown everything into confusion. We had to go through with the reservations as they were and we polled the full Republican strength on every vote but one where we lost a single vote.

Looking to the future, Lodge predicted that the president would resubmit the treaty; Lodge was equally certain that the reservations would be accepted substantially as they stood. As for the merits of the League, Lodge allowed that many people thought it would never amount to anything in practice and would really be quite harmless; others, of whom Lodge was one, thought it contained menacing possibilities, not only for the United States but for the peace of the world: a loosely drawn instrument and, therefore, perilous.[4] For the present, however, the next move was Wilson's, though Lodge considered the president incapable of making any move. He believed Wilson's condition to be much worse than the White House bulletins indicated.

Wilson's invisibility was the heart of the difficulty. He did not read letters sent to him; Hitchcock had seen him only twice; House was not allowed to see him at all. Lodge saw no prospect of a solution and assumed that the other powers would now go ahead with the League without the United States. He also complained that "a regency of Tumulty and Barney Baruch . . . was not contemplated by the constitution."[5]

The so-called friends of the treaty, the genuine loyalists, refused to be discouraged and were ready with advice for the president should a vote again come up. In the aftermath of the disastrous events in the Senate on November 19, Joseph Tumulty forwarded to Wilson a letter from Alabama senator Oscar W. Underwood. Underwood was writing to assure the president, first of all, that the treaty was not dead in the Senate, as Mr. Lodge had asserted. Underwood predicted that the people of America believed that it would in some way be ratified, that "the only thing that can kill it is the direct effort of the Republican majority to destroy it."[6]

On November 22, Senator Hitchcock also reassured Wilson that the situation in the Senate "is not a defeat, but only a deadlock."[7] Two days later, writing from Omaha, the senator broached the subject of compromise. He was disposed to believe that a settlement of the treaty by Christmas was reasonably possible and that there was time "to work up a compromise." He was taking the liberty of submitting by mail one or possibly two suggestions as a reservation on Article X. Back in Washington, when Hitchcock turned up in Tumulty's office on the afternoon of November 29, to discuss the future of the treaty, he waited thirty minutes without seeing either Wilson or Tumulty. On December 1, Tumulty would remind Edith Wilson that Hitchcock "still insists upon seeing the President." The next day the *New York Times* reported that those close to President Wilson said his health was improving steadily, that his shorthand notes made in composing his annual message and other writings were said to be extremely clear and unwavering. Even so, there was uneasiness in the Senate and House over the president's prolonged unavailability, which only stoked rumors of his serious disability.[8]

Of all those concerned, no one was more zealous than Colonel House in his efforts to salvage the League and the president's reputation, which he profoundly believed to be intertwined. House's attempt at rescue began with a letter to Edith Wilson, signed "Your Sincere Friend," on November 24:

> You can never know how long I have hesitated to write to the President about anything while he is ill, but it seems to me vital that the Treaty should pass in some form. His place in history is in balance. If the Treaty goes through with objectionable reservations it can later be rectified. The essential thing is to have the president's great work in Paris live.

House enclosed a typewritten letter addressed to "Dear Governor." He hesitated to intrude his views at such a time, he told Wilson, but he felt he would be doing less than his duty if he did not do so. Since so much depended on the president's decision in regard to the treaty, "its failure would be a disaster not less to civilization than to you." A great many people, Democrats, Progressives, and Republicans, had talked with House about ratification, and they were all pretty much of one mind regarding the necessity for its passage with or without reservations. To the ordinary man, the distance between the treaty and the reservations was slight. Of course, House reassured Wilson, "the arguments are all with the position you have taken and against that of the Senate, but, unfortunately, no amount of logic could alter the situation."

House advised Wilson to call Hitchcock and tell him he felt that he, the president, had done his duty and fulfilled his every obligation to his colleagues in Paris by rejecting all offers to alter the document that had been formulated there—and he would turn the treaty over to the Senate for such action as it might deem wise to take. Then, House continued, Wilson should advise Hitchcock to ask the Democratic senators to vote for the treaty with such reservations as the majority might formulate and let the matter rest with the other signatories. Further, House would have the president say to Senator Hitchcock that, if the Allied powers were willing to accept those reservations, he would abide by the result, conscious of having done his full duty. House allowed that the Allies might not take the treaty with the Lodge Reservations as they now stood, and this would be Wilson's vindication. But if they should take them, even with slight modifications, "your conscience will be clear."

After an agreement was reached, House said, it could easily be shown that the Covenant in its practical workings in the future would not be seriously hampered and that time would provide a workable machine. In conclusion: "The supreme place which history will give you will be largely because you personify in yourself the great idealistic conception of a league of nations. If this conception fails, it will be your failure. Today, there are millions of helpless people throughout the world who look to you and you only to make this conception a realization."

When House did not hear from the president in response to this letter, he wrote to Edith Wilson on November 27, obviously determined to reach the president regarding this momentous issue. "May I trouble you again with another letter to the President. I am afraid that I did not make myself altogether clear in my last one. I feel that if he understands the suggestion as I have it in mind, he will approve it." Addressing the Dear Governor, House said he wished to emphasize that he did not counsel surrender. Rather, the action he advised would make the president's position "consistent and impregnable." Asking Wilson to bear in mind that "everyone who is in close touch with the situation admits that the Treaty cannot be ratified without substantial reservations," House assured him that he need not be party to these reservations—if the Senate refused to ratify the treaty as it was made in Paris, the Allies could determine whether they would accept them. In this way he felt certain that Wilson's attitude would receive universal approval. "On the one hand your loyalty to our Allies will be commended and, on the other, your willingness to adopt reservations rather than have the Treaty killed will be regarded as the act of a great man."[9]

As weeks went by, his letters unanswered, House pondered his exile, sadly noting that, as Edith Wilson failed to deny stories about his break with the president, he was forced to conclude that she was willing to have those stories credited. He felt helpless, and the only course, he concluded, was to remain aloof until he received some direct word from the president—though he feared that Wilson was in a condition "totally unfit to appreciate the situation as it has developed."[10]

House could not have known, however, that his letters to Wilson remained unopened until they reached the Library of Congress in 1952, and that Wilson had, presumably, never known of their existence. Sounding the death knell of House's career, the British newsman Arthur Willert had already reported to the London *Times*: "Poor Colonel House is a statesman and did his best. But today he is powerless." The cabinet was jealous of House; so was the president's immediate entourage. "Their pleasure," he suggested, consisted of but one thing, "keeping House on the outside."[11]

* * *

Though Edith Wilson had canceled Senator Hitchcock's scheduled meeting with the president on November 30, she had no choice but to welcome him and Republican senator Albert Fall—a subcommittee of two
from the Foreign Relations Committee—to the president's bedside on
the afternoon of December 5. The precarious Mexican situation, with a
possibility of U.S. intervention, was the official reason for the talks.
Relations between the countries had blundered into crisis, as they
chronically did, being subject to Mexico's successive dictatorships and to
America's oil investments. The U.S. consular agent in Puebla, Mexico,
had been robbed and kidnapped and then charged with conspiracy in his
own kidnapping in order to discredit the Mexican government of President Venustiano Carranza.[12]

   The prospect of the meeting worried both Grayson and Tumulty, who
feared Fall's discovery that the president was much weaker and less
capable than their reports to the press had indicated. Edith mentioned
that the meeting was precipitated by "some little incident with Mexico."
Privately, she believed that the real object of what she characterized as a
"maneuver" was not to discuss the Mexican situation but to judge the
extent of her husband's disability and to see whether he was mentally
capable of administering his office. Washington was on edge, ripe with
gossip over the president's continued silence, the authenticity of his signature, the authorship of his annual message to Congress, the accuracy
of the bulletins reporting his improving health, and the truth of Senator
George Moses's allegation that Wilson had suffered a brain lesion. Lansing's revelation that neither he nor any member of the State Department had consulted the president about Mexico since his return from his
Western tour may have served as the final catalyst for the requested
White House interview.

   Ike Hoover would speak of countless deceptions carried on at the
White House during Wilson's illness. The strange part for him was the
president's participation in them "in his feeble way," such as in the masterful staging of the December 5 meeting with Hitchcock and Fall when
the "great camouflage took place."[13] Wilson had been sitting up in his
rolling chair, but when the time came for the subcommittee to arrive, he
was put to bed. The room was darkened, only one light on the bedside
table left burning. Bolstered by pillows, he was covered over entirely,
except his head and right arm. It was quite impossible for someone coming in from a well-lighted part of the house to see anything clearly.
Edith Wilson stood at the foot, the nurse at the side of the bed, Dr.
Grayson in the doorway, which was left open, and Hoover behind

Grayson, "and everyone was happy afterwards that nothing more serious had happened."[14]

Admiral Grayson greeted the two senators (Wilson referred to them as the "Smelling Committee") and escorted them to the president's bedroom; the *New York Times* said that Senator Hitchcock was chosen as a friend, while Fall represented the Republican critics of the president. Senator Fall entered the room and told Wilson, "Well, Mr. President, we have all been praying for you." "Which way, Senator?" inquired the president with a chuckle. Mr. Fall laughed, Edith concluded, "as if the witticism had been his own."[15] More than likely it was hers, as it is not quoted in any of numerous versions of this meeting, either by participants or observers, nor in Edith's original notes. Loathing the senator as she did, she had taken the precaution, she admitted, to carry a pad and pencil so she would not have to shake hands with him. She then sat on the other side of the bed and carefully wrote down what passed between the men. At last, Fall said, "You seem very much engaged, madam." "Yes," Edith said, "I thought it wise to record this interview so there may be no misunderstanding or misstatements made."

If Edith did not capture every word—and abbreviated, crossed out, or omitted some—her crude record does contain on six pages of White House stationery the gist of the forty-minute meeting. Later that same day, as he had promised the president, Fall sent over by messenger the typed fifteen-page draft of his investigation of Carranza's revolutionary efforts. Fall's report was prefaced by a page inscribed "The President, The White House," with his own name written in the upper right-hand corner, "New Mexico" printed at the lower right. Edith, in preserving her notes of the meeting, simply appropriated Fall's title page, unwittingly perhaps demonstrating her disdain not only for state documents but for Senator Fall. She crossed out "New Mexico" and wrote along the outer edge in three vertical lines: "Notes taken when Senator Fall called on the President in his bedroom at the White House"; she added a fourth line: "Taken by EBW."

Fall made a colorful enemy for Woodrow Wilson, and consequently for Edith. Born in Kentucky, he had lived in Texas and Mexico, moving to territorial New Mexico in 1886. He had pounded a miner's drill, read law, and been elected and appointed to several territorial positions, first as a Democrat and later as a Republican. In 1912 he was one of the two Republican senators the newly admitted state elected to the U.S. Senate. He wore a black, broad-brimmed Stetson hat and was noted for his soft drawl, bronzed complexion, bombastic and scathing oratorical style, and above all, for his resolute commitment to the Republican Party. Considered an expert on Mexican affairs and on American oil and mining interests in that country, he consistently pressed for intervention to right the wrongs suffered by U.S. citizens in Mexico. In 1913, he had advocated annexation of the northern Mexican states.

Fall opposed Wilson's policies on Mexico and on the recent war in Europe. Fall had bitterly disagreed with Wilson's initial stance of "watchful waiting." Wilson had fought Fall's reelection in 1918: the president's telegram, which was reprinted in an Albuquerque newspaper, had cautioned that "no one who wishes to sustain me can intelligently vote for him. If that is the issue the voters of New Mexico wish to vote upon, it is easily determined." Fall won with the help of Theodore Roosevelt, but the New Mexico senator never forgave Wilson for his public attack, especially as it came at the time when his son and one of his three daughters died of the prevalent influenza. As one of the irreconcilables, Fall, shrewdly inverting Wilson's recent verbal taunts, insisted he could not "with my 'limited horizon' and possibly 'pigmy' mind" see his way to ratify the president's proposals as contained in the treaty and covenant for the league, and at the same time ". . . not betray the United States and its people."[16]

The meeting was generally regarded as a success for Wilson—astonishingly so. Fall sat a little to one side of the president's bed, "in a shaded portion of the room,"[17] noting that the president's articulation seemed thick during the entire conference but that he, Fall, could understand perfectly his every word. The senator explained what had taken place in Mexico, but found Wilson already surprisingly well informed, picking up and laying down a printed copy of the Senate's resolution that Fall had sent him. Their talk was interrupted by the announcement that the American consular agent had been released, his bail provided by the unsolicited help of a fellow American.

When the two senators emerged from the White House after the conference, Hitchcock, smiling broadly, reported that the president was mentally most alert, physically greatly improved. Wilson had shaken hands with his right hand and used both hands freely in picking up and laying down a printed copy of Senator Fall's resolution; in fact, the president's paralyzed left hand had lain hidden under the bedcovers. Senator Fall added that the president seemed to him to be in excellent trim, both mentally and physically, for a man who had been in bed for ten weeks. Unfortunately, the story of the senators' meeting, despite the exceedingly positive account in the *New York Times,* was alarmingly distorted in other publications and gave rise to wild rumors that the two men had forced their way into the sickroom where Fall had brutally pulled back the president's bedclothes. Fall was haunted by this tale for the next ten years. It was said to have prejudiced his fate when, in frail health at the age of sixty-eight, he was tried for accepting a $100,000 bribe as secretary of the interior in 1921 under President Warren Gamaliel Harding, in the so-called Teapot Dome scandal, fined $100,000, and sentenced to a year in jail. At that time, seeming to regard Fall's disgrace as her private revenge, Edith was indignant as she recalled, "This was the man Mr. Henry Cabot Lodge had delegated to pass on the mentality of Woodrow Wilson."[18]

From Grayson's distorted perspective of the critical meeting at the White House, the interview had proved especially gratifying. Describing the day as gloomy outside but bright with electric lights inside the president's bedroom, he was relieved that the meeting had put an end to rumors, to "a campaign of innuendo and 'whispering slander.' " No longer would the scandalmongers' lies mislead sane Americans to believe that the president's sickness was far more serious than Grayson had indicated in any of his bulletins.[19] Elated by the outcome of the meeting, and probably unaware of the gravity of Wilson's illness, Navy Secretary Josephus Daniels congratulated Edith Wilson on "the clear and convincing statements of the President [that] confounded even Senator Fall" and spoke of his hope that they would silence "the amateur key-hole diagnosticians."[20]

Scarcely a scandalmonger or an amateur, the respected thirty-seven-year-old British journalist Arthur Willert remained distinctly apprehensive over Wilson's isolation and secrecy. Nothing, it seemed, could dispel Willert's pessimism over America's "chaotically inefficient government," coping clumsily at best with problems posed by Bolshevik Russia, the Mexican dilemma, the coal miners' continuing strike, and most frightening, the "everything or nothing" attitude of the president regarding the League. Fondly recalling the time of his first visit thirteen years earlier "when the country was swinging ahead under Roosevelt's great presidency," Willert was saddened as he reported to H. Wickham Steed, editor of the London *Times,* on December 6:

> There are no positive influences here. Washington is torn between
> the hatred of the Senate and the White House, between the jeal-

ousy of the State Department and the White House, and the Cabinet is quite incapable of pulling things together . . . Republicans, flouted by the President, kept in ignorance by him in every possible way, knowing nothing of what went on in Paris, of the need for compromise and cooperation if the war is not to be the least of the trials that the Germans have condemned us to, are taking the only natural course of pandering to the old spirit of isolation and of keeping the country out of a mess which they don't understand beyond the fact that one of the chief figures in it is the man whom of all others they distrust and dislike.

The fact remains, Willert said, "that everything is going at half speed."[21]

In the second week of December, the "government a welter of disorganization,"[22] Edith Wilson held firm as the disabled president's administrator, censor, guard, all-powerful broker, and courier, in this last capacity routing documents as she saw fit. Nor, of course, could anyone see him without her consent. Vice President Marshall observed that during the two months when he had been trying to meet with the president without success, others "had access to him who should be properly in jail."[23]

Supervising the concerns of the United States in her husband's virtual absence, Edith appeared unaware of the ramifications of Joseph Tumulty's support in this endeavor. Had she been able to manage on her own, she would probably have dismissed him. For his part, serving her was a means of serving his beloved, stricken president. His efforts to anticipate and expedite important matters were untiring and utterly sincere, if at times overextended. Monitoring the conclusion to the United Mine Workers' plans to strike—postwar demands for a 60 percent wage increase would be settled at 14 percent—Tumulty suggested to Edith Wilson that it would be wise if the president sent a message to the acting head of the union, John L. Lewis. The response, "the President says alright," this time in Ike Hoover's handwriting, paved the way for the telegram sent in Wilson's name on December 11: "May I not express to you and, through you, to the other officers of your organization, my appreciation of the patriotic action which you took at Indianapolis yesterday? Now we must all work together to see to it that a settlement just and fair to everyone is reached without delay."

By return telegram Lewis, honored and reassured by the president's purported message, was able to promise "sincere cooperation will be given . . . that the final settlement will comprehend every element of justice and right."[24]

Even when deliberately excluded by the Wilsons, Tumulty, sensitive to the controversial issues regarding the peace treaty, refused to turn his back on them. Initially, he was stunned to read Wilson's pronouncement in the *New York Times* on December 15 that the president had in mind no compromise or concession of any kind, but intended that the Republican leaders of the Senate "shall continue to bear the undivided responsibility for the fate of the treaty and the present condition of the world in consequence of that fate." Tumulty immediately made known to the president's wife that Sunday's statement "was a body blow . . . a brave, audacious thing to do," and that he thought it would cleanse and purify the murky atmosphere surrounding the whole situation. He also suggested that its immediate effect would be to precipitate harsh criticism and the antagonism of enemies and indifferent friends. In this forecast, he did not exaggerate. Democratic senators did not take easily to the fact that they were now pledged to an obviously lost cause on their final vote in March. Inwardly seething, it was said, over the president's position, they wondered whether the statement was written by Wilson "or by some cheap politician assuming to speak the President's mind."

Despite some inevitable sense of defeat, Tumulty persevered. Acting as intermediary for Hitchcock, he asked Edith Wilson, on December 18, to tell the president that the senator wanted to know whether the president would look with favor on any effort on his part "to soften the Lodge reservations and avoid splitting the party." Edith's response might have discouraged a less dedicated soul than Tumulty: "The President was clear," she reported on her discussion with him on the matter, "that it would be a serious mistake for him (or for our side) to *propose* anything."[25]

Ever mindful of problems beyond the treaty, Joe Tumulty—while remaining deferential—prodded Mrs. Wilson: "Please don't think I am trying to crowd you or to urge immediate action by the President, but I thought it would help you if you could have before you a list of matters that at intervals the President might wish to have presented to him for discussion and settlement." Beginning at the top of the page, Tumulty listed: message as to railroads, if any; recognition of Costa Rica; selection of commission to settle miners' strike. Under the heading of appointments: secretaryships of the treasury and the interior; assistant secretaryship of agriculture; action upon Secretary Lansing's recommendation of William Phillips for Holland. Page two listed five resignations from various commissions, seven vacancies on the Waterways Commission alone, more on three rent commissions, and eight vacancies in the diplomatic corps.[26]

Tumulty also informed Edith of a legitimate difference of opinion about the date on which the railroads, taken under federal authority on March 21, 1918, should be returned to their owners, a step promised for December 31, 1919. Walker Downer Hines, the railroads' director general, wrote an anguished letter to Wilson pleading for postponement in the best interest of all classes—railroad employees, executives, and the general public. With Congress in recess until January 5 and temporary legislation unsettled regarding rates, Hines feared that the termination of federal control on January 1 would create conditions of a "most chaotic character, both financially and in an administrative sense." Tumulty, to strengthen Hines's argument for postponement, wrote Edith Wilson a note telling her that Justice Brandeis of the U.S. Supreme Court was emphatic—by Hines's report—that it would be unjustifiable and unwise, and seriously injurious to the public interest, to return the railroads on December 31.

Wilson was annoyed. Feeling pressured by his secretary, he wrote "Dear Tumulty," on lined, blue paper. The probable "You" at the start of his curt sentence is inked out, and the message reads: "must let me alone about the RRs. I've announced that the roads go back to their owners January 1 and that cannot be altered."[27]

Much as Wilson resented doing so, however, he did agree subsequently to a postponement. A press release written by Tumulty and stamped "Woodrow Wilson" (with "approved," possibly in Edith's handwriting) announced that, because the railroad and express companies were not organized to receive and manage their properties on December 31 without raising serious financial and legal complications, the transfer of possession would become effective at 12:01 A.M., March 1, 1920.[28]

On December 20, Wilson was wheeled out for an airing on the snow-covered grounds of the White House, and Dr. Grayson announced that, given the president's marked improvement, Dr. Dercum would discontinue his weekly Saturday consultations and make visits at indefinite periods. Grayson's incorrigible optimism was obviously unwarranted and clouded by the last sentence in the *New York Times'* report: "Mr. Wilson will eat Christmas dinner in his room and there will be no Christmas tree at the White House this year." Despite Grayson's announcement, Dr. Dercum had arranged to maintain representation in the White House, not only weekly but daily, with the help of a therapist, R. A. Rogers, whom he employed to work with his stroke patients.

Rogers's two confidential letters to Dercum reveal a disturbing analysis of the ravages of the president's illness—he suffered not only periods of forgetfulness but spells of dizziness, was very weak and tired easily. The therapist was also suspicious of Wilson's caretakers—they were absolutely inadequate and, he complained, had no system at all. It didn't take long for Rogers to realize that "Mrs. Wilson runs the case" and "Dr. G. is afraid to speak to patient or Mrs. W.," he wrote December 13/19, 1919. That the therapist conceded that Dercum was "right" in his first statement seemed to imply that the physician may have conveyed his dismal opinion of the way the president was being cared for.[29]

The first of Rogers's two letters to Dr. Dercum (he actually tore up his very first for fear that it would be "held up," possibly confiscated, by "some malicious person") clearly suggests that he must have been recommended in such a manner that Edith Wilson had no choice but to consent to his installation in the gloomy, mysterious White House, where he was made to feel superfluous if not unwelcome. Rogers waited for four days after his arrival to be introduced to the patient, when he was told that there was absolutely nothing to do for the president but hand him the urinal occasionally. When at last he was favorably received, to the surprise of "the opposition party" (undoubtedly Edith Wilson and Grayson), he set to work to compensate for the president's not having received any therapy. At this time, when Wilson was so disabled that it took three people to get him out of bed, Rogers warned that if they didn't get busy soon with treatments, "you might as well close the book as they will do no good later."[30]

Therapy, as planned by Dr. Dercum and executed, if permitted, by Rogers, included frequent baths, passive exercise, and massages, particularly of the patient's left arm and left leg from toes to groin. In an amazingly short time Rogers could report that the president was making steady progress. He could stand on his right leg and, with support, throw the left leg out and put some weight on it for a few steps. A bit stronger now, he could hold himself a little better and was therefore not quite so heavy to lift. Rogers also hoped that Wilson would be strong enough to use the commode soon and, as Dercum had recommended, to sit up for one meal in a chair. Rogers hoped the doctor would excuse his long letter, but seemed to think Dercum would appreciate the information because "you never knew how things were running here."[31]

Edith Wilson, who was initially dismissive of therapy, eventually did recognize the benefits of Rogers's treatments, so the therapist reported to Dercum. Six months later, however, in June 1920, it was still impossible to apply the physician's method with any precision. New to the case, another of Dercum's therapists, David C. Williams, said it was not exactly the work one had to do that was hard, but the way in which it had to be done. In an atmosphere thick with secrecy, Williams did not know how Rogers had endured it all these months—unable to talk to anyone, having to be guarded about what one wrote and to whom. He hoped that it would later be possible to faithfully follow Dr. Dercum's prescribed regimen.[32]

During what was for Wilson a joyless Christmas season, the president, crippled not only physically but emotionally, grew increasingly unpredictable, a worry to his friends who were aware, ever since his statement of no compromise, of his sinking popularity. Even the New York *World* and the *New York Globe*, which had stood by Wilson throughout, had turned lukewarm. Infuriated by members of Congress who dared to oppose his wishes—those who had voted in November for the Lodge Reservations or against the Underwood resolution for consent without any reservations—Wilson made a crude and aborted effort to bypass the Senate by attempting to hold a national referendum on the League of Nations. To this end he drafted a letter challenging fifty-six senators—mistakenly including three who had opposed the Lodge resolution—to resign their seats and take immediate steps to seek reelection on the issue of their record with regard to the ratification of the treaty. He promised that at the finish, if all of them or a majority were reelected, he would resign the presidency. Edith followed up this letter with one of her own, sent directly to Attorney General A. Mitchell Palmer, to check on the effects of the proposed resignations in thirty-five states and to inquire whether the interim successors would be chosen by their governors or by election. Possibly on advice that the plan was legally indefensible, the Wilsons seem not to have pursued it.[33]

Even so, Woodrow Wilson did not run out of ways to express discontent with his lot in life. On December 22, he abruptly wrote to his former great friend Princeton president John Grier Hibben that "the big table which was in the study at Prospect when I left . . . and which I assume to be there still, is not the property of the University." He had bought it out of his own pocket, and it could therefore fairly be said to be his; it would be most serviceable at the White House. Would Hibben send it, and of course, Wilson planned to pay for the cost of the crating and shipment. In a genial note, Hibben responded two weeks later to say that he hoped the president would allow the university the privilege of delivering the table to him in Washington, a note Wilson seems not to have acknowledged.[34]

On the same day, Wilson also wrote to a Mrs. Young, proprietor of Glencove in Bermuda, where he had vacationed with his wife, Ellen, and his daughters after his election in 1912. The letter, painfully manifest of his erratic mood swings, told Mrs. Young that he was beginning to hope, after being confined to the house for several months by illness, to rent Glencove in February and March. He knew of no house in which they could be more comfortable, "and it would be a great joy" if she found it was convenient to let them have it.[35]

Frank Polk, undersecretary of state, returned from France to Washington and wrote to Wilson, on December 23, that he would be only too glad to have the opportunity of seeing him in order to report, but that probably "Mrs. Wilson and your doctors do not wish you to waste your time with unnecessary visitors." Three days later, Polk told Tumulty that one matter he really wished, if possible, to be brought to the president's attention was the question of recognition of Costa Rica. Edith Wilson, ignoring the suggestion of a meeting, wrote Polk that his letter gave the president much pleasure and that he joined her in a hearty welcome.

With every dinner table in Washington feasting on speculation about the president's isolation, a former cabinet member, Franklin Lane, chairman of the Railroad Wage Commission, boasted that "no country except the United States could have survived such a condition without anarchy and revolution."[36] As for fathoming the logic of the president's immutable position regarding the treaty, Raymond Fosdick, his former student and trusted representative abroad and at home, suggested that he might prefer to lose, if necessary, in the belief that history would ultimately vindicate his position "and mark him as a prophet who lived before his time."[37] Virtually resigned to the inevitability of the president's defeat, Tumulty found himself, in late December, musing about Wilson's place in history—"if he had [died] when [he] brought the treaty home it would have let him loom larger."[38]

CHAPTER 29

The White House snubs the British ambassador

What came to be known as the Craufurd-Stuart affair, as the post-war issue of the League of Nations awaited a solution in the winter of 1919, illuminated the desolate state of the presidency under Edith Wilson's subjective sense of diplomacy. Opinionated and outspoken on so many themes, she was silent about "one of the most amazing and wholly unprecedented episodes in Washington diplomatic annals" in which she played a critical part.[1] Although characterized as "front page history of the most-far-reaching consequences,"[2] in which honorable purposes were trivialized by petty behavior, this freakish episode escapes mention by Edith, as though snuffed from her memory.

The temporary appointment of Sir Edward Grey, Viscount Grey of Fallodon, as British ambassador in Washington should have pleased Edith Wilson and, in accepted diplomatic practice, should have been the occasion of an invitation to the White House—most particularly to accompany the prince of Wales on his visit to the Wilsons. Grey, His Majesty's Ambassador Extraordinary and Plenipotentiary on Special Mission,[3] was held in greatest honor and reverence by his countrymen for his firm English qualities and love of his country, his instinct for quiet self-sacrifice and active devotion to principle.

Woodrow Wilson had, at an earlier period, respected House's friendship for this revered statesman and, on first learning of the possibility of Grey's appointment, had welcomed it wholeheartedly. Writing to House on August 15, 1919, Wilson had called Grey "the one available statesman whose reputation for honor and loftiness of purpose made him ideal" and had looked forward "with great pleasure to being associated with him."[4] Wilson, who had met Grey in London at the time of the Peace Conference, was aware not only of the nobleman's political interests but of his private hobbies—his love of fishing, of nature, and especially of birds. Grey had sent Wilson the books he had written on these themes. Wilson was especially sympathetic to the widowed Grey's bereavement; and while mourning his own loss at Ellen's death, he had more than once spoken of Grey's earlier tragedy. Wilson had also expressed concern for Grey's loss of sight.[5]

Grey was appointed to succeed the affable Viscount Reading, who had withdrawn from his post, in June 1918, to return to his previous responsibilities as lord chief justice of Great Britain. As special ambassador, Lord Grey was officially assigned to confer with President Wilson on three subjects: the League of Nations, the policy on armaments, and the bitter question of Irish secession. Instructions regarding the foundation of the League were precise: "It should be the constant effort of Your Lordship to convince the United States Government that this is the desire of His Majesty's Government just as the latter are convinced that the same desire animates the government of the United States."[6]

Phrased more candidly by the current foreign secretary, Lord George Nathaniel Curzon, Britain's informal instructions urged Grey to assure and reassure the United States on the necessity of its membership in the League, and to counter American apprehensions that Great Britain was the evil genius of the Peace Conference. Extolling the new ambassador, the *Observer* of London claimed that only a European could make America understand how much she must mean to Europe, and no European could speak to America with the same political authority and moral earnestness as Lord Grey. His country was sending her best to America.

Grey sailed for New York on the SS *Mauretania*, accompanied by his secretary, Sir William Tyrrell, a former assistant undersecretary of state in the Foreign Office. Grey's equerry, Major Charles Kennedy Craufurd-Stuart, came highly recommended by Lord Reading, whom he had served in Washington. Grey was fifty-seven years old, spare, sinewy, and broad-shouldered with high cheekbones and thin lips that creased into a gentle smile. His virtually sightless eyes were deep set; his expressionless stare was concealed by dark glasses. He had fastidiously packed three cases of a special blend of tea in his luggage, having been advised that this was unprocurable in the United States.

Grey disembarked in New York on September 26, 1919—the day on which Wilson had collapsed near Pueblo—and proceeded to the British embassy in Washington.[7] He did not look forward to this assignment, but had felt that he could not refuse it. "You know the definition of Life," he had told a friend: "'one damned thing after the other.'"[8] Less than three months later, on December 12, the *Times* of London gave notice that Lord Grey, having been greatly embarrassed by his inability to see the president, was returning to England, "the first instance in the history of the U.S. when an Ambassador or Minister from Great Britain has not been formally received by the President."[9]

The *Times* was invoking a 134-year-old diplomatic tradition originating in the recognition of John Adams, on February 24, 1785, as the first American minister accredited as plenipotentiary from the United States of America to the Court of St. James. Adams's appointment had signaled a new era for a new nation. Reciprocal courtesies had automatically been extended ever since between Britain and the United States.

In 1929, in his posthumously published memoir, Sir Cecil Spring-Rice, Lord Reading's predecessor as British ambassador, remembered Wilson as "a rather Olympian personage . . . shrouded in darkness from which issue occasional thunderbolts." Having been posted in Russia, Germany, Turkey, and Persia—countries all popularly supposed to be under autocratic rule—Rice had never known any so autocratic as Wilson's presidency.[10] Antagonism was apparently mutual: disliked by Wilson, Spring Rice was recalled by his government. The diplomatic difficulties encountered during Reading's term in Washington were not attributable to any failings on the ambassador's part, but to the offenses of his equerry, who had barely escaped censure for his allegedly unflattering remarks about the Wilsons in the winter of 1918. Major Craufurd-Stuart's errors were compounded by his implication of Bernard Baruch during an investigation of a suspected German spy, May Ladenburg, and resulted in the major's being declared persona non grata in the United States.[11] However, a tactful resolution allowed the major to remain in his position at the British embassy until the spring of 1919, when he accompanied Lord and Lady Reading back to England. His transgressions remained, of course, unforgotten and unforgiven at the White House. And his return to Washington with Grey in the autumn of 1919 was regarded as an astonishing breach of diplomatic etiquette that, under pressure from Edith Wilson and Baruch, would cause the president of the United States to ignore the British ambassador, in an unprecedented international rebuff.

Lord Grey's ambassadorial mission had begun very differently. Quite unaware of either the year-old spying scandal or the alleged defamation by Craufurd-Stuart of the president and his wife, Grey had written on his arrival in Washington in late September to Secretary of State Robert

Lansing to say that he was anxious to present his credentials to the president in person; but that, having read, with deepest regret, of Wilson's ill health, he refrained from requesting a definite appointment. He transmitted a copy of King George's letters, including one expressing the king's hope that Lord Grey's eminent talents and devoted service would find favor with the president.[12]

On October 4, after Wilson's collapse, Grey wired the first of a series of telegrams to London, informing foreign secretary Lord Curzon that "everything was in suspense" due to the president's illness, that there was little use in discussing matters of prime importance with any official other than the president, that there was no precedent for the temporary replacement of the presidency, and that the business of the state and Congress could hardly be expected to carry on automatically for more than ten days or so.[13]

Frustrated by his inability to see Wilson and the suspension of all official and public activity in Washington, Grey now conveyed, in messages, marked private and secret, the nuances of the opposition to the peace treaty and drew attention to the six-vote power held by Britain and its dominions in contrast to the United States' single vote in the League Assembly. What was needed, the ambassador explained, was an assurance that, in any controversy involving the British Empire, Britain and its dominions must, in terms of voting power, be regarded as a whole. On October 7, Grey wrote that he was again informed by the State Department that there was no possibility of Wilson's receiving official visitors for at least six weeks or two months.[14] Three days later, Grey was accorded provisional recognition as Ambassador Extraordinary and Plenipotentiary on Special Mission, formal recognition to be granted when the president received him in audience.[15]

Grey's next contact with the State Department was in regard to an entirely different matter, one that Lansing predicted might have explosive results, giving substance to rumors that a certain member of Ambassador Grey's staff was persona non grata.[16] Lansing, authorized by the president, with Admiral Grayson as the latter's intermediary, instructed his assistant secretary of state, William Phillips, at a reception, to request that Lord Grey send away his equerry, Craufurd-Stuart. Hurt and angered that this curt message was the first word of any kind he had received from the president since his arrival from Britain, Grey reported to Lord Curzon on November 2 that owing to "a tiresome incident"[17] he must send Craufurd-Stuart home. Grey explained that while in Washington with Reading, the equerry had supposedly, at a private dinner party prior to Wilson's departure for Paris, expressed his opinion that it was a mistake for the president to go to Europe. Grey had checked with Craufurd-Stuart, who denied the year-old charges.[18] While pursuing the matter further, Grey once again received word that the president insisted on Craufurd-Stuart's removal. Aware of Wilson's feeble condition, Grey could hardly believe that the president was concerned in the matter, "but such is the message."[19]

In defense of his equerry, the ambassador wrote Curzon that Craufurd-Stuart took care of him admirably, and that, owing to his blindness and his solitary life since his wife's death, he was particularly dependent on the major's assistance. In addition, Craufurd-Stuart was engaged to an American lady and planned to live with the father of his fiancée. Grey did not see how even the president could, in these circumstances, turn Craufurd-Stuart out of the country and could see no reason why the young man should not stay with him here in Washington in an unofficial capacity. Grey appealed to the French ambassador, Jean Jules Jusserand, who was dean of the diplomatic corps, to adjudicate. In the event of an unsuccessful outcome, Curzon must be prepared for Grey's own returning home as he had not "come out of private life to put up with this indignity and nonsense," which, a colleague said, "savored of old Berlin."[20] Meanwhile, in an effort to mollify the president, the State Department was notified of Grey's request that Craufurd-Stuart's name be omitted from the next diplomatic list as he had ceased to be a member of the official embassy staff.[21] Grey nevertheless refused to send the equerry home without a hearing, feeling that such a move would terminate the major's career and was, in his view, unjustified. Failure to prove the first round of charges had inclined him to believe that his equerry was a victim of a conspiracy.[22]

The man whom Grey sympathetically defended was a bachelor, a ubiquitous presence at Washington's social parties, who cut a dashing figure in his vivid Indian army uniform with purple satin trousers. Craufurd-Stuart may have appeared to be a gadabout and gossip, dismissed as one of wartime's "temporary gentlemen," but he could not so easily be shunted aside. A brave soldier who had won the Distinguished Service Order at Gallipoli, he had served with the military police in Burma and had been "on special service" in the Sudan before arriving in Washington, in February 1918, as private secretary to the then newly arrived ambassador, Lord Reading. Craufurd-Stuart had other talents: he had exhibited at the London Salon of Photography, was a sportsman who enjoyed both polo and archery, and had composed popular songs.

Following further talks with British and American colleagues, Curzon reported to Grey that he had heard that Craufurd-Stuart's offense was of a more serious nature than initially described. The major was rumored not only to have cast aspersions on Wilson's mission to Paris, but also to have dined out, during the closing months of 1918, on an off-color remark—on which Curzon did not elaborate and which must have bypassed Grey's ear entirely, but which had continued to resound deep inside the White House. Craufurd-Stuart, it was claimed, had enjoyed a brief triumph at dinner tables by saying that "when Wilson proposed to the second Mrs. Wilson, she was so surprised that she nearly fell out of bed."[23] The major was also reported to have insinuated that Edith Wilson had no position in America, but had wanted to shine socially by going to London—that would be the only way she would see the queen. Another time he was credited with a vague remark about Mrs. Wilson buying off Mrs. Peck. The British soldier had done little to retrieve his errors when, in response to a Washington hostess's query as to why he was so popular in America, he had replied, "Perhaps because I am middle class myself."

Beyond Craufurd-Stuart's allegedly slanderous remarks about Edith Wilson, his fatal mistake, and one that undoubtedly sealed his fate, was to incur the enmity of Bernard Baruch. Although it was generally acknowledged that the major had proved invaluable in organizing the British embassy's domestic staff, took admirable care of Lord Reading, and was especially solicitous of the handsome though deaf Lady Reading, the major's duties included a clandestinely official side. He also served as liaison and courier for Sir William Wiseman, the U.S. head of the British intelligence service. Goaded by British complaints that secret information was being leaked from the United States into Germany, Craufurd-Stuart alerted American military intelligence on May 15, 1918, that he had found the source of the espionage.

This was the young and beautiful May Ladenburg, to whom her supposed admirer Bernard Baruch—the handsome man, tall, quick, and spare, whom Wilson called Dr. Facts[24]—was said to reveal state secrets. The case against Baruch was predicated on his earlier relationship with Mrs. Archibald White, the former actress Olive Moore, whose recent three-year liaison with Count von Bernstorff had been interrupted by the German ambassador's recall. Baruch, according to British military intelligence files, had been seen in the company of Olive Moore and her financier husband and with von Bernstorff on more than one occasion in the summer of 1916. Baruch's reputation was tarnished further by virulent anti-Semitism, exemplified in the ugly commentaries of *Town Topics*.[25]

As his alleged coconspirator, May Ladenburg was a model for the heroine or villainess of a classic spy story: "by far the most vivid and exciting of all the visitors brought by the war." A delightful hostess, charming in face and figure, interesting and intelligent and "an enigma," this celebrated newcomer was soon a favorite with old and young.[26] She was the daughter of the former Emily Stevens and of Adolf Ladenburg—partner in the German banking firm of Ladenburg, Thalmann and Company—who had died mysteriously at sea in 1896.[27] The heiress to a $6 million fortune, the daughter was, apparently, largely suspect on grounds of her paternal German lineage. It was said that she had been confused with another young woman by the name of Marie von Ladenburg, although even the writer of a relevant memorandum in the American military intelligence file realized that such a confusion "seems hardly possible."[28] Given the hysterical climate of mistrust in wartime Washington (the German-born bride of one of the president's chauffeurs did not escape surveillance, and even the oranges crated to von Bernsdorff were rumored to be rubber filled with secret messages), it was perhaps inevitable that May Ladenburg should prove a magnet for investigation.

In this imbroglio, the British embassy successfully enlisted American authorities to conduct a counterespionage operation, which was set afoot at Ladenburg's house, at 1831 M Street, NW, in Washington, under the supervision of Brigadier General Marlborough Churchill, director of military intelligence for the War Department, who despite his British name was an American graduate of Harvard. Churchill asked Alice Roosevelt Longworth for help—affording her, she said, an opportunity to serve her country. All she was asked to do, she later explained, "was to look over transoms and peep through keyholes. Could anything be more delightful than that?" Apparently not for Mrs. Longworth, uninhibited by the fact that the young May Ladenburg was "a friend of all of ours." Mrs. Longworth's cousin, Assistant Secretary of the Navy Franklin Delano Roosevelt, was enlisted to prepare false documents about naval maneuvers so that Ladenburg might convey misleading information. Mrs. Longworth readily agreed to help Churchill and his colleagues hide hearing devices in the house and studio, to which

Craufurd-Stuart had surreptitiously gained advance admittance by charming the maid during her mistress's absence.

"So I went," Longworth said, "and looked and told them that there was an upper balcony with . . . not exactly a hammock but a kind of mattress on a swing that I thought . . . might be a good place for one of the devices, so they put one there and connected it to the studio." Longworth would report gurgling noises and revelations that were astounding but indisputable, having heard May ask, in between sounds of kissing, how many locomotives were being sent to Romania. "Of course," Longworth acknowledged later, she and Franklin "were doing a most disgraceful thing in the name of looking after the affairs of our country, but it was sheer rapture."[29]

Although the story was recounted on innumerable occasions over more than seventy years, and never more capriciously than in Longworth's version in 1981, the nature of the Baruch-Ladenburg conversation remains unknown. The recording was reputedly handed by the major to Lord Reading and then to Secretary of War Newton Baker, who made the enigmatic pronouncement that the content was "not very bad." An American intelligence officer, who later claimed possession of the recording and knowledge of its contents, said that, among other things, Baruch had told his companion that "he expects to rank in history as the greatest of all Jews." In Baruch's opinion, Disraeli was then the greatest, but times were so different that, given modern opportunities, Baruch felt he could eclipse Disraeli. Baruch thought the president was the greatest man in the world and he intended to be the next greatest.[30]

Despite this inconclusive evidence, the injurious accusations persisted and were echoed abroad—reaching Baruch when he was attending the Peace Conference in Paris in the summer of 1919. In consequence, when Craufurd-Stuart made his unwelcome reappearance in Washington as aide to Lord Grey, Bernard Baruch set himself to square accounts by enlisting the authority of the White House and the eager cooperation of both Edith Wilson and Cary Grayson. Believing herself a victim of the major's taunts, Edith, with her habitual recklessness, savored revenge. At the price of endangering British-American relations, her terms were implacable: Lord Grey's admittance to the White House depended on Craufurd-Stuart's dismissal.

Sir William Wiseman, and subsequently Grey's secretary, Sir William Tyrrell, tried to intervene on Grey's behalf. Aware that Edith Wilson alone held the key to access to the president, both men sought the help of her secretary, Edith Benham, in appealing to the president's wife. Convinced that Lord Grey's mission was important, Benham wanted to do her part and approached "Mrs. W." immediately. The secretary had relied on Mrs. Wilson's sense of fairness and justice, "which at times was very well developed," to perceive the injustice being done to the major. Benham sensed immediately that her attempt to mediate was going badly, and that the strain of the president's illness had induced a querulousness that at times made his wife unlike her normal self. Clearly displeased, Edith Wilson sternly reprimanded her secretary for having seen the Sir Williams at all. Contending that the matter should have been settled by the State Department, Edith Wilson insisted that "she never interfered in political matters!"

From intimate exposure to conditions at the White House, Edith Benham knew the latter claim to be untrue. The secretary wrote in her diary that Edith Wilson "was the mouthpiece for the President," actively "transacting a great deal of the business of the Government at that time, and her influence decided the P. in the few decisions which were brought up to him." Though the conversation between the two women ended pleasantly, with Edith Wilson promising to speak to the president and to pass on his decision, the secretary had reason to be discouraged. "Speaking to the P. meant," she knew, "that she would have him say no." Benham waited four days without an answer. Five days after their initial conversation, Edith Wilson declared that the message to rid the British embassy of the major had come from the president, who, according to Mrs. Wilson, had said, "As for me Stuart cannot go too quickly."[31]

Initially sympathetic to Grey's dilemma, the British foreign secretary, Lord Curzon, was justifiably exasperated that the amity between two great nations—and the personal convenience of Britain's ambassador—should be disturbed by such "trumpery incidents."[32] Grey responded that there was more to the situation than he could fully explain. Those close to the president decided arbitrarily who might see him; and owing to Grey's intimacy with Colonel House, who was now out of favor, this adverse situation worked against him. If Wilson should recover sufficiently to resume real control, conditions might be changed, but there was no imminent prospect of that. Thus, the very conditions that had made Grey seem especially suitable for the mission to Washington were now a definite disqualification. The intrigue was not pleasant, and the sooner Grey withdrew the sooner it would cease. Having acquired considerable understanding of the position in the Senate, and of some aspects of American opinion that he could convey on returning home, he was sure that his decision to depart was right.[33]

Two weeks before Grey's sailing on January 3, Edith Wilson was approached timorously by the secretary of state, Robert Lansing, through Tumulty. Edith was reminded that Grey was returning to England, and that he had not been received by the president. While an appointment could not be requested—not only because of the president's illness, but because several other ambassadors and ministers had been waiting still longer—it was felt that it would be most appropriate for the president to receive Grey informally. Forwarding Lansing's letter to Edith, Tumulty asked, "What shall I say?" Three days later Tumulty again asked Edith Wilson to let him know if the president had decided whether he would see Lord Grey. Neither Lansing nor Tumulty received an answer.

On the day before the ambassador left the city, Mrs. Wilson asked Lansing to call on her. Edith Wilson then asked of Lansing whether the major had been sent home, as the president had requested. Lansing replied no. Edith said that the president so understood and thought Lord Grey had treated his wishes with little consideration. By ignoring Wilson's request, Grey had hardly merited special treatment. Lansing spent three-quarters of an hour trying to persuade Mrs. Wilson otherwise. However, when she said that she would do what she could, but that the president felt personally indignant and might not be willing to concede an appointment, the secretary went away feeling little hope of success.

Efforts to reach the truth of the Craufurd-Stuart brouhaha intensified after Grey's departure. Perhaps Sir William Wiseman came closest to an accurate appraisal of the labyrinthine episode. Though he had resigned from the British intelligence service by August 1918, he stated in a later interview that he was thoroughly familiar with the Craufurd-Stuart–Ladenburg affair. The story was true but not nearly so melodramatic as some renditions had made it. He did not believe there could have been anything morally wrong in the relationship between May Ladenburg and Baruch as she was his niece of whom he was fond. Wiseman did not think "Miss L." was disloyal, but merely indiscreet and eager to appear knowledgeable. In a somewhat ambivalent defense of Bernard Baruch, Wiseman, who questioned the financier's integrity and his value as a public servant, doubted that Baruch could have told any important secrets in 1918, as he did not have any to tell.[34]

Both May Ladenburg and Bernard Baruch, humiliated by the charges of spying, embarked on campaigns to salvage their reputations. Their forays were made separately, and at the highest levels of authority. Through Baruch's influence—which is to say, his access to Edith Wilson, Grayson, and therefore the president—Ladenburg was able to approach Brigadier General Marlborough Churchill and Secretary of War Newton Baker. She told the general that the defamatory accusations could not remain unchallenged, and that her family naturally felt strongly that the slander must be traced back to its original source so that steps might be taken to disprove it.[35] To Secretary Baker she wrote that she would be extremely grateful if he would look up any recording claimed to have been made in her house that supposedly reflected on her patriotism. He could easily understand, she believed, her wish to have very definite proof with which to refute untrue and humiliating accusations.

Churchill was accommodating. The general sent a note by messenger two days later, reassuring his supplicant that he had no information that would justify anyone in making a statement that she was a German spy.[36] Newton Baker also assured her that the War Department had never had "any evidence of any disloyalty or lack of patriotism on your part, or reflection on your moral character."[37] This was on March 8, 1920. Three days later, in a handwritten letter marked "Confidential," Baker granted President Wilson's request, relayed as usual by his staunch emissary, Admiral Grayson, to deliver to the president certain papers in Baker's personal possession of which the two had previously spoken. Since Baker avoids names, only a handwritten notation at the end certifies them as "the May Ladenburg papers delivered to President personally." Some thought had obviously been given to their destruction. The war secretary wrote to the president that "there must be some way of ridding the public files of papers which like these have no military or public significance," but that the judge advocate general had advised him some time ago that this could only be done by reporting to Congress and with papers over a specified age and of no further value. Baker himself was not satisfied with that conclusion and was, therefore, working on the legal question, about which he would have word in a few days. Meantime, from various quarters he had been hearing "agitation" about these papers. While their confidential character was a complete privilege, "the present destruction of the papers, even if we had a right to do it, would be unwise, as it would deprive innocent persons," he counseled the president, "of the protection which the record gives against wild accusation."[38]

On the same day that he wrote Wilson, Baker also returned papers to General Churchill—again, only a note at the end identifies them as the May Ladenburg file. Baker's desire to state officially the proper limits of action of the War Department in such matters took the form of a stiffly worded reprimand that suggests that he might have been carrying out instructions, from within the White House, relayed through Dr. Grayson: "The collateral matters which appear in these papers are not the concern of the War Department; they should be regarded as arising incidentally and their further pursuit should not be undertaken."[39] Successfully negotiated by Edith Wilson, through Baruch's influence, the Ladenburg papers were reconstituted in a new file, the old one banished apparently beyond recall.[40]

As for Baruch, he tried to minimize this insulting and embarrassing episode. He used his considerable power to influence the press to ignore the role of Craufurd-Stuart as an intelligence officer, and to stress instead Grey's refusal to dismiss his gadfly attaché as a violation of diplomatic tradition and as the underlying reason for Lord Grey's having been ignored by President Wilson. In short, the major was insulting, and Grey was an incompetent diplomat. "British Attaché's Slur Led to Snub for Grey," Frederic William Wile proclaimed in Philadelphia's *Public Ledger*, on February 19, 1920, "White House Coldness to Ambassador Was Caused by His Refusal to Send Home Man Who Spoke Slightingly of President." At last it was possible, the paper boasted, to lift the veil and to clear up the mystery of President Wilson's refusal to receive Viscount Grey.[41]

Three weeks after Lord Grey's return to London, his letter to the editor of the London *Times* was heralded as "probably unique in the history of diplomacy." Signed Grey of Fallodon, published on Friday, January 31, 1920, and reprinted the next day in the *New York Times*, it was the culmination of persistent efforts by London *Times'* astute journalists—Arthur Willert in Washington, and Wickham Steed in London—to wrest an exclusive statement from Grey on the situation in the capital.[42] Not a word in the letter betrayed the frustration of Grey's humiliating experience in Washington, where, as he confided to Steed, the president was practically a prisoner at the hands of his wife, Grayson, and Tumulty, and under the control of Baruch.[43]

This nearly blind diplomat showed flawless vision in his recognition that disagreements between the United States and Great Britain could only be settled in "the clear light of right understanding." By illuminating aspects of the U.S. position regarding the League of Nations that were not wholly understood in Great Britain, he intended not only to educate his countrymen, but also to crystallize issues for the Americans themselves, or at least for those who chose to listen. In what was justly called "an act of fine courage and broad statesmanship,"[44] Grey reviewed the American Senate's independent role and explained that for some Americans the League of Nations was not merely a plunge into the unknown, but a plunge into something of which its historical tradition positively disapproved: foreign, and particularly European, entanglements.

Acknowledging the crisis, he also granted that without U.S. membership, the League would have neither overwhelming physical nor moral force behind it. Without a League of Nations, the old order of things would revive, the old consequences would recur, and there would be yet another great catastrophe of war in which the United States would find itself compelled to intervene for the same reason and at no less or even greater cost than in 1917. He concluded that it would be better to have the United States enter the League as a willing partner with limited obligations than as a reluctant partner who felt that her hand had been forced.

Having addressed the specific grievances between Lodge and Wilson, with the League's future in crisis, Grey asked for understanding, help, and compromise. He had come to believe that if the Senate offered to cooperate in the League of Nations, it would be the greatest mistake to refuse because of conditions attached to such a proposal. A wise and gracious man, and a seasoned diplomat, Grey urged that "when that cooperation is accepted, let it not be accepted in the spirit of pessimism."

At that moment, when all the world was calling for action on the peace treaty, Lord Grey's letter was not only the sensation of the hour, but elicited an inundation of transatlantic newspaper articles, editorials, and discussions. In one stroke, Grey's assurance that Britain was openly amenable to reservations shattered Wilson's primary arguments against the Lodge Reservations to the treaty—the premise that the whole thing would have to be renegotiated, and that it was unthinkable to confront such a long and risk-laden process; and that any modification would dishonor him and the government and people of the United States.[45]

This was substantially the message of the Massachusetts *Springfield Republican*, which Tumulty sent to Mrs. Wilson with a note saying, "I know the President will not be pleased with some parts of this editorial, but I hope that you will have a chance to read it to him." Urgently advising conciliation, the paper pointed out that Grey's letter undeniably weakened the president in his struggle for a treaty as nearly as possible like the treaty that he had signed, but did afford him time for taking stock. In the belief that the president could not have lost all of his old suppleness and dexterity of mind, the editorial expressed hope that he might find opportunity to reconsider the Lodge Reservations; while the worst of them were, on paper, destructive, in practice they would probably be innocuous.

Optimism regarding Grey's conciliatory overture was punctured almost immediately. A five-line paragraph at the top of an otherwise blank paper in the Wilson files records "a report that the President was displeased at Grey's letter to the London *Times* re the attitude of the United States Senate on the Treaty appeared in the *New York Times* February 6, 1920." The truth is more vivid: the Englishman's letter infuriated both the president and his wife—assuming that the erratic scrawl of Edith's response is a barometer of the couple's mood. Reputedly dictated by Wilson, who regarded Grey's letter as the conspiratorial effort of David Lloyd George and Clemenceau in addition to Grey, the original, livid note bristles with assurance "that had Lord Gray ventured upon any such utterance while he was still at Washington as ambassador (a post which he had just left—with the intimation that he was on leave) his government would have been promptly asked to withdraw him."[46]

Wilson's blunt rejection of Grey's letter provoked an outpouring of bitter criticism stemming from the conviction that, in this twentieth century, at this critical stage in world affairs, there was no reason for the nation to be subject to an invisible government emanating "not from a throne, but apparently from a bed."[47] *Harvey's Weekly* accused Wilson of being intolerant of Grey's letter because it told the truth and swept into limbo the fantastic fabric of pretenses the president had erected to bolster his doctrinaire ambitions. Indeed, Grey's letter made it quite clear that the president might submit the treaty with the reservations to the Senate without the slightest fear of rejection. Above all, *Harvey's* pointed out, the letter demonstrated that despite the president's insistence that it would break the heart of the world, at least—as Lord Grey perceived it—"the heart of the world resolutely refuses to be broken."[48] Ray Baker sorrowfully commented on the tragic plight of the president now willing to kill his own child rather than to have it misborn in the world. It was "the old old tragedy of a man's dearest desire thwarted by the defects of his own temperament, and his own physical weakness."[49]

The repercussions of the Wilsons' reaction to Grey's letter were judged to be grave. That the letter brought "scathing comment from Mrs. Wilson," the historian Arthur Walworth has written, "thus intro-

509a

When comment was asked for at the Executive office upon Viscount Grey's extraordinary attempt to influence the action of the President & the State, it at once became evident that the Executive had been as completely taken by surprise as the general public itself by Lord Grey's utterance.

It may safely be assumed that had Lord Grey ventured upon any such utterance while he was still at Washington as Ambassador (a post which he had just left with the intimation that he was on leave) his Government would have been promptly asked to withdraw him.

duced another obstacle to an understanding that might have resulted in the Senate's approval of the peace treaty."[50] Arthur Willert meanwhile believed that the impact of the personalities involved had "changed the whole course of subsequent history," the implication being that "but for the obstinate President and his wife," the United States would have signed on with the League.[51] In fateful assessment of Wilson's rejection of Grey's overture, the *New York Times* on February 8, 1920, predicted that "the real League of Nations will come after the next war."

CHAPTER 30

"Wilson's last mad act"

At noon, the vast East Room of the White House, eighty-two feet long, was not only desolate but pitch-dark, its curtains closely drawn and its crystal chandeliers opaque so that the stricken president might view his daily movie more distinctly. Loneliness was even more pervasive as the rare visitor continued from the Green to the Red Room and on to the dining room, footsteps echoing on barren floors where rugs had been removed to ease the path of the president's wheelchair. Below, in the pressroom, White House reporters filled empty hours playing cards. Except for a trickle of occasions, such as December's visit of the Senate's "Smelling Committee," they were faced with the president's mostly vacant calendar from Monday, October 20, 1919, through February and a blank March. Words such as *abandoned, deserted, solemn, forsaken,* were irrepressible. As the White House was increasingly perceived as a place of gloomy secrets and impostures, sympathy dampened into cynicism, outrage, and slander.

The principal complaint was that Wilson was invisible, the only proof of his existence being his wife's word or his secretary's or his physician's—his daughters went unmentioned. The president was senile; he had a venereal disease; he spouted nursery rhymes about pelicans. Proof of his insanity was that his doctors had nailed bars to prevent him from throwing himself out of the White House windows (in fact, these bars had been installed for the safety of Teddy Roosevelt's young children). After long months of invisible government, the White House claim that Woodrow Wilson's mind was as clear as a bell met with the disdainful response "But bells are sometimes cracked."[1]

Edith Wilson remained in denial. She quoted doctors as saying that the president's recuperative "ascent" thus far was marvelous. His improvement, though gratifying and steady, was slow, she explained to a friend, "owing to the nature of all nervous troubles."[2] The most cheering "bulletin" was Edith's own glowing countenance, noted at a mid-

January charity ball. At the ball, a benefit for the Children's Hospital, "she entered with vim into the spirit of the occasion and, though she did not linger long, she looked more content than anyone has seen her since the tragic return to Washington." The historian William E. Dodd congratulated Edith, on January 4, 1920, on her admirable direction of the affairs of the White House and was sure that "it could hardly have escaped the country that you are one of its important servants . . ."[3]

A lunchtime visit at the White House and a private talk with Edith Wilson set Ray Stannard Baker to wondering whether there was ever "such a situation in our history!" The journalist despaired over Wilson's prolonged illness—now of four months' duration—and thought the meaning of his isolation all too apparent. Though Baker claimed to be impressed with Edith Wilson's sound good sense, her understanding of the difficulties, and her eagerness to help, he noted with dismay that "everything must come through one over strained woman!" . . . that "everything of importance is handled by Mrs. Wilson."[4]

Baker was alluding most immediately to the peace treaty, which, though critical, was only one of a mass of pending issues needing presidential attention. In January 1920, the State Department urged recognition of Finland and Costa Rica, called attention to the fact that the Turkish Treaty, and the settlement on Fiume and the sensitive Adriatic situation, would be discussed in Paris in the near future, and that the first meeting of the Council of the League of Nations would take place at the Quai d'Orsay on Friday, January 16, at 10:30 A.M. Clemenceau's telegram to the U.S. government raised the question of exchange of goods with Russia.

International problems themselves were losing urgency in the face of unprecedented domestic strife within a floundering nation grown weary of countrywide strikes and especially a horrifying series of politically instigated bombings in late April, May, and June of 1919. Wilson himself, on his fatal speaking tour, had warned that "the poison of disorder, the poison of revolt, the poison of chaos," had already forced their way "into the veins of this free people."[5] He did not venture to name the perpetrator of the poison, but a paradoxical Quaker with presidential aspirations—the attorney general, A. Mitchell Palmer (whose own home was bombed on June 2, 1919)—felt compelled, in a nation growing more insular by the moment, to specify the originators of the poison: alien Bolsheviks. In an era of fanatical chauvinism, he led the deportations delirium of 1920 to purge the nation of radicals and foreign-born aliens.

Judge George W. Anderson denounced the tragedy of the xenophobic "Palmer raids" on supposed bastions of communism and anarchism as a violation of civil liberties, "a more lawless proceeding hard for anyone to conceive."[6] Their reflection on the pitiful state of Wilson's presidency both astonished and dismayed Walter Lippmann, the young journalist who found it "forever incredible," he wrote to War Secretary Newton Baker on January 17, 1920, "that an administration announcing the most spacious ideals in our history should have done more to endanger fundamental American liberties than any other group of men for a hundred years." The raids, in his opinion, had instituted a "reign of terror in which honest thought is impossible, in which moderation is discountenanced, in which panic supplants reason."[7]

To combat the so-called Red menace, Mitchell Palmer led the raids with the help of the twenty-four-year-old director of the radicals division of the Bureau of Investigation, and future director of the Federal Bureau of Investigation, J. Edgar Hoover. The raids began more meagerly on November 7, 1919, with attacks on the clubhouses of the Federation of Unions of Russian Workers in New York, Chicago, Philadelphia, and several other cities. They culminated in the gigantic roundup of January 2, 1920. An estimated five thousand men (the figures vary broadly) were arrested in forty cities across the nation. Fifteen hundred were released while thirty-five hundred were held in federal or state custody for days and weeks in crowded cells. Some of them, it was reported, were marched in chains through the streets. As word of the brutalities spread, "Palmerism" drew sharp criticism from, among many others, a group of twelve lawyers that included the Harvard Law School professor Felix Frankfurter. Their published report, "To the American People: Report on the Illegal Practices of the United States Department of Justice," charged Palmer with violation of at least three amendments to the Constitution—arresting and seizing people without warrants, administering cruel and unusual punishment, and denying prisoners the right to counsel.[8] Ultimately, 556 of the approximately five thousand arrested were deported.

The subject of the raids was discussed at the cabinet meeting in April 1920, the first Wilson attended since his stroke, at which time he cautioned Palmer "not to let the country see red." According to the editors of Wilson's papers, however, there was "no evidence that Wilson knew anything about the Palmer raids prior to this Cabinet meeting."[9] This indication of the president's ignorance of such fateful departures from accepted constitutional practice—which had been widely reported in the nation's press—confirms the severity of his disability, and the outrage

visited on the country's institutions. It certifies as well Edith's absolute control of the presidency.

Those closest to the White House seemed adrift in deference. Tumulty tried, with much circumspection, to focus Edith Wilson's attention on the American government's continued failure to recognize Costa Rica's government. That failure meant Costa Rica would not be represented at the forthcoming Pan American financial conference.

"I am embarrassed about this letter and leave it to your discretion to say what is to be done," Tumulty wrote Edith Wilson.

"Nothing at present" was the answer, initialed WW.[10]

Secretary of State Lansing's suggestions of replacements for retiring ambassadors to Italy, China, the Hague, Switzerland, and Siam were ignored. When Lansing went to the White House to remind Edith Wilson of the necessity to act on such pressing matters, he was curtly informed, "The President does not like being told a thing twice."[11]

Tumulty would have better luck when he approached Mrs. Wilson on February 10 on behalf of Director General of Railroads Walker Downer Hines, over the transfer of ownership of the railroads. Three months earlier the two men had failed miserably to engage her attention. Now she appeared to listen. Tumulty wrote of his talk with Hines about the pending disaster. Hines followed up the next day with the specifics of the railroad employees' terms, and again one day later with two recent letters from chief executives of principal railroad organizations. Hines advised the president to signal his intention to form, at the earliest possible date, a tribunal with power to resolve an imminent emergency.

On the morning of February 13, the president, dressed in his old sweater and golf cap and swathed in a blanket, was wheeled into a meeting with a committee representing the railroad workers. He shook hands and "passed facetious remarks" for about ten minutes. Unable to sustain a lengthier conference, he then handed a letter to each member signed in his name but authored by Walker Hines. The *Times* reported that Tumulty and Mrs. Wilson were present during the conference and that Dr. Cary T. Grayson dropped by to inquire about the president's health; also, that the "President Shows Old Form in Talk with Railroad Men."

The next day a telegram prepared by Walker Hines at Tumulty's suggestion was submitted to Edith Wilson with the hope that she might read it to the president. If it met with his approval, it might immediately be sent to A. E. Barker, president of the recalcitrant Brotherhood of Maintenance of Way Employees and Railway Shop Laborers, with the

request that he at once take the necessary steps to withdraw the strike orders and to make sure that no interruption to transportation occurred. Giving Hines and Tumulty grudging approval, Edith wrote in answer, "The President regards this as poorly expressed—but says let it go, as he agrees to the subject matter.[12]

By return telegram Barker informed Wilson that the strike called for February 17 by his union had been "indefinitely postponed."

Wilson's ghostwriters and editors stood by faithfully. In myopic devotion to the leader Wilson had once been and might be again, they appeared to confuse the preservation of the incumbent with the well-being of the presidency itself and of the nation. Incapacitated as he was, Wilson stubbornly ventured on an incongruous foray of his own during this period, with the assistance of the compliant Tumulty and the resolute Edith. Too ill to address the Democrats who would attend the annual Jackson Day banquet, Wilson was determined that the message read in his name at the gathering should further the cause of the League of Nations. The message delivered on January 8, 1920, created a sensation. David Lawrence was not alone in believing that it had been prepared by others.

Tumulty's draft of the Jackson Day message was based on Wilson's letter draft of December 17 challenging fifty-six senators to resign and immediately seek reelection on the issue of their records regarding the ratification of the peace treaty. If a majority were reelected, he would resign the presidency. The vice president authorized Wilson to say that he too would resign in such a case. Quite obviously, while Wilson's plan was never realized, the idea revealed, historian John Morton Blum would write, "the deterioration of a once effective talent."[13]

After consultation with several cabinet members on January 6, and a warning from Secretary of Agriculture David Houston that Wilson's message would arouse wide adverse comment, irritate the Allies, and make the treaty a partisan issue in the next election, Tumulty attempted to soften the president's position—so that he appeared more accommodating to reservations of an "interpretative" character. However, Tumulty's were not to be the final words.

The final draft—addressed to and read by the chairman of the Democratic National Committee, Homer S. Cummings—read on January 8 before an audience of fifteen hundred crowded into the Willard and Washington Hotels, and three weeks prior to U.S. publication of Lord Grey the Viscount of Fallodon's letter advocating compromise, confirmed that the president had chosen to use the Democratic caucus as the place to insist on a treaty without reservations of any kind. In Edith Wilson's pasted addition to the Houston redraft—she had scrupulously monitored the speech from start to finish—Wilson held firm: "Personally, I do not accept the action of the Senate of the United States as the decision of the Nation. . . . We cannot rewrite this treaty. We must take it without changes which alter its meaning, or leave it, and then, after the rest of the world has signed it, we must face the unthinkable task of making another and separate treaty with Germany."[14]

What did the letter mean? The question echoed from Washington across the Atlantic. Did Wilson wish to postpone the settlement of the treaty beyond the November elections? Raymond Fosdick took his former professor's message as a sign that illness had so isolated him from reality that he did not realize how deeply the misrepresentations of the Senate debate had aroused fear in the United States about the purpose of the League of Nations.[15] Democratic senator Henry Ashurst concluded that by making the Versailles Treaty the issue, Wilson "gives the campaign of 1920 an unusual feature to wit, we know now in advance what will be the result"—that theirs was a lost cause.[16]

In the third week of January, Wilson contracted what Grayson believed to be a sharp attack of the flu, rampant in Washington, from which he suffered nausea, vomiting, severe headaches, sweats, chills, and high temperature.[17] The president's condition made Grayson uneasy, though with careful nursing Wilson would soon recover. As to what Grayson enigmatically referred to as Wilson's "other condition," the physician wrote Stockton Axson that the president was improving slowly and steadily.

Apart from Edith and Wilson's daughter Margaret, no one knew of this influenza attack. He was responding to treatment so quickly that Grayson decided not to issue any announcement, for fear of an exaggerated response. Yet Wilson himself must have been gravely troubled about his health for him to talk, as Grayson claimed, of his possible resignation—a step that the physician now strongly advised, but to which Edith Wilson objected.[18] In April, Wilson told the doctor that he was seriously thinking about his duty to the country on account of his physical condition, and that his personal pride must not be allowed to stand in the way of his duty. When he was well, he explained, he felt "eager for work. I judge my condition because now I do not have much desire for work."[19]

The president's health was said to improve in early February, and with improvement "came euphoria and a surge of energy"—according to contemporary psychoneurologists, a euphemistic description of aggressive, irascible, and pugnacious behavior, now diagnosed as "the accentuation of what might be called his temperamental defects by his stroke during the recovery period."[20] During this period, Wilson, less than a week after reading the reprint of Lord Grey's letter in the *New York Times* on February 1, abruptly fired Secretary of State Robert Lansing. With the situation possibly exacerbated by what Edith mistakenly perceived as Lansing's unsympathetic role in the British ambassador's frustrated mission, the president used the issue of the cabinet meetings Lansing had called many months earlier to justify his dismissal. Wilson also threatened the prime ministers of France and England with withdrawal from the treaty with Germany if their countries made any concession to Italy regarding Fiume. Despite sporadic claims from his various physicians that the president was mentally alert and high-spirited, able-bodied and tranquil, a more recent and truthful evaluation maintains that "Wilson's intransigence in all matters now became pervasive."[21]

Rumors of the president's displeasure with his secretary of state had of course circulated almost from the time of the appointment. Lansing had disapproved of Wilson's going abroad, thought the League and the Covenant might more easily be dealt with separately from the treaty with Germany, and had been quoted by William Bullitt in such a way as to raise a question of his loyalty. "To all this Mrs. W. probably added this last perfidy," Edith Benham wrote in her diary on February 18, "that Mr. L. wanted to supersede him by the Vice President."[22]

The tone of the president's letter to his secretary of state—the correspondence between the two was made public the evening of February 13—was shocking to Lansing's friends and to his enemies: "this sudden & violent action . . . the petulant & irritable act of a sick man."[23] It led another critic to observe that thrombosis "evidently has not affected the President's kicking foot."[24] Wilson's letter, for which there was not a glimmer of constitutional support, bluntly asked Lansing, was it true, as Wilson had been told, that during his illness Lansing had frequently called the heads of the executive departments of the government into conference? If it was so, Wilson felt it his duty to call Lansing's attention to considerations that Wilson did not care to dwell upon until he'd had confirmation from Lansing of the allegation.

Wilson wrote, "Under our constitutional law and practice, as developed hitherto, no one but the President has the right to summon the heads of the executive departments into conference, and no one but the President and the Congress has the right to ask their views or the views of any one of them on any public question."[25]

Lansing was seared by this "brutal and offensive" letter, the first he had received from the president since Wilson's illness that was actually signed by him. He considered the president's question about the cabinet meetings—twenty-five or possibly twenty-seven in all—"superfluous," as Wilson had been informed on at least two occasions about the meetings and had even inquired about them. As for Wilson's "dilating" on the dangers of disregarding constitutional law and practice and of departing from custom and precedent—in view of the utter disregard that the president had shown to law as well as precedent, Lansing pronounced this part of the letter "ludicrous, were it not so tragic."

Far more discreet in his actual reply than in his memo to himself, Lansing admitted to frequent informal conferences with the heads of the executive departments of the government. He explained that after Wilson was taken ill in October, certain members of the cabinet felt that, since they were denied communication with Wilson, it was wise to confer informally on interdepartmental matters and those requiring immediate attention. In view of the mutual benefit derived, the practice was continued. Lansing could assure the president, however, it never for a moment entered his mind that he was acting unconstitutionally or contrary to Wilson's wishes. Certainly, Lansing had no intention of assuming powers and exercising functions that under the Constitution are exclusively confided to the president. "If, however, you think that I have failed in my loyalty to you and if you no longer have confidence in me and prefer to have another conduct our foreign affairs, I am of course ready, Mr. President, to relieve you of any embarrassment by placing my resignation in your hands."[26]

Wilson's acceptance of this offer two days later, on February 11, suspended all traces of the reasonable statesman. From the perspective of his sickroom he summarily discounted Lansing's explanation: "I have to remind you, Mr. Secretary, that no action could be taken without me by the Cabinet, and therefore there could have been no disadvantage in awaiting action with regard to matters concerning which action could not have been taken without me." Worse, since his return from Paris, Wilson had been struck by the number of matters in which the secretary of state had acted first and asked for Wilson's approval when it was impossible for him to form an independent judgment. In this most self-incriminating part of the letter, Wilson unwittingly revealed that in arguing lack of "opportunity to examine the circumstances with any degree of independence," he admitted to lacking ability, the physical and mental capacity, to evaluate and judge matters of state. Lansing submitted his resignation the next day.[27]

In her *Memoir*, unable to avoid the subject of Lansing's dismissal, Edith was bound to render her own interpretation of that clumsy event. The secretary, she insisted, was guilty of what she considered the cardinal sin, of being an ambitious usurper of her husband's power. When at length Wilson learned of this, he acted promptly.

Lansing was to analyze, review, question, and defend his course of action as secretary of state to the end of his life. His precise record of the "Cabinet Meetings Held During the President's Illness," written on February 23, 1920, notes the dates and hours of the twenty-five or more meetings he had conducted. He also specifies the subject matter of each, ranging from the impending coal strike, returning the railroads to the owners, the Mexican situation, and the Jackson Day dinner speech, to the detention of the German *Imperator* and tankers and negotiations with the British over their provisional allocation. In his bleak summation of that period he concedes, "It was an unsatisfactory method of government, but there seemed to be no other possible."[28]

In his defense he might also have said that during this extraordinary period from October 1919 to his resignation in February 1920, the president never saw his secretary of state. Instead, Lansing was reduced to relying on Joe Tumulty's help in routing his memorandums, letters, and pleas for attention and decisions. Whether the president actually saw these papers only Mrs. Wilson, Admiral Grayson, and Secretary Tumulty could tell.

Lansing would call Friday, February 13, twenty-four hours after his resignation, his lucky day. He was free at last from the intolerable situation in which he had labored so long. He regarded the opening that the president had given him to tell the truth as "simply amazing." Hoping for recognition, he went so far as to compare the publication of the texts of Wilson's letter and his response, in the *New York Times*, February 13, to the explosion of "a pretty good-sized bomb . . . which will cause a tremendous racket in this country and find an echo abroad."[29]

Public acquittal exceeded even Lansing's greatest expectations. Telegrams and letters by the hundreds congratulated the former secretary of state on his resignation, commended him for his services, and condemned the president for his harsh and unjust treatment. Heartened by the reaction, Lansing thought no man had ever received a greater reward for striving to do his duty than he had in the past seven days. He was not vain enough, he said, to suppose that it was his ability or the value of his services that had caused the outburst of popularity: it was the injustice of the president's act.

Robert Lansing was not a man to arouse staunch loyalties. Fifty-six years of age, dignified, thoughtful, knowledgeable, and precise, he tended to be dismissed as an amiable person who lacked vitality.[30] He revealed to his wife and to a few close friends the underlying fury of the civil letter of resignation he had sent to the president. He confined his rage to the pages of his private diary, to his confidential memorandums, and to what he labeled "Strictly Private Notes." Within those parameters he shows himself an intensely vulnerable man, who was also an astute legal scholar, and sometimes eloquent on the theme of the U.S. Constitution. An astringent critic of Wilson's (Ray Stannard Baker suspected that if Lansing ever put his real feelings in his diary, "there'll be holes burned in the pages!"),[31] he had pondered history's verdict as to Woodrow Wilson's part in the great drama of the day. "Will his accomplishments or his failures win the higher place in the judgment of posterity? Where will his name be placed in the roll of great men who stand forth in the annals of history? True and fair verdict cannot be given," he concluded, "until this generation has passed away."[32]

The president's conduct—his dismissal of Lansing and his refusal to meet with Ambassador Grey—was generally regarded as brutal. The New York *Evening Globe* called the president's action "an amazing error"; the Syracuse *Journal* said it was his "biggest blunder"; according to the *Los Angeles Times*, it was "Wilson's last mad act."[33] On February 15, the *New York Times* was indignant. Of all men in the United States, President Wilson should have been the most wary of raising the question of the cabinet meetings, as it was known early in October that he could not attend them. "If Congress had accepted the theory which Mr. Wilson now propounds, that the Cabinet could do nothing without his presence, and consequently that the Government business was at a standstill, Congress might have felt it to be its duty to ascertain whether in respect to the president the condition described in Article II, section 1 of the Constitution as 'inability to discharge the powers and duties of the said office' actually existed.'" Abroad, the *Echo de Paris* said that Wilson had dismissed Lansing in a tone that no Russian despot ever employed toward his most faulty minister. On a more temperate note, the British

Pall Mall Gazette judged the quarrel as a possible prelude to some piquant revelations of history.[34]

In the week of that controversy, two radically different appraisals of the president's health intensified the confusion. On February 10, the *Baltimore Sun* published an interview with Dr. Hugh H. Young, a consultant from Johns Hopkins Hospital, who found "the greatest reason for encouragement." Though Wilson was diagnosed as suffering from cerebral thrombosis that had affected his arm and leg, his mental vigor was "simply prodigious," and indeed, in many ways he was in better shape than before the illness. His eyes were bright, his complexion glowed, and if he was rarely seen outside the White House, "only the weather is to blame."[35]

Five days later, on February 15, the *Philadelphia Press* reported that the universal interest in the condition of President Wilson, revived by the publication of his correspondence with Lansing and his curt dismissal of his secretary of state, had prompted an inquiry for an authentic medical opinion on the subject. One did not have to read beyond the headlines to share the dismal prognosis advanced by Dr. Arthur Dean Bevan, ex-president of the American Medical Association, professor of surgery at Rush Medical College:

PRESIDENT WILL NEVER RECOVER,
IS VIEW OF DR. BEVAN
Ex-President of American Medical Association
Declares Brain Will Always Be Affected.
Should Resign, He Feels
'Not Competent to Act as Nation's Executive
and Head of Defenses.'[36]

On the morning of February 26, 1920, twenty-one members of the House Judiciary Committee of the 66th Congress heard Congressman Martin B. Madden from Illinois state his concern that it was increasingly important that legislation should be enacted to provide for someone to conduct the business of the country during any period of disability on the part of the president.[37] What had triggered the gathering was Wilson's pronouncement in his letter to Lansing that cabinet meetings could not be held in the absence or inability of the president—a statement that, Madden said, left the executive branch of the government "functionless." If Wilson's edict was observed, no future secretary of state would be likely to call the cabinet together, even informally, whatever the crisis, without direct authority of law. To prevent what he foresaw as government paralysis, of a cabinet going into decay, the bill he was introducing made it the secretary of state's legal duty to call the cabinet in case of the inability of the president.

In the next two hours the committee's attempt to define Article II, section 1, clause 5, of the Constitution (relative to disability, removal from office of the president of the United States) seemed to result in more questions than answers. Did Congress have the responsibility and power under the Constitution to legislate and to prescribe the method of determining that disability? Ought cabinet appointees judge the question of the disability of officers elected by the people? And what about the ability of cabinet members to be impartial when they owed their position to the man whose ability they were weighing? Were members of the Supreme Court or Congress more competent? What about the propriety of submitting the question to a board of physicians of some kind?

Massachusetts representative John J. Rogers immediately pointed out that the question of presidential succession was as old as the Constitution itself. No answer was given at the outset or when it was first put to test, during the period after President James Garfield was shot and lingered between life and death from July 2 until September 19, 1881. During those suspenseful months, eminent scholars, jurists, and lawyers had explored and printed much material in an effort to determine the meaning of the constitutional provision. All had reached different conclusions, all aware of the age-old complexity surrounding the issue of disability.[38]

Despite the ratification, in 1967, of the Twenty-fifth Amendment to the Constitution, answers to the tantalizing questions of medical and moral judgment remain elusive. The amendment, which addresses the transfer of power in case of presidential illness or death, provides for the president to declare in a letter to Congress that he is unable to discharge his duties. The vice president then becomes acting president until the president declares, again in writing to Congress, that he is able to resume his duties. As late as the Reagan presidency (given the questions of his fitness to govern after the attempt on his life and during the possible onset of Alzheimer's disease), implementation of the amendment remained unclear on many counts. Because of the challenge of determining unimpeachable evidence of mental or physical disability, coupled perhaps with an instinctive reluctance to do so, governance in circumstances of presidential disability still remains at risk. As an antidote to White House cover-ups of the past, a Stanford University professor of radiology, Herbert L. Abrams, has proposed that Congress (presumably within the framework of the existing Twenty-fifth Amendment) create a medical advisory committee on the health of the president, whose "independence, breadth of expertise, lack of conflict of interest, availability, and credibility . . . would assure the public of an objective appraisal and would preclude inaction by the executive branch in the face of disability."[39] Such a provision has yet to be enacted.

In hindsight, Edith Wilson wished that her husband had phrased his acceptance of Lansing's resignation differently. Had he to do it over again, she would have had him stress "the accumulation of disloyalty" instead of the secretary's "infringement on Executive prerogatives." Initially, for fear that Wilson might appear "small," she had begged her husband, or so she claimed, to give his reasons for accepting Lansing's resignation—that in spite of liking Mrs. Lansing and having great respect for her father, he considered Lansing's disloyalty intolerable.[40] Lansing's wife, Eleanor, had her own perspective on her husband's humiliating dismissal. She held Edith Wilson responsible for most of the trouble, said that Edith wished to dominate the entire situation and estranged the president's friends. So wounded by the situation that "I cannot write what is in my heart," Eleanor Lansing confided to Edith Benham, "What hurts more than anything is to go without a word from your chief to whom you have tried to be faithful and loyal. Mais c'est fini."[41]

CHAPTER 31

Edith Wilson as "foremost statesman"

Recognition of Edith Wilson's exercise of authority now spread widely. "Nothing more startling has been disclosed in this week of endless sensations at Washington," the London *Daily Mail* reported on February 22, 1920, "than the fact that the wife of President Wilson has for months past been acting President of the United States." It was her so-called "Tea-Table Decisions" that caused her to be anointed as "acting ruler."[1] Though the White House refused to acknowledge the significance of intimate afternoon tête-à-têtes between the president's wife and a series of illustrious men, their purpose was for Mrs. Wilson to personally negotiate the recent reorganization of the president's cabinet.[2]

Since January, Edith had been offering these posts in the president's name. One Sunday, Secretary of Agriculture David Houston responded to a telephone message that Mrs. Wilson wished him to call at the White House that afternoon. Greeting him, she said, "Of course I did not ask you to come merely to drink tea. The President asked me to tell you he is anxious for you to become the Secretary of the Treasury."[3] On Houston's immediate acceptance of his new position, he was not only urged to suggest his own successor but also someone for secretary of the interior, vacant owing to Franklin Lane's retirement. This post was courteously rejected at tea on February 9 by Henry Robinson, former member of the United States Shipping Board and present member of the Coal Commission, and accepted two weeks later by Judge John Payne. It was said that Edith's "persuasive and statesmanlike presentation" at her tea table was responsible for recruiting Admiral William Benson, retired chief of naval operations, to take Payne's newly vacated chairmanship of the United States Shipping Board with the charge of creating America's new merchant marine.

Until now, Edith Wilson had generally been assumed to be a charming woman with gracious Southern manners, and a bright way of telling an anecdote or a "darky" story. That she should develop, as it seemed, overnight into a trained nurse, and an experienced diplomat, was what had astonished.[4] Recognition of her influence as her husband's spokesperson, intermediary, and interpreter required a revision of the more conventional view of the president's second wife. The press—respectful, supportive, and even awed—recognized Edith Wilson's authority "as a buffer—and a very effective one—between her invalid husband and the great affairs of the state." It was understood that no person, however distinguished or urgent his business, could cross the threshold of the White House without her sanction. It was not only understood but expected that she could ignore the most insistent demands and enforce her rule with an iron hand.

The Canton, Ohio, *Daily News* announced on March 12, 1920, that "one of the foremost statesmen in Washington is a woman—Mrs. Woodrow Wilson, wife of the President of the United States."[5] The Baltimore, Maryland, *Star*, March 16, admiringly gave its view that "there is in America today a woman to whom we believe that literature will yet do justice." The paper congratulated Edith on her deferential feminine qualities, on avoiding the spotlight from the beginning of her career as wife of the chief executive, eschewing newspaper interviews, evading leadership in organizations, shunning social prestige, positively disliking affairs of state and never interfering in such things. Forced to do what she had never thought of doing before, with world messages passing through her hands at her husband's dictation, she merited "nothing but the greatest deference and admiration as 'Mrs. Wilson, the acting President.' Whereas the idea of a President Jane Addams or a President Carrie Chapman Catt is as annoying as it is ridiculous."[6]

The image of a reluctant but informed Edith Wilson rallying to the responsibilities of the presidency had its following. One of her admirers was a fellow Virginian, Carter Glass, who had resigned as secretary of the treasury in the previous November to serve as senator: "She showed from the first a grasp of affairs that surprised us all. . . . She never intruded, yet she was always there, ready and able to write a good letter, see an important caller, convey the President's view to this or that official."[7]

Edith was indeed always there for the favored few, absolute in her control of the White House and of access to the ever-narrowing path to the president. A shrinkage of the White House staff augmented her authority. The stenographer Gilbert Close, in permanent limbo since the president's stroke, had accepted a job with the Commonwealth Steel Company of St. Louis. When, on March 4, Edith learned that Edith Benham had suffered a complete nervous breakdown and had to take indefinite leave, she felt terrible, she said, but was far from stranded. She took no steps to replace her companionable secretary.[8] Instead, after she'd tackled the first day's consignment of mail herself, she arranged with Mr. McGee, Miss Benham's typist, to draw up answers to subsequent correspondence from a choice of form letters she devised. When none applied, however, she took the time, even late at night when she was almost too weary to hold a pencil, to write a special response and had the humility to wonder how McGee deciphered her scribbles. Saluted by *Collier's* as the president's "most intimate counsellor," as the country's "Executive by Proxy," Edith "not only proved herself a real mistress of the White House, but mistress of a situation unique in American political life."[9]

Edith's steel grip on presidential access was reinforced by her polite but firm request that Tumulty issue express directions that no document or paper of any kind be sent from his office to her that was not in a sealed envelope. "I think you will see the reasons for this suggestion without my dwelling upon them," she added. In this furtive White House atmosphere, Mrs. Wilson, instead of the secretary of state or any member of the State Department or the cabinet, oversaw the study of papers relating to the pending negotiations on the peace treaty and the League of Nations. On January 5, 1920, demanding secrecy, she wrote to Senator Hitchcock: "The President asks me to ask you to send him a copy of the memorandum he gave you last Summer [September 3, 1919], but he also asks that you allow no one else to see it. So, knowing what a busy person you are, I suggest—if agreeable to you—that you send me the original and let me make the copy and return the original to you. Will you address it to me, as then I can return it to you promptly."[10]

The memorandum Hitchcock unearthed, the basis for his "Proposed Substitute Reservations" forwarded to Edith Wilson on November 13, had been written just before Wilson left Washington to canvass the West on behalf of votes for his League. Titled "Suggestion," it was one of Wilson's works of wish fulfillment. Proposing language to be adopted by Congress, sweeping aside all differences of opinion on the extent of America's international obligations, he declared, "The Senate of the United States of America advises and consents to the ratification of said treaty . . ." Wilson next illuminated his understanding of Articles I, X, XV, and XXI, of the Covenant, which dealt specifically with the acceptance of the authority of the League regarding U.S. army, navy, and air force commitments to fight on behalf of all other members of the League, and submission to arbitration in case of disputes. Satisfied with his interpretation—ignoring the opposition represented by Henry Cabot Lodge—Wilson concluded with reference to Article XXI that "nothing contained in the covenant shall be interpreted as in any way impairing or interfering with the application of the Monroe Doctrine in the American Hemisphere."[11]

Hitchcock, with Grayson as courier, returned the president's September memorandum to Edith on the day of her request, with the addition of a letter of his own. Rereading Wilson's positions on the League deepened the senator's conviction of the need for concessions, and his awareness that he had, as he wrote to the president's wife, as yet "little encouragement from the President to make them." The president, Hitchcock told Edith, might be interested in his analysis of the Republican situation in the Senate. Of the forty-nine Republicans, fourteen had voted against ratification in any form and would do so again; of the remaining thirty-five, probably fifteen, but certainly twelve, sincerely desired a compromise but were unable to budge Lodge from his position. Conscious that Senator Borah, the Supreme Irreconcilable (so named as a member of a group of opponents of the League), would lead fifteen or more Republicans in revolt against compromise with the Democrats, Lodge, in Hitchcock's opinion, merely dallied and trifled with the moderate Republicans to keep them quiet, always promising them that enough Democrats would surrender.

The goal then, said Hitchcock, was to increase that dozen who wanted a compromise to twenty so that, Lodge or no Lodge, the Senate could send the treaty to the president with reservations he might accept, even if he found them not entirely satisfactory. Concessions were in order, and in his concluding sentence, Hitchcock warned that "public opinion is strong for compromise as well as for ratification."[12]

Meanwhile, Tumulty was working faithfully to penetrate the mental and physical barriers blinding the president to the fate of his endangered treaty. As messenger, correspondent, ghostwriter, adviser, and publicist, Tumulty was barely tolerated by Edith Wilson. Her ragged notes contain the essence of his suggestion to enlist the help of Gilbert Hitchcock to encourage the president to adopt a conciliatory mood on negotiations for the League, indicating that the idea had, at least, captured her attention. The notes possibly originated during a telephone conversation with Tumulty.

Basically, Hitchcock was to ask Wilson to write a letter stating his ideas on interpretive reservations and expressing willingness to discuss the Lodge Reservations in a general way, and demonstrating that "for the sake of the peace of the World & the magnitude of the Treaty you are willing to accept them if the Senate accept interpretive reservations."[13]

With the assistance of cabinet members, Tumulty prepared a letter that Wilson might, if he agreed, send to Hitchcock. In his covering letter, submitted to Mrs. Wilson, Tumulty emphasized that the document drew upon the president's Western speeches and on proposals made by Senator Hitchcock. According to this draft, Wilson was glad to have Hitchcock inform his Democratic and Republican colleagues who desired an early ratification of the peace treaty that Wilson agreed that the delay was unfortunate. On behalf of those who sincerely wanted the treaty ratified, Wilson urged that every effort be made to accomplish that result promptly. Conciliatory on the subject of the inflammatory Article X, the draft assured the senator that it ought to be clearly understood that whenever the employment of military or naval forces was recommended by the League of Nations, the power of the Congress of the United States to accept or reject such a recommendation was inviolate. "Action along the lines suggested in this letter," Tumulty concluded, "would make the issue clear and clean-cut and remove from the President's shoulders the responsibility for a seeming unyielding attitude."[14]

On the following day, January 16, convinced that an endorsement from respected David Houston might enhance the cause with the president's wife, Tumulty forwarded the cabinet secretary's approval of the proposed draft. The draft appeared to cover the situation admirably and would appeal, Houston predicted, to the good sense of the American people. He also felt that it would force speedy ratification of the treaty and put full responsibility for delay on the Republicans. Tumulty now persisted with Edith, repeating to her that the "psychological moment" was approaching when the president could strike with force along the lines suggested in the letter to Senator Hitchcock, which would be delivered within weeks. In another note, he told Edith that he felt that she would want to read to the president a friendly editorial from the *Oregon Journal*. The biting response "I would not be willing" was penciled beneath Tumulty's signature.[15] In the face of blatant insults, Tumulty continued to send his insistent, thoughtful, and unwelcome letters.

On January 15, Tumulty had informed Mrs. Wilson that efforts were being made in the Senate to work out a compromise. Hitchcock, with

Democratic senators McKellar, Owen, Simmons, and T. J. Wal[.]
begun to confer with the Republicans Kellogg, Lenroot, Lodge, and
On January 22, four days into the bipartisan conference in Senator S[.]
mons's office, rumors that Lodge was weakening on the fiery Article
gave rise to "uproar within the Republican ranks" and the apparen[t]
instigation of a bizarre mission. Appalled that agreement might be imminent, the leaders of the Republican irreconcilables were reputed to have
sent an emissary who brashly interrupted the conciliatory proceedings
and provoked Lodge's "hasty and compulsory withdrawal" from the
conference. In vague justification of his abrupt departure, Lodge was
said to claim that he had approached by men who protested against
any change in the Reservations, which were already at an "irreducible
minimum." While reports of a threat by the arch-Republican Borah to
replace Lodge as majority leader may be exaggerated, it is clear that, after
that precipitate encounter, the fires of compromise were effectively
smothered. The bipartisan conference did not meet again until January
26; its talks broke off completely yet inconclusively on January 30.[16]

On the subject of compromise on the treaty, Edith Wilson's position
seems confused. She had confided to Ray Baker on January 23 that she
was in favor of speedy ratification of the treaty on the best terms available, but that the president was not of her way of thinking. The journalist told her, "So much hangs on this issue, possibly the very existence of
a League." "I know," she replied, even as she defended her husband's
stand. She admitted that people thought him stubborn and, in an effort
to correct this impression, maintained that the president, with his favorable reception in the West still in mind, believed that the people were
with him. Commenting on his talk with Edith Wilson, Baker identified
the root of this impasse: the president did not know what was going on
and yet, even in this seclusion, continued to wield immense power. It
seemed clear to Baker that, while Mrs. Wilson agreed on the necessity of
an important conciliatory gesture, she could do nothing to move the
president: "He simply did not want to hear what was going on."[17]

In response to Baker's offer to publish a strong and sympathetic article about the League crisis, Edith acknowledged that, four months after
his stroke, her husband (evidently unable to talk to Baker himself) was
still physically and mentally disabled and could neither help nor be
helped in his cherished cause.

Whatever she thought privately, Edith remained stalwart in support of
her husband's categorical position. However cautiously or reasonably

ม, the letters advising compromise were usually ignored. Senator s oblique hope for compromise was at least refused with courtesy.[18] February 9, 1920, the senator urged Wilson to accept former president Taft's reservation to Article X, under which the United States assumed no obligation to preserve the territorial integrity or political independence of any other country or to interfere in controversies between other nations—"unless in any particular case the Congress, which under the Constitution has the sole power to declare war or authorize the employment of the military and naval forces of the United States, shall by act or joint resolution so declare."[19] In this way, Glass argued, the defeat of the treaty would rest with Lodge and his Republican associates. The Democrats could go to the country pointing to their willingness to accept a reservation drafted by a Republican ex-president of the United States that had been rejected by those who proposed to endanger the world out of spite against a Democratic president.

Wilson's response again demonstrated the futility of attempting to convert him. As his amanuensis, Edith, on five small handwritten pages, left no doubt that her husband's judgment was "decidedly against the course Senator Glass proposes." Article X was the backbone of the Covenant: "This is the Presidents clear judgment after repeated & careful considerations of the whole situation & he believes that absolute inaction on our part is better than a mistaken initiative."[20]

On February 27, after talking with Democratic senators, Tumulty again warned Wilson that their forces were disintegrating. People were tired of the endless Senate debate; the man on the street yearned for peace, for an early settlement, and for ratification even with the Lodge Reservations. Showing now some desperation in his proposal and weighing salvation of the treaty against Wilson's pride, Tumulty advised acceptance of ratification with the Lodge Reservations followed by a presidential address contrasting the flaws in Lodge's position with the integrity and logic of his own. "If we pocket the Treaty, will we not be responsible for all the consequences and all the perils that may come because of the failure to bring about peace?"[21]

Tumulty's advice was again ignored. He appears, at this stage, to have relinquished the quest for compromise and, as his biographer John Blum contends, embraced his chief's extremist position. Perhaps the abrasive tone, as well as the Wilsonian cadences, of an eventual presidential letter to Hitchcock, dated March 1, 1920, reflect the secretary's effort to remain in the president's good graces, even at the price of reversing his own convictions.

Tumulty may also have been antagonized by Sir Edward Grey's provocative comments in February on the deadlock between the president and the senate. "You will notice," Tumulty wrote to Edith Wilson regarding his latest draft of the letter to Hitchcock, "I have added a gentle slap at Sir Edward Grey's unwarranted interference in our policies." He called particular attention to an italicized passage concerning the leadership of reactionary elements of the Old World who, "having failed to enforce their will when the treaty originally was framed, now were endeavoring to regain their lost ground and *brazenly thrusting themselves into our politics, avowing their support of such a reservation and who, in anticipation of its passage and the consequent nullification of the League force their imperialistic purposes into the peace settlements themselves.* . . . . We cannot accept such a leadership and please God, we will not."[22]

Wilson himself, it has been suggested, may have been largely responsible for the ultimate letter to Hitchcock and for its confrontational nature. In "The Aftermath of Wilson's Stroke," Dr. Bert E. Park writes that the president's resistance to compromise reflected the ravages of his stroke on October 2. The letter to Hitchcock, of March 8, 1920, is a paean to Article X, "in poignant if tragic prose," and, Park concludes, "effectively ended any hope of winning the Senate's consent to the ratification of the Versailles treaty when it voted for a second time on March 19, 1920."[23]

Appearing in the press on March 9, 1920, Wilson's lengthy letter to Senator Hitchcock did indeed clarify his position. He was pronounced an "affirmative irreconcilable" by the *Washington Post.* Concession and compromise were no longer considerations. Wilson said, "We can dismiss from our minds the idea that it is necessary to stipulate in connection with Article X the constitutional methods we should use in fulfilling our obligations under it. We gain nothing by such stipulations and secure nothing which is not already secured." He welcomed the opportunity to throw light on a subject that had become singularly beclouded. He held the doctrine of Article X to be the essence of Americanism. He was sorry to say that the reservations that had come to his notice were, almost without exception, not interpretations but virtual nullifications of those articles.

In expressing his "unwillingness to trust to the counsel of diplomats the working out of any salvation of the world from the things which it has suffered," Wilson now provoked speculation that he wanted to carry the treaty fight into the presidential campaign and was considering running for a third term. He trusted to himself, rather than others, to work things out. Most certainly, he wrote, he did not trust the French, citing a militaristic party seeking to gain ascendancy in French government councils.

The immediate effect of the letter was destructive, arousing suspicion, sarcasm, and outright hostility. "Of the many extraordinary utterances of the White House," the *New York Tribune* wrote, March 10, 1920, "the latest, it will scarcely be denied, is the most extraordinary. Instead of returning physical vigor softening the President's weaknesses of temper, his unreasonable acerbity seems to grow." The *New York Times* was somber in its prediction of the consequences: the gulf between the president and Senator Lodge was unbridgeable. "In his new letter," the French ambassador Jusserand reported from Washington to Paris, "everything and everyone is thrown overboard"—including Hitchcock, Republicans of goodwill, extreme radicals, and finally, France herself. Jusserand also complained privately to a State Department official that when one has such criticism to make about a country that is not an enemy state, one goes to its ambassador and not to the press. "But wrongly motivated, seeing no one, not having shown his letter to anyone before making it public"—here Jusserand was mistaken—"he has acted totally in the wrong way."[24]

The long-suffering Hitchcock made one more gesture at reaching the president—presuming that he would fail even as he did so. Lodge, he pointed out, had offered a substitute for Reservation No. 2, which some Democratic senators thought Wilson might accept. To the opening sentence "The United States assumes no obligation to preserve the territorial integrity or political independence of any other country," Lodge had added, "by the employment of its military or naval forces, its resources, or any form of economic discrimination." As Lodge's insertion made the reservation more specific, Hitchcock had been correct in expecting Wilson's negative reaction. The senator's assumption "that you would not accept it" received the taut response "You are quite right," initialed W.W.[25]

"I do not believe," said Senator Robert Latham Owen, one of Wilson's staunchest supporters, in the final speech before the roll was called on Friday, March 19, "that there is a single Democratic Senator who would not vote for this resolution of ratification if it were not for the belief of such Senators that the President of the United States desires them to defeat the resolution of ratification now pending and would regard their failure to do so as a refusal to follow his view as a party leader."[26] Despite his sensitivity to the president's wishes, Owen was among the twenty-one Democrats along with twenty-eight Republicans who voted for ratification with the so-called Lodge Reservations. Twenty-three Democrats and twelve Republicans voted in opposition; three Democrats and nine Republicans were not present or did not vote. Lacking the necessary two-thirds vote, the treaty was rejected by the Senate by a vote of forty-nine to thirty-five.

The defeat was attributed directly to the president. The treaty's embittered supporters recognized that, had he sought his party's vote for the treaty, accepting the Lodge Reservations with twenty-three Democrats gained instead of lost, it would have been ratified by a vote of seventy-two to twelve. Hitchcock, in a letter to Wilson on March 20, apologized for being unable to make a better report on the treaty ratification. "But," he wrote in a provocative footnote, "it required most energetic efforts on my part to prevent a majority of the democratic senators from surrendering to Lodge and his reservations."[27]

William Jennings Bryan called the president's rejection of the League "a colossal crime." For the British journalist Arthur Willert, it was a tragic disappointment. The Wilsonian crusade in world affairs was over, and America was again in isolation. Willert had hoped that America would come into the League and remain there long enough to help in the reconstruction of Europe. Antipathetic though he had always found Wilson, he felt some sympathy for the president: "As a politician he had earned his defeat. As an idealist he had deserved better things. There was no taint of self-seeking about him. In foreign affairs ignorance had been his bane. Good intentions over the League had been frustrated by bad judgment, bad management, and bad health."[28] Others were not so readily appeased. Connecticut's Republican senator Frank Brandegee commented that the president "has strangled his own child."[29]

Edith informed her husband of the result on the morning following the vote. The president was downcast. He had both won and lost. He had worked hard for this outcome, the defeat of the treaty with the Lodge Reservations. Even so, in his troubled mental state, he may have entertained a hope of its unencumbered passage, free of his enemies' restrictions. He sighed, "I feel like going to bed and staying there." That night, though quiet, he was restless. At about 3 A.M. Wilson turned and said, "Doctor, the devil is a busy man." Later he asked Grayson to get the Bible and read from Second Corinthians, chapter 4, verses 8 and 9: "We are troubled on every side, yet not distressed; we are perplexed, but not in despair; Persecuted but not forsaken; cast down, but not destroyed." Wilson said, "If I were not a Christian, I think I should go mad, but my faith in God holds me to the belief that He is in some way working out His own plans through human perversities and mistakes."[30]

Two weeks later, Wilson was dour and confused: "I don't know whether it is warm or cold. I feel so weak and useless. I feel that I would like to go back to bed and stay there until I either get well or die. I cannot make a move to do my work except by making a definite resolve to do so." During this period, he spoke bitterly of the League's antagonists. "Those who oppose it," he predicted, "will be gibbeted and occupy an unenviable position in history along with Benedict Arnold." As the spring advanced, his anger was unabated. He "vigorously if not viciously" talked to Josephus Daniels about the men who had killed the treaty. "It is dead," he said, "and lies over there. Every morning I put flowers on its grave."[31] Edith was adamant in her condemnation: Henry Cabot Lodge had put the world back fifty years, and "at his door lies the wreckage of human hopes and the peril to human lives that afflict mankind today."[32]

On the morning on which Lodge had left his house for the Capitol to vote on the ratification of the treaty, he had, in fact, been in a positive frame of mind. He told his annual houseguest, Theodore Roosevelt's sister, Corinne Roosevelt Robinson, that he hoped to have in his pocket, on his return that evening, a draft of the U.S. ratification of the treaty, with reservations. "Are you quite sure?" Mrs. Robinson had asked. "Yes," he replied. "I am positive that I now have enough Democratic votes added to my Republican votes to make this possible."

That afternoon, Mrs. Robinson, back from tea at the British embassy, found Lodge in his spacious library lighting the fire. Sensing that he was dispirited, she decided to say nothing about the treaty unless he opened the subject. After a moment, he turned around to face his visitor. He remembered that she had doubted the possibility of ratification: "You were right—just as I thought that I had everything settled and that my number of Democratic votes was ample in every way, a sinister, unseen hand came out from the White House and drew away many votes, and I could do nothing."[33]

* * *

Angry but undefeated, Edith Wilson had stated, one month earlier, that it might be necessary for her husband to run for the presidency for a third term.[34] Political gossip in Washington already associated the president's wife with influences urging that he offer himself as candidate for a third term. "If the President yields to their pressure," the journalist F. W. Wile reported from Washington, "he will stand as the embodiment of the League of Nations and, to use his own words, die fighting for it if the fates so decree."[35]

CHAPTER 32

Wilson for a third term

Outside his circles of political intrigue, it was undreamt of that President Wilson had any thought of a third-term nomination in 1920. The very suggestion was a grave mistake, "at once relegated to the unthinkable." In the light of reports on his appearance just three months before the Democratic National Convention, the *New York Times*, on March 27, pronounced the idea "absurd."[1]

Accounts of Wilson's first meeting with his cabinet on April 14, after a seven-month hiatus, were discouraging. Called hastily at the suggestion of Dr. Grayson, obviously with the approval of Edith Wilson, its purpose was to bolster a despondent president, whose rambling bedside confidences dwelt on his contempt for the disorganization of the U.S. Senate, the double-dealing of certain senators, and of Henry Cabot Lodge in particular. Wilson was disappointed in Colonel House, whom he had not seen since Paris, and with others who had failed him. At this juncture, Grayson persuaded Wilson to hold a cabinet meeting: "A personal contact with your advisers," Grayson consoled Wilson, "will reassure you of your ability to continue to handle the situation."[2]

On the designated morning, Wilson was seated behind a desk at the far end of the old Cabinet Room of the White House. That each member, well known to Wilson, was announced by name as he entered the room suggested to one participant the extent to which the president's eyesight might be impaired. Wilson's lips were thicker, his face longer, his jaw tended to droop to one side as he tried to speak, and his voice was weak and strained. He shook hands, told several jokes, and fell silent. It became clear that he was not going to take the initiative. He seemed to have difficulty initially concentrating on the discussion—undoubtedly, as David Houston correctly speculated, because he knew little about the subjects raised by Attorney General A. Mitchell Palmer: the wildcat strikes of the railroad workers, the suggested Bolshevik influences, and the role of the Communist labor party. Discussion dragged on for over an hour until interrupted by Dr. Grayson and Edith Wilson. The president's wife looked disturbed as she suggested that everyone leave, saying, "This is an experiment, you know." David Houston wrote later that to look at Wilson, old, worn, and haggard, one of his arms useless, was enough to make one weep.[3]

Pity for the president in some quarters was countered by hostility in others. The Pennsylvania Republican senator Philander Knox reminded Congress on May 5 that more than seventeen months had passed since the last shot was fired in the great war; and for the welfare and safety of the nation, its property, its free institutions, and even its lives, he demanded peace. To that end he had called a meeting of the Foreign Relations Committee on April 12 to consider a resolution (introduced in the House on April 1 and passed on April 9) declaring the state of war with Germany at an end. Deploring the months during which the country had been a rudderless ship, he also denounced the ship's captain, the president, who insisted on thwarting every attempt on the part of the Senate, the Congress, or the people to take any action on the provisions of the Treaty of Versailles, and who had preferred, instead, to maintain the country in a theoretical state of war rather than to abate "one jot or tittle of the full measure" of his isolated will.

The need for governance was by now an emergency. Rife with industrial and social problems, the nation required statesmanship from a leader robust in mind and body. Instead, as critics said openly, their president was a broken reed, dependent on a deficient few for his imperfect knowledge of the conditions of the country over which he presided.[4] The question of where a new leader was to come from exacerbated the dilemma. Within three months of the Democratic National Convention there seemed no coherent proposal as to who would be nominated for president on either ticket.

Courageously—considering that his advice had consistently been ignored—Joseph Tumulty took the initiative concerning the matter of the president's own candidacy. In view of the defeat of the treaty and the proximity of the convention, Tumulty wondered, as he wrote to Edith Wilson on March 23, whether the president should now make a conclusive statement concerning a third term—*"In my opinion this is the time to act"*[5]—to refute the Republican claim that the president was attempting to make the League of Nations a reason for demanding a third term. A statement of withdrawal would strengthen every move the president wished to make during the remainder of his second term and would also keep the issue of the League of Nations alive. Having proposed such a

message, Tumulty elaborated on its presentation: It should be intimate
and generous in character, embodying the president's best feelings about
the League. It should also refer to his fight for the League and Covenant,
the damage of Lodge's reservations, the fact that no selfish motive
underlay his purpose: the League of Nations was not his idea but the
dream of statesmen across the centuries.

The president should, in Tumulty's view, say unequivocally that he
wished his name not to be considered in connection with a third term.
Were he nominated, he would decline. He intended to employ all his
energies for fulfillment of the great purpose behind the League, whether
in or out of office. Tumulty's appeal was wise and realistic, and patently
sincere in its intention to exalt Woodrow Wilson. Edith did not bother to
acknowledge it. She did, however, show the letter to Wilson, who then
discussed its theme with Dr. Grayson.

Wilson saw no reason to come out against a third term. It was presumptuous and in bad taste to decline a possibility not offered him. It was
best to keep the world guessing for the time being. With present turmoil
in the United States and throughout the world, the Democratic convention in San Francisco might be hamstrung; and, Wilson told Grayson,
it might then become imperative that the League of Nations and the
treaty be made the dominant issue. If the convention became deadlocked
on candidates, there might be a near-universal demand for someone to
lead delegates out of the wilderness. If so, Wilson himself was the logical
choice to champion that cause. In such circumstances he would feel
obliged to accept the nomination even if he thought it would cost him his
life. Grayson notes in his memorandum dated March 25 that Wilson
assured him he would rather lead a fight for the League of Nations "and
lose both my reputation and my life than shirk a duty of this kind if
absolutely necessary."[6] As he had at the beginning of his Western tour,
Wilson felt that he had only to go to the people and they would understand the facts. It was his sole purpose to see that the treaty was not
rejected or emasculated. By the following morning, Wilson found consolation in the thought that the country was evidently unready to accept
the League. It might be, he told Grayson, that it would be necessary to
"break the heart of the world and the pocketbook of the world before the
League will be accepted and appreciated."[7]

On April 12, 1920, Wilson rehearsed his first campaign message in a letter that touched on the question of a third term. Jouett Shouse, the assis-

tant secretary of the treasury, was leaving to attend his state convention, and Wilson availed himself of the occasion to send a cordial greeting to the Democrats of Kansas. In Wilson's view, the party was to be congratulated on confronting a year of exceptional opportunity and duty. It had a duty to raise with the voters nothing less than the honor of the United States and the redemption of its solemn obligations—to its associates in the great war and to mankind, to whom it had pledged itself to establish a concert of nations to guarantee a permanent peace based on justice. "One of the great issues that has fallen to a party to fight for, it now falls to the Democratic party to push to victory."[8]

The month of May found Wilson in campaigning mood. Was it important to nominate candidates pledged to ratify the Versailles Treaty without the Lodge Reservations? the chairman of Oregon's Multnomah County Democratic Central Committee, G. E. Hamaker, had wired on May 9. Wilson answered fiercely that it was "imperative that the party should at once proclaim itself the uncompromising champion of the nation's honor and the advocate of everything that the United States can do in the service of humanity. It should therefore endorse and support the Versailles treaty and condemn the Lodge reservations as utterly inconsistent with the Nation's honor and destructive of the world leadership . . ."[9] Both the Shouse and the Hamaker "speeches" may have been written for Wilson by Tumulty, just as David Houston drafted Wilson's message, submitted to Congress unsigned on May 13, vetoing the legislative, executive, and judicial appropriation bill.

By May it became clear that Wilson, in a receptive mood, was convinced that he would be nominated for a third term. Those who did encourage him, whether out of sentiment or cynical calculation, could scarcely have hoped to delude the convention. Most amazing to Ike Hoover was that Edith Wilson and Grayson seemed to enter into the planning. They had put over so many subterfuges, Hoover guessed, that "perhaps they believed this might be just one more opportunity to exhibit their magic prowess."[10]

Hoover was not the only one in the White House to be amazed that Edith Wilson supported her husband's ambition to serve another term. The Secret Service man Starling said that no one knew better than she how unqualified he was for such a task. She knew intimately the invalid's routine. She followed each painful moment from the time when he, ensconced in his wheelchair, descended to the basement and was rolled into the garden on the east side of the grounds to the protected corner formed by the jutting end of the east window, where it was usually warm and sunny, and where he might enjoy a fine southern view. She undoubtedly timed his automobile rides, which made use of the newly built platform in the driveway at the south entrance, which brought him level with the floor of the car. There, standing at last, Wilson was lifted into his seat, his cape and cap adjusted so that he did not appear an invalid to the passersby on the street. On his return, a group was organized to cheer him as he passed through the White House gates. (The first time this occurred, when he was lifted out from the car, there were tears in his eyes. "You see," he told Mrs. Wilson, "they still love me!"[11])

Wilson took his first car ride on a balmy March 3 and soon proved an irascible passenger. He had the notion that no auto should pass his—despite that his car slowed purposely to fifteen or twenty miles an hour so he could enjoy the scenery. When his presidential limousine was to be serviced, he canceled Edith's plans for him to ride in a Secret Service car and, on the grounds that he had not been consulted, insisted instead on riding in a horse-drawn carriage. At this point, Wilson had grown so cantankerous, his staff complained, he begrudged them their vacations.

Wilson was discouraged by his stultifying routine. By the end of May he would manage to walk from the bedroom to the study at 9 A.M. He would work at his desk until about ten-thirty or eleven, after which he was wheeled into the White House gardens in his Atlantic City rolling chair. He would watch a movie from twelve to one, take lunch, rest in bed from two to three, tend to official matters, take a motor ride, read, and be read to. On June 7, he sat at the downstairs dining room table for the first time since his stroke.

Official pronouncements to the contrary, he was a painful sight to the rare outsiders—to the foreign ambassadors, for example, whose presentation of their credentials could not diplomatically be postponed. At an awkward ceremony, the British ambassador, Sir Auckland Geddes, found himself confronted in late May with the sixty-three-year-old invalid president. Wilson was a tired old man whose left arm gave not a sign of movement, Geddes reported to his prime minister, David Lloyd George. "It was quite evident that on the Democrats' side, Wilson had been the whole show and the real trouble now was that there was nobody with the brain power to supply the imagination needed to meet the difficulties facing America. The deadlock was so complete that one would almost be justified in saying that the United States had no government..."[12]

The report of the new Swiss minister to the United States, Marc Peter, was still more somber. Wilson's air of senility seemed to disappear once he spoke and his eyes lit up, but Peter pitied this motionless figure and questioned the president's logic on many counts, most urgently on his indifference to other opinions. Wilson seemed not to take account of the opposition of the Senate, the public, or the press. His isolation, his apparent intention to live out his life in the White House, which had become his ivory tower, was disturbing.[13]

Wilson was, of course, ill mentally as well as physically. Grayson refers to Wilson's bouts of depression, as well as to his nervous cough, loss of appetite, and bladder trouble. There was no air in his lungs, he told the physician. He complained of asthma and talked slowly. He had "prostatic trouble—blue," Grayson wrote in his diary on May 19, in reference to Wilson's distressing bladder infection and glum mood. On May 20, Wilson was "Depressed and Much depressed" and told Grayson, "This may be my last day."[14]

During this period Edith sent her husband three letters (there may have been more) reminiscent, in sentiment and vocabulary, of the couple's early love letters during their courtship. Tender and encouraging, they may have been written in an effort to cheer him during those trying days. On a new White House stationery engraved with the presidential seal, Edith wrote, "I love and adore you." Wilson's response, from "Your own Boy," came the same day: "This is beautiful paper—almost fine enough for the loveliest woman in the world, whom I love to distraction."[15]

On May 24, 1920, on the same gilt-embellished White House stationery, Edith wrote "My own Precious Boy":

I must tell you what a day of gold this has been despite its grey sky—for I have felt your dear love expressed in tender ways— ways that cost effort and sacrifice—which in spite of your suffering and heartache you did for me.

Dear little Boy—I can not express the love & gratification this thrills me with—but I believe you know—and, because you know, you will struggle on and on until this valley of sorrow is over and together we will stand on the height and look back upon it. Both stronger for the lesson it has taught—and surer of our great love.

Remember I want to share everything with you—and that will

make it easier to see beyond the cloud & doubt. Keep a stout heart under your jacket, little Boy Lover and we will win!![16]

On June 5, 1920, Edith wrote to "My own precious One":

> When you asked me if I had faith in you it was like asking if I believed the sun gave light.
>
> You are to me the tangible evidence of all that is strong, fine and true! I trust you unquestionably and have faith in you beyond words.
>
> Sometimes you tell me I am strong or, as you put it, "great"— don't you see little boy—that it is the contact with you and your greatness that lifts me up and if there is merit in me, it is because I am your mirror in which your fineness is reflected.
>
> You are so splendid your self that the very fact makes you blind to itself and I would not have it otherwise.
>
> Always remember dear One that you are not only strong your self but that by your example you make us so—and that any one who is with you as I have been absorbs all wholesome things and becomes better from the inspiration! I love you—always, E.B.W.[17]

Edith Wilson hovered solicitously over Wilson as he met with the national chairman and keynote speaker for the Democratic National Convention, fifty-year-old Homer Cummings, on the morning of May 31. Wilson's eyes seemed unnaturally large; he was unusually subdued and listened more. His hands shook and it seemed as if his right hand picked at the fingers of his immobile left hand as though finding it numb or prickly. In this reduced state, his displeasure over any reference to his illness was surprising to Cummings, who, after a movie and lunch, retired to the library with Edith to work out a code that would secretly keep the president abreast of the convention.

There were further signs that Wilson was a candidate for president. In talk of the convention and the leading candidates, he expressed no preference. He said he did not want to take the position of dictating to the party. Of course, he told Cummings, some candidates might be seriously objectionable, but that bridge should be crossed when they got to it. When Wilson did speak of a candidate, it was as though he were defining a rival: there was always some reservation. John Davis was a fine man but a formalist; if you wanted to stand still he was just the man to nominate. Senator Glass would make a fine president, but Wilson doubted whether he would make a good candidate. Nonpartisan Herbert Hoover, lacking the courage to stand by the Democratic Party, had followed the line of least resistance by joining the Republicans. "He is not fit for it," Wilson said of his son-in-law, former secretary of the treasury McAdoo. As for Ohio's Governor James Cox—his nomination "would be a fake." Wilson dismissed entirely the logical candidate: "It would be fatal to let Marshall have anything to do with the framing of the Democratic platform."[18]

Wilson would not see McAdoo on any of the five occasions, in mid-May, on which his son-in-law sought an interview. Wilson would not even speak to the aspiring Mitchell Palmer during a cabinet meeting. The president's stenographer, Charles Swem, said that Wilson believed both were rival nominees. Palmer's sin was to have publicly announced that the president realized there was some sentiment throughout the country against a chief executive running for a third term. In response, Wilson said it showed a lack of character for a cabinet officer to seek to supersede his chief.[19] During the convention in San Francisco, Wilson's rivalry with his son-in-law was acutely demonstrated when Postmaster General Albert S. Burleson's interest in McAdoo's nomination precipitated Wilson's recommendation that Burleson be excluded from the leadership's more intimate counsels.

Wilson's reelection aspirations are reflected in his random notes pertaining to a possible third term. Wilson's questionnaire of June 10, entitled "THE GREAT REFERENDUM and ACCOUNTING of your GOVERNMENT," posed three questions: Does the reader wish to make use of Wilson's services as president for another four years? Does he approve of the way in which the administration conducted the war? Does he wish the Treaty of Versailles ratified? And in this latter regard, does he approve of the League of Nations as organized and empowered under the Treaty of Versailles, and does he wish the United States to play a responsible part in it? At the end of this document, Wilson listed his slate for his "3rd Administration," including Bernard Baruch for secretary of commerce and four nominees for secretary of the treasury. As there was no mention of a vice president, possibly he intended to retain Marshall after all.[20]

Wilson did not, of course, name his wife to any post. But she was omnipresent, in the bedroom, in the office, at mealtimes, on his automobile rides, and at his meetings. She was her husband's campaign manager, as well as his devoted wife. In May she entertained prominent women at a series of White House teas that included wives of various ambassadors. She made a charming picture in her summerish dress—on one occasion a soft gray mull with frills of cream lace and a loose cluster of sweet peas tucked in at the belt. Miss Bertha Bolling, her sister, was by her side at these gatherings of twenty-five ladies. Also present was her old Negro mammy, who had come back—as *Town Topics* expressed it—to "Miss Edif" when she'd married Norman Galt.[21]

Edith's mastery of public relations was displayed in her promotion of a White House interview with the reporter Louis Seibold, which, on June 17, advised readers of the New York *World* of Wilson's resurgence of health. Controlled by Edith, the results surpassed the previous December's performance, when Senators Fall and Hitchcock were convinced that Wilson was fit to retain his office. Six months later, with a possible third term in view, the Wilsons agreed to the *World* interview, from which it was intended that Wilson would emerge as the uniquely qualified candidate: a master of politics, whose concepts outsoared those of all rivals.

Louis Seibold saw the interview, as he told Joseph Tumulty, as an opportunity for the president to "visit" with the citizens of the United States. Tumulty found the idea fortuitous, as did the Wilsons. Planned for publication six days after the nomination of Harding for president at the Republican convention, and ten days before the opening of the Democratic convention, the interview had several goals. For Seibold, there was prestige in being the first reporter to interview the president since his collapse in October. To Tumulty, it afforded Wilson a chance to define himself in such a way as to strengthen the Democratic platform.

In preparation for the interview, Tumulty set forth questions and answers on foreign policy, the peace treaty, the League, Mexico, labor, taxes, and the Volstead Act and submitted these to Edith for approval. He also proposed a long-sought objective that Edith had chosen to ignore: that Wilson use the occasion to renounce any desire for renomination. This time Edith returned an unmistakable refusal. Nothing but "exaltation" of her husband would be permitted.[22]

Seibold was not the first journalist beguiled by power. He referred to the White House as "the nearest approach to an official palace" in America and was awed in the presence of its principal resident. Having covered Wilson's Western tour, Seibold was sympathetic to Wilson personally, as well as to his cause. On the June morning of the White House interview, Seibold found the president and his wife on the south balcony overlooking a green lawn hedged with spruces, maples, and dogwood. Mrs. Wilson was standing: the first lady of the land, mild, charming, and smiling.

Wilson, wearing a Panama hat, was seated in an office chair. He extended his right hand in a hearty grip. Seibold described "the smiling chatelaine of the White House" with her left hand on the back of her husband's office chair and using her right to arrange some document in a square desk basket. The party was joined by Dr. Grayson, Tumulty, and Swem. The president excused himself to turn to some official business, and Mrs. Wilson presented papers requiring the president's attention. Tumulty supplied the president with explanations of certain documents. Dr. Grayson excused himself to attend to professional business elsewhere. The president disposed of matters with the same deliberation that had always characterized his official methods.

At noon, the group moved to the East Room, where Seibold watched a movie with the Wilsons—Bill Hart in *Sand*. Before lunch, the president having disappeared on official business, Dr. Grayson informed the reporter that Wilson had gained twenty pounds in the last two months. He was nearly back to normal in that respect, and he had performed a great deal of work since he had reestablished himself at the White House proper, rather than in the adjoining office building. Following lunch, the president went to prepare for the cabinet meeting. The next afternoon, as Seibold called to say good-bye, Wilson, about to go for a motor ride, emerged from the elevator. He was wearing a natty sailor straw hat with a dark blue ribbon, a short, blue flannel coat, white flannel trousers, white canvas shoes. He looked like a man ready for a stroll on the beach. As the car departed, the president raised his hat with his right hand in acknowledgment of the reporter's parting salute.

During Tuesday's interview Wilson had declined to respond to Seibold's question as to the type of man the Democratic Party should choose as its candidate. He had not come forward in the promotion of any Democratic presidential nomination. He was, however, clear on the chief issue. The League of Nations was too great a concept for mere political skulduggery. There could be no doubt of his opinions on his Republican adversaries, Senators Lodge and Johnson. "One of these gentlemen is disingenuous and evasive and the other candidly hostile."[23]

The *World* carried two articles by Louis Seibold: one, a report of a visit to the White House; the second, a report of an interview. The first concentrated on the president's physical state, the other on his political positions. On the basis of a three-hour interview on Tuesday, June 15, and a half hour on Wednesday, the "best loved and most hated man in the world" was all but deified. His face was that of a man who had endured his suffering with a stoicism born of fine courage; his eyes were unmistakably the Wilson eyes, keen, searching, and snappily intelligent; despite his slight tendency to favor his left side, contrary to reports his arm did not hang helplessly at his side. The cane he used to walk from the White House elevator to the garden was merely the sort of stick he had used to thrash through the turnip patches when he was president of Princeton. Altogether, nine months of courageous battling had neither daunted the spirit nor impaired in the slightest degree his splendid intellect, his facility of expression, his directness of meaning. Nor had the passing months modified the intense devotion to principles for which he had fought against the grasping statesmen of Europe and the political obstructionists of his own country.

An accompanying photograph (credited to Harris and Ewing, fireplace in the background) showed Wilson at his desk, peering through his pince-nez full face and pointing to file cards held by Edith, standing and dressed in her lawn and lace. According to the *New York Times,* June 18, the couple had achieved their goal: "His Interview Called Bid to Hold Party Leadership." But the story went further. In Republican circles the character of the president's interview, as well as the emphasis that Seibold laid on the improved health of the president, was "susceptible of an interpretation that the President is ready to run for a third term."[24]

The interview benefited not only the Wilsons. Its author was rewarded with a Pulitzer prize for "a historic first in journalism." There was intense professional interest in Seibold's work, the Columbia University Press would write in 1974, because the exclusive presidential interview was a rarity at the time. It was well understood that the *World*'s reporter had been favored because the paper had fought hard for the League of Nations and because the interview conveyed Wilson's warning to the Democratic National Convention not to sidestep a pledge for the League. However, the propaganda content of the interview did not detract from Seibold's importance.[25] Given her iron will and erratic judgment, obscured by her fabled Southern charm, Edith Wilson was successful at staging the interviews that portrayed her husband's supposed health and well-being. Members of the press such as Louis Seibold, and the White House Associated Press correspondent Lionel Probert, who could be counted on to write agreed untruths, were granted privileged access. Stories that fell below her demands for flattery—as in the case of an article in which the British journalist Wilfred Steed touted House over her husband—did not go unpunished. If Edith was not the first angry first lady in regard to the press, she may have been the most manipulative. While Seibold remained on cordial terms with the Wilsons, assiduously courting Edith's good graces with praise of her husband, those less obsequious fared differently.

The Democratic National Convention opened in the Civic Auditorium in San Francisco at noon on June 28. A giant searchlight illuminated the flag-draped portrait of President Wilson. The crowd went wild, men and women climbing on chairs, yelling, waving, and whistling. Chairman Cummings's keynote address accused the Republicans of carping criticism of the war effort—and of the president, whose bout of illness was attributed to the malicious slanders of his opponents. In a coded telegram, Cummings reassured Wilson, "There can be no doubt that the Convention is with you and for the League of Nations overwhelmingly." Two days later, the message read, "Situation as to candidates much confused. Palmer . . . cannot be nominated. Cox campaign has been badly managed . . . Chances of McAdoo appear best . . . Everything thus far has moved off beautifully . . . It is a Wilson convention in spirit and purpose."[26]

Despite this flattery, Wilson was wary. The reassurance he sought was in fact lacking. It might be a Wilson convention in spirit, but where did he stand as a candidate? He had been encouraged to believe he had a chance. A few weeks earlier, he had been oddly gratified to have Senator Glass tell him that he would rather follow Wilson's corpse through a campaign "than the live bodies of some of the men mentioned for the nomination," a remark the senator chose, more oddly still, to repeat.[27]

Wilson called Grayson at 3 A.M., July 1, to complain that his lungs again felt airless. With Grayson by his bedside, he discussed the pros and cons of the candidates. Less than twenty-four hours later, at 2:30 A.M., Grayson treated him for an asthmatic attack. On the following afternoon, Bainbridge Colby, Lansing's successor as secretary of state, wired Wilson in code that, in view of a deadlock, he was going to place Wilson's name in nomination. Believing that such a step would sweep the convention, he told Wilson "the outstanding characteristic of the convention is the unanimity and fervor of feeling for you." By return wire, Edith Wilson dictated her husband's positive response. On July 3, at 3:15 A.M., Grayson gave Wilson news of the balloting. There was talk of dark horses, of McAdoo, Palmer, and Cox. "If they nominate Cox," Wilson responded, "he is one [of] the weakest of the lot."[28]

Wilson's hopes evaporated. On July 4, at a hastily called and contentious meeting, Colby's colleagues, including Glass, Cummings,

Burleson, Ray Stannard Baker, and Secretary of the Navy Daniels, persuaded Colby that from all standpoints—health, platform, the general resentment of a third term, and the vagaries of practical politics—Wilson's candidacy was not feasible. A successful nomination of Wilson would be tantamount to signing his death warrant. An adverse vote would result in his humiliation.

When informed by telegram from San Francisco of Colby's intentions to nominate Wilson, Tumulty dared to repeat to Edith his cogent objections to a third term for the president: "As his devoted friend I am still of the same view, for I firmly believe it would mar his place in history."[29] That same day a chastened Colby conceded the failure of his plan—and was made, he said, to feel like a criminal. Humble in his apology to Wilson for withdrawing his candidacy, it was the belief of his friends, Colby took care to explain, that Wilson's name might not command sufficient votes for the nomination.

The balloting resumed on Monday, July 5, the votes teetering between McAdoo and Cox. On the thirty-ninth ballot it was 440 votes for the president's son-in-law against 468½ for Cox, whose lead gradually increased. On the forty-third ballot Cox received a majority of the votes, 568 to McAdoo's 412; on the forty-fourth ballot, state after state switched its votes to Cox; and McAdoo's manager moved that Cox be nominated unanimously. Wilson was bitter over his own defeat. Between Cox and McAdoo, Wilson preferred Cox, "solely," as the stenographer Swem believed, "out of jealousy toward McAdoo."[30]

The way the convention had played itself out both saddened and angered Ike Hoover. The process had been cruel and unpatriotic and could have been avoided. The proposal to nominate Wilson had been a whim, a hoax, concocted from pretenses and falsehood. The president, in his enfeebled condition, had taken it seriously. His official as well as his private family had persuaded him that the country owed him reendorsement and that he had a right to fool the people as to his physical condition—when they all knew, Ike Hoover said, there was no possibility whatever of President Wilson's becoming the candidate of his party for a third term.

Wilson, humiliated, was pitiful in his complaints that all his circle, including Grayson, and even his wife, had lost interest in him because he was now judged hopeless. He responded coolly to his returning cabinet members, as though they were individually responsible for his failed nomination. With the aid of Dr. Grayson, Josephus Daniels was the first to receive acceptance. Edith Wilson was a help to Colby. However, since "poor old Burleson," as Hoover referred to the postmaster general, had fatally demonstrated his disloyalty by telephoning from San Francisco to ask Wilson's endorsement of McAdoo (and had also presumed to read a proposed prohibition platform plank in the president's name), he was nearly fired from the cabinet. His earlier recommendation that Wilson agree to modification of the Lodge reservation on Article X contributed to his becoming an outcast around the White House.

Wilson grew increasingly suspicious. He had kept the code developed with Cummings secret from Tumulty and would now advise Colby that all State Department communications must be addressed to him personally and not to his secretary, as a "great deal of time and roundabout traveling of papers will thereby be saved."[31] Even Grayson was not immune. "Just a word in your ear," Wilson confided to Secretary of the Navy Daniels, asking that he communicate with Wilson directly rather than through Dr. Grayson and others, as "communications through third persons lead to all sorts of delays [and] all sorts of vagueness." Wilson was sure Daniels would understand and acquiesce.[32]

On the hot Sunday morning of July 18, the candidates James Cox and Franklin Delano Roosevelt paid a call on Woodrow Wilson. The sight of him seated in his wheelchair on the south portico of the White House, with a shawl draped over his left shoulder and arm, brought tears to Cox's eyes. Cox, who had previously announced that he would urge the ratification of the League of Nations, repeated this commitment to the president, affirming that he was "a million percent with you, and your Administration, and that means the League of Nations." The president looked up and in a scarcely audible voice said, "I am very grateful," then repeated, "I am very grateful." Allegiance to Wilson was, however, tantamount to disaster. By embracing the doctrine of the League, the presidential candidate of the Democratic Party, according to *Town Topics*, had "signed the death warrant of his aspirations to the Chief Magistracy of the United States."[33]

Unable to conceal his despondency, Wilson was trying to contemplate the future with Edith after departure from the White House. On finishing a chart of prospects that included Baltimore, Washington, Richmond, Boston, and New York, the couple rated each city according to climate, friends, opportunities, freedom, amusements, and libraries. Though Washington would afford no freedom whatever, they settled on the nation's capital primarily because, as Edith explained, the Library of

Congress offered her husband the facilities needed for a long-planned book and, second, because the city was home to her. Wilson would prefer a house in bungalow style, but had to keep up the appearances and dignity of a former president. He also needed space for four thousand books.

From the start Edith clearly preferred a house of dignity, beauty, and size. She wanted open fireplaces, a beamed ceiling, a broad entrance door, an elevator, ample closets, a servants' dining room, and space for the tapestry that was a personal gift from the French government. On July 15, she wrote to Henry White, telling him how much they missed him. She spoke of the decision to remain in Washington, if a suitable house could be found. She asked whether White wished to sell his lovely house and if so, at what figure. She concluded by wishing they could have a long, gossipy talk and told him that Washington was "almost deserted by Society (with the big 'S') but we of the 'Working Class' stay on," and that her patient did not seem to mind the heat.[34]

In August, informed that Harklakenden was for sale, Wilson felt nostalgia for his cooling summers in New Hampshire. The availability of the house was a great temptation, since as he wrote to the real estate broker George A. Foster, he admired it very much. There were, however, many obstacles in the way of his buying the property. He asked for an idea of the average annual cost of upkeep, and whether the furnaces provided adequate winter heat.[35]

Looking back on the tense days of the Democratic convention in the summer of 1920, Josephus Daniels pondered why Wilson, though partially paralyzed, would have been willing to defy the old three-term jinx to accept the nomination. One reason, Daniels thought, was that Wilson had regarded the possible nomination as a command to protect his imperiled League, and since his views were well known, he would have believed that personal campaigning was unnecessary. A second reason had applied to all presidents since Andrew Jackson: not one had willingly left the White House. The office of the president, and the White House itself, imposed their hold on even the least ambitious incumbent; and all subsequent life became anticlimactic. Daniels concluded that "no man stung by the Presidential bee ever quite recovers." The same might have been said of the president's wife, at least in the case of Woodrow Wilson.[36]

CHAPTER 33

"*Pecuniary anxieties*"

From the start of the 1920 presidential campaign Tumulty eagerly sought Wilson's intervention on behalf of the Democratic candidate, James Cox, and stressed the urgency of Wilson's support. It was up to the president, Tumulty informed Wilson on September 16, to lay the whole cause of the Democratic Party before the public, and to begin from early October to issue a weekly address to the American people. One month later he reported to Wilson "a slight drift towards Cox," but "unless you take advantage of it and speed it up, there is very little hope." Obviously annoyed, Wilson told Tumulty, "Of course I will help. I was under the impression that I was helping. But I will do it at my own time and in my own way." Despite the testy response, Tumulty reminded the president later in October of their previous discussion: if ever he was going to write the letter in praise of Cox, "now is the time."

Cox now wrote on his own behalf (in tacit recognition of her pivotal role, directly to Edith) to invite the couple to a meeting in New York. Wilson, not Edith, immediately responded. The candidate might be sure they would come "if it were physically possible," a painful admission.[1] It was one thing for Wilson to be unable to campaign actively for his possible successor, but quite another to be unable to attend a luncheon on his own premises. At the White House on October 10, Edith Wilson referred to her husband's "nervous dread of people" by way of apology for his inability to see their guest, the newly retired U.S. ambassador to the Court of Saint James. "A curious inaccessibility," John W. Davis would comment in his diary that same day, "for the leader of a great party & Chief Magistrate of a nation."[2]

Logic was not Edith's strong point, nor, in regard to his health, was it Wilson's. The rare visitors—a reporter, a delegation of pro-League Republicans—were shocked by the president's appearance. Misled by press reports, they were unprepared to find such a "mournful object," the ravages of his stroke all too visible. Yet, even now, Wilson denied the nature of his underlying illness. Flattered by comments that it was a pleasure to find him looking so well, he replied, "When a man is suffering from nervous prostration, he doesn't always show it."[3]

As illusory as his statement on his health was the manner in which he kept his promise to help Cox. In Wilson's first formal statement, reported in the *New York Times* on October 28, 1920, he did not even mention Cox. He chose instead to emphasize Article X as the crux of the present campaign. The fate of parties was a matter of indifference; the candidacy of every aspirant for office must be tested by this question: "Shall we or shall we not redeem the great moral obligation of the United States?"

On November 2, Harding and Coolidge were elected by 61 percent of the popular vote, a landslide total of 16,152,000 votes to 9,147,000 for Cox and Roosevelt. The electoral vote was 404 to 127; Harding carried thirty-seven states, Cox only eleven, all Southern. The Republicans took ten Senate seats from the Democrats, making for a majority of twenty-two; they carried 303 seats in the House of Representatives against 131 for the Democrats. Neither the outcome of the election nor its magnitude was ever in doubt. With the overturn of three great empires, Germany, Austria-Hungary, and Russia, and their satellites facing anarchy and chaos, the world cried for peace. Yet those closest to Wilson remembered him as stone-deaf to myriad warnings, insisting that the American people would never elect Harding. They remembered too his confidence in a Democratic victory, his reprimand to faithless cabinet members.[4] Now friends echoed Edith's fears that Cox's defeat, synonymous in her mind with the League's defeat, would have a very adverse effect on her husband.

Wilson's second daughter, Jessie Sayre, sensing the effect of Tuesday's landslide on her father's mental and physical well-being, was consoled by her uncle Stockton Axson. She was not to feel that her visits were useless. While any reciprocal show of affection was lacking, at moments her father said "a little—never much—about your mother and you girls and old times which show how deep it all lies in his heart." Axson told Jessie, "Your father loves you dearly—and is getting much better in health," and that Grayson believed Wilson would be on the golf course in another year playing chiefly with his right arm.[5] During this same period, the physician, in a confusing evaluation, claimed that the president "seems much better after the election" and, simultaneously, was a shattered human being whose "trouble is more of his nerves . . . more easily loses control of himself & when he talks is likely to break down & weep."[6]

Edith—wary of adverse publicity, and of all references to Wilson's invalid state—favored Ray Baker with invitations to the White House in appreciation of his loyalty, hearteningly demonstrated in his recent book, *What Wilson Did at Paris*, and in his flattering assurance that "nothing is more certain than the great place the President is to have in history."[7] She implicitly commanded editorial privileges over his work, among them the right of refusal, which she did not hesitate to exercise. It was with this understanding that Baker proposed writing an article about Wilson, based on his noon visit to the White House on November 28. Baker meant to reflect everything exactly as he saw it.

Through the door of the parlor, Baker saw them lifting up and laying aside the heavy red rug of the main hall. The president was slowly approaching, with a cane, over the smooth marble floor. His left arm hung inert; his eyes were extraordinarily large and brilliant; he was faultlessly dressed. To one who remembered vividly his singularly active step, the alert, listening poise of the head, the sight produced a shock of intense compassion, which instantly gave way to amazement at the indomitable spirit of the man. It was in every line of his face, sharpened and deepened with suffering, it shone in his eyes . . . as he stood there, a broken, stooped, gray-faced, white-haired man.

The president passed on down the hall into the great ballroom of the White House, empty except for half a dozen chairs. He took his seat, Mrs. Wilson next, then Mrs. Wilson's niece, Admiral Grayson, and Baker. A picture flashed on a screen at the end of the room, one of five newsreels of Wilson's epic European venture that the president, the undisputed star, had sat through at least seven times for his captive audience of three daughters, Grayson, and even Dr. Dercum. Baker felt himself transported to "a brave, brilliant world, full of wonderful and glorious events," sailing into the harbor at Brest, the ships beflagged, the soldiers marshaled on the quay, the airplanes skimming through the skies, and the president himself, smiling from the bridge, erect, tall, lifting his hat to the acclaiming crowds.

In the darkened White House ballroom, the president leaned forward to watch his pictured triumphs in Europe, practically silent except for his weary comments on the fleeting scenes. Though Edith Wilson and Grayson kept up a steady stream of light remarks to cheer the invalid,

Wilson never seemed to notice. When the film ended, figures emerged out of the surrounding darkness, one to place a foot against the president's foot so that he did not slip in rising. Then, with his cane, he shuffled painfully out of the room.

Despite his wish to provide a true picture, Baker could scarcely describe how the sight of the president had affected him. He could not get over the look of the broken, elderly, shuffling man, the fingers of his left, lame arm drawn up like a claw, the left side of his face sagging. His voice did not sound human, gurgling in his throat, like that of an automaton. At luncheon, Baker observed Edith caring for her husband as if he were an infant. They had a silent grace. Wilson talked little, yet seemed alert, grinding ceaselessly in a vacuum. "Poor tragic figure; poor president! He was so late in heaven, now in hell."[8]

Baker thought he had succeeded in writing the article he had discussed with Edith Wilson, an intimate and sympathetic portrait of the president: the man with a "powerful, active, intense mind . . . imprisoned thus in a ruin." If anyone could see that sight without a passion of anger at the personal and slanderous attacks of insect-minded enemies, soured friends, and envious rivals, then, Baker concluded that person "has no soul, nor any power of imagination."[9]

Baker showed his draft to Tumulty, who said it was truthful and thought it ought to be published. Grayson and Edith Wilson thought otherwise. Edith apologized to Baker for her typewritten note, but she was anxious to get it off immediately. His article was really inspired, a vivid picture straight from the heart, which she would personally value. From the public point of view, however, she thought it would come as an absolute blow. To those personally aware of her husband's great improvement, it would strike the wrong note. She did not withdraw her support or dampen Baker's initiative for further writings on her husband's behalf. Much in the article could, she thought, be worked into another effort "which would attain the end I think you seek."[10]

Baker thanked Edith for reading his small, inadequate article and for expressing her opinion so frankly. He promised that he would do nothing further with the piece in its present state. He would like, later, to set down his own feeling about how the president had suffered and come through so courageously in the last terrible months and to give Wilson's views about present responsibilities and opportunities in America. Baker's adulation of Wilson was not lost on Edith. His official appointment as the presidential historian would come later and enable him to expand his earlier, small work on the events in Paris into a three-volume eulogy, *Woodrow Wilson and World Settlement*.

By December 16, after a search for a future home, the Wilsons settled on a commodious, Georgian-style, redbrick mansion at 2340 S Street, NW. Although it was not her first choice, Edith was satisfied that this "unpretentious, comfortable, dignified house [was] fitted to the needs of a gentleman's home."[11] Ownership of the S Street house entailed a deposit of $5,000 and payment of $150,000 in cash to Henry Parker Fairbanks and his wife, Frances Lewis Fairbanks, from whom Edith would obtain the deed on January 31, 1921. Extensive alterations involved the valet's and chauffeur's quarters, stacks for Wilson's library, the placement of a fireplace, staircase, bathrooms, elevator, and garage. Possibly it was therapeutic for Wilson to be absorbed in these details, which he followed assiduously.

Edith in her *Memoir* touched lightly on the subject of money, but Grayson was aware of her concern. Unlike Roosevelt, who had a fortune of his own, augmented by income from writings, and unlike Taft, who had regular profitable sources of funds, Wilson was largely dependent on his salary. His previously handsome royalties from books had slumped, but that was counterbalanced by the circumstances of his presidency, which enabled him to save from an annual salary of $75,000, earned during his eight-year tenure. As a result of the suspension of social functions during wartime, one newspaper estimated that the former president's pocketbook was at least $250,000 richer since he had not been called upon to wine and dine numerous official persons.[12] In the past December, Wilson had been honored with the Nobel Peace Prize "as First Head of a State, [who] promulgated the thought of an international organization" as the only remedy toward general pacification. The accompanying monetary award of over 133,000 Swedish crowns, amounting to $40,000, had augmented the president's savings.[13]

Nevertheless, to free the president from any financial pressure, and to smooth his transition from the White House to S Street, his physician turned to Wilson's philanthropic admirers, and to friends, colleagues, and wealthy Democrats, for help. A group led by Wilson's Princeton classmate and friend Cleveland Hoadley Dodge would collect $3,500 so that the president might take the White House Pierce-Arrow touring car into retirement with him; but the car was merely part of a "larger scheme" to raise $100,000—two-thirds of the price of the S Street house. Two years later, loyal donors, including Dodge, Jesse Holman Jones, Cyrus McCormick, Thomas Davis Jones, and Bernard Baruch, would reach a formal agreement to provide an annuity for Wilson of $10,000 for the remainder of his life, prompted in part by the conviction that they were doing what Congress ought to do for all retiring presidents (an official pension would only be granted with passage of the Former Presidents' Act in 1958), and by their "sense of fairness and justice to this great man for his patriotic and unselfish life."[14]

Dodge and Jesse Jones notified Wilson on October 1, 1923, of the creation of the trust. The next day, Dodge explained that, because he himself, and two or three other friends, wanted Wilson to feel at ease for the rest of his life in regard to financial matters, Dodge was enclosing the first quarterly payment, a check for $2,500. On receipt of the first annuity payment, in January 1924, Wilson drew Jones's graceful acknowledgment of his thanks. ("You have," Jones wrote, "rendered a service to mankind impossible to measure, and I am proud beyond expression of having so large a share of your friendship.") Relieved of pecuniary anxieties on January 13, Wilson wrote, "Your generous letter . . . comes to me like a benediction . . ."[15]

Financial stress might have been eased earlier had the president been able to accept several lucrative proposals to write and publish made to him before he left the White House. Edith's concern now centered, however, on finding some other means of giving Wilson "something definite to accomplish" to sustain him.

To this end, she permitted him to receive Ralph Pulitzer, in July 1920, on the theme of writing for the New York *World*. Wilson rejected Pulitzer's offer, however—as he did that of Arthur Krock, editor of the *Louisville Times* and a subsequent *New York Times* columnist, who proposed a fee of $75,000 a year, presumably for Wilson to write a column. It went against his grain, Wilson told Grayson, to accept such a big offer for so little in return. Wilson also turned down the opportunity to write two articles a month on current political and social topics for which *The Independent* magazine would be glad to pay $1,000 each. His negative response to the George H. Doran Company was more vague. For the rights to any book by Wilson on the period of his presidency, and particularly the past five years and the great ethical and altruistic principles involved, Doran proposed to pay $100,000 in advance and $100,000 on delivery of a manuscript of not less than 150,000 words and 20 percent on all books sold in the United States, with foreign royalties to be adjusted.

In his rejection, Wilson explained that he felt obliged to postpone all plans until he had settled to a new method of life and "found what it is possible for me to find time and opportunity to do."[16]

By mid-August, he appeared to develop a more favorable attitude toward publishing. Either the financial prospects suggested to Edith by George Creel, journalist, editor, author, publicist, and quasi-diplomat, were too alluring to reject, or she and Wilson realized their need for help in negotiations with Harper & Brothers for a suggested but unspecified translation (presumably into a foreign language) of a volume of his published speeches. Edith was responsive to Creel's offer to act as her husband's literary agent. The former editor of Denver's *Rocky Mountain News*, chairman of the wartime Committee on Public Information responsible for the notorious censorship policy embracing the 1917 Trading with the Enemy and Espionage Acts and the 1918 Sedition Act, had accompanied the Wilsons to Paris and won their trust. With delicacy and shrewd practicality, Creel assured the president's wife that, although he knew her husband would shrink from any idea of commercialization, the fact remained that there was money to be made from his work— which he could either view as a free gift to publishers or use to provide for himself and his family.

Months later, Creel unveiled to Edith his ambitious plans for Wilson's retirement and for the publishing industry he himself was to head. He was even more convinced, he wrote Edith Wilson on February 15, that the president owed to himself, to those who followed him, and to the world a history of the Peace Conference. There was also his story of the war, told from the White House, from August 1914 to the armistice, in addition to an updated version of Wilson's *History of the American People*. To help the president Creel recommended retaining the services of Wilson's stenographer Swem and the employment of two trained historians, the dean of the University of Minnesota, Guy Stanton Ford, and a professor of history at the University of Indiana, Samuel Bannister Harding.

Creel had dazzled Edith with visions of sales to magazines, serial publications in newspapers, of a shelf of books. What he now needed was the president's decision to write. Edith's disappointing though cordial response indicated that Wilson had reservations about the proposal but failed to mention his alternative plans. Edith did not reveal that Ray Baker had already been chosen as Wilson's historian.

The distinguished editor and historian William Edward Dodd, whose biography *Woodrow Wilson and His Work* was published in 1920, revered Wilson and was awed by his strenuous religious training. It was precisely Wilson's brand of firm faith in prayer that had made America a great country, that had given the president the strength to survive the cynical atmosphere of Paris, and that would place him second only to George Washington in the country's history. Dodd was candid in his disapproval of Baker. He was disturbed not by Baker's character but by the fact that, as the appointed authority on the Wilson presidency, he lacked historical knowledge. Wilson had no need of "defenses"—by which the historian presumably meant the perpetual ennoblement he foresaw as the hallmark of Baker's partisan accounts. Dodd urgently repeated his recommendation (he wrote to Edith as well as to Wilson and to his daughter Margaret) that the presidential papers be given to the Library of Congress.

Despite Edith's allusions to settling in Washington for its proximity to the Library of Congress and Grayson's assurance to Dodd of Wilson's plans to do a good deal of writing, Wilson clearly could not write. He could barely muster the concentration to edit what was written for him. He excused himself from writing about the Paris Peace Conference on grounds that nothing came with such bad grace "as narrative of that sort," since "it would be as bitter as the memoirs of John [Quincy] Adams."[17] In this, Wilson spoke truthfully, for he was vitriolic in his criticisms and, not infrequently, brutal to those with whom he disagreed or profoundly distrusted. Herbert Hoover, who had served creditably as chairman of the American Relief Committee in London and of the Belgian Relief Commission, and as U.S. food administrator during the war (as a private citizen he would direct relief operations throughout the great Russian famine of 1921), was a "fakir" and Wilson would not "assist him in any way in any undertaking whatsoever." The journalist Albert Fox was "a skunk"; Lloyd George, "a slippery character." Wilson readily named many others he profoundly distrusted.[18]

Wilson and Edith did, however, realize that there must be a written record of their views of the Wilson presidency, and the choice of Baker as their historian was in its way logical. A virtual member of their presidential family since the Paris days, Baker promised exaltation. He now reminded Wilson that he, Baker, had raised the possibility in Paris of being allowed access to the full records, and Wilson had let him have the reports of the Council of Ten, on which Baker had drawn for his "small book" *What Wilson Did at Paris,* 1919. He had not seen the more important records of the Council of Four and many other essential documents.

He now suggested, deferentially, that he might be helpful in setting the record straight—if for any reason Wilson did not intend to write it fully himself, which of course would be the greatest thing of all.[19]

Wilson could not refuse such an eager and flattering disciple. Almost immediately, the president alerted Baker that he had in effect won the job. By Wilson's own painful admission it was not possible to write anything himself, but he believed that Baker could do it admirably. In January 1921, Wilson presented Baker with the three large trunks into which he had shut up the Paris documents, including minutes of the various councils; reports, memos, letters; important diaries kept during the conference by Colonel House, Robert Lansing, and the chief of staff of the U.S. army, General Tasker Bliss. Wilson explained to Baker that he had had to conceal his private papers because the servants in the house in Paris were spies.

In February, Baker complained about learning "in a left-handed way" of the arrangements that Wilson had made with Creel. Equally in the dark was Creel, to whom the president had referred the previous September in a letter to Harper & Bros. as his "agent and spokesman in matters of publications in the months to come." Creel acknowledged to Edith Wilson that the decision to give Baker exclusive rights at this time to a significant portion of the president's material was "a bitter blow." At Wilson's request, Creel and Baker, with Edith and her brother John Randolph Bolling, met and agreed to a division of the proceeds for all involved.[20]

To Creel's disappointment, Wilson refused to adopt his plan for an advisory committee in connection with his papers. Creel was, however, relieved to come to terms with Baker on the scope of the work. The book was to be entirely about the Peace Conference. It would not contain personal controversy nor sound a note of defense, apology, or attack. It was to rely entirely upon the presentation of facts, supported at every point by facsimile documents. In the event, this plan went predictably askew. Baker's readers would be informed, for example, of the "Beginning of Coldness Between President Wilson and Colonel House," a hint of the author's campaign against House, and others—in which he was firmly supported by Edith Wilson.

Meanwhile, William Dodd tried to convince Edith that her husband's papers belonged in the Library of Congress, where they would be accessible to scholars and safely cared for. Baker's inadequacies were implicit in the belief, expressed by Dodd to Wilson, that there could be "perversions of history by the most respectable characters."[21] With magisterial evasion, Edith thanked Dodd for his suggestions and assured him that when Wilson resumed his literary activity, he hoped to arrange these matters along the lines proposed by Dodd.[22]

Both Wilsons, it was obvious, intended to deposit the presidential papers where and with whom they chose. On March 1, a warm spring day, Edith appeared in Baker's office at the White House with a large bundle of documents and letters discovered in a White House safe. They dealt with the years 1915 through early 1918. Baker said that while they involved more work, "they let in new light on the roots of the war."[23]

At Wilson's last cabinet meeting on Tuesday, March 1, 1921, he apologized for his tears: due to his weakened condition he could not control his emotions as in the past. Pitying him, David Houston—who had served through the eight years of Wilson's presidency—could conceive of no greater trial than this for a Scotch Presbyterian whose entire philosophy of life was self-control. Tumulty, observing the president groping his way with his cane, was dismayed at the thought of his pending separation from the man whom he had served, through peace, war, and illness, for over ten years. A highly sentimental man, Tumulty, who had repeatedly been wounded by Edith Wilson, could not depart without telling the president's wife of his deep admiration and affection: her devotion to the president had touched him more than he could say.

Edith Benham Helm too assured Edith Wilson of continued friendship and assistance after the White House. She wept over their departure, not because they were leaving the White House but out of thankfulness that they were now going to their own lovely house, which, "please God, will bear out the promise of those first years."

As the old administration ended, the *New York Times* reported, on March 3, that Woodrow Wilson and Bainbridge Colby were to start a law firm. The idea had casually been initiated by Wilson one month earlier, and Colby was confident that it would work out well. Wilson's name was the most valuable that a law firm could have, and Colby was continually struck with Wilson's remarkable skill. There need be no anxiety about undue demands on his energy: it was unnecessary for him to keep fixed office hours. Edith was pleased by Colby's flattery as well as with the offices, which would be located at 1315 F Street in Washington, and at 32 Nassau Street in New York City.

The pathos of the transition escaped no one. The *Detroit News* maintained, "When all the pages of history of his time are written, it probably would be said of [Woodrow Wilson] that no American has ever carried himself and the nation to such heights of world commendation" nor "with the possible exception of Andrew Johnson, ever retired from the office with less of good feeling and regret on the part of his countrymen." There was something heartrending, the *New York Times* reported, about the broken frame of the man who hobbled from the White House to accompany his successor to the Capitol. Warren Harding and his wife arrived at the White House at 11 A.M., where cabinet members, aides, and official guests had gathered. Woodrow and Edith Wilson met the Hardings in the Blue Room. Wilson was determined to walk that day, to go out the front door followed by Harding. Policemen stood by to enforce the rule against photographs being taken before the president was seated in the car, a feat he negotiated precariously, without his now accustomed platform and with the help of Ike Hoover, the Secret Service man Richard Jervis, and the valet Arthur Brooks.

Edith Wilson rode with Florence Harding, whom she found too rouged, too voluble, and with her high, sharp voice and Western twang, "a perfect picture of this new, small-town, middle-western woman transported suddenly into great place."[24] The women followed in their official car along Pennsylvania Avenue, which was banked with crowds. The clatter of cavalry hoofs resounded all the way to the Capitol. Although it was traditional for the president and his successor to walk together up the Capitol steps to the Senate chamber, Harding went alone. The car then proceeded to the freight entrance of the Senate wing, where a platform had been provided, and where Brooks waited for Wilson with a wheelchair, which he rolled to a private elevator. Wilson limped the rest of the way into the President's Room, sat at his desk, signed bills, offered congratulations. In a sudden hush, the spade-bearded Henry Cabot Lodge appeared. As chairman of the Foreign Relations Committee he had one final, formal exchange with the president. "I beg to inform you," said Senator Lodge, "that the two houses have no further work and are prepared to receive any further communications from you." The president listened to the report. Then he said simply, "Tell them I have no further communication to make. I thank you for your courtesy. Good morning, sir."

The Richmond, Virginia, *News Leader* reported "Wilson's Snub to His Enemy Was Dramatic" and that the final finishing "Good morning, sir," addressed to Lodge, "cut the air with its finality and coldness." Wilson's face flushed, his eyes fixed on the eyes of Senator Lodge, "these two men stood face to face in the final scene of what has been perhaps the greatest of battles in American history over the ratification of a treaty."[25]

Wilson did not stay to see Vice President Coolidge sworn in. He apologized with some sarcasm (the *Times* said it revealed his human side) for his inability to go through the entire inaugural ceremony: "Well, the Senate threw me down before, and I don't want to fall down myself now."[26] Wilson left on the arm of Edith, walking ahead of a sad little procession made up of Tumulty and Grayson, two Secret Service men, and twelve newspapermen assigned to accompany the now former president to his home. The policemen bowed, the marines stood motionless; two motorcycle policemen led Wilson's car along Pennsylvania Avenue, past the White House and around Madison Place to Seventeenth Street, Massachusetts Avenue, and Sheridan Circle.

It was not a happy ride for Edith. Infuriated by the "performance," as she referred to it, Edith stressed Harding's "abandonment" of her husband and his thoughtlessness. She had apparently dismissed Harding's kindly letters from Florida the previous month offering to observe the inaugural ceremonies in whatever way Wilson found most convenient. She chose to nurture her grievances. There could never be respect or courtesy enough for her husband. Neither the award of the Nobel Peace Prize,[27] the establishment of the Woodrow Wilson Club at Harvard, a proposed statue at the University of Texas, nor letters of congratulations, praise, and flattery from former pupils, family, colleagues, and friends could appease her bitterness.[28]

Reaching the house on S Street, Margaret Wilson and Edith's sister Bertha helped Wilson out of the car into his wheelchair and into the elevator. Throughout the afternoon, people called and sent flowers. More than five hundred people stood on the sidewalk cheering when the Wilsons appeared at a third-story window. The couple acknowledged the informal procession of League advocates and other admirers who halted in front of their home. Edith raised the window sash. Wilson smiled, bowed, waved his right hand. The cheers subsided in expectation of a speech. Wilson waved again, but did not speak and withdrew. When he returned to the window, a hush fell over the crowd. He raised his right hand to his throat with a gesture indicating that he found himself unable to respond. Smiling and bowing, he again left the window. The crowd disappeared only after policemen told them that there would be no speech.[29]

★ Part V ★

Retirement

Wilson & Colby

To ease her husband's transition to private life, Edith set about dupli-
cating his White House bedroom as far as possible, with his easy chairs,
his footrests, the tables that would hold his books (detective stories—
including E. Phillips Oppenheim, *The Great Impersonation*—and multiple Jane Austens), reading lights (he hated the dark), and his very worn
Bible. He had grown accustomed to the Lincoln bed in what had been his
White House sickroom, and Edith ordered its reproduction, eight feet six
inches long by six feet two inches.[1]

The marble-floored center hall opened to the left on to the household
office she called "the dugout," with other rooms beyond. Living room,
dining room, and library occupied the second floor. Four bedrooms were
on the third floor, and servants' quarters and a laundry on the fourth.
With the gentle and sympathetic care of their household servants Isaac
and Mary Scott, "the best of the old-time colored Virginia stock"—and
Edith's brother John Randolph Bolling as private secretary—it seemed
to Edith that they had lived on S Street for years.

In the late spring of 1921, Wilson was visibly depressed. He took little
exercise, declining even to walk around his back garden. Stockton Axson
believed that Wilson was in sore need of systematic mental occupation,
which he hoped Wilson's intended practice of law with Bainbridge Colby
would provide. Axson, however, expressed his doubts about the outcome
to Princeton's John Grier Hibben: "Maybe he will get interested in
that—God grant it!"[2]

Randolph Bolling was of inestimable assistance in the establishment of
that firm. Staunch friend, overseer, and mediator, Bolling was capable and
ambitious. Frail as their sister Bertha and hunchbacked, he was skilled at
reinforcing Edith's public myth of a healthy and sage Woodrow Wilson.
Bolling succeeded Grayson as a bearer of optimistic tidings regarding
Wilson's health. Ignoring the realities of his brother-in-law's despon-

dency, Bolling concluded his letters with reports "that the rest Mr. Wilson is taking is doing him a great deal of good" and "Mr. Wilson is again in his old time form."

As Wilson's secretary, Bolling—aided by his stenographer, Edward Kriz—advised the Woodrow Wilson Clubs and Foundation and the Democratic National Committee on matters of organization and the intricacies of fund-raising. With his sister, he worked in the dugout of the S Street house to prevent unseemly news from reaching Wilson—to spare him, for example, the substance of business arrangements with George Creel, while reassuring him that they were satisfactory. Meticulously sorting and culling each day's mail, Bolling roughed out appropriate answers for Edith's approval before piling these papers on her own bulky rolltop desk that also stood in the dugout. By August, Wilson, unable to bear the strain of writing by pen with his one working hand, found himself dependent on Bolling for maintaining even a most tentative control of his still voluminous correspondence. On August 26, 1921, he dictated a letter for Bolling to sign to intimate friends, explaining that it was difficult for him to use a pen at all, and sometimes painful. To ease her brother's burden, Edith listed forty-two standardized opening sentences—"Mr. Wilson asks me to acknowledge"; ". . . desires me to acknowledge"; ". . . directs me to ask"; ". . . to thank"; ". . . to reply"—that might facilitate Bolling's replies.[3]

Wilson had not practiced law since 1883 and had been admitted only before the bar of the Superior Court of Georgia. Preparing him for his law practice in Washington was Bolling's foremost task. He arranged for Wilson to be admitted to the Washington bar, to take the oath and sign his name in the court register on Saturday, June 25, 1921. Colby's private contacts secured the passage of a special bill in the New York State legislature, by means of which Wilson was admitted to the bar of the State of New York on June 29, 1921.[4]

Bolling organized the completion of the offices of Wilson & Colby in the American National Bank building at 1315 F Street, adjacent to the Adams Building, the site of the former home of President John Quincy Adams. Bolling contended with striking carpenters, painters, plasterers, and electricians. He advised on five thousand notices to be sent to potential clients, many of them eminent in governmental and academic circles.

On August 17 the *Times* reported on what was to be Woodrow Wilson's sole visit to his spacious law office. Though the office was handsomely furnished, the bookshelves were empty and the walls bare.

Wilson's friends were quoted as being gratified by his interest in his law practice and were said to believe that his new activities would have a beneficial effect on his health.[5] That same day, perhaps because these promising horizons momentarily distracted him, Wilson was moved to write a note to his wife: "Beloved, You have filled these two years with happy memories. W."[6]

In April, 1921, Wilson received a request from Louis Wiley of the *New York Times* for a letter to be included in a book commemorating two landmark celebrations—that of Adolph Simon Ochs's twenty-five-year tenure as publisher of the newspaper, and the seventieth anniversary of its founding. His negative response, Wilson informed Wiley, arose from his conviction that he was quite unfamiliar with the part the publisher had played in shaping the paper's character and policy: what he would write "would be so vague as to be of no significance whatever."[7]

The tone of his refusal was another manifestation of the ravages of his illness. This acid, lonely old man—whose petulance was typical, according to medical diagnosis, of the organic brain syndrome, aggravated by "selective amnesia"—was incapable of a small gesture of generosity to honor the publisher of the newspaper whose support he had cultivated and effusively acknowledged in the past.[8] Wilson's memory no longer recorded the long span of his heartfelt association with Adolph Ochs.

Aware that a letter from Wilson would mean much to Ochs, Wiley did not give up his quest. Bernard Baruch, who had close ties to Ochs as well as to Wilson, was asked to intervene, only to have both his attempts meet with refusal.[9] A year later, however, with Wilson in a more receptive mood (there was talk of his possible leadership of the Democratic Party), Wilson's attitude changed. He had apparently recovered his memory of what the paper had meant to him in the past; or he thought, given his still smoldering political ambitions, it might be of value to him in the future. On November 22, 1922, he wrote to the *Times*, to Ochs's nephew Julius Ochs Adler, that he was "always proud of any editorial commendation you may be generous enough to give me, for I know how sincere and generous you are. It is such friendship and approval that keep a man in heart."[10] However, on January 8, 1924, almost three years after the *Times'* initial request, Wilson wanted no part of Adolph Ochs's anniversary album. Despite a final plea on grounds that the publisher, even with the passage of time, did not consider the album complete without the former president's contribution, Wilson insisted that "he has not followed Mr. Ochs's career closely enough to be prepared to write an intelligent estimate of him."[11]

The promise of a regenerated Wilson household reached its apogee in September 1921 when the *New York Tribune* reported, "Wilson, Stricken 2 Years Ago, Now Puts In Healthy Man's Day." Following the ways of a retired gentleman with a lively interest in the world's affairs, he lives a full day, sleeps for eight hours, works for eight hours, relaxes for eight hours, "and keeps to the schedule pretty well." The article goes on to describe Wilson's active days, ending, "He will be 65 in December . . . and his eyesight is good [that he is blind in one eye goes unmentioned] . . . his appetite too robust to please his physicians."[12]

Edith would have readers of her *Memoir* remember Woodrow Wilson in an extraordinarily peaceful setting. In summer sitting near the window, at other times by the fireplace, how he loved this quiet hour, with the curtains drawn and a low reading light, which, illuminating his table and his book, did not dull the flicker of the flaming logs. However, random notes, jotted on scraps of paper and on an envelope, tell another version—of his devotion to and need of Edith, and of the profound loneliness of his sickly isolation. Much confined to his bedroom, solitary at mealtimes, he asks, "Dear Heart Bring S. up when lunch is over, please," and again, "Beloved I sh. like, when you have finished lunch, to speak a word to Colby from my bed." Childlike, on a day when he feared to be deprived of his favorite activity and possibly too ill to leave his bedroom, he wrote, "Dearest, A Question before I sleep. I suppose there can be no drive this afternoon. Can there?" During a period of acute illness, he might ask Isaac Scott, his personal servant, to take a reassuring message to Edith, who was perhaps entertaining luncheon guests. "Darling, I thought you w'd like to know that I had some relief," he wrote on a small, lined card. Or, "Dearest, I think I'd better not come down. I am suffering a good deal 'in my midst.'" And another time: "My darling, I have gone to bed, to be beforehand with the nausea I felt coming on, but there is nothing to be concerned about further. Your devoted, if stupid Lover."

There is a wistful, self-pitying letter written on yellow, lined paper: "My Darling: Whenever I fail to live up to the great standards which your dear love has set for me a passion of sorrow, and remorse sweeps over one which my self-control cannot always withstand."[13]

By the time of President Harding's invitation to the Wilsons to join him on Armistice Day, November 1921, Edith had become intolerant of the slightest difference of opinion. In regard to President Harding's invitation, her host and his delegated authorities were, in her view, inconsiderate, inefficient, and possibly insulting. Harding had asked the Wilsons to meet him and his party at the Arlington Memorial amphitheater for ceremonies for the burial of an unknown soldier who had served in the late World War. Wilson thanked his prospective host for his courteous suggestion and in several letters told him that he wished to pay his respects to the dead by appearing in the procession, but, due to his disability, he could not take part in the Arlington service. Instead, he wished to drive in an open carriage and accompany the body of the unknown soldier all the way to Arlington Cemetery.

The secretary of war's orders were, though conciliatory, quite firm, and not to Wilson's liking. Wilson, granted his carriage, was to arrive opposite the main east entrance to the Capitol at 8:25 A.M., where an officer would guide him to the appointed place in the procession, immediately preceding the associate justices of the Supreme Court. When the procession reached West Executive Avenue, the president, vice president, and members of the cabinet would turn left and leave, proceeding afterward by motor car via the highway bridge to Arlington. In issuing final orders to Wilson, the secretary of war was "constrained" to ask that Mr. Wilson conform to the arranged plans. She was amazed, Edith Wilson said, that her husband accepted the dictum of the War Department. But only, she might have added, for lack of an alternative.[14]

On November 9, Wilson called the newsman Louis Seibold to S Street to discuss the arrangements for the burial of the unknown soldier in Arlington and to turn over his frustrating correspondence about it, with the request that it be published. Advised by the reporter against making the letters public, Wilson reluctantly accepted the conditions imposed by the War Department without public comment.

On November 11 the Wilsons mounted their victoria, which was drawn by two horses, with their servant Scott in the box beside the coachman. Wilson, in dark suit and high silk hat, wore a small red poppy—then, and for years thereafter, the symbol of remembrance of the First World War—in his lapel. Edith also was dressed in dark clothes, dark fur, and a black hat. In place of her signature orchid, she had pinned a large red poppy on her breast. Throughout the journey to the Capitol, Wilson constantly raised his hat to acknowledge the salutes of his friends. As the carriage entered the parade, a volume of applause swept the length of Pennsylvania Avenue until the carriage turned out of line after passing the White House. "The pale face of the man who gave his health and strength to uphold the same ideals for which the Unknown Soldier died seemingly unleashed the pent-up emotions of the watchers," the New York *World* would report the following day.

Home again, Wilson appeared at his door shortly after 3 P.M. For ten minutes, cheers for the League of Nations and for the greatest soldier of them all, Woodrow Wilson, echoed through the neighborhood. Wilson wept. His right hand sought his wife's, and she too burst into tears. As the crowd sang "My Country 'Tis of Thee," the couple turned away and stepped into the house. The next day, Wilson told Louis Seibold, "Your counsel saved me from a very stupid blunder, and I thank you with all my heart." Seibold answered, "My Dear Boss: The dear, dead Unknown private was no better soldier than his beloved Commander-In-Chief proved himself in a very trying situation. I always knew you were a good sport. Affectionately."[15]

Edith remained critical. Readers of her *Memoir* would learn that President Harding was again insensitive, the officials in charge were rude and overbearing, 8:30 A.M. was "no little effort for an invalid," the police were without instructions, and no parade official could be found to take an interest in their plight. Even she was pleased, however, that thousands of people had gathered in S Street to cheer the "Known Soldier."

That heartfelt reception had unquestionably buoyed Wilson's spirits. In thanks for a copy of the revised edition of his biography *Woodrow Wilson and His Work*, he wrote to the author, William Dodd, that he should very much like to get out a revised edition of the physical Woodrow Wilson, much needed for private and public circulation. Dodd replied to Randolph Bolling, "If Mr. Wilson were to have that physical revision of which he speaks in his letter he would literally be drafted for the Presidency." Bolling, in turn, told Dodd, "Your comment about Mr. Wilson being drafted for the presidency—should his health improve to the point where he felt he could again undertake such a task—bears out the prediction of literally thousands who have written him in the same vein since his appearance on Armistice Day."[16]

CHAPTER 35

Wilson & Colby folds

Wilson acknowledged that his wonderful wife could not work miracles. They could only give each other mutual support and await what Providence had in store. So he told his cousin in Peoria, Illinois, in January 1922. He did not add that for months he had been actively attempting to bring "every legitimate influence to bear" to make American membership in the League of Nations the dominant issue of the presidential campaign of 1924.[1]

Wilson now was, to all appearances, moribund. He could barely hold a book, let alone a pen, because one hand was paralyzed and the other feeble; he could see out of one eye only. But nothing could temper his obsession with the League and with the dominant role that he planned to assume in the coming election—a role that would be nothing less than leader of the Democratic Party, if not its presidential candidate.

In June 1921, after leaving the White House, he had engaged a sitting Supreme Court justice in a flagrantly political undertaking—asking Louis Brandeis, with the help of Bainbridge Colby and the Wall Street lawyer Thomas Lincoln Chadbourne Jr., to help draw up a statement of progressive principles for the Democratic Party. Secretly intended to define the platform on which he would run for a third term in 1924, it would evolve, through many versions, into The Document: a twenty-six-article constitution reflecting his frustrated mission to make the Covenant inseparable from the League. "How would the following do for one broadside," Wilson asked Brandeis: "We insist upon the early resumption of our international obligations and leadership . . . lost by the rejection of the Treaty of Versailles. . . . We condemn the group of men who brought this sinister thing about as the most partisan, prejudiced and unpatriotic coterie that has ever misled the Senate of the United States, and declare that the country will never be restored to its merited prestige until their work is undone."[2]

Although The Document was developed in relative secrecy, Wilson's aspirations for the League and for party leadership, sustained almost to his last breath, were transparent. He spoke positively about the time "when the Democrats come in" and gave Ray Stannard Baker the impression, confirmed in a chat with Dr. Grayson, that he was contemplating still another campaign. Baker remarked, "The sheer spirit of the man! Here he is, paralyzed, blind in one eye, an invalid, sixty-six years old and sees himself leading a campaign in 1924."[3]

Edith Wilson appeared as optimistic as her husband, convinced that "there are great things ahead of him."[4] She was notably visible in the cause. In one of her rare public appearances since Wilson's collapse two and a half years earlier, she "came out of her hole" to attend a gathering of the Woman's Democratic National Committee, as Daisy Fitzhugh Ayres reported in the *Louisville Courier-Journal* in May 1922. She was a brilliant success. In gray crepe and lace, wearing a black picture hat and the inevitable orchids pinned to her waist, she was modest and gracious. Everybody fell for her, no one more heartily than Daisy Ayres herself.[5]

In December 1922, Edith delivered two messages to the Democratic Women's Club in Baltimore: her husband was improving in health; and she and the former president had a strong interest in the activities of Democratic women in Maryland. Rumors persisted that the former president remained unalterably opposed to the candidacy of his son-in-law, the perpetually thwarted William McAdoo. While no man could devise initiatives more imaginatively, or put them into operation with greater vigor, the former secretary of the treasury was not, as Wilson complained, a reflective man. For years Wilson had also expressed doubts about other possible contenders. He had told Stockton Axson two years earlier that neither of the two bygone cabinet members, Newton Baker and David Houston, had the qualities of a winning candidate. In reference to the coming election, it was said that while nobody knew whether Mr. Wilson was actively in favor of any particular candidate for president at this time, "there has leaked out of his tightly sealed house . . . the names of two men he is not for." One was McAdoo; the other, James M. Cox, the party's unsuccessful nominee in the 1920 election.[6] The mystery of his preference would not be solved until a Democratic leader left a conference on S Street with the conviction, as the *New York Times* reported on September 19, 1923, that "Mr. Wilson might even permit himself to be drafted as a candidate for the Presidential nomination."

*   *   *

Though Wilson professed a wish to be of service to the Democratic Party, he again refused the request of Joseph Tumulty, who had opened his own law firm, to send words of support for James Cox, whom Wilson patronizingly referred to as "our failed candidate"—this time at the Jackson Day banquet in Dayton, Ohio, in January 1922. That evening Tumulty, friend and booster of Cox, took the liberty of telling the Dayton audience that "expressions of devotion and affection . . . evidenced tonight are comforting to Woodrow Wilson," a remark that evoked no response from S Street. But a second inoffensive statement would precipitate the final break between Tumulty and his old chief.[7]

In April, Tumulty again prodded Wilson to send a message ("It would hearten and inspire everybody") to be read at the National Democratic Club's annual Jefferson Day dinner in New York City. Wilson's refusal was immediate; a message from him would be quite meaningless unless it included a serious expression of his views on the present national situation, and he did not find the present occasion appropriate for breaking silence.[8] Tumulty, determined not to leave Washington empty-handed, called on the president a few days later and left feeling confident of success.

On Saturday evening, April 8, at the Commodore Hotel, James Cox urged the country to continue the fight to join the League as the only hope for a stable posterity and attacked the Harding administration for its failure to cooperate in this humanitarian movement. A message from Wilson was then read assuring the Democrats of New York that he was ready "to support any man who stands for the salvation of America, and the salvation of America is justice to all classes." On the following day the press heralded the results of the dinner: "Cox Boom Launched on Wilson Keynote of Justice for All / Ex-President Sends Greetings."[9] Unfortunately for Tumulty, the headlines would soon be harshly contradicted.

Bristling as though his name had been sullied by association with Cox's, Wilson informed Tumulty of his deep distress that the dinner was interpreted as a boom for Cox, whose renomination, in Wilson's judgment, would be "an act of deliberate suicide" for the party. He would be grateful if Tumulty could discover the source of the alleged message. Wilson also dictated the first of two letters to Louis Wiley, editor at the *New York Times*, relating his distress over the "telegram," which he called "an absolute fabrication." By Thursday the headlines were altered to Wilson's satisfaction: "Doubt Is Cast on Wilson 'Message' to the Cox Dinner / Not a Direct Telegram, but a Typewritten Slip Presented by His Former Secretary."[10]

Tumulty tried unavailingly to speak with Wilson. He wrote "Dear

Governor," on April 12, that he was sorry for the misunderstanding and accepted full responsibility. He reviewed the events of the afternoon at S Street, when Wilson had given him the purported "message." Privately, he consoled himself that, no matter how keenly he might feel the injustice of his beloved boss's public rebuke, "I will not wince under the blow nor shall I grow in the least faint-hearted or dispirited."[11]

Tumulty's memorandum, entitled "Statement by Mr. Tumulty," written, presumably, to clarify the events but never released, reveals a grievously wounded man who consoled himself with the thought that in dealing with greatness "we must consider that we are merely insignificant atoms." The rebuke contained in Woodrow Wilson's letter was characteristic of his greatness, showed that he played no favorites and allowed no personal feelings to influence him in the least where he saw his duty. Tumulty therefore found solace in believing that Wilson, in his large heart, had regretted the necessity of this action.[12]

Wilson was implacable. At his request, the *Times* published the former president's letter, dispelling all doubt: "I did not send any message whatever to that dinner nor authorize anyone to convey a message."[13] It was Wilson who attracted public disfavor. His acrimonious conduct had transformed his former secretary, the Cleveland *Plain Dealer* reported, into a "momentary hero."[14] Washington was "stirred as it had been by no political sensation" since Robert Lansing's dismissal. Even Tumulty's critics, according to the *Plain Dealer*, were fully aware that he had served his great chief "with all the ardent devotion of which his emotional Celtic nature was capable." The chief correspondent for the St. Louis *Post-Dispatch* called Wilson's unexplained repudiation of the devoted Joe Tumulty's "innocuous little message" an example of the former president's "ruthlessness," finding "Brusque Treatment of Secretary Largely Traceable to His Long Illness" as well as to his lack of "Publicity Sense."[15] The correspondent, Charles G. Ross, did not reveal that Wilson was his own preferred nominee.

Wilson told Grayson that, while he hated to punish his former secretary, he had to correct the wrong impression given by the newspapers. Had Tumulty been his own son, he would have rebuked him. Always in precarious standing with Edith, Tumulty had already diminished the Wilsons' goodwill by publishing a memoir, *Woodrow Wilson As I Know Him*, in the previous year. Written, it was said, because Tumulty needed money to underwrite his legal career, the book breathed devotion in every line, yet irritated the Wilson household. A reviewer, E. W. Osborn in the New York

World, December 18, 1921, thought that future historians might find the chapter "Wilson—the Human Being" useful. Tumulty described Wilson as a man of cheerful impulses whom critics persistently "gloomed," and a man of companionable good cheer. Osborn ranked the work as one of the important books of the year and bound to endure.

Edith differed. Her own appraisal was given frankly to Tumulty: the book was a mere repetition of what had been said many times. While she knew of no more sympathetic and generous spirit than Tumulty's, "still W's passionate love of privacy makes him dread even a sympathetic invasion of it."[16] Elsewhere, Edith acknowledged that she had "never liked Tumulty."[17] A reconciliation with Wilson never took place.

On March 7, 1924, James Kerney, editor of the *Trenton Evening Times*, would type out a copy of a letter Wilson had sent him five months earlier that Kerney was including in an article he had written for the *Saturday Evening Post*. Having rejected Kerney's suggestion that he run for the Senate from New Jersey, the former president recommended that Kerney not overlook Tumulty as a possible candidate: It "would make some of the reactionary senators sit up and take notice of the arrival of modern times and circumstances."[18]

But Edith Wilson, having learned from an advertisement in a prior *Post* issue of the contents of the upcoming Kerney story, protested that she alone had rights, for which she was in the process of seeking legal affirmation, to all the president's letters and refused permission to reprint this one. Edith left no doubt of her disdain for Tumulty. While she took less than two pages of her *Memoir* to relate the story of Robert Lansing's supposed betrayal of her husband, she allotted seven in recounting the former secretary's "preposterous camouflage."[19]

She chose to remember Tumulty with a poisonous anecdote—as untrue as it was unfair—concerning the presidential campaign of 1920. She portrayed him as a racist in his attempt to blackmail the Republican candidate, Warren Harding, while the 1920 campaign was under way.[20] Actually, Tumulty had done his best to prevent the spread of the unfounded rumors of Harding's Negro lineage and informed zealous Democrat would-be perpetrators "that under no consideration would the White House lend its influence" to the scheme.[21] But for readers of her *Memoir*, Edith ennobled her husband at Tumulty's expense.[22]

In the summer of 1922, Wilson monitored the midterm congressional campaigns, offering his caustic opinions of the candidates, including those of his own party. He tried to persuade the leading Democrats in

Massachusetts that Sherman Whipple was an unfortunate choice as candidate for the Senate: "not of our intellectual breed" and, from what he could judge, "just about as much interested in human progress broadly and concretely conceived as a hog is in the grand opera." As for James K. Vardaman, Wilson thought him untrustworthy: it would be detrimental to Mississippi and the nation if Vardaman was returned to the Senate.[23]

When Wilson was not campaigning against Democrats, he was working on The Document. He enlisted the help not only of Justice Brandeis and Colby but also of former cabinet members. He was articulate to the point of insult on any suggestion of compromise regarding membership in the League. His present formula was that "the world has been made safe for democracy but democracy has not yet made the world safe from irrational radicalism and revolution, and our task is to remove by rational and enlightened reform the soil in which such weeds grow."[24]

Of concern during the summer and fall of 1922 was the problematic survival of the firm of Wilson & Colby, already endangered by the difficulties of operating within moral confines imposed by the former president, who had cautioned his partner "to keep free from all association with commercial and pecuniary interests of any kind." Wilson made known his unhappiness with a succession of prospective clients—including Ecuador, in quest of a $12 million loan from the United States, and the putative government of the Western Ukrainian Republic. When Colby mentioned the likelihood of working with former senator George Sutherland, "a man of unusual ability," Wilson countered that the senator had seemed to him "one of the most thick headed and impenetrable of the Senate partisans."[25]

In September, Colby wrote to Wilson of his deepened respect—but speaking as a man who had spent his life in the rough-and-tumble of the legal profession, it made him a little dizzy to toss away business that one's professional colleagues were bending every energy to obtain. "But it's a fine game," Colby concluded, "and worth the candle as long as we can hold out."[26] The candle dimmed two months later. Pressed to finance a personal investment, Colby could not afford his partner's lofty code of operation. Two months later, signaling the demise of the law firm, he wrote to Wilson of limitations he could not now avoid and apologized for not having done more, given the great prestige of Wilson's name and the powerful aid of his constant interest and accessibility. He was relying, he added, on Wilson's understanding to secure his letter from any misconstruction.

Fortunately, though inadvertently, Wilson's fighting Armistice Day speech, given two weeks earlier, would provide a theme for the press release announcing the termination of the Wilson-Colby partnership. Wilson's statement before a crowd of five thousand assembled beyond his doorstep inspired journalists from Boston to Kentucky to predict that the former president was "About to Come Back" and to have "a decisive influence on the selection of the Democratic nominee for the presidency in 1924."[27] Wilson's spirits soared, his ambition nurtured not only by the press and Edith, but by a coterie of admirers.

Encouraged to believe that he might regain political power, Wilson divested himself of his law partnership on November 24, thereby releasing Colby to accept the sort of business, he said, with which he himself, due to his years of public service, could not be associated. Capitalizing on the positive press predicting Wilson's complete recovery, Colby's announcement terminating their law firm, which appeared on the front page of the *New York Times* on December 13, praised his partner's "disciplined power and effectiveness as a lawyer." Wilson explained that, in view of the steady gain in his health during recent months, he was turning his energies once more "to subjects which have long invited him and the importance of which cannot be overestimated."

The concluding words of Colby's statement, however, disturbed and angered Wilson. He disliked the suggestion that his supposed "Come Back" would be recorded as "one of the most remarkable incidents in modern history." Nor the assumption that his improved physical condition was insufficient to warrant his renewed candidacy for the presidency, but merited some somewhat secondary role. "Hence the opinion, widely and strongly entertained," the Washington *Evening Star* declared, that "the object of his activity is control of the next Democratic national convention in the interest of a man of his choice and the adoption of a platform of his construction."

Chagrined by the editorial,[28] Wilson turned to the newsman Frank Irving Cobb for advice. To counteract demeaning publicity he wondered, with The Document in mind, whether he ought to give out "a program" now. Three days later he received affirmation of his position and power: "Everybody knows that no Democratic candidate in 1924 will have a ghost of a chance unless he is acceptable to you," Cobb told Wilson, adding that "without your support and co-operation the ticket would be doomed to defeat." Meanwhile, Cobb advised, the situation might be allowed to "stew in its own juice for a while."[29]

Stockton Axson, who had loved and respected his sister Ellen, seems to have been fascinated by her successor. He was one of many who credited

Edith with the salvation of her husband's health. Public recognition of her role now came in full measure. J. W. Rixey Smith had written in October 1922 in *Collier's National Weekly* that Edith's story was, in essence, "the record of an American woman's sense of duty to her husband; of her heroism and of her patriotism." At his side, barring the door against the world, saving the hurt man from the venomous thrusts of a nation he had done what he thought best to serve, stood a woman, and how "strange that America could not see all this then!"

Then was intended to refer to a time of poisoned whisperings about petticoat government in Washington, and to past accusations that the nation was leaderless and the country drifting because of "the woman in the White House." *Then* was a time when the country "was full of mixed hates and prejudices, blended with the curious, quick, senseless anger at many things. . . . The land seethed with feelings that were part reptilian partisanship and part reaction from war strain." Now, however, the nation was beginning to see the situation clearly. "Mrs. Wilson was wife, super-nurse and super-secretary" of the sick man of the White House "when he needed these services more than he needed anything else in the world."[30]

In early December, Grayson publicly allowed that most of the credit for Wilson's remarkable progress went to Mrs. Wilson: "a most patient nurse, absolutely insisting on the long period of seclusion." B. V. Oulahan would report in the *New York Times* that none of the trained nurses had worked harder than Mrs. Wilson to keep life in her husband's stricken body. Always there, day in, day out, she deserved a large share of credit in winning the battle for the restoration of the former president.[31]

As a gesture of appreciation for The Woodrow Wilson Foundation, a new organization celebrating her husband, and as his representative, Edith attended a dinner in the ballroom of the Hotel Astor in New York, at which Lord Robert Cecil was also honored, receiving $25,000 for his outstanding labors on behalf of peace. Gratified by her brief trip—the longest absence from her husband in three years—she enjoyed sitting next to Cecil in a room festive with flags, flowers, candles, and music; and spending a night as the houseguest of the Bernard Baruchs. She told Baruch that she felt that "you had waved a magic wand and I had stepped into a new world which has been in eclipse so many many months."[32] In her *Memoir*, she wrote glowingly of Cecil, referring to him as a partner of her husband in the creation of the Covenant. What pleased her most was the Englishman's unfaltering endorsement of the League as it stood.

Unfortunately, after tea in Washington with the Wilsons, Cecil's feelings were hardly reciprocal: Edith, it would appear, had misinterpreted his position on the League.

On the afternoon of April 20, 1923, Cecil visited the Wilsons at S Street in what he would describe as "a smallish house." Led to believe that Wilson's health had improved, he was dismayed to find his host feeble, with his left side definitely paralyzed. Wilson was short of breath as he told anecdotes in his old way ("none remarkably good but some amusing"). Cecil had come to believe that it was essential to have the United States in the League even at the cost of important concessions. He found Wilson's insistence, to the contrary, tragic ("Remember we are on the winning side and make no concession"). Cecil feared that Wilson, the repository of a great idea—who up to a point had done so much to carry that idea into effect, and then done everything to destroy it— remained highly influential and might ultimately direct the policy of his party negatively. Cecil also observed Mrs. Wilson, who seemed to him "quite definitely a foolish woman," sitting there throughout "interposing banal observations."[33]

CHAPTER 36

"To my incomparable wife"

In the spring of 1923, Edith Wilson quietly attempted to "market" her husband's brief essay "The Road Away from Revolution." Wilson, obsessed by this article, sometimes called his wife at three or four in the morning to dictate a single sentence. His shadow of an outline intimated the grandeur of his intentions: a preface, a forward, sections called "The Destiny of the Republic," "The Vision," and "Purpose of the Founders."

The essay that evolved was pitifully fragmentary, repetitious, and something of a sermon. The "road ahead," Wilson wrote, "seemed darkened by shadows." Attempting to assess the causes of the world's distress, Wilson concluded that civilization could not survive materially unless it was redeemed spiritually. It could be saved only by becoming permeated with the spirit of Christ. Prefacing a book he would never write, the dedication was saddening: "To my incomparable wife, Edith Bolling Wilson, whose gentle benefits to me are beyond all estimation, this book, which is meant to contain what is best in me, is, with deep admiration and gratitude, lovingly dedicated."[1]

In April, Wilson sought the advice of George Creel, his sometime literary agent. In the belief that his essay included certain vital suggestions, Wilson was anxious for as wide a circulation as possible and would send Creel a copy. Ten days later, Creel tried as delicately as possible to convey his disappointment at the essay's lack of "body." He thought it fell short of what would be expected from the former president's first publication and was in danger of inciting "a very ugly reaction." Sound critic that he was, Creel was also a protective, sensitive friend. He discussed his predicament with Edith, in the hope of saving her husband from embarrassment.

Creel sent Edith two letters—one for her eyes only, the other to be shown to Wilson. In both he mentioned the importance of safeguarding Wilson's reputation from the crass commercialization of a huckstering campaign. To Edith alone, he was explicit: under different circumstances he would advise with all his conviction against publication. Given the circumstances, however, and the risk of crushing Wilson's confidence, Creel could not follow his own inclination. He had therefore approached Richard John Walsh, editor of *Collier's*, who felt as Creel did about the article but was ready to pay $2,000. Creel was comfortable with the *Collier's* offer, which averted the danger of a huckstering campaign by a newspaper syndicate and would at the same time give a fair return and almost the same amount of publicity. Apologetic, Creel wrote, "You can understand how painful it is for me to write this letter. It leaves me sick at heart, and yet I would be less than honest and less than a true friend if I did not lay these opinions before you."

By contrast, Creel's second letter, intended for Wilson's eyes, omitted any hint of criticism. He had surveyed the possibilities of publishing the article and come up with *Collier's* offer of $2,000 and the assurance of their tasteful handling and advertisement in such manner as to gain widest possible circulation. The alternative, of newspaper syndication, meant $1,000 more in money, but entailed a huckstering campaign that would undoubtedly have many disagreeable aspects. He therefore suggested the acceptance of *Collier's* offer and awaited decision.[2]

Wilson did not see either of Creel's letters. Instead, Edith spoke to him of the negative response to his article during an automobile ride in the company of Stockton Axson. She reported that someone—she avoided Creel's name—had said that the article needed expansion. It didn't do justice to Wilson: the old touch wasn't there, and for his own sake, it was better not to publish. Wilson's reaction was all that Edith had dreaded. He was adamant: he had done all he could and did not want anyone badgering him. After the ride Wilson went upstairs. Axson, lingering in Randolph Bolling's office, was suddenly aware of Mrs. Wilson, "that strong woman," sobbing in the hallway. Axson, moved—it was the only time he had ever seen her break down—asked to see the article. He read it carefully, pronounced it too long rather than too short, and advised cutting several paragraphs. At Edith's prompting, Axson repeated his suggestions to Wilson, who readily asked that they be put into effect.[3]

Edith informed Creel that Wilson disagreed with suggestions of the need for a fuller work: he was simply writing a short essay in the form of a challenge. The proposed payment and exposure were inadequate. She thought that *Collier's* offer of $2000 might seem a good price for an obscure author, but was not commensurate with her husband's dignity and with the article's significance as Wilson's first writing in years. She did not consider *Collier's* the proper vehicle; and her husband had reminded her that the *Atlantic Monthly*, the publisher of nearly all his essays, was his personal preference. Could Creel get in touch with the editor of the *Atlantic Monthly*? Creel apparently could not or would not. Politely, he suggested that she approach the magazine independently. He warned, however, that he would be greatly surprised if Wilson received an offer of $250. Edith, perceiving Creel's impatience, regretted troubling him, assured him that she would handle the matter, and wanted him to know that it was not the amount paid for the article that concerned her, but that it should receive proper respect and appear in the right context.

Wilson eventually concluded negotiations for publication in the *Atlantic Monthly* for the sum of $200. Edith, clinging to her earlier ambitions, enlisted the help of her brother. At her prompting, Randolph Bolling wrote to Ellery Sedgwick, editor of the magazine, to ask if he would be interested in publishing Mr. Wilson's essay in book form. If so, Bolling thought that a letter from the editor to Wilson with this suggestion and mention of a satisfactory royalty would secure Sedgwick rights to the essay. The proposal was accepted and elicited the hoped-for response from Wilson. He was flattered that the magazine felt his little essay was worthy of such attention.

Negotiations over the publication of "The Road to Revolution" had not pleased Edith. She disliked having Creel question her judgment and, resenting that his predicted payment had proved accurate, she altered the truth in recounting the tale of the essay's publication. In her version, instead of Wilson's having approached Creel, it was Creel who had begged that he be named agent without pay to negotiate with publishers and get a good price for the article. Rather than Creel warning Edith of the danger of a huckstering campaign to sell the essay, it was Creel who offered to "shop around," and Wilson who told the agent that he did not want his work "hawked" about for the highest bidder.[4]

Brief dispatches announced on Monday, August 27, 1923, that Edith Wilson had left her husband's side for a week's rest for the first time in four years, except for an overnight visit to New York City for the Wilson Foundation dinner. Exhausted, and feeling that she might break down, she accepted an invitation from Washington friends, the Charles Sumner Hamlins (he was a governor of the Federal Reserve Board), to visit them at their vacation home on the western shore of Buzzards Bay in Mattapoisett, Massachusetts. She was accompanied by her former secretary Edith Benham Helm.

On this visit to New England, Edith wrote Wilson daily. In a tender, enthusiastic tone reminiscent of her earliest letters, she told her "Dearest One" about the music she heard, the gardens and houses she visited, the company she met, which ranged from the seven-year-old daughter of the pretender to the throne of Portugal to all the "old dowergers of the 400."[5] Wilson's letters in turn, to his adorable "Sweetheart," are kindly and affectionate though revealing of an apprehensive, fretful, ailing man who suffered severe bouts of illness, one of which he described as "a bit of a knockout" on the day of her departure.

An earlier correspondence conveys the great strain of the invalid household on S Street, as well as Edith's close relations with her brother, who was serving as Wilson's secretary. She kept no secrets from Randolph, who was infinitely helpful in the care of her husband. Randolph also shared responsibility for the well-being of their mother and their sister Bertha, an unfortunate and impoverished pair who had moved the shabby contents of their furnished room in Washington, at the Hotel Powhatan, to The Hadleigh.[6]

By August of 1923, concern had centered on Edith herself and her need for a respite from S Street. Uncharacteristically vulnerable and dependent as she thanked her brother "a thousand times" for making her trip possible, she referred to him as her "anchor," wrote to him fondly, and was fully aware that, but for his willingness to undertake her task in all its demanding routine, she would never have been able to leave the side of her invalid husband. Randolph's "log" of his daily letters, his telephone calls, and his telegrams was consistently reassuring and almost cheerful. In response to his sister's protestations of feeling selfish at inflicting her responsibilities on him, he made light of the relentless monotony: the mornings when Wilson dictated two or three letters, his fifteen-minute walk back and forth in the house, his "electricity" to treat paralysis caused by the strokes,[7] his lunch with Grayson or Bolling. As Randolph preferred to walk by himself, he chose to "duck" the afternoon ride, if he could substitute another member of the Bolling family, or Axson or Grayson, to keep Wilson company. Randolph generously urged his sister to lengthen her visit to Massachusetts, an offer she gratefully accepted.[8]

Edith returned to Washington on Wednesday, September 5—and was immediately preoccupied with the imminent departure of Jessie, Wilson's second daughter, for Bangkok with her three children and her husband, Frank Sayre, who was to serve as adviser on international law to the court of Siam. Refreshed by her New England visit, Edith claimed a new outlook on the world. The same, she sadly admitted, could not be said for her husband. Despite Randolph's optimistic reports, Wilson seemed to have grown increasingly depressed during her absence. The ten-day interval had given her a painful perspective. With clearer eyes she now saw and faced the reality of how much her husband was failing. Returning to his side, she was determined to help maintain some semblance of his former life.

The *New York Times* reported that Great Britain's wartime prime minister David Lloyd George, visiting S Street that October, had found Wilson "alert of mind and displaying the most vivid interest in the European situation, which he has been following closely in all its recent developments." Privately, Lloyd George was struck by Wilson's grudging anger, the bitterness of his nature, his concentrated hatred of people—France's former president Raymond Poincaré was "a cheat and a liar"; mention of the newly sworn president, Calvin Coolidge—successor to Harding, who had died unexpectedly on August 2—elicited a similar outburst. "Here was the old Wilson with his personal hatreds unquenched right to the end of his journey." Their talk, terminated at a signal from Grayson, was the last Lloyd George saw of "this extraordinary mixture of real greatness thwarted by much littleness."[9]

Nothing seemed to inhibit Wilson's ambitions. In late October 1923, he invited Raymond Fosdick, now a trustee of the Rockefeller Foundation, to S Street to discuss the possibility of educational work, to help American universities attain the standards of Oxford and Cambridge. When Fosdick indulgently referred to Wilson's proposal as "the nostalgic dream of an old and crippled warrior," he was probably unaware that the "dream" was merely an alternate plan, secondary to the possible declaration of Wilson's candidacy for a third presidential term.[10] James Kerney heard Wilson express his passionate belief that the liberals of the world were looking to him to lead them: he confidently expected to dictate to the zero hour the paramount issues of the coming presidential campaign in 1924.[11]

An invitation to speak over the radio on November 10 on "The Significance of Armistice Day" fueled Wilson's plans and, consequently, Edith's. There were two weeks of preparation, which for the old Woodrow, Edith said, would have been an eternity. Now, with failing energy and eyesight, each and every sentence was haltingly constructed word by word, both day and night. On the evening of the address, Wilson suffered a blinding headache. He rose from his sickbed, put on his dressing gown, and walked down the third-floor stairs to his library, where the transmission equipment had been set up. Insisting that he could talk only while standing, he leaned heavily on his cane as he faced the microphone. Edith stood behind him, fortified with a carbon copy of the speech in case he should lose his place while reminding his audience of the nation's withdrawal into a "sullen and selfish isolation which is deeply ignoble because manifestly cowardly and dishonorable."[12]

At two-thirty the next afternoon, at his front door, Wilson addressed the third Armistice Day pilgrimage of five thousand people crowded on both sides of S Street. Edith, in a rose-colored hat and a moleskin cape, again hovered protectively. The former president's face twitched and his voice was weak, but his message was clear. He was "not one of those that have the least anxiety about the triumph of the principles I have stood for. I have seen fools resist Providence before. I have seen their destruction, as will come upon these again—utter destruction and contempt." As the band played "Onward Christian Soldiers" and "Dixie," Wilson savored the moments before Edith helped him indoors. "An extraordinary ovation to an extraordinary old man," the Lewiston, Idaho, *Weekly Tribune* would report. His visionary faith undimmed by physical infirmities and the adversities of political fortune, "he rests his case on what to him is higher ground than the temporary mood of the people."[13]

Wilson was warmly complimented, also, by his coterie of acolytes. Heartened by their support, he agreed that it was a relief once more to speak his mind. His hatred of the French premier, "that skunk Poincaré," whose leadership he thought reckless, was now almost uncontrollable. He told a colleague that he was sorry for Germany and hoped she would "wipe [France] off the map." As for his critic Frederick Edwin Smith, the first earl of Birkenhead, who had said that Wilson had come to the Paris Peace Conference "with a noble message of hope; but unhappily, in the sequel, hope proved to be his principal equipment," Wilson dismissed him as an "egregious ass," with "a crude and insincere intellect."[14]

Loyalists ignored the malevolent aspect of Wilson's character because of congruent political opinions or excused it on grounds of ill health. They remained ardently committed. Ray Baker, for one, focusing on the forthcoming presidential elections, talked about a "Back to Wilson" movement as essential to the country. Wilson's economic and political adviser, and staunch friend, Norman Davis, suggested that Wilson advise members of the Democratic Party that he was prepared to render further service to his country on vital questions. A ludicrous attempt to revive

Wilson's writing career was made by Randolph Bolling and Stockton Axson, who knew intimately the wretched state of Wilson's health.[15]

On his birthday, December 28, 1923, Wilson was formally presented with a specially constructed Rolls-Royce by those members of the Woodrow Wilson Trust who provided him with the annual gift of $10,000. In expressing his appreciation, Wilson said he was quite over-whelmed by the wonderful kindness and generosity shown him, felt himself unworthy of "this ideal act of confidence and friendship." He was unanimously elected president of the American Historical Association. The former president responded cordially to these gifts and honors, but his main preoccupation was the coming election.

In the new year, Wilson's telegram brought greetings to those attending the Democrats' Jackson Day dinner in Pittsburgh and his congratulations to the party "to which must be entrusted the redemption of the nation from the degradation of purpose into which it has in recent days been drawn." He announced his hope for a role in that redemption, advising that he would "be glad to take part in so distinguished a service."[16]

To his satisfaction, the Democratic Party officially launched the 1924 campaign with an endorsement of the "incomparable" achievements of Woodrow Wilson's great administration and with a two-hundred-member pilgrimage in pouring rain to the "shrine of peace" on S Street.[17] Visitors were greeted by Edith before passing into the library to shake hands with Wilson, who was seated in an easy chair by the fire. Four days later, Wilson decided to air the terms formulated in The Document and wrote to his former cabinet member Newton Baker to ask his opinion of the final draft.[18] Randolph Bolling, with Edith's advice, decided against sending the letter, writing instead to suggest to Baker that he call to discuss these matters when he was next in Washington at the end of January. Newton Baker took away a copy of the new platform; he would return it to Edith Wilson on July 11.

On January 21, 1924, fourteen days before his death, Wilson planned for his own reelection, sketching out not only his acceptance speech as the Democratic Party's candidate, but also his third inaugural address. Clinging to life and to the cause of the League, he wrote that "in the High Court of Honour and true Loyalty it must be held to be as deep and heinous a treason that a great and holy cause . . . should be betrayed in the moment of its triumph as that the armies of the nation should be betrayed on the field of battle." Ever the evangelist, he summoned, in his "Notes and Passages for a Third Inaugural Address," the counsel and support "of every man and every woman who loves justice and believes no sacrifice too great which promises to set it up as the rule of life in the community, whether local or national."[19]

Four days later, on January 25, Wilson made provision for posterity by choosing his biographer. Ray Baker, already commissioned to write on the Peace Conference, had long and openly expressed, in terms highly flattering to Wilson, his consuming ambition to make a comprehensive study of the former president's career. Such a work, Baker said, would and must be undertaken. He hoped that Wilson would not misinterpret him when he said, "I think I'm the man." And he was: Wilson was glad to promise him that, with reference to personal correspondence and similar papers, he regarded Baker "as my preferred creditor, and shall expect to afford you the first,—and if necessary, exclusive access to those papers."[20] This letter, in turn, was also withheld, at Edith Wilson's discretion. Only one year later, on the date of Edith's confirmation of his appointment as authorized biographer, would Baker be told of its contents.

Dr. Cary Grayson left for a shooting trip in South Carolina on Saturday, January 26, with the understanding that, if Wilson needed him, he could be reached by telegram. Rushed back to Washington the following Thursday, the physician told Randolph as well as the reporters clamoring at the door that the former president was suffering from "one of his old indigestion attacks," and while he seemed very unwell, Grayson did not regard his condition as alarming. By Friday morning Edith Wilson, feeling that her husband was dying, told Randolph to notify his daughters. Crowds gathered outside the house. Bulletins noted Wilson's steady weakening until Grayson sorrowfully read the last of them, attributing the death of his beloved patient at eleven-fifteen on Sunday morning, February 3, to "his ill-health, which began more than four years ago, namely arteriosclerosis and hemiplegia. The immediate cause was exhaustion following a digestive disturbance."[21] The next day the *New York Times* reported that "his wife was at the dying man's bedside until the end. Her name was the last word to pass his lips and his last sentence, 'I am ready,' he had spoken [the previous] Friday."

S Street was transformed from a street of waiting to a street of mourning. President and Mrs. Coolidge were among the first callers; Altrude Grayson, the doctor's wife, arrived with Helen Bones, their faces veiled in black. The next day Edith sent two letters of contrasting tone, both of them related to her plans for her husband's funeral.

On February 4, in response to Coolidge's note of sympathy, she assured the president that he and his wife were welcome if they wished to come to a short service on Wednesday afternoon at S Street before leaving for the National Cathedral. It would be a pleasure to have them and every provision would be made for their comfort and protection. The second letter was addressed to Henry Cabot Lodge, who would out-live Wilson by only nine months. Having read in the newspapers that the Bostonian had been designated by the Senate of the United States as one of those to attend the funeral service of Mr. Wilson, she wrote: "As the funeral is private, and not an official one, and realizing that your presence there would be embarrassing to you and unwelcome to me I write to request that you do not attend."

Lodge's gentlemanly response was immediate. He explained that when the Senate committee was appointed he had no idea that it was expected to attend the private services at her house, and he had supposed that the services at the church were open to the public. "You may rest assured," he concluded, "that nothing could be more distasteful to me than to do anything which by any possibility could be unwelcome to you." Publicly it was reported that Lodge was suffering from a sore throat and because of doctor's orders was unable to attend the service for the former president. Shortly after Wilson's death, however, the New York *World* noted that the senator's "beneficent affliction" might not have been wholly responsible for his absence from the funeral services but undoubtedly contributed to that act of good taste.[22]

Flags flew at half-mast over Washington. February 6 was a raw day, the overcast sky hinting at a storm as guests, at Edith Wilson's invitation, filed into S Street for the private memorial service preceding the public one at the National Cathedral. The *New York Times* named, among early arrivals, the many cabinet members, Bernard Baruch, cousins of the first Mrs. Wilson as well as her brother Stockton, the Galt family, George Creel, Princeton classmates, the White House staff, Ike Hoover, Edmund Starling, Charles Lee Swem, and Joseph Tumulty. The former secretary had been omitted until William McAdoo intervened and saw to it that Cary Grayson's wife telephoned an invitation. The absence of Wilson's once closest colleague and friend Colonel House was not noted by the press.

House had arranged to go to the funeral but hesitated to do so when he learned that it was to be somewhat private and that a special permit was required. He telephoned several people before asking Bernard Baruch to find out from Grayson whether he would be admitted. That

evening, after receiving an evasive response, House concluded that he
would not be welcome. Instead, he remained home. As a member of the
vast audience attending a service for Wilson at Madison Square Garden,
he heard Rabbi Stephen S. Wise's fierce denunciation of those who had
struck down "the hope-bringer of mankind" and "broke the heart of the
world!"

In his exclusion, House remained generous. While the ceremony at
Madison Square Garden lacked historical tradition, he had never, he
wrote in his diary on February 9, witnessed a more impressive and
touching service than that given for Woodrow Wilson. House also
entrusted his personal eulogy to those pages: "It was the ending of one
of the great careers of which the world has record—a career intertwined
with the best and most active years of my life—a career upon the success
of which I had placed all the desires, hopes and dreams for a better and
more understanding world. It was not alone my interest in the success of
his undertaking, but I had a deep and abiding affection for the man
which all that has happened on June 28, 1919 [the day in Paris of their
last conversation] has not shaken."[23] One last attempt, a few weeks earlier, to reconstitute the friendship between House and Wilson had been a
miserable failure. Cyrus McCormick, Wilson's generous benefactor, had
approached Edith for help in attempting to heal the misunderstanding
between the two men—an issue, he felt, as did Cleveland Dodge, "of
great moment not only to the two but to the cause of Democracy generally." McCormick very much wanted to speak to her and Randolph, and
then to Woodrow, on the matter. "Can it be managed?" McCormick
asked Edith on January 13, 1924. By a return note that same day, the
answer was, it could not. She would keep an open mind, but since seeing
McCormick, Edith wrote, she had learned things that did not incline her
to change her opinion that the present status was the only one possible.[24]
When Colonel House was questioned years later, at the age of seventy-
eight, about his relationship with Edith Wilson, he said that it remained
precisely what it always had been: "We never were close friends: we are
not now. We never have been enemies: we are not now."[25]

Still another person closely connected to Wilson in earlier times was
missing from the funeral services in Washington. This was Mary Allen
Hulbert Peck, Wilson's epistolary confidante—whom he had met in
Bermuda, seen rarely in later years, and received for a last time during
his tour of California. In letters he had loved her deeply and had revealed
himself intimately. Living in Manhattan at the time of Wilson's death,
she knew that Sunday, as she entered the doors of the Christian Science

Church she had adopted, that Wilson had died. After the service, she walked home in the Sabbath quiet to her tiny apartment, where she took the copy of the *Oxford Book of Verse* that he had given her and read, as they had on the south shores of Bermuda years ago, "For power must fail, / And the pride must fall, / And the love of the dearest friends grow small—/But the glory of the Lord is all in all."[26]

From the pulpit of the National Cathedral on Mount St. Alban in Washington, the congregation heard Dr. Sylvester Beach pay tribute to Woodrow Wilson for "his courage in the right as God gave him to see the right; for his unflinching integrity; for the fervor of his patriotism." Edith herself was not without encomiums, coincidentally published on the morning of her husband's death. "Not even the receptions accorded to her during the peace conference and in the capitals of the great allied power would have been sufficient to recompense Mrs. Woodrow Wilson," Betty Edwards wrote on February 3 in the *Washington Daily News*, for the more than eight years she was constantly by his side. "During the last months of his presidency Mrs. Wilson had acted as the intermediary between the vast machinery of government and the stricken Executive. Her intelligence and unusual memory enabled her to grasp the intricate affairs of state and present them to her husband. With energy and tact, she shielded her invalid husband from anything that might have proven a strain for him after he had retired to private life."[27] Recognition was expressed more succinctly by Wilson's old friend Nancy Toy, who wrote Edith, "He couldn't 'carry on' a day without you, could he?"[28]

As guardian of her husband's "posthumous fame,"[29] as writer, researcher, editor, censor, lobbyist, fund-raiser, preservationist, publicist, and propagandist, Edith Wilson would devote the rest of her long life to nurturing, defending, commemorating, and mythologizing her husband's goals and reputation as ennobled prophet, warrior, and statesman. In her messianic cause, she paid to ensure that her husband's burial place within the somber walls of the National Cathedral in Washington was suitably impressive, supervising the execution of a Mankato cream stone sarcophagus and iron grill. As the driving force and fund-raiser for Staunton, Virginia, she was, in her persistence, responsible for the rehabilitation of Wilson's birthplace. She insistently lobbied the Eisenhower administration to celebrate the centennial of her husband's birth. Rewriting history in her prejudiced and untruthful *Memoir,* she saw to it that Hollywood's filmed version was, in turn, faithfully flawed. The apogee of her influence was achieved with her implacable control of her husband's papers. The person she confirmed as her husband's biographer, and subsidized in that task, was to use those papers, she would make certain, "to enshrine Wilson in literary stained glass."[30]

Edith Wilson was intolerant of those who pondered the personality, character, and judgment of the twenty-eighth president of the United States. She dismissed those who questioned whether he was the hero or the villain of the League of Nations, or who suggested the possibility, as did the writer Mark Sullivan, that the course of history would have been altered, and U.S. membership in the League assured, had Wilson not been so obdurate—if he had met with Lodge and had not allowed himself to be dominated by hatred of the Bostonian.[31] Most certainly, Edith Wilson would try to stifle the grim charge that Wilson "did more to get us *in* and more to keep us *out* of the League than any other man," that he was a failure as a statesman "because through self-will, inflexibility, egotism, failure to distinguish between the essential and inessential, he successfully defeated his own and the country's *purpose.*"[32]

Negative thoughts would be admitted to Ray Stannard Baker's volumes only when they related to people other than Wilson. Consideration of Wilson's temperament, judgment, second marriage, shortsightedness, and autocracy was irrelevant. There was no need to look further than Raymond Fosdick to justify the canonization of Woodrow Wilson. In his ideals, Fosdick claimed, the twenty-eighth president of the United States represented "a new hope for the future," who "stood at a cross-road in history and pointed out a new path," which, because of his wife's vigilance, would be strewn with roses and remain evergreen.[33]

CHAPTER 37

Edith Wilson on her own, 1924–61

Now, as Woodrow Wilson's widow, a grande dame, Edith once again sailed for Europe as she had in 1910 as the widow of Norman Galt. This time, in July 1925, she was accompanied by Bernard Baruch's daughter Belle and Belle's friend Evangeline Johnson. They remained until November. Fashion being a sustained interest, Edith was fascinated by the new look of the twenties. She reported home that women were cutting their hair short as a man's and using much brilliantine, wearing long coats and skirts to the knee, appearing with very red lips and tiny felt hats: "There are millions like that!"[1] Her visit that summer at the Palazzo Cantarini Accademia in Venice was delightful, a perfect rest— the girls added to her comfort and happiness and so spoiled her that, to tell the truth, she wrote in effusive appreciation to Baruch, she was afraid she could never again settle down to looking out for herself in prosaic Washington.[2] Her extended stay allowed her to accept Belle's invitation to Fetteresso Castle in Scotland, and to visit Geneva—where even one day in the Swiss city that had become the home of the League of Nations would have justified her trip "if every other pleasure had been eliminated."

Gratified that all those men with whom Woodrow had worked in Paris had gone out of their way to pay him tribute, Edith in Geneva clarified her future role as self-designated ambassador of the memorial realm of Woodrow Wilson. Newspapers acclaimed her reverence for her husband's memory, and for allowing nothing to disturb her tranquillity of spirit or her determination to pursue quietly the mission that she had assigned to herself and which she held sacred, the study of the League of Nations.[3] She was elated: all the years of pain and heartbreak for her great husband were worthwhile. She wrote to Bernard Baruch that, while she ached for Woodrow to see what she was seeing, she felt that he knew and was satisfied and happy.[4]

Edith made three more trips to Europe with Belle Baruch, and eleven with other companions. On those occasions, she always stayed in Geneva and attended meetings of the Assembly of the League of Nations. In 1926, she took tea with Queen Marie of Romania at the Hôtel Ritz in Paris. In August 1929, on a three-month tour, she arrived in Peking by way of Egypt, Turkey, India, and Hong Kong, then continued on to Japan—which she visited again in 1932 for her niece's wedding. Though she protested to her biographer Alden Hatch that, in keeping with her policies, she traveled as an obscure tourist, without pomp or demand for extra service, her arrivals were not unheralded. She had achieved sufficient recognition in Japan to be invited to dinner by the emperor's brother and by the American ambassador to Japan and, in November 1929, to attend the chrysanthemum garden party given by the emperor. In 1931, there was the invitation of the president of Poland, the pianist Ignacy Paderewski, to the dedication of the Wilson Memorial at Poznan. Traveling with her niece Lucy Moeling and with Bernard and Belle Baruch (with a stop in Paris for the Grand Prix), she was met in Warsaw by the Polish minister of foreign affairs and by the American ambassador and his wife and was lodged at the president's palace, built by Kaiser Wilhelm.

In Washington, more privately, Edith was known as a bridge addict whose friends often let her win,[5] who gave and went to luncheons and enjoyed outings at the horse races. Publicly, she was a complex figure, an object of reverence and gossip, an icon of devout widowhood who was said to visit her husband's tomb several times weekly. On October 2, 1925, when the Baltimore *Sun* reported, "Mrs. Wilson Silent on Romance Rumor," she neither denied nor affirmed her supposed engagement to her family friend and physician, Dr. Sterling Ruffin. There was also the announcement of her foray into politics.

In the summer of 1927, Edith Wilson, who was backing Governor Alfred E. Smith for president, was talked of as the Democratic candidate for vice president. As evidence of her own popularity—or of Wilson's lingering fame—Democratic women who said she "would grace the office and would fill it capably" were making an effort to obtain her nomination.[6] Highly visible at various Democratic gatherings, including the once contentious Jackson Day dinner, she called for party harmony when she spoke briefly at the Democratic National Convention in the twenty-thousand-capacity Sam Houston Hall in Houston, Texas, on June 25, 1928, and was hailed as the party's first lady, a majestic figure to whom Democrats paid homage "as if she were the Statue of Liberty."[7] The factotum journalist George Creel may have defined her life as Wilson's widow when he wrote, "Former First Lady Lives Largely with Past, Yet Watches Present."[8] And with an eagle eye, he might have added.

Her rejection of her husband's loyal and capable stenographer Charles Swem was an early indication of Edith's intentions regarding her husband's letters. Within days of Wilson's funeral, she dismissed the memoir Swem had submitted for her approval. She wrote to Swem on February 12, 1924, that she doubted the legitimacy of the quotations— she couldn't conceive that her husband would have given permission to make them ad libitum from his correspondence. Also, quotations of certain things should be excluded out of loyalty. She concluded, "This random selection and publishing of parts of things would destroy the big coordinated work."[9]

But Edith's negation of Swem's effort to memorialize Wilson's presidency did not mean that she forfeited his resources altogether. In the same letter, she assured Swem that rejection of his manuscript was not meant to imply any defect on his part. She could, in fact, think of nothing more valuable, at a later stage, than his notebooks of transcriptions of letters and speeches, which would assist in compiling the chronicle of Wilson's life and work. "I know your friendship and loyalty to him would make you eager to further such work." Cowed, Swem conceded the next day: he was glad to have her opinion and "shall not quote from any of Mr. Wilson's letters. I shall not write a book at all."[10] Edith was deeply touched, she claimed. His letter showed the fine feeling she felt sure he always had, and his ready response, she told him, showed her that when the time came, he would be ready to help—with his personal notes or memories of close associations.

The following month, Edith took legal steps to reinforce her position. As executrix of her husband's estate, with the advice of her family attorney, Mrs. Woodrow Wilson asserted her legal rights in the publication of her husband's letters and manuscripts.[11] Edith was moved to take legal steps—at the same time she objected to James Kerney's use of a letter about Tumulty—by an advertisement for William Allen White's forthcoming, two-part article for *Liberty Magazine* that quoted Wilson's letter to Mary Allen Hulbert Peck about his chances for the presidency.[12] If Edith thought, however, that her legal position would influence Mary Peck's subsequent series for the same publication, she would find herself disappointed. As though Wilson had never written a letter to her, Mrs. Peck ingeniously cited other sources that appeared immune to legal intervention: "According to my diary" or "I recall his words of one evening in 1911" or "Such were his very words as I later jotted them down" or "I am translating from my diary."[13]

Having staked her legal boundaries, Edith never relented. Tactfully or rudely, she permitted no exceptions. Neither flattery nor reason would persuade her to permit writers of articles and books about their Wilson-related years to make use of letters they had safeguarded in their private files and desk drawers. She claimed all the letters as her rightful property. With or without the use of direct quotations from her husband's letters, literary efforts in general, apart from the authorized biography, were discouraged, and those who dared to breach her position even marginally risked a blistering reprimand and, in one case, the threat of litigation.

When the *Memoirs of William Jennings Bryan*, published in 1925, included three letters Wilson had exchanged with his former secretary of state on their differing positions on neutrality, Edith was incensed. She would have taken the matter to court had it not been for Bernard Baruch, who advised her to avoid a fight with Bryan's wife, the book's editor and author. Baruch also cautioned Edith on the impracticality of the case. To attempt on legal grounds to recall the Bryan *Memoirs* would have involved lawsuits with individual booksellers across the country. Mrs. Bryan's subsequent letter, explaining to Edith that she had published the letters to "justify my husband," was only a further irritant. "I do not feel that is sufficient reason for breaking down our own position," Edith wrote Baruch on February 7, 1926, and she was sorry she had not made a public statement on the matter.[14]

Her obsessive concern about any reference to her husband only deepened with time. She was angered not only by attempts to publish Wilson's letters, but also by the publication of letters others had written about him. She responded with scarcely suppressed fury to Edith Benham Helm's invitation to read her series "The Private Letters of the Wilsons' Social Secretary" prior to publication in Hearst's *International-Cosmopolitan*. These were Mrs. Helm's letters to her fiancé during the great days of the Paris Peace Conference. Since the contract was in hand, reading would have been only, in effect, an empty gesture and possibly cause embarrassment. In a frosty tone Edith added that she sincerely hoped the monetary reward compensated for "what must be a natural shrinking from giving to the public such intimate letters written when you were in the confidential position of my Secretary, and a member of our household."

Mrs. Helm tried to defend herself. She did not understand why Mrs. Wilson was surprised. Her understanding was that Edith had always

known of her intentions to publish the letters when they were in a satisfactory, edited version, and that Edith had given her approval to do so.
Edith's handwritten reply assured Mrs. Helm that she was quite mistaken. To the contrary, she had always assumed that Mrs. Helm felt they
could not be published because of the conflicting position she occupied in
the president's home, and that the secretary meant to preserve the letters as a private link in the events of that historic time. As requested,
Edith Wilson continued, she had kept the secretary's manuscript (the
first draft or copy of the letters) in the vault and taken it out at Mrs.
Helm's request to read it to the president. Because it was unwise, during
those pulsating days in Paris, to put him under such emotional strain,
she had read only the first few pages, had not felt herself at liberty to
verify the secretary's quotations, and thought it a bold thing for anyone
to have done. Quoting from her social secretary's letter in which she
said, "They were written with a heart full of love for you and the President," Edith concluded, "I cannot conceive of your writing otherwise for
I had always counted you a real friend and tried in every relation to
serve you in that rare capacity."[15]

In April 1924, more than two months after Wilson's death, even as Ray
Stannard Baker waited anxiously in the wings, Edith decided to postpone any decision regarding the choice of her husband's biographer
until the entire field had been canvassed. She was certain, however, that
it was not a moment too soon to start on her own the research, to collect
the material—meaning all pertinent documents and personal letters—
from persons associated with her husband's administration and hold it
until she had found the best available writer.

In gathering everything possible relating to Mr. Wilson's life and
work, she sent out a number of letters, asking two favors of the recipients: to write and forward the history of the work done with or for the
president and to send his letters (Wilson frequently wrote without keeping copies), which she would return after photographing them at her
expense.[16] In her amiability, she avoided mentioning the extent of the
authority she meant to enforce over use of these materials. However,
Wilson's friends and colleagues soon learned that his widow's restrictions were immutable.

On January 5, 1925, Edith at last delivered the letter her husband had
been too ill to sign just nine days before his death, the one "coming truly
like a voice from the clouds," which allowed the heir apparent, Ray

Baker, to call himself Woodrow Wilson's "authorized biographer."[17] Simultaneously, she left no doubt as to who would be the final arbiter of what appeared in print. There was one point, she added in her covering note, that she was sure Baker would understand: she would like to read all the material before it was sent to the publisher "to check anything I know to be inaccurate."[18] That she would pay the writer a regular fee until his royalties developed was not likely to lessen her case. For Edith's purposes, her choice of this press officer whom she had come to like and trust in Paris was ideal. The "chief historical architect of the Wilsonian epic,"[19] Ray Baker was the very man to exalt her husband's fame as "prophet, warrior, and statesman."

Baker had first seen and heard Woodrow Wilson at dinner at the Hotel Astor in New York on January 21, 1910. The forty-year-old newsman, novelist, and essayist had been impressed at once with Wilson's Whitmanesque expanse and moralistic yearnings. No one he had ever heard, in fact, had made an impression "quite so vivid and clear-cut."[20] Baker, who had abandoned Michigan Agricultural College and the study of law at the University of Michigan, was both a crusading journalist and an autodidactic psychologist. He was sentimental, and a reformer at heart. First for *McClure's* and then for *The American*, as a member of the famed circle of muckrakers[21] that included Lincoln Steffens and Ida Tarbell, he wrote on the most critical issues of the day, on politics, labor, and race relations. Under the pen name David Grayson, he had won a *Collier's* prize for a best short story and had given comfort to hungry hearts and minds with *Adventures in Contentment* and *Friendship and Understanding*. Admirers claimed that Baker offered "something positive in terms of human need . . . something in the way of national uplift."[22]

The biographer did not exaggerate when he said that meeting Wilson was a "truly determinative experience." He thought the fifty-three-year-old president of Princeton had the finest mind in the field of statesmanship. When Wilson received the nomination for president, Baker became a complete convert, helping to organize Wilson clubs, and writing and speaking about him. After Wilson's election, he wrote *Wilson, Man of Action*, the *New Spirit in Washington*, and *A Thinker in the White House*. By the time he published *Wilson—after Twenty Months*, he was concerned that his enthusiasm precluded objectivity toward the newly widowed president.[23] However, irresistibly drawn to Wilson, Baker had extolled the president's clear exposition of his policies, his forthrightness and sense of inner discipline, and the kind of self-confidence that convinces and inspires.

With the outbreak of the Great War, Baker emerged from his independent muckraking tasks as a Woodrow Wilson partisan. Moved by the president's "great wind of noble thoughts,"[24] he echoed and amplified Wilson's message and his oratorical style. War was a moral crusade, the art of the great human game; war lifted us a little out of our prejudices and conventions; war warmed us with a new sense of common purposes, of loyalty to something above and outside ourselves. Eager to serve and appointed special agent of the State Department in February 1918, Baker sailed for England as a foreign correspondent and, at Wilson's request, stayed on to organize a press bureau in Paris channeling information from delegates to the Peace Conference to more than 150 American correspondents. The opportunity for daily contact with Wilson was not lost on Baker. As Wilson's apologist, he insisted that the president was not cold, aloof, arrogant, but intensely engrossed. Wilson's stubbornness was the courage of conviction. Like Wilson, Baker believed that "compromise was the enemy." Preferring glorious failure to moderate success, he wrote that the only hope left for the Peace Conference was for Wilson to emerge with a "terrific blast for his principles and their *specific application,* and go down in the ruin." ("*I fear he won't*" was his great dread.)[25]

Returning to the United States, Baker helped the president to parry personal attacks. Working as an independent journalist during Wilson's Western tour, Baker published a series of favorable articles that appeared in *McClure's,* a magazine estimated to reach about 10 million people. Republished in the *Congressional Record,* the articles were collected as a book in 1919, under the title *What Wilson Did at Paris.* Baker was thanked by Edith Wilson for making "such a splendid effort to interpret to the American people the stupendous difficulties that confronted the President in Paris."[26] Given his devoted service to the president abroad and at home, the journalist was, for the Wilsons, the logical person to entrust with the three trunks and more of papers that resulted in *Woodrow Wilson and World Settlement* in 1922. Two years later he was joint editor with Professor William E. Dodd, later U.S. ambassador to Germany, of Wilson's public papers, which Baker—unaware of Tumulty's and others' authorship—perceived as bearing the touch of a master craftsman in the English language, of an orator who never used ghostwriters.

Rumblings in scholarly circles about the writer's lack of qualifications to write the "big coordinated work"[27] were bitterly challenged: Baker vowed to examine as many documents as possible. He was convinced, however, "that truth lies in what I remember, not in the facts of the documents. Documents crush out truth!"[28]

A giant yellow and red van labeled "Federal Storage and Freight Service No. 7," hired by Edith Wilson to deliver over eleven tons of her husband's papers, stirred quite a commotion as it lumbered into Ray Baker's peaceful hometown of Amherst, Massachusetts, on March 6, 1925. The mountain of papers derived from S Street, and from sealed storage rooms in a Washington warehouse. The lode the basement catacombs of the White House included sixty-seven dusty steel cases packed with 5,516 folders containing a total of 200,000 assorted letters and documents.

Baker started immediately to assess the papers, which were stored in the fireproof top-floor quarters at the Jones Library of Amherst College and in a fireproof basement vault in his own house. Despite their great bulk, the substantial portion of the president's correspondence with Edward House was lacking, letters which Wilson had typed himself and whose originals—presumably the sole copies—were filed among the colonel's papers now held by Yale University. Baker also took note of those who were "ambushing my innocent progress."[29] Though he did not name these obstructions, it is likely that he thought of the forty-year-old Charles Seymour (who, with House, had jointly edited a collection of essays, *What Really Happened at Paris*). Then in the process of editing *The Intimate Papers of Colonel House*, Seymour was determined that this four-volume work would include Wilson's letters to the colonel.

Ray Baker greatly resented his dependence for the House papers on Seymour, who was Sterling professor of history at Yale and would be the university's future president. "I tremble until I get the letters; they are simply invaluable," Baker would confide to Edith Wilson.[30] Protracted negotiations among Seymour, Baker, House, and most significantly, Edith herself in consultation with Randolph Bolling and Bernard Baruch were inaugurated by Seymour's letter, which emphatically stated his understanding of a reciprocal arrangement. "I gather," Seymour had written Baker on October 5, 1925, "that you and the Colonel agreed we ought to be mutually helpful and that he would be glad to let you have copies of the President's letters which you lack and to permit the publication of his own letters to the President, on the understanding, naturally, that I might publish the President's letters to the Colonel which would fit into my book."[31]

Bernard Baruch helped Edith frame her rejection of Seymour's subsequent direct request for permission to use the communications House had received from Wilson: she had established at considerable legal expense her right to control the publication of all of Mr. Wilson's letters, and she could not in justice to others and to herself make an exception in his case. Seymour made no secret of his disappointment. The omission of Wilson's letters would, he wrote to Edith, lessen the image of strength and virility of the president in *The Intimate Papers*. Seymour did not say that the damage would be far greater to House: without Wilson's letters, it would not be possible to substantiate the depth of the colonel's influence. Seymour also noted forlornly, as though in disbelief and perhaps in hope of the decision's being reversed, that "the plan of co-operation seems to have been abandoned . . . for [Baker] now asks permission to publish Colonel House's letters to the President although reciprocal privileges are denied."[32]

The word *permission* unnerved the president's widow. She seemed to discount any possibility that the colonel might legally be entitled to rights over his own letters. She insisted that Seymour had "misunderstood" Mr. Baker and that there was some "confusion" in House's mind. The idea, she wrote the colonel on December 2, 1925, was "preposterous"—neither Mr. Baker nor she had any idea of asking for permission to publish his letters to Mr. Wilson—in view of her position "not to allow the publication of any of Mr. Wilson's letters by any one."[33] What she was asking and what had been discussed was just what she had written him and all of the old friends and associates of her husband's in June 1924—the privilege of having copies of all letters and memorandums written by Mr. Wilson, or any other data he could give her that would assist a future biographer. In return, she was willing to cooperate in any way should House's own files be incomplete—an exchange of whose inequities Edith seemed oblivious. Though Wilson frequently typed letters without keeping a carbon, House's files were intact. Indeed, the colonel's secretary, Frances Denton, the fastidious Miss Fanny, had not only kept the papers in meticulous order but had protected them "in true Texas style" with a small revolver she carried in her reticule.[34]

Seymour was sorry, as he courteously told Edith, to have "misunderstood" Baker. When he had got his book *The Intimate Papers of Colonel House* off to the publisher, he would await Colonel House's wishes as to the next move—he was strictly bound by the terms of the colonel's gift as to the copying of papers in the Yale collection.[35] Negotiations extended over a year. House obviously capitulated and Edith would have it both ways: jurisdiction over Wilson's letters to House and the use of the colonel's letters without his permission. On November 10, 1926, a jubilant Baker wrote to Edith, "I feel like throwing up my hat and giving three cheers! The first lot of the House letters came yesterday, bringing us down to Feb. 1917." Other letters would soon arrive. Reaffirming his earlier appraisal of their value, Baker pronounced these letters of Wilson to House "of the utmost value and importance."[36]

Commenting on the ban on printing Wilson's letters in Charles Seymour's four volumes of *The Intimate Papers of Colonel House,* the colonel's friend and editor of *Life* magazine, Edward Martin, supposed that the prohibition would be lifted at some future time. He wrote to Ray Baker that he did not know the particulars of the law on which it rested, "but it is not in the interest of the truth of history that it should be possible for anybody's widow—especially a second wife—to control permanently the publications of all his private papers in whatever hands." Baker was defensive: Of course it wasn't a permanent arrangement. Mrs. Wilson was merely anxious "to try to secure the chance for an orderly and truly interpretive presentation of the material before the papers are open to general use."[37]

Achieved "order" came at a staggering cost. Reasonable judgment and any concept of objectivity were set aside in Baker's partial and prejudiced portraits of Wilson and House. He would march Wilson on to monumental fame and relegate House to a tainted oblivion. In tribute to his puritanical hero Woodrow Wilson, all the facts would be there, but Baker's task, as an artist, was to make them lose their "awkwardness, offensiveness, vulgarity," by relating them to the whole picture, and "thus finding out where they will be beautiful."[38]

While the biographer peppered his volumes with quotations from House's letters, he repeatedly questioned the colonel's methodology, intelligence, purpose, and honesty as well as his writing skill. Whereas Wilson's letters were analogous to engravings, unsullied by a doubtful or indistinct word, House's were "curiously paragraphed, disconnected."[39] Disparaging House's "mission" abroad as though it had been less than legitimate, Baker also raised questions about the intellectual abilities of this confidential diplomat. The "clear-headed Sir Edward Grey," he pointedly mentioned, received a letter from House that was "so vaguely framed and so little an answer . . ." One must be skeptical, Baker said, about trusting House. "As Wilson made no notes of his conversations with the Colonel, one had to depend," Baker warned, "on a [one-sided report of] what occurred."[40]

In response to a comment about his prejudiced treatment of House, Baker admitted his culpability. His colleague was probably right—but, he explained, in the colonel's case, he felt under no compulsion to be impersonal. Betraying overwhelming animus, he said there was "so much that is smug, not only in House's assumptions but in Seymour's treatment of them, so much plain bunk, that it is difficult to be temperate."[41]

Edith Wilson claimed she wrote the first part of her *Memoir* on a train: she was so mad, she told her biographer Alden Hatch, after reading Colonel House's book she "just started in writing furiously, and continued at home but never expected to publish it."[42] In April 1925, Holcombe Bolling had suggested to his aunt Edith that she write "some answering statements" to Mary Peck's articles published in *Liberty Magazine* in the preceding December and January. Doing so would mean putting the "cards on the table," giving personal reminiscences, definite statements of her opinions, and photographs that, he acknowledged, she might not be willing to make public. However, the nephew believed that such a rebuttal would be timely and effective in view of the Wilson "revival" that seemed currently in the air.[43]

When Bernard Baruch asked to see her manuscript—written over ten years—Edith demurred: it was badly written, it was illegible. She did take his advice, however, and had it retyped. Baruch sat up all night reading it and told her that she must publish it. She complained that she did not know how to write: it wasn't good enough. Nonetheless, according to Edith, Baruch insisted: "I command you to." Marquis James was helping Baruch with his own book, and the financier would send this prominent biographer to help her. James came to S Street, stayed several days, and finally said, "I can't change it. It is yours and I would spoil it. Just leave out the nasty remarks you have made about House and some of the others." *The Saturday Evening Post* paid Edith Wilson $40,000 for eleven installments beginning December 17, 1938.[44]

When it came to collecting the articles in book form, the author's stiletto pen posed problems of taste and judgment, some of which were, possibly, legally actionable. The publisher suggested changes. On November 19, 1938, Randolph Bolling was found writing to assure D. L. Chambers, president of Bobbs-Merrill, the publishers, that he had persuaded Mrs. Wilson to omit certain of the "dirty digs" in her manuscript. While

Chambers was most cordial in leaving the choices up to Mrs. Wilson—"her wish is law, of course"—he instilled some fear of repercussions. Mrs. Wilson said that she did not think her editor would allow her to publish anything that even bordered on libel, but she would be grateful to have the galleys read carefully from that point of view and would be pleased to delete whatever might be construed as libelous.[45]

In a broadcast on March 24, 1939, Irita Van Doren, the literary editor of the *Herald Tribune*, reported that the reviews and comment on *My Memoir* ran the whole gamut from praise to disapproval. It was called, simultaneously, the most devastating self-portrait ever written, and "a fascinating Cinderella-like tale." Friends of Woodrow Wilson's protested its publication as a desecration of his memory; other good friends felt that he was here vindicated for the first time.[46]

As the poet and novelist Stephen Vincent Benét put it, the *Memoir* was the story of a devoted wife, a fierce partisan whose husband was always right—which was natural, "but it followed that the other men were always wrong."[47] A less magnanimous review in the Providence, Rhode Island, *Journal*, March 12, 1939, called the book "trivial, and at once acid and saccharine . . . her hates so sharp" about House, McAdoo, Lodge, Lansing, and John Singer Sargent "that they instill in the reader doubt about the author."

No one survived more gracefully Edith Wilson's minefields, in or outside her *Memoir*, than Bernard Baruch. A towering figure in morning coat and impeccable silk top hat, elegant and affluent, he not only "distinguished himself during the War by his brilliant service as the head of the War Industries Board," but was the one, Edith wrote, whom the president and she counted "as a friend and counsellor and learned to regard with personal affection."[48] As a widow, she echoed these sentiments. She basked in his hospitality and generosity, was often dependent on his advice, and followed his "able direction." Edith's trust and respect, enhanced by Baruch's financial assistance, which was both personal and philanthropic, by his understanding of her mercurial temperament, and by his readiness to be helpful, nurtured the unique bond between them. He had met Edith—who was two years his junior—before she knew Wilson, probably through his connections with her brother Rolfe, a banker.[49]

Edith sought Baruch's judgment and intervention regarding her most vital concerns: the working details of the Wilson biography (including the research, permissions, financial arrangements with Baker, and his

possible replacement due to illness); the question of the Woodrow Wilson Foundation turning over to Princeton University all of its funds
for the establishment of the Woodrow Wilson School of International
Relations; the safekeeping and disposition of the Wilson papers; the
restoration of Wilson's birthplace, Staunton. Before leaving for Japan at
the end of August 1932, she sent Baruch a most affectionate letter,
enclosing a reminder about the missing deed to the seventy-five hundred square feet, three lots' worth, with 25-foot frontage on Massachusetts Avenue, contiguous to her S Street house, which he had bought for
her to protect her privacy.[50]

She also sought advice on personal matters, always wishing, she said,
that he be in touch with her plans.[51] She knew how reluctant he was to
give advice about financial matters, especially to women. However, having implicit confidence in his judgment, she appealed to him in October
1933 for help in a matter of some concern, her investment in Federal Land
Bank bonds.[52] In rare instances—when, for instance, she planned to cruise
around South America aboard the German liner *Bremen*—Baruch did not
wait to be asked for his advice. Fearing for her safety and reputation, he
called to her hotel in New York about noon on February 11, 1939, the date
of her sailing, to tell her that since the *Bremen* was owned by Germany,
he thought her journey most unwise: war might break out between Germany, the ship's home port, and one of the South American countries of
the *Bremen*'s destination, and Edith might consequently be interned or
become the subject of international complaint. With her luggage already
on shipboard, her first response was to say it was too late to change
plans. An hour later, Baruch telephoned again, saying that his conscience
would not allow her to make such a mistake. As a result, after consultation with the State Department, she gave up on her trip and was back
home in Washington by midnight on February 11.[53]

The two played cards together, and she fondly mentions her enjoyment
of their "delightful little talks." A recurrent subject was their shared
interest in politics. Another theme would have been their mutual loathing
of Colonel House. Edith, who grew increasingly restive about the effect of
the publication of the *Intimate Papers of Colonel House* on her husband's
reputation, was consoled by Baruch. Mr. Wilson's future was "perfectly
safe," and, he urgently advised, "the quieter we keep the better" about the
man he referred to as "Judas and his charlatan biographer."[54]

When she asked Baruch that he make the memorial address on
Armistice Day in 1934, she told him that no one else could do it "with
the same distinction and, personally, no one dearer to me." He was her

adviser, patron, and cherished friend. Yet even Baruch stumbled on forbidden territory. Proposing a collection of Wilson's state speeches and
interviews, he had asked Edith if that would interfere with the biographical work in progress. He learned that it would most definitely do so.
Baruch immediately instructed his secretary to telegraph Edith: "The
Work Has Been Stopped."[55]

Baruch's explanation of his early allegiance to Wilson may account for
his unfaltering devotion to the president's widow. Since his first sight of
the newly elected governor of New Jersey, erect, dignified, confident,
smiling, Baruch—a college student wearing his father's made-over clothes
and excluded from a Greek letter society because he was a Jew—had hailed
Wilson's opposition to snobbery and prejudice. His stand against private
clubs at Princeton, among other issues, had convinced Baruch that Wilson
personified the qualities desirable in a man elected to high office.[56] Baruch
would continue to revere Wilson's memory "due to the gallant pioneer-
ing which he did, and to a deepening realization that it was we, the people,
who failed Wilson."[57]

As far back as 1925, Bernard Baruch had encouraged Edith Wilson to
believe that Woodrow Wilson's birthplace at Staunton, Virginia, might
be turned into a dignified and permanent memorial. The project gave
free rein to Edith Wilson's compulsive style. When, in 1938, the
Woodrow Wilson Birthplace Foundation was chartered "to purchase,
preserve, and maintain" the old manse formerly owned by Mary Bald-
win College, it was the start of Edith's exhaustive efforts to create the fit-
ting environment she envisioned for her husband's childhood.

Swiftly at work, she chose colors, rugs, furniture, and wallpapers;
worried about outlets over the fireplace mantels; guided the placement
of sink and stove; passed judgment on promotional material, invitations,
guest lists, the choice of speakers as well as the precise wording and
punctuation of the visitors' guide; and whenever she could, consigned
the memorabilia of the first Mrs. Wilson to oblivion. On May 18, 1941,
she wrote to say that, of all the people in the world she had wished
Baruch and his daughter Belle had been able to attend the dedication of
the birthplace two weeks earlier, and she thanked Baruch with "my love
and deep gratitude for all you did to help in the restoration of the
house."

But the financial aspect of Staunton remained a challenge. The prospective filming of *Wilson*, based on her *Memoir* as well as on Baker's biography, proposed in 1942, helped alleviate the financial strain.[58] In lieu of

any direct payment to her, Edith arranged that the check for $25,000 from the Twentieth Century–Fox Corporation be used "to start an endowment Fund for the Birthplace to insure its protection in the future." She would leave a like sum to Staunton from the same source at her death.

From the start, with Randolph Bolling by her side, Edith had taken a keen interest in Baker's discussion of a proposal to sell the motion picture rights of her *Memoir* and his book *Woodrow Wilson Life and Letters* to the Fox Corporation—the eighth and last volume of his fourteen-year enterprise, published in 1939, acclaimed "a Condensation Made With Obvious Skill."[59] The three agreed to put the matter in the hands of the best literary agent in New York, and Bolling advised Baker that he and his sister thought this might be an opportunity for the biographer "to control the historical part of the motion picture." Whatever was implied by the word *control,* Edith certainly did not mean to forgo her own say in the proceedings. She dismissed Baker's claim that the revised shooting script finally captured a "feeling of greatness beyond anything they had in the former drafts." On the contrary, she read the latest version with increasing disappointment and—if he would forgive her for speaking very frankly—she felt that they have "simply *ruined* what had been an unusually good pen portrait and understanding of the man and," she added with emphatic underlining, "I cannot give my consent to the production of this Sept. 13th, 1943, draft as it stands."[60]

The amended script arrived at S Street on November 5, 1943. Throughout that entire Friday, Edith and Randolph read it aloud in the library. That night, in her room, she reviewed it again, word by word. On the following day, Randolph reread it with Edith's requested changes— "fly specks," as Baker called them. If these minor changes were honored, Edith said, she would have no further comments to make and "to use parliamentary phraseology, 'motion (picture) stands approved.'"[61]

Edith was also anxious about the choice of an actor to take the part of her husband. Geraldine Fitzgerald had been chosen from some twenty-five possible candidates to play Edith's part. While Miss Fitzgerald would not resemble Edith as Alexander Knox did Mr. Wilson, she was a fine actress, with unusual beauty, animation, and charm. Edith was glad to learn of her "alto ego," but she remained skeptical about the actor who would play Wilson. She had heard from a friend that Mr. Knox was nothing like Woodrow in appearance.

When the film, on which Darryl Zanuck was said to have staked his reputation and more than $5 million of his fortune, was given its London premiere, Baker was elated. "It is the beginning of the march around the world," he wrote Edith on January 9, 1945.[62] The winner of five Oscars, but a box office disaster, it was not immune to criticism or to observations such as that of the *New York Post*: "A lot of us are too young to remember the fight between Wilson and the isolationist Senators. But those who are too young to remember Wilson are young enough to be fighting in Guam and Brittany. The history of Wilson's failure has been the history of their lives . . ."[63]

The last letters between Ray Baker and Edith Wilson, in January 1945, were most cordial, and on his part quite chivalrous. Ray Baker invited Edith Wilson's ideas for the foreword of a new printing of *Woodrow Wilson, Life and Letters*, and she acknowledged his overtures almost flirtatiously: "You are a very subtle flatterer to ask a novice such as I to help you, a master author." Baker wrote back, "What a good and prompt collaborator you are." Baker's reference to their mutual involvement was not a casual compliment but rather an accurate description of their financial agreement, revealed in response to queries from the trust officer of the First National Bank of Amherst, Massachusetts, following Ray Baker's death in 1946, at the age of seventy-six, of a severe heart attack. Attesting to her financial acumen (by restricting the use of Wilson's papers she had actually profited personally), Edith wrote, "The arrangement between Mr. Ray Stannard Baker and me was an equal division of all royalties received from the publication of *Woodrow Wilson, Life and Letters*. The method Baker followed was to deposit the checks received from the publishers, and then send me his [check] back for my half, together with the statements of sales sent him by the publishers. After checking the amounts, I returned the statements for his files."[64]

As friends and family died—her brother Rolfe in 1936, her sister Bertha the next year, and Cary Grayson the next—Edith suffered her gravest loss with the demise of her unfailingly loyal brother Randolph in 1951. The mainstay of her household during her extended stays abroad, her occasional escort and traveling companion, Randolph was the recipient of many of her detailed letters of instruction, gossip, and messages, to which he sometimes responded in code and acted on, when required, faithfully and with initiative. Although Edith's own faltering health brought an end to her grand tours, she was always alert for opportunities to enhance the reputation of Woodrow Wilson. She deserved credit for the joint resolution of Congress to establish the Woodrow Wilson

Centennial Celebration Commission in 1956,[65] and in April of that year, she negotiated the landmark status of the S Street house with the National Trust, as a permanent memorial to her husband. In the fall of 1958, she finally sanctioned the official transfer of the Wilson papers to the Library of Congress.

Author and film heroine as she had become, Edith was respected as a former first lady. Innumerable White House events attended by her included the Roosevelts' festivities for Queen Elizabeth and King George in June 1939, and in response to a warm invitation from Mamie Eisenhower, the lawn party held for wounded and disabled servicemen in 1953. John Kennedy sent her a brief note on U.S. Senate stationery on December 28, 1959, to "solicit any thoughts you might have. I appreciate your comments and suggestions and would be very grateful for your support."[66] Completely won over, Edith sat up all night to learn the results of Kennedy's run for president and found his election in November 1960 "thrilling." She also thought Mrs. Kennedy would be a great asset to her husband "as she is so cultivated and charming."[67] Her relations with Vice President Nixon were another matter. When her biographer Alden Hatch drove up to S Street with a Nixon sticker on his car, Edith told him, "Don't ever park in front of my house with that thing on your car again."[68]

In her midseventies Edith suffered from high blood pressure and swelling in the legs and was under such emotional strain, according to a note in her files, that it was recommended that someone sleep in the room with her. Ten years later, her niece Elizabeth Boyd was living with her, as was a young and pleasant secretary and companion, Mrs. Margaret Cherrix Brown. The condition of her sister Gertrude Galt, suffering at age ninety from recurring heart attacks, was a concern to Edith. Herself plagued by illnesses, Edith was fundamentally a resilient woman and seemed, at least to a friend, to acquire new life after surgery.[69] Ten days out of the hospital, she lunched at the home of her former secretary Edith Benham Helm and—being the bridge addict she was—stayed to play with her cronies.

One woman talked of sad memories of her broken friendship with Edith Wilson. There were several such ruptures with friends to whom she had been close. Margaret Wilson, in dire financial difficulty due to a failed enterprise, turned to Joe Tumulty for help: in "very quietly and confidentially" investigating her legal claims on her father's estate, her relationship with her stepmother had become severely strained.[70] Edith

Epilogue

Stricken with a respiratory ailment on Thanksgiving night, 1961, Edith Wilson died one month later, at the age of eighty-nine. Two nieces were at her bedside. On that day, December 29, which was the day after the 105th anniversary of her husband's birth, she was to have dedicated a new bridge, named the Woodrow Wilson, over the Potomac River. The funeral service for Edith was conducted by the Reverend Francis B. Sayre Jr., Woodrow Wilson's grandson and dean of the Washington Cathedral, in collaboration with the pastor of Edith Wilson's St. Margaret's Church. Sayre was almost alone in representing the president's family, Edith having outlived two of her stepdaughters. Sayre's mother, Jessie Wilson Sayre, had died on January 16, 1933. His aunt Margaret Woodrow Wilson—secretary in the last decade of her life to the Indian thinker Sri Aurobindo—had died in Pondicherry, India, in 1944. Aunt Eleanor Wilson McAdoo, who had divorced her husband in 1934, died in 1967.

The *New York Times* obituary noted that Edith Wilson's astute guardianship and care of the twenty-eighth president had caused "so much stir" in official circles. Invoking her version of her husband's illness, the paper reported Edith's account of her consultation with her husband's physicians: when she'd asked if Woodrow Wilson should hand over the reins of government to Vice President Marshall, she was assured of her husband's recovery, if he could be protected from all forms of agitation. The *Times* commented that the president's wife "was regarded in almost as many lights as there were shades of contemporary political opinion." Some thought her the best of all possible wives. Moderate critics had suggested that she carried her fierce protection of her husband too far. "There was no lack of opinions."

Forty years after the death of Edith Bolling Galt Wilson, opinions continue to proliferate, ever more varied, about the role of this Virginian who is regularly referred to as the first woman president of the United States. During Woodrow Wilson's illness, his wife had at times usurped, and more generally shared his position. Edith clearly set herself to win over some of her era's most prominent male figures—physicians, politicians, and journalists, as well as successive generations of historians—

had fallen out with the Hamlins, her fond hosts at Mattapoisett, Massachusetts. There had been a long hiatus in her relations with Edith Benham Helm. Helen Bones's feisty account of their break was more rueful than sentimental: when Arthur Walworth was researching his Pulitzer prize–winning biography of Wilson, Bones advised the historian that Edith Wilson was sensitive about references to the president's first marriage. Bones also warned the author that Edith might insult him, but if she took a fancy to him, she could be utterly charming. Unfortunately, he would have to look to others for an introduction: "Edith Bolling Wilson and I never came to blows," Bones explained, "but she stopped liking me and I certainly stopped liking her toward the last."[71]

In October 1960, Mrs. Wilson declined to attend a meeting at Staunton as "politically unwise" because the Republican president Eisenhower was to be present. In January 1961, at age eighty-eight, as she stood on the reviewing stand at President Kennedy's inauguration, former president Harry S. Truman kissed her on the cheek. That October, at the White House, white-haired but clear-eyed, she sat beside a president less than half her age as John F. Kennedy signed into law the bill establishing the Woodrow Wilson Memorial Commission. A month later President Kennedy named her as one of the trustees of the worldwide Freedom from Hunger campaign.[72]

Edith Helm would mention that, in her younger days, Mrs. Wilson was inclined to what might be called rages. She thought that Edith was not well advised by Randolph, who had many prejudices and seemed to dislike people who were close to his sister. Mrs. Helm was convinced that Edith often repented the loss of friends.[73] In her last months, Edith Wilson saw her former secretary quite frequently. Though she found Mrs. Wilson "a wreck," Mrs. Helm writes poignantly of being glad of the happy memory of "sitting opposite her . . . in the library on S Street and having her hold my hand in hers."[74]

with her representation of wifeliness throughout her husband's last years. At the same time, she was a formidable presence who could bind two reputable doctors to secrecy concerning Woodrow Wilson's paralysis. As we consider the stakes, of peace and war, we must wonder at her persistence in the sustained inventions that were consequential for all the world and at her readiness to leave a distorted record of the two closing years of the Wilson presidency. In recently recovered documents, the original diagnosis of Wilson's physicians confirms the rumors of the time—that the president of the United States was, in the last years of his tenure, physically unfit for office.[1]

Historians have been lenient, attributing the extraordinary lapses in Edith's "phenomenal" memory to amnesia. Even so, they concede that she made two decisions with incalculable political implications—that there should be no disclosure of Wilson's true condition and that Wilson should remain at the White House until the end of his term. Some writers still insist that they have found no evidence that Edith Wilson attempted to direct the government of the United States or ever acted other than as Wilson's amanuensis—even while acknowledging that others had to think and act for a stricken president who was virtually isolated and uninformed, and that almost all of Wilson's correspondence and public statements during that period were composed on his behalf. Other commentators seek to perpetuate Edith's exaltation of Wilson at the expense of one or more of his colleagues—inevitably, Edward Mandell House, Robert Lansing, and Joseph Patrick Tumulty—and persist in darkening the role of the president's arch rival, Senator Henry Cabot Lodge. Outliving all of these men, Edith might have expected to enjoy the last word. However, Colonel House's opinion was made public posthumously, in the *New York Times*, July 28, 1963, when Yale's retiring president, Charles Seymour, revealed the content of a conversation that had, at House's request, been held secret for twenty-five years. The rift that developed between President Woodrow Wilson and Colonel Edward M. House was, in his judgment, largely due "to the President's second wife."

It has been written that Edith Wilson, "in her quiet, ignorant, misguided way did much damage at Paris, and even more at Washington,"[2] where Wilson, disabled and isolated, rendered the Senate's ratification of the League impossible through his absolute refusal to compromise on what the British economist John Maynard Keynes regarded as the "disastrous blots" on the Covenant.[3] In that hour, when Colonel House's talents for conciliation were supremely required, his efforts were frustrated by the first lady. One wonders today at her disregard of that counsel; Clemenceau was only one of many European leaders who lauded the "supercivilized" Texan "who sees everything, who understands everything," and whose "keen, enlightened intelligence" was of "such assistance."[4]

One also wonders how Wilson's first wife, Ellen Axson Wilson, an educated, thoughtful, and idealistic woman, might have reacted the October night of her husband's stroke. We cannot imagine that Ellen, tactful but principled, and with a "very judicial . . . rather critical mind,"[5] would have distorted the physicians' diagnosis and deceived or defamed her husband's staff and colleagues. Edith, on the other hand, willfully betrayed the public interest when she made her implicit case against Marshall as Wilson's logical successor.

Wilson's absolute need for compliance and devotion now recoiled fatefully upon him and on history. At the time of his first marriage, he had acknowledged to Ellen—though without misgiving—his imperative requirements of uncritical adherence and unquestioning love. We have seen how Ellen, emerging from her first timid adulation and observing the dangers of her husband's inflexibility, discreetly sought to modify these ill effects, particularly after Wilson attained a position of great influence and power. Edith, on the contrary, had encouraged the president in his categorical positions—to a degree that became, at times, sheer assertiveness, arousing Wilson's own resistance. As infirmity overcame him, the power to claim obedience, in the name of loyalty, passed to her, and unreflectively, she exerted it.

It is conceivable that Wilson, with a more farsighted spouse, might have been prevailed upon to withdraw in favor of sixty-six-year-old Vice President Marshall. An able, self-deprecating man who presided over the Senate with discretion, and a strong advocate for the League of Nations, Marshall might well have accepted a modified Senate version of the Treaty of Versailles and the United States would then have participated in the League.[6] The reality is that Woodrow Wilson remained in office, and that the League, lacking American participation, was born in weakness and effectively disintegrated in 1935, unable to halt Italy's invasion of Ethiopia. In 1945, the League of Nations metamorphosed into the United Nations. The new charter was, admittedly, as imperfect as the old; the great powers assured their own hegemony, but the rationale was, at least in principle, more liberal, and compromises were required of many nations. It was, in 1945, as it had been in 1920: a matter of getting "half a loaf or no bread."[7]

* * *

Wilson, naive participant in the vast transformation of the face of Central and Eastern Europe, remains admired, by many, as a messiah, a prophet, and even as "the old warrior." And indeed, for his determined pursuit of that elusive humanitarian ideal of the ages, the building of an enduring peace, he was awarded the Nobel Peace Prize. His detractors, however, wonder whether the nurturing of one great idea is sufficient to warrant the ennoblement of Woodrow Wilson, whose own intransigence undermined the very purpose of his labors. While Wilson was capable of delivering sermons on the Fourteen Points, John Maynard Keynes suggested that he was untutored in the crucial issues, that the perils of the future lay not in frontiers or sovereignties but in finance and economics, in food, coal, and transport. Given the "extraordinary story of hopes, ideals, weaknesses, failures, and disappointments, of which the president has been the eponymous hero," Keynes asked, "Was Hamlet mad or feigning; was the President sick or cunning?"[8]

Henry Cabot Lodge had little patience for what he called "idealism on the loose"; although he admired practical idealists who succeeded in converting ideals into realities. It was his belief that these practical idealists had, in addition to a keen sense of existing conditions, "a full and abiding comprehension of their own limitations and shortcomings which breeds both wisdom and tolerance." Lodge cited Lincoln as a leader who succeeded as few men have done in putting his ideals into practice by recognizing the world as it is and proceeding accordingly. Thus Lincoln was able to replace "what is by what ought to be."[9] This required a measure of selflessness, a mature integrity that Wilson could appreciate but could not command.

The essential task of creative statesmanship, Keynes has written, is to understand and work with "the grain of the times." At critical intervals finding a rational path through the turbulent years of educational, industrial, and social revolution, Wilson's first wife, Ellen, and Wilson's intimate and trusted counselor Colonel House had acted—as did Wilson's true friends at Princeton earlier in his career—with tact to "save Woodrow from himself," and to encourage him to control his declamatory and self-approving zeal.

During the supreme challenge to his leadership in 1919, the president had by his side neither Ellen Wilson nor Edward House but a companion unqualified to reconcile him to the necessity of wooing the "simian public" or of suffering fools patiently. Edith fatally divided her husband from House, who, in his intelligent devotion to the best interest of his country, might have helped Wilson save the treaty on which Wilson had staked his career and his stature, and unfortunately, his egotism.

To a skeptical poet at home, Wilson was a "chilly looking college professor"[10] who, despite his legislative achievements—his introduction of an income tax, reorganization of banking institutions, antitrust legislation—failed in his promise to be president of all the people. An ingrained Southerner, Wilson tolerated discrimination against blacks.[11] His support for women's suffrage was belated and tenuous. He failed to comprehend, at the onset of his illness, the evil and hysteria of the "Red Menace" deportations, which left their legacy on the dark side of America's history.

Edith Wilson's long life leaves, at its close, no sense of completion. On her vigorous temperament, introspection never cast its ripening light. She had been at the center of momentous events to which she brought, with much energy and assertive courage, a provincial gaze and little humility. Her preeminence in the president's life was little directed at the nurturing of his larger qualities and too often fostered pettiness and indignation. Her impassioned devotion to Woodrow Wilson and the self-denying care she gave throughout his final years are inevitably clouded in the historian's eye by the imposture of which Mrs. Wilson was the chief author and with a sense of the influence wielded over great decisions by a woman of narrow views and formidable determination. In public life, we continue to crave exemplars and shrink from the realities of human imperfection. The Wilsons' story, with its shrouded conclusion, recalls to us the underlying drama of private character in all human existence: "Between the idea / And the reality / Between the motion / And the act / Falls the shadow"—we may be wiser for the truth of their tragedy.[12]

Notes

In the case of the persons, libraries, or documents that I name with some frequency in the end notes, I have used abbreviated references as follows:

Stockton Axson: SA
Ray Stannard Baker: RSB
Bernard Mannes Baruch: BMB
John Randolph Bolling: JRB
Cary Travers Grayson: CTG
Irwin Hood Hoover: IHH
Edward Mandell House: EMH
Robert Lansing: RL
Henry Cabot Lodge: HCL
Mary Allen Hulbert Peck: MAH
Theodore Roosevelt: TR
Joseph P. Tumulty: JPT
Arthur C. Walworth: ACW
Edith Bolling Galt Wilson: EBG, EBW
Ellen Axson Wilson: EAW
Woodrow Wilson: WW

Harvard University Library, Houghton Library: HL
Library of Congress, Manuscript Division: LC
New York Times: NYT
Princeton University Library: PL
Yale University, Manuscripts and Archives: YL

The Papers of Edith Bolling Galt Wilson, deposited with and without the Galt name, in the Library of Congress: EBGW.
The Papers of Woodrow Wilson, sixty-nine volumes published by Princeton University Press: *PWW*
The Papers of Woodrow Wilson, unpublished, on microfilm, held by the Library of Congress: WWP

PREFACE

1. EBW, *My Memoir*, 289, 286.
2. Ibid., 288.
3. Winston S. Churchill, *The Aftermath*, 118–19.
4. "The President Becomes Normal," *Harvey's Weekly*, February 21, 1920, vol. 3.
5. August Heckscher, *Woodrow Wilson*, 728.
6. *PWW*, 64: ix.
7. Ibid.
8. Arthur S. Link to author, January 8, 1994.
9. *PWW*, 64:ix.
10. Arthur S. Link, *Washington Post*, November 25, 1990.
11. Frederick Lewis Allen, *Only Yesterday*, 34.
12. Caroline Thomas Hamsburger, *Mark Twain at Your Fingertips*.

1. "A GREAT CAPACITY FOR LOVING THE GENTLE SEX"

1. EMH to WW, May 29, 1914, Charles Seymour, *Intimate Papers of Colonel House,* 1:248.
2. Ibid.
3. Winston Churchill to Clementine Churchill, July 28, 1914, Mary Soames, ed., *Winston and Clementine.*
4. "The phrase . . . was on every lip," Winston Churchill, *The Gathering Storm,* 3.
5. Description, Grey of Fallodon, *Twenty-Five Years,* 20. George Macaulay Trevelyan, *Grey of Fallodon,* vi; HCL to Moreton Frewen, September 10, 1919, Papers of Moreton Frewen, cont. 36, LC.
6. *NYT,* August 4, 1914; RSB, *Woodrow Wilson,* 5:3.
7. Probably Burton Stevenson, *Poems of American History* (Boston and New York: Houghton Mifflin, 1908).
8. Memorandum of conversations with Dr. Stockton Axson on February 8, 10, 11, 1925, and August 28, 1931, RSB Papers, reel 70.
9. Eleanor Wilson McAdoo, *The Woodrow Wilsons,* 13, 28.
10. Randolph Axson wrote to his niece Ellen, June 12, 1883, *PWW,* "[t]he place and manner" of her father's death are inexpressibly sad: but you cannot doubt his 'acceptance in the Beloved.' It was a dark cloud which had settled upon his reason." Record of his admission to the Central State Hospital, Milledgeville, Georgia, January 13, 1884, in the Georgia State Archives also suggests suicide: "Lunatic from Chatham Co. Ga. . . . Duration of insanity about four weeks . . . Has always been a very nervous man, easily excited. Lost his wife about a year ago, which seemed to grieve him a great deal. Slight suicidal tendency. Is disposed to be violent occasionally. Has been in the habit of taking chloral at night." Dr. Edwin A. Weinstein, *Woodrow Wilson: A Medical and Psychological Biography* 67; n. 33, 35.
11. WW to EAW, October 11, 1883, RSB Papers, reel 69. While at law school, determined to find a "lady-love if possible," Wilson again proposed to his cousin Harriet Woodrow, a student at Augusta Female Seminary, who had rejected him two years earlier. But his social life in Atlanta was not entirely arid. He frequented the W. D. Grant mansion at the corner of Peachtree and Pine Streets, "where the charming Sara Frances lived" and also spent nights reading aloud with Katie Mayrant at the home of her aunt, where Wilson was a boarder. *Atlanta Constitution,* February 26, 1956, quoted by George C. Osborn, "Woodrow Wilson as a Young Lawyer, 1882–1883," *Georgia Historical Quarterly* 41, no. 2 (June 1957): 126–42. Courtesy Patricia O'Toole.
12. WW to EAW, December 22, 1883, RSB Papers, reel 69.
13. SA Papers, PL.
14. ACW to author, October 5, 1999; RSB, *Woodrow Wilson, Life and Letters,* 1:20–21.
15. WW to EAW, April 20, 1888, RSB Papers, reel 77.
16. Isabella Jordan to RSB, June 10, 1927, RSB Papers, reel 77.
17. WW to EAW, April 19, 1888, RSB Papers, reel 69.
18. Edwin A. Weinstein, James William Anderson, and Arthur S. Link, "Woodrow Wilson's Political Personality: A Reappraisal," 593.
19. RSB, *Woodrow Wilson,* 1:131.
20. WW to EAW, December 7, 1884, RSB Papers, reel 69.
21. Ibid.
22. WW to EAW, April 22, 1884, RSB Papers, reel 69.

23. WW to EAW, November 6, 1883, RSB Papers, reel 69.

24. Thomas W. Wilson, "Cabinet Government in the United States," *International Review,* August 1879.

25. *New Princeton Review,* March 1887.

26. *Political Science Quarterly,* June 1887.

27. WW to EAW, February 15, 1885, RSB Papers, cont. 69.

28. Edwin A. Weinstein, "Woodrow Wilson's Neurological Illness," 330.

29. Signed X, *The Princetonian,* June 7, 1877, 42; RSB, *Woodrow Wilson,* 1:93 n. 1.

30. Ibid.

31. Mary W. Hoyt to RSB, RSB, *Woodrow Wilson,* 1:104 n. 3.

32. WW to R. Heath Dabney, May 31, 1881, RSB, *Woodrow Wilson,* 1:129.

33. WW to EAW, February 27, 1885, RSB Papers, cont. 69.

34. WW to EAW, November 8, 1884, RSB, *Woodrow Wilson,* 1:236.

35. Ibid., 1:238–39; Frances Wright Saunders, *Ellen Axson Wilson,* 62.

36. *PWW,* April 13, 1885, 4:484–85; April 15, 1885, 4:488; April 16, 1885, 4:494.

2. "AMONG THE FOREMOST THINKERS OF HIS AGE"

1. RSB, *Woodrow Wilson, Life and Letters,* 1:252.

2. WW to EAW, March 1, 1885.

3. Ibid.

4. EAW to WW, May 18, 1886, RSB Papers, reel 69.

5. EAW to WW, November 22, 1884, RSB Papers, reel 69.

6. EAW to WW, August 27, 1902, RSB, *Woodrow Wilson,* 2:67.

7. WW to R. Heath Dabney, November 7, 1886, RSB, *Woodrow Wilson,* 2:276–78.

8. Arthur S. Link, *Wilson: The Road to the White House,* 21.

9. WW to Robert Bridges, August 26, 1888, RSB, *Woodrow Wilson,* 1:295 n. 2.

10. *PWW,* 1:172.

11. WW to Joseph Ruggles Wilson, March 20, 1890, and WW to Robert Bridges, February 13, 1890, Arthur C. Walworth, *Woodrow Wilson,* 1:53 n. 2.

12. The family lived at 48 Stedman Street, called Library Place, and six years later the Wilsons built a home on an adjacent lot bordered by meadows and looking out to distant hills. Wilson drew the plans for the house, in Norman style, of fieldstone and timber-patterned stucco, at 50 Library Place, while Ellen created a three-dimension model in clay to settle a long discussion about the line of the roof. She bought a head of Hermes for the mantel of the fireplace in the hall. Representations of the Apollo Belvedere and the Winged Victory stood on adjacent pedestals. Wilson's impeccably orderly study was hung with portraits of men he admired: Washington, Webster, Gladstone, Bagehot, and Edmund Burke, all drawn in crayon by Ellen.

13. EAW to WW, April 3, 1892, RSB Papers, reel 69.

14. EAW to WW, June 29, 1892, RSB Papers, reel 69.

15. EAW to WW, February 23, 1896, RSB Papers, reel 69.

16. Link, *Wilson,* p. 31.

17. RSB, *Woodrow Wilson,* 2:104.

18. Edwin A. Weinstein, James William Anderson, and Arthur S. Link, "Woodrow Wilson's Political Personality: A Reappraisal," 588.

19. WW to EAW, March 20, 1884, RSB Papers, reel 69.

20. Edwin A . Weinstein, "Woodrow Wilson's Neurological Illness," 325–51.

21. EAW to WW, June 15, 1896, RSB Papers, reel 69.

22. Eleanor Wilson McAdoo, *The Woodrow Wilsons.*

23. WW to EAW, August 10, 1902, RSB, *Woodrow Wilson*, 2:138.

24. EAW to Florence S. Hoyt, June 28, 1902, RSB Papers, reel 65.

25. *PWW*, 1:282–83; RSB, *Woodrow Wilson*, 2:35.

26. RSB, *Woodrow Wilson*, 2:139.

27. Ibid., 141.

28. EAW to Florence Hoyt, RSB Papers, reel 65.

29. Weinstein, "Woodrow Wilson's Neurological Illness," 334.

30. RSB, *Woodrow Wilson*, 2:215–16.

31. Ibid., 2:147.

32. Ibid., 2:183.

33. Ibid., 326.

34. Eleanor Wilson McAdoo, *The Woodrow Wilsons*, 48.

35. WW to Hibben, September 15, 1899, memoir of a conversation with President Hibben of Princeton, June 18, 1925, RSB Papers, reel 77, LC.

36. Ellen claimed that Wilson's subsequent illness was brought on by grief and disappointment over Hibben's alleged betrayal. Congratulating Hibben on his eventual accession to the presidency of Princeton in 1912, Ellen wrote to their once beloved neighbor, friend, and colleague, "You are ideally fitted for what is expected of you since conditions which to others would be a burden too grievous to be borne will be to one of your temperament a source of unalloyed pleasure." EAW to John Hibben, February 10, 1912, *PWW*, 24:149–50.

37. WW to MAH, November 2, 1908, Woodrow Wilson Collection II, Special Correspondence, MAH Papers, box 33, folder 3.

38. WW to MAH, February 28, 1910, MAH Papers, box 33, folder 4.

39. Ibid.

40. Ibid.

41. Ibid.

42. RSB, *Woodrow Wilson*, 2: 195–96; 3:39.

43. *PWW*, 2:100.

44. Ibid.

45. Samuel Eliot Morison, *The Oxford History of the American People*, 839.

46. McAdoo, *Woodrow Wilsons*, 120.

47. RSB, *Woodrow Wilson*, 3:82.

3. "Turn a corner and meet your fate"

1. RSB, *Woodrow Wilson, Life and Letters*, 3:218.

2. JPT quotation, Stockton Axson Papers, PL.

3. WW to MAH, March 5, 1911, Woodrow Wilson Collection II, Special Collection, MAH Papers, box 33, folder 6.

4. EAW to George Harvey, November 12, 1910, William G. McAdoo Papers, box 8.

5. EAW to Judge Robert Ewing, January 12, 1912, McAdoo Papers, box 8.

6. Ibid.

7. WW to MAH, January 3, 1911, MAH Papers, box 33, folder 5.

8. WW to MAH, January 10, 1911, MAH Papers, box 33, folder 5.

9. Ibid.

10. RSB, *Woodrow Wilson*, 3:203, 205, 209.

11. Ibid., 3:210.

12. Eleanor Wilson McAdoo, *The Woodrow Wilsons*, 114.

13. WW to MAH, July 6, 1912, August 25, 1912, MAH Papers, box 33, folder 7, PL.

14. RSB, *Woodrow Wilson,* 3:394.

15. Ernest Samuels, *Henry Adams,* 442.

16. Immediately after graduation from medical school he became an intern at Columbia Hospital, Washington, D.C., and did additional postgraduate work with the famed Dr. William Osler at Johns Hopkins, Baltimore. He served on the staff of the Naval Medical School Hospital and aboard the *Mayflower* and from December 1912 until February 1921 as aide to the president of the United States at the White House. He retired in 1928 from the Medical Corps of the navy. Thereafter he had a flourishing medical practice in downtown Washington with Dr. Walter Bloedorn. He served as chairman for the American National Red Cross from 1935 until his death on February 15, 1938. Navy Historical Center, Navy Office of Information; Cary T. Grayson Jr. to author, June 30, 1999.

17. McAdoo, *Woodrow Wilsons,* 205.

18. Ellen Maury Slayden, *Washington Wife,* 199–200.

19. Jonathan Daniels, *The End of Innocence,* 86.

20. Francis B. Sayre to RSB, RSB Papers, reel 82.

21. WW to MAH, July 27, 1913, MAH Papers, box 33, folder 8, PL.

22. WW to MAH, March 16, 1913, MAH Papers, box 33, folder 8.

23. WW to MAH, July 27, 1913, MAH Papers, box 33, folder 8.

24. WW to MAH, October 12, 1913, MAH Papers, box 33, folder 8.

25. WW to MAH, June 7, 1914, MAH Papers, box 33, folder 8.

26. Statement of Dr. Cary T. Grayson, WW Papers of Others, Charles L. Swem, PL.

27. EAW to Margaret Wilson, undated, William G. McAdoo Papers, box 8, LC.

28. Diagnosis of EAW: Edwin A. Weinstein, "Woodrow Wilson's Neurological Illness," 338.

29. WW to MAH, August 2, 1914, MAH Papers, box 33, folder 8.

30. Papers of Isabella Hagner; RSB, *Woodrow Wilson,* 4:467–68.

31. William Howard Taft to Mabel Boardman, August 10, 1914, Henry F. Pringle, *The Life and Times of William Howard Taft,* 2:872, n. 9.

32. CTG to EBG, August 15, 1914, EBGW Papers, box 19.

33. CTG to EBG, August 5, 1914, EBGW Papers, box 19.

34. CTG to EBG, September 21, 1914, EBGW Papers, box 19.

35. Helen Bones to ACW, April 21, 1950, ACW Papers, YL

36. Francis B. Sayre to RSB, August 5, 1931, RSB Papers, reel 82; Helen Bones to ACW, January 26, 1950, ACW Papers, YL.

37. WW to MAH, September 20, 1914, MAH Papers, box 33, folder 8.

38. WW to Nancy Saunders Toy, November 9, 1914, *PWW,* vol. 31.

39. Worth, the Paris couturier, is repeatedly mentioned, including Diary, July 27, 1907, Papers of EBGW, box 1, and *My Memoir,* 13, 56. Charles Frederick Worth, an Englishman by birth, is credited with officially founding the Paris couturier in 1858. Though especially celebrated for the elaborate ballgowns worn by royalty in their portraits by Winterhalter, Worth's salon came to be a requisite stop for every affluent American tourist of the era.

40. Edith often referred to them simply as "Beauty," as she does in her Diary, July 22, 1907, EBGW Papers, box 1; she mentions "blood red roses," June 9, 1915, EBW to WW, EBGW Papers. Also, Edwin Tribble, ed., *President in Love,* 30.

41. TR quoted, *American History Illustrated,* 6 (June 22, 1971): 46; WW to EA(W), October 11, 1883, RSB Papers, reel 69.

42. IHH Papers, cont. 5–6, LC.

43. EBW, *My Memoir*, 53–56.
44. Ibid.

4. "Anyone can do anything they try to"

1. IHH Papers, cont. 5–6, LC.
2. Ibid.
3. EBG to Annie (Mrs. Rolfe) Bolling, March 23, 1915, EBGW Papers, series 20, box 1.
4. IHH Papers, cont. 6, undated.
5. WW to EBG, April 30, 1915, EBGW Papers, box 1.
6. WW to EBG, May 6, 1915, EBGW Papers, box 1.
7. WW to EBG, June 5, 1915, EBGW Papers, box 1.
8. WW to EAW, October 2, 1882, RSB Papers, reel 69.
9. IHH Papers, cont. 6.
10. EBW, *My Memoir*, 60.
11. EBG to WW, May 4, 1915, EBGW Papers, box 1.
12. EBG to WW, May 10, 1915, EBGW Papers, box 1.
13. EBG to WW, May 11, 1915, EBGW Papers, box 1.
14. EBW, *My Memoir*, 54–55.
15. Ibid., 58.
16. EBG to WW, May 11, 1915, EBGW Papers, box 1.
17. EBW, *My Memoir*, 1.
18. "The Wilson Administration Commencing March 4, 1913," Isabella Hagner James Papers, Office of the Curator, the White House.
19. Edith enjoyed recalling her descent from a rallying figure of early America's history, the legendary Indian woman Pocahontas, King Powhatan's daughter, who, seven generations earlier, had married the Oxford-educated scholar John Rolfe, and whose grandchild Jane had married the prosperous Colonel Robert Bolling. Edith could claim the third president of the United States as brother-in-law to her great-great-grandfather John Bolling, who had married Thomas Jefferson's sister, Martha. Proud of her Indian forebear, Edith was silent about the long line of bewigged Bollings who had, since their arrival in Virginia in October 1660, amassed huge tracts of land and served honorably as commanders of militia, as justices of the peace, and as members of the House of Burgesses. Edith was possibly unaware that the Bolling name was recorded in the Domesday Book—the survey of landowners dating back to William the Conqueror. She may not have known of the existence of Bolling Hall, the family's massive, towered country seat since the time of Edward IV, near Bradford, in Yorkshire, England. Nor, perhaps, had she read Robert Bolling's *Memoir of a Portion of the Bolling Family in England and Virginia*, written first in French and published in English in Richmond, Virginia, in 1868.
20. Richard Tillinghast, *Sewanee in Ruins* in *Our Flag Was Still There* (Middletown, Conn.: Wesleyan University Press, 1984), 24.
21. Archibald Bolling died in 1860, one year before the first shot of the Civil War was fired at Fort Sumter. The battle of Lynchburg was fought a few miles from Rose Cottage on June 17 and 18, 1864. General Robert E. Lee surrendered his Confederate forces at nearby Appomattox on April 9, 1865. In July 1873, Bolling's widow, Ann E., would sell the property on Wigginton Road, less a quarter acre for a family burial ground, for $3,000 "in hand paid." Deed dated July 28, 1873, Wythe County Court.
22. EBW, *My Memoir*, 1.

23. "Appraiser's List of the personal Estate of Dr. A. Bolling." Will Book, Bedford County, Va., p. 28.
24. EBW, *My Memoir*, 12.
25. *Wytheville Times*, July 9, 1859; February 18, 1860.
26. Wythe County, Va., Clerk's Office.
27. EBW, *My Memoir*, 3.
28. *Southwest Virginia Enterprise*, July 29, 1874.
29. Wytheville was named for George Wythe, revered law professor and the first Virginian to sign the Declaration of Independence.
30. EBW, *My Memoir*, 10.
31. "Edith Bolling lived next door to Governor and Mrs. E. Lee Trinkle. Helen Trinkle talked a lot about Edith and her sad and poor early life. Edith's mother took in boarders as well as cooking, cleaning, etc., for the extended family. In the South at that time this was not unusual." Betty Francis Freeman to the author, June 28, 1989, Roanoke, Va. And see *My Memoir*, 21: "two paternal aunts, a cousin" probably includes Sallie Bolling's half sister, Lizzie Logwood, who lived with the Bollings until her marriage to General James G. Field, and Mary Jefferson Bolling Teusler and her son, Rudolph Jr.
32. Dr. W. R. Chitwood, September 12 and November 7, 1989, to author.
33. Puzzling over why the family appeared so impoverished, Betty Francis Freeman suggests that Judge Bolling's legal work for the Norfolk & Western should have been profitable. His appointment to the University of Virginia Board of Visitors, on the other hand, entailing financial donations, might have caused hardship. If Judge Bolling "built a facade of prominence," she adds, "this was not unusual at that time." Freeman to author, June 28, 1989.
34. EBW, *My Memoir*, 4, 5; Archibald Bolling to Ann Bolling, December 7, 1914, EBGW Papers, box 1.
35. Alden Hatch Papers, University of Florida Library.
36. EBW to Randolph Bolling, September 8, 1913, EBGW Papers, box 1.
37. E. David Cronin, ed., *The Cabinet Diaries of Josephus Daniels, 1913–1921*, 267.
38. EBW, *My Memoir*, 21.
39. EBG to WW, August 12, 1915, EBGW Papers, box 1.
40. EBW, *My Memoir*, 13.
41. Ibid.
42. Virginius Dabney, *Richmond: The Story of a City*, 230–31. Description based on photographs in the Valentine Museum, Richmond, Va.
43. EBG to WW, August 12, 1915, EBGW Papers.
44. WW to EBG, August 13, 1915, EBGW Papers.
45. EBW, *My Memoir*, 16.

5. "A NEW WORLD" FOR EDITH GALT

1. EBW, *My Memoir*, 13, 17.
2. EB to Norman Galt, undated, EBGW Papers, box 1.
3. Ibid.; Alden Hatch Papers, University of Florida Library.
4. Mrs. Wm. H. Bolling to "My Precious Children," September 23, 1903, EBGW Papers, box 1.
5. Wilmer Bolling to EBG, September 24, 1903, EBGW Papers, box 1.
6. Annie Bolling (Maury) to EBG, September 25, 1903, EBGW Papers, box 1.

7. Bertha Bolling to EBG, September 23, 1903; EBG to Mrs. Wm. H. Bolling, EBGW Papers, box 1.

8. Mrs. Wm. H. Bolling to EBG, September 28?, 1903, EBGW Papers, box 1.

9. My lengthy correspondence with various hospitals, a Washington agency, and calls to the Galt family cemetery in Georgetown have failed to produce any record of the specific birth date, name, or burial place of the baby born to Edith and Norman Galt.

10. Norman Galt to EBG, June 27, 1904, EBGW Papers, box 1.

11. Norman Galt to EBG, June 25, 1904, EBGW Papers, box 1.

12. EBG to Bertha Bolling, July 4, 1906, EBGW Papers, box 1.

13. EBG Diary, September 4, 1907, EBGW Papers, box 1.

14. Mrs. Wm. H. Bolling to EBG, July 1, 1906; EBG to Mrs. Bolling, February 18, 1907, EBGW Papers, box 1.

15. *Washington Star*, January 28, 1908, 2. According to the paper, Normal Galt had succeeded his uncle William Galt as a director of the Arlington Fire Insurance Company.

16. EBGW Papers, box 56.

17. EBW, *My Memoir*, 22–23.

18. Ibid., p. 46.

19. EBG to "Dersia," August 23, 1913, EBGW Papers, box 1.

20. EBW, *My Memoir*, 55.

21. Herbert Biggs to Bertha Bolling, July 27, 1911, EBGW Papers, box 1.

22. Warren Van Slyke to EBG, July 25, 1911, EBGW Papers, box 34. One of the first attorneys to bring suit against Germany on behalf of relatives of passengers drowned in the sinking of the *Lusitania*, Warren Van Slyke served as a lieutenant commander in naval intelligence and after World War I was decorated with the naval Distinguished Service Medal and the French Legion of Honor. At the time of Edith's engagement to President Wilson he cordially congratulated the couple, reminding Edith that he must be numbered among the prophets who had forecast her wonderful future, "once the shadows were removed." He also ventured one more prophecy, that it would fall to President Wilson to establish "a permanent world people and to shape an international policy which will for all times prevent a repetition of those awful years." Warren Van Slyke, 1880 census for Kingston, Ulster County Genealogical Society, Hurley, N.Y.; obituary, *New York Herald Tribune*, April 8, 1925.

23. Papers of WW, supplement series 20, no date.

24. EBW to "Dearest Trio," September 21, no year, EBGW Papers, box 1.

6. "THERE IS SUCH A THING AS A MAN BEING TOO PROUD TO FIGHT"

1. IHH Papers, cont. 5–6, LC.

2. WW to EBG, May 27, 1915, EBGW Papers.

3. Ibid.

4. Ibid.

5. WW to EBG, June 9, 1915, EBGW Papers.

6. WW to EBG, June 18, 1915, EBGW Papers.

7. Ibid.

8. EBG to WW, June 18, 1915, EBGW Papers.

9. EBG to WW, June 10, 1915, EBGW Papers.

10. James Kerney, *The Political Education of Woodrow Wilson*, 459.

11. Arthur S. Link and William M. Leary, Jr., eds., *The Diplomacy of World Power: The United States, 1889–1920*, 115.

12. *Papers Relating to the Foreign Relations of the United States*, 1915, 121–23.

13. RSB and William E. Dodd, eds., *The Public Papers of Woodrow Wilson*, 3:287–288.

14. Ibid., 3:197–98.

15. Ibid., 3:299–300.

16. Ibid., 3:303–6.

17. Isabella Hagner James Papers, working notes for 1915: April 7, 10, 14, 19, 23, 27, 29, 30.

18. RSB, *Woodrow Wilson, Life and Letters*, 5:327.

19. EBG to WW, May 5 and 6, 1915, EBGW Papers.

20. Winston Churchill, *The World Crisis*, 348; Walter Hines Page to Arthur Page, *The Life and Letters of Walter Page*, 2:5.

21. Edwin Tribble, ed., *President in Love*, 17.

22. WW to EBG, May 9, 1915, EBGW Papers.

23. Address at Naturalization Ceremonies, May 10, 1915, *The Messages and Papers of Woodrow Wilson*, 1:117.

24. WW to EBG, 9 P.M., May 11, 1915, EBGW Papers.

25. Ibid.

26. "First note to Germany on sinking of the *Lusitania*," May 13, 1915, *Presidential Messages*, 1:239–43; WJB to WW, May 12, 1915, Mary Baird Bryan, *The Memoirs of William Jennings Bryan*, 399–400.

27. Bryan, *Memoirs of Bryan*, 395–96.

28. Ibid., 400–402.

29. WW to EBG, May 15, 1915, EBGW Papers.

30. EBW, *My Memoir*, 63.

31. EBG to Anne Stuart (Mrs. Rolfe) Bolling, May 16, 1915, EBGW Papers.

32. EBG to WW, May 24, 1915, EBGW Papers.

33. EBG to WW, May 27, 1915, EBGW Papers.

34. *Foreign Relations of the U.S.*, 1915, suppl., May 28, 1915, 419–21.

35. WW to EBG, May 28, 1915, EBGW Papers

36. WW to EBG, May 29, June 1, 1915, EBGW Papers.

37. EBG to WW, June 2, 1915; WW to EBG, June 3, 1915, EBGW Papers.

38. WW to EBG, June 3, 1915, EBGW Papers.

39. EBW to WW, June 7, 1915, EBGW Papers.

40. WW to EBG, June 8, 1915, EBGW Papers.

41. RSB, *Woodrow Wilson*, 5:320 n. 22.

42. *Department of State, Diplomatic Correspondence and Belligerent Governments*, 2:171–72; Samuel Flagg Bemis, ed., *American Secretaries of State and Their Legacy*, 56.

43. Samuel Flagg Bemis, ed., *American Secretaries of State*, 57.

44. Bryan to WW and WW to Bryan, June 8, 1915, *Memoirs of Bryan*, 406–7.

45. EBG to WW, June 9, 1915, EBGW Papers

46. WW to EBG, June 9, 1915, EBGW Papers.

47. WW to EBG, June 11, 1915, EBGW Papers.

48. EBG to WW, June 9, 1915, EBGW Papers.

49. WW to EBG, June 12, 1915, EBGW Papers.

50. EBG to WW, June 9, 1915, EBGW Papers.

51. WW to EBG, August 13, 1915, EBGW Papers.

7. THE PRESIDENT'S MOST TRUSTED ADVISER, COLONEL HOUSE

1. Patrick Devlin, *Too Proud to Fight*, 302.
2. WW to EBG, June 9, 1915, EBGW Papers.
3. David F. Houston, *Eight Years with Wilson's Cabinet*, 1:141.
4. Barbara Tuchman, *The Zimmerman Telegram*, 63, 172–73.
5. William McAdoo, *Crowded Years*, 339.
6. A. W. Lane and L. H. Wall, eds., *The Letters of Franklin K. Lane*, 175.
7. IHH Papers, cont. 5–6, LC.
8. Ibid.
9. Ibid., January 24, 1927, cont. 6–7.
10. Margaret L. Coit, *Mr. Baruch*, 95.
11. Ibid.
12. Ibid., 26–28.
13. John Dos Passos, *Mr. Wilson's War*, 158.
14. Edith Gittings Reid, *Woodrow Wilson*, p. 167.
15. Charles Seymour, *The Intimate Papers of Colonel House*, 1:6.
16. ACW to author.
17. EMH Diary, March 17, 1914, vol. 10.
18. Arthur D. Howden Smith, *The Real Colonel House*, 29.
19. House's Dutch ancestors—the original name was Huis—emigrated to England and then, after three hundred years, to America—to Texas, where House's father, Thomas William House, acquired sugar plantations and undeveloped lands and founded several banks. Asked about blockade-running during the Civil War, House wrote, "My Father did considerable running of the blockade out of Galveston but he used ships which he owned. One of these was the celebrated *Harriet Lane*, captured by the Confederate Government. They sold a half interest in the *Harriet Lane* to Father with the understanding that he should have the outgoing cargo consisting of cotton and they have the incoming cargo which consisted of munitions of war. There was considerable difficulty after the war about this ship since Father sold her in Havana at the close. Later he had to refund the price to the Federal Government." EMH to Arthur D. Howden Smith, March 20, 1932, WW Collection, Papers of Andre De Coppet, PL.
20. Seymour, *Intimate Papers*, 1, 40.
21. Ibid., 1:44.
22. Ibid., 1:45.
23. Conversation with Colonel House, week of October 13, 1930. George S. Viereck Papers, box 4, folder 2, YL.
24. Ibid.
25. Seymour, *Intimate Papers*, 1:247.
26. Ibid., 1:209.
27. Ibid.
28. WW to EMH, January 17, 1915, RSB Papers, reel 65.
29. Ibid.
30. EMH to WW, May 9, 1915, Seymour, *Intimate Papers*, 1:450.
31. WW to EMH, June 1, 1915, RSB Papers, reel 65.
32. WW to EMH, June 22, 1915, RSB Papers, reel 65.
33. EMH Diary, vol. 7, June 24, 1915.

34. Ibid.
35. Ibid., July 10, 1915.
36. EMH to WW, October 1, 1915, WWP, reel 72.

8. "FIT FOR COUNSEL AS ANY MAN"

1. IHH Papers.
2. Ibid.
3. WW to EBG, July 20, 1915, *PWW*, vol. 34.
4. Ibid.
5. WW to EBG, July 21, 1915, *PWW*, vol. 34.
6. Ibid.
7. EBG to WW, August 4, 1915, EBGW Papers.
8. WW to EBG, August 7, 1915, EBGW Papers.
9. WW to EBG, August 20, 1915, EBGW Papers.
10. WW to EBG, August 7, 1915, EBGW Papers.
11. EBG to WW, August 7, 1915, EBGW Papers.
12. EBW, *My Memoir*, 72.
13. WW to EBG, August 9, 1915, EBGW Papers.
14. Ibid.
15. EBG to WW, August 13, 1915, EBGW Papers.
16. WW to EBG, August 7, 1915, EBGW Papers.
17. Ibid.
18. Newspapers quoted in Edwin Tribble, ed., *President in Love,* 121. See also Charles Seymour, *Intimate Papers of Colonel House,* 1:223. The thirty-five-year-old dictatorship of Porfirio Diaz had been succeeded in 1911 by the reformist regime of Francisco Madero, who in turn was overthrown by Victoriano Huerta—who, after Wilson took office, was vanquished by the counterrevolutionist Venustiano Carranza, an old Madero supporter. Wilson had initially backed Carranza in his quest for a regime based on law and representative of the majority of the Mexican people. For further bloodletting, a general named Francisco "Pancho" Villa was waiting in the wings to push America to the brink of war with Mexico the following year.
19. WW to EBG, August 12, 1915, EBGW Papers
20. WW to EBG, August 10–11, 1915, EBGW Papers.
21. EBG to WW, August 13, 1915, EBGW Papers.
22. Ibid.
23. WW to EBG, August 15, 1915, EBGW Papers.
24. Ibid.
25. WW to EBG, August 13, 1915, EBGW Papers.
26. WW to EBG, August 14, 1915, EBGW Papers.
27. Ibid.
28. WW to EBG, August 19, 20, and 24, 1915, EBGW Papers.
29. EBG to WW, August 19, 1915, EBGW Papers.
30. EBG to WW, August 26, 1915, EBGW Papers.
31. WW to EBG, August 28, 1915, EBGW Papers.
32. Ibid.
33. Ibid.
34. Ibid.
35. Ibid.

36. John A. Garraty, *A Great Life in Brief,* 103.

37. Josephus Daniels, *The Wilson Era,* 454; Jonathan Daniels, *The End of Innocence,* 181.

38. John M. Blum, *Joe Tumulty and the Wilson Era,* 116–17, 293 n. 24; EBG to WW, August 28, 1915, EBGW Papers.

39. Isabelle W. Anderson, *Presidents and Pies,* 171.

40. MAH to WW, June 16, 1915, WWP, reel 71; September 3 and 7, 1915, reel 72.

41. EBG to WW, September 21 and 22 and 26, 1915; September 26, 1915, EBGW Papers.

9. "The awful Earthquake"

1. Edwin Tribble, ed., *President in Love,* 172.

2. WW to EBG, September 13, 1915, EBGW Papers.

3. WW to EBG, September 6, 1915, EBGW Papers.

4. WW to EBG, September 12, 1915, EBGW Papers.

5. EBG to WW, September 3, 1915, EBGW Papers.

6. EBG to WW, September 17, 1915, EBGW Papers.

7. EBG to WW, September 12, 1915, EBGW Papers.

8. Ibid.

9. WW to EBG, September 12, 1915, EBGW Papers.

10. WW to EBG, September 18, 1915, EBGW Papers.

11. EBG to WW, September 18, 1915, EBGW Papers.

12. EMH, Diary, vol. 7, September 22, 1915.

13. WW to EBG, September 19, 1915, EBGW Papers.

14. EBG to WW, September 19, 1915, EBGW Papers.

15. WW to EBG, September 19, 1915, EBGW Papers.

16. WW to EBG, September 20, 1915, EBGW Papers.

17. Ibid.

18. EBG to WW, September 20, 1915, EBGW Papers.

19. *PWW,* 34:496–97, and see note 1, p. 497: "the date assigned . . . is somewhat conjectural."

20. WW to EBG, September 21, 1915, EBGW Papers.

21. EBG to WW, September 21 and 22, 1915, EBGW Papers.

22. Ibid.

23. Ibid.

24. EBW, *My Memoir,* 75–78.

25. Edwin A. Weinstein, *Woodrow Wilson: A Medical and Psychological Biography,* 292.

26. Helen Bones to ACW, November 10, 1949, ACW Papers.

27. Memorandum of talk with Dr. Stockton Axson, August 28, 1931, RSB Papers, reel 70.

28. Hatch, Allen, *Edith Bolling Wilson,* 5.

29. EBG to WW, September 22, 1915, EBGW Papers.

30. Ibid.

31. EMH, Diary, vol. 7, September 22, 1915.

32. Ibid.

33. Ibid.

34. WW to EBG, September 23, 1915, EBGW Papers.

35. Ibid.

36. EMH, Diary, vol. 7, September 22, 1915.
37. Ibid.
38. EMH, Diary, vol. 7, September 24, 1915.
39. Ibid.
40. Ibid.
41. EBG to family, September 23, 1915; WW to EBG, September 24, 1915, EBGW Papers.
42. WW to EBG, September 26, 1915, EBGW Papers.
43. WW to EBG, September 30, 1915, EBGW Papers.
44. Ibid.
45. EBG to WW, September 30, 1915, EBGW Papers.
46. David Lawrence, *The True Story of Woodrow Wilson*, 134.
47. The appointment of Brandeis as associate Supreme Court justice in 1916, depending on the source of gossip, was owed to Wilson's bid for the German, Jewish, and radical vote or to Wilson's appreciation for the lawyer's role as mediator in the payment of $7,500 for the purchase of the Peck letters. But, as Josephus Daniels would point out, there was no evidence of blackmail and consequently "no evidence that Brandeis had anything to do with the lady or the case." Jonathan Daniels, *The End of Innocence*, 190.
48. EMH, Diary, vol. 7, November 22, 1915.
49. *Liberty Magazine*, December 29, 1924.
50. Francis W. Saunders, "Love and Guilt, Woodrow Wilson and Mary Hulbert," 77.

10. MARY PECK, THE DEAR FRIEND HE FOUND IN BERMUDA

1. William Allen White, "Woodrow Wilson," *Liberty Magazine*, December 20, 1924.
2. Mrs. Francis B. Sayre to RSB, October 20, 1928, RSB Papers, reel 82.
3. WW to MAH, January 22, 1922; November 2, 1908, WW Collection II, Special Correspondence, MAH Papers, box 33, folder 7, PL.
4. Ibid.
5. Ibid.
6. WW to MAH, April 13, 1909, MAH Papers, box 33, folder 7.
7. White, "Woodrow Wilson," pt. 2, November 22, 1924; WW to MAH, January 10, 1911, MAH Papers, Box 33, folder 5.
8. *PWW*, 64:506 n. 11.
9. MAH , "Bermuda," undated, MAH Papers, box 33, folder 10, 6–7.
10. WW to EAW, January 30, 1907, RSB Papers, reel 69.
11. WW to EAW, January 26, 1908, RSB Papers, reel 69.
12. Ibid.
13. WW to MAH, June 26, 1909, MAH Papers, box 33, folder 3.
14. WW to MAH, January 10, 1922, MAH Papers, box 33, folder 3.
15. Helen Bones to ACW, January 1 and 19, 1950, ACW Papers.
16. MAH, *Liberty Magazine*, December 27, 1924.
17. John S. Monagan, "The President and Mrs. Peck," 19–32.
18. MAH, "The Woodrow Wilson I Knew," *Liberty Magazine*, January 3, 1925.
19. Edwin A. Weinstein, *Woodrow Wilson: A Medical and Psychological Biography*, 185.
20. Francis Wright Saunders, *Ellen Axson Wilson*, counted according to Wilson's references in his letters.
21. WW to EAW, July 20, 1908, *PWW*, 18:371–73.
22. WW to MAH, October 25, 1908, MAH Papers, box 33, folder 11.

23. WW to MAH, November 2, 1908, MAH Papers, box 33, folder 3.

24. WW to MAH, June 26, 1909, MAH Papers, box 33, folder 3.

25. Helen Bones to ACW, ACW Papers, YL.

26. A. W. Tedcastle to RSB, May 21, 1925, RSB Papers, reel 83.

27. EAW to WW, February 24, 1910, *PWW*, 20:172.

28. Eleanor Wilson McAdoo, *The Woodrow Wilsons*, 131.

29. EAW to WW, February 24, 1910, *PWW*, vol. 20.

30. Helen Bones to ACW, January 19, 1950, ACW Papers.

31. MAH to WW, February 22, 1910, WWP, S series, collection 1187, LC.

32. EAW to WW, July 18 and August 2, 1913, *PWW*, 28:43, 103 n. 7.

33. WW to MAH, August 1, 1909, WW Collection, box 33, folder 4.

34. WW to MAH, September 29, 1912, WW Collection, box 33, folder 7.

35. White, "Woodrow Wilson," pt. 2, November 22, 1924.

36. WW to MAH, February 19, 1913, MAH Papers, box 33, folder 7.

37. WW to MAH, September 21, 1913, MAH Papers, box 33, folder 7.

38. WW to MAH, July 20, 1913, MAH Papers, box 33, folder 7.

39. WW to MAH, September 21, 1913, MAH Papers, box 33, folder 7.

40. MAH to WW, August 7, 1914, WWP, S series, collection 1187, LC. (Early letters are signed Mary Allen Peck; after her divorce she resumed the name of her first husband, thus signing letters as Mary Allen Hulbert. For the sake of consistency, I have, in the notes, tried uniformly to refer to her as MAH.)

41. WW to MAH, December 6, 1914, WWP, reel 533.

42. Ibid.

43. Ibid.

44. WW to Nancy Toy, December 12, 1914, *PWW*, vol. 31.

45. WW to MAH, December 27, 1914, MAH Papers, box 33, folder 9.

46. WW to MAH, January 10, 1915, MAH Papers, box 33, folder 9.

47. MAH to WW, February 12, 1915, WWP, S series, collection 1187.

48. Talk with Mr. and Mrs. A. W. Tedcastle, May 21, 1925, regarding Mrs. Hulbert, RSB Papers, reel 83.

49. MAH, "The Woodrow Wilson I Knew," (first of a series of articles to February 14, 1925) *Liberty*, December 20, 1921.

50. WW to MAH, March 14, 1915, MAH Papers, box 33, folder 9.

51. WW to MAH, April 4, 1915, MAH Papers, box 33, folder 9.

52. WWP, reel 533, series 14.

53. MAH to WW, June 16, 1915, WWP, S series, collection 1187, reel 71.

54. MAH to WW, June (undated) 1915, WWP, reel 71.

55. WWP, reel 14. "Received from Mary Allen Hulbert the following mortgages and bonds covering the properties listed below: Property located in the Bronx and designated, house numbers 1988 and 1990 Cruger Ave.; property known as 419 East 239th Street; lots known as 148 and 149 on the west side of the Macomb's Road about 63.32 feet south of 174th St." A letter dated July 28, 1915, from Horace Herbert Clark, a Pittsfield acquaintance, referred to as the Hulberts' sales manager, confirmed the purchase, enclosed a promissory note for $7,500 signed by Mrs. Mary Allen Hulbert, bearing interest and maturing in six months. Clark wrote again on August 6, 1915, to say that he had repeated Wilson's suggestion of purchasing the mortgages outright and that Mrs. Hulbert had asked Clark to write that she would find it most agreeable if it was convenient for Wilson to do so and that,

after suggested deductions, Wilson would owe $7,097.50 and that the interest would be twenty-two days at 6 percent or $27.50.

56. WW to MAH, October 4, 1915, MAH Papers, box 33, folder 9.
57. MAH to WW, October 11, 1915, WWP, S series, collection 1187, reel 72.
58. WW to MAH, November 10, 1915, MAH Papers, box 33, folder 9.
59. MAH, "The Woodrow Wilson I Knew," *Liberty*, February 7, 1925.
60. EBG to MAH, undated, MAH Papers, box 33, folder 9.

11. A WEDDING ON DECEMBER 18, 1915

1. IHH Papers, cont. 5–6, LC.
2. Ibid.
3. Memorandum of a conversation with Charles L. Swem, July 16, 1925, RSB Papers, reel 83, LC.
4. RSB, *Woodrow Wilson, Life and Letters*, 6:51–52.
5. Patrick Devlin, *Too Proud to Fight*, 364.
6. Frank Parker Stockbridge to RSB, December 11, 1927, RSB Papers, reel 83.
7. HCL to TR, December 20, 1915, *PWW*, 4:42 n. 52.
8. IHH Papers, cont. 5–6.
9. Ibid.
10. Ibid.
11. Colonel Edmund W. Starling, *Starling of the White House*, 58.
12. IHH Papers, cont. 5–6.
13. Ibid.
14. WW to Edith G. Reid, December 5, 1915; RSB, *Woodrow Wilson*, 6:21.
15. RSB, *Woodrow Wilson*, 6:21–22.
16. IHH Papers, cont. 5–6.
17. Edwin Tribble, ed., *President in Love*, EBG to WW, November 30, 1915.
18. Ibid., WW to EBG.
19. *Town Topics*, November 25, 1915.
20. EBW, *My Memoir*, 84.
21. Ibid., 85.
22. Sir Edward Grey to EMH, August 10, 1915, Charles Seymour, *The Intimate Papers of Colonel House*, 2:87. The concept of a league had been eagerly and eloquently embraced by both House and Great Britain's Sir Edward Grey.
23. EMH Diary, vol. 7, December 25, 1915, YL.
24. WW to EMH, December 24, 1915, RSB, *Woodrow Wilson*, 6:138.
25. Ibid., 6:138–39.
26. Tribble, ed., *President in Love*, 209.
27. EBW, December 19, 1915, EBGW Papers, box 1.
28. EBW to "Dearest Bert," December 26, 1915, EBGW Papers, box 1.
29. EBW to IHH, December 29, 1915, IHH Papers, cont. 6.
30. EBW to "Bert," EBGW Papers, box 2, undated.
31. Helen Bones to EBW, "Christmas Day 1915," EBGW Papers, box 10.

12. "THE WORLD IS ON FIRE"

1. WW to Margaret Randolph Axson Elliott, *PWW*, 35:393.
2. JPT to WW, January 2, 1916, *PWW*, 35:419.
3. RL to WW, January 3, 1916, *PWW*, 35:422.

4. RSB, *Woodrow Wilson, Life and Letters,* 6:66.

5. *Congressional Record,* 64-I, p. 1636, quoted *Woodrow Wilson,* 6:67.

6. JPT to WW, January 7, 1916, *PWW,* 35:492–93.

7. *The Messages and Papers of Woodrow Wilson,* 1:66, pp.162–168.

8. *Evening Wisconsin,* January 31, 1916, WWP, reel 503.

9. Ibid.

10. *Milwaukee Daily News,* February 1, 1916.

11. *Milwaukee Sentinel,* February 1, 1916.

12. *Ohio Syndicate Letter,* February 24, 1916.

13. *St. Louis Globe Democrat,* February 4, 1916.

14. *Courier-Journal,* December 7, 1916.

15. Golf score from *Starling of the White House,* 66.

16. EBW, *My Memoir,* 90.

17. EMH to WW, January 7, 1916, Charles Seymour, *The Intimate Papers of Colonel House,* 2:117.

18. House wrote in his diary, January 28, 1916: "The beer did not apparently affect him, for his brain was as befuddled at the beginning as it was at the end. Into such hands are the destinies of the people placed." Seymour, *Intimate Papers,* 2:142.

19. Ibid., 2:157.

20. Ibid., EMH to WW, February 3, 1916, 2:157.

21. Ibid., Memorandum of Sir Edward Grey, Foreign Office, February 22, 1916, 2:201, 202 n. 1.

22. EMH Diary, Series 2, vol. 8, April 10 and 11, 1916.

23. Ibid.

24. *Foreign Relations,* 1916, suppl. 232–37.

25. *War Memoirs of Robert Lansing,* 139; RSB, *Woodrow Wilson,* 6, 188.

26. *War Memoirs,* 138–39.

27. EMH Diary, Series 2, vol. 8, March 30, 1916.

28. Ibid., vol. 10, March 3, 1917.

29. Ibid., March 28, 1917.

30. Ibid., June 10, 1916.

31. Ibid., April 6, 1916.

32. Seymour, *Intimate Papers of Colonel House,* November 16, 1912, 1:113.

33. Josephus Daniels, *The Wilson Era,* 513.

34. EMH diary, Series 2, vol. 10, January 12, 1917.

35. Josephus Daniels, *The Wilson Era,* 518.

36. Jonathan Daniels, *The End of Innocence,* 191–92.

37. Shadow Lawn was offered to Woodrow Wilson as a summer residence by a delegation of prominent citizens of New Jersey.

38. EBW, *My Memoir,* 107.

39. Adolph S. Ochs typed memo, October 17, 1916, "Private for the family only," *NYT* Archives, Woodrow Wilson file, 1901–1950. Courtesy of Susan Dryfoos.

40. WW to Adolph Ochs, November 20, 1916; WW to Adolph Ochs, May 25, 1921; Adolph S. Ochs Papers, *NYT* Archives.

41. EMH to WW, October 20, 1916, Seymour, *Intimate Papers,* 2:379: "Dear Governor: If Hughes is elected—which God forbid—what do you think of asking both Lansing and Marshall to resign, appoint Hughes Secretary of State, and then resign yourself? This would be a patriotic thing to do. . . . Such a procedure would save the situation from danger and embarrassment . . . Affectionately yours."

42. Notation on November 19, 1919, re WW to RL, Seymour, *Intimate Papers,* 2:380, and 2:378–80 re colonel's proposal, WW to RL, November 5, 1916; undated memo signed AHS (probably on or about June 16, 1931), *NYT* Archives.

43. RSB to A. W. Dulles, August 7, 1931, Adolph S. Ochs Papers, *NYT* Archives.

44. *Louisville Courier-Journal,* WWP, reel 503, no date.

45. *Washington Post,* March 1917, WWP, reel 503.

46. *The Star,* November 10, 1916.

47. *Louisville Courier-Journal,* December 9, 1916.

13. "A PEACE WITHOUT VICTORY"

1. Memorandum of James W. Gerard to RSB, RSB, *Woodrow Wilson, Life and Letters,* 6:362.

2. EBW, *My Memoir,* 113.

3. The meeting took place in August 1918 according to interviews with Sir William Wiseman, April 26, 1952, May 1, 1954, and April 22, 1957; ACW Papers, YL.

4. *Official German Documents,* 1:420–21, 2:1077; *NYT* quoted in RSB, *Woodrow Wilson,* 6:392 n. 2.

5. Tentative draft on WW's own typewriter, undated, presumably December 14, in RSB, *Woodrow Wilson,* 6:394 n. 2.

6. *Foreign Relations,* 1916, suppl., 97–99; in RSB, *Woodrow Wilson,* 6:399.

7. *War Memoirs of Robert Lansing,* 187–89.

8. EBW, *My Memoir,* 123.

9. RL, "President's Attitude toward Great Britain and Its Dangers," September 1916, quoted in Thomas Henry Hartig, *Robert Lansing,* 225, 389 (n.16).

10. *War Memoirs,* 187–90.

11. EMH Diary, Series 2, vol. 11, September 10, 1917.

12. *Foreign Relations,* December 19, 1916, suppl., 102; RSB, *Woodrow Wilson,* 6:407.

13. *New York American,* January 23, 1917.

14. RSB and William E. Dodd, eds., *The Public Papers of Woodrow Wilson: The New Democracy,* 2:407–14. Walter Lippmann to RSB, September 24, 1932, writes of his "enormous surprise" at finding Wilson's use of the phrase "peace without victory," which apparently originated in the title of the journalist's article in the *New Republic,* December 23, 1916. Lippmann continues, "I do not know how the article was brought to the President's attention except that I do know that at that particular time he read the *New Republic* constantly.... The article itself ... did not advocate a peace without victory, but rather attempted to show that the German offer, if accepted, would constitute a peace without victory." RSB Papers, reel 75.

15. Memo of conversation with Vance C. McCormick, July 18, 1928, RSB Papers, reel 79, p. 12.

16. EMH Diary, vol. 10, January 12, 1917, YL.

17. David Lawrence to ACW, interview, May 22, 1953, ACW Papers.

18. New York *Call,* in "Joe Tumulty Pulls the Strings," *Current Opinion,* April 1913, 285–86, quoted in Douglas M. Bloomfield, "Joe Tumulty and the Press," 414.

19. Memo on Kerney's *Political Education of Woodrow Wilson,* from A. Howard Meneely, RSB Papers, reel 80.

20. WW to Ida M. Tarbell, "Talk with the President of the United States," *Collier's Weekly* 58, no. 6, quoted in John Morton Blum, *Joe Tumulty and the Wilson Era,* 60.

21. Ibid., 3.

22. JPT to William Allen White, January 27, 1925, JPT Papers, LC. Tumulty was sensitive to being portrayed in stark contrast to Wilson. Though Tumulty understood, he told William Allen White, the journalist's intention to emphasize the austerity and scholastic quality of Woodrow Wilson's background as opposed to his own, he pointed out politely, even deferentially, its imprecision. "Some of the devices for making this dramatic contrast come naturally enough to so good a writer as yourself, but they are just far enough away from the literal facts as to cause me a certain amount of trouble." Friends, he said, took exception to White's characterization of him as "one Roman Catholic who played a square hand with a Presbyterian." They also objected to his being given an alien vocabulary—he had never, for example, called his father "papa." Those close to him disagreed too with the suggestion that Tumulty's education was limited in comparison with Wilson's and called attention his being a "duly-authenticated Master of the Arts." In the event of a second edition of White's work, Tumulty hoped that he might be given an opportunity to make the words literally his own.

23. Ibid.

24. JPT, "A Close-Up View of Woodrow Wilson," *Current Opinion*, December 1920, 789–94, in Bloomfield, "Joe Tumulty."

25. WW to EBG, August 28, 1915, Edwin Tribble, ed., *President in Love*, 165.

26. Reverend J. Gheldof to JPT, February 17, 1916, RSB, *Woodrow Wilson*, 6, 67 n. 8.

27. JPT to WW, March 15, 1916, quoted in Blum, *Joe Tumulty*, 93

28. Reverend R. H. Tierney, "Mr. Tumulty and Mexico," *America*, 14, (December 4, 1915): 173–74, quoted in Blum, *Joe Tumulty*, 93.

29. Ibid., 89.

30. Conversation with Lindley M. Garrison, November 30, 1928, RSB Papers, reel 75.

31. Blum, *Joe Tumulty*, 115.

32. JPT to WW, November 18, 1916, WWP.

33. Memo of a conversation with Vance C. McCormick, July 18, 1928, RSB Papers, reel 79.

34. John M. Blum, *Joe Tumulty*, 125–29.

35. JPT to Mrs. T. F. Logan, February 9, 1917, JPT Papers; Blum, *Joe Tumulty*, 128–29.

36. Copies of "Rome in the Government," Tract No. 7, were sold at 237 Michigan St., Room W, Toledo, Ohio; EBW to JPT, undated, JPT Papers, box 46.

37. EMH Diary, Series 11, vol. 10, January 12, 1917.

38. Ibid., January 3, 1917.

39. Ibid., March 5, 1917.

14. "Nothing less than war"

1. *Courier-Journal*, March 24, 1917, WWP, reel 503.

2. On March 12, as Lansing was about to announce the order for arming American ships, Wilson urged that regulations governing the arming of merchant vessels prepared by Daniels be kept secret: "I would be very much obliged if you would give the most emphatic orders that no part of any of this is to be given even the least publicity. I should feel justified in ordering a court martial for disobedience to such an order." RSB, *Woodrow Wilson, Life and Letters*, 6:488–89.

3. E. David Cronin, ed., *The Cabinet Diaries of Josephus Daniels*, 109.

4. EBW, *My Memoir*, 131–32; *Foreign Relations*, 1917, suppl. 1, p. 171.

5. John L. Heaton, *Cobb of "The World,"* 268–70, and see RSB, *Woodrow Wilson*, 6:507 n. 1.

6. EBW, *My Memoir*, 132–33.

7. The note, intercepted by the British, proposed, in case of war with the United States, an alliance with Mexico with "an understanding on our part that Mexico is to reconquer the lost territory in Texas, New Mexico, and Arizona." Mexico was also to extend an invitation to Japan to join forces. *Foreign Relations*, 1917, suppl. 1, 1147–48.

8. "Wilson's Address to Congress Advising That Germany's Course Be Declared War Against the United States," delivered in joint session, April 2, 1917, *The Messages and Papers of Woodrow Wilson*, 1:372–83.

9. EBW, *My Memoir*, 134.

10. Ibid., 146.

11. *The Ladies' Home Journal*, October 1921.

12. EBW to EMH, May 1, 1918, RSB Papers, reel 65.

13. Marianne Means, *The Woman in the White House*, 154; Alden Hatch Papers, p. 55.

14. Alden Hatch Papers, p. 73.

15. "Never enthusiastic," quoted in Memorandum of Conversations with Stockton Axson, February 8, 10, 11, 1925, RSB Papers, reel 70; EBW quoted in Means, *Woman in the White House*, 154.

16. Quoted in *Suffrage*, exhibition at the Woodrow Wilson House on S Street, Washington, D.C.

17. June 17, 1916, RSB, *Woodrow Wilson*, 6:261.

18. WW to E. W. Pou, May 14, 1917, RSB, *Woodrow Wilson*, 6:68–69.

19. Inez Haynes Irwin, *Uphill With Flags Flying*, 208.

20. EBW, *My Memoir*, 138.

21. WW to Mrs. Carrie Chapman Catt, October 13, 1917, RSB, *Woodrow Wilson*, 7:306.

22. At Harvard, Theodore Roosevelt favored women's suffrage and independence. In his senior thesis he wrote, "A cripple or a consumptive in the eye of the law is equal to the strongest athlete or the deepest thinker, and the same justice should be shown to a woman whether she is or is not the equal of a man. . . . As regards the laws relating to marriage, there should be the most absolute equality preserved between the two sexes. I do not think the woman should assume the man's name . . . I would have the word 'obey' used not more by the wife than the husband." Thesis courtesy of Emme Deland.

23. WW to Mrs. George Bass, January 22, 1918, RSB, *Woodrow Wilson*, 7:489.

24. Ellen Maury Slayden, *Washington Wife*, 320–21.

25. WW to Robert Bridges, February 4, 1918, RSB, *Woodrow Wilson*, 7:525.

26. EBW, *My Memoir*, 148–50.

15. Fourteen Points

1. WW complained on July 21, 1917, to EMH, 7:181 and to Mrs. Francis B. Sayre, 7:182, RSB, *Woodrow Wilson, Life and Letters*.

2. *NYT*, September 9, 1917, *PWW*, reel 503.

3. WW to EMH, June 1, 1917, RSB Papers, reel 65.

4. Conversation with Colonel House, November 17, 1930: This quotation is crossed out, and written in the margin is a question mark and this notation: "You had better say that." George Sylvester Viereck Papers, box 4, folder 7, YL.

5. Dr. Isaiah Bowman to Charles Seymour, *The Intimate Papers of Colonel House*, 3:325 n. 1.

6. Viereck interview with EMH, November 13, 1920, George Sylvester Viereck Papers, box 4, folder 6.

7. WW may have written more frequently, but on record he wrote to EMH the summer and fall of 1917: June 1, 15; July 21; August 16, 22; September 19, 22, 24, 26; October 1, 7, 13.

8. WW to EMH, June 1, 1917, Seymour, *Intimate Papers*, 3:134 n. 1.

9. WW's Flag Day address, June 14, 1917, *The Messages and Papers of Woodrow Wilson*, 1:411–18.

10. Sir William Wiseman to EMH, August 11, 1917, Seymour, *Intimate Papers*, 3:151–52.

11. EMH to WW, August 15, 1917, Seymour, *Intimate Papers*, 3:153–54.

12. WW to EMH, August 16, RSB, *Woodrow Wilson*, 7:218.

13. Ibid., 7:231

14. EMH to WW, August 24, 1917, Seymour, *Intimate Papers*, 3:164.

15. WW to EMH, August 22, 1917, Seymour, *Intimate Papers*, 3:166–67.

16. Lord Robert Cecil to EMH, cablegram, August 27, 1917, Seymour, *Intimate Papers*, 3:167; "written in pencil," RSB, *Woodrow Wilson*, 7:237.

17. Seymour, *Intimate Papers*, 3:168.

18. William Phillips to EMH, May 19, June 6, 1917; EMH to WW, September 21, 1917, Seymour, *Intimate Papers*, 3:169 n. 2.

19. Wiseman memorandum on the Inquiry, June 5, 1928, Seymour, *Intimate Papers*, 3:172, and see 170–73.

20. WW to David Lawrence, October 5, 1917, RSB, *Woodrow Wilson*, 7:294.

21. Walter Page to WW and RL, October 8, 1917, RSB Papers, reel 65.

22. WW to EMH, September 24, 1917, RSB, *Woodrow Wilson*, 282.

23. EBW, *My Memoir*, 144–45.

24. Lloyd George to EMH, September 4, 1917; A. H. Frazier to EMH, October 12, 1917; Arthur Balfour to EMH, October 14, 1917; Seymour, *Intimate Papers*, 3:187–88, 195–96, 197.

25. EMH to WW, September 24, 1917; EMH to Lloyd George, September 24, 1917; Seymour, *Intimate Papers*, 3:195 n. 1, 188–89.

26. George F. Kennan, *Russia Leaves the War*, 28–29.

27. EMH to WW, October 27, 1917, RSB, *Woodrow Wilson*, 7:329.

28. WW to EMH, October 28, 1917, RSB Papers, reel 65.

29. "Wilson's Address Before the American Federation of Labor," Buffalo, N.Y., November 12, 1917, *Messages and Papers of Woodrow Wilson*, 1:439.

30. Seymour, *Intimate Papers*, 3:217.

31. EMH to WW, November 13, 1917, Seymour, *Intimate Papers*, 3:219.

32. RSB, *Woodrow Wilson*, 8:354,

33. Roger Aycock, *All Roads to Rome*, 318.

34. EMH to WW, November 23, 1917, Seymour, *Intimate Papers*, 3:251–53.

35. EMH to WW, December 2, 1917, Seymour, *Intimate Papers*, 3:284–85.

36. EMH to WW, November 30, 1917, Seymour, *Intimate Papers*, 3:281.

37. WW to EMH, December 1, 1917, RSB, *Woodrow Wilson*, 7:387.

38. EMH Diary, December 1, 1917, Seymour, *Intimate Papers*, 3:283–84.

39. EMH, December 1, 1917, Seymour, *Intimate Papers*, 3:286.

40. WW to EMH, RSB, *Woodrow Wilson*, 7:389.

41. EBW, *My Memoir*, 154.

42. *NYT*, January 22, 1918; Seymour, *Intimate Papers*, 3:292 n. 1.

43. RSB, *Woodrow Wilson*, 426.

44. *Washington Times*, November 14, 1917, WWP, reel 503. Involved were 173,000 employees, including 35,000 passenger-train employees, 85,000 freight-train men, and 53,000 yardmen asking for an aggregate increase of $48 million. According to the *Washington Times*, an end to strikes and walkouts in all industries in the United States was predicted on November 14, 1917, when the American Federation of Labor in Buffalo directed a committee to meet with President Wilson to settle the differences between employers and employees.

45. RSB and William E. Dodd, eds., *The Public Papers of Woodrow Wilson*, 5:150–54, in RSB, *Woodrow Wilson*, 7:451 n. 1.

46. Seymour, *Intimate Papers*, 3:325.

47. RSB, *Woodrow Wilson*, 7:453–54.

48. Seymour, *Intimate Papers*, 3:321.

49. January 8, 1918, *The Messages and Papers of Woodrow Wilson*, 464–72.

50. EBW, *My Memoir*, 157.

51. *New York Tribune*, January 9, 1918.

52. EBW, *My Memoir*, 157.

16. "SHE KNOWS WHAT HER HUSBAND KNOWS"

1. RSB, *Woodrow Wilson, Life and Letters* 7:509–10 n. 1.

2. EMH Diary, vol. 13, January 27, 1918.

3. EMH to WW, January 31, 1918, Charles Seymour, *The Intimate Papers of Colonel House*, 3:355.

4. Martin Gilbert, *The First World War*, 427 n. 1.

5. *NYT*, February 12, 1918; RSB, *Woodrow Wilson*, 7:538 n.2.

6. WW to EMH, July 8, 1918, RSB, *Woodrow Wilson*, 8:266.

7. Carl W. Ackerman to EMH, February 4, 1918, Seymour, *Intimate Papers*, 3:357.

8. Seymour, *Intimate Papers*, 3:354, 365.

9. WW to EMH, February 26, 1918, RSB, *Woodrow Wilson*, 7:567.

10. "President Wilson's Address to Congress, 'Analyzing German and Austrian Peace Utterances,'" February 11, 1918, *The Messages and Papers of Woodrow Wilson*, 1:472–79.

11. EMH to A. J. Balfour, March 1, 1918, Seymour, *Intimate Papers*, 3:378.

12. Lord Robert Cecil to EMH, February 16, 1918, Seymour, *Intimate Papers*, 4:8–9.

13. WW to Theodore Marburg, March 8, 1918, RSB, *Woodrow Wilson*, 8:17; Seymour, *Intimate Papers* 4:5, 16.

14. WW to EMH, March 22, 1918, RSB Papers, reel 65.

15. *The Real Colonel House*, by Arthur D. Howden Smith, was published in book form by George H. Doran, New York, 1918.

16. Ibid., 36.

17. *Town Topics*, May 2, 1918, 13.

18. Ibid., June 27, 1918, 11.

19. WW to EMH, May 6, 1918, RSB Papers, reel 65.

20. EBW to EMH, May 6, 1918, RSB Papers, reel 65.

21. EMH Diary, vol. 14, September 24, 1918.

22. Henry A. Forster to RSB, July 18, 1926, RSB Papers, reel 75. Forster writes: "I have always doubted personal grounds having anything to do with the alleged rupture.

But Smith, (the author,) who speaks for Colonel House, says that they did cause it. . . . It is regrettable if it is true that personalities caused any of these differences. I hope Smith is wrong, but fear he knows the facts."

23. WW to EMH, July 8, 1918, *Life and Letters,* 266.

24. EMH to Lord Robert Cecil and EMH to WW, June 25, 1918, Seymour, *Intimate Papers,* 4:20–21.

25. RSB, *Woodrow Wilson and World Settlement,* second and third draft, 3:100–110, 117–29; 1:215.

26. WW to EMH, July 8, 1918, RSB Papers, reel 65.

27. EMH Diary, vol. 14, August 18, 1918.

28. Ibid., August 19, 1918.

29. Sir William Wiseman to John Murray, August 30, 1918, Arthur C. Murray, *At Close Quarters,* 39–42.

30. EMH Diary, vol. 14, September 8, 1918.

31. "President Wilson's Address 'Opening the New York Campaign for the Fourth Liberty Loan,'" September 27, 1918, *Messages and Papers of Woodrow Wilson,* 1:520–32.

32. *Daily News,* October 8, 1918, quoted in Seymour, *Intimate Papers,* 4:73.

33. EBW, *My Memoir,* 169

34. Seymour, *Intimate Papers,* October 16, 1918, 4:87.

35. EMH Diary, vol. 14, October 14, 1918.

36. EMH to Viereck, October 13, 1930, Papers of George Sylvester Viereck, YL.

37. EBW to RSB, RSB, *Woodrow Wilson,* 8:510 n. 1.

38. "President Wilson's Appeal to the Voters, to Return a Democratic Congress," October 24, 1918, *Messages and Papers of Woodrow Wilson,* 1:557–59.

39. RSB, *Woodrow Wilson,* 8:487.

40. Ibid., 8:514; Theodore Roosevelt, *Selections from the Correspondence of Theodore Roosevelt and Henry Cabot Lodge,* 2:542 ; RSB, *Woodrow Wilson,* 8:514 n. 1.

41. RSB, *Woodrow Wilson,* quoting Frank I. Cobb and Vance C. McCormick, 8:513–14 n. 1.

42. *Town Topics,* November 28, 1918.

43. Ibid., October 24 and 31, 1918.

44. Seymour, *Intimate Papers,* 4:68 n.1.

45. Winston Churchill, *The Aftermath,* 125.

46. *Town Topics,* November 14, 1918.

47. Jonathan Daniels, *Time Between the Wars,* 17.

48. Seymour, *Intimate Papers,* 4:225. Candidates mentioned included Henry Cabot Lodge, Gilbert M. Hitchcock, Supreme Court chief justice Edward D. White, Senators Philander Knox, Brandegee, Borah, Root, Taft.

49. *Town Topics,* November 7, 1918, vol. 80; RSB, *Woodrow Wilson,* 8:481.

50. EMH to WW, October 31, 1918, Seymour, *Intimate Papers,* 4:174; WW to EMH, October 31, 1918, RSB, *Woodrow Wilson,* 8:539.

51. EMH to WW, November 10, 1918, Seymour, *Intimate Papers,* 4:142.

52. RSB, *Woodrow Wilson,* 8:580.

53. Daniels, *Time Between,* 5.

17. "Such a Cinderella role"

1. Elizabeth Jaffray, *Secrets of the White House,* 65.

2. H. G. Wells, in Jonathan Daniels, *The End of Innocence,* 284.

3. *Town Topics*, November 28, 1918, vol. 80; North American Review's *War Weekly* (also called *Harvey's Weekly*), November 23, 1918.
4. Ibid., November 30, 1918.
5. WW to EMH, November 16, 1918, Charles Seymour, *The Intimate Papers of Colonel House*, 213–14.
6. The article carries Cunliffe-Owen's byline but no source, which is, probably, either the *Washington Times* or *Washington Post*, WWP, reel 503.
7. *Washington Times*, December 3, 1918.
8. *The Hatchet*, December 11, 1918, WWP, reel 504.
9. Ellen Maury Slayden, *Washington Wife*, 351.
10. EBW to "Dearest Mother," December 4, 1918, Papers of EBGW, box 11.
11. *The Hatchet*, December 7, 1918, WWP, reel 504.
12. Ibid.
13. WW to Robert Bridges, April 29, 1883, in George C. Osborn, "Woodrow Wilson as a Young Lawyer, 1882–1883," 140–41.
14. George F. Kennan, *Russia Leaves the War*, 30–31.
15. RL, appendix to Diary, "On Board SS *Washington*," December 8, RL Papers, cont. 66–67, reel 1.
16. Raymond B. Fosdick, "Diary of a Trip on the *George Washington*," Raymond B. Fosdick Papers.
17. Charles Seymour to his family, December 12, 1918, *PWW*, vol. 53.
18. EBW, *My Memoir*, 174.
19. Ibid., 6.
20. Associated Press, December 13, 1918.
21. EBW, *My Memoir*, 178.
22. EBW to "Dearest Ones," December 15, 1918, EBGW Papers, box 2.
23. The estate was demolished, and 28 rue Monceau is now the address of Électricité France. Only a side lane bears the name of Prince Murat.
24. Charles Lee Swem to Daisy Swem, December 23, 1918, Diary and notebooks of Charles Lee Swem, WW Collection.
25. EBW to Bert, January 14, 1918, "Poor Colonel House has gallstones (secret)," EBGW Papers, box 2; Seymour, *Intimate Papers*, 4:273; Charles Seymour, "End of a Friendship."
26. *Town Topics*, January 6, 1919.
27. *New York Herald*, European edition, December 15, 1918; EBW, *My Memoir*, 177.
28. Daniels, *End of Innocence*, 171.
29. As of September 1918, Pershing was designated "General of the Armies of the United States."
30. David Lloyd George, *Memoirs of the Peace Conference*, 139.
31. Winston Churchill, *The World Crisis*, 1:234.
32. Charles T. Thompson, *The Peace Conference Day by Day*, 18.
33. North American Review's *War Weekly* (also called *Harvey's Weekly*), December 21, 1918.
34. CTG Diary, part 1, p. 10, PL.
35. IHH, *Forty-Two Years in the White House*, 79.
36. *The Messages and Papers of Woodrow Wilson* 1:581–82.
37. Ibid., 1:584; John Dos Passos, *Mr. Wilson's War*, 451.
38. CTG Diary, part 1.
39. Diary of Lady Wigram, quoted by Kenneth Rose, "Albany at Large," *Sunday Tele-*

graph, March 25, 1990; Rose to the author, April 20, 1990; Lloyd George, *Memoirs,* 1:182.

40. EBW to Bertha Bolling, January 4, 1919, EBGW Papers, box 2.
41. *The Messages and Papers of Woodrow Wilson,* 1:594–613.
42. Thompson, *Peace Conference,* 69.
43. IHH Papers, cont. 6–7, LC.

18. "Is it a League of Nations or a League of notions?"

1. EBW to "Dearest Ones," January 11, 1919, EBGW Papers, box 2.
2. Edith Benham Helm, "The Private Letters of the Wilsons' Social Secretary," *Hearst's International Cosmopolitan,* August 1930, Edith B. Helm Collection, box 8, LC.
3. *Town Topics,* January 23, 1919.
4. Ibid.
5. Helm, "The Private Letters," January 22, 1919, Helm Collection.
6. EBW to mother, Bert, Randolph, January 20, 1919, EBGW Papers, 1919–24, box 2.
7. Charles Thaddeus Thompson, *The Peace Conference Day By Day,* 1.
8. Helm, "The Private Letters," January 12, 1919, Helm Collection.
9. Thompson, *The Peace Conference Day by Day,* 121; *The Messages and Papers of Woodrow Wilson,* 2:614–15.
10. RSB, *Woodrow Wilson and World Settlement,* 1:252.
11. EBW to mother, Bert, Randolph, January 20, 1919, EBGW Papers, 1919–24, box 2.
12. EBW, *My Memoir,* 233.
13. Ibid.
14. Helm, "The Private Letters," January 12, 1919, Helm Collection.
15. Ibid.
16. Ibid.
17. Thompson, *Peace Conference,* 140.
18. Alfred Capus, *Le Figaro,* February 10, 1919, quoted in Thompson, *Peace Conference,* 187.
19. Ibid., 191.
20. Ibid., 196.
21. EBW, *My Memoir,* 227.
22. "At the Peace Conference, Presenting—as Chairman—the Report of the Commission on the League of Nations," *Messages and Papers of Woodrow Wilson,* 2:623–38.
23. Charles Seymour, *The Intimate Papers of Colonel House,* 4:318–19.
24. Jonathan Daniels, *The Time Between the Wars,* 17–18.
25. *Town Topics,* February 13, 1919.
26. RL, *The Peace Negotiations,* 208–9; RL, *The Paris Peace Conference, 1919,* 11:547–48.
27. EBW, *My Memoir,* 237.
28. U.S. State Department, *Papers Relating to the Foreign Relations of the United States,* 1919, 3:1003–4.
29. Arthur C. Walworth, "Considerations on Woodrow Wilson and Edward M. House," 79–86.
30. EMH Diary, v. 15, February 14, 1919.
31. Frederick Palmer, *Bliss, Peacemaker,* 386; RL Strictly Private Notes. Appendix 34.
32. EMH to Edward S. Martin, February 7, 1919, Mrs. Edward S. Blagden Papers.

19. PARIS TO WASHINGTON, AND BACK . . .

1. EBW, *My Memoir*, 241.
2. Joseph P. Lash, *Eleanor and Franklin*, 216.
3. Ibid., 231.
4. Eleanor Roosevelt, *This Is My Story*, 280.
5. Ibid., 234.
6. EBW, *My Memoir*, 241.
7. JPT, *Woodrow Wilson As I Know Him*, 317.
8. Archibald Hopkins to HCL, February 19, 1919, HCL Papers, box 50.
9. Calvin Coolidge to HCL, February 19, 1919, HCL Papers, box 50.
10. Charles Seymour, *The Intimate Papers of Colonel House*, 4:332
11. *The Paris Peace Conference*, Papers Relating to the Foreign Relations of the United States, 1919 suppl., 11:509.
12. "Address of President Wilson at Boston, Mass., on His Return from Europe," February 24, 1919, *The Messages and Papers of Woodrow Wilson*, 2:638–47.
13. Jonathan Daniels, *The Time Between the Wars*, 25.
14. Notes for *My Memoir*, EBGW Papers, box 49, notebook 15.
15. CTG Diary, February 26, 1919.
16. *NYT*, February 27, 1919, *PWW*, 55:268–76.
17. New York *Sun*, in *Congressional Record–Senate*, 4528–30.
18. Diary of Chandler Anderson, March 10, 1919, LC.
19. Daniels, *Time Between the Wars*, 25–26.
20. EBW, *My Memoir*, 241–42.
21. HCL, *The Senate and the League of Nations*, 100.
22. HCL to Archibald Hopkins, February [?], 1919, HCL Papers, box 50.
23. HCL to Henry White, in Allen Nevins, *Henry White*, 390–91.
24. HCL to Calvin Coolidge, February 24, 1919, HCL Papers, box 50; *Congressional Record–Senate*, February 28, 1919, 4525–28.
25. "Remarks to Democratic Committee," *PWW*, 55:322–34.
26. HCL, *Senate and the League*, 121.
27. *PWW*, March 4, 1919, 55:408–9. Before the November 5, 1918, election, the Democrats outnumbered the Republicans—Senate: 53 Democrats, 42 Republicans; House: 216 Democrats, 210 Republicans. After the election—Senate: 49 Republicans; 47 Democrats; House: 240 Republicans, 190 Democrats (3 others).
28. Colonel Edmund W. Starling, *Starling of the White House*, 133.
29. Seymour, *Intimate Papers*, 4:332; *Paris Peace Conference*, 11:511–23. House cabled to Wilson on February 19, twice on the 20th, twice on the 23rd, again on February 24, 25, 26, 27, twice on March 1, again on March 4, 7, and 10.
30. WW to EMH, February 20, 1919, Seymour, *Intimate Papers*, 4:336 n. 1.
31. EMH to WW, February 25, 1919, Seymour, *Intimate Papers*, 4:350.
32. EMH to WW, February 26, 1919, Seymour, *Intimate Papers*, 4:350–51.
33. EMH to WW, February 27, 1919, Seymour, *Intimate Papers*, 4:351–52.
34. March 1, 1919, *Paris Peace Conference*, 11:518–19.
35. Interview with Charles Swem, February 17, 1949, Papers of ACW, YL.
36. WW to EMH, March 4, 1919, Seymour, *Intimate Papers*, 4:352–53. This quote is noted as a "Paraphrase of the President's Cablegram to Colonel House."
37. EMH to WW, March 4, 1919, *Paris Peace Conference*, 11:521.

38. RSB, *Woodrow Wilson and World Settlement,* chap. 17, "While Wilson Was Away," 1:295–313.

39. EBW, *My Memoir,* 246, elaborating on earlier RSB volume.

40. F. B. Brandegee to HCL, March 1919, Conwell Papers #5, HCL Papers, box 50.

41. Address of President Wilson at New York City, March 4, 1919, *Messages and Papers of Woodrow Wilson,* 2:647–58.

42. Ibid.

43. Notes for *My Memoir,* EBGW Papers, box 49, notebook 15.

44. *Messages and Papers of Woodrow Wilson,* March 4, 1919, 2:654.

45. Samuel Gompers, *Seventy Years of Life and Labor,* 486.

46. Daniels, *Time Between the Wars,* 29.

47. The actual quotation from Robert Green Ingersoll reads: "I would rather have been a French peasant and worn wooden shoes . . . than to have been that imperial impersonation of force and murder known as Napoleon the Great." John Bartlett, *Familiar Quotations,* 603.

48. Notes for *My Memoir,* EBGW Papers, box 49, notebook 15. The spelling of the word *underwater* is incomplete ("underwa") and partially crossed out.

20. THE PREACHER AND THE BRAHMIN

1. Henry Adams, *The Education of Henry Adams:* "he had stood up for his eighteenth century," 353.

2. Alden Hatch, *The Lodges of Massachusetts,* 128.

3. Ibid., 2.

4. Ernest Samuels, *Henry Adams,* 102

5. Ibid., 164.

6. Henry Adams to HCL, June 2, 1872, Worthington Chauncey Ford, ed., *Letters of Henry Adams,* 228.

7. Samuels, *Henry Adams,* 380; Patricia O'Toole, *The Five of Hearts,* 208.

8. Adams, *Education of Henry Adams,* 353.

9. Ibid.

10. Henry Adams to Elizabeth Cameron, February 16, 1915, J. C. Levenson et al., eds., *Letters of Henry Adams,* vol. 6.

11. Harold D. Cater, ed., *Henry Adams and His Friends,* cv.

12. HCL to TR, February 22, 1917, HCL Papers, box 75, HL.

13. HCL to TR, February 1, 1915, HCL Papers, box 75.

14. HCL to TR, March 1, 1915, HCL Papers, box 75.

15. HCL to TR, February 19, 1915, HCL Papers, box 89.

16. HCL to Robert N. Washburn, February 14, 1918, HCL Papers, box 57, in which he quotes the last line of Robert Browning's "A Toccata of Galuppi's."

17. HCL to TR, May 28, 1917, HCL Papers, box 90.

18. HCL to TR, January 26, 1917, HCL Papers, box 90.

19. HCL to TR, March 20, 1917, HCL Papers, box 90.

20. William J. Miller, *Henry Cabot Lodge,* 419

21. Josephus Daniels, *The Wilson Era,* 1:535.

22. William C. Widenor, *Henry Cabot Lodge and the Search for an American Foreign Policy,* 209 n. 153.

23. HCL speech, Washington, December 31, no year given, HCL Papers, box 75.

24. HCL to Senator George W. Norris, February 6, 1915, HCL Papers, box 89.

25. *Congressional Record,* 63rd Congress, 3rd session, 1915, 3558, in William C. Widenor, *Henry Cabot Lodge,* 208.

26. HCL to TR, September 17, 1917, HCL Papers, box 90.

27. HCL to Emlen Hare Miller, January 30, 1919, HCL Papers, box 51.

28. HCL to Emlen Hare Miller, April 23, 1917, HCL Papers, box 51.

29. HCL to TR, April 23, 1917, HCL Papers, box 89.

30. HCL to TR, December 9, 1918, HCL Papers, box 89.

31. Ibid.

32. Ibid.

33. HCL to TR, December 20, 1915, TR Papers, LC.

34. Inman Barnard to HCL, February 9, 1919, HCL Papers, box 50.

35. Edith Wharton to HCL, March 4, 1919, HCL Papers, box 49. Wharton was writing from the Hôtel du Parc, Hyères, and spoke here of her preference for the "Society of Nations, which, in its practical application, would be simply an alliance of the big democratic peoples; and unless that is formed I don't see what is to save France or civilization." Nor did she see how peace terms could be settled (considering the capacities of some of the smaller allies) until some sort of League of Nations had been worked out first to which all had to agree, whether they liked it or not. She claimed that she didn't think she ever had "the presumption to write a political letter before, and it seems the height of irony to address my first attempt to you! Don't be indulgent, please," she begged Lodge.

36. L. J. Maxse to HCL, February 3, 1919, HCL Papers, box 51.

37. Rudyard Kipling to HCL, March 15, 1919, HCL Papers, box 52A.

38. Lord Charnwood to HCL, June 15, 1919, HCL Papers, box 50.

39. HCL to Rudyard Kipling, April 8, 1919, HCL Papers, box 52.

40. HCL to Edith Wharton, April 8, 1919, HCL Papers, box 49.

41. HCL to Robert L. Raymond, February 20, 1919, HCL Papers, box 51.

42. HCL to Moreton Frewen, April 7, 1919, Moreton Frewen Papers, LC.

43. "Joint Debate on the Covenant of Paris," March 29, 1919, World Peace Foundation, *League of Nations* (Boston), 96–97.

44. CTG Diary, pt. 2, March 11, 1919.

45. Charles Seymour, *The Intimate Papers of Colonel House,* 4:357–59.

46. Ibid., WW to EMH, March 10, 1919, 4:358 n. 2.

47. EMH Diary, vol. 15, March 3, 1919.

48. EBW, *My Memoir,* 245.

49. Eleanor Roosevelt, *This Is My Story,* 298.

21. A DIFFERENT PRESIDENT . . . A DIFFERENT PARIS

1. Winston S. Churchill, *The Aftermath,* 191, 164.

2. Ibid., 121.

3. EMH Diary, vol. 15, March 14, 1919.

4. David Lloyd George, *Memoirs of the Peace Conference,* 160.

5. ACW, "Considerations on Woodrow Wilson and Edward M. House," 79–86.

6. EMH Diary, vol. 18, July 21, 1924.

7. EBW, *My Memoir,* 245, 246; Colonel Edmund W. Starling, *Starling of the White House,* 135.

8. EMH to WW, February 24, 1919, *The Paris Peace Conference, 1919,* Papers Relating to the Foreign Relations of the United States, 1919, 11:513–14.

9. CTG Diary, March 13, 1919, *PWW*, 55:486–89.
10. EMH Diary, vol. 15, March 14, 1919.
11. *PWW*, Arthur Link's footnote, 55:488 n. 2.
12. Edwin A. Weinstein, *Woodrow Wilson: A Medical and Psychological Biography*, 292: "In her memoir . . . Mrs. Wilson gives a highly fictitious account" of the possible disclosure of letters the president had written to Mary Peck. "Confabulations," Weinstein continues, "are not only fictitious recollections of past events" but may, with the passage of time, "become anxiety-relieving when placed in another symbolic context." Weinstein also refers to Mrs. Wilson's "amnesia," which "shielded" her from the memory—that is, the truthful recollection—of two painful events of her life.
13. ACW, "Wilson and House," 81.
14. Ibid., 152.
15. EMH to WW, March 4, 1919, *Paris Peace Conference*, 11:511–13, 521.
16. Frederick Palmer, *Bliss, Peacemaker*, 386.
17. Margaret Ayer Cobb to ACW, ACW Papers, YL.
18. CTG, "The Colonel's Folly and the President's Distress," *American Heritage*.
19. RSB notebook, April 4, 17, 1919, RSB Papers, LC.
20. RSB, *Woodrow Wilson and World Settlement*, 1:307.
21. RSB Diary, April 3, 1919, RSB Papers.
22. Churchill, *Aftermath*, 203.
23. Lloyd George, *Memoirs*, 159.
24. Ibid.
25. Ibid.
26. "Interesting Comment of One Near the President on Situation," June 5, 1919, Private Memorandum, RL Papers, conts. 66, 67, LC.
27. ACW, "Wilson and House," 81.
28. EBW, *My Memoir*, 247.
29. On the southeast corner at rue Amiral d' Estaing, it looks onto the small green where Bartholdi's effusive sculpture celebrates an earlier diplomatic alliance, that of Washington and Lafayette.
30. IHH Papers, cont. 6–7, LC.
31. EMH Diary, vol. 15, March 14, 1919.
32. CTG Diary, pt. 2.
33. JPT to WW, March 16, 1919, *Woodrow Wilson As I Know Him*, 520.
34. Ibid.
35. EBW, *My Memoir*, 247–48.
36. JPT, *Woodrow Wilson*, 520.
37. Charles T. Thompson, *The Peace Conference Day by Day*, 247.
38. Edith Benham Helm, March 22, 1919, "The Private Letters of the Wilsons' Social Secretary," *Hearst's International Cosmopolitan*, September 1930, Edith B. Helm Papers, LC.
39. EBW to Dearest Ones, April 3, 1919, EBGW Papers, box 2.

22. WILSON SUFFERS A "FLAREBACK"

1. RL to John Davis, April 11, 1919, RL Papers, box 5, LC.
2. Ibid.
3. EBW, *My Memoir*, 249–50.
4. "Wilson's Neurologic Illness At Paris," *PWW*, 58:622 n. 57.
5. JPT to CTG, April 9, 1910, JPT, *Woodrow Wilson As I Know Him*, 524.

6. London *Times*, April 7, 1919 , *PWW*, 56:533.

7. EBW, *My Memoir*, 250–51.

8. Ibid.

9. *PWW*, 56:558, final paragraph n. 1.

10. Ibid., 64:499 n. 5; vol. 58, appendix.

11. "A Statement by Dr. Grayson," October 15, 1919, *PWW*, 64:497–98.

12. A. J. P. Taylor, ed., *David Lloyd George: A Diary, by Frances Stevenson*, 277.

13. Printed in *NYT*, October 5 and 13, 1919; *PWW*, 63:567–68.

14. James F. Toole, "Some Observations on Wilson's Neurologic Illness," *PWW*, 58:636.

15. Bert E. Park, "The Impact of Wilson's Neurologic Disease During the Paris Peace Conference," *PWW*, 58:614. More specifically, Park writes: "Given the presence of untreated hypertension in Wilson's clinical history as early as 1906, at which time significant involvement of the retinal vessels of the eye was already manifest (considered an *end-stage* of the accelerated phase of the disease), it is not surprising that thirteen further years of the untreated condition predisposed Wilson to the development of incipient hypertensive multi-infarct dementia long *before* his viral illness in early April 1919 and his devastating large-vessel atherosclerotic strokes in September and October of the same year."

16. *PWW*, 56:558.

17. Louis Brandeis to RSB, March 23, 1929, in *PWW*, 58:613 n. 6.

18. CTG Diary, May 1, 1919.

19. EMH Diary, June 10, 1919.

20. Park, "The Impact of Wilson's Neurologic Disease," 58:613–14.

21. Ibid., 58:613.

22. Edwin A. Weinstein, "Woodrow Wilson's Neuropsychological Impairment and the Paris Peace Conference," *PWW*, 58:633.

23. David Lloyd George, *Memoirs of the Peace Conference*, 139–59.

24. Ibid.

25. Ibid.

26. Ibid.

27. Queen Marie of Romania, "My Mission," *Cornhill Magazine*, December 1939, 722–32. Courtesy of Hannah Pakula.

28. General Tasker Howard Bliss to Eleanora Anderson Bliss, Frederick Palmer, *Bliss, Peacemaker*, 400.

29. John Maynard Keynes, *The Economic Consequences of the Peace*, xvii; 24–27.

30. Lloyd George, *Memoirs*, 153.

31. CTG Diary, pt. 2, April 7, 1919.

32. RSB Papers, April 22, 1919; *PWW*, 57:585.

33. CTG Diary, pt. 2, May 3, 1919.

34. CTG to JPT, April 10, 1919, in CTG Diary, pt. 2.

35. CTG, "The Colonel's Folly and the President's Distress," 94–101.

36. CTG Diary, pt. 2, April 9, 1919, p. 92.

37. Stephen Bonsal diary, undated 1919 (May 3?), quoted in Robert H. Ferrell, *Woodrow Wilson and World War I*, 279 n. 27.

38. Memorandum by Colonel A. L. Conger, *The Paris Peace Conference, 1919*, 12:131.

39. J. C. Smuts to David Lloyd George, May 22, 1919; J. C. Smuts to WW, May 30, 1919, reprinted, RSB, *Woodrow Wilson and World Settlement*, 3:458–68.

40. George B. Noble to Joseph Grew, May 15, 1919, *Paris Peace Conference*, 11:572.

41. William C. Bullitt to WW, May 17, 1919, *Paris Peace Conference*, 11:573. Techni-

cally, Bullitt was assistant in the Department of State, attaché to the American Commission to Negotiate Peace.

42. EBW, *My Memoir*, 257.
43. WW cable to JPT, June 28, 1919, *Congressional Record*, 58, pt. 2, pp. 1952–53, reprinted in *Paris Peace Conference*, 11:604
44. EMH to Ralph Martin, July 15, 1919, Mrs. Edward S. Blagden Papers, HL.
45. RL, "The Signing of the Treaty of Peace With Germany at Versailles on June 28th, 1919," *Paris Peace Conference*, 11:603.
46. Edmund W. Starling, *Starling of the White House*, 146.
47. Conversation with EMH, December 1, 1930, George Sylvester Viereck Papers, YL.
48. Conversation with EMH, October 13, 1930, George Sylvester Viereck Papers.
49. Ibid.

23. A Congress "Frothing at the Mouth"

1. Jonathan Daniels, *The Time Between the Wars*, 47.
2. Michael Teague, *Mrs. L., Conversations with Alice Roosevelt Longworth*, 169.
3. *PWW*, 61:359 n. 1.
4. RL to Frank L. Polk, June 4, 1919, RL Selected Papers, LC.
5. Ibid.
6. EBW, *My Memoir*, 272.
7. *Courier-Journal*, July 13, 1919, WWP, Series 9, reel 505.
8. Ibid.
9. *The Messages and Papers of Woodrow Wilson*, 2:709.
10. Diary of Henry Fountain Ashurst, July 11, 1919, *PWW*, vol. 61.
11. Ibid.
12. Thomas A. Bailey, *Woodrow Wilson and the Great Betrayal*, 79.
13. Ibid.
14. *NYT*, July 14, 1919, *PWW*, vol. 61.
15. *Washington Post*, July 22, 1919; *New York Times*, July 22, 1919, *PWW*, vol. 61.
16. Bert E. Park, "Wilson's Neurologic Illness during the Summer of 1919," *PWW*, 62:628–29.
17. EBW to Henry White, August 4, 1919, Henry White Papers, LC.
18. Henry White to William Phillips, May 8, 1919, in Allan Nevins, *Henry White*, 447.
19. Ibid.
20. Park, "Wilson's Neurologic Illness," 62:629.
21. HCL to WW, July 15 and July 22, 1919, *PWW*, vol. 61.
22. WW to HCL, July 25, 1919, *PWW*, vol. 61.
23. Park, "Wilson's Neurologic Illness," 62:631.
24. William Shakespeare, *Macbeth*, act 1, sc. 7, l. 5.
25. Park, "Wilson's Neurologic Illness," 62:638.
26. HCL to John T. Morse Jr., August 18, 1919, HCL Papers, box 52A, Massachusetts Historical Society.
27. RL, August 2 and 11, 1919, Private Memoranda, RL Papers, conts. 66, 67.
28. RL testimony before the Senate Committee on Foreign Relations, Senate Document 106, pp. 139–252, and see "Hearing Before the Senate Committee on Foreign Relations," August 7, 1919, Private Memorandum, RL Papers. Newspapers quoted in Thomas H. Hartig, *Robert Lansing*, 290.
29. R. C. Lindsay to Lord Curzon, August 8, 1919, Public Record Office, Kew.
30. HCL to Right Honorable Viscount Bryce, August 9, 1919, HCL Papers, box 52.

31. HCL to John T. Morse Jr., August 18, 1919, HCL Papers, box 52A.

32. Ibid.

33. The sixteen senators included Lodge, McCumber, Borah, Brandegee, Fall, Knox, Harding, Johnson of California, New, Moses, Hitchcock, Williams, Swanson, Pomerene, Smith, and Pittman.

34. David Lawrence, *The True Story of Woodrow Wilson*, 270

35. *NYT*, August 19, 1919.

36. Park, "Wilson's Neurologic Illness," 62:631.

37. *NYT*, August 20, 1919.

38. Park, "Wilson's Neurologic Illness," 62:634.

39. Senator Key Pittman to WW, August 15, 1995, *PWW*, vol. 62.

40. Private memorandum, August 20, 1919, RL Papers, conts. 66, 67. Park, "Wilson's Neurologic Illness," 62:631, writes: "Yet, as is so typical of individuals with evolving organic brain syndromes what he was not disposed to do was to change in the face of advice from senators of both parties who told him that he simply did not have the votes for ratification unless he accepted reservations to the treaty." Rating the impairment of the whole person, it is concluded that Wilson would conservatively have been certified as 15 to 45 percent impaired as to a percentage of the whole man by September 1919, according to the American Medical Association, *Guides to the Evaluation of Permanent Impairment*, 2nd ed. (Chicago: 1982); also see Bert E. Park, "Presidential Disability: Past Experiences and Future Implications," *Politics and the Life Sciences* 7 (1988): 50–66 in *PWW*, v. 62:634 n. 17.

41. *PWW*, 62:631.

42. *PWW*, 62:633.

43. WW, *Constitutional Government in the United States*, 139–41, in *PWW*, 62:632 n. 14.

44. RL to Frank Polk, July 26, 1919, RL Papers, box 5.

45. Sir William Wiseman to Charles Seymour, Charles Seymour, *The Intimate Papers of Colonel House*, 4:515 and n. 2.

46. New York *Sun*, August 27, 1919.

47. WW to EMH, August 29, 1919, *PWW*, vol. 62.

48. EMH to Gordon Auchincloss, August 31, 1919, EMH Selected Correspondance, box 7, Group 466, YL.

49. Gordon Auchincloss to EMH, August 28, 1919, EMH Selected Correspondance, box 7, Group 466.

50. London *Times* (dateline, New York, December 10), December 12, 1919.

51. *Evening Standard*, December 12, 1919.

52. Park, "Wilson's Neurologic Illness," 62:636.

53. Samuel Eliot Morison, *The Oxford History of the American People*, 882.

54. EBW, *My Memoir*, 274.

24. WILSON'S GREATEST PUBLICITY CAMPAIGN

1. RSB Diary, *PWW*, 63:619.

2. CTG Diary, pt. 3, September 4, 1919, PL.

3. *Los Angeles Examiner*, September 3, 1919, *PWW*, 2:103.

4. Key Pittman to JPT, September 8, 1919, *PWW*, vol. 63.

5. *Congressional Record*, 66th Cong., 1st sess., pp. 4493–501, in *PWW*, vol. 63, p. 5 n. 4.

6. Address to the Columbus Chamber of Commerce, September 4, 1919, *Messages and Papers of Woodrow Wilson*, 2:727–43; *PWW*, 63:7.

7. Address in the Indianapolis Coliseum, September 4, 1919, *Messages and Papers*, 2:743–54, *PWW*, vol. 63.
8. William Bayard Hale, *The Story of a Style*, 256–303.
9. Address to the Columbus Chamber of Commerce, September 4, 1919, *Messages and Papers*, 2:727–43; *PWW*, vol. 63; quoted under heading "National Republican," without date, WWP, 2:105.
10. Rudolph Forster to JPT, re Norris complaint, September 7, 1919, *PWW*, vol. 63.
11. WW to George William Norris, September 11, 1919, *PWW*, vol. 63.
12. Luncheon address in Portland, September 15, 1919, *Messages and Papers*, 2:949–54; *PWW*, vol. 63.
13. JPT to Rudolph Forster, September 7, 1919, *PWW*, vol. 63.
14. Columbus, Ohio, *Dispatch*, September 4, 1919, WWP, series 9, reel 505.
15. *Kansas City Post*, September 6, 1919, WWP, series 9, reel 505.
16. *NYT*, September 14, 1919, WWP, series 9, reel 505.
17. Louis Adamic, *American Mercury*, 21 (October 1930): 138–46; *PWW*, 63:239 n. 1.
18. Thomas Marshall to RL, October 6, 1919, RL Papers.
19. Richard H. Hansen, *The Year We Had No President*, 29; Thomas Marshall to RL, October 6, 1919, RL Papers.
20. John D. Feerick, *From Falling Hands*, 176.
21. *NYT*, September 15, 1919.
22. JPT, *Woodrow Wilson As I Know Him*, 441–43.
23. *Treaty of Peace with Germany: Hearings before the Committee on Foreign Relations, United States Senate*, 66th Cong. 1st sess., Sen. Doc. No. 106 (Washington, 1919), p. 1233, in *PWW*, 63:338 n. 1.
24. Henry White to HCL, September 19, 1919; HCL to White, October 2, 1919; HCL Papers, box 53, Massachusetts Historical Society.
25. William Phillips to RL, September 13, 1919; followed by note September 15, RL Papers, vol. 46, LC.
26. RL to Acting Secretary of State William Phillips, September 15, 1919, RL Papers, vol. 46.
27. RL to John W. Davis, September 21, 1919, RL Papers.
28. Eleanor Lansing Dulles to author, February 22, 1989.
29. RL to WW, September 17, 1919, WWP, series 2, reel 105.
30. Breckinridge Long Papers, LC.
31. JPT, *Woodrow Wilson*, 441–43; *PWW*, 63:338–40.
32. RL to John W. Davis, September 21, 1919, RL Papers.
33. Edith Benham Helm Papers, cont. 19A, LC.
34. RL to Honorable James Hamilton Lewis, April 7, 1919, RL Papers.
35. Ibid. On October 6, 1919, RL wrote, "How can I resign at the present time?" and see JPT, *Woodrow Wilson*, 441–43.
36. *NYT*, September 15, 1919; *New York Sun*, September 15, 1919.
37. EMH to Gordon Auchincloss, September 15, 1919; Auchincloss to EMH; EMH Papers, series 1, box 7, YL.
38. Mary Allen Hulbert, "The Woodrow Wilson I Knew . . . My Last Meeting with Woodrow Wilson," *Liberty Magazine*, February 21, 1925, 25–27; a slightly different version in Mary Allen Hulbert, *The Story of Mrs. Peck*, 267–77, and *PWW*, 63:419–21.
39. Edmund W. Starling, *Starling of the White House*, 150.

40. *NYT,* September 18, 1919.
41. Starling, *Starling of the White House,* 150.
42. *NYT,* September 26, 1919.
43. CTG Diary, pt. 2.
44. *PWW,* 63:527
45. EBW, *My Memoir,* 285.
46. *NYT,* September 27, 1919.
47. David Lawrence, *The True Story of Woodrow Wilson,* 279.
48. *NYT,* September 29, 1919.
49. Ibid., September 27, 1919.
50. Ibid., September 29, 1919.
51. CTG Diary, pt. 3.
52. CTG to Harry Garfield, October 1, 1919, *PWW,* vol. 63.
53. *NYT,* September 28, 1919.
54. EBW, *My Memoir,* 286.

25. "The beginning of the deception of the American people"

1. IHH Papers, cont. 6–7, reel 7, LC.
2. Editors' note: "To us, Hoover's account has the ring of truth"; "Hoover impresses us as an intelligent and sturdily honest witness"; *PWW,* 63:542 n. 1.
3. IIH Papers, cont. 6–7, reel 7, LC.
4. The names given are Miss Harkins and Miss Ruth Powderly, *PWW,* 64, 509.
5. "The Truth About Wilson's Illness," IHH, *Forty-Two Years in the White House,* 97–108.
6. EBW, *My Memoir,* 288.
7. Dr. Bert E. Park's evaluation, circa 1990, "Woodrow Wilson's Stroke of October 2, 1919," based on the seventy-year-old medical records and current interpretations, in the 1990 edition of *PWW,* 63:646.
8. *NYT,* October 3, 1919.
9. White House Diary by IHH.
10. Josephus Daniels Diary, *PWW,* 63:548.
11. RL Memorandum, written after resignation, February 1920, *PWW,* vol. 61.
12. Thomas Jefferson, *A Manual of Parliamentary Practice. For the Use of the Senate of the United States* (Washington, D.C.: 1801).
13. JPT, *Woodrow Wilson As I Know Him,* 443–44.
14. RL to Professor Julius W. Pratt, June 14, 1928, 6–7. RL Papers, LC.
15. Josephus Daniels, *The Wilson Era,* 559. "Those nearest the President believed death a certainty after [Wilson's] first stroke. Therefore they did not inform Thomas R. Marshall lest he prematurely assume presidential power. Instead, they decided to warn Marshall unofficially through his friend, J. Fred Essary, the *Baltimore Sun's* Washington correspondent. "Government by Proxy," *Century,* February, 1926, 481–82, in Ruth C. Silva, *Presidential Succession,* 60 n. 36.
16. Richard H. Hansen, *The Year We Had No President,* 40. This was intended as a humorous comment, provoked during a tiresome senatorial debate about the needs of the country.
17. Daniels, *Wilson Era,* 558, 562.
18. Henry L. Stoddard, *As I Knew Them,* 547.
19. Thomas R. Marshall to RL, October 6, 1919, RL Papers.

20. John D. Feerick, *From Failing Hands,* 176.
21. *Washington Post,* October 6, 1919; *PWW,* 63:553.
22. EBW, *My Memoir,* 289.
23. *PWW,* 64:ix.
24. The papers were given to the editor of the *PWW,* Arthur S. Link, by CTG's sons, James Gordon Grayson and Cary T. Grayson Jr., and see *PWW,* 63:ix, 507 n. 1.
25. CTG to Louis Seibold, October 9, 1919, *PWW,* vol. 64.
26. CTG Statement, undated, *PWW,* 64:497–99.
27. Ibid.
28. Dr. Bert E. Park, *PWW,* 62:629.
29. CTG Memorandum, *PWW,* 64:507–8.
30. Francis Xavier Dercum to CTG, with enclosure "Dr. Dercum's Memoranda," October 20, 1919, *PWW,* 64:500–505.
31. Ibid., 503.
32. "A Memorandum by Dr. Grayson," undated, *PWW,* 64:510
33. Ibid.
34. Ibid.
35. EBW, *My Memoir,* 290.
36. Edwin A. Weinstein, *Woodrow Wilson: A Medical and Psychological Biography,* 360.
37. Daniels, *Wilson Era,* 2:512.
38. RSB Diary, November 5, 1919, *PWW,* vol. 63.
39. *NYT,* October 7, 1919.
40. CTG Memorandum, October 6, 1919, *PWW,* vol. 64.
41. Stoddard, *As I Knew Them,* 547.

26. "The President says"

1. EBW, *My Memoir,* 288.
2. Charles Swem to ACW, ACW Papers, YL.
3. JPT to William Bauchop Wilson with enclosure, October 6, 1919, *PWW,* vol. 63. See vol. 62, WW to Samuel Gompers, September 3, 1919, for origin of conference to confer "on the great and vital questions affecting our industrial life."
4. Alden Hatch Papers, University of Florida Libraries.
5. CTG, *Woodrow Wilson,* 55.
6. Josephus Daniels to WW, October 1, 1919, and George A. Sanderson to WW, October 6, 1919, regarding the resolution of the Senate of the United States of September 30, 1919, no. 198, WWP, 2:105.
7. EBW, *My Memoir,* 286.
8. Breckinridge Long Diary, October 7, 1919, LC, in *PWW,* vol. 63.
9. Margaret Woodrow Wilson to Edith Gittings Reid, October 16, 1919, *PWW,* vol. 63.
10. Memo for the secretary of the navy, no date, WWP, reel 2:105.
11. EBW to Josephus Daniels, October 7, 1919, WWP, reel 2:105.
12. Sir Arthur Willert, *Washington and Other Memories,* 132.
13. Newton D. Baker to Joseph C. Hostetler, October 7, 1919, in Frederick Palmer, *Newton D. Baker,* 396.
14. *NYT,* October 12 and 13, 1919.
15. *San Francisco Bulletin,* October 14, 1919, WWP, reel 505.
16. *Harvey's Weekly,* October 25 and November 1, 1919.
17. Franklin Knight Lane to JPT with enclosure, October 19, 1919, *PWW,* 63:582–87.
18. *PWW,* 63:588–90.

19. EBW to JPT, undated, but note by JPT says, "Wrote Mr. Barnes 11/10/19" and "Papers sent to Mr. Barnes—inc. letter from Secy State," WWP.

20. JPT to EBW, November 10, 1919, JPT Papers, box 46, LC.

21. JPT to EBW, November 24, 1919, JPT Papers, box 46.

22. JPT to EBW, December 2, 1919, incl. *Washington Star*, December 2, JPT Papers, box 46.

23. The Constitution, art. 1, sec. 7: "If any bill shall not be returned by the President within ten days (Sundays excepted) after it shall have been presented to him, the same shall be a law, in like manner as if he had signed it, unless the Congress by their adjournment prevent its return, in which case it shall not be a law."

24. *PWW*, 63:602 n. 1.

25. RL to Frank Polk, October 3, 1919, *The Paris Peace Conference, 1919*, 11:650.

26. RL to Polk, November 14, 1919, RL Papers, LC.

27. RL to WW, November 4, 1919, and JPT to EBW, November 5, 1919, WWP, 2:105.

28. EBW, no date, WWP, 2:105.

29. RL to WW, November 6, 1919; EBW on note of JPT to "Dear Governor," November 11, 1919, WWP:105.

30. In EBW handwriting, WWP, 4:182.

31. RL to JPT, November 21, 1919, and message at bottom, JPT to "Dear Mrs. Wilson" and EBW response, "The President says," undated, WWP, 4:182.

32. Gilbert F. Close to ACW, May 7, 1951, ACW Papers.

33. *Town Topics*, October 16, 1919, 9.

34. *Harvey's Weekly*, November 22, 1919, 10.

35. Robert K. Murray, *The Harding Era*, 3, 75, 84.

36. "A Statement," October 25, 1919 n. 3, *PWW*, vol. 63.

37. JPT to EBW, November 11, 1919, and EBW handwriting, no salutation or date, WWP, 2:105.

38. *Harvey's Weekly*, November 1919; EBW, *My Memoir*, 300.

27. LODGE'S OLIVE BRANCH

1. For the evolution of Article X and its final draft, see RSB, *Woodrow Wilson and World Settlement*, 3: 179 final text.

2. *Congressional Record*, 66th Cong., 1st sess., November 1919.

3. Gilbert M. Hitchcock (signed G. M. Hitchcock) to EBW, November 13, 1919, with encl. "Proposed Substitute Reservations. To take the place of those Proposed by Sen Lodge," *PWW*, vol. 64.

4. Arthur Willert to H. Wickham Steed, October 27, 1919, London *Times* International Record Office.

5. Raymond B. Fosdick, *Letters on the League of Nations*, October 24 and 29, 1919, November 7, 1919.

6. Ibid.

7. Interview with EBW, Alden Hatch Papers, University of Florida Libraries.

8. H. H. Kohlsaat, *From McKinley to Harding*, 220.

9. EBW, *My Memoir*, 293.

10. IHH Papers, LC.

11. *Town Topics*, September 25, 1919.

12. "Refused," Edith Benham Helm Papers, cont. 19A, LC.

13. Public Records Office, F.O. 371, U.S. Files, 23017–85083:4250, July 18, 1919–November 22, 1919.

14. EBW, *My Memoir*, 292–95.
15. HCL to Henry White, October 2, 1919, HCL Papers, box 53, HL.
16. HCL to Lord Bryce, October 8, 1919, HCL Papers, box 52A.
17. Ibid.
18. HCL to Henry White, November 3, 1919; White to HCL, October 11, 1919, HCL Papers, box 52A.
19. *Congressional Record*, 66th Cong., 1st sess., reel 136, p. 6600, October 9, 1919.
20. David Hunter Miller, *My Diary at the Conference of Paris*, 20:569–93.
21. Thomas A. Bailey, *Woodrow Wilson and the Great Betrayal*, 176.
22. Stephen Bonsal, *Unfinished Business*, 247, 258, 253.
23. Ibid., 250, n. 1.
24. Ibid., 261.
25. EBW to Loulie Hunter House, October 17, 1919, *PWW*, vol. 63 (parenthesis left unclosed).
26. EMH to EBW, October 22, 1919, *PWW*, vol. 63.
27. EMH to EBW, November 17, 1919; EMH to "Dear Governor," November 17, 1919, and encl., *PWW*, vol. 64.
28. EBW to EMH, November 18, 1919, *PWW*, vol. 64.
29. *NYT*, November 8, 1919; Gilbert M. Hitchcock, speech, January 12, 1925, Nebraska Historical Society.
30. Gilbert M. Hitchcock to EBW, November 13, 1919, *PWW*, vol. 64.
31. *PWW*, 62:621 n. 1.
32. Gilbert M. Hitchcock to EBW, EBW to Hitchcock, November 15, 1919, *PWW*, vol. 64.
33. Gilbert M. Hitchcock to EBW, November 17, 1919, encl. "A Suggestion," undated, WWP 2:105, no. 112035.
34. Ibid., EBW edited version.
35. EBW, *My Memoir*, 296–97.
36. *Congressional Record*, 66th Cong., 1st sess., November 19, 1919, reel 137, 8779.
37. JPT to EBW, November 21, WWP, 4:182.
38. Herbert Hoover to "The President," November 19, 1919, WWP, 4:182.
39. November 18, 1919, HCL Papers, box 51.
40. Thomas A. Bailey, *Woodrow Wilson and the Great Betrayal*, 190–92; Henry Fountain Ashurst Diary, November 19, 1919, *PWW*, vol. 64.
41. *PWW*, vol. 64, November 19, 1919.
42. "A Draft of a Statement," c. November 19, 1919, *PWW*, vol. 64.
43. HCL, undated, HCL Papers, box 51.
44. HCL, *The Senate and the League of Nations*, 222–25; speech, August 12, 1919, appendix.
45. EBW, *My Memoir*, 297.

28. The "smelling committee" pays a visit

1. *Harvey's Weekly*, November 22, 1919.
2. Ibid., November 29, 1919. Wilson's quotation is from *Congressional Government*.
3. Elihu Root Jr. to HCL, December 1, 1919, HCL Papers, box 52A, Massachusetts Historical Society.
4. HCL to Lord Bryce, December 2, 1919, HCL Papers, box 52A.
5. HCL to Root, quoted in ACW, *Woodrow Wilson*, 378.
6. JPT with encl. from Oscar Wilder Underwood to EBW, November 21, 1919, *PWW*, vol. 64.

7. Gilbert M. Hitchcock to WW, November 22, 1919, *PWW*, vol. 64.

8. Oscar Wilder Underwood to WW, November 21, 1919; Gilbert Hitchcock to WW, November 22 and 24, 1919, WWP, 4:182.

9. EMH to EBW and enclosure to "Dear Governor," November 24 and 27, 1919, WWP, 2:105. ACW writes, "It is not known whether Wilson ever knew of them," *Woodrow Wilson*, 387.

10. EMH Diary, January 31, 1920, YL.

11. Arthur Willert to H. Wickham Steed, December 6, 1919, London *Times* International Record Office.

12. On December 1, Tumulty wrote Mrs. Wilson a note telling her of his talk with Lansing and the latter's promise that nothing radical would be done in Mexico without consulting the president, that his justification for sending "stringent" notes was to forestall congressional action. On December 3, Fall proposed Senate Concurrent Resolution 221: "Resolved by the Senate, the House of Representatives concurring, that the action taken by the Department of State in reference to the pending controversy between this Government and the Government of Mexico should be approved; and, further, that the President of the United States be, and he is hereby, requested to withdraw from Venustiano Carranza the recognition heretofore accorded him by the United States as existing between this Government and the pretended government of Carranza." *Congressional Record*, 66th Cong., 2nd sess., 73.

13. "The facts about President Wilson's illness," IHH Papers, cont. 6–7, LC.

14. Ibid.

15. EBW, *My Memoir*, 299.

16. Stratton, David H., "The President's Smelling Committee," *The Colorado Quarterly* vol. 5, no. 2, 165–68.

17. Albert Fall quoted in the *NYT*, December 6, 1919, *PWW*, 64:133.

18. EBW, *My Memoir*, 299.

19. CTG Memorandum, December 5, 1919, *PWW*, vol. 64.

20. Josephus Daniels to EBW, December 5, 1919, WWP, 2:105.

21. Arthur Willert to H. Wickham Steed, December 6, 1919, *Times* International Record Office.

22. Ibid.

23. EMH Diary, December 22, 1919, YL.

24. JPT to EBW, December 11, 1919; WW to John L Lewis; Lewis to WW; *PWW*, 64:179–80.

25. JPT to EBW, December 18, 1919; EBW to JPT, December 19, 1919; *PWW*, vol. 64.

26. JPT to EBW, December 18, 1919, JPT Papers, LC.

27. Walker Downer Hines to WW, December 23, 1919, *PWW*, vol. 64; JPT to EBW, December 23, 1919, JPT Papers, box 46; WW to JPT, December 24, 1919 (in WW's disjointed handwriting), though it may have been written the previous day, JPT Papers, box 50.

28. Statement, December 23, 1919, JPT Papers, box 46.

29. R. A. Rogers to Dr. Francis Dercum, December 13/19 and 17/19, 1919, Francis Xavier Dercum Papers received from Dr. Steven Lomazow, *PWW*, 67:611–14

30. Ibid.

31. Ibid.

32. David C. Williams to Mrs. Baer, June 1, 1920, *PWW*, 67:618–19.

33. Draft of a public letter, c. December 1919; EBW to Alexander Mitchell Palmer, December 18, 1919; *PWW*, vol. 64.

34. WW to John Grier Hibben, December 22, 1919; Hibben to WW, January 6, 1919; *PWW*, vol. 64.
35. WW to Mrs. Young, December 22, 1919, *PWW*, vol. 64.
36. Franklin Lane to George Lane, A. W. Lane and L. H. Wall, eds., *The Letters of Franklin K. Lane*, 330.
37. Raymond B. Fosdick to Sir Eric Drummond, December 30, 1919, Raymond Fosdick, *Letters on the League of Nations*, 91.
38. E. David Cronon, ed., *The Cabinet Diaries of Josephus Daniels*, 473–74, December 22, 1919.

29. THE WHITE HOUSE SNUBS THE BRITISH AMBASSADOR

1. Frederic William Wile, *Public Ledger*, February 19, 1920, National Archives, F60324.
2. George Egerton, "Diplomacy, Scandal and Military Intelligence," *Intelligence and National Security*, October 1987, vol. 2, no. 4, 111.
3. Grey of Fallodon to RL, October 3, 1919, Grey's title spelled out in presentation of paper with King George's appointment, National Archives, 701. 4111.
4. WW to EMH, August 15, 1919, RSB Papers, reel 65, LC.
5. Ibid.
6. National Archives, 701.4111/box 6296.
7. Charles Seymour, *The Intimate Papers of Colonel House* 4:496.
8. Grey to Moreton Frewen, August 13, 1919, in Frewen to HCL, August 15, 1919, HCL Papers, box 52A.
9. Joyce Grigsby Williams, *Colonel House and Sir Edward Grey*, 129 n. 59.
10. Cecil Spring Rice, *The Letters and Friendships of Sir Cecil Spring Rice*, 2:374, 372.
11. Lord George Nathaniel Curzon (Earl Curzon of Kedleston) to Grey, November 25, 1919. In further consultations with both British and American colleagues, Curzon learned that Wilson had mentioned in Paris his objection to the major. The British Library, India Office Library and Records, f. 112 / 211.
12. Grey to RL, October 3, 1919, National Archives, 701.4111/289.
13. Grey to Curzon, October 4, 1919, *Documents of British Foreign Policy*, first series, vol. 5, 1919, pp. 1004–5.
14. Grey to Curzon, October 7, 1919, *Documents of British Foreign Policy*, first series, vol. 5, 1919, p. 1007.
15. RL to Grey, October 10, 1919, National Archives, 701.4111/289.
16. RL quoted in Willert to Steed, October 27, 1919, *Times* Newspapers Limited.
17. Grey to Curzon, November 2, 1919, India Office Library and Records, British Library.
18. In a typed statement on British embassy stationery, dated November 4, 1919, Craufurd-Stuart explained that the one topic of conversation at the dinner party a year earlier at the home of Mrs. James McDonald, the handsome widow of the Standard Oil magnate, was the president's approaching departure for Paris. A good many people gave their opinion, but the major had not given his but had merely asked a guest if she had seen an article in that morning's *Tribune* that was critical of the president's powers and ability in comparison with those of the British officials Balfour, Asquith, and Lloyd George. The opinion was not his, he pointed out in his statement, and he added that after dinner he had not joined the ladies but played the piano. India Office.
19. Grey to Curzon, November 2, 1919, India Office.

20. Willert to Steed, December 6, 1919, *Times* Newspapers Limited. Two documents among the British embassy files in Washington, at least one of which was initiated by the French ambassador, prove that the reinvestigation of Craufurd-Stuart's remarks was conducted most seriously. In one, the hostess of the dinner party wrote to say that the major did not give any opinion on his own but that one of the guests who had not read the article in the paper, the topic of conversation at the moment, asked the major what it was and what paper it was in. The other statement, referred to in note 18, was from Craufurd-Stuart himself. Cover letter, Isabelle McDonald to Sir William Tyrrell, November 2, 1919 (with Robert Lansing's notation: "Handed me by French Amb. Nov. 4/19"), and statement, November 4, 1919, signed C. Kennedy Craufurd-Stuart, Major, National Archives, 701.4111/3122–1/2.

21. R. C. Lindsay to William Phillips, November 9, 1919, National Archives, 701.4111/305.

22. Ibid.

23. Sir Robert Bruce Lockhart, *Giants Cast Long Shadows*, 77.

24. John Dos Passos, *Mr. Wilson's War*, 226.

25. *Town Topics*, found in Charles Seymour Papers, 1920, box 64, folder 119. Avoiding mention of Bernard Baruch's name, the columnist asks, seeing "Old Glory being dragged into oblivion," if there are "representatives of the Hebrew race in offices that control our Government" and whether to classify them among those "who would do anything and everybody—his own people as well as everybody else—for selfish and personal gain."

26. Charles Hamlin Papers, cont. 347, LC.

27. *NYT*, August 10, 1937, 19. Emily Stevens Ladenburg was the daughter of Alexander H. Stevens, a descendant of Albert Gallatin, secretary of the treasury under Thomas Jefferson, a cousin of Admiral Samuel Eliot Morrison's, and the president of the Sixth National Bank of New York. In February 1896, Mr. Ladenburg was ill and went to Nassau in the Bahamas to recuperate. On his return to New York City on the Ward liner *Niagara*, he is believed to have been washed overboard by a heavy sea. The couple lived at 13 East Thirty-eighth Street. May's full name was Eugenie Marie. Two-thirds of Adolf Ladenburg's estate of $10 million was left to May, one-third to her mother. According to her obituary, *New York Times*, September 20, 1975, May (Ladenburg) Davie, widow of a lawyer, was active in the Republican Party in 1932 and wrote "Our American Way of Life" for the *New York Herald Tribune*.

28. Military Reference Branch, Textual Reference Division, No. 60324, May 15, 1918, National Archives.

29. Michael Teague, *Mrs. L., Conversations with Alice Roosevelt Longworth*, 162.

30. EMH Diary, March 25, 1920 (copy in Baruch Papers, Mudd Library, Princeton University). During his visit with Colonel House in the spring of 1920, Henry Wheelwright Marsh not only claimed possession of the Dictograph record but confided its contents. Marsh was the flamboyant founding partner in 1906 of the prospering insurance firm of Marsh and McLennan, located on the twentieth floor of 80 Maiden Lane in New York City. In 1917 the partners were serving in Washington, McLennan, at the invitation of his friend and colleague Bernard Baruch, on the War Production Board. Harry Marsh, who had left Harvard in 1885, a born detective who had relished his secret Manhattan office compartment from which he could eavesdrop on staff conversations, served in the Military Intelligence Division, an obvious outlet for his interests and skills. "Marsh & McLennan," courtesy of Pamela Newman to author.

31. Edith Benham Helm dictated her impressions of the events of the autumn of 1919 to her husband, who recorded them in longhand. The typed version, "The Craufurd Stuart Affair," is dated October 1929. Edith Benham Helm Papers, cont. 19A.

32. Curzon to Grey, November 22, 1919, f. 112/211, India Office.

33. Grey to Curzon, December 9, 1919, f. 112/211, India Office.

34. Conversation with Sir William Wiseman, April 9, 1946, Charles Seymour Papers, folder 119, YL.

35. May Ladenburg to General Marlborough Churchill, no date (February 2, 1920), Military Reference Branch, PP F 60324, National Archives.

36. Churchill to Ladenburg, February 6, 1920, Military Reference Branch, PP F 60324.

37. Newton Baker to Ladenburg, March 8, Newton D. Baker Papers, cont. 12, LC.

38. Baker to WW, March 11, 1920, Baker Papers, cont. 12.

39. Baker to Churchill, March 11, 1920, Marlborough Churchill Papers, RG. 165 E 65 (MID), box 3723, file 100560–376, National Archives.

40. Years after the fact, the Craufurd-Stuart affair remains a tantalizing tale. By 1929, Edith Benham (then Mrs. Helm) concluded that Craufurd-Stuart had been the victim of a conspiracy involving Dr. Grayson and a man with whom Grayson had a devoted friendship, obviously Bernard Baruch. One version has the recording of the Baruch-Ladenburg conversation remaining with Secretary of War Newton Baker. But according to the British journalist Wickham Steed, the wax rolls were turned in to the Department of Justice in Washington, stolen, hawked about to various New York newspapers, and eventually bought for $10,000 by Adolph Ochs, publisher of the *New York Times,* who was said to have burnt them. This last account is somewhat plausible, given the familial ties—Baruch's father, Dr. Simon Baruch, being the Ochs family physician. Disappointingly, Ochs's papers bear no trace of this transaction, and this tape and its contents continue to elude historical reckoning.

41. Egerton, "Diplomacy, Scandal and Military Intelligence," 132 n. 70, suggests that newspaper reports of February 19 based on information in the *Public Ledger,* and the New York *World,* etc., may have originated with Baruch, who had close contacts with the press.

42. Willert to Steed, December 6, 1919, *Times* International Archives.

43. Steed to Northcliffe, January 19, 1920, Steed Papers, *Times* Archives; Egerton, "Diplomacy, Scandal, and Military Intelligence," 132 n. 67.

44. John Quinn to Sir William Tyrrell, February 3, 1920, f. 371/4547, Public Record Office, Kew.

45. Leon E. Boothe, "A Fettered Envoy," 93.

46. WWP, 2:106, both original and typed version, dated February 6, 1920.

47. Ibid.

48. *Harvey's Weekly,* February 14, 1920.

49. RSB Diary, February 3, 1920, *PWW,* vol. 64.

50. ACW, *Woodrow Wilson,* 381.

51. Sir Arthur Willert, *Personality in Politics,* 158–59.

30. "Wilson's last mad act"

1. *Town Topics,* February 19, 1920, v. 83.

2. EBW to John Wesley Westcott, December 28, 1919, *PWW,* vol. 64.

3. William E. Dodd to EBW, January 4, 1920, WWP, 2:106.

4. RSB Diary, January 23, 1920, *PWW,* vol. 64.

5. Stanley Cohen, *A. Mitchell Palmer: Politician*, 210.

6. Ibid., 238.

7. Walter Lippmann to Newton Baker, January 17, 1920, Ronald Steel, *Walter Lippmann and the American Century*, 167.

8. "To the American People: Report on the Illegal Practices of the United States Department of Justice" (Washington: National Popular Government League, 1920), in Donald Johnson, "The Political Career of A. Mitchell Palmer," 345–70.

9. *PWW*, 65:186, and 188 n. 6.

10. JPT to EBW, January 5, 1920, *PWW*, vol. 64 (enlarged signature possibly WW's).

11. EMH Diary, January 3, 1920, in *PWW*, vol. 64.

12. EBW to Rudolph Forster, undated, in answer to Forster's forwarding, at Tumulty's request, a draft of a telegram prepared by Hines, February 14, 1920, JPT Papers, box 46, LC.

13. John Morton Blum, *Joe Tumulty and the Wilson Era*, 232.

14. A Jackson Day Message, January 8, 1920, *PWW*, vol. 64.

15. Raymond B. Fosdick to Sir Eric Drummond, January 10, 1920, Raymond Fosdick, *Letters on the League of Nations*.

16. Diary of Henry Fountain Ashurst, January 9, 1920, *PWW*, vol. 64.

17. RL to John Davis, February 1, 1920. The State Department was riddled with the flu, though RL said the present epidemic was a less malignant type than in the previous two years. It has also been suggested that WW was suffering instead from a viral infection. RL Selected Papers, LC.

18. RSB Diary, November 28, 1920, *PWW*, vol. 64, and John W. Davis Diary, September 2, 1920, 363 n. 1.

19. CTG Memorandum, April 13, 1920, courtesy James Gordon Grayson and Cary T. Grayson Jr., *PWW*, 64:363 n. 1.

20. Bert E. Park, "The Aftermath of Wilson's Stroke," *PWW*, 64:527.

21. Ibid.

22. Edith B. Helm Collection, cont. 19A, LC.

23. RSB Diary, February 15, 1920, *PWW*, vol. 64.

24. Thomas Bailey, *Woodrow Wilson and the Great Betrayal*, 248–49.

25. WW to RL, February 7, 1920, WWP, 2:106.

26. RL to WW, February 9, 1920, *PWW*, vol. 64.

27. WW to RL, February 11, 1920, *PWW*, vol. 64.

28. "Cabinet Meetings . . . ," RL Confidential Papers, cont. 66, 67.

29. "My Resignation and Some Thoughts on the Subject," February 13, 1920, RL Confidential Papers, conts. 66, 67. The exchange of letters was given to the press at seven-thirty that evening.

30. Lansing was in truth physically weak, a diabetic since his midtwenties. Sickly during his entire term as counselor and secretary of state, he managed, under his doctor's supervision, to control his disease through diet and rest. Insulin would be available to him only in two years' time, in 1922.

31. RSB Diary, February 5, 1920, LC; *PWW*, vol. 64.

32. "The Year 1919 and the President," January 1, 1920, RL Confidential Papers, conts 66, 67.

33. Thomas H. Hartig, *Robert Lansing*, 311.

34. *Pall Mall*, February 15, 1920; *Echo*, February 16, 1920.

35. *PWW*, 64:394–96.

36. Ibid., 432–33.

37. "Hearings Before the Committee on the Judiciary," House of Representatives, *Congressional Record*, 66th Cong., 2nd sess., February 26 and March 1, 1920.

38. The lawyer Henry E. Davis, writing in 1881 on the "Inability of the President—A Monograph on What Constitutes and Who Decides the Inability of the President to Service," analyzed the question from three angles, asking: What is inability? By whom is the fact of its existence to be decided? What is its effect, once established, on the president in office? Initially, the summation of the 1881 discussions seemed to provide a practical guide. In the first paragraph, quoting Professor Theodore W. Dwight, it stated clearly and positively that inability was to be judged on "strict intellectual incapacity" established by legal evidence that Congress was competent to prescribe, and when such inability was properly established, the vice president was to fulfill the president's four-year term. Dwight's next paragraph was less reassuring, alerting the reader that the fault with disability lies not so much in its recognition but in its acknowledgment: the people of the United States will not, in the absence of the clearest evidence of mental inability, be satisfied to part with the services of a president, at the present day, practically of their own choice. Though this article was prepared by Mr. Davis, a member of the Washington bar, immediately after the death of Garfield, it was not printed as a Senate document until 1918. Ibid.

39. Herbert L. Abrams, "Can the Twenty-Fifth Amendment Deal with a Disabled President?" Recognizing his close personal relationship and friendship with his physician, "President Jimmy Carter . . . seriously doubts that White House physicians can be depended on to convey important information about medical conditions such as strokes, changes in mental status, and other incapacitating illnesses without the full consent of the president, any more than the president's wife and the White House staff could be expected to do so. Carter has opined that there would have been a strong inclination to conceal Reagan's condition if he had developed Alzheimer's disease while in the White House." Ibid., 119, James Carter, comments at Conference of the Working Group on Disability in United States Presidents, Carter Center, Emory University, Atlanta, Ga., January 28, 1995. When George Bush suffered from an irregular heartbeat, "atrial fibrillation," it was "difficult to assess the President's condition because of the Administration's decision to withhold definite medical information." Barbara Bush, after spending the night in the hospital with the president, announced, "Doctor I'm not, but he looks fabulous." *NYT*, May 6, 1991.

40. EBW, *My Memoir*, 301.

41. Eleanor Lansing to Edith Benham, Edith B. Helm Collection, undated.

31. EDITH WILSON AS "FOREMOST STATESMAN"

1. *Daily Mail*, February 22, 1920, WWP, series 9, reel 505.

2. "How the White House Patient Was Preserved from Annoyance," F. W. Wile, *Weekly Dispatch*, February 22, 1920, WWP, series 9, reel 505.

3. David F. Houston, *Eight Years with Wilson's Cabinet*, 60.

4. New York City *Evening Mail*, September 4, 1920, WWP, series 9, reel 505.

5. Canton, Ohio, *Daily News*, March 12, 1920, WWP, series 9, reel 505.

6. Baltimore, Md., *Star*, March 16, 1920, WWP, series 9, reel 505.

7. New York City *Evening Mail*, September 4, 1920, WWP, series 9, reel 505.

8. EBW, *My Memoir*, 302. Edith Benham married Admiral James Meredith Helm on

April 20, 1920. EBW attended the wedding and the following July 15 wrote Henry White, "The lady has recovered I think in spirit and body . . ." EBW to Henry White, July 15, 1920, *PWW*, vol. 65.

9. *Collier's*, quoted in *Harvey's Weekly*, March 20, 1920.
10. EBW to Gilbert Hitchcock, January 5, 1920, *PWW*, vol. 64.
11. "Suggestion," September 3, 1919, *PWW*, vol. 62.
12. Gilbert Hitchcock to EBW, January 5, 1920, *PWW*, vol. 64.
13. EBW notes, undated, probably January 15, 1920, WWP, 2:107.
14. The possibility is that Edith may have spoken to Tumulty before he wrote the January 15 letter: *PWW*, January 15, 1920, and n. 1.
15. JPT to EBW and return, January 17, 1920, WWP, 2:107.
16. Gilbert Hitchcock to JPT, January 26, 1920, *PWW*, vol. 64 and n. 2; Carter Glass to WW, February 9, 1920, *PWW*, vol. 64; Thomas A. Bailey, *Woodrow Wilson and the Great Betrayal*, 232.
17. RSB Diary, January 23, 1920, *PWW*, vol. 64.
18. A. S. Burleson to JPT, March 5, 1920, *PWW*, vol. 65.
19. Carter Glass to WW, February 9, 1920, *PWW*, vol. 64; William Phillips to WW, September 22, 1919, *PWW*, vol. 63 n. 2. "Representatives of the League to Enforce Peace reports that the following reservation has been agreed upon by the mild reservationists with Senator Lodge: "The United States assumes no obligations under the provisions of Article X to preserve the territorial integrity or political independence of any other country or to interfere in controversies between other nations whether members of the League or not or to employ the military and naval forces of the United States under any article of the treaty for any purpose unless in any particular case the Congress, which under the Constitution has the sole power to declare war or authorize the employment of the military and naval forces of the United States, shall by act or joint resolution so declare."
20. Draft, undated, *PWW*, attributed February 11, 1920, vol. 64.
21. JPT to EBW, February 27, 1920, *PWW*, vol. 64.
22. JPT to EBW, March 1, 1920, *PWW*, vol. 65.
23. Bert E. Park, "The Aftermath of Wilson's Stroke," *PWW*, vol. 64, appendix, "intransigence," 527; "effectively ended," 526–27.
24. Jean Jules Jusserand to Frank L. Polk, March 11, 1920, *PWW*, vol. 65, and to the foreign minister, No. 124, March 16, 1920, vol. 65, n. 1.
25. Gilbert M. Hitchcock to WW, March 11, 1920, *PWW*, vol. 65.
26. *Harvey's Weekly*, March 27, 1920.
27. Gilbert M. Hitchcock to WW, March 20, 1920, *PWW*, vol. 65.
28. Sir Arthur Willert, *Washington and Other Memories*, 134.
29. "own child," *PWW*, 65: 71 n. 3.
30. A Memorandum by CTG, March 31, 1920, courtesy, James Gordon Grayson, Cary T. Grayson Jr., *PWW*, vol. 65; CTG, *Woodrow Wilson: An Intimate Memoir*.
31. Diary of Josephus Daniels, April 20, 1920, *PWW*, vol. 65.
32. EBW, *My Memoir*, 303.
33. HCL Papers, typed notation of HCL conversation as recalled by Mrs. Corinne Roosevelt Robinson, dated "In March or February 1920," HL.
34. E. David Cronon, ed., *The Cabinet Diaries of Josephus Daniels*, February 20, 1920, 497.
35. F. W. Wile, "How the White House Patient Was Preserved from Annoyance," *Weekly Dispatch*, February 22, 1920, WWP, reel 505, series 9.

32. WILSON FOR A THIRD TERM

1. *NYT,* March 27, 1920.
2. CTG Memorandum, April 13, 1920, *PWW,* vol. 65.
3. Josephus Daniels Diary, April 14, 1920, *PWW,* vol. 65; David F. Houston, *PWW* 65: 186, n. 1.
4. RL to John Davis, May 22, 1920, RL Selected Papers, LC.
5. JPT to EBW, March 23, 1920, JPT Papers, LC.
6. CTG Memoranda, March 25, 1920, *PWW,* vol. 65.
7. CTG Memoranda, March 26, 1920, *PWW,* vol. 65.
8. WW to Jouett Shouse, April 12, 1920, *PWW,* vol. 65.
9. WW to G. E. Hamaker, May 9, 1920, *PWW,* vol. 65.
10. "The Facts about President Wilson's illness," cont. 66–67, reel 7, IHH Papers, LC.
11. Edmund W. Starling, *Starling of the White House,* 157.
12. Auckland Geddes to David Lloyd George, June 4, 1920, *PWW,* vol. 65.
13. Marc Peter to Giuseppe Motta, May 28, 1920, *PWW,* vol. 65.
14. CTG Diary, May 19 and 20, 1920, *PWW,* vol. 65.
15. WW to EBW, May 14, 1920, *PWW,* vol. 65; EBGW Papers, series 20, box 2.
16. EBW to WW, May 24, 1920, EBGW Papers, series 20, box 2.
17. EBW to WW, June 5, 1920, EBGW Papers, series 20, box 2.
18. WW re McAdoo, Josephus Daniels, *The Wilson Era,* 553; WW re Cox, Carter Glass, Memorandum, June 19, 1920, *PWW,* vol. 65; WW re Marshall, CTG Diary, July 3, 1920, *PWW,* vol. 65.
19. Charles Lee Swem Diary, May 17, 1920, *PWW,* vol. 65.
20. WW, Random Notes, c. June 10, 1920, *PWW,* vol. 65.
21. *Town Topics,* June 17, 1920.
22. John M. Blum, *Joe Tumulty and the Wilson Era,* 242–44 n. 33: questions, answers, were attached to Seibold and Tumulty memorandums. According to *PWW,* 65: 401 n. 1, these papers, found by Blum in a warehouse in northeastern Washington in 1947–48, have been lost or destroyed.
23. *World,* June 17, 1920, in *PWW,* 65: 416.
24. *New York Times,* June 18, 1920, *PWW,* 65: 426.
25. John Hohenberg, *The Pulitzer Prizes,* 38. Seibold's favored relationship with the Wilsons was sustained at least through 1921. He sent flattering references to "the Boss" and the League of Nations from China and Japan He rejoiced to see the Boss in fair fighting trim, he wrote Edith Wilson on May 10, 1921, and would be very happy to come and be of assistance if Wilson should decide that he would like to make public his views at any time. Seibold would "see that the matter approved by him" would be given to all the other newspapers. Louis Seibold Papers, LC.
26. "crowd went wild," *NYT,* June 29, 1920 *PWW,* vol. 65, n. 1; "Convention is with you," Homer Cummings to WW, June 28, 1920, *PWW,* vol. 65.
27. Carter Glass Memorandum, June 19, 1920, *PWW,* vol. 65.
28. Bainbridge Colby to WW, July 2, 1920; CTG Diary, July 3, 1920, *PWW,* vol. 65.
29. JPT to EBW, July 4, 1920, *PWW,* vol. 65.
30. Charles Lee Swem Diary, c. July 6, 1920, *PWW,* vol. 65.
31. WW to Bainbridge Colby, August 16, 1920, Swem Papers, box 78, PL.
32. WW to Josephus Daniels, August 28, 1920, *PWW,* vol. 66.
33. *Town Topics,* August 12, 1920, 13.
34. EBW to Henry White, July 15, 1920, *PWW,* vol. 65.

35. WW to George A. Foster, August 21, 1920, *PWW*, vol. 66.

36. Josephus Daniels, *The Wilson Era—Years of War and After*, 557.

33. "PECUNIARY ANXIETIES"

1. JPT to WW, October 20, 1920; Cox to EBW, October 21, 1920; WW to Cox, October 22, 1920; *PWW*, vol. 66; EBG, *My Memoir*, 321.

2. John W. Davis Diary, October 10, 1920, *PWW*, vol. 66.

3. William Hawkins, September 17, 1920, *PWW*, vol. 66.

4. David F. Houston, *Eight Years with Wilson's Cabinet*, 2:93.

5. Stockton Axson to Jessie Sayre, November 4, 1920, *PWW*, vol. 66.

6. RSB Diary, December 1, 1920, *PWW*, vol. 66.

7. RSB to EBW, November 2, 1920; RSB Diary, November 28, 1920; *PWW*, vol. 66.

8. RSB Diary, November 28, 1920, *PWW*, vol. 66.

9. RSB to EBW, November 29, 1920, *PWW*, vol. 66.

10. RSB Diary, November 28, 1920, "A Draft of an Article by RSB"; EBW to RSB, November 30, 1920; *PWW*, vol. 66.

11. EBW, *My Memoir*, 312; WW to Charles Z. Klauder, December 16, 1920, Charles L. Swem Papers, box 78, PL.

12. *New York Tribune*, September 27, 1921.

13. Alfred Hermann Fried to WW, December 16, 1920, *PWW*, vol. 66.

14. "A Memorandum of an Agreement," October 1, 1923, *PWW*, vol. 68.

15. WW to Jesse Jones, January 4, 1923; Jones to WW, January 9, 1924; WW to Jones, January 13, 1924; RSB Papers, reel 65, LC.

16. WW to George Henry Doran, November 26, 1920, *PWW*, vol. 66.

17. Charles L. Swem Diary, December 18, 1920, *PWW*, vol. 66.

18. WW to Norman Davis, December 9, 1920; WW to Carter Glass, December 11, 1920; WW to Secretary of War Baker, December 14, 1920; Charles L. Swem Papers, box 75.

19. RSB to WW, December 16, 1920, *PWW*, vol. 66.

20. WW to Thomas Bucklin Wells, September 30, 1920, *PWW*, vol. 66.

21. William Dodd to EBW, May 10, 1921, *PWW*, vol. 67.

22. EBW to William Dodd, May 22, 1921, *PWW*, vol. 67.

23. RSB Diary, March 1, 1921, *PWW*, vol. 67.

24. RSB Diary, March 24, 1921, *PWW*, vol. 67.

25. David Lawrence quoted in Richmond, Va., *News Leader*, March 5, 1921, WWP, 9:506. A version appears in Lawrence's *True Story of Woodrow Wilson*, 309.

26. "A New Report," March 4, 1921, *PWW*, vol. 67.

27. The official announcement was made on December 11, 1920.

28. EBW, *My Memoir*, 318–19.

29. *NYT*, March 5, 1921.

34. WILSON & COLBY

1. *Sense and Sensibility* and *Persuasion* were taken from the library in March and April 1922; EBW, *My Memoir*, 321.

2. SA to John Grier Hibben, June 11, 1921, *PWW*, vol. 67.

3. "Form dictated by W.W. August 26, 1921 for me to sign to intimate friends," presumably JRB; two-page typed list of approved acknowledgments, undated, both, WWP, series 12, Misc. Docs. Fragments, reel 527.

4. Sidney Gribetz, "The Strange Case of Woodrow Wilson's Admission to the Bar," *New York State Bar Journal*, February 1997.

5. *NYT*, August 16, 1921.

6. WW to EBW, August 17, 1921, EBGW Papers, box 20.

7. Louis Wiley to WW, April 21, 1921; JRB to Louis Wiley, May 25, 1921; Adolph S. Ochs Papers, *NYT* Archives, courtesy of Susan Dryfoos.

8. Bert E. Park, "The Aftermath of Wilson's Stroke, " *PWW*, 64:526–27

9. BMB to WW, August 10, 1921, Ochs Papers, *NYT* Archives.

10. WW to "My dear Adler," November 22, 1922, Ochs Papers.

11. JRB to Louis Wiley, January 8, 1924, *PWW*, vol. 68. One year earlier, on January 8, 1923, Henry Morgenthau wrote Wilson that, when he had visited Ochs, who had undergone a serious prostate operation, the publisher had told him that "the main worry on his mind was that Wilson had not written him a congratulatory letter on his twenty-fifth anniversary" and that he regarded his "Silver Book of Testimonials" as incomplete without that contribution; *PWW*, 68:268. Wilson's erratic, irrational position on Ochs was not lost on Bernard Baruch, who nonetheless remained protective of the former president. Twenty-three years after the incident, in September 1947, Baruch informed Ochs's son-in-law, Arthur Hays Sulzberger, then publisher of the *Times*, that, going over his old correspondence, he had found two letters (one was Wilson's answer as to why he was unwilling to write a congratulatory letter; the second was Baruch's reply about the *Times* having shown itself a good friend) that he would like to give Sulzberger for safekeeping as Baruch feared they might be misinterpreted if they fell into improper hands. The letters should be returned if the paper ever desired to make them public. Following Baruch's call, Sulzberger, who found the letters provocative enough to warrant comment, wrote a memo to his children. Sulzberger agreed with Wilson that the editorial policy of the *Times* had been much too conservative and offended other citizens as well as Mr. Wilson. For the rest, Sulzberger was hardly conciliatory. He thought the former president showed a mean and petty spirit, for he never had more loyal support than that of the *Times*. He thought Wilson could have ignored controversy and concentrated the contents of a congratulatory letter on appreciating the *Times'* support of the League. Sulzberger also thought Wilson disingenuous in claiming ignorance of the part Mr. Ochs had played in shaping the *Times*. On November 20, 1950, Baruch had a change of heart. He wrote to Sulzberger that he thought it a mistake for the *Times* to have the letters, which might create a bad impression; and he suggested they be sent back. Returning the letters two days later, Sulzberger was sorry that they should have given Baruch concern and attached a copy of the memorandum filed with the papers for his children's edification. The last paragraph noted that "Bernard Baruch's father was my mother's family physician and brought me into the world. I think Mr. Baruch, for that reason, has always had a special affection for me—which he most certainly displayed at this time." Memorandum, Arthur Hays Sulzberger, September 24, 1947, *New York Times* Archives.

12. *New York Tribune*, September 26, 1921, *PWW*, vol. 67.

13. WW to EBW, undated, 1921, EBGW Papers, series 20.

14. EBW, *My Memoir*, 330.

15. WW to Louis Seibold, November 12, 1921; Louis Seibold to WW, November 14, 1921; *PWW*, vol. 67.

16. JRB to William Edward Dodd, November 19, 1921, *PWW*, vol. 67.

35. WILSON & COLBY FOLDS

1. WW to Hamilton Holt, November 5, 1922, WW and EBW Papers, Rutgers University Library.
2. WW to Louis Brandeis, June 20, 1921, *PWW*, vol. 67.
3. RSB Diary, April 4, 1922, *PWW*, vol. 67.
4. Ibid.
5. *Courier-Journal*, May 13, 1922, WWP, 9:506.
6. Edmund G. Lowry, "The Outs Who Want to Get In . . . ," *Collier's National Weekly*, in *PWW*, 68:476 n. 3.
7. John M. Blum, *Joe Tumulty and the Wilson Era*, 262–63.
8. JPT to WW, April 5, 1922; WW to JPT, April 6, 1922; *PWW*, vol. 67.
9. *NYT*, April 9, 1922, *PWW*, vol. 68.
10. WW to JPT; JRB for WW to Louis Wiley, April 12, 1922; JPT Papers, box 99, LC. *NYT*, April 12, 1922, *PWW*, vol. 68.
11. JPT to WW, April 12, 1922, *PWW*, vol. 68; "Statement by Mr. Tumulty," JPT Papers, box 45.
12. Ibid.
13. WW to editor of the *NYT*, April 12, 1922, *PWW*, vol. 68.
14. *Plain Dealer*, April 13, 1922, JPT Papers, box 99.
15. Charles G. Ross, *Post-Dispatch*, April 16, 1922, JPT Papers, box 99.
16. EBW to JPT, no date, JPT Papers, box 79.
17. "I never liked Tumulty, but got along with him in spite of that," Alden Hatch Papers, University of Florida Libraries.
18. James Kerney to JPT, March 7, 1924, includes WW to Kerney, October 30, 1923, JPT Papers. Curiously, while Edith vilified Tumulty, it would seem as though Wilson, apart from his deliberate attempts to exclude his secretary in certain matters, had cared enough to seek some means of providing for him after their White House years together. At the end of July 1920, Wilson offered to appoint Tumulty as chief justice of the Customs Court of Appeals in Washington at the yearly salary of $8,500, work Tumulty would not have to take up until the following March. Tumulty thanked Wilson graciously ("you always know best how to do the pleasing and cheering thing") on August 5, said he would need time to think it over, and if it was in the public interest to fill the position in the meanwhile to do so. On December 17, 1920, he asked Edith Wilson to inform the president that he had decided not to accept the offer, that the only fair thing to his family was to resume the practice of law, that he did not intend to form a partnership but merely to "hang out my shingle on my own hook," eventually at 1317 F Street, NW, in Washington, D.C., JPT to EBW, June 3, 1921, JPT Papers, box 79.
19. *The Saturday Evening Post*, upon receiving Mrs. Wilson's protest, revamped Kerney's Wilson story to exclude the letter in question, but it was too late to prevent its being carried in the Western editions. JPT to William Allen White, editor, *Emporia Gazette*, March 19, 1924, JPT Papers, box 79.
20. EBW, *My Memoir*, 339.
21. Memorandum, October 19, 1920, signed by Tumulty, John M. Blum, *Joe Tumulty*, 250.
22. EBW, *My Memoir*, 305–6.
23. WW to Bainbridge Colby re Whipple, June 20, 1922; WW to James F. McCaleb re Vardaman, July 8, 1922, *PWW*, vol. 68.
24. WW to Frank Cobb, November 15, 1922, *PWW*, vol. 68.

25. WW to Bainbridge Colby, August 23, 1922, *PWW*, vol. 68.

26. Bainbridge Colby to WW, September 2, 1922, *PWW*, vol. 68.

27. David Lawrence, *Detroit News*, November 14, 1922, WWP, 9:506.

28. WW to Frank Cobb, with newspaper encl., December 15, 1922, *PWW*, vol. 68.

29. Frank Cobb to WW, December 19, 1922, *PWW*, vol. 68.

30. J. W. Rixey Smith, *Collier's National Weekly*, October 21, 1922 (acknowledges material from Charles A. Selden in *Ladies' Home Journal*); New York *Evening World*, December 6, 1922, WWP, 9:506.

31. *NYT*, June 19, 1923, WWP, 9:506.

32. EBW to BMB (marked 1923), BMB Papers, PL.

33. Lord Robert Cecil Diary, April 21, 1923, *PWW*, vol. 68.

36. "TO MY INCOMPARABLE WIFE"

1. WW per EBW, April 26, 1923, WWP, series 12, Misc. Docs. 1916–28, reel 526.

2. George Creel to EBW, April 19 and 24, 1923; EBW to George Creel, April 20, 24, 25, 1923, *PWW*, vol. 68.

3. Memorandum of a talk with Dr. Stockton Axson, August 28, 1921, RSB Papers, reel 70, LC. The account in *PWW*, 68:349, is prefaced: "The following incident Dr. Axson does not wish to have used in the book in any way."

4. EBW, *My Memoir*, 343.

5. EBW to WW, August 30 through September 4, 1923, *PWW*, vol. 68.

6. Bertha Bolling to Randolph and Edith, October 4, 1921, EBGW Papers, box 2, folder 1919–24.

7. The "electricity treatment" of stroke-induced paralysis involved the application of an electrical current through electrodes placed on the skin above the affected muscles. Widely accepted by the early twentieth century, electric stimulation shocked paralyzed muscles into motion and hastened recovery. Because the electric current also stimulated nearby nerves, however, the treatment could have been quite painful. Ellen R. Kuhfield, "Return with us now to those shocking days of yesterday," in Proceedings of the Fourth International Symposium on Biologically Closed Electric Circuits. Courtesy of Anne Emanuelle Birn. Ph.D, Assistant Professor of Health Policy and History, New School University.

8. EBW to JRB, JRB to EBW, August 27 through September 4, 1923, EBGW Papers, box 2, folder 1919–24.

9. David Lloyd George, *Memoirs of the Peace Conference*, 154–55.

10. Raymond B. Fosdick, *Chronicle of a Generation*, 230–31, in *PWW*, 68:452 n. 1.

11. Report of two interviews by James Kerney, *PWW*, 68:588–90.

12. Radio address, November 10, 1923, *PWW*, vol. 68, printed in *New York Times*, November 11, 1923.

13. *Weekly Tribune*, November 15, 1923, WWP, 9:506.

14. John R. Mott's notes of a conversation, December 19, 1923, *PWW*, vol. 68.

15. JRB to Richard Gillmore Knott with SA encl., November 23, 1923; JRB to Knott, December 18, 1923; *PWW*, vol. 68.

16. WW to Mr. Joseph F. Ouffey, January 6, 1924, WWP, 9:506.

17. *Washington Star*, January 16, 1924, WWP, 9:506.

18. Final draft of The Document (c. January 20, 1924); JRB to Newton D. Baker, January 21, 1924; WWP, 9:506, and n. 1, *PWW*, vol. 68.

19. Notes and Passages for an Acceptance Speech, c. January 21, 1924, *PWW*, vol. 68.

20. WW to RSB, January 25, 1924, RSB *American Chronicle*, 508.

21. Memorandum by JRB; CTG announcement, February 3, 1924; *PWW*, 68:548–50, 567.

22. EBW to HCL and HCL to EBW, February 24, 1924, and clipping, EBGW Papers, box 54.

23. EMH Diary, vol. 18, February 9, 1924.

24. Cyrus Hall McCormick Jr. to EBW and return, January 13, 1924, *PWW*, vol. 68.

25. EBGW Papers, box 54, newspaper clipping, "Wilson and House Parted by Bedroom Circle," no date.

26. MAH, "The Woodrow Wilson I Knew," *Liberty Magazine*, February 21, 1925; Richard Doddridge Blackmore (1825–1900), "Dominus Illuminatio Mea," stanza 4.

27. *Washington Daily News*, February 3, 1924, WWP, 9:506.

28. Nancy Toy to EBW, February 1, 1924, WWP, 9:506.

29. George Sylvester Viereck, *The Strangest Friendship in History*, 6.

30. Richard Marius, *Harvard Magazine*, March/April 1992.

31. Mark Sullivan to BMB, April 21, 1923, BMB Papers, PL.

32. Dr. Abraham Flexner to Raymond Blaine Fosdick, February 5, 1924, in Raymond B. Fosdick, *Letters on the League of Nations*, 140–41.

33. Fosdick to Flexner, February 6, 1924, in Fosdick, *Letters*, 140–41.

37. EDITH WILSON ON HER OWN, 1924–61

1. EBW to "Dearest Viola," August 29, 1925, EBGW Papers, box 2.

2. EBW to BMB, July 25, 1925, BMB Papers, PL.

3. *Boston Globe*, September 9, 1925, WWP, reel 50.

4. EBW to BMB, undated; EBW to BMB, September 18, 1925; BMB Papers.

5. Edith Benham Helm to Bertie Hamlin, Bertie Hamlin Papers, LC; Mrs. Walter C. Lescure, former president, Woodrow Wilson Birthplace Foundation, Inc. to author.

6. Lois M. Buell, South Bend, Indiana, *Mirror*, November 5, 1927; Associated Press, Des Moines, Iowa, 1927, WWP, reel 509.

7. Houston *Press*, June 25, 1928; Houston *Post Dispatch*, June 26, 1928; EBGW Papers.

8. George Creel, WWP, reel 509.

9. EBW to Charles L. Swem, February 12, 1924, EBGW Papers, folder 1915–31.

10. Charles L. Swem to EBW, February 13, 1923; EBW to Swem, February 14, 1924; EBGW Papers, folder 1915–31.

11. Those rights were part of the revised statutes of the United States which at the time provided, Section 4967: "Every person who shall print or publish any manuscript without . . . the consent of the author or proprietor first obtained, shall be liable to the author or proprietor for all damages occasioned by such injury." *Evening Star*, March 12, 1924, WWP, series 9, reel 510. Famously, the status of personal letters was brought into question in 1987 when the reclusive novelist J. D. Salinger won an injunction against use of unpublished personal letters on deposit in university libraries by his would-be biographer Ian Hamilton. Publishers, biographers, and scholars protested the decision of the U.S. Court of Appeals for the Second District on grounds that the Salinger decision prevented responsible scholars, among others, from citing primary sources and suppressed information. An argument in favor of the Salinger decision raised the possibility that Salinger might someday write his autobiography that would be in competition with Hamilton's biography and therefore the infringement would deprive him of income. *NYT*, July 19, 1991; *Los Angeles Times*, December 8, 1991.

12. "Woodrow Wilson," *Liberty Magazine*, November 15 and 22, 1924.
13. "The Woodrow Wilson I Knew," *Liberty Magazine*, December 20, 1924, to January 17, 1925.
14. Three letters, WW to William Jennings Bryan, May 13, (2) and May 14, 1915, Mary Baird Bryan, ed., *Memoirs of William Jennings Bryan*, 400, 401, 403. Early in World War I, Bryan, standing for mediation, considered Germany's submarine attacks inhumane, but held that England was no less culpable when she cut off food supplies from innocent people. Concerned about America's position, he told Wilson "that the administration was lacking in neutrality—not in commission, but in omission; not the notes which were written, but the notes not written, threw the delicate machinery out of balance and made the work of the Secretary of State increasingly difficult."
15. EBW to Mrs. James M. Helm, May 5, 16, 1920, EBGW Papers, box 20.
16. EBW to BMB, April 26, 1924, BMB Papers.
17. RSB to Breckenridge Long, April 10, 1925, RSB Papers, reel 79, LC.
18. EBW to RSB, January 5, 1925, RSB Papers, reel 79.
19. Robert Bannister, *Ray Stannard Baker*, 240.
20. RSB, *American Chronicle*, 272.
21. Like the "Man with the Muckrake" in Bunyan's *Pilgrim's Progress*, according to William Archer, *British Fortnightly Review*, May 1910, the term signified honesty and truth in a journalist.
22. Frank Prentice Rand, *The Story of David Grayson*, 92–93.
23. RSB, *American Chronicle*, 279.
24. Bannister, *Ray Stannard Baker*, 174.
25. Ibid., 185.
26. RSB, *American Chronicle*, 464.
27. Previously quoted, EBW to Charles L. Swem, February 12, 1924, EBGW Papers, folder 1915–31.
28. RSB, *American Chronicle*, 490, quoted from journal in Bannister, *Ray Stannard Baker*, 304.
29. RSB, *American Chronicle*, 511.
30. RSB to EBW, October 25–26, 1925, EBGW Papers, box 6.
31. Charles Seymour to RSB, October 5, 1925, RSB Papers, reel 82.
32. Charles Seymour to EBW, November 18, 1925, Charles Seymour Papers.
33. EBW to Seymour, December 2, 1925, Charles Seymour Papers, box 15, YL; EBW to EMH, December 2, 1925, Charles Seymour Papers.
34. Charles Seymour, "End of a Friendship," 7 n. 1.
35. Seymour to EBW, December 7, 1925, Charles Seymour Papers, box 15.
36. RSB to EBW, November 10, 1926, EBGW Papers, box 6.
37. Edward Martin to RSB, February 11, 1926; RSB to Martin, February 11, 1926; RSB Papers, reel 79.
38. RSB Journal 40, January 1925, 112–13, 138, in Bannister, *Ray Stannard Baker*, 251.
39. RSB, *Woodrow Wilson, Life and Letters*, 1:xxii.
40. Ibid., 6:126 n. 2.
41. RSB to Howard Meneely, November 23, 1931, RSB Papers, reel 80.
42. According to her *Memoir*, although she had never written a line for publication, EBW decided to yield to the importunities of editors and friends to write of the deep experiences it had been her privilege to share with her husband, Alden Hatch Papers, University of Florida Libraries.

43. Holcombe Bolling to "My dear Aunt Edith," April 7, 1925, EBGW Papers, box 1.

44. Notes of interview with EBW, Alden Hatch Papers.

45. JRB to D. L. Chambers, November 19, 1938; Chambers to JRB, December 14, 1938; JRB to Chambers, December 5, 1938, EBGW Papers.

46. Irita Van Doren, March 24, 1939, Marquis James Papers, box 25.

47. Stephen Vincent Benét, *Herald Tribune Books,* March 12, 1939, Marquis James Papers, box 25.

48. EBW, *My Memoir,* 111, 150.

49. Subsequently, the two men shared and staunchly weathered the sensational headlines in the *New York Times,* January 31, 1917: "Peace Note 'Tip' Traced to Washington; Bolling Denies All Knowledge of It; Baruch Tells How He Made $476,168."

50. EBW to BMB, August 30, 1932, BMB Papers; "Memo. for Mr. B.M. Baruch," January 13, 1926, EBGW Papers, box 9.

51. EBW to BMB, June 6, 1926, BMB Papers.

52. "Practically all of my income is derived from investment in Federal Land Bank 4½, 4¼ and 5% bonds, and a few municipals. A well-intentioned friend advised me the other day that she had been told it was wise to sell securities, such as I have mentioned, and re-invest the funds in dividend paying common stocks."

"Mr. Wilson regarded the Federal Land Bank bonds as one of the safest and best investments he could make but in these days of the changing value of the dollar I have thought it best to ask what you think I had best do; i.e., leave the investment as it is, or change to different securities.

"Please forgive my asking, but it means my ability to carry on." EBW to BMB, October 25, 1933, EBGW Papers, box 9.

53. Alden Hatch Papers.

54. BMB to EBW, February 10, 1926, BMB Papers; BMB to EBW, September 2 (no year) , EBGW Papers, box 9.

55. EBW to BMB, June 26, 1920, BMB Papers; telegram authorized by BMB and signed M. A. Boyle, to EBW, September 2 (no year), EBGW Papers, box 9.

56. Marquis James papers, box 35.

57. "Woodrow Wilson After 25 Years," BMB to editor, Dallas *Times Herald,* March 12, 1945, BMB Papers.

58. EBW to Mrs. Smith, July 25, 1944, Woodrow Wilson Birthplace, Staunton, Va.

59. Charles Willis Thompson, June 24, 1939, New York *Sun,* Charles Seymour Papers, box 2, folder 51. The early volumes were issued as syndicated series in many newspapers, but the later ones, less timely as interest in Wilson had waned, appeared only in book form. RSB, *American Chronicle,* 515.

60. JRB to RSB, October 30, 1942, EBGW Papers, box 8.

61. EBW to RSB, November 8, 1943; EBW to RSB, October 19, 1943, EBGW Papers, box 8.

62. RSB to EBW, January 9, 1945, EBGW Papers.

63. *New York Post,* 5, quoted in EBW to RSB, January 1, 1945, EBGW Papers.

64. EBW to B. O. Moody, September 11, 1946, EBGW Papers.

65. Authorized by the Eighty-third Congress, 2nd sess., final report, *Woodrow Wilson Centennial, 1956,* according to the *New York Times*: "It was long the fashion among the fearful, the cynical and the narrow-headed wise to sneer at some of Woodrow Wilson's phrases and ideas. Now we know the world might have been made safe for democracy . . . now we know it will have to be made so or civilization will perish. President Wilson was not wrong, he was just ahead of his

time. . . . The man is dead along with his minor faults and his shining virtues. . . . His career set a new high standard of public service. No greater tribute can be paid to any man."

66. JFK to EBW, December 28, 1959, EBGW Papers, box 9.

67. EBW to Mrs. Emily Pancake Smith, November 17, 1960, Woodrow Wilson Birthplace, Staunton, Va.

68. Alden Hatch Papers.

69. Edith Benham Helm to Bertie Hamlin, February 22, 1962, Bertie Hamlin Papers, LC.

70. Margaret Woodrow Wilson to JPT, no date, JPT Papers, box 79, LC. Also JPT to BMB, February 7, 1927, distressed by "the Margaret Wilson article": "We all ought to get together and take care of the matter," BMB Papers. Margaret Wilson, disenchanted with political life and the White House scene and in need of spiritual help, turned to the Vive Kananda Center in New York City, where she worked on a translation of the gospel of Robert Krishna. Margaret Wilson's friend Seyril Schochen to author, courtesy of William Greaves.

71. Helen Bones to ACW, April 20, 1950, ACW Papers.

72. Associated Press, December 29, 1961.

73. Edith Benham Helm to Bertie Hamlin, February 22, 1962, Bertie Hamlin Papers.

74. Ibid.

EPILOGUE

1. "A Statement by Dr. Grayson," *PWW*, 64:510.

2. A. Lentin, "What Really Happened at Paris?" 271.

3. John Maynard Keynes (referring to Articles V and X), *The Economic Consequences of the Peace*, 164.

4. George Clemenceau, *Grandeur and Misery of Victory*, 75.

5. "Mrs. Ellen Wilson and Mrs. Edith Wilson," Stockton Axson Papers, PL.

6. Daniel M. Smith, "Lansing and the Wilson Interregnum," 161.

7. "World Security," *The New Republic*, April 30, 1945, 608.

8. *The Peace of Versailles*, quoted in Mark Sullivan, *Our Times*, vol. 5.

9. Henry Cabot Lodge, *The Senate and the League of Nations*, 222–24.

10. Stephen Vincent Benét, *New York Herald Tribune*, book review, March 12, 1939.

11. John Morton Blum, *Woodrow Wilson and the Politics of Morality*, 10, 115: "Throughout the South the discharge or demotion of Negro federal employees attended the New Freedom."

12. T. S. Eliot, "The Hollow Men."

Bibliography

MANUSCRIPT SOURCES

BERMUDA ARCHIVES
Island news of Woodrow Wilson and Mary Allen Peck

UNIVERSITY OF FLORIDA LIBRARIES, RARE BOOKS AND MANUSCRIPTS
Papers of Alden Hatch, biographer of Edith Bolling Galt Wilson

THE BRITISH LIBRARY, INDIA OFFICE LIBRARY AND RECORDS
Private correspondence between Lord Curzon and Grey of Fallodon, November 2, 1919, to December 9, 1919, regarding Major Charles Kennedy Craufurd-Stuart

LIBRARY OF CONGRESS, MANUSCRIPT DIVISION
Papers of Ray Stannard Baker (microfilm) includes journals, interviews, correspondence relating to Woodrow Wilson
Papers of Irwin Hood Hoover, chief usher of the White House
The Robert Lansing Papers, confidential memorandums and notes, 1864–1928; desk diaries, strictly private notes
Papers of Theodore Roosevelt
Papers of Woodrow Wilson (microfilm) encompass:
  Papers of Edith Bolling Galt Wilson, diary notes, family and general correspondence, including letters to and from Woodrow Wilson, restricted until fifteen years after her death in 1961
  Papers of Mary Allen Hulbert: S series, collection 1187, reels 69 through 74; letters to Woodrow Wilson, February 25, 1907, to November 22, 1915
  Wilson-McAdoo Papers, box 8, including letters of Ellen Axson Wilson to Colonel Harvey and to her daughter Margaret, and William McAdoo to Edith Bolling Wilson
  Papers of Joseph P. Tumulty
Papers of others:
  Chandler Parsons Anderson Diary, includes notations on the vice-presidential role in the face of presidential disability
  Newton D. Baker
  General Tasker H. Bliss
  Stephen Bonsal
  George Creel
  Josephus Daniels
  Raymond B. Fosdick
  Moreton Frewen
  Bertie Hamlin
  Charles S. Hamlin
  Edith B. Helm Collection
  Marquis James
  Breckinridge Long Diary
  William Gibbs McAdoo
  Louis Seibold
  Warren Van Slyke
  Henry White
  William Wiseman

HARVARD UNIVERSITY, HOUGHTON LIBRARY
Henry Cabot Lodge Papers include Corinne Roosevelt Robinson's notes of Lodge's position regarding the possible ratification by the United States of the League of Nations on final vote in the Senate
Edward Mandell House correspondence with Edward S. Martin, Papers of Mrs. Edward S. Blagden

MASSACHUSETTS HISTORICAL SOCIETY
Papers of Henry Cabot Lodge, include wide correspondence regarding his position on League of Nations
Papers of James Ford Rhodes in reference to Lodge

NATIONAL ARCHIVES
Papers and correspondence regarding appointment of Sir Edward Grey as ambassador to the United States, and statements in reference to Major Charles Kennedy Craufurd-Stuart
Military Reference Branch: Military Intelligence Division
    Confidential and personal papers regarding investigation of spy charges against
        Bernard M. Baruch
News International PLC Record Office, *Times* (London), London Observations of Washington by British newsman Arthur Willert

THE NEW YORK TIMES ARCHIVES
Papers of Adolph S. Ochs include references to Woodrow Wilson, Edith Bolling Galt Wilson, and to Bernard Baruch

PRINCETON UNIVERSITY LIBRARY (FIRESTONE AND MUDD LIBRARIES)
Stockton Axson, "Memoir of Woodrow Wilson," unpublished (courtesy of Arthur S. Link)
Cary Travers Grayson Diary (courtesy of Arthur S. Link)
The Mary A. Hulbert Collection
The Robert Lansing Selected Papers
Woodrow Wilson Special Correspondence Collections, "Papers of Others":
    Bernard M. Baruch
    Gilbert Close
    Andre De Coppet
    Raymond B. Fosdick
    David F. Houston
    Arthur Krock
    David Lawrence
    Charles Lee Swem
    Charles Willis Thompson

PUBLIC RECORD OFFICE, KEW
Correspondence and official documents relating to Sir Edward Grey and to British views of the USA

THE WOODROW WILSON BIRTHPLACE, STAUNTON, VIRGINIA
Correspondence regarding Edith Wilson's role as founder
YALE UNIVERSITY LIBRARY, MANUSCRIPTS AND ARCHIVES
Gordon Auchincloss
John W. Davis

Colonel Edward Mandell House, diaries
Vance C. McCormick
Frank L. Polk
Charles Seymour
George Sylvester Viereck
Arthur Clarence Walworth, Wilson biographer, includes notes of significant interviews
Sir William (George Eden) Wiseman

WHITE HOUSE, OFFICE OF THE CURATOR
Papers of Isabelle Hagner
OTHER SOURCES
Bedford (city/county) Museum, Bedford, Va.
Berkshire Atheneum, Pittsfield, Mass., Public Library
Jones Memorial Library, Lynchburg, Va.
Kingston Area Library, Kingston, N.Y.
Nebraska State Historical Society, Lincoln
The New York Historical Society
The New York Public Library
University of North Carolina Library, Manuscripts Department
Rice University, Fondren Library, Houston
Rome-Floyd, Ga., County Library
Rutgers University Library, N.J.
Ulster County Genealogical Society, Hurley, N.Y.
Valentine Museum, Richmond, Va.
University of Virginia, Special Collections, Alderman Library, Charlottesville
Virginia Historical Society, Richmond
Wythe County Historical Society, Wytheville, Va.

PRINTED MANUSCRIPT SOURCES

Baker, Ray Stannard. *Woodrow Wilson and World Settlement*. 3 vols. Garden City, N.Y.: Doubleday, Page, 1922.
———. *Woodrow Wilson, Life and Letters*. 8 vols. Vols.1 and 2, Garden City, N.Y.: Doubleday, Page, 1927. Vols. 3 through 8, Garden City, N.Y.: Doubleday Doran, 1931–39.
Baker, Ray Stannard, and William E. Dodd, eds., *The Public Papers of Woodrow Wilson*. 6 vols. New York: Harper & Brothers, 1925–27.
Bemis, Samuel Flagg, ed., *American Secretaries of State and Their Legacy*, Vols. 9–10. New York: Pageant Book Co., 1958.
Bolling, John Randolph. *Chronology of Woodrow Wilson*. New York: Frederick A. Stokes, 1927.
Congressional Record (microfilm). 66th Cong., 1st sess., Senate, September 1919 to March 25, 1920. Washington, D.C.: Government Printing Office.
Congressional Record. 66th Cong., 2nd sess., House of Representatives, Hearings before the Committee on the Judiciary, "Relative to Disability, Removal from Office, etc., of the President of the United States."
German White Book: Concerning the Responsibility of the Authors of the War. New York: Oxford University Press, 1924.
The Lansing Papers, 1914–1920. U.S. State Department, suppl., *Papers Relating to the Foreign Relations of the United States*. Washington, D.C.: U.S. Government Printing Office, 1940.

Link, Arthur S., ed., *The Papers of Woodrow Wilson.* 69 vols., Princeton: Princeton University Press, 1966 to 1993.

The Messages and Papers of Woodrow Wilson. 2 vols. New York: The Review of Reviews Corporation, 1924.

Paris Peace Conference, 1919. Vols., 1–3, 5, 11, 12, including messages of Woodrow Wilson to Congress, December 7, 1920; April 12 and December 6, 1921. *Papers Relating to the Foreign Relations of the United States.* Washington, D.C.: Government Printing Office, 1947.

Seymour, Charles. *The Intimate Papers of Colonel House.* 4 vols. Boston: Houghton Mifflin, 1927–28.

Ward, A. W., and G. P. Gooch. *The Cambridge History of British Foreign Policy.* New York: Octagon Books, 1970.

Woodward, E. L., and Rohan Butler, eds., *Documents of British Foreign Policy.* 1st ser., vol. 5, chap. 2, 1919; "The Mission to Washington of Viscount Grey of Fallodon." London: Her Majesty's Stationery Office, 1954.

NEWSPAPERS

Associated Press
Atlanta Constitution
The Baltimore *Sun*
Columbus, Ohio, *Dispatch*
Dallas *Times Herald*
Echo de Paris
The Evening Standard
The Evening Wisconsin
Kansas City Post
Le Figaro
London *Daily Mail*
Los Angeles Examiner
Louisville Courier-Journal
The Milwaukee Daily News
The Milwaukee Sentinel
New York Herald Tribune
New York *Sun*
The New York Times
Philadelphia *Public Ledger*
Philadelphia *Record*
Richmond *News Leader*
St. Louis Globe Democrat
Town Topics
The Washington Post
The Washington Times
The World

PERIODICALS

American Heritage
The American Historical Review
American History Illustrated
American Mercury
Canadian Historical Review

Century
Christian Science Monitor
Collier's
Cornhill Magazine
Current History
Current Opinion
Diplomatic History Documents
Harper's
Hearst's International Cosmopolitan
The Historian
The International History Review
Journalism Quarterly
The Journal of American History
The Ladies' Home Journal
Liberty Magazine
The New Republic
New York University Law Review
The North Carolina Historical Review
The North American Review's *War Weekly,* by George Harvey
Presidential Studies Quarterly
The Princetonian
Reviews in American History
Saturday Evening Post
Town Topics
The Yale Law Journal

BOOKS

Ackerly, May Denham, and Lula Eastman Jeter Parker. *Our Kin.* Harrisonberg, Va.: C. J. Carrier, 1976.

Adams, Henry. *The Education of Henry Adams.* Boston and New York: Houghton Mifflin, 1918.

——. *Letters of Henry Adams.* Ed. Worthington Chauncey Ford. Boston and New York: Houghton Mifflin, 1930.

——. *The Letters of Henry Adams.* Vol. 6. Eds. J. C. Levenson et al. Cambridge, Mass., and London: The Belknap Press of Harvard University Press, 1988.

Alderman, Edwin Anderson. *In Memoriam Woodrow Wilson.* Washington, D.C.: Government Printing Office, 1925.

Allen, Frederick Lewis. *Only Yesterday.* New York: Harper and Row, 1931.

Ambrosius, Lloyd E. *Woodrow Wilson and the American Diplomatic Tradition.* Cambridge: Cambridge University Press, 1987.

Anderson, David D. *Woodrow Wilson.* Boston: Twayne Publishers, 1998.

Anderson, Isabelle. *Presidents and Pies.* Boston and New York: Houghton Mifflin, 1920.

Andrews, Mariette Minnegerode. *My Studio Window.* New York: E. P. Dutton, 1928.

Annin, Robert Edward. *Woodrow Wilson, a Character Study.* New York: Dodd Mead & Company, 1924.

Asquith, Margot. *An Autobiography.* 4 vols. New York: George H. Doran, 1922.

Axson, Stockton. *"Brother Woodrow."* Princeton: Princeton University Press, 1993.

Aycock, Roger. *All Roads to Rome.* Rome, Ga.: Rome Area Heritage Foundation, 1981.

Bagehot, Walter. *The English Constitution.* London: Oxford University Press, 1949.

Bailey, Thomas A. *Woodrow Wilson and the Great Betrayal.* New York: The Macmillan Company, 1945.

Baker, Newton B. *Why We Went to War.* New York: Harper for the Council on Foreign Relations, 1936.

Baker, Ray Stannard. *American Chronicle: The Autobiography.* New York: David Grayson, Charles Scribner's Sons, 1945.

———. *What Wilson Did at Paris.* Garden City, N.Y.: Doubleday, Page & Co., 1919.

Balfour, Arthur James. *Retrospect.* Boston and New York: Houghton Mifflin, 1930.

Bannister, Roger. *Ray Stannard Baker.* New Haven, Conn.: Yale University Press, 1966.

Bartlett, John, *Familiar Quotations.* Boston: Little, Brown and Company, 1951.

Baruch, Bernard M. *Baruch: The Public Years.* New York: Holt, Reinhart & Winston, 1960.

Battey, George Magruder, Jr. *A History of Rome and Floyd County.* Atlanta, Ga.: Webb and Vary Company, 1922.

Beers, Burton F. *Vain Endeavor.* Durham, N.C.: Duke University Press, 1962.

Bell, H. C. F. *Woodrow Wilson and the People.* Garden City, N.Y.: Doubleday & Company; reprint, Archon Books, 1968.

Bender, Robert J. *Woodrow Wilson.* New York: United Press Associations, 1924.

Bertie, Lord. *Diary of Lord Bertie of Thame.* London: Hodder and Stonington, 1924.

Blum, John Morton. *Joe Tumulty and the Wilson Era.* Boston: Houghton Mifflin, 1951; reprint, Archon Books, 1969.

———. *Woodrow Wilson and the Politics of Morality.* Boston: Little, Brown, 1956.

Boller, Paul F., Jr. *Presidential Wives.* London: Oxford University Press, 1988.

Bonsal, Stephen. *Suitors and Suppliants.* New Jersey: Prentice-Hall, 1946.

———. *Unfinished Business.* London: M. Joseph Ltd., 1944

Bryan, Mary Baird, ed. *Memoirs of William Jennings Bryan.* Chicago, Philadelphia, Toronto: The John C. Winston Company, 1925.

Carter, Morris. *Isabella Steward Gardiner and Fenway Court.* Boston: Gardner Museum, 1925.

Cater, Harold D., ed. *Henry Adams and His Friends.* Boston: Houghton Mifflin, 1947.

Catt, Carrie Chapman, and Lettie Rogers Shuler. *Woman Suffrage and Politics.* New York: Charles Scribner's Sons, 1923.

Churchill, Winston S. *The World Crisis, 1915.* New York: Charles Scribner's Sons, 1923.

———. *The World Crisis, 1916–1918.* 2 vols., Charles Scribner's Sons, 1927.

———. *The Aftermath, 1918–1928.* Charles Scribner's Sons, 1929.

———. *The Gathering Storm.* Boston: Houghton Mifflin, 1948.

Clemenceau, George. *Grandeur and Misery of Victory.* New York: Harcourt, Brace and Co., 1930.

Cohen, Stanley. *A. Mitchell Palmer: Politician.* New York: Columbia University Press, 1963.

Coit, Margaret L. *Mr. Baruch.* Boston: Houghton Mifflin, 1957.

Colby, Bainbridge. *The Close of Woodrow Wilson's Administration.* New York: Mitchell Kennerley, 1930.

Commager, Henry Steele, ed. *Documents of American History.* New York: Appleton-Century-Crofts, 1963.

Cooper, John Milton, Jr. *The Warrior and the Priest.* Cambridge, Mass, and London: The Belknap Press of Harvard University, 1983.

Cooper, John Milton, Jr., and Charles E. Neu, eds. *The Wilson Era: Essays in Honor of Arthur S. Link.* Arlington Heights, Ill.: Harlan Davidson, Inc., 1991.

Corwin, Edward S. *The President: Office & Powers*. New York: New York University Press, 1940.

Creel, George. *The War, the World, and Wilson*. New York and London: Harper & Brothers, 1920.

Crisspell, Kenneth R., and Carlos F. Gomez. *Hidden Illness in the White House*. Durham, N.C.: Duke University Press, 1988.

Dabney, Virginius. *The Story of a City*. New York: Doubleday, 1976.

Daniels, Jonathan. *The End of Innocence*. Philadelphia, N.Y.: J. B. Lippincott, 1954.

———. *The Time Between the Wars*. Philadelphia, New York: J. B. Lippincott, 1954.

Daniels, Josephus. *The Life of Woodrow Wilson*. Chicago, Philadelphia, Toronto: John C. Winston, 1924.

———. *The Wilson Era—Years of Peace*. Chapel Hill: University of North Carolina Press, 1944.

———. *The Wilson Era—Years of War and After*. Chapel Hill: University of North Carolina Press, 1945.

———. *The Cabinet Diaries of Josephus Daniels*. Ed. E. David Cronin. Lincoln: University of Nebraska Press, 1963.

Dawes, Charles G. *A Journal of the Great War*. Boston and New York: Houghton & Mifflin, 1921.

Devlin, Patrick. *Too Proud To Fight*. New York, London: Oxford University Press, 1975.

Dodd, W. E. *Woodrow Wilson and His Work*. Garden City, N.Y.: Doubleday, Page & Co., 1920.

Dos Passos, John. *Mr. Wilson's War*. Garden City, N.Y.: Doubleday, 1962.

Dulles, Eleanor. *Chances of a Lifetime*. New Jersey: Prentice-Hall, 1980.

Dunn, Arthur Wallace. *From Harrison to Harding*. New York and London: G. P. Putnam's Sons, 1922.

Duroselle, Jean-Baptiste. *From Wilson to Roosevelt*. Cambridge, Mass.: Harvard University Press, 1962.

Dyer, Walter A. *David Grayson: Adventurer*. Garden City, N.Y.: Doubleday, Page & Co., 1926.

Edel, Leon, *Henry James*. 2 vols. Philadelphia: J. B. Lippincott, 1962.

———. ed. *The Henry James Reader*. New York: Charles Scribner's Sons, 1965.

Farnsworth, Beatrice. *William C. Bullitt and the Soviet Union*. Bloomington and London: Indiana University Press, 1967.

Feerick, John D. *From Failing Hands*. New York: Fordham Press, 1965.

Ferrell, Robert H. *Woodrow Wilson and World War I*. New York: Harper and Row, 1985.

Floto, Inga. *Colonel House in Paris*. Princeton: Princeton University Press, 1980.

Fosdick, Raymond B. *Letters on the League of Nations*. Princeton: Princeton University Press, 1966.

Freud, Sigmund, and William C. Bullitt. *Thomas Woodrow Wilson*. Boston: Houghton Mifflin Company, 1967.

Fromkin, David. *A Peace to End All Peace*. New York: Avon Books, 1989.

Furman Bess. *White House Profile*. New York and Indianapolis: Bobbs-Merrill, 1951.

Gann, Dolly. *Dolly Gann's Book*. Garden City, N.Y.: Doubleday, Doran, 1933.

Gardiner, A. G. *The War Lords*. New York: J. M. Dent & Sons, E. P. Dutton & Co., 1913.

Garraty, John A. *Henry Cabot Lodge: A Biography*. New York: Alfred A. Knopf, 1953.

———. *Woodrow Wilson: A Great Life in Brief*. New York: Alfred A. Knopf, 1956.

George, Alexander L., and Juliette L. George. *Woodrow Wilson and Colonel House*. New York: Dover Publications, 1964.

Gerard, James W. *My Four Years in Germany.* New York: George H. Doran Company, 1917.

[Gilbert, Clinton W.] *The Mirrors of Washington,* by Anonymous. New York: G. P. Putnam's Sons, 1921.

Gilbert, Martin. *The First World War.* New York: Henry Holt and Company, 1994.

Gompers, Samuel. *Seventy Years of Life and Labour.* New York: E. P. Dutton and Company, 1925.

Gould, Lewis L. *Progressives and Prohibitionists.* Austin: Texas State Historical Association, 1992.

Grant, James. *Bernard M. Baruch.* New York: Simon & Schuster, 1983.

Grayson, Rear Admiral Cary T. *Woodrow Wilson: An Intimate Memoir.* New York: Holt, Rinehart and Winston, 1960.

Greene, Theodore P., ed. *Wilson at Versailles.* Boston: D. C. Heath, 1957.

Grey of Fallodon. *Fly Fishing.* London: J. M. Dent and Company, 1920.

———. *Twenty-Five Years, 1892–1916.* 2 vols. New York: Frederick A. Stokes, 1925.

Hale, William Bayard. *The Story of a Style.* New York: B. W. Huebsch, 1920.

Hamerton, Philip Gilbert. *Round My House.* London: Seeley, Jackson and Halliday, 1876.

Hamsburger, Caroline Thomas, ed. *Mark Twain at Your Fingertips.* New York: Beechhurst Press, 1948.

Hankey, Maurice Pascal. *The Supreme Control at the Paris Peace Conference.* London: G. Allen and Unwin, 1963.

Hansen, Richard H. *The Year We Had No President.* Lincoln: University of Nebraska Press, 1962.

Harriman, Florence Jaffray (Mrs. J. Borden). *From Pinafores to Politics.* New York: H. Holt & Co., 1923.

Hartig, Thomas H. *Robert Lansing.* New York: Arno Press, 1982.

Hatch, Alden. *Edith Bolling Wilson, First Lady Extraordinary.* New York: Dodd, Mead, 1961.

———. *The Lodges of Massachusetts.* New York: Hawthorn Books, 1973.

Heaton, John L. *Cobb of "The World."* New York: E. P. Dutton, 1924.

Heckscher, August. *Woodrow Wilson.* New York: Charles Scribner's Sons, 1991.

Hendrick, Burton J. *The Life and Letters of Walter H. Page.* 2 vols. Garden City, N.Y.: Doubleday, Page & Co., 1924.

Hohenberg, John. *The Pulitzer Prizes.* New York and London: Columbia University Press, 1974.

Hoover, Herbert, *The Ordeal of Woodrow Wilson.* New York: McGraw-Hill Book Company, 1958.

Hoover, Irwin Hood. *Forty-Two Years in the White House.* Boston and New York: Houghton Mifflin Company, 1934.

House, Edward Mandell. *Phillip Dru.* New York: B. W. Huebsch, 1912.

House, Edward Mandell and Charles Seymour, eds. *What Really Happened at Paris.* New York: Charles Scribner's Sons, 1921.

Houston, David F. *Eight Years with the Wilson Cabinet.* 2 vols. Garden City, New York: Doubleday, Page & Co., 1926.

Hulbert, Mary Allen, *The Story of Mrs. Peck,* New York: Minton Balch and Company, 1933.

———. *Treasures of a Hundred Cooks.* New York and London: D. Appleton and Company, 1927.

Hurley, Edward N. *The Bridge to France.* Philadelphia and London: J. B. Lippincott Company, 1927.

Irwin, Inez Haynes. *Angels and Amazons.* Garden City, N.Y.: Doubleday, 1933.

————. *Uphill with Banners Flying*. Penobscot, Maine: Traversity Press, 1964.

Jaffray, Elizabeth. *Secrets of the White House*. New York: Cosmopolitan Book Corporation, 1927.

James, Henry. *Autobiography*. New York: Criterion Books, 1956.

Jessup, Philip C. *Elihu Root*. Vol. 2, Dodd, Mead, 1938; reprint, New York: Anchor Books, 1964.

Kegley, Mary B. *Wythe County, Virginia: A Bicentennial History*. Marceline, Md.: Walsworth Publishing, Inc., 1989.

Kennan, George F. *Russia Leaves the War*. Princeton: Princeton University Press, 1956.

Kennedy, David M. *Over There: The First World War and American Society*. New York: Oxford University Press, 1980.

Kerney, James. *The Political Education of Woodrow Wilson*. New York and London: Century Co., 1926.

Keynes, John Maynard. *The Economic Consequences of the Peace*. Vol. 2 of *The Collected Writings*. New York: St. Martin's Press, 1971.

Knock, Thomas. *To End All Wars*. Princeton: Princeton University Press, 1992.

Kohlsaat, H. H. *From McKinley to Harding*. New York: Charles Scribner's Sons, 1923.

Lane, A. W., and L. H. Wall, eds. *The Letters of Franklin K. Lane*. New York and Boston: Houghton Mifflin, 1922.

Lansing, Robert. *The Peace Negotiations*. Boston and New York: Houghton Mifflin, 1921.

————. *War Memoirs of Robert Lansing*. Indianapolis and New York: Bobbs-Merrill, 1935.

Lash, Joseph P. *Eleanor and Franklin*. New York: W. W. Norton, 1971.

Lawrence, David. *The True Story of Woodrow Wilson*. New York: George H. Doran Co., 1924.

Lerner, Laurence, ed. *The Victorians*. New York: Holmes and Meier, 1978.

Levin, Gordon N., Jr. *Woodrow Wilson and World Politics*. New York: Oxford University Press, 1968.

Lewis, R. W. B. *Edith Wharton*. New York: Harper & Row, 1975.

Licht, Sidney. *Therapeutic Electricity and Ultraviolet Radiation*, New Haven, Conn.: Licht, 1959.

Link, Arthur S. *Wilson: The Road to the White House*. Princeton: Princeton University Press, 1947.

————. *Woodrow Wilson and the Progressive Era, 1910–1917*, New York: Harper & Brothers, 1954.

————. *Wilson: The New Freedom*. Princeton: Princeton University Press, 1956.

————. ed. *Woodrow Wilson and a Revolutionary World, 1913–1921*. Chapel Hill: University of North Carolina, 1982.

Link, Arthur S., and William M. Leary, Jr., eds. *The Diplomacy of World Power: The United States, 1889–1920*. New York: St. Martin's Press, 1970.

Lippman, Walter. *Men of Destiny*. New York: Macmillan, 1927.

Lloyd George, David. *Memoirs of the Peace Conference*. 2 vols. New Haven: Yale University Press, 1939.

Lockhart, Sir Robert Bruce. *Giants Cast Long Shadows*. London: Putnam, 1960.

Lodge, Henry Cabot. *The Senate and the League of Nations*. New York and London: Charles Scribner's Sons, 1925.

Longworth, Alice. *Crowded Hours*. New York and London: Charles Scribner's Sons, 1933.

Loth, David Goldsmith. *Woodrow Wilson: The Fifteenth Point*. Philadelphia and New York: J. B. Lippincott Company, 1941.

MacMahon, Edward B., M.D., and Leonard Curry. *Medical Cover-Ups in the White House.* Washington, D.C.: Farragut Publishing Company, 1987.

Mantoux, Etienne. *The Carthaginian Peace: Or the Economic Consequences of Mr. Keynes.* Pittsburgh: University of Pittsburgh Press, 1965.

Margulies, Herbert F. *Senator Lenroot of Wisconsin.* Columbia: University of Missouri Press, 1977.

McAdoo, Eleanor Randolph, with Margaret Y. Gaffey. *The Woodrow Wilsons.* New York: The Macmillan Company, 1937.

McAdoo, Eleanor Wilson. *The Priceless Gift.* New York, Toronto, London: McGraw-Hill, 1962.

McAdoo, William Gibbs. *Crowded Years.* Boston: Houghton Mifflin, 1931.

McCombs, William Frank. *Making Woodrow Wilson President.* New York: Fairview Publishing Co., 1921.

Meagher, Margaret. *History of Education in Richmond.* Richmond, Va.: [s.n.], 1939.

Means, Marianne. *The Woman in the White House.* New York: Random House, 1963.

A Memoir of a Portion of the Bolling Family in England and Virginia. Richmond, Va.: W. H. Wade & Co., 1868.

Miller, David Hunter. *My Diary at the Conference of Paris.* Vol. 20 of 21 volumes. New York: Appeal Printing Company, 1924.

Miller, William J. *Henry Cabot Lodge.* New York: James H. Heineman, 1967.

Morison, Elting E., ed. *The Letters of Theodore Roosevelt.* Cambrdige, Mass.: Harvard University Press, 1954.

Morison, Samuel Eliot. *The Oxford History of the American People.* New York: Oxford University Press, 1965.

Morley, John. *The Life of William Ewart Gladstone.* London: Macmillan, 1903.

Mulder, John M. *Woodrow Wilson: The Years of Preparation.* Princeton: Princeton University Press, 1978.

Murray, Arthur C. *At Close Quarters.* London: John Murray, 1946.

Murray, Robert K. *The Harding Era: Warren G. Harding and His Administration.* University of Minnesota Press, 1960.

Nesbitt, Henrietta. *White House Diary.* Garden City, N.Y.: Doubleday & Co., 1948.

Nevins, Allan. *Henry White: Thirty Years of American Diplomacy.* New York: Harper & Bros., 1930.

Nicholson, Harold. *Peacemaking, 1919.* London: Constable and Co., Ltd., 1933.

O'Toole, Patricia. *Five of Hearts.* New York: Clarkson Potter, 1990.

Pakula, Hannah. *The Last Romantic: Queen Marie of Roumania.* New York: Simon & Schuster, 1984.

Palmer, Frederick. *Bliss, Peacemaker.* Freeport, N.Y.: Books for Libraries Press, 1934.

Parks, William Rogers, with Frances Spatz Leighton. *My Thirty Years Backstairs at the White House.* New York: Fleet Publishing Corporation, 1961.

Patterson, A. W. *Personal Recollections of Woodrow Wilson.* Richmond, Va.: Whittet & Shepperson, 1929.

Phillips, Ulrich Bonnell. *American Negro Slavery.* Baton Rouge: Louisiana State University Press, 1966.

Phillips, William. *Ventures in Diplomacy.* Boston: The Beacon Press, 1952.

Pringle, Henry. *The Life and Times of William Howard Taft.* 2 vols. New York: Farrar and Rinehart, 1929.

Pusey, Merlo J. *Charles Evans Hughes.* 2 vols. New York: Macmillan, 1951.

Rand, Frank Prentice. *The Story of David Grayson.* Amherst, Mass.: The Jones Library, 1963.

Reid, Edith Gittings. *Woodrow Wilson.* London and New York: Oxford University Press, 1934.

Rhodri, Jeffreys-Jones. *American Espionage from Secret Service to CIA.* New York: Free Press, 1977.

Roosevelt, Eleanor. *This Is My Story.* New York and London: Harper and Bros., 1937.

Roosevelt, Elliott. *F.D.R.: His Personal Letters, 1905–1928.* New York: Duell, Sloan and Pearce, 1948.

Roosevelt, Theodore. *Selections from the Correspondence of Theodore Roosevelt and Henry Cabot Lodge, 1884–1918.* 2 vols. New York: Charles Scribner's Sons, 1925.

Rosenman, Samuel, and Dorothy Rosenman. *Presidential Style.* New York: Harper & Row, 1976.

Ross, Ishbel. *Power with Grace.* New York: G. P. Putnam's Sons, 1975.

Rowbottom, Margaret, and Charles Susskind. *Electricity and Medicine: History of Their Interaction.* San Francisco Press, 1984.

Samuels, Ernest. *Henry Adams.* Cambridge, Mass., and London: The Belknap Press of Harvard University Press, 1989.

Saunders, Francis Wright. *Ellen Axson Wilson.* Chapel Hill and London: The University of North Carolina Press, 1985.

[Scanlan, Nelle M.] *Boudoir Mirrors of Washington,* by Anonymous. Philadelphia and Chicago: The John C. Winston Co., 1923.

Schwarz, Jordan A. *The Speculator: Bernard Baruch in Washington.* Chapel Hill: The University of North Carolina Press, 1981.

Seymour, Charles. *American Neutrality.* New Haven, Conn.: Yale University Press, 1935.

Shachtman, Tom. *Edith and Woodrow.* New York: G. P. Putnam's, 1981.

Shotwell, James T. *The Autobiography.* Indianapolis and New York: The Bobbs-Merrill Company, 1961.

Silva, Ruth C. *Presidential Succession.* Ann Arbor: University of Michigan Press, 1951.

Slayden, Ellen Maury. *Washington Wife.* New York: Harper and Row, 1962–63.

Smith, Arthur D. Howden. *The Real Colonel House.* New York: George H. Doran, 1918.

Smith, Daniel M. *Robert Lansing and American Neutrality, 1914–1917.* Berkeley: University of California Press, 1958.

Smith, Gene. *When The Cheering Stopped.* New York: William Morrow, 1964.

Smith, Ira R. T., with Joe Alex Morris. *Dear Mr. President.* New York: Julian Messner, 1949.

Smith, Rixey, and Norman Beasley. *Carter Glass.* New York and Toronto: Longmans, Green and Co., 1939.

Soames, Mary. *Winston and Clementine.* Boston: Houghton Mifflin, 1998.

Spring Rice, Sir Cecil. *The Letters and Friendships of Sir Cecil Spring Rice.* 2 vols. Boston and New York: Houghton Mifflin, 1929.

Starling, Colonel Edmund W., as told to Thomas Sugrue. *Starling of the White House.* New York: Simon and Schuster, 1946.

Steed, Henry Wickham. *Through Thirty Years.* Garden City, N.Y.: Doubleday, Page & Co., 1924.

Steel, Ronald. *Walter Lippman and the American Century.* Boston and Toronto: Atlantic Monthly Press Book, Little, Brown and Company, 1980.

Steffens, Lincoln. *The Autobiography of Lincoln Steffans.* 2 vols. New York: Harcourt, Brace and Company, 1931.

Stein, Charles W. *The Third-Term Tradition.* New York: Columbia University Press, 1943.

Stoddard, Henry L. *As I Knew Them*. New York and London: Harper & Brothers, 1927.

Stone, Ralph A., ed. *Wilson and the League of Nations*. New York: Holt, Rinehart and Winston, 1967.

Sullivan, Mark. *Our Times: The United States, 1900–1925*. Vol. 5. New York and London: Charles Scribner's Sons, 1933.

Tardieu, Andre. *The Truth About the Treaty*. New York: Bobbs-Merrill, 1921.

Taylor, A. J. P., ed. *Lloyd George: A Diary by Frances Stevenson*. New York: Harper and Row, 1971.

Teague, Michael. *Mrs. L.: Conversations with Alice Roosevelt Longworth*. Garden City, N.Y.: Doubleday & Company, Inc. 1981.

Thompson, Charles Thaddeus. *The Peace Conference Day by Day*. New York: Brentano's, 1920.

Thompson, Charles Willis. *Presidents I Have Known*. Indianapolis and New York: Bobbs-Merrill, 1929.

Trevelyan, George Macauley. *Grey of Fallodon*. Boston: Houghton Mifflin, 1927.

Tribble, Edwin, ed. *President in Love: The Courtship Letters of Woodrow Wilson & Edith Bolling Galt*. Boston: Houghton Mifflin, 1981.

Tuchman, Barbara W. *The Guns Of August*. New York: Macmillan, 1962.

———. *The Zimmerman Telegram*. New York: Viking Press, 1958.

Tumulty, Joseph. *Woodrow Wilson As I Know Him*. Garden City, N.Y.: Doubleday, Page, 1921.

Vansittart, Lord. *The Mist Procession*. London: Hutchinson & Co., 1958.

Viereck, George Sylvester. *The Strangest Friendship in History*. New York: Liveright, 1932.

Walworth, Arthur C. *Woodrow Wilson: American Prophet* vols. I and II. New York, London, Toronto: Longman Green and Company, 1958.

———. *America's Moment: 1918*. New York: W. W. Norton, 1977.

———. *Wilson and His Peacemakers: American Diplomacy at the Paris Peace Conference, 1919*. New York: W. W. Norton, 1986.

Watson, James E. *As I Knew Them*. Indianapolis and New York: Bobbs-Merrill, 1936.

Weinstein, Edwin A. *Woodrow Wilson: A Medical and Psychological Biography*. Princeton: Princeton University Press, 1981.

Wharton, Edith. *A Motor Flight Through France*. New York: Charles Scribner's Sons, 1908.

White, William Allen. *Woodrow Wilson*. Boston and New York: Houghton Mifflin, 1929.

Widenor, William C. *Henry Cabot Lodge and the Search for an American Foreign Policy*. Berkeley: University of California Press, 1980.

Willert, Arthur. *Washington and Other Memories*. Boston: Houghton Mifflin, 1972.

Williams, Joyce Grigsby. *Colonel House and Sir Edward Grey*. Lanham, Md., and New York: University Press of America, 1984.

Wilson, Edith Bolling. *My Memoir*. New York: Bobbs-Merrill, 1939.

Wilson, Woodrow. *The State*. Boston and New York: D. C. Heath & Co, 1898.

———. *The New Freedom*, Garden City, N.Y.: Doubleday, Page & Company, 1912.

Wise, Jennings C. *Woodrow Wilson, Disciple of Revolution*. New York: The Paisley Press, 1938.

Young, Hugh, M.D. *A Surgeon's Autobiography*. New York: Harcourt, 1940.

ARTICLES

Abrams, Herbert L. "Can the Twenty-Fifth Amendment Deal with a Disabled President? Preventing Future White House Cover-Ups." *Presidential Studies Quarterly* 29, no. 1 (March 1999).

Ambrosius, Lloyd E. "Woodrow Wilson's Health and the Treaty Fight, 1919–1920." *International History Review* 9 (February 1, 1987).

Auerbach, Jerold S. "Woodrow Wilson's 'Prediction' to Frank Cobb: Words Historians Should Doubt Ever Got Spoken." *The Journal of American History* 54, no. 3 (1967).

Bagby, Wesley M. "Woodrow Wilson, a Third Term, and the Solemn Referendum." *American Historical Review*, April 1955.

Bloomfield, Douglas M. "Joe Tumulty and the Press." *Journalism Quarterly*, summer 1965.

Boothe, Leon E., "A Fettered Envoy: Lord Grey's Mission to the United States, 1919–1920. *Review of Politics* 33 (January 1971).

Bragdon, Henry. "The Woodrow Wilson Collection." *Princeton University Library Chronicle* 7, no. 1 (November 1945).

Cutler, Charles L., Jr. " Dear Mrs. Peck." *American History Illustrated* 6 (June 22, 1971).

Egerton, George W. "Britain and the 'Great Betrayal': Anglo-American Relations and the Struggle for United States Ratification of the Treaty of Versailles, 1919–1920," *Historical Journal* 21, no. 4 (1978).

———. "Diplomacy, Scandal and Military Intelligence: The Craufurd-Stuart Affair and Anglo-American Relations, 1918–20." *Intelligence and National Security* 2, no. 34 (October 1987).

"Genealogies of Virginia Families." *Virginia Magazine of History* (Genealogical Publishing Co., Baltimore [1981].

George, Juliette L., Alexander L. George, and Michael F. Marmor. "Issues in Wilson Scholarship: References to Early 'Strokes' in the *Papers of Woodrow Wilson*." "Communications." *Journal of American History* 70 and 71 (March 1984, June 1984).

Grayson, Admiral Cary T. "The Colonel's Folly and the President's Distress." *American Heritage*, October 1964 (originally written in 1924).

Hulbert, Mary Allen. "The Woodrow Wilson I Knew." *Liberty Magazine*, series of weekly articles, December 20, 1924, to February 14, 1925.

Johnson, Donald. "The Political Career of A. Mitchell Palmer." *Pennsylvania History* 25, no. 4 (October 1958).

Kuhfeld, Ellen R. "Return with Us Now to Those Shocking Days of Yesterday," in Proceedings of the Fourth International Symposium on Biologically Closed Electric Circuits. Bloomington, Minn.: October 26–29, 1997.

Lentin, A. "What Really Happened at Paris?" *Diplomacy & Statecraft*. (London) 1, no. 2 (July 2, 1990).

Link, Arthur S. "The Case for Woodrow Wilson." *Harper's* 234, no. 1403 (April 1967).

Lodge, Henry Cabot. "The Treaty Making Power of the Senate." *Scribner's Magazine*, January 1902.

Loth, David Goldsmith. "The Woodrow Wilson Foundation and the Centennial of Woodrow Wilson, 1856–1956."

Queen Marie of Romania. "My Mission." *Cornhill Magazine*, 160, no. 958 (October–December, 1929).

Maxse, L. J. "Too Much Wilson." *National Review*, (London) 72 (September 1918–February 1919).

Monagan, John S. "The President & Mrs. Peck." *The Bermudian*, February 1984.

Neu, Charles E. "The Search for Woodrow Wilson." *Reviews in American History* 10, no. 2 (1982).

Osborn, George C. "Woodrow Wilson as a Young Lawyer, 1882–1883." *Georgia Historical Quarterly*, 41, no. 2 (June 1957).

de la Pena, Carolyn Thomas. "Powering the Body." *Favourite Edition* (New York Academy of Medicine) 2, (spring 2000).

Rintals, Marvin. "Woodrow Wilson," a review of *The Papers of Woodrow Wilson*, vol. 2, 1881–1884. *Review of Politics* 31 (October 1969).

Rogers, Lindsay. "The Power of the President to Sign Bills After Congress Has Adjourned." *Yale Law Journal* 30, no. 1 (November 1920).

Saunders, Francis W. "Love and Guilt: Woodrow Wilson and Mary Hulbert." *American Heritage.* April/May, 1979.

Saunders, Richard. "History, Health and Herons: The Historiography of Woodrow Wilson's Personality and Decision Making." *The Presidential Studies Quarterly,* winter 1994.

Selden, Charles H. "Mrs. Woodrow Wilson." *Ladies' Home Journal,* October 1921.

Seymour, Charles. "End of a Friendship." *American Heritage* 14, no. 5, August 1963.

Schlesinger, Arthur., Jr. "Back to the Womb." Foreign Affairs 74, no. 4, July–August 1975.

Smith, Daniel M. "Lansing and the Wilson Interregnum." *Historian,* 21 (February 1959): 161.

Smith, Elizabeth A. "A Wanderer's Journal." New York: Privately Printed, 1889.

Smith, Ira R. T., with Joe Alex Morris. "My Fifty Years in the White House." *Saturday Evening Post,* January 8, 1949.

Stratton, David. H. "President Wilson's Smelling Committee." *The Colorado Quarterly,* 5, no. 2, (autumn 1956).

Thomas, John D. "Tales of Marsh & McLennan." *M* 14, no. 32, (1987). Archives of Marsh & McLennan Companies.

Thompson, Charles Willis. Review of *Woodrow Wilson, a Character Study,* by Robert Edward Annin. *New York Times Book Review,* March 23, 1924.

Trow, Clifford W. "Woodrow Wilson and the Mexican Interventionist." *Journal of American History* (Ballentine Hall, Indiana, Hall), 58 (June, 1971).

Walworth, Arthur C. "Considerations on Woodrow Wilson and Edward M. House: An Essay Letter to the Editor." *Presidential Studies Quarterly* 24, no. 31 (winter 1984).

Weaver, Judith L. "Edith Bolling as First Lady: A Study in the Power of Personality, 1919–1920." *Presidential Studies Quarterly* 15, no. 1 (winter 1985).

Weinstein, Edward A., James William Anderson, and Arthur S. Link. "Woodrow Wilson's Political Personality: A Reappraisal." *Political Science Quarterly* 93, no. 4 (winter 1978).

Weinstein, Edwin A., and Robert L. Kahn. "Personality Factors in Denial of Illness." *American Medical Association Archives of Neurology and Psychiatry,* March 1953.

———. "Woodrow Wilson's Neurological Illness." *The Journal of American History* 57 (1970).

White, William Allen. "Woodrow Wilson." *Liberty Magazine,* November 15 and 22, 1924.

Williams, Joyce G. "The Resignation of Secretary of State Robert Lansing." *Diplomatic History* 3, no. 3 (summer 1979).

Wimer, Kurt. "Senator Hitchcock and the League of Nations." *Nebraska History* no. 3 (September 1963).

———. "Woodrow Wilson and a Third Nomination." *Pennsylvania History* 29, no. 2 (April 1962).

Acknowledgments

White House chief usher Irwin Hood Hoover's prickly rendering of Edith Bolling Galt Wilson in *Forty-Two Years in the White House*—a gift from my daughter Kate—first propelled me, a number of years ago, to the Library of Congress. There I found Edith's baroque love letters to Woodrow Wilson (the equal of his), family correspondence, notes from her journal and for her *Memoir*, and detected something beyond her rapt commitment to Wilson, such as overtones of curiosity and ambition and possessiveness; also innuendo about his friends and colleagues. On further reading, including her nervously scribbled instructions regarding the disposition of state papers, I was committed to finding the truth about the "White House Mysteries."

Fortunately, and sometimes overwhelmingly, it seems as though everyone associated with Woodrow Wilson, sensing the grandeur of his quest, and the momentous possibilities of his messianic mission, wrote and preserved, far above and beyond the administration's official documents, hundreds of personal letters and dozens of private diaries and journals, which are readily available, if not in the original, on what appear to be miles of microfilm. And by everyone, I do mean not only Wilson's closest associates, his secretary of state, numerous ambassadors, members of Congress, "brain-trust" professors, and journalists, but also his stenographer, his Secret Service men, the White House chief usher, the housekeeper, and Edith Wilson's secretary, among many others.

With the helpful interest of Mary Wolfskill, head of Reference & Reader Services of the Manuscript Division of the Library of Congress, I began reading Edith Bolling Galt Wilson's own papers, available by the terms of her will, fifteen years after her death in 1961. I am also indebted to Maja Keech, reference specialist, and Debra Evans and Bonnie Coles in the library's Prints and Photographs Division. Once the pebble was cast, the circle seemed never to stop growing.

Starting with Edith Bolling Galt Wilson's early life in Virginia, as grateful recipient of public documents, private correspondence, and photographs, I am beholden to Carter Beamer, chairman of the Wythe County Historical Society; to Dr. W. R. Chitwood; Kathleen Ewald; Abby Endres, curator, Bedford (city/county) Museum; to Betty Francis Freeman; Mary B. Kegley; Jeanne D. Mead, researcher, Jones Memorial Library; Agnes Graham Sanders Riley; Teresa Roane at the Valentine Museum; Mary K. Sine and Ella Gaines Yates at the Virginia State Library and Archives.

Judith Ann Schiff, chief research archivist, Yale University Library, proved to be the beneficent ringleader of what I think of as the crucial Yale connection. In her wisdom, she introduced me to Arthur Clarence Walworth, the independent scholar whose biography *Woodrow Wilson: American Prophet* was awarded the Pulitzer prize in 1959. My manuscript is far sounder for his opinions and suggestions and for research materials, both archival and of the moment, that he so generously provided. Owing to Walworth, I share his cherished friendship with Edward House Auchincloss, grandson of Colonel Edward Mandell House, who led me to Gaddis Smith and the sage critique of Yale's Larned professor of history emeritus.

I am indebted to Louis Leonard Tucker, former director, and to Peter Drummey, of the Massachusetts Historical Society; to the patient staff of the New York Society Library; to Betty Monkmon, curator of the White House; to Katharine L. Brown, former executive director, the Staunton Birthplace; to Allene Hatch, who, quite serendipitously, presented me with the notes of her husband, Alden Hatch, Edith Wilson's biographer. Thanks to Susan Dryfoos, I read the papers of Adolph S. Ochs held in the *New York Times* archives. Eleanor Lansing Elliott introduced me to Eleanor Lansing Dulles, who recalled the Paris Peace Conference during World War I. Cary T. Grayson Jr. shared with me family photographs and the diary of his mother, the beautiful Alice Gertrude Gordon, Edith's young traveling companion; in an interview at his Upperville, Virginia, farm, he talked about his father's relationship with the Wilsons. Virginia Colby, president of the Cornish Historical Society, wrote to me about the Wilson's retreat in Cornish; William Zuill, president of the Bermuda Historical Association, spoke of Mary Allen Hulbert Peck's presence on the island. From Paris, Veronique Brown Claudet wrote of the signing of the first Charter of the League of Nations Society at the Crillon Hôtel.

At Brown University, librarian Margaret Mutter resolved an ornery accredation. During my encampment on Arthur S. Link's doorstep at Princeton's Firestone Library, his administrative assistant, Ilse Mychalchyk's midmorning and afternoon tea trays were a blessing. Christine W. Kitto also made the difference at Princeton.

At the Woodrow Wilson House on S Street in Washington, on my seemingly innumerable visits, Frank J. Aucella proved himself a remarkably astute as well as hopitable historian. Thanks also to his colleagues, to Meg Nowack and to Helen Murphy, a delightful consultant on a number of occasions.

At the Museum of Modern Art, Charles Silver, curator of film, gave me a private showing of *Wilson*. I appreciate also the support and friendship of Christina and Tony Melian, of Li Zhang and David Li, Eliot Roland, Ralph Alswang, Linda Kulman, Barbara Dubivsky, Grace Glueck, the late Janet Bewster Murrow, Pamela Newman, Michael Leahy, Albert DeStefano, William Schwalbe, Linda Caristo, William Greaves, Aldelira Prince, Ann Thorne, and Joanne Stern. For research on the "electricity treatments" administered to Woodrow Wilson, I am hugely indebted to Anne Emanuelle Birn, Ph.D. Not a day went by that I wasn't grateful to Walsh and Marian MacPhail McDermott for the gift to my family of their library of Wilsonia and related subject matter.

As for the evolution of the manuscript, I cannot even begin to count the ways to express my profound appreciation to Geraldine Sheehen for her labors on behalf of *Edith and Woodrow* from conception to final resolution. I feel myself as woefully inadequate in thanking Shirley Hazzard Steegmuller. In her masterly surveillance of *Edith and Woodrow*, I was moved by her generosity of spirit and profoundly inspired by the wisdom of her flawless judgment and taste.

One especially lucky day my sister and brother-in-law, Marjory and Mortimer Berkowitz, introduced me to Sterling Lord, who became my agent and who, in turn, introduced me to my editor, Lisa Drew, notable for her skill, integrity, and not to be underestimated, her enthusiasm. Her assistant Jake Klisivitch has been of constant help. I am appreciative of Laura Wise's watchful production editing.

And now my family. I am especially beholden to Kate for her always honest and constructive thoughts on early and late versions of *Edith and Woodrow*, and for her infinite, around-the-clock support of the entire enterprise. Anna's fine legal eye repeatedly clarified fuzzy details. Peter outdid Hercule Poirot in tracking down recalcitrant footnotes. My loving thanks then to John Levin and Louisa Swift, to Anna and Peter Levin, to Emme and Jonathan Deland, to Kate Levina and Mark di Suvero. Collectively, they have performed services of amazing breadth, both erudite and mundane, on behalf of *Edith and Woodrow*. Whether it has been a matter of style, grammar, technology, or morale, or moving my office, they have never wavered in their interest and support. Clearly, I am forever indebted to my husband, Bill Levin, for his faithful company on this arduous journey.

Index